Best wishes always to:

Michael E. Summers –

A Soldier Reports

W. C. Westmoreland

Dec. 10, 1976

As I look back on my life, I thank God for the opportunity that was given to me to be a soldier. If given that opportunity again, I would with the same pride and even greater humility raise my hand and take once again the soldier's oath.

From the author's remarks
upon retirement, June 30, 1972.

A Soldier Reports

General William C. Westmoreland

Doubleday & Company, Inc.   Garden City, New York   1976

ISBN 0-385-00434-6
Library of Congress Catalog Card Number 74-27593
Copyright © 1976 by William C. Westmoreland
All Rights Reserved
Printed in the United States of America

To

Kitsy

Stevie, Rip, and Margaret

and to

the valiant men and women of the
United States and other nations
who served the cause of freedom
in South Vietnam

Preface

Serving one's country as a military man is a rewarding experience. It is nevertheless a life of constraint. A military man serves within carefully prescribed limits, be it as enlisted man, junior officer, battalion commander, division commander, even senior field commander in time of war. The freedom to speak out in the manner of a private citizen, journalist, politician, legislator has no part in the assignment.

Perhaps that is one reason why generals who have hung up their uniforms traditionally turn to the pen, seek an opportunity for free expression that they long have properly denied themselves, to report to the people they have served. In these pages I have tried to exercise that prerogative that in the end is mine, while at the same time seeking to make an objective and constructive contribution to the history of a dramatic era. In the idiom of the time, I have tried to tell it like it was.

This is my personal story, yet inevitably it represents more than that; for my story is inextricably involved with the stories of those who served with me during thirty-six years in the United States Army—from wooden-wheeled artillery to antiballistic missile, from horse to spaceship, from volunteer army to draftee army in three wars and back to volunteer army. My story is particularly involved with the stories of those who served with such valor and sacrifice in the Republic of Vietnam. My hope is that in telling my story I have in some manner done justice to theirs, that I have to some degree contributed to an appreciation by the American people of arduous, imaginative, valiant service in spite of alien environment, hardship, restriction, frustration, misunderstanding, and vocal and demonstrative opposition.

One of the unanticipated pleasures in writing my story has been enthusiastic support from my former colleagues. So many have assisted that I am obliged to list them separately in an appendix.

I owe a particular debt of gratitude to a former General and President, the late Dwight D. Eisenhower, for urging me early in my service in Vietnam to keep a diary in order to maintain a record of the unique experiences I was undergoing. That diary has been of special help in writing this account.

I also take particular note of the help of my dear Kitsy, who, as always, contributed selflessly, and of the historical offices of all the military services. I owe appreciation also to my secretary, Charles M. Montgomery; my editor, Stewart Richardson; and a former aide, Paul Miles.

In a special category is the help of a distinguished military historian, Charles B. MacDonald, who took leave of absence from his usual duties to assist.

Contents

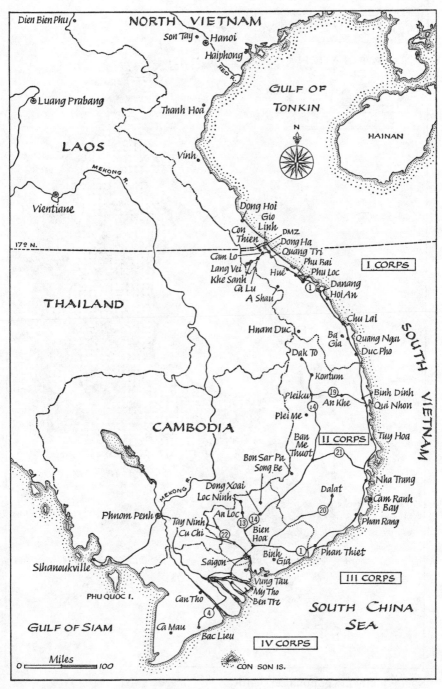

Southeast Asia, showing Tactical Zones for I, II, III, and IV Corps

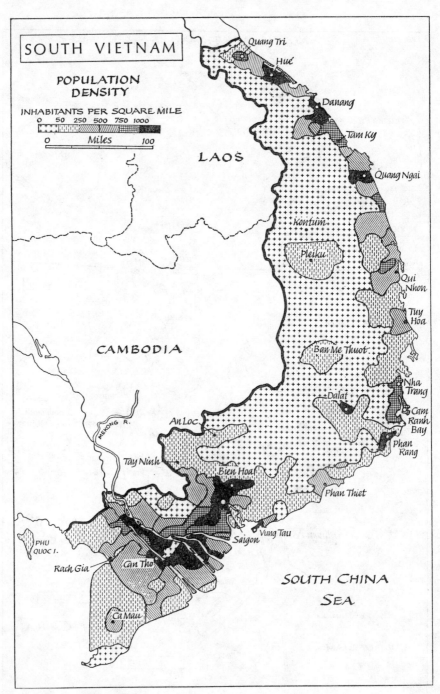

South Vietnam—population density

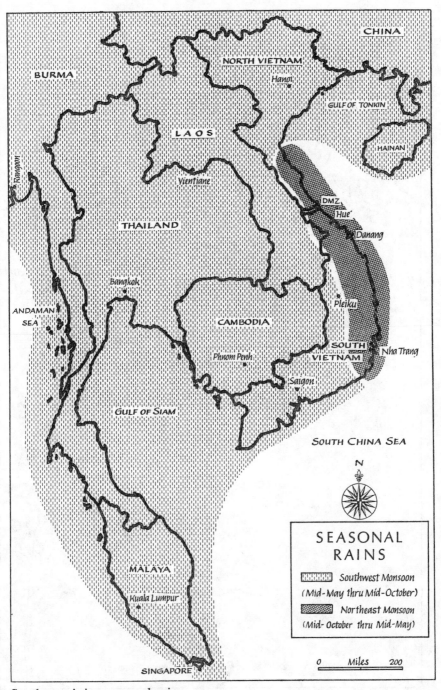

Southeast Asia—seasonal rains

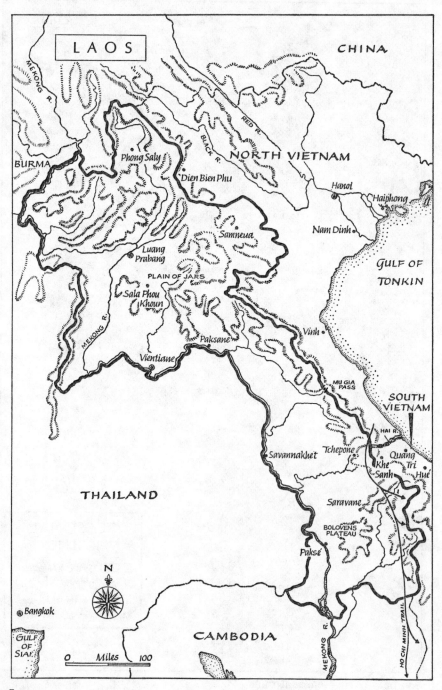

Laos

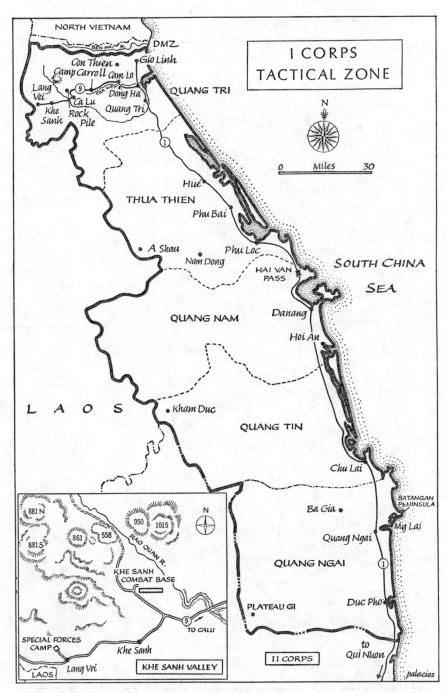

I Corps Tactical Zone (*Inset:* Khe Sanh Valley)

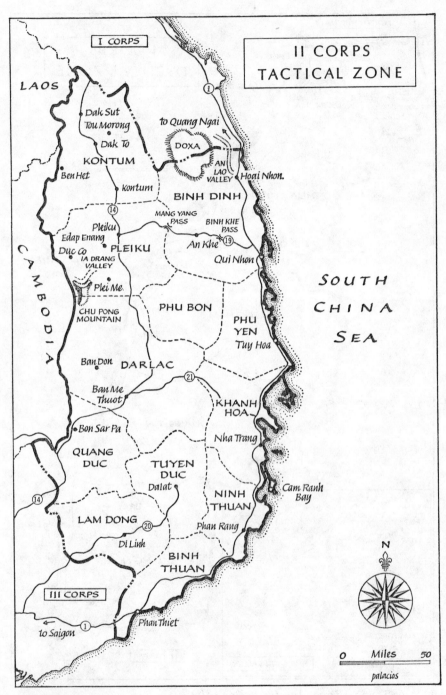

II Corps Tactical Zone

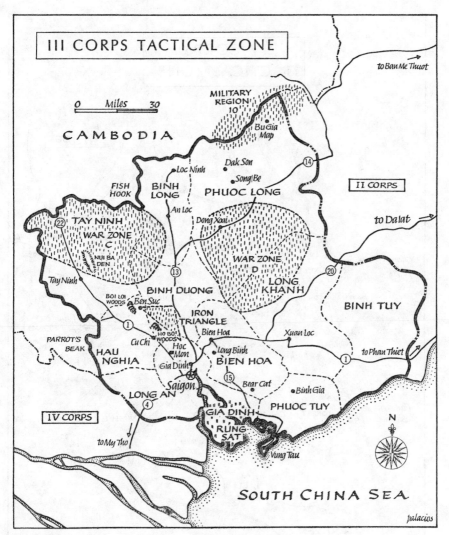

III Corps Tactical Zone

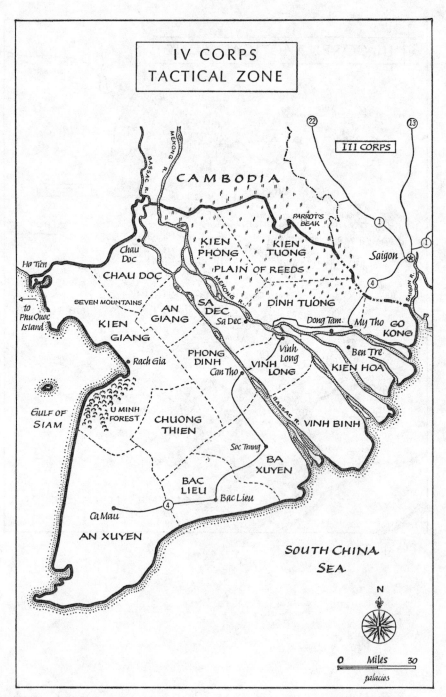

IV Corps Tactical Zone

Chapter I
Example and Apprenticeship

The old soldier spoke with carefully measured words. "Westmoreland," he said, "I know you realize that your new assignment is filled with opportunities but fraught with hazards."

With that he firmly shook my hand. It was to be my last meeting with a man whom I admired tremendously, General Douglas MacArthur. He was referring to my assignment to join the United States Military Assistance Command in Vietnam.

The first inkling I received that I might be going to Vietnam came late in December 1963, when the telephone rang in my office at Fort Bragg, North Carolina, where I commanded the XVIII Airborne Corps. It was the United States Army's Chief of Staff, General Earle G. Wheeler, known throughout the service by the nickname "Bus." He wanted to talk with me, General Wheeler said, on a subject he preferred to discuss in person.

As I entered General Wheeler's office in the Pentagon the next morning, he told me immediately that I was to go to Vietnam. I was to be deputy to General Paul D. Harkins, known by the imposing acronym COMUS-MACV, for Commander, United States Military Assistance Command, Vietnam, the officer responsible for the American forces serving in an advisory role to the Republic of Vietnam. It was probable that in time I would succeed General Harkins. The Secretary of Defense, Robert S. McNamara, wanted me to depart as soon as possible.

My only commitment, difficult to cancel, was a speech to the cadets at the United States Military Academy at West Point. In any case, I wanted to fill that engagement. As I prepared to assume what obviously would be a trying assignment, possibly the most difficult and complex of my career, it seemed somehow apt and comforting that I visit the institution that had exerted such a profound influence on my life and my career.

My father, James Ripley Westmoreland, was indirectly responsible for

my attending the Military Academy. The local manager of a textile operation, Pacolet Mills, near Spartanburg, South Carolina, a man of strong character, industrious, thrifty, scrupulously honest, intolerant of unreliability
and immorality, he more than anyone tried to instill in me respect for those
virtues for which I later learned West Point stands. Informed and well
read, he encouraged me in a broad range of activities, from my high school
studies to boxing and playing the flute. By enabling me at the age of fifteen
to attend a world Boy Scout jamboree in England, he triggered in me a love
of travel that in due time turned me toward West Point.

It was my father's friend James F. Byrnes who got me there. As a young
man, my father—"Wawa," my sister and I called him—had roomed in a
boarding house with Mr. Byrnes, who subsequently was a United States
senator, governor of South Carolina, special assistant during World War
II to President Franklin D. Roosevelt, Secretary of State, and Supreme
Court Justice. I came to know him early in my youth.

Wawa had no military experience, but since he was a graduate of The
Citadel, the military college of South Carolina, I was almost foreordained to
go there, although not with a view toward a military career. Having been
thwarted in his own desire to become a lawyer, my father aspired for me,
an only son, to achieve what he had missed. Expecting to obtain a liberal arts
degree as a preliminary to the study of law, I entered The Citadel in 1931.

I soon grew restless. Memories of my exciting trip to Europe kept coming
back, including recollection of a meeting during the trip with a group of
midshipmen from the United States Naval Academy at Annapolis. What
better way, I deduced, to see the world than to become a naval officer?
Receiving no encouragement from my father, I nevertheless outlined my
plan to Senator Byrnes: if I could receive an appointment to the Naval
Academy, I could see the world during my obligatory tour of duty, then
later enter the law school at Yale University.

Although sympathetic, Senator Byrnes suggested that with what I had in
mind, West Point would be more appropriate. He considered the curriculum
there to be broader and less technically oriented. Yet he had already made
his allotted nomination for the year. He nevertheless named me an alternate, and when the principal nominee failed to qualify academically, I took
his place.

That was the end of my father's aspirations to have an attorney in the
family and of a conflicting ambition on the part of my mother that I become
a doctor. It was the start of a long and rich association with the United
States Army, an association that spanned an era of incredible change. I entered an army that still relied heavily on the horse; in one brief career span,
I departed an army that relied instead on powerful motor transport, aircraft, and helicopters and possessed such sophisticated weaponry as guided
missiles with atomic warheads.

As I entered the Military Academy in July 1932, I had already learned
from my experience as a Boy Scout and as a cadet at The Citadel that I en-

joyed challenge and discipline, so much a part of military life. My days at West Point were long and often difficult, ranging from early struggles with English grammar and composition to later responsibilities in the post of First Captain. Yet they were rewarding days, replete with lasting friendships and with gainful associations with competent and moral officers, some of whom later joined the ranks of America's most distinguished soldiers.

Most rewarding of all was the appreciation and respect I gained for the code of ethics for which the Military Academy stands and which its honor system exemplified. The importance of the veracity of an officer's word had already been underscored for me by an incident during my year at The Citadel. When the college's new president, General Charles P. Summerall, World War I commander of the 1st Infantry Division and recently retired as the U. S. Army's Chief of Staff, made his first appearance before the state legislature, some senator accused him of inaccurate statements about the budget he had submitted. Shocked that his integrity should be questioned, General Summerall announced forcefully that that had never before happened to him and he was unable to tolerate it. Stating his intention to resign, he walked briskly from the chamber. That night the corps of cadets gathered outside his residence on the campus and by their support prevailed upon him to remain as president. Which he did, for nineteen years, but he had made his point.

An officer corps, my West Point education emphasized, must have a code of ethics that tolerates no lying, no cheating, no stealing, no immorality, no killing other than that recognized under international rules of war and essential for the military victory. Yet I also learned to my chagrin that there are those who fail the standards and that the code must be constantly policed. I saw failures at West Point, and for all my preventive efforts, I also saw failures among those who subsequently served under my command. Yet if an officer corps is to serve the nation as it should, firm dedication to a high moral code must always be the goal.

One of the most exciting events of my plebe year was the commencement address by the Army Chief of Staff, General MacArthur, who as much as any man extolled such a code. Already a distinguished soldier even before World War II and the Korean War, General MacArthur spoke at a time when pacifism and economy imperiled the military services and the nation's security. While warning against misguided pacifism and politically inspired economy, he spoke of West Point as "the soul of the Army." "The military code that you perpetuate," he said, "has come down to us from even before the age of knighthood and chivalry. It will stand the test of any code of ethics or philosophy."

Another who impressed an eager plebe was the commandant of cadets, Lieutenant Colonel Simon Bolivar Buckner, destined to die on Okinawa as a general officer commanding the Tenth Army. A muscular man with a big frame, bulging thighs, and a barrel chest, he was proud of a reputation as an outdoorsman and of the father for whom he was named, Kentucky's Confederate General Buckner, who had surrendered at Fort Donelson, Tennessee, to his old friend Ulysses S. Grant. No matter how cold the weather—and it can be bitter chill along the Hudson River—he never wore an overcoat, and rumor had it among the cadets that even though there was a Mrs. Buckner, he slept alone on a cadet cot with a hard mattress and only a sheet as cover.

As acting cadet adjutant during yearling summer camp, I had to read the Declaration of Independence on the Fourth of July from Battle Monument, a memorial to regular soldiers of the Union Army, which overlooks the Hudson. I read poorly, Colonel Buckner told me bluntly, and mispronounced three words. Never was I more conscious of the shortcomings of my regional accent.

That same summer, while inspecting cadet tents during encampment at Fort Clinton on the Hudson, Colonel Buckner was displeased to find perfumed shaving lotion on some of the toilet shelves. An order forbidding it was quick to come; only witch hazel was allowed. "I say to you, gentlemen," our commandant told us, "if you have to smell, smell like a man."

I also remember Colonel Buckner's definition of Army life. He called it genteel poverty.

Returning home on leave following my second year at West Point, I called on a great-uncle who had joined the Confederate Army at the age of sixteen and had fought in a number of major Civil War battles, including Gettysburg, and had been with Robert E. Lee at Appomattox. My Uncle White was the younger brother of my grandfather. He hated Yankees and Republicans, not necessarily in that order, and talked derisively about both. When I visited, he was seated in a wheel chair, in grudging acquiescence to the infirmities of age. Tobacco juice decorated his shirt and stains around a spittoon on the floor testified to the inaccuracy of his aim. Flies buzzed through screenless windows.

"What are you doing with yourself, son?" Uncle White asked.

I answered the old veteran with trepidation. "I'm going to that same school that Grant and Sherman went to, the Military Academy at West Point, New York."

Uncle White was silent for what seemed a long time.

"That's all right, son," he said at last. "Robert E. Lee and Stonewall Jackson went there too."

As graduation neared for the class of 1936, it fell my lot as First Captain to communicate to the superintendent the desires of the class for a commencement speaker. In the intervening years since General MacArthur's address, we had heard President Roosevelt and former Secretary of War Newton D. Baker, but it was MacArthur, the military man, who had impressed us most. I was pleased when my classmates accepted my suggestion that we invite the World War I commander, General of the Armies John J. Pershing, on the occasion of the fiftieth anniversary of his own graduation. Standing in the required full-dress uniform, including white gloves, in the superintendent's office I myself was later to occupy, I found the superintendent receptive. He later gave me General Pershing's letter of acceptance as a memento.

Considerably older than MacArthur, General Pershing lacked the fire and enthusiasm that General MacArthur had communicated. Yet his words for young officers were lucid and cogent. Maintain your own morals at a high level, he said, and you will find them reflected in the morals of your men. Decisiveness, initiative, determination, a concern for the individuality of your men—those, he said, were essentials of leadership. He stressed the importance of the small-unit leader, a point that perhaps never had more relevance than in the war in which I was to find myself engaged more than a quarter of a century later. I thought back to that graduation day with a pang when in Vietnam I noted one morning on the list of those killed in action the name of General Pershing's grandson Second Lieutenant Richard W. Pershing.

As graduation neared, neither my classmates nor I could know, of course, that World War II was in the offing. It was destined to expose us to trying and often tragic events. My roommate, Billy Hulse, a flier, disappeared on a training mission over the Great Lakes, his body never recovered. A close friend, Frank Oliver, died in the fighting in Normandy soon after the invasion. Buist Dowling killed in Normandy while leading a patrol. One of the better football players, Jock Clifford, killed as a regimental commander on Okinawa. Bill Priestly, aide to the high commissioner of the Philippines, electing to stay when the fighting started in the islands, also killed. Those and more.

A number of classmates were to rise to important positions during the war and later. Another football player, Casey Vincent, commanded an air wing in Claire Chennault's Flying Tigers in China and became a brigadier general before he was thirty. The first man in the class academically, Oliver Hayward, held an important post in the Manhattan Project, which developed the atomic bomb. In later years, Joe Nazarro commanded the Strategic Air Command and subsequently the United States Air Forces, Pacific. Mike Michaelis was commander of the United Nations Command and the Eighth Army in Korea after the war there was over; Bruce Palmer commanded American troops in a crisis in the Dominican Republic and later became Vice Chief of Staff; Jim Lampert became the forty-sixth superintendent of the Military Academy and the last U. S. High Commissioner of Okinawa; A. P. Clark became the sixth superintendent of the U. S. Air Force Academy; Benjamin O. Davis, Jr., became the first black general officer and subsequently commanded the 13th Air Force; Howell Estes commanded the Military Airlift Command during the war in Vietnam; and Johnny Heintges was my deputy in Vietnam, as was Creighton W. Abrams, who succeeded me both in Vietnam and as Chief of Staff of the United States Army.

Some who served on the faculty during my cadet days also rose to high positions: The graduate manager of athletics, Jacob L. Devers, became commander of the 6th Army Group during World War II in Europe and a full general. The adjutant, Robert L. Eichelberger, commanded the Eighth Army in the liberation of the Philippines. Alfred M. Gruenther, who as a lieutenant—which in those days of slow promotion he had been for eighteen years—taught me chemistry, served as Supreme Allied Commander in Europe with the North Atlantic Treaty Organization. Clyde D. Eddleman, a tactical officer, became Vice Chief of Staff of the Army. Orval R. Cook, who taught aeronautics and physics, became a four-star Air Force general. The commandant of cadets before Colonel Buckner, Robert C. Richardson, Jr., later commanded U. S. Army forces in the Central Pacific. Three others with whom I was associated became lieutenant generals: Clovis E. Byers, a tactical officer; Lemuel Mathewson, who taught Spanish; and T. Francis Farrell, who taught English. Finally, I became closely acquainted with an instructor in tactics who later became one of our few five-star generals, Omar Bradley.

Graduation over, second lieutenant's bars in place, two of my classmates, Al Peck and Larry Laurion, and I departed on a semiofficial mission to Ecuador, invited by that country's acting ambassador to the United States, whom I had met while performing my welcoming duties as First Captain. Aside from an opportunity to travel, to observe a Latin-American army, and to see such sights as the headwaters of the Amazon River, the trip afforded a lesson in diplomats and diplomacy that was to serve me well in later years. It also taught me that there is no one more vain than the second lieutenant who has yet to experience the wrath of a superior officer.

Welcomed in the port city of Guayaquil with a round of official parties that involved multiple toasts, we aroused the ire of the German-born American consul. Having read exaggerated newspaper accounts of remarks we had made in responding to toasts, the consul asked me to call. Judging from the remarks, he said, we—mere second lieutenants—were presuming to speak officially for the United States. Furthermore, if my mission was semiofficial, it behooved me to check in on arrival with him, which I had failed to do. He was going to inform Washington, he said angrily, and, even before I had reported to my first duty station, "ruin" my career.

As we toured the country with Ecuadorian Army Captain Garnef as escort, we received an invitation to come the next evening for dinner with the U.S. ambassador in the capital of Quito. When Captain Garnef told me that our itinerary made it impossible to reach Quito in time for dinner, I asked him to send a message of regret. When we did finally arrive, our Ecuadorian hosts escorted us to call on the President. When at last I found time to call at the U. S. Embassy, the first secretary gave me a strangely cool reception.

The next day I received a curt note from the ambassador summoning me to the Embassy. In the ambassador's eyes, I had sinned on two counts. First, he told me bluntly, I had called on the President of Ecuador without going through the U.S. ambassador, who properly should have accompanied me. Second, I had failed to attend a dinner given in my honor, "disappointing" the Minister of Defense and several other members of the President's Cabinet. An invitation from the Embassy, I learned, took precedence over all other activities.

My first official duties as an officer had, quite clearly, come a cropper. Yet not all was lost. Before we left Ecuador, we managed to get Captain Garnef promoted to major.

Having failed to qualify for service in the Army Air Corps because of a minor sight impediment, I chose the Field Artillery, which brought me a first assignment in the fall of 1936 at the home of the Field Artillery School at Fort Sill, Oklahoma. I joined the 18th Field Artillery, a regiment that served as demonstration troops for the school. Our guns in that era of penury were horse-drawn Model 1897 French 75s with steel-rimmed wooden wheels.

The private soldier's pay in those days was $21 a month, that of a second lieutenant, $125. On pay day it was standard practice to give all privates a three-day pass, because the soldier was bound to head for town to squander his money with or without permission. It was a special occasion when a unit obtained a recruit who was a high school graduate, for that meant getting a man who could be taught special skills.

In that day of a small army of only some 160,000, Fort Sill was an isolated post, the closest town, Lawton, little more than a village to which Indians in colorful dress repaired on Saturdays. With fellow officers I went from time to time for weekends in such cities as Dallas, Fort Worth, and Oklahoma City. That was in keeping with the second lieutenant's "flagpole rule," which decreed that if you have to raise hell, get off the post and away from the gossips.

In the main, our activities were confined to the post where social life was sometimes as demanding as the military duties. At dinner in the evenings, an officer had to wear a civilian dinner jacket with black bow tie. Aside from formal dinners and dances at the officers' club and amateur theater, much of the social activity centered around the horse: shows, hunter trials, polo, and colorful Sunday morning hunts with riders attired in traditional pink coats. The hunts were usually followed by lengthy hunt breakfasts where plentiful beer sparked the singing of colorful hunt songs and ballads.

On one of my first hunts I spotted a nine-year-old girl at the head of the field, pigtails flying, riding as if the horse was a part of her. I learned later that she was Katherine Van Deusen, daughter of the post executive officer, Lieutenant Colonel Edwin R. Van Deusen, who clearly had passed along his own renowned prowess on horseback to his daughter. Known as "Kitsy," she was a precocious child, witty, always quick with saucy remark. Since "Van" and "Kay" Van Deusen—one of the most popular couples on the post—lived only a few doors from my BOQ (bachelor officers' quarters), I observed Kitsy often, an active child with sparkling personality.

Just over two years later, as I prepared for reassignment to Hawaii, the girl on the post whom I had been dating married another officer, which brought me considerable sympathy from the ladies of the post. Shortly before my departure, as I sat in the officers' club, apparently looking dejected, an eleven-year-old Kitsy perched on the arm of my chair. "Cheer up, Westy," she said. "Don't worry. I'll be a big girl soon. I'll wait for you."

For all the emphasis on social events, duties at Fort Sill were demanding: maneuvers, firing demonstrations for the Artillery School, experimenting as new, improved weapons gradually became more than a promise. Breaking remounts was a particularly trying assignment, hard on various portions of the anatomy as a bucking horse forced an inevitable spill. The second lieutenant's summer task of supervising horses while they grazed was dull but became for me on one occasion an exhilarating experience. Apparently frightened by a snake, the horses stampeded. Because the herd headed for a narrow iron bridge across a deep-cut creek, where in the crush many would likely be hurt or killed, my sergeant and I raced on our mounts to outrun and turn them. Succeeding only at the last minute, we were almost crushed in the process.

Noncommissioned officers were knowledgeable and helpful to neophyte lieutenants, but they also were often crusty and unafraid to speak up. Once when my battery made several mistakes in a firing exercise, I held the men for extra drill on a Saturday afternoon. First Sergeant "Bull" McCullough dutifully executed my orders, but when the punishment was over, he came to my office.

"Lieutenant," McCullough said with an air of sadness, "the morale of the battery is shot." Several of our best NCOs, he told me, wanted to "buy out," i.e., terminate their enlistments by paying the official dollar price. Although by Monday morning the mood had passed, I had learned indelibly that mass punishment is no way to promote discipline.

The NCOs could also display considerable ingenuity. Apparently peeved that in tugs of war occasionally staged between teams of horses and mules, the heavier horses usually won, a stable sergeant devised a scheme to insure a victory for the mules. Over several months he trained the mules to recognize that when he banged on a tin pan in the stables, their oats were ready. On the day of the big contest, the sergeant maneuvered the animals so that when the mules began to pull, they would be headed toward their stables. When an accomplice in the stables began at the strategic time to bang on a pan, the struggle was over. Leaning into their collars, pulling in unison, the mules dragged the proud horses backward across the field. Only a soldier who was "horse-drawn" could know the full extent of the disgrace.

One who particularly impressed me during my days at Fort Sill was a colonel, Sherman Miles, an urbane, polished, scholarly officer with a keen interest in military history. Having served in a number of attaché assignments, he had an appreciation of international relations. He had developed a checkers-type war game based on the principles of war, which the two of us would play for long hours. In retrospect, I attribute the awakening of my own interest in military history and international affairs to Colonel Miles's influence.

In sharp contrast was my battery commander, who occupied himself with minutiae while I as executive officer and First Sergeant McCullough virtually ran the battery. On one occasion he called me in to read my efficiency report. Although it was mediocre, I made no protest until he told me that I deserved better, but because he as a young officer never received a better report, he would rate no one higher. "If that is your criterion," I said, "I take official exception and request permission to speak to the battalion commander." Although the battalion commander refused to change the report, I suppose, as I look back over my career, that the report did no lasting harm.

Arriving in Hawaii in late 1938, I joined the 8th Field Artillery, a regiment equipped with British 3-inch guns towed by trucks. It was still very much a peacetime army, although Adolf Hitler's posturing and threatening in Europe was becoming more and more disturbing. The *Anschluss* with Austria occurred early in the year, the capitulation of the democracies at Munich, over Hitler's seizure of the Sudetenland in Czechoslovakia, in September.

Yet in the idyllic setting of Hawaii, war or the possibility of it seemed remote. There was still much time for sports: again polo and horse shows, but also sailing and surfing. Some months after my arrival, Colonel Van Deusen assumed command of a sister artillery regiment and with him and the rest of his family was Kitsy, then entering her teens. She was an awkward teen-ager but played tennis well and remained an expert horsewoman. To my chagrin, she beat me in several horse show events.

After I and my automobile were the subjects of three official reports for exceeding the fifteen-mile-per-hour speed limit on the post, my regimental commander, Colonel Donald G. McDonald, announced that he was "grounding" me for a month. Without access to a car, my accustomed frequent trips from Schofield Barracks into Honolulu virtually ceased until I discovered that Colonel McDonald's beautiful eighteen-year-old blonde daughter made an excellent chauffeur. When the colonel found out, he was furious, although he failed to ground his daughter.

While at Schofield Barracks, I was assigned to cooks and bakers school, a common practice to teach junior officers how to handle their company messes. Although I was later an instructor at the Army War College and at the Command and General Staff College, that and the parachute school later, at Fort Benning, were the only service schools I ever attended, so that in later years I was amused when people would accuse me of doing things "by the book."

Still interested in the Air Corps, I took commercial flying lessons, but again a minor problem with my eyes prevented me from entering that branch. After months of special eye-muscle exercises, I corrected the problem, but by that time—1939—world crisis was real. War had come to

Europe, and in the Pacific the Japanese had moved into French Indochina. When my transfer orders came, I regretted that no shift to the Air Corps was involved, but took comfort in the thought that if war came for the United States, my five years' artillery experience probably would enable me to be more useful in that branch. Traveling back to the United States on the battleship *Maryland* and gaining knowledge of the Navy, I moved in mid-1941 to Fort Bragg to join an artillery unit of the 9th Infantry Division, destined to be one of the first American divisions to take the offensive in World War II.

Early in World War II, I found myself, as a lieutenant colonel, commanding the 34th Field Artillery Battalion, the 9th Division's general support regiment of 155-mm howitzers, in North Africa and Sicily; next as executive officer of 9th Division artillery in France; then as a colonel, chief of staff of the division in Germany. In the latter position, the division commander, Major General Louis A. Craig, an exceptional officer and good tutor, invested me with considerable responsibility and gave me broad authority. A superb division, the 9th compiled an enviable record through eight campaigns.

My first combat experience in February 1943 followed a four-day forced march from a position just inside Algeria to the village of Thala in Tunisia, over generally unpaved roads through the Atlas Mountains, slippery with ice and mud. The Germans, under Field Marshal Erwin Rommel, had launched an offensive in Tunisia in what became known as the Battle of the Kasserine Pass, and American troops had fallen back under the impact. Although trucks and howitzers slid off the steep, serpentine roads with frustrating frequency, my battalion and the rest of the 9th Division artillery under a red-haired commander, Brigadier General S. Leroy Irwin, arrived in time to help thwart what looked to be a decisive German breakthrough.

General Irwin was a quiet, cultured man who spent much of his spare time reading and writing poetry. He assigned his subordinate commanders mission-type orders and gave them considerable leeway. His example impressed me with the necessity of avoiding oversupervision, a disease that tends to plague the military. On the other hand, inadequate supervision entails considerable risk. While a commander must avoid overcontrol, it behooves him to know what goes on at least two echelons of command below him.

Despite a number of near misses, I came through the war unscathed. In Tunisia a shell hit my vehicle but without harm to me, and in Sicily an exploding mine blew up my vehicle, but I was thrown clear. On the Roer River in Germany, just as I got out of my jeep and entered a company command post, a mortar shell struck my vehicle. In the Remagen bridgehead on the Rhine a shell demolished a latrine moments after I had departed. Somehow none of the enemy's shells had my number.

In crossing into the Remagen bridgehead, I became probably one of the few Americans to cross the Rhine lying flat on his belly. When the 9th Division was ordered to provide hurried reinforcement for the bridgehead, I crossed at night with a truck convoy. So dark was the night that when we reached the captured railroad bridge, I had to lie on my belly on the lead jeep and direct the driver by voice commands. It was no easy task in the darkness to negotiate the wooden ties between the rails of the bridge that the enemy had attempted to destroy before capture.

In the closing chapter of the war in Europe, the 9th Division reached the confluence of the Mulde and Elbe rivers, whence platoon-sized patrols probed across the Elbe toward Berlin, fifty miles away. In view of what amounted almost to a welcome by the Germans, some patrols got into the outskirts of the Berlin suburb of Potsdam, and I was convinced the division could have proceeded to Berlin. Yet there were considerations at higher levels of which I was unaware. We had to pause to await arrival of the Russians.

Russians and vodka, I soon learned, were virtually synonymous. Twice I accompanied my division commander, General Craig, to parties with his Russian opposite beyond the Elbe. Since General Craig was an abstainer, his aides had to exercise considerable ingenuity to dispose of the vodka from his glass in nearby flower pots. The Russian general several times did the same. I noted an unwavering peculiarity about the Russians: we always had to go to them; never would they come to visit us or even meet us halfway.

During the military occupation of Germany after the Allied victory, overcoming acute shortages was a severe test for American commanders. Responsible as commander of the 60th Infantry Regiment for administering five Bavarian *Landkreise* (districts) that contained half a dozen camps for displaced persons, a prisoner of war camp for SS troops, and a detention camp for former Nazi officials, I was hard put to prepare these facilities for winter. Cutting logs for fuel was simple; procuring glass to replace broken window panes and obtaining clothing for the DPs was more trying.

With the help of my ingenious supply officer, Major Jack Coulter, I learned that glass factories in neighboring Austria and Czechoslovakia were languishing for lack of sodium carbonate. Yet that was in ample supply back along the Rhine. My regiment's trucks soon were hauling sodium carbonate into the neighboring countries and bringing back the glass we needed, virtually cornering the glass market in Bavaria. When our needs were met, we used the glass to exchange for other goods required for the DPs.

For clothing, my military government officer one day posted notices in the principal city of Ingolstadt asking voluntary contributions from the people, but during the night somebody defaced the notices with black swastikas. That kind of defiance, I decided, required prompt action. Ordering previously released Nazi officials rounded up and confined, I imposed a strict night curfew in the city and posted American guards to enforce it. Then I sent teams of Americans and Germans into the homes of former members of the Nazi party to take from their wardrobes the clothes that were needed. The Germans were for the moment unhappy but thereafter cooperative.

Being in Germany in the 1940s brought back recollections of my first visit long before as a Boy Scout, when I had had my first encounter with German appreciation of dueling. As a child I had been cut severely on the left cheek when thrown through the windshield of my father's car in a head-on collision, and a prominent scar remained. Traveling in Germany as a youth, I was perplexed when college students would tip their beanie caps as they passed until at last I discerned that they mistook the scar on my cheek for a dueling scar.

During the war years, it was my privilege to associate on a number of occasions with prominent personalities, such as Senator Harry S Truman, for whom my battalion staged an artillery demonstration when he visited Fort Bragg in 1941. When I invited him to fire, he did so with confidence. Shaking my hand as he departed, he said that as an old artilleryman he recognized that the fire mission was uncomplicated and that, even so, he suspected the crews helped him hit the target. "I enjoyed it anyway," he said. When I was in Vietnam, a then former President Truman wrote me a letter of encouragement.

Among a stream of visitors to the 9th Division in England, while it was preparing for D-Day during the early months of 1944, was Prime Minister Winston Churchill. When he arrived to address the assembled troops, he went at first not to the speaker's stand but behind a small outbuilding. He reappeared minutes later deliberately buttoning his fly, making sure no one missed the reason for the delay. The troops loved it.

Soon after arriving in Sicily during the summer of 1943, I learned that the 82d Airborne Division's headquarters were nearby. Electing to call, I found the commander, Major General Matthew B. Ridgway, and his artillery officer, Brigadier General Maxwell D. Taylor, in conference. Under orders to pursue the enemy swiftly, the division was short of transportation. I spoke up. My battalion, I explained, had worked out what I called a "blitz" formation that would enable me to provide the 82d with artillery support while at the same time lending the division forty trucks and jeeps. That sold my battalion's services, and we joined the attack. It was my first acquaintance with two men with whom I was to serve and whom I was to admire in later years. Both later headed the United Nations Command and the Eighth Army in Korea and both served as the U. S. Army's Chief of Staff. My association with General Taylor in Vietnam was to be close.

While in Sicily, I re-established an earlier acquaintance with a dynamic young colonel commanding one of the 82d Airborne's parachute infantry regiments, James M. Gavin, who later commanded the division. When the war was over, General Gavin asked my transfer to the division to command the 504th Parachute Infantry. Since I had yearned to be a paratrooper ever since serving at Fort Bragg in proximity to the first American airborne units, I was delighted with the assignment. I learned much from General Gavin in his capacity as a division commander, particularly on leadership qualities and maintaining the morale of the troops. More than any other commander under whom I served, he impressed me with the necessity for a commander to be constantly visible to those he leads.

Soon after the war—Jim Gavin told me to our amusement—the commandant of the Air War College, Major General Orvil A. Anderson, introduced him as guest speaker. Anderson was a pioneer flier and balloonist, later fired from the Air Force by President Truman for preaching preventive war. "We were never more privileged," General Anderson intoned, "than we are today to have this distinguished speaker, one of America's great soldiers, one of the greatest since Lee, Grant, Pershing, a man who is going down in history as a tactician and strategist, one of the great soldiers of all time." Then General Anderson began to slow down. "One of the great soldiers of all time," he repeated. By that time it was apparent he was stalling. "One of the great soldiers of all time," he said again. Turning to Gavin, he asked in exasperation: "What the hell is your name anyway?"

I first met George S. Patton, Jr., before World War II when he was a lieutenant colonel at Fort Sill, and in North Africa, when he was a general, I saw him often. Almost every day he would head for the front, standing erect in his jeep, helmet and brass shining, a pistol on each hip, a siren blaring. For the return trip, either a light plane would pick him up or he would sit huddled, unrecognizable, in the jeep in his raincoat. His image with the troops was uppermost with General Patton, and that meant always going forward, never backward.

General Patton had two fetishes that to my mind did little for his image with the troops. First, he apparently loathed the olive drab wool cap that the soldier wore under his helmet for warmth and insisted that it be covered; woe be the soldier whom the general caught wearing the cap without the helmet. Second, he insisted that every soldier under his command always wear a necktie with shirt collar buttoned, even in combat action.

At the 9th Division headquarters at El Guettar, Tunisia, enemy planes bombed and strafed incessantly, so that the security normally associated with a headquarters in the rear was missing. Although officers and men alike dug deep, even in foxholes they could get little sleep. One day a small convoy of vehicles arrived, sirens alive, Patton standing in the lead vehicle. While the division commander, Major General Manton Eddy, rushed to greet him, the staff pondered what fault Patton was going to find this time.

"Manton, Goddamn it," Patton shouted in his high-pitched voice, "I want you to get these staff officers out front and get them shot at!" Having been bombarded day and night by enemy planes, having had no sleep for days, a young personnel officer went berserk and had to be evacuated for medical treatment.

Several weeks before General Patton died in a command car accident in 1945, he visited my headquarters at Ingolstadt. Over lunch he remarked on a recent visit he had made to the United States where the press had castigated him for referring to the Nazis as a political party "like Republicans or Democrats." "Westy," he told me solemnly, "don't forget when you return to the States, be careful what you say. No matter what, they'll put it in the newspapers." It seemed remote advice at the time for a young, inauspicious colonel, but I was to have ample reason in later years to reflect on his counsel.

A commander who particularly impressed me was General J. Lawton ("Lightning Joe") Collins, who commanded the VII Corps in France and Germany in World War II and subsequently was the U. S. Army's Chief of Staff during the Korean War. Joe Collins' aggressiveness and enthusiasm were inspirational. Even though my division was engaged in hard fighting and was taking high casualties in the Siegfried Line, General Collins as the corps commander could come close to convincing us that only a bunch of tired old policemen was holding us up. During my time in Vietnam, I was to think often of the effect of his positive presence on others.

A commander clearly is the bellwether of his command and must display confidence and resolution. Even the slightest pessimism on his part can quickly pervade the ranks. Years later, in Vietnam, I was confident, so no play-acting was involved in showing this, yet at the same time I was sharply conscious of the need to demonstrate it.

In the Remagen bridgehead in February 1945 I saw a clear example of the difference an individual commander can make in a combat situation. So irresolute was the III Corps commander, so lacking in confidence, that I feared for the safety of the bridgehead. Indeed, the corps commander virtually abdicated his responsibilities to my division commander, General Craig. When the First Army commander, General Courtney H. Hodges, visited the bridgehead, I as the division's chief of staff saw an opportunity to alert him to the problem, which I feared a commander as loyal as Craig would fail to do.

With General Hodges was an aide, Major Billy Sylvan, whom I had known as a youth when I visited cousins in Columbia, South Carolina. I called Sylvan aside and told him my concern. Although I cannot know what weight my intervention had, General Hodges soon thereafter relieved the corps commander. Battlefield reliefs are trying, almost always traumatic to both officers involved, yet the senior commander must bear in mind that the welfare of the command is the essential criterion, and he must act with decision, however unpleasant the responsibility.

A superb officer, Major General James A. Van Fleet, assumed command of the III Corps in the bridgehead. What a difference his presence made. He seemed indefatigable, constantly visiting subordinate units, exuding confidence, pointing to the map and issuing orders on the spot: do this, do that. When I commanded an airborne combat team under General Van Fleet in Korea, he had lost none of his decisiveness. With him a subordinate knew exactly where he stood, precisely what was expected.

Replacement of commanders may be necessary even after the trial of combat passes, as I discovered during the early months of the occupation of Germany while commanding the 9th Division's 60th Infantry Regiment. The temptations for officers and men alike in the turbulent, decadent atmosphere of a defeated nation were great, accentuated by the vast territory that every unit had to administer and the attendant isolation from senior headquarters. I had to relieve two battalion commanders for improper conduct and to prefer charges against a captain for stealing furs from a warehouse. War and the aftermath of war produce a climate conducive to illegality and immorality, and the man who lacks sufficient character to withstand the temptations must be replaced or corruption will soon infect the entire command.

For my return to the United States in 1946, I commanded a skeleton 71st Infantry Division, which I preceded by plane. On the long flight I reflected on my many months of war and almost twelve months of peace in an occupation force and considered that there were at least three matters that had been given insufficient emphasis or had been done poorly.

We had failed, I believed, to provide our troops at the tactical small-unit level sufficient information on what the job they were being called upon to risk their lives for was expected to accomplish and what was expected of them when doing it. I also believed that our inspector-general system broke down, particularly near the end, because of insufficient attention to ferreting out trouble before it surfaced. My third point was a corollary of the second: I found our military criminal investigation inadequate in quality and in numbers of investigators. Those thoughts were to return to me often in Vietnam.

At Fort Bragg, after commanding the 504th Parachute Infantry for just over a year, I served for three years as chief of staff of the 82d Airborne Division under three different commanders, each with a highly distinctive style of command: Jim Gavin, Major General Clovis E. Byers, and one of the truly irascible characters of the immediate postwar army, Major General Williston B. Palmer. Willie Palmer was a crusty, meticulous bachelor, figuratively wedded to the military profession, an artilleryman who developed into a logistician of the first order. I was later to be closely associated with him again in the Pentagon.

As I parachuted at Fort Bragg one day from a new C-82 transport aircraft under test, a metal connector link that ties the parachute's shroud lines to the risers and harness hit me in the back of the head. I came to earth unconscious. Although I soon got to my feet, I was temporarily out of my head. Of the first officer who approached me, I asked, "Are we fighting the Russians?"

Flown back to Fort Bragg, I entered a hospital with amnesia. When I came to the next day, I saw with shock that I was in a detention ward with bars over the windows. As I underwent tests for the next week to determine if brain damage was involved, a psychiatrist interviewed me daily. Did I want, the psychiatrist asked repeatedly, to continue jumping? Each time he posed the question, I responded with an emphatic affirmative. Each time the psychiatrist appeared puzzled.

All effects of my accident having passed, I asked the ward doctor to release me. That would be impossible, I learned; I was to be transferred to a general psychiatric hospital.

With concern, I telephoned the 82d Airborne Division surgeon, Lieutenant Colonel Robert Hunter. The psychiatrist, I told him, had apparently concluded that because I wanted to jump out of airplanes, I was crazy.

Colonel Hunter laughed. My analysis was no doubt correct; he had had similar problems with the same psychiatrist, who fortunately was about to depart the service. Hunter took steps immediately to arrange my release.

In the fall of 1946, my personal life underwent a marked change that had its origins in a Sunday morning hunt ten years earlier at Fort Sill.

My telephone rang.

"This is Kitsy," a female voice said. "Remember me?"

Hesitating briefly, I said I did and asked, "Are you a big girl now?"

"Why don't you come," she answered, "and see for yourself?"

I was scheduled for dinner that evening at the Gavins'. Aware that the ladies of the post had just about despaired of my ever marrying (I was all of thirty-two), I thought Mrs. Gavin might welcome my bringing a date. When I called her, she was delighted.

When I again set eyes on Kitsy, I found the pigtails gone, the little girl who had led the chase changed into a beautiful young woman.

Seven months later, on May 3, 1947, in St. John's Episcopal Church in Fayetteville, outside Fort Bragg, we were married.

Chapter II
Preparation for Command

As the Korean War began, in 1950, I was an instructor at the Command and General Staff College at Fort Leavenworth; that was followed by two years in a similar position at the Army War College at Carlisle Barracks in Pennsylvania. Although I had never attended either institution as a student, on the basis of the breadth of my instruction at the War College, covering such subjects as airborne and airmobile warfare, psychological warfare, and strategic planning, I was awarded a diploma.

I was particularly struck by the contrasts in the style of the commandant and deputy commandant of the War College, both of whom were superior officers. The commandant was Major General Joseph M. Swing, former commander of the 11th Airborne Division, a rough, gruff paratrooper, a classmate of General Eisenhower's. The deputy commandant was Brigadier General Arthur G. Trudeau, polished, intellectually active, highly personable, one of the finest minds I encountered during my military service.

My opportunity to serve in Korea came in mid-1952 when I assumed command of the 187th Airborne Combat Team, known as the "Rakissans," which in Japanese means "umbrella men." Although the unit had seen action earlier in the war, the men had for long been in reserve in Japan and needed refresher training. An event the morning after my arrival pointed up how much still remained to be done.

To observe an exercise that was to involve live firing, I stood on a hilltop with the battalion commander. When he called for preplanned defensive fire, mortar rounds began to land all over the hill. A lieutenant standing at my side was severely wounded, along with a machine gunner and several other men. I quickly ordered all firing to cease.

An investigation revealed that the errant rounds were from a 4.2-inch mortar. Checking with the warrant officer in charge, I found that he was unqualified to command a mortar platoon. The incident enabled me to cadge ten more days of intensive training before the combat team went into action.

The training involved a number of parachute exercises. As the new commander, I jumped with each battalion. I was rusty in any case, for even though I had previously made more than fifty jumps, it had been more than a year since my last one. On my second jump I made a poor exit from the aircraft, and my parachute failed to open. Not until I was about 300 feet above the ground did I finally succeed in shaking it loose. It blossomed just in time. I should have pulled my reserve chute; I had flirted needlessly with death.

Because truce talks with the North Koreans had been underway for almost a year, the role of all American ground forces at the time was essentially defensive. For my first combat experience with an infantry regiment, I drew the assignment of blocking a broad valley leading toward the South Korean capital of Seoul. Yet the role was not altogether passive. Patrolling to capture prisoners to keep abreast of enemy intentions demanded ingenuity and emphasis on small-unit leadership. My unit was attached to the 7th Infantry Division, commanded by Major General Wayne C. Smith, whose pear-shaped build accounted for his nickname, "Shaped Charge."

After the combat team pulled back in the fall of 1952 to constitute a reserve in Japan, the Communist Chinese in the summer of 1953, in anticipation at last of an armistice, began a major offensive. The U. S. Eighth Army commander, General Taylor, hastened the 187th back to Korea by air.

That commitment led to one of the few serious disputes over an order from a superior officer that I experienced during my career. It arose soon after the 187th reached the front, attached to the 2d Infantry Division. When a Chinese Communist attack drove a salient into the lines of two adjacent units, it left my combat team holding a critical shoulder of the salient. In the middle of a black, rain-sodden night, the 2d Division commander, Major General William L. Barriger, telephoned to direct me to withdraw one of my battalions from a hill that I considered a key to my entire defensive position.

I objected. I had been to the hill that afternoon, I informed General Barriger, and the troops were well dug in and fully capable of holding. Neither did I consider it advisable to move without reconnaissance into a new position in the middle of such a night, and the proposed move would expose my own headquarters, which would also have to be moved. Yet General Barriger was adamant. When I insisted that I deemed the move ill-advised, he became irate and issued what he called a "direct order" to withdraw the troops immediately. It was such a grave mistake, I believed, that I again asked him to reconsider. When he threatened to relieve me, I had no choice but to obey, but I made clear that I followed the order only under protest.

Under miserable conditions, the battalion commander, Major Frederick J. Kroesen, later to serve as a general officer in Vietnam, executed a withdrawal that only experienced troops could have accomplished, and to assure the integrity of the combat team's position, I had quickly to organize a provisional battalion made up of cooks, clerks, and drivers to occupy a blocking position. Fortunately, American counterattacks eliminated the enemy salient before the Chinese could take advantage of the key terrain feature my men had been forced to abandon.

Paratroopers are magnificent soldiers, but they are also a very lively lot and require firm discipline and regimented activity if they are to be held in check. Since building new defenses along an armistice line failed to sap all their energy, I began a demanding physical conditioning program under the slogan "Every Man a Tiger." Calisthenics, long runs before breakfast, athletic competitions in the evening.

Upon learning in the fall of 1953 that the 187th was to return to its former base in Japan, I thought it prudent to begin a "de-tigerization" program, easing up on the physical routine, lecturing and counseling on what to expect among Japanese people who had recently been restored their full sovereignty. As the men boarded a transport for Japan, a cartoonist in the unit newspaper twitted me handsomely: one drawing depicted me exhorting troops with growling tiger faces; a second showed men climbing a gangplank, tiger faces placid; a third pictured men debarking with the faces of lambs.

That my concern was valid was apparent when we reached Japan; on the march to the camp, thousands of happy American sailors on shore leave lined the streets of the city of Beppu to heckle. My men were furious. I immediately contacted the senior naval officer in the area and arranged a program to bring soldiers and sailors together with informal visits, joint military police and shore patrol details, talks by commanders, and athletics. Incidents, much to my relief, were few. My men got their revenge for the heckling when they defeated the Navy boxers overwhelmingly: seven knockouts for the Army boxers and one draw.

On the occasion of Beppu's centennial celebration as a separate city I was asked to make remarks during ceremonies in a local auditorium. After long hours of rehearsing phonetics with my interpreter, I spoke in Japanese. The amusement of my audience was quite apparent, but the people also appeared to be flattered by my effort. When Japanese reporters began an interview later, they quickly became aware of just how big an effort it had been, and everybody was relieved to revert to English.

Wearing a beautiful kimono presented by Japanese friends, it was Kitsy who was the true center of attention. Japanese reporters described her as a "black-eyed beauty." Kitsy wore the kimono in deference to the wives of Japanese officials, but to her surprise, they appeared in Western dress in deference to her.

Returning to the Pentagon in late 1953 as a brigadier general, I headed the Army's manpower office, a position that enabled me to be privy to top-level conferences as the staff, in 1954, pondered the possibility of intervention in support of the French who were struggling with their rebellious colonies in Indochina. The U. S. Army Chief of Staff, General Ridgway, strongly opposed any form of intervention. Air and naval forces alone, General Ridgway believed, would be insufficient to rescue the French, and so many American ground troops would be required as to strain other world-wide commitments. Inherent in General Ridgway's argument was a belief that to commit American troops on behalf of a colonial power was wrong.

I agreed with that rationale at the time; the difference in the later American commitment was that the stigma of French colonialism was removed. I do recall taking exception to a briefing by the Surgeon General that had a strong influence on the staff. He presented a gloomy picture of an environment in Vietnam so replete with vermin, reptiles, heat, and disease that westerners would be unable to survive. I wondered how the French had managed to do so for close to a hundred years.

The Pentagon assignment provided an opportunity for me to attend the advance management program of the Harvard University Business School, which afforded insights into the management techniques of civilian business and some indication of the motivation of senior business executives. I can trace a number of management ideas that I used in later years to that experience. It also enabled me to establish friendships with civilian businessmen destined for top positions.

The nature of my Pentagon assignment also meant long hours before congressional committees, much of the time before Representative Gerald R. Ford's Army Review Panel of the House Appropriations Committee. I had first met Jerry Ford when he visited Korea in 1952 with Secretary of the Army Robert T. Stevens. Our association during committee hearings resulted in a warm friendship.

On one occasion while testifying in Congressman Ford's committee room just off the balcony of the House of Representatives, I was startled to hear a series of shots. As the congressman opened the door to find out what was happening, a group of men ran past. Puerto Rican terrorists, we learned later, had opened fire from the balcony on the congressmen on the floor of the House.

In the summer of 1954 Ford and I traveled together to Europe to inspect American troops and installations in Germany, including West Berlin. After being officially entertained by the Lord Mayor of Berlin one evening, we decided to see some of the city's night life. Time slipped by rapidly. Emerging from the last club, we found to our surprise that the sun was up. With some chagrin we passed through the security post surrounding the American military commandant's house in full daylight. As we parted to try to get a few hours' sleep before our first official engagement, I told the congressman facetiously that the soldier at the guard post might be from his home district of Grand Rapids, Michigan. I got the impression later that Jerry Ford slept restlessly.

On the way back to the United States, our commercial plane developed trouble after leaving Newfoundland and had to turn back, much to Representative Ford's concern because he had a speaking engagement early the next day in the United States. Checking with local U. S. Air Force headquarters in Newfoundland, I found we could hitch a ride on a C-54 that was deadheading back to the United States after having delivered a load of monkeys to Europe. Why monkeys, I have no way of knowing; what I do know is that the interior of the plane reeked.

On the way home Ford and I talked at some length about our aspirations for the future. In response to my question, Ford said he wanted to be Speaker of the House of Representatives. He had no ambition to be President.

My testifying on Capitol Hill also meant appearances before the defense subcommittee of the House Appropriations Committee, which was always something of a lark because of the irreverent directness of one of the members, Representative Daniel Flood of Pennsylvania. Rank held no awe for Congressman Flood. At one hearing he said to General Ridgway: "Skipper, you didn't win those four stars in a crap game. Now give us the straight dope." Later he turned to me: "Hey, Buster, what have you got to add to what the Skipper has said?"

Many years later when I again served in Washington as the United States Army's Chief of Staff, my duties brought a renewal of my congressional associations. One member of Congress whom I recall with particular affection is Senator Allen Ellender of Louisiana, who at the time was Chairman of the Senate Appropriations Committee. Eighty years old but still running for re-election, Senator Ellender invited me to accompany him to a testimonial dinner in his honor in Leesville, Louisiana. Seeking to convince the voters to ignore his age, he stressed the seniority he had built up over 35 years in the Senate. He had entered the Senate in 1936, he announced to the dinner guests, the year a young man named Westmoreland had been commissioned in the Army, one who was now the Army's Chief of Staff. Even ten years ago, he remarked, it would have been difficult for him to get an appointment with any top official of the Executive Branch, including the Army's Chief of Staff. Now, after thirty-five years, he had a hard time keeping Westmoreland and the others out of his office.

Following duty with the Army's manpower office, my next assignment, in 1955, was as secretary of the General Staff, in effect a kind of chief of staff to the Chief of Staff, General Taylor. As it turned out for me, it was also a kind of apprenticeship for the position of Chief of Staff. For three years I was associated with virtually all the Chief of Staff's activities during an interesting era of President Eisenhower's administration when John Foster Dulles was Secretary of State and Charles ("Choo-Choo") Wilson was Secretary of Defense.

The Vice Chief of Staff was my old commander from Fort Bragg, Willie Palmer. Dedicated to efficiency, General Palmer made a fetish of using minimum numbers of words and would spend hours with a red pencil condensing memoranda. When he sought to save money by ordering elimination of horses used in ceremonial military funerals, he incurred the wrath of a lover of ceremony, Representative Carl Vinson, chairman of the House Armed Services Committee. Eliminate the horses, Congressman Vinson telephoned the Secretary of Defense, and the Army's appropriations would be sharply cut.

Seemingly everything connected with the military was somebody's sacred cow. Still seeking ways to economize, General Palmer directed that Christmas cards not be exchanged among officers and civilian officials on the staff who associated with each other daily. Deeming the Chief of Staff, General Taylor, responsible, the Washington *Post* ran a cartoon depicting General Taylor as a Scrooge. Never having heard of General Palmer's directive, General Taylor was surprised but upon learning the true facts behind the cartoon, chose to make no change in General Palmer's action.

My first active command of a division began inauspiciously with a tragic incident in a maneuver only a week after I joined the 101st Airborne Division at Fort Campbell, Kentucky, in 1958. As any parachutist would be, I was concerned about proper wind conditions and assigned my most experienced airborne officer, Brigadier General Reuben Tucker, to check conditions on the drop zone. When he released a green smoke signal, men of the 502d Parachute Infantry Regiment began to jump. I followed.

As I came to earth, an unanticipated wind approaching twenty miles per hour dragged me joltingly across the ground. Even though I managed on occasion to get to my feet, gusts threw me down again and again. The wind dragged me several hundred yards before others who had landed ahead of me were able to collapse my parachute. Only later did I learn that the wind had dragged seven men to their deaths.

Since training even under adverse conditions is essential to a unit's preparation for battle, I wanted to continue the maneuver the next day; but with wind conditions for a jump still doubtful, I decided to make the first jump myself and on my experience base a decision whether to proceed. After a hard landing, the wind again seized my parachute and dragged me across a rough field until some of my men succeeded in collapsing the chute. Conditions were clearly unsatisfactory. I called off the jump and moved the men by truck to join the ground portion of the maneuver.

An incident related to the tragedy at Fort Campbell, I learned later, occurred at Fort Benning, Georgia, and told something of the courage and determination of the American soldier. Since the Army's basic parachute school was at Fort Benning, the commander of the school was concerned about the effect the event at Fort Campbell might have on the trainees. Assembling them, he gave them details of the accident. Jumping was a hazardous business, he remarked, and any man who wanted to withdraw from parachute training should have that opportunity. When he asked those who wanted to pull out to step forward, not a man moved.

As lamentable as was the tragedy, it had one lasting effect for the better in that it led directly to development of a quick-release parachute device designed to disconnect risers from the canopy under windy conditions. All U. S. Army parachutes are now so equipped.

As the uneasy peace in Indochina that followed the Geneva Accords of 1954 was being broken by ever-growing insurgency in South Vietnam, I began to focus the training of the 101st on counterinsurgency warfare, with emphasis on small-unit operations. An early maneuver that pitted the 101st against the 82d Airborne Division produced no abject failure in small-unit tactics but nevertheless pointed up a need for more small-unit training and the development of resourceful small-unit leaders. Performance by squad leaders was particularly inadequate.

That prompted me to create a special divisional school, which I named RECONDO, an amalgamation of the words "reconnaissance" and "dough-boy" and also "reconnaissance" and "commando." An imaginative officer, Major Lewis L. Millett, who as a captain had been awarded the Medal of Honor for a gallant bayonet charge in Korea, first headed the school. The training unit was the small independent patrol. For two weeks the men underwent mental and physical hardship, rappelling down cliffs, maintaining direction with or without compass, surviving in the woods with minimum rations, and practicing such field expedients as crossing streams with rafts made from rifles and halves of pup tents. The course ended with a three-day exercise that taxed the men's endurance. Upon graduation a man received a special patch to be superimposed on his divisional insignia: the black and white symbolized night and day and the arrowheads pointing up and down, air and ground operations. The patch soon became a mark of prestige within the division.

In addition to working to improve the division's combat readiness, I concentrated on improving the productivity of post maintenance and administrative services and on bettering relations with nearby communities. I introduced work-measurement practices into the division's maintenance units, with such success that I was asked to come to Washington to brief officials of the Bureau of the Budget in the executive offices of the White House. I also stressed a theory that I called "the stretch," encouraging soldiers and the civilian employees to extend themselves beyond normal work achievement, to stretch to do more. Since morale is the essence of achievement, when people achieve more than they think they can, morale soars.

Commanding the 101st Airborne Division afforded me an opportunity to work with the radically new concept of the "Pentomic Division," which the Army Chief of Staff had recently proposed in an effort to meet the need for dispersing troops on the battlefield in the nuclear age. Under the concept, infantry and airborne divisions would have five battle groups of 1,400 men each, each one therefore larger than a battalion but smaller than a regiment, which could be employed in battle singly or in combination. Since the battle group replaced both the battalion and the regiment, one echelon of command was eliminated in the organization, which cut down on staff overhead.

Because the Pentomic Division was a creature of the Chief of Staff, few in the Army were about to criticize it. During its test period with the 101st, the slogan was: "Our job is not to determine whether it *will* work—it is to *make* it work!" Because test officers were reluctant to tell their bosses that the organization was unsound, the concept was adopted and remained standard for several years, a prime example of the difficulty that "yes-men" can cause.

As I prepared to relinquish command of the 101st Airborne in 1960, I recommended abolishing the Pentomic Division, primarily because I had found that control of the five separate battle groups by the division headquarters and five companies by a battle group headquarters was difficult. I recommended re-establishing a regimental level headquarters, additional artillery, and better communications as necessary to give the division essential staying power. That was basically what the Army eventually adopted. In view of the way the Army had to operate in Vietnam—that is, with units large enough to counter the enemy's large units and to fight sustained combat while still able to break down when appropriate into multiple patrols—we would have been in real trouble with the Pentomic Division.

Named in 1960 to become superintendent of West Point, I relished the assignment. Aside from my pleasure at returning to a place I loved and respected, I was anxious to carry on the good work of my predecessor, Lieutenant General Garrison Davidson, in modernizing an educational institution that I consider vital to an effective United States Army.

When President Eisenhower made the appointment, he sent word that he wanted to talk with me before I reported for the assignment. When I walked into his office in the Oval Room of the White House, it was the first time I had seen him since 1946 when as Chief of Staff he had visited the 82d Airborne Division at Fort Bragg. I had first met him when he visited the 9th Division in 1944 shortly before the Battle of the Bulge.

As he had been as a general, President Eisenhower remained warm and cordial in a way that made a visitor feel relaxed and comfortable. As I sat by his desk, he reminisced fondly about his days as a cadet at West Point and his love for the Academy and what it stood for. He himself, he confided, had always wanted to be superintendent of the Academy but had never had that pleasure. Not until I rose to depart did he give advice or instructions. Walking to the door with me, he shook my hand. "The only thing I specifically charge you to do, Westmoreland," he said, "is to buck up that football team." Unfortunately, I failed in the charge. Football success at West Point means beating the Naval Academy, and my tenure coincided with the career of a great Navy quarterback and later professional star, Roger Staubach. Army won not once.

I next saw President Eisenhower when he visited West Point in 1961 to receive the Sylvanus Thayer Award, given annually by the Alumni Association to that American deemed best to personify the Academy's motto: "Duty, Honor, Country." Kitsy and I visited with him and "Miss Mamie" in their suite at the Thayer Hotel where again the President reminisced about his cadet days. He was a poor cadet compared to many, he said, inclined to be indifferent to the system. Older than his classmates, he had been somewhat intolerant of the customary hazing. Although he had longed to play football, an injured knee had ruled that out.

Presenting the Thayer Award was General Anthony C. McAuliffe, a man whom I had known since he was a captain at Fort Sill during my first tour of duty. As commander of the 101st Airborne Division at Bastogne in the Battle of the Bulge in December 1944, he had refused a German demand for surrender with one word, "Nuts!" The President in his response spoke extemporaneously, with warmth and sincerity, and stressed the responsibilities inherent in the Academy's motto. Duty, he said, was "the sublimest word in our language." That was a quote from Robert E. Lee, one fully familiar to me as a favorite of my father's. After my father's death, my mother and I had it inscribed on his tombstone.

I met Vice President Lyndon B. Johnson for the first time when in June 1961 he visited West Point to deliver the commencement address. As we drove from a nearby air base, he said he was unhappy with the speech his writers had prepared and wanted my advice as to whether he should put the manuscript aside and "speak from the heart." Unwilling to pass judgment on an unseen speech, I said only that I was confident that if he spoke from the heart, he would be well received.

The Vice President began with his prepared text. He warned of extraordinary times involving extraordinary challenge. "The Communists will find," he said, "that a nation which produced Davy Crockett and Daniel Boone and Jim Bowie is afraid of no forest and no swamp and no game of fighting, however toughly it is played." Then he put aside his manuscript. In his travels around the world, he said, he had sensed a deep yearning for freedom. He spoke of poverty, the need for education, improved nutrition, medical care. The class of 1961, he said, faced a challenge of helping all people who genuinely love freedom. He was confident that the class would "nail the coonskins to the wall."

The Vice President spoke with obvious sincerity, but I could discern that the cadets were essentially unmoved. As my friendship with him grew over the years, I came to realize that his desire to speak from the heart into the hearts of others was profound, but he had difficulty in some cases—as in that one—in communicating the depth of his feeling.

At a luncheon following the address, I saw an irrepressible politician at work. Pulling souvenir pens from a pocket, Johnson passed them to everybody at the table. That few of the recipients displayed more than casual interest appeared to escape him. Without prompting, he collected place cards from the table and carefully autographed them.

When the Vice President departed, Sergeant Willie Daniels, who was in charge of arrangements, asked Kitsy what to do with the place cards, for almost everybody had left his behind. Unaware, of course, that Mr. Johnson was a future President and was eventually to become a respected friend, Kitsy said to throw them away.

Still another speaker at the Academy during my tenure was the Nobel Prize-winning author William Faulkner, in the spring of 1962 in one of his last public appearances before his untimely death. In the course of a crowded day of appearances, Faulkner remarked that at the Military Academy he had expected to find "a certain rigidity," yet he was "pleasantly astonished to find that the questions I got came from human beings, not from third classmen or second classmen or first classmen, but from human beings . . ."*

Another man destined to be Vice President but at that time the governor of New York, Nelson Rockefeller, was among the stream of visitors which it was my duty as superintendent to receive and entertain. Taking a great interest in the Academy, he was helpful in many ways, such as rallying the New York congressional delegation behind a plan to expand the Academy.

When introducing Governor Rockefeller for a speech, I found an opportunity to needle him. When he had visited West Point years before as a member of the Dartmouth College soccer team, I reminded him, a newspaper photographer had taken a picture of the team, but young Nelson was nowhere to be seen. His father, it developed, had decreed that if he saw his son's picture in the paper, he would cut off his allowance. From all I could discern, I concluded, he had guarded his allowance well, but I detected that he was now making up for his college days by seizing every opportunity to get his picture published.

Another visitor was one of the great ladies of American history, Mrs. Eleanor Roosevelt. Over the years I developed a warm and personal relationship with her and her son John, who were living across the Hudson at the late President Franklin D. Roosevelt's estate in Hyde Park, New York. She entertained contingents of cadets and Kitsy and me on several occasions at Hyde Park following wreath-laying ceremonies at the late President's tomb. Not long before her death in 1962 I had a long conversation with her aboard John's boat, in which she had come down the Hudson and docked at West Point.

The most memorable of all visits during my tenure at the Military Academy was that of an aging General MacArthur in 1962 to receive the Thayer Award. The visit began on a potentially jarring note. Aware that the

* Joseph L. Fant III and Robert Ashley, eds., *Faulkner at West Point* (New York: Random House, 1964), p. 107.

old elevator in the Administration Building was cantankerous, I had a warrant officer insure that it was waiting to take the general and me without delay to the superintendent's office on the second floor. The doors closed smartly, but the elevator went not up but down, faster than I had ever known it to go. To the basement. The doors opened to reveal a heap of garbage. At last we headed up, but not to the second floor: all the way to the attic, where doors at the rear of the elevator opened and the general almost fell backward. Not until after a second unprogrammed trip to the basement did we finally arrive at the second floor. General MacArthur was amused. The elevator, he said, dated from his day.

We entered my office, the office he had occupied as superintendent following World War I. It, too, had not changed, he said. Sitting in his old chair, he leaned back and lost himself in thought.

When we moved to the parade ground for a review by the Corps of Cadets, news photographers complained to me that the general's unfashionable broad-brimmed hat—he was wearing civilian clothes—prevented them from getting unobstructed shots. The photographers, I told him, would like him to remove his hat. "Don't pay any attention to them," he replied. "I will take off my hat when I am ready." A few minutes later, standing in the back of a jeep, he passed before the Corps of Cadets. Removing his hat with a flourish, he placed it over his heart.

The general's physical condition, aggravated by a recent bout of flu, disturbed me throughout the visit. At lunch in the cadet mess, where he was to address the Corps, he ate little. Toward the end of the meal, he pulled a pencil from his pocket and with a shaking hand made a few notes on his place card; but when he moved to the rostrum, he left the notes behind. Standing at the lectern, his shakiness disappeared. Speaking without notes, he was a man of composure and purpose. With unabashedly colorful rhetoric, he hypnotized his audience.

General MacArthur spoke with emotion of his years in uniform, his love of West Point, his respect for the Academy's motto. To the cadets he charged: "Your mission remains fixed, determined, inviolable—it is to win our wars. Everything else in your professional careers is but corollary to this vital dedication. This does not mean that you are warmongers. On the contrary, the soldier, above all other people, prays for peace, for he must suffer and bear the deepest wounds and scars of war."

He concluded with touching emotion. "The shadows are lengthening for me. The twilight is here . . . I listen vainly for the bewitching melody of faint bugles blowing reveille, of far drums beating the long roll. In my dreams, I hear again the crash of guns, the rattle of musketry, the strange, mournful mutter of the battlefield." As his remarks neared an end, he paused between words with dramatic effect. "Today marks my final roll call with you, but I want you to know that when I cross the river, my last conscious thoughts will be—of the Corps—and the Corps—and the Corps."

As thunderous applause began, the general turned to the balcony, caught the eyes of his lovely wife, Jean, and threw her a kiss. The significance of that little exchange escaped me at the moment, but I learned later that it had a meaning. For all the apparent spontaneity of the general's address, Mrs. MacArthur confided later, he had rehearsed it time after time in the weeks before, using Mrs. MacArthur as an audience.

Although that was General MacArthur's formal farewell, he came again the following spring of 1963, to make a quiet, unpublicized visit to the Academy cemetery. I met him there and wandered with him among the headstones. He wanted, he said, to be among his old friends. For an hour I followed him and listened as he reminisced aloud about distant military heroes and his own colleagues: about Winfield Scott, who carried the burden of an unpopular war with Mexico; about George Goethals, who built the Panama Canal; about an officer who served with him in World War I; about another who commanded a division in the South Pacific; about still another who served in Korea; about another who had been an All-American center on the football team. He departed reluctantly only as dusk fell over the Hudson.

One of my goals as superintendent was to increase the size of the Corps from approximately 2,400 cadets to 4,400, roughly the strength of the Brigade of Midshipmen at the Naval Academy. Since President Eisenhower, on advice of the Bureau of the Budget, had disapproved a similar request early in his tenure, I delayed proposing it again until after the inauguration of a new President, John F. Kennedy, in 1961.

Aside from having to convince the federal bureaucracy of the need to increase the size of the Corps, the expansion also involved demonstrating to the Academy's alumni that the concomitant increase in the physical plant would do no damage to a site that they looked upon as a national shrine. Armed with a plan that satisfied me, I visited General MacArthur at the Waldorf-Astoria Hotel in New York to gain his support, then flew to the West Coast to see former President Eisenhower at Palm Springs. Acknowledging that he had earlier disapproved expansion, he said I had made such a good case that he now would support it. As an afterthought he advised me to obtain General MacArthur's blessing and was pleased when I told him he had already approved it with enthusiasm.

As the former President knew, General MacArthur's abiding hobby was football, and he had an intense love for the Army team. As a cadet he had been the team manager, and as superintendent he had developed a plan to expand the athletic facilities to include a huge football stadium along the Hudson that would be accessible to fans traveling from New York by boat. When I discussed the prospect of increasing the size of the Corps of Cadets with him, MacArthur noted that even the football team would benefit.

As I prepared to get the expansion bill started on the long trek through bureaucracy, a discussion with President Kennedy at the Army-Navy football game in December 1962 gave me an opportunity to make my point in person to the Commander in Chief. During the second half, as Navy punished Army, President Kennedy turned to me, possibly at the instigation of his military aide, a classmate of mine, Major General Chester V. ("Ted") Clifton. "General," he said, "why are there so many more midshipmen at the game than cadets?" I pointed out that the two academies operated under separate statutes, which allowed the Naval Academy 2,000 more men. "That, of course, is inequitable," I said, "and certainly unjustified on the basis of differing requirements for officers." Besides, I added quickly, "it gives the Navy 2,000 more men to draw from for a football team." That, I said with a smile, "is one reason we are getting the hell kicked out of us today."

After a further exchange during the game, the President assured me he would support an expansion bill for the Military Academy, which had to be passed by Congress. In 1963, soon after I left the Academy to command the XVIII Airborne Corps at Fort Bragg, he approved it.

I had first met President Kennedy the preceding June when he came to West Point to deliver the commencement address. He seemed particularly pleased on that occasion when the class of 1962 made him an honorary member of the class and presented him a class ring.

The night before the President's arrival, Kitsy and I assembled our three children in the hallway close to a side entrance through which, I told them, the next morning I would escort the President of the United States. All I asked of them was that they dress as nicely as they would for Sunday School.

As I entered the door with the President, Kitsy was standing with our two daughters, Katherine Stevens ("Stevie"), age thirteen, and Margaret, age six, both resplendent in new dresses, but our son, Rip, age seven, was absent. I hoped the President would fail to notice.

"General," President Kennedy asked, "is this all your family?" I sensed that I was about to be trapped, but I had to answer that there was another child.

"Boy or girl?"

"Boy, Mr. President."

"Where is he?"

"Mr. President," I answered, "you have finally backed me into a corner. Last night I told the children I looked forward to introducing them to you but that they had to dress properly for the occasion. The girls were delighted, but my young son wanted to wear his baseball uniform. I told him he would have to wear a coat and tie. 'Under those circumstances,' he said, 'I am not interested.'"

A father himself, the President roared with laughter.

Another event during my stay at West Point involving my son, Rip, then age seven, sticks in my memory. The superintendent's quarters where my family and I lived was a house built in 1820, when Sylvanus Thayer was superintendent, a house that alumni revere as a historic landmark and which Kitsy planned to restore and renovate. One day when Kitsy returned home, she smelled smoke. Investigating, she found it came from the basement. There to her consternation she found that Rip and two of his little friends had built a bonfire that already was searing the timbers supporting the floor above. Save for her chance return, there might have been no Thayer house for restoration, not to mention the fate of Rip and his friends. When I returned home that evening, Kitsy had already administered the strap, but Rip was prepared for me to repeat the punishment.

In addressing the cadets, President Kennedy's wit was winning. He began by exercising his prerogative as Commander in Chief to remit all existing cadet punishments. It might be, he said, that some cadet undergoing punishment might some day head the Army, and he was "glad to have the opportunity to participate in the advancement of his military career."

Turning serious, he predicted that the coming decade would afford West Point graduates unparalleled opportunities for service.

"Yours are not strictly military responsibilities," he said. "Therefore, they will require a versatility and an adaptability never before required in either war or peace." He spoke of "another type of war, new in its intensity, ancient in its origin—war by guerrillas, subversives, insurgents, assassins, war by ambush instead of by combat, by infiltration instead of aggression, seeking victory by eroding and exhausting the enemy instead of engaging him.

"Where there is a visible enemy to fight in open combat," he went on, "the answer is not so difficult. Many serve, all applaud, and the tide of patriotism runs high. But when there is a long, slow struggle, with no immediately visible foe, your choice will seem hard indeed. . . ."

As the President spoke, I recalled the stirring words he had uttered at his inauguration, words that the American military around the world had taken to heart as expressing the national objective for which the military was to strive:

> Let the word go forth from this time and place, to friend and foe alike, that the torch has been passed to a new generation of Americans—born in this century, tempered by war, disciplined by a hard and bitter peace, proud of our ancient heritage—and unwilling to witness or permit the slow undoing of those human rights to which this nation has always been committed, and to which we are committed today at home and around the world.
>
> Let every nation know, whether it wishes us well or ill, that we shall pay any price, bear any burden, meet any hardship, support any friend, oppose any foe to assure the survival and the success of liberty.

Yet however much those words had stirred American military men and those in the diplomatic service, there remained the inherent horror over the prospect of nuclear confrontation and proliferation. Was there no alternative to that kind of Armageddon? Following the uncomfortable years of living with John Foster Dulles' policy of massive retaliation, military and diplomatic thinkers had long sought some other way, as exemplified by Maxwell Taylor's book *The Uncertain Trumpet*† and another by a Harvard University professor, Henry Kissinger, *Nuclear War and Foreign Policy*.‡ President Kennedy in his commencement address also appeared to be searching for that alternative; and I am confident that when he made his subsequent decision to increase American commitment in Vietnam, he had in mind the concern that if aggression went unopposed in its embryonic stage, it would enhance the prospect of nuclear confrontation.

The President in 1962 and the Vice President the year before had outlined a philosophy and a challenge that were to have profound effect on the young men who heard their remarks. "Another type of war," the President had said, " . . . a long, slow struggle, with no immediately visible foe." It would be a kind of warfare that would "seem hard indeed." It was the Vice President, the man upon whom fate in the end would bestow the onus of the long, arduous struggle in Vietnam, who reiterated the pledge to help all people who genuinely love freedom.

Of those two graduating classes, eighty-one were destined to be wounded in Vietnam, thirty-two to die there.

Throughout my days as superintendent, I had an intuitive feeling that eventually I would go to Vietnam. Convinced that Communist insurgency was to be the dominant military challenge of the future, I read all I could on the subject. During my last months at the Academy in 1963, I sponsored a counterinsurgency conference at which Walt W. Rostow, later to become deeply involved in Vietnam policy as a special adviser to the White House, was the keynote speaker. Professor Rostow warned that to defeat armed insurgency, you must go on the offensive. "If you wait passively," he said, "you will be cut to ribbons."

Some six months later, my commitment to speak at West Point as commander of the XVIII Airborne Corps completed and orders for Vietnam in my pocket, I called on General MacArthur at his apartment in the Waldorf-Astoria in New York. For an hour and a half the old general talked of the situation in Southeast Asia, the personalities involved, how to deal with the Oriental. Characteristically, he expected a visitor to listen, not talk, although he would pause on occasion to solicit a nod of the head or an expression of understanding.

I would be working with a young, insecure nation, General MacArthur noted, a nation with limited military background and marginal leadership. "How should you treat the Vietnamese officers?" he asked rhetorically. "Treat them as you did your cadets: be understanding, basic in your advice,

† New York: Harper & Brothers, 1960.
‡ New York: Harper & Brothers, 1957.

patient, work with them to develop their sense of responsibility and their ability to make decisions."

Do not overlook the possibility, he concluded, that in order to defeat the guerrilla, you may have to resort to a scorched earth policy. He also urged me to make sure I always had plenty of artillery, for the Oriental, he said, "greatly fears artillery."

Our young President and the nation were becoming increasingly sensitive to the situation in South Vietnam before his tragic assassination in Dallas, Texas. Few disagreed when the New York *Times* printed on November 3, 1963:

> . . . the loss of South Vietnam to the Communists could raise doubts around the globe about the value of U.S. commitments to defend nations against Communist pressure . . . the impact on revolutionary movements throughout the world would be profound. At best, neutralism in the East-West struggle might spread. In much of Asia there might be a feeling that the Communists—under the leadership and inspiration of Peking—represented "the wave of the future."*

When I went to Washington for a final briefing before departing for Vietnam, Kitsy accompanied me for orientation by the Departments of Defense and State on distaff problems and responsibilities. As we returned to Fort Bragg, the pilot of our small propeller-driven aircraft was unable to lower the landing gear. While he circled to allow ground crews time to spread the landing strip with foam, my aide, Captain Richard Woods, moved from the seat facing me to the one facing Kitsy. Unknown to me at the time, it was a calculated action lest the plane crash and he be thrown against me. General Westmoreland, he told Kitsy, was more important to the country than she was. Kitsy bridled, but took the judgment with her usual graceful humor.

The landing tore much of the bottom from the plane, but no one was hurt. Even from the first, my new assignment was, as General MacArthur had put it, fraught with hazards.

* Quoted in *Foreign Affairs,* Vol. 53, No. 4 (July 1975), p. 653.

Chapter III
The View from Saigon

Flying into Tan Son Nhut airport on the fringe of Saigon in a commercial airliner in late January 1964 was a strange experience, a swift plunge from a comfortable, peaceful world into an alien environment, neither peace nor war but with the trappings of war. Because enemy fire had hit a commercial plane a week or so earlier, pilots of Pan American Airways DC-707s had taken to making incredibly steep, stomach-churning descents to the runways. As the plane taxied to a stop, the accouterments of war were conspicuous. It seemed odd that the pretty stewardesses, the other passengers, and I, all dressed in civilian clothes, some obviously tourists going on to other destinations, should be set down abruptly in such a setting.

Stepping from the plane, I received a less-than-impressive introduction to Vietnamese leadership. In addition to General Harkins, the U.S. commander, and a sizable group from the Saigon press corps, a representative of the Vietnamese government met me: Huynh Van Cao. As a corps commander under President Ngo Dinh Diem, I learned later, General Cao* had excelled at reporting only the good news and at avoiding battle lest casualties evoke Saigon's wrath. Father of a dozen children, he was timid and constantly afraid for his life. On two occasions during attempted *coups d'état* he was to try to take refuge in my quarters. He was one of a minority of Vietnamese who had taken comfort in the French presence years before and frequently urged that I assume command of the Vietnamese military forces and do the job for them.

With me as I arrived was a new aide, Captain David Palmer. When I had interviewed Palmer earlier at Fort Bragg, he had impressed me with his

* The Vietnamese first name, rather than the last, is the family name, but in keeping with Western practice, Americans used the last name. The Vietnamese tolerated it with commendable good grace. Because the ranks of Vietnamese general officers changed frequently, I have chosen for reasons of simplicity to refer to all grades of Vietnamese general officers as "General."

forthrightness. He told me plainly that he had no wish to be my aide because he was scheduled for a tour in Vietnam. Unable at the time to reveal that I too was headed there, I waited until after the White House made the announcement before I pinned him down. "Do I meet your requirements now, Captain?" I asked him. He allowed that I did.

Already struck with the beauty of Vietnam from the air, I was impressed as we rode into Saigon with the charm of the capital and the aura of Paris that the French had imparted to it. Spreading shade trees alleviated shimmering heat in the streets and wide boulevards. Delicate bougainvillea grew on walls surrounding pastel-colored villas and here and there clumps of colorful hibiscus. Slender, black-haired women riding bicycles displayed an impressive dignity, their *ao dai* (a kind of skirt split at both sides and worn over pajamalike slacks) flowing in the breeze. Yet the incongruity of fortifications intruded upon me in the city as it had at the airport. Atop many of the walls were concertinas of barbed wire. Chicken wire protected some sidewalk cafés against grenades. At bridges and the entrances to some buildings armed soldiers stood guard in concrete sentry boxes reinforced with sand bags.

I had lunch with General and Mrs. Harkins at a villa they occupied near the Cercle Sportif, a former French swimming, tennis, and social club. Following General Harkins' departure later in the year, the same villa was to become my home for the next four years: No. 60 Tran Quy Cap, the street named for a Vietnamese scholar and nationalist whom the French had beheaded early in the twentieth century.

Following a courtesy call on the American ambassador, Henry Cabot Lodge, I occupied temporary accommodations in the Rex Hotel, one of several downtown hotels requisitioned as bachelor quarters for American officers and men. Given housekeeping responsibility for all American services in Saigon, the U. S. Navy operated messes in the hotels and ran a small post exchange and commissary. Americans whose wives and children were present lived in rented villas throughout the city.

For all the threat posed by the enemy insurgents, the Viet Cong (a contraction of a derogatory term meaning Vietnamese Communists), life in Saigon in those days was curiously lethargic. Amid knowing nods and smiles, General Harkins was given to frequent quoting of Rudyard Kipling's dictum:

> The end of the fight is a tombstone white
> with the name of the late deceased,
> And the epitaph drear: "A Fool lies here
> who tried to hustle the East."

The South Vietnamese simply called off the war—or ignored it—on weekends and holidays and took long siestas at lunch time. At first glance there seemed little point in Americans keeping different hours, since most of the work involved dealings with the Vietnamese. Yet much more could be accomplished with longer hours and, it was hoped, the practice might impart a helpful sense of urgency. When I later assumed command, I decreed longer hours, including weekend duty, and the Vietnamese gradually went along.

Kitsy arrived in mid-February with Rip, then age ten, and Margaret, nine. (Our other daughter, Stevie, in boarding school in the United States, joined us in June.) At the kind invitation of Ambassador and Mrs. Lodge, we moved into a guest house on the grounds of the ambassador's residence until a villa being prepared for us was ready.

The Lodges were exceedingly kind to us. At our first meeting the ambassador asked me to call him Cabot, the beginning of a rewarding friendship. Both he and Emily Lodge impressed the Vietnamese with their aristocratic, urbane manners. Speaking excellent French, the ambassador developed a warm rapport with Vietnamese leaders.

Cabot Lodge himself told me with amusement of an incident that happened a few days before my arrival. Touring the Saigon zoo with the zoo's director, he was looking at a magnificent male tiger when the animal suddenly raised a leg and urinated on the ambassador. But what a diplomat was the zoo director! He began to pump the ambassador's hand, all the while congratulating him effusively. How fortunate it had happened! In Vietnam it was a sign of good luck and long life.

Ambassador Lodge had a keen sense of humor. Indeed, had it not been for a sense of humor all of us might have drowned in our tears. One of the few times the ambassador apparently saw no humor in an untoward event was when the pilot of his helicopter neglected to check his fuel gauge and had to make an emergency landing at a remote little outpost beside a river deep in enemy-controlled territory. With night coming on, there was insufficient time for a replacement helicopter to bring the ambassador back to Saigon. He had to spend the night on an LST anchored in the river.

The ambassador was sensitive to language. Noting that the U. S. Mission was using the names that the North Vietnamese called themselves and thus promulgating the propaganda inherent in them, he directed a change. No longer were we to speak of the "People's Army of Vietnam" but simply the "North Vietnamese Army." No longer the self-styled "Democratic Republic of Vietnam," but simply "North Vietnam."

One member of my family was for a time missing, which precipitated something of a crisis. That was Hannah, part beagle, part uncertain ancestry, acquired when we were at West Point. At a family conference before my departure, we had decided that Hannah was to be given to friends, but after I had left something happened to that decision. Traveling at my expense by commercial air, Hannah somehow got diverted from Saigon; she finally showed up in Bangkok, much to Rip's, Margaret's, and Kitsy's relief.

My family arrived in Saigon in the midst of a campaign of terror aimed at

Americans, even though the American role in 1964 was still strictly advisory. It had begun on February 3 with the first direct attack on an American installation in Vietnam, a strike by a small band of terrorists against a compound housing U. S. Army advisers to a South Vietnamese Army force in Kontum City in a remote region known as the Central Highlands. One building burned and one American soldier was wounded.

A few days later a bomb exploded in a Saigon bar, killing five American soldiers. Two days after that a length of pipe filled with explosive nearly demolished the bleachers at the Pershing Sports Field, an American recreational facility in Saigon. The explosion occurred during a baseball game when many wives and children were in the stands. Although numbers of Vietnamese normally attended those games, not a one was present that day, which gave one the uneasy feeling that our hosts knew more than they told us. The explosion killed two Americans and wounded twenty-five, but the toll could have been higher had not two additional lengths of pipe failed to go off.

The day before Kitsy and the children arrived, terrorists killed an American military policeman on guard at the Capitol Kinh Do theater in downtown Saigon where Americans and Vietnamese guests were viewing a Sunday afternoon movie. The terrorists then planted an explosive charge in the lobby. Suspecting what was about to happen, Marine Captain Donald E. Koelper jumped to the stage and warned everybody to get down. Ironically, Captain Koelper was one of the two men killed in the explosion. Fifty others, including women and children, were wounded. The American community gathered at plane side the next day to pay final respects to Captain Koelper, posthumously promoted to major, and watch as the Navy Cross for valor was placed ceremoniously on his casket.

The flurry of terror against Americans stopped almost as suddenly as it had begun, giving rise to the theory in some circles that the Viet Cong, or VC, had started it without approval from their supporters in Hanoi, capital of North Vietnam. Not yet ready for a confrontation with the United States, the Communist leaders had probably ordered a halt.

Yet that theory lost some credibility when on May 2 a shaped charge blew a hole in the hull of the U.S.S. *Card,* a World War II escort carrier being used as an aircraft and helicopter ferry, which sank at its Saigon dock. The next day a terrorist riding a bicycle threw a grenade into a crowd watching salvage operations on the *Card,* wounding a Vietnamese civilian and eight Americans. The incident occurred minutes after Ambassador Lodge had left the scene.

Shortly before Secretary of Defense McNamara landed at Tan Son Nhut for a visit in May, Vietnamese police found terrorists rigging detonating wires beneath a bridge along a street that the Secretary was sure to use on his way into Saigon. McNamara was visibly upset and his confidence in the Saigon regime he had come to embrace was obviously shaken.

All security, including protection of American installations, was at the time a Vietnamese responsibility, for the Americans had only a handful of military police. It was more luck than efficiency that the explosives under the bridge were found.

Except for a Vietnamese guard at my villa, I had no special security arrangements during my first months in Saigon. I rode about the city fairly inconspicuously in an old black Chrysler that had been sent from Cambodia after the government there had ousted an American military assistance group.

Once I had taken over from General Harkins, my security was entrusted to the Vietnamese Military Security Service. At first a jeep with guards in civilian clothes preceded my car, another following. So rude were the guards, blowing whistles and yelling at people to get out of the way, that I insisted on a single policeman on a motorcycle, acting quietly and courteously, to precede me with any guards the Vietnamese deemed necessary following in a jeep. That was the usual arrangement, but sometimes two jeeploads of guards would show up at my quarters. Then I would know that the Security Service had received recent word that I was high on the Viet Cong's assassination list.

(Following Kitsy's departure from Vietnam in 1965, she was driving in Honolulu when she heard over her car radio that I had been assassinated. She pulled up and telephoned the radio station, but the staff could be of no help. Only after headquarters of the Commander in Chief, Pacific, cabled Saigon did she find out that the report had been a misinterpretation of an Associated Press dispatch noting that I was on the assassination list, something Kitsy had long known.)

My driver when I first arrived was a Vietnamese named Vinh. After my former driver from Fort Bragg, Sergeant Al Boman, arrived in Saigon, he replaced Vinh, but Vinh and his colleagues soon contrived to make the sergeant lose face. When Boman called for me at a Vietnamese social function, the Vietnamese told him I had already departed, so that when I did leave, I had no car. Since Boman wanted to join the U. S. Army Special Forces anyway, we agreed that I would give in and bring back Vinh. Although the Vietnamese never informed me, I knew that Vinh, who spoke English and Chinese in addition to his native tongue, was actually a captain in the Military Security Service and no doubt reported frequently on my activities. Since I kept no secrets about my travels from Vietnamese or Americans, that made no difference to me.

Neither Kitsy nor the children had special security arrangements at first. Kitsy drove herself around Saigon in my private car, a Ford Falcon shipped from the United States, but after I became COMUSMACV in June 1964, the Vietnamese furnished an armed guard to accompany her. A guard also went with the children when they left the house. American military policemen and a nurse rode the bus that carried the children to the American Community School near Tan Son Nhut. Wire mesh covered the windows as protection against grenades, and military police maintained a twenty-four-hour guard at the school, rifles at the ready. Kitsy said years later that the experience must have made an indelible impression on Margaret because it has taken a figurative gun at her back ever since to make her go to school.

One of Rip's first essays at school told, with some exaggeration, of his impressions. "We ride on a bus with wire on the windows so grenades won't get us and soldiers with real guns so the VC won't get us. When the bus stops, we march in front of two lines of soldiers. Guards are all around us and a big one on the roof with a machine gun to shoot down the VC planes."

As a professional soldier, I have seldom feared for my own life, and I have had to accept the grim fact that men under my command get killed. Having my family constantly exposed to death was another matter. Seldom have I been as nervous as on those occasions when the children were for some reason delayed in getting home.

For all the terror and concern, the American community tried to live as normally as possible but as time passed had to give up certain amenities. When military police discovered unexploded bombs in plant pots around a swimming pool used by Americans, I decided I had to close the pool. When I found it necessary to close motion picture theaters, Kitsy often showed films for groups of children in our villa. When departing for their homes, the youngsters dutifully left in twos and threes, avoiding either being alone or walking in large groups that would present a ready target.

Despite the presence of military police, the American Community School was an island of normalcy. Started two years before my arrival, the school met requirements of American accrediting associations. The students—who included some Vietnamese who elected to pay tuition to attend—had such activities as a glee club, drama club, honor society, athletic teams, and a Junior-Senior prom. The thirty-one-member class of 1964 made a senior trip to the coastal resort of Nha Trang, although for security reasons travel had to be by air. The yearbook was *The Gecko,* named for a Vietnamese lizard that croaks, "Gecko, gecko."

The Vietnamese have it that if a gecko outside your house croaks nine times straight, you will have good luck. Quite a colony of geckos lived around our villa, but no matter how many times I counted, no gecko of mine ever got beyond eight. Maybe they were trying to tell me something.

My concern for the safety of American dependents went beyond the Viet Cong, for the seething local political turmoil in Saigon also posed a threat. Demonstrations, sometimes violent, by students and religious radicals, Buddhists and Catholics, were the order of the day.

Since my house was near a pagoda used as a headquarters by a militant group known as the An Quang Buddhists, some of the demonstrations occurred on my street, Tran Quy Cap. During one demonstration the Vietnamese police guarding our grounds threw down their weapons and fled, leaving the gates to the grounds flung wide. In my absence Kitsy and the children—and Hannah—ran to close the gates, then retired to watch in concern lest the demonstrators storm the house.

The incident prompted me to devise an expedient for their protection. Reluctant to call on American soldiers to guard the villa lest I show lack of confidence in the Vietnamese, I obtained gas masks for all of us and stored them along with a supply of tear gas on the second floor. If the demonstrators charged, I was prepared to flood the house with tear gas.

On another occasion Kitsy was shuttling children home in her car when she found the street ahead blocked by demonstrators. Herding a dozen children and Hannah on foot ahead of her, she took refuge with them in the nearby house of the deputy ambassador, U. Alexis Johnson. When the demonstrators finally passed and she made it back home, she was piqued to find that rather than my pacing the floor in concern, I was sleeping, unaware that a demonstration had occurred. She woke me and insisted that I suffer through every detail.

The city was particularly turbulent with demonstrations the night Kitsy and I went to a special showing of the U. S. Information Agency's film on President Kennedy's death, *Years of Lightning, Day of Drums*. Watching the film in an auditorium in the center of Saigon, I became aware near the end that tears were filling my eyes. Although I can be emotional on occasion, I am usually more controlled. I looked about me to find the ambassador's eyes also moist and tears flowing down Kitsy's cheeks. Almost as one, we realized that our reaction was not to the film, however sad, but to tear gas. The movie's soundtrack had concealed the noise of demonstrators and police efforts to quell them.

On another occasion Kitsy was attending services in a small Episcopal church near our home where the officiating American minister was noted for his lengthy sermons. On that day he had hardly begun to speak when an explosion in the nearby British Embassy shook the church. "In the name of the Father, the Son, and the Holy Ghost," the minister intoned, "the American Church is dismissed." It was a sermon that set a record for brevity.

In typical fashion, Kitsy early in her stay threw herself into a heavy schedule of activities. She was hostess for innumerable dinners for the ambassador, deputy ambassador, heads of other U.S. agencies, visiting congressmen and senators, entertainers, Vietnamese officials. I often filled out the guest list with young American officers on leave in Saigon after long months in the field, both to provide them a pleasant evening and to give the others some feeling of what it was like where the fighting went on.

Kitsy did her own cooking for a while but later employed a chef named Trung, who was lazy but skilled in both French and Chinese cuisine. Trung and the other servants lived on the grounds with their wives and a pack of children that constantly increased in numbers. Living with his fifth wife, Trung had twenty-one children, although not all, thank heavens, were living with him. One of the maids shaved her head bald to prove to her boyfriend that she loved him. The Number One Boy, Hai, was particularly devoted, always waiting for me in the foyer no matter what hour I returned. Although the Vietnamese government provided the servants, I supplemented their pay and paid the wives whenever they worked.

Aside from activities with American children of all ages, Kitsy often worked as a Red Cross nurse's aide at a small U. S. Navy hospital in Saigon and one day a week flew to Nha Trang to work in a U. S. Army field hospital. Concerned lest some serious VC incident at some time overwhelm the little Navy hospital with patients, she fitted out our guest house with cots and air mattresses so it could be used as a temporary infirmary. With the wives of other officers, she formed a unit of Red Cross nurse's aides among the wives of senior Vietnamese officials. Although the Vietnamese ladies were appalled at first that the American wives would work at menial tasks, they soon joined in. Kitsy became particularly close with Madame Khanh, wife of the Vietnamese Premier, and often worked with her at a leprosarium in Saigon. When a disastrous flood struck the northern part of the country, she flew with Madame Khanh and her husband in a Vietnamese plane to survey the damage and exhibit the South Vietnamese government's concern.

Kitsy and I both had some difficulty adjusting to Vietnamese food, notably to *nuoc mam,* a pungent fermented sauce made of drippings from sun-cured fish, which the Vietnamese eat on their rice as a basic source of protein. As Kitsy put it, you ate it in self-defense as the only way to be able to tolerate the odor of it on everybody else. A bottle of *nuoc mam* once broke on my plane, and we almost had to don gas masks in order to survive.

On my first trip outside Saigon, the chief of Phu Yen province fed me a delicious salad of huge langouste-type lobsters covered with delicious mayonnaise, but either the flies that also fed on it or something else about it gave me the first of many bouts with dysentery. The ubiquitous flies disturbed Kitsy particularly at the start. At her first Vietnamese tea, a Vietnamese lady delicately shooed the flies off a cake, then passed it graciously to an unbelieving Kitsy. For a while Kitsy carried a large purse where she would slip food when no one was looking, but in time she became as adept as the next one at shooing off the flies before passing a plate.

Ranks of the American community increased in the summer when dependent sons and daughters attending college in the United States came for visits. They had to pay their way to California but were entitled to one round trip per year from the West Coast to Saigon by military aircraft on a space-available basis.

Perhaps the most difficult problem connected with our children was one Kitsy brought on us herself. Determined that Margaret should have a pony, she ordered one sight unseen shipped by rail from Nha Trang. It turned out to be a stallion with no love for anything or anybody. He kept the grounds around our villa well fertilized and harassed the guards by rushing the gates whenever an automobile horn sounded. Another of his favorite tricks was biting, at which he excelled. When he finally bit Margaret, even Kitsy had had enough. We had to get rid of him or he would have destroyed us all.

After seeing a movie called *The Great Escape* about British prisoners of war in World War II in Germany, Rip took to tunneling. One evening I crawled inside his tunnel for a look and came out horrified. He had practically dug under the wall surrounding the grounds of the villa. I had to put a stop to the enterprise.

Fortunately for my peace of mind, another of Rip's escapades came to my attention only after it was over. Dressed in green fatigues and carrying an AKS—an automatic rifle with a folding stock used in those days by the VC—he climbed atop the wall around the grounds of the villa. One of the guards spotted him. Convinced by size, dress, and weapon that the figure on the wall was a VC, he raised his weapon to fire. Only at the last second did he realize it was Rip.

Aware that I was to assume Paul Harkins' position, I spent as much time as possible during my early months traveling in South Vietnam in order to get to know the country, the people, the military forces, and the nature of the fighting. Except in Saigon and its immediate environs, where I moved by car, I usually traveled by helicopter or in a C-123 cargo plane converted for passenger use, the *White Whale,* a name that carried no special connotation except that the plane had a big belly and was painted white. In the hope of improving relations, which had sunk to a deplorable low, between the U. S. Army and the American press and television, I usually took along a reporter selected from a roster maintained by the MACV (Military Assistance Command, Viet Nam) information officer.

As the Vietnamese like to remark, Vietnam resembles two baskets borne on either end of the Oriental peasant's bamboo carrying pole. Constituting the baskets are two of the world's most densely populated and richest rice-producing regions: in the north, the delta of the Red River; in the south, the delta of the Mekong River. The pole is the narrow curved central portion of the country, composed of jungle-covered mountains and a constricted fertile coastal strip.

Under the century-long rule of France, the country was divided into three parts. The northern basket was a protectorate known as Tonkin with Hanoi the capital; the carrying pole was a protectorate known as Annam—called by the Vietnamese "the Center"—with the capital the ancient imperial city of Hué; the southern basket was a colony known as Cochin China with Saigon the capital. With Laos and Cambodia to the west, those divisions made up what was known as French Indochina.

With the actual—though intended to be provisional—creation of two Vietnams by the Geneva Accords of 1954 which ended the French Indochina War, the dividing line was roughly the center of the pole at the 17th parallel, not far from the site of a wall that early in the seventeenth century had separated two dynastic factions vying for supremacy over long years before the French conquest. A demilitarized zone (DMZ) extended five kilometers on either side of the demarcation line.

A newcomer to South Vietnam at that time was struck from the first by the social fragmentation of the population, a fact that sharply complicated the American role. The divisions are attributable to a number of factors: history, geography, underdeveloped communications, and religious and ethnic differences. The contrast with North Vietnam was sharp, for in the North the people are more homogeneous and Communist rule permitted no dissent.

The history is replete with disparity and dissension, a 2,000-year heritage of subjugation, occupation, rebellion, division, and internal disorder. By dividing Vietnam into three entities, the French throughout their rule consciously promoted division in order to discourage nationalism. About the only things that united the three parts of the country during the French era were a common heritage, a common language, and a common hatred of the master. The last was the strongest bond, which had enabled a minuscule minority of Communists under a charismatic leader with the *nom de guerre* of Ho Chi Minh to rise at the conclusion of World War II and forge a military arm called the Viet Minh capable of defeating the French in 1954 at a place known as Dien Bien Phu.

Even when separated from the north, South Vietnam is an elongated country, approximately the same length as California but only half as wide, a fact that contributes markedly to the society's fragmentation. Saigon is 500 miles from Hué. Using a military comparison, the country is a third again as long as the Western Front in World War I. At the time of my arrival, approximately 80 per cent of the 16 million people lived on but 40 per cent of the land. Some 40 per cent of the land was uninhabited and covered with jungle, scrub brush, elephant grass, or swamps, an ideal setting for nourishing guerrilla warfare.

In addition to the fertile flatlands of the Mekong Delta stretching southwestward from Saigon, a thin strip of arable lowland extends along the coast almost the entire length of the country. A notable exception is south of Hué where the precipitous chain of the Annamite Mountains dips with haunting beauty into the sea. Access from the south to South Vietnam's two northernmost provinces of Quang Tri and Thua Thien and to the cities of Hué and Quang Tri is by a single road hugging the coast and crossing the lofty Hai Van Pass, so that the northern provinces of South Vietnam are in effect cut off from the rest of the country. Unhappy over the Geneva Accords, the North Vietnamese leaders were particularly piqued that they failed to get Quang Tri and Thua Thien provinces.

The most rugged terrain in South Vietnam is in the northwest where the Annamite Mountains reach heights of 8,000 feet. Jungle covered, sometimes with a double or triple canopy of growth, the mountains extend spinelike southward across nearly two thirds of the country, finally dissipating below Dalat, a town which the French developed as an Alpinelike resort with impressive hotels and villas. The mountains are broken in the center of the country by the Kontum Plateau, usually called the "High Plateau," and farther south by the Darlac Plateau. The entire center region of South Vietnam is usually called the Central Highlands. A small, isolated outcropping of high ground is to be found far to the southwest alongside the Cambodian border, known as the Seven Mountains.

South Vietnam was divided into forty-four provinces, which may be likened to American states, although considerably smaller, each headed by a province chief. The provinces were subdivided into 246 districts, similar to American counties, each with its government located in a "district town." The level of government with which the peasant identifies was the village, which consists of several hamlets and might contain 10,000 people or more. The country had about 2,500 villages and 16,000 hamlets. Even during the long-departed halcyon days of the imperial court at Hué, with its historic and exotic trappings, few people had associated themselves with a national government, for real rule was exercised in a kind of enlightened despotism by local mandarins. To the peasant a central government had long meant foreigners or Vietnamese who acted like foreigners.

The country's underdevelopment, particularly in communications, was a major factor in its fragmentation. Major highways, for example, are few. The most important is Route 1, following the coast from Saigon all the way up to the DMZ. Route 14 winds north from Saigon over the Darlac and High Plateaus. Route 20 south from Dalat is the avenue for transporting vegetables grown in the highlands to Saigon, while Route 4 is the lifeline for moving rice from the Mekong Delta to the capital. Few major roads traverse the width of the country. The principal railroad is a narrow-gauge single track generally paralleling Route 1. However, the country has over 3,500 miles of navigable canals and rivers, mostly in the Mekong Delta, which constitute a primary mode of transportation. The Vietnamese peasant with his weather-beaten face beneath conical bamboo straw hat propelling his sampan along the waterways is a traditional and picturesque sight.

As South Vietnam emerged as an entity, the country had only one major port, Saigon, connected with the sea by the Saigon River, although the second largest city, Danang, in the north, had some port facilities. The only major airfield was Tan Son Nhut. Through the French period Vietnam had existed almost solely to fill the coffers of Paris, and few were the efforts to bring it into the modern era.

Crossed by several arms of the Mekong River, the low-lying delta in the south, like the river valleys all along the coast, is subject to flooding, particularly when typhoons strike. While the climate year round is tropical, it can be chilly at night in the high country and in the northern provinces. The climate is critically affected by the monsoons or seasonal winds. Between mid-May and mid-October, the southwest monsoon covers most of the country with low-lying clouds and drenches it with rain, but the high mountains shield the northern coastal regions from the rains. Between mid-October and mid-May, the northeast monsoon brings dry and cooler winds from the Asian mainland. So little rain falls during that season in most of the country that rice paddies dry up and cracks crease the soil. Yet during this same period the northern provinces get most of their precipitation, usually in the form of drizzle accompanied by fog, a condition that the French knew as *crachin*.

The Vietnamese people in the North and South are descendants of several Mongoloid tribes who lived in southern China and gradually moved southward, reaching the lowlands of the south late in the seventeenth century and driving out native Cambodians. Much of the social structure and cultural traditions are of Chinese derivation, but the Vietnamese have retained a strong, distinct ethnic identity. Yet because of later settlement, the Vietnamese of the south have fewer ties to national traditions than do those in the north, and speech accents are distinctly different.

Religious divisions in South Vietnam are sharp. Although some 12 million of the people are nominally Buddhist, only about 5 million actively practice the faith, but they were well-organized in a Unified Buddhist Association with a large militant faction, the An Quang. The roughly 2 million Catholics are a legacy of the French era, many of whom were among some 900,000 northerners who fled North Vietnam in 1954 upon conclusion of the Geneva Accords. To many South Vietnamese, the number of northern Catholics holding positions of authority in their armed forces and their government was a source of considerable discontent.

Two minority religious sects wielded a political influence out of proportion to their size. Both were militantly anti-Communist and for many years maintained autonomous armies, in effect constituting separate states within the state.

The larger is the Cao Dai, whose close to 2 million adherents are most numerous northwest of Saigon adjacent to Cambodia in Tay Ninh province. On the outskirts of Tay Ninh City stands one of the most bizarre temples I have ever seen, decorated with plaster cobras and dragons in brilliant birthday-cake colors. The nave is dominated by a single giant staring eye. The religion has drawn on various other religions, including Buddhism and Catholicism, and the practitioners revere such diverse saints as Jesus, Buddha, William Shakespeare, Victor Hugo, and Winston Churchill.

Less numerous are the Hoa Hao, located in the Mekong Delta southwest of Saigon, who practice a kind of reform Buddhism appealing to the poor. The religion dates only from the World War II era, founded by an individual named Huynh Phu So, whom the Viet Minh ambushed and killed in 1947. Accompanied by Secretary McNamara, I once called on Huynh Phu So's aging mother, whose "palace" was a modest thatched-roof dwelling in the steaming delta alongside a canal in An Giang province. Members of the sect cared for her as if she were a queen bee.

Because political parties were long outlawed throughout Vietnam by the

French, those that were formed clandestinely were militantly nationalist and established an antigovernment tradition that was slow to dissipate. Most of these parties had originated in North Vietnam and the leaders were still mainly North Vietnamese who had come south after the Geneva Accords, which to many South Vietnamese made the parties' leaders suspect. The two that had maintained appreciable influence in South Vietnam were the VNQDD, so called from the party's initials in Vietnamese, and the Dai Viet. During the politically turbulent early months of my stay in South Vietnam, the Dai Viets provided many of the leaders contributing to the unrest. Also active was the Can Lao, a party begun originally as a kind of intelligence arm of the South Vietnamese government. In addition to these, there were scores of splinter parties, and both students and labor were active politically, sometimes militantly.

Politics and political parties in South Vietnam were in the main confined to the towns and cities, for the Vietnamese peasant is in general apolitical, anxious to be left alone to pursue a simple life that seldom affords much wealth but, in a benign climate and a fertile land, little hardship either. Having undergone long foreign occupations—Chinese, French, Japanese—the people are strongly xenophobic.

Adding to divisiveness in South Vietnam is the presence of ethnic minorities totaling over 2 million people, including a million Chinese who live mainly in an adjunct of Saigon known as Cholon and exercised a paramount role in the nation's business. One unusual group of Chinese was known as the "Sea Swallows," several hundred Catholics who fled Communist China in the early 1950s, stopping temporarily in Thailand before being authorized to settle deep in the Ca Mau peninsula of the Mekong Delta. Their leader, Father Hoa, spent most of his time in Saigon soliciting funds. Because of favored treatment by the government and considerable publicity, many Vietnamese in the vicinity resented them.

Another large group is the Khmers, ethnic Cambodians, numbering some 800,000, who live mostly in the Mekong Delta and practice a form of Buddhism. Smaller groups are the Chams, ethnically Vietnamese but Moslems and Hindus, and the Nungs, a Thai tribe of Chinese origin, refugees from North Vietnam and mainly animists. Among the ethnic groups there is little social intercourse or intermarriage, thus perpetuating the differences.

The most intriguing of the ethnic groups are the Montagnards, ethnically Indonesian, who number about 700,000 in some thirty-five tribes and inhabit the thinly populated Central Highlands. A primitive people, they live in quaint "long houses" and practice "slash-and-burn" agriculture, moving on to a new area when productivity of the land declines. Most are animists who worship the sun and stars and are highly superstitious. Vietnamese contempt for them as *moi,* meaning savages, has left a tradition of distrust and unrest among the tribes.

On one of my first visits to a Montagnard village, the tribesmen honored me with an age-old ritual inducting me into their ranks. The men, wearing only loin cloths, and their women, who were topless long before the practice caught on elsewhere, formed ranks leading to a large clay urn filled with potent rice wine. I was to sip from the urn with a straw while an attendant constantly poured more wine to keep the level high.

Having no desire to drink the stuff and possibly invite another round of dysentery, I merely went through the motions of sipping. Since the level of the wine failed to go down, the toothless old chief figured something was wrong with my straw. He took it, tested it with betel nut-stained lips, and passed it back. I had no choice at that point but to drink some of the wine.

That accomplished, the village's prettiest young woman approached and fixed on my arm a copper bracelet, symbol of tribal membership. I was a tribesman; she was my wife. I left before our relationship reached a point that could incite Kitsy's concern.

Following the Geneva Accords, approximately 90,000 southerners moved to North Vietnam, mainly Viet Minh activists and their families, while Communist political cadres stayed behind. Thus a framework on which to hang an insurgency was present when in 1956 the South Vietnamese government—which had refused to accede to the Geneva Accords—declined to go along with a proviso of the Accords for nationwide elections. In mid-1957 the insurgency began according to long-established pattern: terrorism to impress the people with the insurgents' strength and to coerce them either to join the revolt or to refuse to co-operate with the government; murder and kidnapping of government officials and school teachers; tax collection by coercion; destruction of bridges, schools, government installations—anything to disrupt the orderly functioning of government.

As practiced by the Viet Minh against the French and destined to be repeated by the Viet Cong against the South Vietnam government, the insurgency was predicated on three phases in keeping with precepts developed by the Chinese Communist leader Mao Tse-tung. The man who headed Ho Chi Minh's armed forces, a former school teacher, Vo Nguyen Giap, had studied the precepts during a period of hiding in China.

In Phase One, the insurgents remain on the defensive but work to establish control of the population and conduct terrorist and guerrilla operations. In Phase Two, regular military forces are formed, guerrilla attacks increased, and isolated government forces engaged. In the climactic Phase Three, large insurgent military units go on the offensive to defeat the government's large units and to establish full control of the population. A peculiarly Vietnamese aspect of the final stage is the *khoi nghai,* the general uprising, wherein the people theoretically arise and overthrow the government.

The *khoi nghai* remained a major part of Vietnamese Communist theory, though no uprising had occurred against the French. It had, in fact, been unnecessary because a war-weary France had given in following two tactical defeats. The first was in May 1954 in northwestern Tonkin at Dien Bien Phu, where the French had elected to hold with a garrison of 13,000 men and were overwhelmed after a Viet Minh siege. The other was in the Central Highlands near the town of An Khe in the summer of 1954 where the Viet Minh trapped one of the better French units, Groupement Mobile 100, only recently redeployed from Korea. As the French tried to fight their way to the coast, the Viet Minh staged one ambush after another along Route 19 and even after conclusion of the Geneva Accords destroyed the last survivors in a brutal massacre at the Chu Dreh pass. Those two victories were destined to color the thinking of the Communists in the new insurgency in South Vietnam and were always on my mind as a reminder of Communist tactics and methods.

By the time I reached Vietnam, the Viet Cong's organization and methods were well established. From at least mid-1959 the North Vietnamese had begun to export their organizational knowledge and revolutionary expertise by means of southerners formerly in the Viet Minh who had gone north after the Geneva Accords. They joined the political cadres left behind in the south to create an infrastructure, or shadow government, in hamlets and villages. Supervisory echelons were established at district and province levels and in five "military regions." In late 1960 the Communists created a front organization, the National Liberation Front, designed to attract antigovernment dissidents of whatever persuasion. Over-all control was exercised from North Vietnam by means of the Lao Dong (Communist) party's regional committee for South Vietnam, known as the Central Office for South Vietnam, or COSVN (pronounced "cosvin"). Both political and military operations were under COSVN's control.

The Viet Cong's methods were both violent and political. The more visible was the violent, but it was only an adjunct to the political, a way to coerce recalcitrants, eliminate effective government officials, and demonstrate strength. The focus was on enlisting the masses in hamlets and villages so that in time the government centers in the towns and cities would be surrounded and choked. Only after political organization was complete was the insurgency to move into the predominantly military second and third phases.

The military arm of the Viet Cong gradually evolved into three parts: guerrilla, local, and main forces. The guerrillas comprised two types: village guerrillas, who by their presence put a village on the side of the VC, and combat guerrillas, younger men who might roam far from their home villages to do the dirty work of sabotage or assassination. The local force companies existed at the district level, local force battalions at the province level. The main forces, composed of battalions and later regiments and divisions, were organized at the interprovince level.

VC companies usually put about eighty-five men in the field and VC battalions about 350, which made them roughly comparable in size to units of the South Vietnamese Army. The American units that later joined the battle were larger, an Army company usually containing about 130 men, a battalion, 650; U. S. Marine Corps units were still larger.

Whereas the infrastructure and guerrillas could hide among a population that was either sympathetic, apathetic, or cowed, the regular VC units had to have safe base areas or sanctuaries. There they could rest, conduct training and indoctrination, and prepare for operations. The bases were usually located within a reasonable distance of densely populated areas and often had elaborate, literally underground facilities, such as hospitals, command posts, kitchens, and printing plants, all connected by vast tunnel complexes. No one has ever demonstrated more ability to hide his installations than did the Viet Cong; they were human moles. Some base areas dated from the days of the Viet Minh and were vast and well fortified, such as War Zone C northwest of Saigon in Tay Ninh province, where headquarters of COSVN was for long reputedly located; War Zone D in a vast woods north of Saigon; and the "Iron Triangle," in an angle formed by two rivers a few miles northwest of Saigon, convenient for operations against the capital.

The political atmosphere that developed in South Vietnam during the early years of the republic's life was conducive to the growth of insurgency. Heading the government as self-proclaimed President, a respected nationalist, Ngo Dinh Diem, both a mandarin and a Catholic, ruled authoritatively and employed oppressive police methods. Despite pressure from the United States for reforms in exchange for continued military and economic aid, Diem changed little. More and more he and his family, with which he surrounded himself, alienated large segments of the population. The fall of 1961 saw a sharp upswing in VC attacks that included for the first time temporary capture of a provincial capital, Phuoc Vinh, in Phuoc Long province where the VC decapitated the province chief and put his head in a commode. That same province, ironically, was destined to serve as the test case when the North Vietnamese in 1975 began wholesale violation of the 1973 Paris cease-fire agreement, apparently seeking to measure how the United States would respond.

President Kennedy in 1961 reacted by increasing the size of the small American advisory group that was supporting the South Vietnamese Army, known as the ARVN (pronounced "arvin"), for "Army of the Republic of Vietnam." He provided more advisers, including some U. S. Army Special Forces (Green Berets) and for the first time, a few logistical support units. By the end of 1963 American military strength in South Vietnam had risen to about 16,000.

Although increased American contributions made a difference in the fight against the VC, the political situation in Saigon grew worse and worse in a drama played out before the sharply critical eyes of American newspaper men and television camera teams. In the course of a nationwide antigovernment demonstration by Buddhists in mid-1963, American television screens shocked their audiences with graphic footage of Buddhist monks dousing themselves with gasoline and setting themselves afire.

As it became evident that a group of South Vietnamese generals was contemplating a *coup d'état* to oust Diem, Ambassador Lodge, having pretty much despaired of Diem's being able to run the country, interposed no objection. General Harkins for his part still had confidence in Diem; in any event, where was the alternative to him? In a notable interregnum while President Kennedy was away for the weekend, officials in Washington passed word to Saigon to the effect that the United States would make no objection to Diem's removal. The *coup d'état* occurred on November 1, 1963. Despite having anticipated Diem's ouster, American officials in Saigon and Washington were dismayed that in the process Diem and his brother, Ngo Dinh Nhu, were murdered. It was a pivotal event: however negative or even neutral the American role, the United States had played a part in the internal governmental affairs of South Vietnam. That inevitably contributed to a feeling of obligation among American officials in Washington.

Just over three weeks later, President Kennedy, too, died at the hands of an assassin.

The objective of the American Military Assistance Command in Vietnam was

> To assist the Government of Vietnam and its armed forces to defeat externally directed and supported communist subversion and aggression and attain an independent South Vietnam functioning in a secure environment.

Although the exact wording of that objective might change from time to time, it remained essentially the same throughout American involvement. A key to achieving it was to create viable South Vietnamese armed forces by means of military aid and advice.

In the first years of American aid beginning in late 1954, with the conventional invasion of Korea still fresh in mind, the Pentagon's thinking was to create a South Vietnamese Army capable of resisting an invasion long enough to enable an international force to intervene in order to circumvent overt aggression. That led inevitably to the creation of a conventional force organized into divisions and corps. When an insurgency rather than conventional invasion developed, many observers condemned the United States Army for having created an army in its own image.

I disagree. What was the alternative—small mobile units not unlike guerrilla units? That would be to ignore the fact that in combatting an insurgency, the government's forces are of necessity on the strategic defensive. By very definition the insurgents have the initiative, capable of striking where, when, and in such strength as they wish and are able to muster, unless government forces can intercept them in advance. Responsible for defending multiple installations, the government must have forces strong enough either to defeat the enemy's attacks or to hold out long enough for larger reaction forces to arrive. Except for some special units, government forces, unlike guerrillas, cannot be elusive.

As I learned early, the insurgents recognize no rule confining them to small guerrilla units, and if the government's forces are small or fragmented, those forces are peculiarly vulnerable. There is nothing to prevent larger units from being broken down into smaller, more mobile forces when the occasion demands; it is considerably more difficult suddenly to transform small, disconnected units into large cohesive ones.

That is not to say that counterinsurgency warfare requires no special training. Men must learn patrolling, how to fight at night, how to turn the enemy's ambush tactics to advantage. All those operations put a premium on small-unit leadership. The government must also have local militia capable of taking much of the burden of static defense off the regular forces and a mobility well in excess of that of the guerrillas.

When I arrived, South Vietnam was divided for purposes both of military operations and of regional government into four corps zones: The I ("Eye") Corps Zone consisted of the five northern provinces. The II Corps Zone, largest but least populous, consisted of the twelve central provinces. The III Corps Zone consisted of eleven provinces around Saigon, although the capital and its immediate environs (Gia Dinh province) formed a separate command, the Capital Military District. The IV Corps Zone consisted of all the sixteen provinces of the Mekong Delta. The corps commanders were also regional governors, responsible for civil administration as well as for military operations.

Although the armed forces served under the Defense Ministry, the Chief of State was Commander in Chief. A Joint General Staff stood above headquarters of the four services, and in theory the Chief of the Joint General Staff was the military head of all the armed forces and directly in charge of the ARVN; but in reality, except when the Chief of State was nominal, real power remained with and was routinely exercised by him from the palace. That made it vital that the head of the American military command have direct access to the palace. Similarly, in theory, the South Vietnamese Air Force, Navy, and Marine Corps had separate commanders reporting to the Chief of the Joint General Staff.

The ARVN in early 1964 had 192,000 men organized in nine divisions, an airborne brigade, and four ranger battalions. There was also a separate marine brigade, which with the airborne brigade served as a general reserve under the Joint General Staff, while each of the ranger battalions was earmarked as a reserve for one of the corps. The South Vietnamese Air Force had 190 aircraft, mainly armed T-28 training planes, while the United States provided an additional 140 planes (mainly fighter-bombers) and 248 helicopters. The South Vietnamese Navy had a small number of landing craft, patrol boats, and minesweepers.

An additional 181,000 men were in the militia, which consisted of two components, the Self-Defense Corps and the Civil Guard, later to be designated Regional Forces and Popular Forces, respectively. The Popular Forces were part-time soldiers for local defense of hamlets and villages, while the Regional Forces might be employed throughout a province. Some 18,000 other men were in company-size civilian irregular defense groups (CIDG), first created by the U. S. Central Intelligence Agency (CIA) but later transferred to the U. S. Army Special Forces. Those were composed mostly of Montagnards or other inhabitants of remote regions and in the early 1960s manned twenty-five fortified outposts known as CIDG-Special Forces camps, primarily charged with border surveillance.

For all the best efforts of the small band of Americans that had preceded me to Vietnam, the South Vietnamese armed forces were poorly trained and poorly led, and the Regional and Popular Forces even more so. Even after the French, late in their stay, had created a national army, they themselves had provided most of the officers and noncommissioned officers, so that little leadership tradition or experience existed among the South Vietnamese. That is impossible to create in a day. The troops had American World War II weapons and equipment, which were adequate at the time against a grab-bag assortment of weapons used by the VC, but that was soon to change.

The American role was strictly advisory. The MACV at first furnished advisers at all levels down to provinces and regiments, covering not only combat operations but other of the diverse functions of military forces such as budgeting, training, schools, logistics. Only later, beginning in 1964, were there enough advisers to extend down to district and battalion levels. The South Vietnamese officer and his American opposite were known as "counterparts." In addition to advising, training, equipping, and developing the local armed forces, the United States by 1964 was also providing some combat support, primarily by means of a few helicopters.

My first combat operation in Vietnam was less notable for anything that happened to me than for my introduction to one of the more colorful characters in the United States Army, Brigadier General Joseph W. Stilwell, Jr. "Young Joe," as he was known, in deference to his famous father, the late General "Vinegar Joe" Stilwell, who gained renown in Burma and China during World War II, had either inherited or cultivated his father's temper and acid tongue. He commanded the U. S. Army component of MACV, known as the U. S. Army Support Command. Flying with General Stilwell into the Mekong Delta, I watched in surprise as he took over as one of the door gunners. Young Joe was apparently never happier than when he was manning a machine gun in a helicopter, piloting a plane, or making freefall parachute jumps. However adept he was at those jobs, they were hardly proper assignments for a senior officer who had other responsibilities.

When I was inspecting the billets of one of Joe Stilwell's units, he provided a lesson in one-upmanship. Struck by the fact that the official company bulletin board was located against a backdrop of female pin-ups, I spoke to the company commander.

"Lieutenant," I said, "do you require your men to read this bulletin board?" When he replied that he did, I rebuked him for so locating it that the men might be distracted by the pictures. "Somebody," I commented, "might object."

General Stilwell suddenly broke in. "By God, sir," he said, "you are right. I never thought of it that way. We'll poll the unit, and if we find somebody who objects, we'll have him transferred."

In a parachute jump some time later in the United States, General Stilwell incurred multiple bone fractures that kept him in a hospital for months, yet he still returned to jumping. In 1966, while hitching a ride across the Pacific in an outmoded Thai aircraft, which I suspect he piloted, the plane disappeared, never to be found.

On the hazards of air travel in Vietnam, I received an early lesson. The sharp crack of small-arms fire coming close or hitting a helicopter became a fairly common occurrence, but weather too posed problems. On a trip with Ambassador Lodge to a northern province in a Caribou, a small cargo aircraft, the pilot found the airstrip weathered in under a ceiling of only 300 feet. Since the airstrip was alongside a railroad, he flew above the trace of the railroad until he found a small hole in the cover, dropped through it, and followed the railroad at a level so low that the wings often were below the tops of nearby trees. So harrowing was the flight that the ambassador's knuckles and those of some of the accompanying reporters were white from gripping the arms of their seats.

That particular trip introduced me to Lodge's skill in dealing with the South Vietnamese. When we reached a village where Premier Nguyen Khanh was to speak, he did so from beneath a canvas awning, while the villagers listened in discomfort full under the tropical sun. En route to the next village, the ambassador suggested that Khanh should share the conditions of the people. At the second appearance, Khanh dutifully left the shade and read his speech while standing in the sun. An improvement, Ambassador Lodge told him, but the next time he should throw away his speech, move among the people, and talk with them like a friend. At the third village, Khanh followed the instructions all the way.

Close calls in helicopters or planes occurred with regularity. Flying one day through the *crachin* weather of the northern provinces, my pilot suddenly pulled back on the controls to avoid a mountainside by the narrowest of margins. When I was taking off on another occasion from an American base, the pilot of another helicopter failed to see my helicopter and headed straight for it. My pilot pulled up only at the last second with just enough vertical lift to save us.

My closest call happened early in my stay when with Barry Zorthian, head of the Joint United States Public Affairs Office (JUSPAO), and Alfred

Hurt, deputy chief of the Agency for International Development (AID), I visited a remote outpost in the wild A Shau Valley amid mountainous jungles near the Laotian border. As our Caribou taxied to the end of a crude runway for the turnaround, several enemy riflemen took us under fire.

The first rounds tore through the nose of the plane, demolishing the instrument panel, damaging the mechanism controlling the nose wheel, and slightly wounding pilot and copilot. The two nevertheless managed somehow to swing the plane about and gun the engines for takeoff while bullets ripped the thin walls of the craft and the other passengers and I sat helpless. As we lifted into the air, bullets were still striking the plane, wounding the crew chief and several Vietnamese soldiers and missing Zorthian, Hurt, and me only by inches.

Considering the amount of air time I logged in Vietnam, I was no doubt lucky that my narrow escapes were few. My younger daughter, Margaret, would have it otherwise. When a year or so later I was having dinner with my family in Hawaii, Margaret said a blessing that went on and on. She blessed everybody in the family, plus grandparents, uncles, aunts, cousins, seemingly everybody with whom she was even remotely familiar. When she at last concluded, I rebuked her for engaging in such a long-winded grace.

"But Daddy," Margaret protested, "it works."

Chapter IV
Instability and Uncertainty: 1964–1965

Despite the military nature of my assignment in South Vietnam, it was impossible to keep my activities entirely separate from the political turmoil that soon gripped the country, in large measure because most of those in the center of the turmoil were the military leaders with whom I had to deal. For just over a year Saigon was to seethe with political unrest that was close to chaos and eventually led to a crisis posing the specter of defeat.

Those Americans in Washington and Saigon who had seen removal of Ngo Dinh Diem as a panacea for South Vietnam's political troubles soon possessed clear evidence that they had erred. Indeed, if they interpret the events that followed as I do, they would have to conclude that Diem's downfall was a major factor in prolonging the war. Not for close to two years after Diem's death was real political stability destined to emerge.

The government that succeeded Diem's was a military junta headed by one of Diem's senior generals and perhaps the most esteemed of the lot, General Duong Van ("Big") Minh (so called because he was large for a Vietnamese and because another prominent officer of lesser physical stature bore the same name). The new government quickly proved to be without policy or plan. Despite high-sounding declarations about establishing genuine democracy, the junta was stymied by indecision. Probably the most noteworthy accomplishment was negative—a thorough shake-up of the governmental structure and police and a purge of anybody even remotely suspected of having supported Diem. So cowed were the police that they got the nickname "White Mice."

One general who found himself outside the ruling junta was Nguyen Khanh. Something of a loner among the generals, Khanh himself had been plotting to overthrow Diem when the coup of November 1, 1963, upset his reckoning. Aware of Khanh's machinations, the junta attempted to keep him away from Saigon by shunting him off to command the distant I Corps; but Khanh soon found allies among others who felt put upon by the new rulers, notably General Tran Thien Khiem, who commanded the III Corps surrounding Saigon. Khiem controlled two ARVN divisions, the 5th and 7th, whose locations close to the capital situated them ideally for supporting a *coup d'état*.

By the time I got to Saigon, in January 1964, the temporary gaiety that had followed Diem's downfall had disappeared. The atmosphere fairly smelled of discontent—workers on strike, students demonstrating, the local press pursuing a persistent campaign of criticism of the new government. Possibly planted by Khanh and his fellow conspirators, rumors abounded that the government planned to embrace neutralism, as recently urged in a speech by President Charles de Gaulle of France. Word had it that three pro-French members of the junta were working on a plan to adopt neutralism and negotiate with North Vietnam for an end to the war. To almost everybody, neutralism was the first step to a surrender to the Viet Cong.

On January 28, two days after my arrival, General Khanh slipped into the capital in civilian clothes. The next night, troops, armored cars, and tanks controlled by Khanh's confederate, General Khiem, moved swiftly into the city and surrounded the homes of government leaders and top generals of the junta. Late in the evening Khanh's American adviser, Colonel Jasper Wilson, passed word of what was afoot to General Harkins, who alerted Ambassador Lodge. Neither Lodge nor Harkins elected to interfere, possibly because there was little they might have done at that late stage to alter the outcome. This subsequently gave rise to erroneous speculation that the American leadership had had advance knowledge of the coup and condoned it.

In the middle of the night I hurried to MACV headquarters, there to wait with Paul Harkins for whatever might develop. Before daylight Khanh quietly took over the headquarters of the military high command on the outskirts of the city near Tan Son Nhut. As dawn came, Saigon was quiet, the people moving about their business, Khanh and his allies in full control. The American community was shocked but relieved that the takeover was bloodless.

Khanh put the four leading generals of the junta under comfortable but nonetheless restrictive house arrest in the mountain resort of Dalat, whence the four came to be known collectively as the "Dalat generals." In the months to come they were to serve as a discomfiting astringent in Khanh's struggle to stay in power. To simplify recognition of the new government by foreign countries, Khanh retained Big Minh as an ornamental Chief of State while reserving real power for himself as Premier. He also, in effect, put Minh under house arrest. Ostensibly for Minh's own protection, police surrounded his residence in downtown Saigon, the old imperial palace known as Gia Long. I visited Minh there several times, sometimes playing tennis with him on a court behind the palace, other times finding him contentedly cultivating orchids and exotic birds.

Big Minh was something of an anomaly among South Vietnamese generals. A consummate politician with genuine charisma for the Vietnamese people, he actively shunned the power that others less gifted in human relations avidly sought. Minh was nevertheless intensely patriotic. He always carried an ugly bamboo swagger stick, with which Japanese interrogators had knocked out his front teeth when he was a prisoner during the Japanese occupation; carrying the stick, he said, reminded him of what it was like to lose one's freedom. While shunning the responsibility inherent in power, he would fight anybody who he thought was out to scuttle his country. Lacking what he considered a viable alternative, he would reluctantly accept leadership himself. In the last few days of his country's independent existence, he was destined to come again to power for the sad purpose of presiding over his country's surrender.

As for Khanh, he was relatively unknown to the American community except for those few who had worked closely with him, such as his adviser in the I Corps, Colonel Wilson, who thought highly of him. Khanh was a cocky little man, about thirty-three years of age, who imagined himself a South Vietnamese version of Ramon Magsaysay, who in earlier years had brought stability to the Philippines. He was one of only a handful of officers whom the French had allowed to obtain a classical French military education.

Yet however little we knew of Khanh, Washington was quick to endorse him under the same rationale as always: he was the man in charge, so what choice was there? When Secretary McNamara visited the country soon after the coup, he came with instructions to embrace Khanh both figuratively and literally. At a public appearance in Hué, McNamara actually put his arms around Khanh, a kind of performance for which the undemonstrative McNamara was singularly ill-equipped by nature but which he carried off with some aplomb.

Khanh soon demonstrated considerable energy in visiting the countryside so he could be seen by the people at staged public rallies. He also tried to disassociate himself from any legacy of the French by such acts as changing the French name of the big square near the Catholic cathedral in Saigon to that of John F. Kennedy. Yet the uneasiness that was intrinsic to the South Vietnamese crown soon afflicted Khanh. To mitigate the danger of a *coup d'état,* he altered sector boundaries so that the 7th Division, which was getting something of a reputation as the "coup division," would fall directly under the Saigon high command rather than the III Corps, a headquarters critical to any attempted coup. He also sharply restricted use of the airborne and marine brigades, keeping them as a kind of "Praetorian Guard" to protect him against other troops that might support a coup. Khanh soon took up residence in the old French naval commander's quarters beside the Saigon River, whence in emergency he might escape downstream in a sturdy boat to a villa he maintained at the seaside resort of Vung Tau and from there make his way to France. An airborne infantry company protected his house.

One night Khanh's guards sounded the alarm, triggered by a well-meaning effort by American advisers to avoid interfering with Saigon's heavy daytime traffic by moving incoming tanks from the Saigon port after dark. As the tanks clanked harmlessly through deserted streets near the river, Khanh's guards hustled the general, Madame Khanh—who tripped and bruised herself painfully—and their children into a waiting boat and sped down the river to Vung Tau. It was late into the next day before anybody could determine the Premier's whereabouts. I personally went to Vung Tau and convinced Khanh to return to Saigon. Embarrassed by the incident, he saw it as a loss of face.

Feeling insecure, Khanh wanted to demonstrate that he could and would visit any region of Vietnam, however remote. On one occasion he gathered his close confidants and persuaded General Harkins to accompany the party to Plateau Gi, one of the most remote spots in the country, a Montagnard village with several French buildings at more than 6,000 feet altitude in rugged mountains northeast of Kontum City. Inadequate preparations had been made for the stay, and the party had no blankets and shivered through a cold night.

Still another time a nervous Khanh flew with his immediate entourage to Phu Quoc Island off the south coast in the Gulf of Siam. There the VC learned of his presence and shelled his accommodations. When he tried to flee in his plane, they shelled the runway. Khanh telephoned me in desperation to send a helicopter, but by the time it arrived, workers had repaired the runway and the plane had taken off.

Because Khanh was aware of how effective aircraft could be in supporting a *coup d'état,* he assiduously courted the head of the South Vietnamese Air Force, Air Vice Marshal Nguyen Cao Ky. When Ky in 1964, recently divorced from a French wife, married a beautiful South Vietnamese airline hostess, Khanh staged an elaborate party for bride and groom at an expensive Saigon hotel. Amid Khanh's concern for his personal safety, officials in Washington soon discovered that American endorsement was not in itself sufficient to create political stability, and without that, the wary, insecure Vietnamese people were reluctant to commit themselves to the government. The government forces still controlled all the province and district capitals, but officials and military officers suffered so intensely from a "caserne mentality" that they seldom ventured into the countryside. For anyone to travel the roads without heavy armed guard became increasingly perilous; American dependents were forbidden to travel by any means other than air.

Nor was the South Vietnamese house the only one displaying disorder. Having taken opposite positions on the advisability of the Diem coup, Ambassador Lodge and General Harkins were scarcely speaking. Not long after my arrival, the ambassador showed me a small office alongside his that he wanted me to occupy so that we could work closely together; he appeared taken aback when I reminded him that I was a subordinate responsible to my boss, Paul Harkins.

Some of the antipathy between the two may have resulted from differing views of the gravity of the situation. Ambassador Lodge better understood the immensity of the task, the fact that the United States had yet found no glue to hold the South Vietnamese political patchwork together. So pessimistic was he that he asked me to choose a possible haven to which, in emergency, the Americans might retire for evacuation. (Like Khanh, I selected Vung Tau.) General Harkins, on the other hand, was optimistic to the point of fault, which was the basis for his continuing difficulties with American reporters, who found his enthusiastic appraisals sharply different from the word they received from American advisers in the field.

So exacerbated were relations between American newsmen and American officials that on one occasion a young David Halberstam of the New York *Times* reputedly drove by General Harkins' villa, shook his fist, and vowed to "get" him. Given half an opportunity, Paul Harkins well might have reciprocated.

Perhaps conflict between newsman and official was inevitable. Aside from possessing a native optimism, General Harkins as American commander hardly could have been expected to accent the negative. He and other American officials were in Vietnam to execute national policy made in Washington, and bad-mouthing the Vietnamese was no way to do it. In addition, American officials were guests in a sovereign state and under compulsion to accord at least some honor to the wishes of their hosts. Reporters, on the other hand, were looking for the negative. If one accepts the philosophy that American society expects people to do the right thing, then it is news only when somebody does the wrong thing.

Saigon in those early days was one of the world's less desirable assignments for newsmen. A faraway, alien place, it had little attraction for American readers, so that nothing short of the sensational was likely to gain space in the newsman's home paper. Finding fault was one way to achieve the sensational, and finding fault with an Oriental regime with little background in or respect for Western-style democracy was easy. Furthermore, newsmen were unrestrained by the bonds of official duty that affected American officials. If the regime of Ngo Dinh Diem collapsed, that removed what the reporters saw as an evil, and, unlike American officials, they bore no responsibility for whatever might ensue.

In contradiction to their distinguished colleague Drew Middleton, of the New York *Times,* who observed that a reporter's task is "to report the event, not try to influence the course of events," other American newsmen in Saigon soon confused reporting with influencing foreign policy. When their peers back home rewarded two of them with a shared Pulitzer Prize, the pattern for those who followed was set. To many of their successors, the young iconoclasts were folk heroes whose record demonstrated that the more criticism and the more negativism, the greater the possibility of recognition and reward.

In those early days the newsmen were sometimes closer to the truth than were American officials, for there can be no question but that Paul Harkins was overly optimistic. I recall one exchange, for example, during Secretary McNamara's visit that I found incredible.

"Paul," said McNamara, "how long will it take to pacify this country?"

General Harkins replied: "Mr. Secretary, I believe we can do it in six months. If I am given command of the Vietnamese, we can reverse this thing immediately."

On the occasion of a farewell dinner at the Caravelle Hotel as General Harkins prepared to leave South Vietnam in June 1964, he emphasized that he was an avowed optimist. "I leave Vietnam," he said, "convinced that the tide is going to turn soon."

General Harkins was a gentleman and a popular commander. Having been George Patton's deputy chief of staff during World War II, he had the positive, self-confident approach that had succeeded so well with Patton. South Vietnam, however, was a different kind of war.

An incident that occurred when the former Vice President Richard M. Nixon, under the sponsorship of Pepsi-Cola, visited South Vietnam in February 1964 further exacerbated the relationship between Harkins and Lodge. It was my first meeting with Nixon, although as commander of the 101st Airborne Division in 1958 I had had to send a company to Puerto Rico in case men had to be parachuted into Venezuela to rescue the Vice President and Mrs. Nixon from hostile mobs. I was impressed by his determination to stand fast in Vietnam and by his recognition that some catalyst had to be found to motivate the Vietnamese people. Ambassador Lodge, apparently conscious of the sharp change from his former role as Nixon's Republican running mate in the 1960 presidential election to his current position as a diplomat in a Democratic administration, passed the word that Nixon was not to receive official VIP treatment.

When Nixon asked to visit a Vietnamese village, General Harkins arranged for helicopters for his party and asked me to be the escort. Upon learning that, Ambassador Lodge was disturbed and forbade Harkins to provide air transportation for the press. Yet when our helicopter reached a secure hamlet not far from Saigon (incidentally, Big Minh's birthplace), we found the press corps waiting *en masse,* the reporters and cameramen having driven to the scene by taxi. Nixon was delighted. Lodge was irate.

Some of the disorder in the American house was also attributable to ambiguity in Washington's 1962 directive creating MACV. After considerable bickering between the Departments of Defense and State, General Harkins was charged with "direct responsibility for all U.S. military policy, operations, and assistance," and on "U.S. political and basic policy matters" he was to "consult with" the ambassador. Harkins deemed that this arrangement made him, if not the ambassador's coequal, then not his subordinate either.

The ambiguity remained until President Johnson, in July 1964, assigned retired General Maxwell Taylor to succeed Lodge. The new ambassador was to

> have and exercise full responsibility for the effort of the United States Government in South Vietnam . . . I wish it clearly understood that this overall responsibility includes the whole military effort in South Vietnam and authorizes the degree of command and control that you consider appropriate.

Thus, after I assumed command of the MACV, there was never a question as to my relationship with Ambassador Taylor. He was the boss; I was, in effect, his deputy for military affairs.

Like most diplomats I have known, Ambassador Lodge disliked administration. Whereas most embassy staffs are small and thus require minimal administrative effort by the ambassador, the staff in Saigon, linked as it was with the military and various civilian agencies, was sizable, the responsibilities multitudinous. The U. S. Mission was Washington bureaucracy in minuscule, each agency reporting back to its parent agency and centralization occurring only in Washington in the person of the President himself. Rather than to exercise close control through his staff, Lodge's method of trying to bring the hodgepodge together was to deal personally with a few intimates.

Lacking firm direction from the ambassador, the various activities of the Embassy were inevitably fragmented; the CIA contingent was particularly determined to go its own way. Because all agencies were closely involved in pacification—that vital program designed to bring security and government control and services to the countryside—the need for co-ordination in that field was especially acute. When I assumed command, I urged Ambassador Lodge to make MACV the executive agent for pacification, to which he agreed in principle, but he left the country before ordering it. As so often happened in South Vietnam, long months lengthening into years were to pass before anything was done about putting that important function under tight managerial control.

Pacification was the ultimate goal of both the Americans and the South Vietnamese government. A complex task involving military, psychological, political, and economic factors, its aim was to achieve an economically and politically viable society in which the people could live without constant fear of death or other physical harm. It was an effort to improve the quality of life, to improve sanitation, drainage, roads, pagodas, schools, teachers, dispensaries, communications facilities, administrative offices; and to enable the people to pursue their occupations: fishing, tilling the land, raising water buffalo, chickens, pigs, and bringing produce to market. Fundamental to pacification was security, and as long as insurgents were raiding, robbing, molesting, and killing in South Vietnam, the government forces would have to spend their time keeping the enemy out of hamlets and villages rather than improving the welfare of the people.

In an effort to learn from an earlier pacification experience, I went with Barry Zorthian and Al Hurt to Malaya to study how the British had dealt with the long insurgency there that ended in the mid-1950s. Our escort was Robert Thompson, later knighted, who had been head of the police during the Malayan insurgency and then head of the British Advisory Mission to Vietnam for police operations.

Although it was an enlightening visit, so many were the differences between the two situations that we could borrow little outright from the British experience. While committed to Malayan independence, the British still constituted the government and thus commanded both their own and native civilian officials and military forces. That enabled them to place a unified committee of three officials—political, military, and police—at every level, from the top to the hamlet, with the political official in over-all charge. In addition the insurgency in Malaya had been mounted by ethnic Chinese who, unlike the Viet Cong, were distinguishable from the bulk of the populace. It was also a relatively small insurgency, lacking sanctuaries and major support outside the country. What I did bring back from Malaya was reiteration of the importance of centralized control from top to bottom.

Trying to achieve some measure of co-ordination in pacification, I proposed to Ambassador Lodge's deputy, David G. Nes, that we create a committee composed of the deputies of all agencies, with Nes as chairman. The committee was in the midst of its fifth meeting, achieving, I thought, a considerable degree of essential coordination, when Nes was summoned from the conference room to Lodge's office. He returned red-faced and flustered. "Gentlemen," he announced, "the Nes Committee has just been disbanded. The meeting is adjourned." I have yet to learn why Ambassador Lodge took that step; I had assumed Nes had discussed the arrangement with the ambassador.

After I had become commander of MACV, on June 20, 1964, and Lodge, having won the Republican presidential primary in New Hampshire, had resigned to participate in the upcoming political campaign, I again proposed the concept of MACV as executive agent for pacification; but the new ambassador, General Taylor, rejected the proposal. He opted instead for establishing a Mission Council composed of the heads of all U.S. agencies in South Vietnam, including the military, and chaired by the ambassador.

Meeting weekly, the council was an excellent vehicle for co-ordination, considerably better than the Nes Committee since it had real authority; but it provided no means for concentrating specifically on tight management of pacification. A U.S. team at the province level had military, AID, and CIA advisers but no one man in charge. Only at the lower district level, where a military man performed all advisory duties, was there centralized control. Although later in the year I established within MACV a special staff agency to co-ordinate all military support of pacification, the Embassy still exercised only loose control over the pacification programs of all American agencies. I am convinced we fell a year or more behind what we could have accomplished by failing at that time to establish one head of the program.

After having met Maxwell Taylor in Sicily in 1943, I saw him the following year in England while awaiting D-Day. In the spring of 1944, when he commanded the 101st Airborne Division, he asked me through his assistant division commander, General McAuliffe, to join his division. Having long yearned to be a paratrooper, I was tempted, yet I was reluctant to switch units such a short time before D-Day. Still, it was with mixed emotions that I learned my division commander turned down my release.

Impressed with General Taylor, I regretted missing the opportunity to serve with him, but as it turned out, our postwar careers were to be closely associated, to include my service with him when he was Eighth Army commander in Korea and later the U. S. Army Chief of Staff. As Chief of Staff, General Taylor had to fight desperately to prevent the Chairman of the Joint Chiefs, Admiral Arthur Radford, from decimating the Army in favor of the Navy and Air Force.

In 1959, after his four-year tour as Chief of Staff, General Taylor retired from the Army, unhappy over the Eisenhower administration's policy of "massive retaliation," and presented his views in his lucid book *The Uncertain Trumpet*. President Kennedy, in 1961, called him out of retirement to serve as White House military adviser, during the course of which duty he impressed the President with the need for the Army to be prepared to fight small wars and to counter a Communist strategy of "wars of national liberation." President Johnson subsequently designated General Taylor as Chairman of the Joint Chiefs of Staff.

An excellent choice for the Saigon ambassadorial post, General Taylor brought to the assignment not only vast military experience but also a brilliant intellect and considerable tact, although in the volatile atmosphere of South Vietnamese politics, the latter was destined on at least one occasion to be severely tested. A gifted linguist with knowledge of five foreign languages, he could converse readily with the South Vietnamese in French. When he assumed his duties in early July 1964, he was already familiar with the complexity of the situation, having made a number of official fact-finding trips to South Vietnam from 1957 on, the last two in company with Secretary McNamara as recently as the preceding March and May. He had also been at Honolulu in June when Secretary McNamara, Secretary of State Dean Rusk, and CIA Director John McCone reviewed the Vietnam scene with Ambassador Lodge, the CINCPAC (Commander in Chief, Pacific), Admiral Harry Felt, and me.

During the McNamara-Taylor visits to Saigon and Honolulu, I found the thinking in Washington on increasing the American commitment in South Vietnam, possibly to include bombing North Vietnam and even introducing American combat troops, far more advanced than anything we were considering in Saigon. Despite a serene setting overlooking Pearl Harbor, the Honolulu meeting took place in an atmosphere of considerable gloom. For my part, I reported that "the entire military situation is tenuous but not hopeless." If political stability could be achieved, I believed the South Vietnamese could eventually handle the VC, and at that time an invasion by North Vietnam seemed remote.

Political stability was the big question, for after a brief period of relative calm following General Khanh's *coup d'état,* the political broth had begun to boil in such a way that had it not been so serious and tragic, it would have done credit to the most absurd *opéra bouffe.* The foment centered on the long enmity between Buddhist and Catholic, complicated by all the other divisions in Vietnamese society and possibly by VC influence within the militant Buddhist movement.

With the particular assistance of the New York *Times* and American television cameras, the Buddhists had played a major role in events leading to the downfall of Diem, only to find that Khanh's government afforded them few concessions. Their leaders, such as Thich (for priest, or reverend) Tri Quang, long a militant, clearly wanted a dominant voice in the government. Starting in May, the Buddhists took to the streets of Saigon and Hué, prompting the Catholics in turn to stage counterdemonstrations.

Unlike the situation the previous year when the Buddhists had made a case for religious persecution, they failed this time to convince the American press that their demands were other than political, possibly because Khanh was careful to avoid incidents between demonstrators and police. In any event, no young newspaperman-crusader such as David Halberstam, who had shared a Pulitzer Prize for his provocative reporting during the Diem era, emerged this time to parade their cross before the world.

Yet this time Khanh was inclined to grant the Buddhists considerable concessions, which disturbed his fellow generals. I warned Khanh that he was alienating those who were capable of upsetting his regime, but he was either intimidated by the Buddhists or sincerely believed that by embracing them he might gain a measure of popular support for his government. The generals would have ousted Khanh in a moment had they not been aware of how dotingly Washington embraced him and of how determined the American Embassy was that he last at least until the U.S. presidential election in November.

The crisis was building when on August 2 and 4 incidents occurred in the Gulf of Tonkin between North Vietnamese patrol boats and two American destroyers, the U.S.S. *Maddox* and U.S.S. *C. Turner Joy.* After using the incidents to gain broad authority for military action in Southeast Asia from the Congress, President Johnson decided to launch retaliatory air strikes against the patrol boat bases in North Vietnam. Deeming that those events had put the South Vietnamese people in a mood to accept tighter governmental controls, Khanh devised a plan to form a new government under terms of what became known as the "Vung Tau Charter." With obvious pride, he invited Ambassador Taylor, others of the U. S. Mission, and me to Vung Tau for a polished briefing on it. The charter abolished the Chief-of-State position held by Big Minh, for whom Khanh had no love, and established a President with close to dictatorial powers. A Military Revolutionary Council of senior generals was to elect the President, who was to be Khanh himself. Khanh seemed surprised at the cool reception his plan got from the Americans.

Although the generals dutifully rubber-stamped Khanh's gimmick, Tri Quang and his allies among student militants saw it as a threat to their aspirations. Tri Quang's main demand was withdrawal of the Vung Tau Charter. One demonstration followed another, and again Khanh allowed no interference by either police or troops.

As demonstrations continued, Khanh grew increasingly nervous, fearing assassination. Late in the night of August 26 his emissaries routed the Chief of the Joint General Staff, General Khiem, former commander of the III Corps, from his bed, accusing him of plotting Khanh's overthrow. But the next day Khanh knuckled under to the demonstrators and withdrew the charter. So furious were the senior generals at Khanh that he proffered his resignation, but knowing how Washington felt, the generals were unable to accept it.

As street fighting between Buddhists and Catholics broke out in Saigon and rumors of a *coup d'état* abounded, General Khanh removed himself to the cool climate of Dalat, leaving the government to a caretaker, a Harvard-trained economist, Dr. Nguyen Xuan Oanh. The Americans called Oanh "Jack Owen," a name General Harkins had given him after getting to know him that cold night spent at Plateau Gi.

Hardly had Khanh left the city when Jack Owen called a press conference. Making no reference to the temporary nature of his assignment, he announced that he was in control of the government because Khanh was sick. He was, added Jack Owen, "more sick mentally than physically."

As a general practice, I always tried to maintain an apolitical posture in South Vietnam lest political involvement interfere with my duties as military adviser, but on this occasion Ambassador Taylor asked me to go to Dalat to determine Khanh's intentions. Khanh received me at a time when several senior Vietnamese generals were waiting outside, on the theory, I am sure, that the generals would pass the word of my visit and the apparent implication that the Americans still endorsed him. Still concerned about a possible *coup d'état,* Khanh nevertheless assured me that he would soon return to Saigon. He arrived on September 3 and resumed control from a newly obsequious Jack Owen, but when he announced that he was meeting a Buddhist-student demand for release of the four "Dalat generals," new trouble stirred.

Amid growing rumors of an imminent coup, I went to headquarters of the 7th Division to sound out the attitude of the commander, Colonel Huynh Van Ton, and try to discourage him if he was involved in a new plot. Over lunch, Ton's adviser, Colonel Edward Markham, and I talked at length with Ton. He assured me in sincere tones that I had no cause for concern.

I was sleeping at home as daylight neared on Sunday, September 13. The telephone rang. It was the MACV duty officer. After driving through the night from the Mekong Delta, a young American captain, Raymond R. Rau, had arrived, breathless and excited, with word that several thousand ARVN troops, including tanks, were marching on Saigon to overthrow the government. An adviser to a ranger battalion, Captain Rau had thought at first that his unit was departing on a routine operation, but as he gradually became aware that the kilometer markers along the road revealed an approach closer and closer to Saigon, he grew suspicious. Putting together various incidents he had observed during the night, he realized what was happening: *coup d'état.* General Westmoreland, he decided, should be warned. He and his sergeant inched their jeep forward until they were past the last South Vietnamese vehicle, then gunned it, his sergeant all the while reminding him he would either be a hero or be court-martialed.

When Rau finally found MACV headquarters, it was 5:15 A.M. On the basis of the inconclusive evidence Rau possessed, a colonel who happened to be present refused to allow a telephone call to disturb me at such an hour, but a young major, the duty officer, thought otherwise. Remarking that as duty officer he was in charge, he rang my quarters. I was on the scene within fifteen minutes.

The leaders of the coup were a former III Corps commander and Minister of the Interior, General Lam Van Phat, whom Khanh had recently ousted as one of his concessions to the Buddhists; the commander of the IV Corps, General Duon Van Duc, who had been recalled by Khanh from Paris where he had been working as a waiter; and the man who only a few days before had assured me so vehemently that I had no cause for concern, the commander of the 7th Division, Colonel Ton. I was to recall Ton's duplicity some months later on the eve of what turned out to be another coup, when the Air Force commander, Air Vice Marshal Ky, warned me that I should pay no heed to what a Vietnamese said but should instead judge him by his actions alone.

The rebel forces soon controlled much of Saigon, with machine guns set up in the streets and tanks patrolling, while over Radio Saigon General Phat announced that he had deposed Khanh and taken over the government. Yet the compound of the Joint General Staff and Tan Son Nhut airport remained in the hands of forces loyal to Khanh.

Establishing my Combat Operations Center as an emergency command post, I telephoned Alexis Johnson, Ambassador Taylor's deputy. Johnson was a former ambassador to Thailand, whom Dean Rusk had hand picked to provide Taylor, a military man, with a senior diplomatic assistant. Acting ambassador while Taylor visited Washington for discussions with the President, Johnson joined me at my command post. Through much of the day the two of us were on the telephone to various leaders, including both Duc and Phat, seeking to avoid bloodshed and endeavoring to put an end to the rebellion.

Another whom I telephoned was the Chief of Staff of the Joint General Staff, General Nguyen Van Thieu, while my Air Force assistant sought out Air Vice Marshal Ky, whose attitude toward the coup could prove decisive. Neither Ky nor Thieu, we found, was involved. Indeed, Ky assumed personal command of a squadron of hand-picked pilots and ordered them to hover over Saigon, planes loaded with bombs, as a threat should the troops move against the compound of the Joint General Staff or Tan Son Nhut or should the plotters' reinforcements try to enter the city.

Because telephone communications to the IV Corps command post had been disrupted, it was late in the day before I was able to contact Duc's and Ton's American advisers, but at my bidding they hastened to Saigon to find and try to influence their counterparts. Duc's adviser, Colonel Sammie N. Homan, set out to render General Duc ineffective by getting him drunk on his favorite brand of scotch, but in the process got himself stoned. He staggered into the operations center about 4 A.M., saluted drunkenly, and in a blurred voice stammered: "Sir, mission accomplished!" I sent him to my quarters to go to bed. When he arrived at the house, Kitsy was unable to ascertain from an incoherent Homan or the Vietnamese driver what had happened, but she rallied dutifully to the occasion and with the help of the driver, got Homan to the guest house, took off his shoes, and put him to bed.

The mission was, indeed, accomplished, but probably less from Sammie Homan's unorthodox effort than from the fact that the leaders of the coup failed to get the support they had hoped for from other generals, partly because the others recognized that the American mantle still rested on Khanh's shoulders. Duc, with a severe hangover, had no more fight in him, and Phat and Ton were soon less concerned over seizing power than over saving their skins.

On Khanh's promise of no immediate reprisals, the officers took their troops home. Khanh subsequently relieved all three and made a show of bringing them and their accomplices to trial, but in an effort to maintain harmony in the officer corps, he saw to it that all were acquitted. He nevertheless sentenced all three "for disciplinary reasons" to sixty days in jail.

A footnote followed when Madame Phat sought Kitsy's intercession with me in an effort to get her husband released. Undeterred by the fact that the English language has no verb to denote participation in a *coup d'état,* Kitsy replied: "Madame Phat, your husband should have thought of you and your six children before he went out to coup."

The headquarters over which I assumed command, MACV, was a "joint" command, made up of officers and men from the United States Army, Air Force, Navy, and Marine Corps. Air Force numbers and responsibilities already were sufficient to necessitate a separate air headquarters, the 2d Air

Division, which later became the Seventh Air Force. Although the Navy contingent remained relatively small, Army numbers and responsibilities later required replacement of the small U. S. Army Support Command with a separate headquarters: United States Army, Vietnam. As senior Army officer in Vietnam, I headed that headquarters as well as MACV, although a deputy handled day-to-day duties, which were largely logistical and administrative.

MACV was but one component, albeit the largest, of what was known as the "United States Mission," or "Country Team." Under terms of the Mutual Defense Assistance Act of 1949, the U.S. ambassador headed the Mission. Aside from MACV and the Department of State, other organizations involved were the Central Intelligence Agency; the Agency for International Development (earlier known as the United States Operations Mission); the Joint United States Public Affairs Office, an agency of the United States Information Service (USIS); and the Mission Economic Counselor. It was a complex, awkward arrangement.

When I assumed command of MACV, my senior Air Force officer was Major General Joseph H. Moore, a former high school classmate in South Carolina who had entered service as a flying cadet. Joe Moore and I had a close rapport, but it was only by chance that he was nominated to me. Lest I foster some kind of Westmoreland cult or entourage, I made a point of seldom asking for assignment of specific individuals, electing instead to submit a list of several qualified officers from which officials in the Pentagon might choose. There are advantages in having officers with whom one is familiar, such as capitalizing on mutual confidence previously established, and such senior commanders as Douglas MacArthur have employed the procedure, but I personally would have been uncomfortable with it.

My first deputy in Vietnam was Lieutenant General John L. Throckmorton, an officer who had been a class ahead of me at West Point and had been my assistant division commander with the 101st Airborne Division; but after several months General Throckmorton incurred a slipped disk, so that I reluctantly had to accept his return to the United States for surgery. His replacement was Lieutenant General John A. Heintges, son of a World War I German officer who had married an American. Johnny Heintges dealt well with the Vietnamese and was particularly knowledgeable in small-unit tactics. Aware that my deputy might have to succeed me, I resisted pressure from the Air Force for my deputy to be an air officer. Why place an air officer in a position where he might have to run what was essentially a ground war? I similarly resisted pressures for an equal-quota system for officers of the various services on the MACV staff.

MACV functioned not directly under the Joint Chiefs of Staff in Washington but through CINCPAC. That is to say, that was the prescribed channel; but in practice the Joint Chiefs usually communicated directly with me while sending the same message to CINCPAC. I adhered to the chain of command and sent my messages to CINCPAC but occasionally sent information copies to the Joint Chiefs. The White House seldom dealt directly with me but through the Joint Chiefs.

In view of this command arrangement, seeds of friction not unlike those that had plagued MacArthur and the Navy during World War II were present. As I took command of MACV, the CINCPAC, Admiral Felt, a man of small physical stature who commanded autocratically, was succeeded by one who was as determined as I was to make the command arrangement work: Admiral U. S. Grant Sharp, whom I knew by his nickname, "Oley." Although obviously Navy-oriented, Oley Sharp eschewed parochialism and dealt fairly with all the services. As I was aware that Sharp and his staff were jealous of their prerogatives and that President Johnson seldom brought him into the front rank, despite his position as my boss, I made a point of considering Oley Sharp's views thoroughly.

What many failed to realize was that not I but Sharp was the theater commander in the sense that General Eisenhower, for example, was a theater commander in World War II. My responsibilities and prerogatives were basically confined within the borders of South Vietnam. Admiral Sharp commanded the Navy's Seventh Fleet, over which I had no control, although, through my air component commander, working with a Seventh Fleet liaison officer, I could co-ordinate strikes within South Vietnam by carrier-based aircraft. When the bombing of North Vietnam began in February 1965, Admiral Sharp controlled that too, although I could claim priority on aircraft if a mission in South Vietnam was essential. At my insistence, I also controlled air operations over a small segment of North Vietnam just above the DMZ; known as the "extended battle area," it was important tactically for North Vietnamese operations in the south. I also had authority over limited air strikes authorized later in Laos. The big B-52 bombers that were later employed in South Vietnam were under the Commander in Chief, Strategic Air Command, but I was responsible for selecting targets for final approval by authorities in Washington.

I had one outside responsibility at first, that of commanding a military assistance group in Thailand, although a senior Army officer in Thailand, Major General Ernest Easterbrook, acted as my deputy for routine matters. The arrangement was originally designed to assure one over-all commander in Southeast Asia should North Vietnam or Communist China turn to overt aggression or should American forces become involved in Laos. It was never put into practice.

My task would have been eased had I headed a "Southeast Asia Command." As it was, I had to deal on military policy matters affecting Thailand and Laos with the U. S. Ambassadors, Graham Martin and William Sullivan, respectively. Although gifted and dedicated men, they lacked full understanding of military requirements and were reluctant to yield points that I considered crucial. I often kidded them that the power they held had turned them into field marshals.

When the three of us visited an air base in Thailand and a host of airmen followed us around snapping us with their cameras, Ambassador Sullivan remarked that I appeared to have numbers of devoted followers. "Why would they want a picture of a general," I asked him, "when they can snap two field marshals?"

The possibility of a Southeast Asia Command arose from time to time, once as late as 1967. Had President Johnson lifted political restrictions on operations in Laos and Cambodia, such a command would have been essential, particularly after 1965 when Washington eliminated my command of the military assistance group in Thailand on Ambassador Martin's theory that it was distasteful to the Thais to have military advisers in their country subject to a headquarters in another Asian country. I disagreed, considering that the arrangement enhanced co-ordination, but it was not a thing for which I was going to fall on my sword.

When I lost my double hat involving Thailand, co-ordination with American officials in other Southeast Asia countries technically had to be achieved through CINCPAC or Washington. To obviate that tedious procedure, Alexis Johnson and I promoted an informal Southeast Asia co-ordinating committee composed of the heads of mission in South Vietnam, Laos, and Thailand. The group met at irregular intervals either in Vietnam or Thailand.

It was true that the Thais were politically sensitive. An incident involving one of the first American squadrons of F-100 fighter aircraft to arrive in Thailand illustrated the point. Having trained in the bayou country near Alexandria, Louisiana, the squadron had taken the nickname "Alligators" and had painted an alligator on the nose of each plane. Before departing for Thailand, the crews innocently altered the emblem, putting a cobra in the jaws of the alligator. Landing in Thailand, the planes taxied to a stop alongside a Royal Thai squadron that had cobras painted on the noses of its planes. The Thais were incensed, and the Americans avoided an international incident only by promptly painting out the cobras on their own planes.

Hardly had General Khanh subdued the attempted *coup d'état* of September 13, 1964, when he faced another crisis. An incipient turmoil that was always just below the surface among the Montagnard tribesmen in the Central Highlands erupted.

For some thirty years before French departure from Vietnam, the Montagnards had staged a number of revolts. When the South Vietnamese government, after the Geneva Accords, located some of the refugees from North Vietnam in the region, unrest became endemic, including another revolt in 1958. Yet other Vietnamese continued to move into the region until they constituted some 40 per cent of the population.

One of the larger tribes, the Rhade, was in the forefront of a long struggle for Montagnard autonomy, led by an organization called the Bajaraka Autonomy Movement. After the unsuccessful revolt of 1958, the most prominent Rhade leader, Y Bih,* took to the bush and joined the Viet Cong. A number of other Montagnards were imprisoned by the South Vietnam authorities, including the chairman of the Bajaraka Autonomy Movement, Y Bham, who was second only to Y Bih in importance. Relations between the tribesmen and the Saigon government were still severely strained when General Khanh came to power in early 1964. Bringing a number of Montagnards into governmental positions in an effort to correct some of the grievances, Khanh released Y Bham from jail and named him a deputy chief of Darlac province.

Although Khanh made a legitimate effort to alleviate tension in the highlands, he was frustrated at almost every turn by local officials. One, for example, announced that the solution to the problem was to put the Montagnards in reservations. Yet for all the enmity between the Montagnards and the South Vietnamese government, Montagnards and Americans in Vietnam had a warm relationship. After the American Embassy in 1961 convinced the Vietnamese to arm and train the mountain tribesmen in village defense, men of the U. S. Army Special Forces, operating at the time under the CIA, served as advisers for the CIDG units that as early as 1962 were providing village defense and border surveillance. Officers for the CIDG companies were from the South Vietnamese Special Forces.

Through much of 1964 rumors of a coming Montagnard revolt were common. Under a relatively moderate Y Bham, the highlanders reduced their demand for full autonomy to a demand for a separate governmental structure, their own flag, and separate military forces under Montagnard leadership; but even Khanh's government with its air of amelioration was unprepared to go that far. Apparently reorganizing the Bajaraka Autonomy Movement, Y Bham renamed it United Front for the Struggle of the Oppressed Race, or FULRO, after its French title.† Reports that a revolt was imminent began to surface in early September. Word was on the morning of September 19 that it would come that night, but most Vietnamese officials discounted it.

At midnight on September 19 mainly Rhade tribesmen in four CIDG-Special Forces camps near the Darlac provincial capital of Ban Me Thuot revolted. They disarmed their American Special Forces advisers, seized the village of Dak Mil, taking some sixty South Vietnamese civilians hostage, held South Vietnamese soldiers as hostages and killed seventy-three of them, mostly their Special Forces commanders. Some 2,000 armed tribesmen marched on Ban Me Thuot, surrounded the town, and gained control of the radio station.

The 23d ARVN Division under General Lu Mong Lan reacted swiftly, setting up blocking positions on all roads leading into Ban Me Thuot. Troops of the two sides glared at each other, but nobody fired. When Gen-

---

* In the Montagnard lexicon, "Y" means "son of."
† Front Unifié de Lutte de la Race Opprimée.

eral Lan and the II Corps commander, General Nguyen Huu Co, arrived with their American advisers, including Colonel John F. ("Fritz") Freund, who was destined to play a key role in the denouement, they encountered no difficulty in entering Ban Me Thuot.

Then, suddenly, at noon a jeep belonging to a U. S. Special Forces captain and carrying the captain and several of the rebels dashed into town. As the captain revealed later, he was a hostage of the rebels and forced to do their bidding. Before the South Vietnamese officials could do anything about it, they stopped at Y Bham's house, picked up the Montagnard leader, and left. After they returned to their CIDG-Special Forces camp at Bon Sar Pa, near Dak Mil, Y Bham, the apparent instigator of the revolt, disappeared, presumably to set up a FULRO headquarters across the border in Cambodia and there to carry on a long agitation against the South Vietnamese government.

The presence of the American captain and his jeep upset South Vietnamese officials, including General Khanh, who deduced that the captain was helping the rebels. So close was the rapport between Montagnards and Americans that many Vietnamese were quick to suspect American motives in the highlands. When I learned of Khanh's concern, I immediately sent an officer to Khanh with a letter explaining that I was confident the captain was a hostage and had no choice but to accede to the rebels' demands.

During the afternoon the American Special Forces advisers convinced some of the rebels to return to their camps, while Colonel Freund went to the rebel command post in an unsuccessful effort to convince the Montagnard leaders to call off the uprising. Freund spoke French fluently and had an uncanny ability to establish quick rapport with both South Vietnamese and Montagnards.

The more militant of the rebels were from the camp at Bon Sar Pa. For a time they planned an attack on Ban Me Thuot until Freund and low-flying South Vietnamese fighter planes prompted them to return to their camp. They insisted that Freund go with them to the camp to assure safety from attack by the planes. Meanwhile, the situation in the other camps was tense, most American advisers still deprived of their weapons, but Bon Sar Pa was clearly the key site.

As Freund arrived at Bon Sar Pa, he found the Montagnards holding approximately a hundred hostages. The former camp commander, an officer of the South Vietnamese Special Forces, was tied to a flagpole where he had been since the start of the rebellion. Freund went immediately to the flagpole, cut the officer's bonds, and sent him to a waiting helicopter. The Montagnards grumbled their displeasure but did nothing.

For all Fritz Freund's efforts, the Montagnards refused to release the other hostages and made clear that they considered Freund and nine other Americans who were present as their prisoners as well. Only Freund was allowed to carry a weapon. The Montagnards saw the advisers as insurance against ARVN attack on the camp. Briefed on the situation, I decided to leave the advisers in the camps, at least temporarily, as a stabilizing influence but insisted to the Vietnamese that no attack be mounted against any of the camps.

Colonel Freund was determined to demonstrate that he considered himself no prisoner while at the same time assuring adequate defense of the camp in the event of VC attack. He set out alone to inspect the defense posts and demanded that the rebel leader correct any shortcomings. Yet despite seemingly endless conferences with the rebels, permission to release the hostages never came. Freund also tried to arrange a meeting in Ban Me Thuot between South Vietnamese officials and the Montagnard high command—presumably Y Bham—but the Montagnards doubted the sincerity of South Vietnamese assurances of safe passage.

As the crisis dragged on, I directed preparation of a plan to rescue hostages and U.S. troops from all the rebel camps, should the situation require. A platoon of volunteers from the U. S. Special Forces was to enter each camp by helicopter under cover from other helicopters armed with machine guns.

By the seventh day, September 26, General Khanh and other South Vietnamese officials were becoming so visibly upset at the impasse that I became concerned lest they ignore my warning and attack the camps. While the situation was basically peaceful at three of the camps, it remained delicate at Bon Sar Pa. If the hostages there could be removed, I believed we could end the trouble. The task force assigned to Bon Sar Pa got ready to move the next morning.

The American troops were in the air when Freund assembled the Montagnards at Bon Sar Pa and began to speak to them in French. He reminded them of how much the Americans had helped them, the respect they themselves held for their American Special Forces advisers. The Saigon government, he said, was unable to negotiate so long as South Vietnamese citizens were hostage. If it came to fighting, he warned, the Montagnard cause could be set back seriously.

Time was running out—the airborne task force soon would either have to land or call off the mission to refuel—when Freund dramatically extended his pistol toward the rebel leader.

"I don't want any of you to be responsible for shooting an American," he said to the others. "Let your leader do the shooting."

The leader turned and ran away.

Signaling the task force to descend, Freund explained to the Montagnards what was about to happen. Turning his back on the crowd, he walked to the two buildings where the hostages were held and cut the wires holding the doors. Leading the hostages, he marched past the assembled Montagnards to the helicopter pad. When the helicopters landed, the hostages fell over themselves clambering aboard.

Release of the hostages failed to relieve the tension at Bon Sar Pa. Instead, the tension increased with news that the South Vietnamese, under

Khanh's instructions, were planning to hit the camp with artillery and ground attack early the next morning, September 27. As soon as I heard that, I telephoned General Khanh at his retreat in Dalat, getting him out of bed in the middle of the night, and demanded that he call off the attack. Khanh was noncommittal, but a later check with the American advisory command post at Ban Me Thuot verified that he had telephoned and countermanded the attack order.

My operations officer, Brigadier General William E. DePuy, who was representing me at Ban Me Thuot, nevertheless recommended that the advisers be removed from Bon Sar Pa, and I approved. In early morning of September 27 the advisers assembled at the back gate of the camp. When helicopters landed, the Montagnards made no attempt to interfere.

In mid-morning an ARVN officer who was himself a Montagnard entered the camp with Colonel Freund and General DePuy. The Montagnards at last agreed to relent. When two companies of South Vietnamese troops surrounded the camp, Freund met their commander at the gate, escorted him inside, and introduced him to the Montagnard leader.

General Khanh himself flew to the camp during the afternoon. With Vietnamese and Montagnard troops assembled in ranks facing each other, a band playing, the Montagnards ceremoniously surrendered their arms. The rebel flag went down, the saffron and orange South Vietnamese flag went up.

Chapter V
Chaos Unabated

For all the domestic foment, the U. S. Military Assistance Command during the latter months of 1964 made at least a measure of progress in the basic assignment of providing security for the people and helping defeat the Viet Cong. Progress centered in a program that I code-named HOP TAC, which in Vietnamese means co-operation. It was designed to gradually expand security and government control and services—pacification—outward from Saigon into six provinces that form a kind of horse collar about the city.

For several years, priority for ARVN actions against the VC had been based on wherever the insurgents were strongest. I considered it better to accept temporary setbacks in some regions while using the government's limited resources to secure the more critical areas, such as Saigon and its environs, then gradually to expand outward as those areas were secured.

When I presented this concept at the Honolulu conference in June 1964, I received authority to conduct HOP TAC, and thus in effect obtained for MACV the role of executive agent for pacification around Saigon, the role that I believed the military should have for the entire country. As adviser to the commander of the III Corps surrounding Saigon, Colonel Wilbur ("Coal Bin Willie") Wilson (he got the nickname at Fort Bragg where he had ordered that coal bins be whitewashed) developed the concept and organization, while his successor, Colonel Jasper Wilson, worked out the plan in detail. To assist within my headquarters, I called in Major Robert M. Montague, who had had success in organizing and employing pacification teams in one of the country's southernmost provinces. Montague was in the end to become a specialist in pacification.

Under HOP TAC, a combined military-political effort, military forces were to expand outward from Saigon into zones defined by roughly concentric circles. As larger enemy forces were pushed farther and farther from the city, saturation patrolling and ambushes would further enhance security until the task could be turned over to militia and an expanded police force.

As areas were secured, civilian agencies would move in to institute government control and services, providing everybody with ID cards, police protection, and such amenities as schools, wells, dispensaries, and medical care. The idea was to establish a standard of living perceptibly higher than the Viet Cong could provide. It was, in effect, a "spreading oil spot" concept. If successful around Saigon, similar programs might be conducted in the environs of such other cities as Danang, Qui Nhon, and Can Tho, until eventually all might merge.

Since the military phase of HOP TAC was in some respects different from conventional military operations, I sought expressive terms or phrases to serve as a common terminology among the South Vietnamese and their American advisers. My staff came up with three that I considered more apt than any I had thought of personally.

The first was "clearing," which was either destroying or driving out the guerrillas and other military forces so that the civilian agencies could begin their assignments. The second was "securing," which was holding onto a cleared area by means of outposts and patrols, at the same time attacking any vestiges of the guerrillas and uprooting the secret political infrastructure. The third was "search and destroy," which was nothing more than the infantry's traditional attack mission: locate the enemy, try to bring him to battle, and either destroy him or force his surrender. In the process the troops were to find the secret VC base areas and eliminate them and their supply caches, thereby removing the sanctuaries and supplies to which the enemy always returned following his destructive forays into the populated areas or his attacks against government installations.

Although the Vietnamese appeared to understand the terms, many Americans apparently failed to comprehend "search and destroy," possibly because detractors of the war chose to distort it. Since it is always the basic objective of military operations to seek and destroy the enemy and his military resources, I saw nothing contradictory or brutal about the term, yet as the months passed, many people, to my surprise, came to associate it with aimless searches in the jungle and the random destroying of villages and other property. Some even labeled American strategy in Vietnam a "search-and-destroy strategy," when in reality "search and destroy" was nothing more than an operational term for a tactic.

I was long unaware of how twisted the meaning of the term became and, in retrospect, wonder why some friendly critic failed to alert me of the distortion. Not until early in 1968 did the head of Voice of America, a friend and former television personality, John Charles Daly, call my attention to it. "General," John Daly told me during a visit to my office, "you are your own worst enemy to perpetuate a term that has been so distorted."

Although those who saw the war as a political issue could no doubt have twisted any term, I changed it without fanfare to "sweeping operations" or "reconnaissance in force." Yet the term still stuck in the minds of many.

Some people somehow seemed to believe you could fight one of history's more brutal enemies without hurting or killing.

To assure more regular Vietnamese forces for HOP TAC, I talked with the Chief of the Joint General Staff, General Khiem, about moving a division from some other part of the country to Hau Nghia province, between Saigon and the nearby Cambodian border, a hotbed of VC activity. I suggested a division from the highlands, accepting the possibility, however much I disliked it, of temporarily losing some of that sparsely populated region. Khiem suggested instead moving the 25th Division from Quang Ngai province, far to the north. Since the VNQDD party, composed of dedicated anti-Communists, was strong in Quang Ngai, leaving one of the division's regiments behind and expanding militia forces would make it possible to hold the line there.

The move was a mistake. In all units except the airborne and marine brigades and ranger battalions, most of the South Vietnamese soldiers came from a specific region in the manner of American National Guard units. Move them far away and they quickly became homesick for their families and former homes, and this feeds the desertion rate. Moving the soldiers' families to Hau Nghia was but a partial help, for the families, too, were discontent in a strange region. A full three years was to pass before the 25th Division recovered from the exercise and became fully proficient. We would have done better to have formed an entirely new division.

In launching HOP TAC, I was concerned lest the press overplay it as some conclusive answer to winning the war, as others earlier had pictured a program of locating the people in "strategic hamlets" during the Diem era. Unlike the start of a conventional attack, there could be no dramatic crossing of a line of departure. I saw HOP TAC instead as a slow-starting, gradual thing, from which South Vietnamese and Americans alike would learn as time passed, with escalating achievement as the Vietnamese civilian ministries gained experience. I also wanted it understood that it was a South Vietnamese operation to which Americans contributed only advice and commodities. Yet the press did play it big, as if Westmoreland was staking his reputation on it; and in the uncertain political atmosphere in which many South Vietnamese leaders were reluctant to commit themselves lest they became associated with a program that tomorrow's government might repudiate, many were slow to support it.

To co-ordinate the military and civilian agencies, the South Vietnamese established a HOP TAC council, composed of officials of the HOP TAC region and representatives of the Ministry of Interior, National Police, and South Vietnamese Central Intelligence Organization. Their American counterparts met and worked with them. In keeping with my insistence that HOP TAC was a South Vietnamese program, I required that Americans at the meetings never exceed the number of Vietnamese. For a time I was the senior American on the council, acting as counterpart to General Khanh, but Khanh became so involved with political agitation that he gave HOP

TAC little attention, although he did designate the III Corps commander to chair the meetings as his representative.

I saw HOP TAC—as one of my staff, Brigadier General James L. Collins, later put it—as "a laboratory experiment in pacification." If we were unable to succeed in pacification "in the shadow of the flagpole [Saigon]," in Collins' words, how could we expect to succeed in the farther reaches of the country?

HOP TAC's problems can be summed up in two words: political instability. With everybody at South Vietnamese top levels concerned about the next possible *coup d'état,* few gave more than minimum commitment to the program. Aside from inattention, Khanh himself detracted from it by holding the airborne and marine brigades in their barracks close to Saigon as insurance against political upheaval. He complicated organization by refusing to allow the III Corps to absorb Gia Dinh province, a doughnut in which Saigon is the hole, again lest the military forces in Gia Dinh link with others in the III Corps to support a coup. There were also constant shifts of province officials; a man might develop a certain expertise and get a viable program going, then suddenly be replaced by someone with no experience but presumably more politically reliable.

The performance of the ARVN was also disappointing, not so much by the rank and file as by the leaders at division level and above, who were as beset as other officials by concern over how deeply to commit themselves to a government that might pass in the night. The caserne mentality that for long had afflicted ARVN leaders was still much in evidence. Besides, there were simply insufficient troops to do the job. All these factors contributed to a growing strength of the insurgents and thus to a continuing insecurity that made it difficult for the civilian agencies to function in the villages and hamlets.

From a slow start in September 1964, HOP TAC three months later was nevertheless achieving measured progress. Although police strength failed to increase in the numbers I wanted, it did rise by several thousand, and police morale improved. VC incidents in the capital itself decreased. Agents of the civilian ministries gradually developed experience, and joint American-Vietnamese teams making unannounced inspections spotted more flagrant problems. In the long run, measures became standardized, so that despite slower progress than I had hoped for, HOP TAC became the basis for the pacification program that eventually, after American troops became available to counter the enemy's big units, brought security to much of the country.

In 1965 a new Saigon government put a formal end to HOP TAC, deeming the name too closely associated with the Khanh government, but the essential program remained intact under a new Ministry of Rural Construction. HOP TAC clearly took up some of the slack in pacification caused by failure to co-ordinate all American efforts closely at the top. Without it, I fear the enemy during 1965 might have made critical inroads on government control of the capital area.

A major problem in those early days, as through the entire war, was that Washington policy decisions forced us to fight with but one hand. The most crippling restriction at first was on use of American aircraft. In what was known as the FARMGATE program, American pilots could provide air support only with a Vietnamese pilot aboard, ostensibly executing a training mission.

Because Vietnamese pilots were slow to join their counterparts when a call for a mission came and because Vietnamese flying their own planes were also slow to react, American advisers with ARVN units tended to put little reliance on fighter aircraft. They felt they could count on quicker support from U. S. Army helicopters, even though in those days there were no true helicopter gunships, merely helicopters mounting machine guns.

Trying to improve reaction time, my Air Force colleague, Joe Moore, established a separate air communications net for the advisers. Only time and training could overcome the reluctance of Vietnamese pilots to report for a mission; but in one squadron equipped with the two-seater T-28, in which neither American nor South Vietnamese pilots liked to ride in the rear seat, Moore tried a bit of subterfuge. He had Air Marshal Ky assign him a group of privates who would be on alert at all times to climb into the back seat with an American at the controls in front. That assured quick response while at the same time fulfilling the letter of the requirement for having a Vietnamese along.

Yet the arrangement proved short-lived. Unaccustomed to flying, the privates often got air sick. The way the T-28 was constructed, the vomit would slosh back and forth on the floor of both seat compartments, a discomfiting experience. As one pilot went into a dive, the private fainted and collapsed against the dual control stick. The plane nearly crashed before the pilot succeeded in putting enough pressure on his control stick to offset the weight of his passenger.

Sometimes the only way to save some besieged South Vietnamese ground unit was simply to ignore the requirement for a Vietnamese to be along. As time passed, the entire FARMGATE program with its requirements for Vietnamese participation and Vietnamese Air Force markings on the planes became badly eroded. By mid-1964, when the military situation was deteriorating and when U.S. helicopters were already providing aerial fire support, the program was, in any event, out of date.

The tendency for U. S. Army advisers to rely on helicopters rather than fighter planes contributed to a long-held U. S. Air Force concern that the U. S. Army was trying to usurp the Air Force role. When I was in Washington late in 1964, General Curtis E. LeMay, Air Force Chief of Staff, upbraided me about the way I was using air power, and a few weeks later when he was visiting Hong Kong he summoned General Moore to join him there where he administered a tongue-lashing for what he called failure to uphold Air Force doctrine but what in reality was his discontent that Moore had endorsed installing machine guns on helicopters.

To my regret General LeMay never accepted my invitation to visit Vietnam and examine at first hand how we used air power. Had he done so he might have learned that counterinsurgency warfare required many variations from conventional practices and that there was room enough amid the myriad requirements for close air support in Vietnam for both fighter plane and helicopter gunship.

The naval encounters in the Gulf of Tonkin in August 1964 and retaliatory bombing by American planes raised the question of evacuating American dependents, particularly when a renewed campaign of terrorism against Americans and attacks on American installations began. It started in September when a terrorist tossed a grenade into a jeep a few miles outside Saigon, killing a U. S. Army officer and wounding a civilian AID official.

Having wives and children at hand was unquestionably good for American morale. While those who served in the field with ARVN troops were unable to bring their dependents to Vietnam, they received compensation through shorter tours of duty. When the terrorism started, some Americans voluntarily sent dependents home, but most stayed, a total of about 1,800.

Thinking—as were many in Washington—that the time was approaching when the only recourse to avert defeat of the South Vietnamese was to bomb North Vietnam, both Ambassador Taylor and Admiral Sharp at CINCPAC thought dependents should go lest they provide a ready target for retaliation for the bombing. I was more sanguine—or I may have been engaging in wishful thinking—but I hoped that our continuing efforts would bring improvement in the fight against the VC. I was also concerned lest we communicate to the enemy a sense of impending disaster and worried lest the South Vietnamese interpret departure of dependents as a first step in American withdrawal. So low was South Vietnamese morale that any signal that we were abandoning them might be enough to prompt them to give in, a concern that some ten years later was to prove to be warranted.

American wives were anxious to stay, as Kitsy demonstrated soon after Alexis Johnson arrived to serve as Ambassador Taylor's deputy. Rumor had it that Johnson was to make the decision whether to order dependents out. As my dinner guest his first evening in Saigon, he was talking with Kitsy on the porch while awaiting my arrival when an explosion occurred nearby, rattling the windows of the house. Kitsy remained calm, continuing to talk as if nothing had happened. With the blast of a second explosion, she talked more fervidly than ever. She was determined to demonstrate that the wives were unruffled by whatever went on.

As terrorism continued—searchers in January 1965 found the bodies of four American soldiers who had disappeared while fishing off the coast, weighted and drowned—I subsequently recommended a gradual withdrawal of dependents designed to minimize the impact on South Vietnamese morale and on continuity in American ranks. If dependents left all at once, everybody would become eligible for a one-year tour and would depart around the same time. I suggested that wives with small children leave immediately, whereupon the number of other dependents would gradually diminish as tours ended and newcomers arrived unaccompanied.

As events developed, the decision was not ours to make. President Johnson soon was to make it for us.

In early fall of 1964, several weeks after a squadron of B-57 bombers arrived at an air base at the town of Bien Hoa, north of Saigon, a U. S. Navy bomber crippled by enemy fire landed and with difficulty taxied to the end of the ramp where the B-57s were aligned. As crews from the flight line swarmed about the Navy plane to help, a mammoth explosion occurred at the other end of the flight line. The explosion killed some of the airmen, one man's body totally disintegrating in the blast, and set some of the B-57s afire.

The explosion scattered 500-pound bombs all over the runways. Because many had been armed in preparation for a mission and some were equipped with chemical time fuses that had already been activated, the base had to be evacuated. During the first twelve hours, some of the bombs exploded, but others did not. Anxious to put the base back into service, Joe Moore and his staff were struggling for a solution when a jaunty paratrooper, Lieutenant Colonel Jack O'Shaughnessy, who had served with me in the 82d Airborne Division, volunteered to rig TNT beside the bombs and explode them.

Those on the scene watched nervously as O'Shaughnessy went calmly about his work. Any one of the bombs might go off at any moment. The job done at last, O'Shaughnessy ran for cover. He was subsequently decorated with the Air Force Cross.

When the incident occurred, I was on an inspection trip at an air base in Thailand. Learning of it, I flew back immediately, observing the holocaust at low level before landing at Tan Son Nhut. A subsequent investigation of the incident pointed to sabotage, but it could have been an accident.

There could be no doubt as to the cause of the next incident at Bien Hoa. On the night of November 1, a hundred VC mortar shells rained down on the air base. Two Americans and four Vietnamese were killed and numbers wounded. Five B-57s were destroyed and other planes and helicopters damaged. As so often happened, the raiders got away unscathed. The raid bore some resemblance in miniature to the Japanese attack on Pearl Harbor in that the planes had been lined up close together to ease the task of protecting them against sabotage, seen as the most likely threat. We subsequently gained some protection for aircraft by building revetments constructed first of sandbags and then of earth held in place by metal sheathing.

Just over a fortnight later, an explosion ripped a shack that served as a snack bar at Tan Son Nhut. One Vietnamese and eighteen Americans were wounded. I had been by the shack several times that day.

At noon on a Sunday shortly before Christmas, I received word that my eighty-six-year-old father, who had meant so much to me, had died. As Kitsy held my hand, for the first time since I was a child I cried. Since the children would not qualify under the circumstances for official travel, Kitsy remained with them and I flew back alone for the funeral.

On the way the last letter my father had written me was often on my mind, a letter that expressed consternation and frustration over Vietnam probably shared by many Americans:

> Dear Son: I hardly know what to think about the situation in Vietnam. That condition there has been going on for ten or more years and it seems some solution could have been found by this time . . . If I have the public opinion sized up this country would order all of you home and let that country go to "that place."

While in South Carolina for the funeral, I received orders to return by way of Washington for a conference with the Joint Chiefs. Although I received no invitation to talk with the President or the Secretary of Defense, I assumed at the time that that was attributable to the President's desire to maintain a low profile on the war. When I learned later that at the time of my visit major new steps for escalating the war were under consideration, I deemed it odd that neither the President nor the Secretary had sought my views.

I did have an opportunity to talk with Deputy Secretary of Defense Cyrus Vance about my need for more military police. Vance shocked me by belittling the need. "Mr. Secretary," I demanded, "how can you say that? I am concerned about the security of my installations and my people." The Deputy Secretary subsequently relented, possibly because hardly had I returned to Saigon when the need was cruelly demonstrated.

It happened on Christmas Eve. Kitsy and I were preparing to entertain guests from the field for dinner when a tremendous blast shook the villa. A bomb had exploded at a downtown hotel used as an officers' billet and renamed the Brink Hotel after Brigadier General Francis G. Brink, the first American commander in Vietnam, who had died a suicide while in a mood of depression during a visit to Washington.

While Kitsy changed from her dinner dress into her Red Cross uniform, I hurried to the scene of the bombing and thence to the hospital. An American Navy officer and a civilian were killed. More than a hundred were wounded, including sixty-six Americans. It was a bloody scene.

(Brigadier General Frank Osmanski, the MACV logistical officer, and his wife had left their car in the hotel garage for safekeeping while they visited the United States. Back home they saw it burning on television.)

Kitsy's foresight in arranging to use our guest house as an infirmary was soon apparent. Recruiting her dinner guests to help, she inflated air mattresses with a vacuum cleaner, set up cots, and was ready when ambulances transferred patients from the Navy hospital to make room for victims of the bombing. With the food prepared for fifteen guests, Kitsy performed something of a miracle on the order of the seven loaves and a few fishes to feed in addition thirty-one patients.

American ability to laugh at adversity was demonstrated the next day when comedian Bob Hope and his troupe performed their first Christmas show in Vietnam. A quip that drew one of the biggest laughs was Bob's remark: "As I landed at Tan Son Nhut, I saw a hotel go by." At another show he quipped: "When I landed at Tan Son Nhut, I got a nineteen-gun salute. One of them was ours."

Many months later, when American troops captured thousands of VC documents in the Iron Triangle, which was headquarters for VC operations against Saigon, one of the documents revealed that sappers had set off their charge at the Brink Hotel prematurely. The explosion had been designed to occur just as the Bob Hope troupe arrived at the hotel, where most were to stay. The troupe had been delayed at Tan Son Nhut by the unloading of big boxes of cue cards, known in the trade as "idiot cards."

The Vietnamese political situation remained as shaky as ever. The main result of events following the abortive Phat-Duc coup in September 1964 was not more political stability but the emergence of a dissatisfied, restless group of generals who called themselves the "Young Turks" and constituted another abrasive element within the political structure. In exchange for having remained loyal to General Khanh during the attempted *coup d'état,* they demanded an increasing say in the government. The apparent leaders were Air Vice Marshal Ky and General Nguyen Chanh Thi.

General Thi was an impulsive, enigmatic man, a former paratrooper who had been a leader in an unsuccessful anti-Diem coup in 1960. As deputy to General Khanh in the I Corps, Thi had participated in Khanh's coup and subsequently commanded the 1st ARVN Division in the I Corps, where he displayed a disturbing sympathy for Thich Tri Quang and his militant Buddhists.

Marshal Ky was a soft-spoken, imperturbable man, mustached and suave. A former reputation as a ladies' man had passed with his marriage to the Vietnamese airline hostess. Ky designed his own uniform, which usually included a purple scarf, and once when he accompanied me to an American aircraft carrier, he wore a purple jump suit. An expert marksman, he could split a playing card with a shot from the pearl-handled revolvers that he wore on either hip. His command of English was excellent. A transplant in 1954 from North Vietnam whose home village was Son Tay, where an American force was later to make an unsuccessful effort to rescue prisoners of war, Ky was also a Buddhist, but because of his intense anti-Communism he maintained a close relationship with the more numerous Catholic generals. Joe Moore believed Ky to be innately honest, in no way tainted by the corruption or rumors of corruption that haunted other leaders.

Less obvious as a leader among the young generals but actually the one who wielded the most power was the former Chief of Staff of the Joint General Staff and at the time commander of the IV Corps, Nguyen Van Thieu. An unusually capable military man, Thieu had earlier waged an astute though cautious campaign against the VC as commander of the 5th ARVN Division. Cautious and deliberate, so patient that he was for long content to operate behind the scenes, he was handsome, well-groomed, intelligent, and, above all, shrewd. He was devoted to his family. Once when I visited his home our discussion had to await his tidying his children's toys. Yet at parties with fellow officers Thieu sought center stage by telling dirty jokes.

Thieu had a wry sense of humor, as demonstrated at a conference when one of my officers expressed concern over rumors of a possible coup. Asked where he got the rumors, the officer said they came from the American soldiers' newspaper, *The Stars & Stripes*. Thieu responded with a smile that expressed a total dismissal of responsibility and concern. "That," he said, "is General Westmoreland's newspaper."

As far as I was able to discern, Thieu was an honest man, and over the months to come I became increasingly close to him. When he took parachute training in an attempt to cement relationships with the elite South Vietnamese airborne troops, I resolved to pay him the parachutist's supreme compliment by participating in his qualifying jump. At a reception at the American Embassy the night before, Ambassador Taylor objected to my jumping, but I deemed the opportunity to further a friendship with Thieu well worth any small risk involved.

The next day I found a place in Thieu's plane before his arrival. Seeing me, his eyes widened in surprise, but he was clearly pleased. We jumped—my 121st jump—and came to earth on a field that was so hard from long baking in the tropical sun that the landing jolted me painfully.

As we divested ourselves of our harnesses, airborne troops rushed onto the field with a table covered with a gleaming white tablecloth. We drank a champagne toast—something the Vietnamese had learned from the French and liked to do on almost any occasion—whereupon I presented Thieu with honorary U.S. airborne wings. Furthering the camaraderie, the Vietnamese airborne commander presented me with South Vietnamese paratrooper wings.

As an outgrowth of the governmental crisis in August 1964 associated with the Vung Tau Charter, Khanh had agreed to form a High National Council, composed of revered elder civilians representing a broad spectrum of the society and authorized to draft a constitution and establish a civilian government. This Khanh did in September. So elderly were most of the members that the council came to be known in some circles as the "High

National Museum," and it was soon clear that Khanh would allow a civilian government to be nothing more than a front.

Anticipating the installation of a civilian government, Khanh assured himself a position from which to exercise power behind the façade. Sending General Khiem, then the Minister of Defense and head of the armed forces, out of the country, eventually to become ambassador to Washington, Khanh himself took the position of head of the armed forces. Quite clearly no government could survive but at the whim of the military, and the head of the armed forces controlled the military. When the High National Council on October 24 named a civilian government, Khanh dutifully resigned as Premier in return for confirmation as head of the armed forces.

The High National Council named Phan Khac Suu as a ceremonial Chief of State in place of Big Minh, whom Khanh also dispensed with by sending him on a good-will tour to Europe and eventual exile in Thailand. Suu was an elderly agricultural engineer who wore a goatee, black robes, and mandarin hat in keeping with the ancient mode of Vietnamese dress. Suu in turn named as Premier a former schoolteacher and mayor of Saigon, Tran Van Huong, who had a reputation for honesty but also for inflexibility. Like Big Minh, Huong many years later was destined to play a role in his country's final days of independence.

When Tran Van Huong chose a number of technicians rather than politicians for his Cabinet, he incurred the wrath of both Buddhists and Catholics, but Huong vowed that he was no figurehead and would yield to no pressure. He himself would run the government until, he added with a realistic nod to the facts of Saigon life, such time as the military might force him from office.

Huong's government soon was beset by political strife as noisy and sometimes as violent as that which had racked Saigon and other cities the preceding August. Infiltrated by VC agents, the students took to the streets first, then the Catholics, then the Buddhists; but with General Khanh's endorsement and promise of military backing, Huong held firm and in November declared martial law in the capital.

Unfortunately for Huong, Khanh's promise of military support lacked substance, for the young generals were fast becoming disenchanted with Khanh and more and more reluctant to do his bidding. How deep the discontent was became known to me in late November after I heard from Joe Moore that Marshal Ky was, in Moore's words, "getting restless" and wanted to talk with me. Apparently wanting to speak on delicate matters, he asked to come to my office rather than my following my normal practice of going to his.

Ky told me flatly that if the deteriorating situation in the countryside was to be reversed, there had to be a change in command of the armed forces. Khanh had to go. His compromises with the Buddhists, his reinstatement of the Dalat generals, his handling of the leaders of the Phat-Duc coup—these and other vacillations and compromises had so disturbed division and corps commanders that they had lost confidence in Khanh. Contrary to my own view, he maintained that morale of the men in the ranks was also seriously impaired.

When I told Ky bluntly that the American government would support no change by other than orderly and legal processes, he said he would take no action for three months. If the situation continued to deteriorate, he went on, he would be constrained to act, although any action would be "legal" and would be no embarrassment to the United States. When I asked who should succeed Khanh, Ky hesitated only briefly, then answered: "Nguyen Van Thieu."

Ky was surprisingly frank. That was the time when he told me that Americans should not believe anything a Vietnamese said. Following close on his apparently sincere discussion, the statement perplexed me; but as it turned out, Ky had given me a blueprint of things to come. Although I reported the conversation to the ambassador and to Washington, its significance remained undetected.

A few days later, meeting at Dalat, the senior commanders formed an Armed Forces Council, ostensibly to "assist" Khanh to run the armed forces but in reality to establish firm control over him. Among other responsibilities, the council voted itself veto power over promotions and assignments of officers, a power Khanh had been exercising unilaterally. Word spread that the generals were planning to remove Khanh.

It was to such an atmosphere that Ambassador Taylor returned in early December from another of his periodic visits to Washington. When he sought a forum where he might impress the generals with the gravity with which the American government viewed the continuing chaos, I gave a dinner at my villa on December 8 for a score of senior South Vietnamese commanders, including Thieu, Ky, and the corps commanders. As the first of a series of incidents involving the ambassador and the generals, the event came to be known in Saigon circles as "Westy's steak dinner."

Speaking in French, Taylor made a strong plea for political unity. The recent disorders, he said, had "completely dismayed the staunchest friends of South Vietnam." Political stability, he insisted, was essential for effective use of American aid and "crucial" to any increase in aid. In conclusion he exacted an informal implied pledge from all the generals to work in harmony.

Judging from the actions that followed, few of the South Vietnamese generals took their implied agreement to mean accepting the status quo. Having created the Armed Forces Council, they began to use it as a hammer with which to bludgeon Khanh into submission.

Although I warned Khanh that it would be folly to accept government by committee, he chose to compromise with the generals much as he had with the Buddhists. At the behest of the young generals, he asked the High National Council to require mandatory retirement of all officers with as much as twenty-five years' service, a measure that would get rid of Big Minh, the Dalat generals, and others who outranked the Young Turks. When the elder statesmen refused, Khanh simply disbanded the council.

Precipitated abruptly in the middle of the night of December 20 when several of the young generals burst in on Premier Huong and Chief of State Suu with the news that the council was dissolved, the action left Huong with but three alternatives: resign, compromise, or defy. When Ambassador Taylor recommended defiance, General Khanh, in an interview with a correspondent for the New York *Herald-Tribune,* accused the ambassador of interfering in Vietnam's internal affairs with "activities beyond imagination." Taylor, Khanh said, was "not serving his country well. We make sacrifices for the country's independence and the Vietnamese people's liberty, not to carry out the policy of any foreign country."

Khanh was, in effect, naming the ambassador as *persona non grata.* To which the usually tactful, mannerly Taylor reacted with, as he himself later put it, "calculated asperity," the only time I knew him, when dealing with the South Vietnamese, to drop his diplomatic cloak. When Khanh sent four emissaries to talk with Taylor—Generals Thieu and Thi, Marshal Ky, and the senior Navy officer among the Young Turks, Admiral Chung Tan Cang, Ambassador Taylor and Alexis Johnson greeted them coolly.

"Do you understand English?" Taylor began bluntly. The behavior of the generals, he said, was irresponsible, a kind of suicidal nonsense the United States was unprepared to tolerate again. In the end he expressed regret for having to speak so sharply, and upon departure the two sides shook hands in apparent amity. Yet after reporting to Khanh, the Vietnamese officers complained publicly that the ambassador had treated them like puppets and schoolboys, insulting them and the armed forces. They were hurt—Ky in particular—that Ambassador Taylor had questioned their ability with English.

When Ambassadors Taylor and Johnson called on Khanh the next day, they found him belligerent and unrepentant. Having decided in any case that the United States might better work with someone else, perhaps Big Minh, Taylor told Khanh that he thought he had outlived his usefulness. Seeking to exacerbate his fellow generals, a petulant Khanh told them that the ambassador had said he should "get ready to leave the position of Commander in Chief and to leave the country."

Khanh reported this version and his own account of Ambassador Taylor's meeting with Thieu, Ky, Thi, and Cang to the Chief of State and the Premier, calling on them to "take appropriate measures to preserve the honor of all the Vietnamese Armed Forces and to keep national prestige intact." Following Khanh's signature on the report were the names of four of the young generals, but those of Thieu and Ky were notably missing.

Khanh was obviously trying to demonstrate how well he could resist the role of puppet, thereby hoping to regain control over the generals; but in the process he inevitably revealed that the American mantle was slipping from his shoulders. Men as astute as Thieu and Ky could hardly have missed noting that.

That Ky at least was aware of Khanh's machinations became apparent on Christmas Day 1964 when, at Ambassador Taylor's request, my deputy, General Throckmorton, talked with Ky, Thieu, Thi, and Cang. Ky said that Khanh had been "practically finished" as Commander in Chief three weeks before, but he was using the dispute "to reconsolidate his position." With the exception of Admiral Cang, all revealed that their emotional wounds had healed and they would try to reach an accommodation with Premier Huong.

After considerable negotiation and back-sliding, the officials reached a solution soon after the start of the new year, 1965, but few could see it as anything more than tentative. It involved bringing four generals into the Cabinet, including Thieu and Ky. Although the armed forces reaffirmed faith in a civilian government, Khanh's continuing attestation that the armed forces bore a responsibility to intervene if the government changed course made it clear that any government still would survive only with the generals' forbearance.

Khanh himself appeared to soften to a degree, although I suspected it was another case of a Vietnamese talking in a way different from how he planned to act. Having made another of his nervous retreats to Vung Tau, he asked me to call, ostensibly to discuss military matters but in reality to dwell on the political scene.

He felt no animosity, Khanh said, for Ambassador Taylor and admitted he may have misinterpreted the ambassador's remark about leaving the country. He wanted only to do what was best for Vietnam. He was for the people, and since the Buddhists represented the bulk of the people, he had to consider their demands. He had told the Armed Forces Council, he said, that anytime the council lost confidence in him, he would resign and depart, asking only safe exit from the country for himself and his wife and children. Yet he had cautioned the generals to have a qualified person at hand to succeed him lest the army and then the nation collapse.

As Khanh talked, I noted that he had the beginnings of a mustache and a goatee. Over the months I had observed that whenever Khanh expected some major change or melodramatic event, he would grow mustache and goatee, then when the crisis passed, shave them off.

Khanh soon made his new move: a deal with the Buddhists. Although Buddhist demonstrations were continuing, including a general strike that paralyzed Hué, the numbers of demonstrators and their fervor were lessening, so that Buddhist leaders grew receptive to compromise. Yet not before they tried to revitalize their lagging protests with an anti-American campaign.

On January 23 a mob stormed the U. S. Information Service Library in Hué, destroying thousands of books, while signs denouncing Ambassador Taylor as a lackey of Premier Huong appeared throughout the city. Demonstrators in Saigon shouted anti-American slogans in front of the USIS Library and the Embassy. Khanh presented himself to the other generals as the only figure capable of negotiating with the Buddhists and halting the demonstrations. He had, he said, reached an agreement with the Buddhists. Although Buddhist leaders denied any deal, the demonstrations ceased.

On January 27 the Armed Forces Council did Khanh's bidding, ousting the Huong government and appointing Khanh to form another. As so often happened, the generals acted while Ambassador Taylor was on a trip outside the country. Although Khanh seemed inclined at first to set himself up as a powerful Chief of State, Ambassador Taylor upon his return passed the word to some of the generals that the United States Government would be unable to work with him. Khanh settled for retaining Suu as Chief of State and naming "Jack Owen" as Acting Premier until he could locate another candidate with more impressive credentials. He eventually decided on a medical doctor, Phan Huy Quat, a northerner whom most observers suspected of being in league with the Buddhists.

Dr. Quat had hardly named his cabinet—which included General Thieu—when a new crisis shook the government. Unsuccessful with the coup attempt in September, General Phat tried anew. He again had the support of the erstwhile 7th Division commander Colonel Ton, but the true instigator this time was a kind of professional revolutionary, Colonel Pham Ngoc Thao. Colonel Thao had commanded the tanks that moved on the presidential palace in the overthrow of Diem, but he had failed to gain favor with the ruling military clique and eventually had been shunted off to Washington as a press attaché. Recalled to Saigon in late 1964, Thao saw the recall as a trap, went underground, and began plotting a *coup d'état*.

In early afternoon of February 19, 1965, troops and tanks commanded by Thao seized the Saigon post office and radio station and surrounded the homes of Suu and Khanh, but not before General Khanh escaped in his private plane to Vung Tau. Forces under General Phat meanwhile seized Tan Son Nhut airport, parking tanks to block the runways, and occupied the South Vietnamese Air Force's Operations Center.

Only a short time before the coup attempt began, I had returned to Tan Son Nhut in the *White Whale* from an inspection trip to the Delta in company with one of President Johnson's special assistants, Michael Forrestal. The excitement generated by my plane's having been hit by small arms fire in departing Can Tho was soon forgotten in the turmoil engendered by the coup. I hurried to the Embassy. Reaching Joe Moore by telephone, I told him to go to the South Vietnamese Air Operations Center and to send his assistant, Brigadier General Robert R. Rowland, to stick with Air Marshal Ky. Both were to keep me informed of developments. Having been through coup attempts before, Moore and Rowland were on a list of officers whom I called "coup qualified."

Despite the presence of Phat's tanks, Ky managed to take off from a taxiway for Bien Hoa, where he assumed personal command of his elite squadron. Planes loaded with bombs and buzzing Saigon, Ky threatened to blast the Air Operations Center. Through General Rowland I sent Ky an ultimatum to desist, if for no other reason, because several thousand American troops were quartered in the vicinity. As the buzzing continued, I got Ky on the telephone from the Embassy and personally told him to knock it off. Much to the visible relief of the ambassador and Mike Forrestal, the buzzing stopped.

Within the Air Operations Center, General Moore busied himself with the in-basket at his desk, avoiding any impression of interfering but watching events closely. As several hours passed, General Phat grew nervous. Well he might, for the attempted coup had elicited little support. Venturing outside the Air Operations Center around midnight, Phat discovered that his rebel guards had fled. He hurried back inside, shed his uniform to reveal civilian clothes underneath, pumped Joe Moore's hand abruptly, said, "I go now," and disappeared in a waiting civilian automobile.

As troops loyal to General Khanh converged on Saigon, the rebels gave up. If any shots had been fired, they were blanks. By daylight the attempted coup had collapsed, but a more important development was yet to come. Meeting in mid-morning of February 20, the Armed Forces Council adopted a vote of no confidence in Khanh and elected General Tran Van ("Little") Minh as Commander in Chief, obviously an interim appointment.

After traveling about the country trying to rally support, Khanh landed at Dalat, his plane almost out of gas. I sent Jasper Wilson there to urge Khanh to avoid further crisis by resigning. Khanh obliged. A few days later he left for the United States, allegedly "to report to the United Nations" and to serve as an ambassador at large. Pulling out all stops to help Khanh save face, the generals gave him a ceremonial send-off with bands, flags, honor guard, and a high decoration.

Like all others of the U. S. Mission at the time, I saw the Phat-Thao shenanigan as a genuine attempt at a *coup d'état*. Looking back on it, however, I am convinced it was a staged farce with Thieu and Ky directing the action to demonstrate that Khanh was no longer capable of controlling the armed forces. Indeed, shortly after Khanh's departure, Ky reminded me that he had said earlier that any action against Khanh would be "legal."

Thieu and Ky, I believe now, enlisted Phat and Ton as fronts with a promise of amnesty for their September action and either safe passage out of the country or protection within the country. Both disappeared, and for as long as I was on the scene were never seen or heard from publicly.

As for Colonel Thao, whose apparently genuine machinations served as a convenient vehicle for the make-believe, he too disappeared for a time but emerged again in late May 1965 with another inept attempt at a coup, which the government quickly squashed. After having remarked to General Thieu that I saw Thao as a menace, I was shocked to learn a few days later that Thao had been killed in an argument with someone with whom he had been involved in a traffic accident. Such a number and variety of enemies did Thao have that I have always doubted the announced circumstances of his death.

With Khanh's departure, another act in Vietnam's troubled drama ended. Khanh was a capable man, straightforward and honest in his dealings with me, however devious he may have been in the political arena. While anxious to do what was right for his country, he had come to power in a no-win situation.

As for the young generals—and in particular Thieu and Ky—they could see no stable government under one who constantly temporized with extremist factions. Convinced that stability was essential if United States aid was to continue, they assumed the obligation of doing something through the medium of the nation's only viable institution, the armed forces, to achieve it, within the framework of civilian government, if possible; outside it, if not.

Whether the United States would, in fact, have pulled out of Vietnam in 1965 if the political instability showed no signs of abating is problematical. I think it likely that Washington was already too deeply committed in word and deed to do other than more of the same. Yet so obvious was the bickering, the machination, the inefficiency, the divisiveness among the Vietnamese that I suspect few in the world would have faulted us at that point had we thrown up our hands in despair. When we failed to renege on our commitment under such blatantly exigent conditions, the time when we could have withdrawn with some grace and honor had passed.

Chapter VI
Constant Crisis

The political turmoil in Saigon would have been unsettling under any circumstances. Set as it was against a backdrop of decreasing government control in the provinces, growing enemy strength, and blatant assaults against American installations, it was distressing, a fact demonstrated by growing debate in American circles as to what might be done to avert the defeat of South Vietnam.

It was a paradox that even though government control was sharply decreasing in hamlets and villages and the government simply had to surrender some areas, ARVN troops, when they came face to face with the enemy, more often than not gave as good as they got. When it came to the life-and-death struggle in the field, the political turmoil had little effect on the rank and file. The effect instead was on the upper leadership—division and corps commanders—who were reluctant to take risks or act decisively, to commit their forces until the enemy himself impelled them to move. If you did nothing, the government could hardly say you had done something wrong.

Because of growing enemy strength in units of battalion size or larger, ARVN units often had to abandon their pacification assignments, their relatively static defense of the population, in order to oppose the big units. Ignore the big units and you courted disaster. Failure to go after them in at least comparable strength invited defeat.

That was what happened in the mid-coastal province of Binh Dinh (which, ironically, means "pacification") where the ARVN incurred a serious defeat for which I bear a measure of personal responsibility. At my urging, ARVN leaders broke down their forces into small units, parceling them out to district chiefs to provide protection throughout the province and to patrol extensively in hope of inhibiting VC movement. The tactic worked fine for a while, but in November 1964 two main-force VC regiments came out of the hills and opened a general offensive.

One by one the big VC units defeated the small ARVN and militia detachments. Lacking an adequate reserve, ARVN leaders were powerless to strike back. To help salvage the situation, I gained approval to bring in several U. S. Army Special Forces detachments on temporary duty from Okinawa to retrain the militia and bolster morale. The ARVN units had to be rebuilt and put through a lengthy training program. A long time would pass before the damage in Binh Dinh province could be rectified. It was a lesson to be long remembered, one that I was often to recall in later months as many among my colleagues and in the American press agitated for paying less attention to the enemy's big units in order to assign more troops to the process of pacification.

Despite growing strength and the deterioration in Binh Dinh province, the Viet Cong were in general incapable of holding territory against a determined ARVN effort to retake it. Although the VC sometimes occupied villages and an occasional district town for several days, their eventual ouster was fairly certain. Yet controlling territory was at that stage unnecessary to achieve their goal of controlling population. Through the tested stratagems of coercion, harassment, shelling, kidnapping, murder, and other terrorism—sometimes burning entire hamlets—and through ambushes and attacks that inflicted painful losses on the ARVN, they kept an image of power before the people. No matter that they often failed to swing the people to their side; they still prevented or dissuaded the people from active commitment to the government.

A basic difficulty was that the ARVN simply lacked the numbers to be everywhere at once. If ARVN units sought or chased the enemy's big units, local guerrillas could move in and regain control in the face of a militia that was poorly equipped, poorly led, and poorly motivated. Yet without defeat of the big units there could be no security. As Lewis Carroll's Red Queen put it, it took all the running you could do just to stay in the same place.

An encouraging development was an increase of some 90,000 in strength of the South Vietnamese armed forces, mainly a result of Secretary McNamara having authorized increased resources during his visit in March 1964, followed by a government decree making all males between the ages of twenty and forty-five eligible for service. As with almost everything in Vietnam, a long lead time passed before results began to show; but by the fall of 1964 some 230,000 were serving as regulars and some 270,000 in the Regional and Popular Forces. How many men comprised the ARVN was dependent upon several factors: the manpower base available to the government for recruiting and drafting, the numbers that the government could conscript and that the ARVN training system could profitably absorb, and the funds that the Department of Defense in Washington was willing to dispense.

Based on a tradition that a boy becomes a man at age twenty, the South Vietnamese long resisted lowering the draft age to eighteen. The situation later became lamentable when thousands of American eighteen- and nineteen-year-olds were fighting and dying for a country that refused to draft its own youth of the same ages.

Similarly regrettable was the fact that sons of many South Vietnamese leaders who should have been fighting were sitting out the war in European schools. While insisting that the draft age be lowered, I also prodded the South Vietnamese to end that practice, pointing to sons of prominent Americans who served in Vietnam. Captain Thomas B. Throckmorton, for example, son of my deputy, Johnny Throckmorton, incurred a serious stomach wound while serving as an adviser to an airborne battalion in 1964 and on a second tour was for a time near death from injuries incurred in a helicopter crash. One of Ambassador Taylor's sons, Captain Tom Taylor, later fought with the 101st Airborne Division, and both President Johnson's sons-in-law, Charles Robb and Patrick Nugent, also served. The son of Admiral John S. McCain, Jr., who succeeded Oley Sharp as CINCPAC, was captured when his plane was shot down over North Vietnam; and First Lieutenant Stephen W. Davis, son of Brigadier General Franklin M. Davis, Jr., was killed in 1967 while serving with the 101st Airborne Division at a time when his father was my personnel officer in Saigon.

It was encouraging that some 3,000 Vietnamese were volunteering each month for service. No doubt partly draft-induced, the development also reflected the people's awareness and concern for the nation's plight.

Countering that was the fact that ARVN desertions were running from 5,000 to 7,000 a month. Hardly any of those men were defecting to the enemy; indeed, many were not deserters in a true sense but were taking French leave to look after their families or the rice crop or were re-enlisting in Regional or Popular Forces, so they could serve closer to their families. South Vietnamese record keeping was too rudimentary to reflect those aspects of the problem. Although the government talked a hard line on deserters and draft dodgers, particularly those in Saigon, which was a magnet for them, enforcement in the politically volatile atmosphere was feeble.

VC casualties far exceeded those of South Vietnamese forces: as reported by the government, over 20,000 VC were killed and captured in 1964 against just over 7,000 South Vietnamese. Yet the VC seemed fully capable of absorbing those losses. Another 17,000 VC had surrendered under a *chieu hoi* (open arms, or amnesty) program since the late President Diem started it in the spring of the previous year. Yet the VC still grew rapidly. In a year they increased by some 85,000 to a total estimated strength of 170,000. Most were recruited in the South, reflecting a broadening base of VC control of the population, but the number of North Vietnamese infiltrating into South Vietnam also increased, reaching a total for 1964 of 12,000.

The ambush was the VC forte and the ARVN nemesis. By means of the ambush, the VC on a number of occasions destroyed entire ARVN companies. Although American helicopter strength increased to the point where a U. S. Army aviation company or a U. S. Marine Corps aviation squadron was available for each ARVN division, much ARVN travel still had to be by road. A common VC tactic was to attack an ARVN outpost, then lie in wait for the ARVN reserve coming by land to help.

I constantly exhorted ARVN commanders to find these ambushes by patrolling in advance of movement, then to capitalize on the enemy's vulnerability inherent in his fixed position. Because the enemy was immobile, he could be outflanked and destroyed. To serve as a reminder for American advisers, I distributed small pocket cards that explained how to defeat ambushes, but for all my efforts, it was not until much later, after American units had demonstrated how to do the job, that ARVN units were consistently able to elude and defeat enemy ambushes.

Long a student of the Chinese military philosopher Sun Tzu, who may be called the Clausewitz of the Orient, although he wrote centuries ahead of the nineteenth century German military philosopher, I was conscious that many South Vietnamese officers, as I had found earlier with Korean officers, shared my interest in his theories. So often did the VC evade ARVN encirclement that I suspected an undue obeisance on the part of ARVN leaders to Sun Tzu's dictum to beware lest a surrounded enemy fight like a trapped tiger: "To a surrounded enemy you must leave a way of escape." Yet in the end I concluded that the South Vietnamese were doing their best, but that the VC were simply uncommonly adept at slithering away.

Aside from Binh Dinh province, the most serious erosion of government control was in the I Corps Zone, where there was even less tradition of loyalty to a Saigon government than elsewhere and where student and Buddhist agitation compounded the difficulties. Aside from the cities, about all the government controlled were the villages astride critical Route 1, and even that control was questionable. Only in the HOP TAC area around Saigon was the government expanding its influence.

The village of Phu Hoa Dong in Binh Duong province, north of Saigon, provided an example of what could be accomplished if security could be maintained. Before HOP TAC started, Phu Hoa Dong was virtually dead, containing only 738 people. Six months later the population had increased to 1,800. Before, only forty-seven children had been going to school; six months later, a thousand. Where before there had been no market place, six months later more than a hundred merchants were doing business. Yet for every Phu Hoa Dong there were a dozen other villages elsewhere in the country where the VC roamed freely, if not by day, then surely by night.

The performance of South Vietnamese forces was in many cases inspiring. At Camp Kannach, a U. S. Special Forces outpost in Binh Dinh province north of An Khe, a band of Montagnards of the Hre tribe held off an entire enemy regiment. As I always tried to do after a major engagement, I flew to the camp to find the tiny, primitive tribesmen elated with their performance. Through the bloody fight, women and children had tended the wounded and reloaded ammunition belts. I was emotionally touched by the performance, truly a community victory.

Instances of individual heroism by both Vietnamese and Americans were commonplace. In July 1964, for example, at Nam Dong, a CIDG-Special Forces camp in jungle-clad mountains near the Laotian border, Captain Roger Hugh C. Donlon almost single-handedly held the South Vietnamese forces together in the face of attack by a reinforced VC battalion. Through a welter of enemy fire and shells, Donlon dashed here and there about the perimeter, rescuing wounded Vietnamese, retrieving abandoned crew-served weapons, and killing several of the enemy who had broken through. He refused treatment for multiple wounds from shell fragments until daylight came and the enemy fell back. Captain Donlon still had not been evacuated when I arrived at Nam Dong and presented him the Bronze Star, the highest award for valor that I was authorized at that time to award on the spot. It was subsequently raised to the Medal of Honor, the first to be awarded for action in Vietnam, which Donlon received from the hands of President Johnson.

After the bulk of the 25th ARVN Division had left Quang Ngai province to participate in HOP TAC and the enemy made a determined effort to overrun militia forces near Quang Ngai City, my operations officer, Bill DePuy, arrived at the height of the action and personally shifted units to critical points. Adroit commitment of an ARVN ranger battalion and the individual heroism of the battalion's adviser, Captain Christopher O'Sullivan, saved the day, although O'Sullivan died in the process. He was posthumously awarded both the Distinguished Service Cross and the Silver Star. O'Sullivan's father later wrote me an inspiring letter in which he said he regretted that he had "only one son to give the battle."

On a visit to the district village of Hoi Nhon in Binh Dinh province just after a company of Regional Forces had repelled a VC attack, I met the hero of the action, a Sergeant Truong, who had assumed command after the company's only officer was killed. On subsequent visits I was so impressed with the way Sergeant Truong ran the company that I called him to the attention of General Khanh, who went personally to Hoi Nhon and promoted Truong to second lieutenant. So capable was Truong that the VC in the district openly advertised their intent to kill him.

On yet another visit I found Truong proudly wearing his lieutenant's insignia, but through inept administration, after six months he was still drawing a sergeant's pay. I saw to it that this was corrected in Saigon, but a short time later I received word that the VC had made good on their threat. Lieutenant Truong was killed on patrol.

Truong was typical of many South Vietnamese, fighting for long years against tremendous odds with no end in sight but carrying on with dedication and fearlessness. Touched by his death, I wrote a letter of condolence to his young widow and made a special request to the South Vietnamese government that she be provided for.

Yet however impressive the performances of individuals and ARVN units, recurring defeats marred the over-all picture. A contributing factor was a new family of weapons that the VC began to adopt in 1964, the most important of which was an assault rifle provided by the Soviet Union, the automatic AK-47, a superior weapon whose high cyclic rate of fire produced an emetic sound similar to that of the World War II German "burp gun." The Viet Cong heretofore had mainly used weapons captured from the ARVN or left over from the fighting with the French. In mid-1964 North Vietnam began to provide them with rifles and machine guns of a single caliber, 7.62-mm, brought from the Soviet Union and Communist China. Also provided were modern rocket launchers, mortars, and recoilless rifles. Most of these weapons arrived by sea, smuggled into some of the innumerable coves along South Vietnam's extensive coastline; the South Vietnamese junk force trying to screen the coast had many of the characteristics of a sieve. Although the increased firepower complicated the enemy's resupply of ammunition, that was more than offset by the advantages of standardization and increased effect. Against the new weapons the ARVN still had U. S. World War II models, including the semiautomatic M-1 rifle and, for Regional and Popular Forces, the light semiautomatic M-2 carbine.

Probably the most portentous ARVN defeat of 1964 occurred in late December in Phuoc Tuy province, on the coast little more than a stone's throw from Saigon. Two VC regiments, linked together to form the 9th Division, the enemy's first divisional unit, infiltrated from War Zones C and D to the coast, picked up their new weapons, and retired to the nearby jungle to train. On December 27 the division emerged from the jungle and a rubber plantation and overran the hamlet of Binh Gia, a settlement of some 6,000 North Vietnamese Catholic refugees.

Over the next two days a Vietnamese ranger battalion fought its way into the fringes of the hamlet. When a marine battalion arrived on the third day, the enemy retired to entrenchments in the rubber plantation. There the marines came under sharp attack that lasted until the VC broke off the engagement on New Year's Day. In the course of the fighting the ranger and marine battalions were virtually destroyed. However serious that result, the portentous fact was that the enemy appeared to be moving from guerrilla and small-unit warfare into a new and presumably final phase, attacks by big units that would stand their ground.

That was disturbing enough in itself. We would have been even more concerned had we known at the time that as early as September 1964, the North Vietnamese decided to commit North Vietnamese regiments and divisions in the south, a decision that went beyond mere support of the insurgency to direct intervention by regular units of the North Vietnamese Army.

Since October we had been aware that infiltrators from the north included not only "regroupees" who had departed the south after the Geneva Accords but also regulars and draftees of the North Vietnamese Army. South Vietnamese intelligence experts claimed that the infiltrators constituted separate North Vietnamese units, but my own intelligence specialists saw them as packages formed for infiltration purposes but then broken up as individual replacements for VC units. Yet in either case they were North Vietnamese soldiers.

Whether the North Vietnamese came as units or as individuals was soon moot. The first regular North Vietnamese regiment, we learned later, had arrived in Kontum province in the Central Highlands in December 1964.

In a rising debate in American circles in Saigon and Washington that accompanied the continuing political unrest in South Vietnam and growing enemy strength, I was less bellicose about what was needed to reverse the trend than were some; for I was convinced from the first that there were no easy solutions, that the war would be long and costly. During a talk with Secretary McNamara during his visit in May 1964, when the Secretary was apparently trying to satisfy himself that I was indeed the man to take over from Paul Harkins, I called the situation a "bottomless pit." I warned that it would take a lot of resources and infinite patience on the part of the American people. Only with such patience could we eventually succeed. So important did I consider patience that I urged McNamara to recommend some kind of people-to-people program, to get the American people involved emotionally with the Vietnamese people, to provide an incentive for perseverance that would go beyond any engendered by a strategic American interest in Southeast Asia. McNamara brushed my suggestion aside.

Washington had already decided, I learned later, to play the war in a low key. Nineteen-sixty-four was an election year, with the President's most likely opponent a man who advocated the strongest measures against North Vietnam. Indeed, concerned lest the hawks force acceptance of harsh measures, the Johnson administration long withheld from the public the information that North Vietnamese regular troops were entering South Vietnam. Even after the election had passed, a policy of extreme caution, of minimum rocking of the political boat, of both guns and butter, of war plus the "Great Society" was to continue. Nobody appeared to recall Sun Tzu's dictum: "There has never been a protracted war from which a country has benefited." Nor the Duke of Wellington's admonition to the House of Lords: "A great country cannot wage a little war."

Only days after I reached Vietnam in early 1964, the United States Joint Chiefs of Staff proposed striking at the insurgency's outside base by bombing North Vietnam. Had I been consulted on the proposal, I would have disagreed. Although I had no doubt that North Vietnam was supporting the insurgency and that eventually we would have to do something about it, why take provocative actions that might prompt increased North Vietnamese participation at a time when the South Vietnamese were patently incapable of countering it?

I was particularly concerned lest the North Vietnamese respond to bombing by committing major troop units in the South. Barring direct intervention by the Soviet Union or Communist China—which I considered unlikely —how else could the North Vietnamese react except on the ground? Under increased pressure the fragile structure that South Vietnam was at the time might collapse. Although I believed that with a stable, enlightened government the South Vietnamese could eventually suppress the VC, I had no such illusions should North Vietnam openly intervene.

Firm in that belief, I made no pitch either during Secretary McNamara's visits in the spring or during the Honolulu conference in June 1964 for bombing the north. In presenting my proposal for HOP TAC, I was furthering the policy that Secretary McNamara and the President had decided upon, which was essentially to step up the pacification program while working to increase ARVN strength and capabilities and striving for political stability. Neither I nor officials in Washington had any way of knowing that even without bombing of North Vietnam, the North Vietnamese would decide to intervene.

I had less concern about North Vietnamese reaction to covert operations against the North and against the supply corridor maintained through the Laotian panhandle known as the Ho Chi Minh Trail. Some of those operations had been going on since as early as 1961 with no apparent North Vietnamese reaction other than the specific defensive measures taken against the operations themselves. Although I had serious reservations about how much the covert operations accomplished, they represented probably the only action we could take against the North without provoking a level of reaction which the South Vietnamese would be unable to absorb. Nor did I have any question about the morality of the operations since they were much the same as North Vietnam long had supported against the South.

President Kennedy had authorized the first covert operations in mid-1961, a program that included inserting South Vietnamese agents into North Vietnam, attempting to form networks of resistance in the North, dropping propaganda leaflets, and infiltrating small South Vietnamese forces into the Laotian panhandle to attack Communist bases and supply routes. Late in the year the South Vietnamese with American assistance organized a fleet of motorized junks to search traffic off the South Vietnamese coast for enemy infiltrators and supplies.

Soon after President Kennedy's assassination, President Johnson directed planning for possible increased activity against North Vietnam. From that planning emerged OPLAN 34A, providing for covert operations by South Vietnamese who were to be trained and supported logistically by MACV and the CIA. The theory was that by gradually increasing pressure North Vietnamese leaders might be convinced to end their support of the insurgencies in South Vietnam and Laos, although few associated with the plan held any real hope for such a conclusive result. As approved by Washington, the program began primarily for intelligence purposes but later included such acts as shelling military installations along the North Vietnamese coast.

To plan and execute the operations, MACV established a Studies and

Observation Group, known by the acronym SOG. This was what is known as a "joint unconventional warfare task force" and thus included representatives of all U.S. services and a few liaison personnel from the CIA. Although SOG was a component of MACV, a special office in the U. S. Joint Chiefs of Staff supervised its activities, for from the first Washington exercised the closest control over SOG's operations. Every action had to be approved in advance by the Secretary of Defense, Secretary of State, and the White House.

Antedating SOG, a related program known as DESOTO involved patrols by United States destroyers in the Gulf of Tonkin. As were all U. S. Navy operations outside South Vietnam, the DESOTO patrols were managed by CINCPAC with no participation by MACV. The destroyers *Maddox* and *C. Turner Joy* were operating under that program when they encountered North Vietnamese patrol boats in August 1964 in the Gulf of Tonkin.

SOG conducted its first operations in February 1964, in what the Joint Chiefs called "a slow beginning," but they continued on the theory that they forced the North Vietnamese to expend considerable resources to defend against them. Over the years SOG's operating force increased to some 2,500 Americans and 7,000 South Vietnamese mercenaries. Except for the headquarters staff, all were volunteers. In the case of the Americans, most were from the Special Forces; thus they were in effect triple volunteers, having opted first for airborne training, then for the Special Forces, then for specific SOG missions. It said something for the intrepidity of the American soldier that SOG always had a waiting list of applicants.

One of the first SOG operations in Laos, known by the code name LEAPING LENA, involved parachute drops of five- to six-man South Vietnamese teams to reconnoiter for enemy installations and to harass traffic along the Ho Chi Minh Trail. Few of those first efforts or those of agents inserted into North Vietnam were successful, most of the men being killed or captured, but the record quickly improved. Beginning in 1965 patrols known as PRAIRIE FIRE, consisting usually of nine Vietnamese and three Americans, began operating in the Laotian panhandle. Their basic mission was to gather intelligence: locate likely bombing targets, check enemy troop and supply traffic, capture prisoners for interrogation, place mines and sensors on enemy trails. Yet many ran into the enemy and had to fight and some had destruction missions, such as attacking underdefended command posts or destroying rice or ammunition stocks that were difficult to get at with air strikes. For those missions SOG usually employed Montagnard tribesmen whose people lived on both sides of the frontier.

In later months SOG created two battalions to be used as a reserve, or reaction, force whenever a team got into a fight it was unable to handle alone. Helicopters and fighter planes might be called in first. Calls for help went by radio, relayed from an outpost inside Laos called the "Eagle's Nest," atop a peak so high and steep that every North Vietnamese effort to capture it or shell it ended in failure.

The SOG commanders were an ingenious group. One of the first had been my operations officer in the 101st Airborne Division, Colonel John K. Singlaub. Unknown to me at the time, Jack Singlaub personally reconnoitered the site for the Eagle's Nest to make sure it could be defended. He and his staff developed special clothing and equipment for Americans manning the Eagle's Nest and participating on patrols so that nothing could be traced to its U.S. origin.

Since patrols often stayed out as long as two weeks, Singlaub's staff developed special rations even lighter than the U. S. Army's usual emergency rations. A squadron of C-130 aircraft equipped with special personnel recovery devices, which Singlaub personally tested to demonstrate its effectiveness, supported the patrols. The patrols operated from existing CIDG-Special Forces camps along the frontier or from new camps created for the purpose, such as the one at a place in the extreme northwestern corner of South Vietnam known as Khe Sanh.

SOG also operated radio stations with powerful transmitters, one at Hué known as the "Voice of Freedom" and called a "gray" station because it never revealed its location, and others called "black" stations that professed to be located within North Vietnam and run by dissident North Vietnamese. SOG conducted some black broadcasts from a circling propeller-driven aircraft.

Americans seldom participated in operations in areas under North Vietnamese jurisdiction except for frogmen who might accompany sea-launched patrols or men assisting in land operations to rescue downed American pilots. Colonel Singlaub kept several of his best teams on constant alert for land rescue missions. When a call came for help, they would fly to an American aircraft carrier off the coast, then go into North Vietnam in U. S. Navy helicopters. If one can differentiate among the incredibly brave deeds performed by all the men who served with SOG, those who went on rescue missions were the most intrepid of all. Two in particular—Sergeants Dick Meadows and Jerry Waring—performed with such courage that Colonel Singlaub asked my help to get them commissioned as captains.

Beginning in 1964 SOG used motorized South Vietnamese junks to kidnap North Vietnamese civilians—usually fishermen—and take them to an island off the coast near the DMZ. From the SOG base on the island, run entirely by the South Vietnamese, the fishermen were unable to discern that they were not on the mainland. Representing themselves as Communists but anti-North Vietnamese Communists, the South Vietnamese while querying their prisoners about conditions inside their country would gradually indoctrinate them in anti-Communist thinking. They would keep them from six to eight weeks, feeding them well so that when released their condition would impress their compatriots and they themselves would recognize the limitations of their previous diet. The South Vietnamese also cared for their medical and dental needs and upon release gave them radio sets fixed on SOG and South Vietnamese stations and gifts of clothing, toys, sewing kits, all designed to impress North Vietnamese villagers with South Vietnamese compassion and generosity. Over the years probably about 1,200 North Vietnamese underwent this indoctrination.

How effective SOG operations? That is hard to tell. Judging from North Vietnamese jamming efforts, SOG radio broadcasts clearly rankled. SOG patrols in Laos destroyed large amounts of ammunition and other supplies, forced the North Vietnamese to expend manpower on defense, and pushed our eyes and ears beyond the South Vietnamese borders into regions whence the enemy emerged to launch his attacks inside the country. Whether the indoctrination program had tangible results may never be known. If nothing else, it must have impressed those who went through it with the corruption of their officials, for the officials confiscated the gift kits the South Vietnamese provided. The South Vietnamese countered by providing two kits, one to be confiscated, another to be hidden for later use. In any event, to my mind, in a war that as much as any in history pitted will against will, it was worth a try.

Although President Johnson rejected the first proposal by the Joint Chiefs to bomb North Vietnam, he did authorize contingency planning for reprisals or even greater pressure against the North. Prepared by CINCPAC in the spring of 1964, this was known as OPLAN 37 and involved three proposed phases of operations against enemy infiltration routes in border areas of Laos and Cambodia and against North Vietnam. Phase One provided for pursuit of enemy forces across the borders of Laos and Cambodia; Phase Two, "tit-for-tat" reprisal air strikes, raids, and mining operations against North Vietnam; and Phase Three, increasingly severe and continuing air strikes against the North. All operations were to be by South Vietnamese forces with some help from American planes.

Those of us in Saigon who knew of OPLAN 37 saw little possibility that the President would implement it until after the November election. Indeed, we saw it strictly as a postelection plan. When the President responded to the Gulf of Tonkin incidents in early August with reprisal air strikes, that was a one-shot affair unrelated to OPLAN 37.

Although I agreed with the reprisal strikes, they heightened my concern that the North Vietnamese might react by committing major units in the South before the South Vietnamese were capable of coping with the development. While doubting that Ho Chi Minh would risk an overt invasion and thus expose his forces to air attack, I believed he might step up infiltration, possibly to include some of his regular army units, and with increased strength, attack major U.S. bases at Danang, Bien Hoa, and Tan Son Nhut. Some of my concern was allayed when Washington sent seventy more U. S. Air Force planes to Tan Son Nhut and Danang, moved others to Thailand and the Philippines, placed two Marine Corps battalion landing teams aboard ship in the Gulf of Tonkin, and alerted other units for possible deployment, including a U. S. Army airborne brigade.

Although the enemy failed to attack our bases, another incident occurred in the Gulf of Tonkin the night of September 18, 1964, when the destroyers *Edwards* and *Morton* fired on and apparently sank what appeared on their radar screens to be enemy PT boats. Probably because of doubt as to whether the targets were in reality North Vietnamese craft, Washington this time ordered no reprisal.

Aside from my concern over likely North Vietnamese reaction to bombing the North, I thought at that stage that the only possibility, however remote, of convincing North Vietnamese leaders to halt their support of the insurgency was to demonstrate within South Vietnam that the insurgency was bound to fail. To my mind we could better use our air power to that end by supporting ARVN operations and by hitting the enemy's infiltration route through Laos.

The first use of U.S. aircraft in the Laotian panhandle had begun in May 1964, under a program known as YANKEE TEAM wherein Air Force and Navy carrier planes flew reconnaissance flights over the panhandle and the Plain of Jars in north-central Laos in support of the Royal Laotian Air Force. Under strict rules of engagement prescribed by Washington, U.S. planes could fire only if fired upon and flights over the panhandle were limited to approximately five missions per week.

In late August I asked for approval of combined American-South Vietnamese air strikes against specific targets in the panhandle, but Washington demurred. For a long time the only other authorization for air operations in the panhandle was, in effect, a step-up of the YANKEE TEAM flights, with authority actually to attack targets of opportunity, such as North Vietnamese transport and troop concentrations. Operations began on December 14, 1964. Known as BARREL ROLL, the flights involved only two missions a week, each with four aircraft, so that it was hardly surprising that the North Vietnamese failed to discern that a new program was underway.

For several months I had even less success in obtaining authority to use American planes in support of ARVN forces other than under the restrictive FARMGATE program. On the first of November I asked approval to employ American planes "if and when required," but to no avail. Conscious of the growing number of large enemy units appearing on the battlefield, I renewed my request in late January 1965, intentionally limiting the scope of the requested authority in the hope that that approach would encourage approval. "As a matter of military prudence," I cabled, "I am constrained to ask for authority to employ U.S. jet aircraft in a strike role . . . under emergency situations." This time Washington approved but with the proviso that I personally rule on each mission. I was to authorize strikes only to deny a "major" VC victory, to avoid loss of "numbers" of American lives, or to execute spoiling attacks beyond the capability of Vietnamese planes.

I used the new authority for the first time in mid-February, 1965, with a spoiling attack by two dozen B-57s against a reported VC regiment in the jungles of Phuoc Tuy province, not far from the scene of the bloody fighting

The author as a teen-ager.

The author as a teen-ager.

The author as a cadet during the summer of 1933, with Major Omar N. Bradley, later the United States Army's last surviving five-star general.

The author as a first classman in the spring of 1936 rides at Tuxedo Park, New York.

The author as a cadet receives his diploma in 1936 from General of the Armies John J. Pershing. At right is Major General William D. Connor, Superintendent of the Military Academy.

The author leading troops of the Horse Artillery at his first duty station, Fort Sill, Oklahoma, 1938.

The author (front center) and other officers and men of Battery B, 18th Field Artillery Battalion, at Fort Sill, Oklahoma, in 1938. On the front left is Captain Homer Kiefer; on the front right, Lieutenant John Cone.

The author, second from right, with fellow commanders of the 9th Division before D-Day, 1944.

Wedding at Fayetteville, North Carolina, May 3, 1947.

The author after a training parachute jump in Korea in 1952. *(U. S. Army Photograph)*

The author and Mrs. Westmoreland at West Point, with former President and Mrs. Dwight D. Eisenhower in 1961.

The author and Mrs. Westmoreland with General and Mrs. Douglas MacArthur, on the occasion of General MacArthur's farewell address at West Point, May 1962. (*U. S. Army Photograph*)

President John F. Kennedy's arrival at West Point in June 1962. (*U. S. Army Photograph*)

The author early in 1964, before departure for Saigon, with his father (left), sister, Mrs. N. Heyward Clarkson, Jr., and mother.

No. 60 Tran Quy Cap, Saigon. *(U. S. Army Photograph)*

Old MACV headquarters at 137 Pasteur Street
Saigon. *(U. S. Army Photograph)*

On the occasion of the departure of General Paul D. Harkins from Saigon in late
spring 1964. From left: the author, General Tran Thien Khiem, General Nguyen
Khanh, Ambassador Henry Cabot Lodge, General Harkins, and General
Nguyen Van Thieu.

at the end of 1964 around Binh Gia. Only a few days later, on February 24, 1965, I employed my authority again when the enemy trapped an ARVN ranger battalion and a CIDG company and their American advisers near the Mang Yang Pass on Route 19 between An Khe and Pleiku City, the same area in which the Viet Minh had destroyed Groupement Mobile 100 ten years earlier. Without the support of American jets and helicopter gunships, the small force probably would have been annihilated. Following the air strikes, helicopters extracted everybody without the loss of a man.

With this demonstration of the value of U.S. planes in mind, I again asked broad authority. "The strength, armament, professionalism, and activity of the VC have increased to the point," I reported, "where we can ill afford any longer to withhold available military means to support the counterinsurgency campaign." I asked permission to use American planes inside South Vietnam "as I judge prudent." Yet again Washington slackened the reins only slightly. To use the planes in other than emergency situations or spoiling attacks, I had to get approval of each mission from the Joint Chiefs in Washington.

That, I replied, was "impractical and operationally unsound." "Again," I cabled, "I urge that I be given my head and allowed to use these means in accordance with my best judgment."

At last I succeeded. A return cable removed almost all restrictions. Although the FARMGATE training program was to continue, all aircraft not actually belonging to the South Vietnamese were to bear U.S. markings and might be used for tactical missions without the much-abused proviso of having a Vietnamese aboard. All American planes inside South Vietnam might be used to support ARVN and South Vietnamese Air Force operations except in cases where the Vietnamese were capable of doing the job alone.

Meanwhile, through the fall of 1964, the numbers of American troops increased slightly to a total of approximately 23,000. The increases were mainly in Army helicopter units, aviation support units, signal troops, and Special Forces. Among the new arrivals was headquarters of the 5th Special Forces in October, a result of an earlier request by General Harkins. Also during the fall the South Vietnamese for the first time granted approval for American advisers to operate at battalion level.

As the year neared an end, I remained considerably less disturbed about the military situation than was either Ambassador Taylor or officials in Washington. Like Taylor, I wanted a reprisal bombing for the VC attack in November on our base near the town of Bien Hoa, but I could understand Washington's view that such a change in policy two days before the presidential election might look like a political ploy. I also welcomed word from the Joint Chiefs a few days later to plan reprisals for future attacks; but to espouse tit-for-tat bombing was different from endorsing a continuing air campaign against the North.

I still believed we should wait before beginning sustained bombing until the South Vietnamese government was, as I put it at the time, established "on a reasonably firm political, military, and psychological base before we risk the great strains that may be incurred" by taking steps that might provoke large troop commitments from North Vietnam. While agreeing that hitting the North would have a salutary effect on South Vietnamese morale, I was not a party, I told the Ambassador, "to the thought that this country is despondent at this juncture." I believed we should wait at least until the turn of the year to see how the government was progressing before instituting a tough policy against the North, and I saw the possibility that we might be able to delay that until the spring of 1965. To a Joint Chiefs' proposal that the U.S. military's dependents go home and a U. S. Marine force land at Danang, I replied that either or both would reflect lack of confidence in the Vietnamese and would seriously affect their morale.

For all my objections, both Ambassador Taylor and the Joint Chiefs were coming to think more and more in terms of sustained bombing of the North. Had it not been for my concern over North Vietnamese reaction against an unprepared South Vietnam, I would have agreed, for bombing quite clearly would hamper North Vietnamese support of the insurgency, though to what degree would depend upon the intensity of the campaign. Ambassador Taylor and some civilian officials in Washington were also tending to think of bombing in terms of a gradually escalating campaign, of twisting the enemy's arm with more and more pressure until eventually, so the theory had it, the North Vietnamese leaders would cry uncle.

This eventually became known as a policy of "graduated response." Subsequently adopted, it was one of the most lamentable mistakes of the war.

To my knowledge, the history of warfare contained no precedent for such a policy. Although nations in the past have intentionally kept wars limited, as the United States did in Korea, they have applied pressure in terms of their self-imposed restrictions with full force whenever the means were available. In almost all wars the tempo of operations has gradually increased, but not through any conscious policy of gradual escalation, rather through the gradually increasing availability of means. In World War II, for example, the United States started slowly, but through lack of preparedness rather than design.

Faced with escalating pressure, the North Vietnamese could adapt to each new step and absorb the damage, so that any hope that the enemy's leaders would find the prospect of the next step unbearable was false. The only way bombing the North could convince the North Vietnamese to desist was to hit surely, swiftly, and powerfully, not with everything in the American arsenal, for that would have been overkill, but with sufficient force to hurt and to demonstrate a clear, firm resolve. The strikes would have to be aimed from the first at vital targets, such as the limited but nonetheless important industrial facilities in the vicinity of Hanoi and Haiphong, and would have to include mining Haiphong Harbor. Washington's phobia that sudden heavy air strikes and mining the harbor would trigger Chinese Communist or Russian intervention was chimerical.

Even had Washington adopted a strong bombing policy, I still doubt that the North Vietnamese would have relented. That they made some concessions when President Nixon pursued it in 1972 is another matter, for by that time the condition of the insurgency was far different than it was in 1964 and 1965. To force the North Vietnamese to desist at that earlier time, we had to do more than hurt their homeland; we had to demonstrate that they could not win in the South, and South Vietnam had to make real progress in pacification. In 1964 and early 1965, defeating or even containing the insurgency was a question of political stability, and such tangential benefits as a bombing program might produce were to my mind too minor to justify risking a North Vietnamese reaction that might overwhelm the existing unstable government.

President Johnson took the first step toward a policy of sustained bombing in early December when he conditionally accepted a two-phase program —in effect, the first two phases of OPLAN 37—recommended by an interagency board called the National Security Council Working Group. He approved Phase One, involving increased American air operations in the Laotian panhandle and tit-for-tat reprisals for major VC attacks, and he agreed in principle to Phase Two, gradually escalating air strikes against the North. Yet he withheld authority for Phase Two. That was to be contingent on improved performance by the Saigon government.

The bombing of the Brink Hotel on Christmas Eve 1964 seemed to me and to Ambassador Taylor to be a major attack amply justifying recourse to the new policy of tit-for-tat, but Washington disagreed, citing reasons that may have seemed cogent thousands of miles away but in Saigon were absurd. Such as continuing political turmoil in Saigon, lack of irrefutable proof that the VC had done the deed for all their propaganda claims of credit for it, and the presence of American dependents. The only reason that made sense to me was that Washington delayed so long coming to a decision that the enemy would have been hard put to figure out what we were retaliating for.

President Johnson himself explained the reasons for failing to authorize retaliation for the Brink Hotel bombing in a personal cable to Ambassador Taylor in which he questioned whether we were doing all we could to protect our installations and whether we were communicating effectively with the various political factions within the country. He also expressed doubt that bombing the North represented any panacea, encouraging us instead to think of putting starch into the ARVN by introducing specialized American ground troops, such as rangers and more Special Forces. Stung by the President's implied criticism and disturbed that he saw introducing ground troops as a less serious step than bombing the North, Ambassador Taylor consulted with Alexis Johnson and me in framing his reply. All of us were conscious of the momentous nature and probable long-range consequences of introducing American ground troops and were anxious to avoid it if at all possible.

"We are faced here," Ambassador Taylor wrote the President, "with a seriously deteriorating situation characterized by continued political turmoil, irresponsibility and division within the Armed Forces, lethargy in the pacification program, growing anti-U.S. feeling, signs of mounting terrorism by VC directed at U.S. personnel, and deepening discouragement and loss of morale throughout S[outh] V[iet] N[am]." We had about as many advisers, he went on, as the Vietnamese could absorb. Introducing American combat troops might result in the South Vietnamese letting the U.S. "carry the ball" and, in view of past colonialism, lead to open hostility against Americans. For Americans to provide their own security would require some 75,000 American troops, and even then nobody could guarantee against a repetition of Bien Hoa and the Brink Hotel.

Noting that many factors were beyond U.S. ability to change, such as the unstable government and a general war-weariness, Taylor concluded that "something new" had to be added "to make up for those things we cannot control," something that would contribute to marshaling the various factions in the country behind the government. The only possibility, as Ambassador Taylor saw it, was the old recipe of bombing the North.

Put teeth into the decision for tit-for-tat bombing, he urged, by authorizing joint planning with the South Vietnamese for reprisals and developing a process that would enable retaliation within twenty-four hours of an enemy attack. When those strikes began, he added, we would have a rationale for removing American dependents without that looking like a retreat. Once minimal conditions of stability were established within the Saigon government, go to Phase Two, "graduated" air strikes against the North. "To take no positive action now," he wrote, "is to accept defeat in the fairly near future."

Something quite clearly had to be done to bolster the Vietnamese armed forces and the people. What else could we do? The theory that a graduated bombing campaign would convince North Vietnamese leaders to desist remained more than I could accept, but like Ambassador Taylor, who also had doubts, I could see no viable alternative within current policy restrictions and a reasonable time frame. Noting Ambassador Taylor's reservation that the graduated bombing be delayed until the stability of the South Vietnamese government improved and the strength of South Vietnamese military forces increased, I went along with the recommendation.

A possible alternative that planners in Washington had explored as early as 1961 was introducing an international force to guard against infiltration through Laos and the DMZ. In the spring of 1964 President Johnson had appealed for help from other Free World countries in what became known as the "more flags" program, but it involved only economic and technical aid. President Johnson in December 1964 again raised the subject. I was enthusiastic, for it seemed to me that with troops of nations other than South

Vietnam and the United States committed along the borders, where they could see for themselves the North Vietnamese violation of the South and—if the North Vietnamese persisted—participate in countering the infiltration, the rest of the world would be more likely to accept the fact of the violation and pressure on the North Vietnamese to desist would mount. Yet forming an international force would take time and was no substitute for the dramatic, immediate "something new" needed at the time.

Although Ambassador Taylor's communication to the President produced no major new move, I did receive authority in late January 1965 for joint planning with the Vietnamese for reprisal bombing, and in response to a Taylor recommendation that the President send a personal representative to survey the scene, his National Security adviser, McGeorge Bundy, arrived in Saigon in early February. Bundy was on the last day of his visit when on February 7 the VC attacked the U.S. advisory compound and airfield at Camp Holloway in the Central Highlands near Pleiku City.

Employing mortars and demolitions teams, the VC killed eight Americans, destroyed five aircraft and damaged several others. Done at a time when the Soviet Premier, Aleksei Kosygin, was visiting Hanoi, the attack looked to be a deliberate provocation.

With news of the attack, McGeorge Bundy and Ambassadors Taylor and Johnson joined me in the operations room of my Saigon headquarters. As discussion evolved on what our reaction should be—basically a political decision—I intentionally held back, presenting my views as a military man only when asked.

Bundy himself led the discussion, intense, abrupt, at moments a bit arrogant. He may have been distressed that what he and other civilian officials in Washington had been hopefully predicting would not happen, had now happened and that it had brought us to a kind of Rubicon. Or perhaps, like numbers of civilians in positions of some governmental authority, once he smelled a little gunpowder he developed a field marshal psychosis.

Although Bundy seemed perturbed about reprisal strikes while Kosygin was in Hanoi, he and the rest of us recognized that the targets we would hit were far from Hanoi. Furthermore, the attack had been too blatant to be ignored. Bundy himself telephoned the White House with a recommendation for reprisal. The President quickly approved, subject to South Vietnamese concurrence.

The decision made, I sensed among my colleagues a feeling of immense concern tempered by relief: by God, we had acted and this was a turning point! Since it was a reprisal action, I failed to share their belief that it was so momentous. I also doubted that the bombing would have any effect on the North Vietnamese, but I deemed it would at least help South Vietnamese morale.

Having already begun joint planning with the Vietnamese for reprisal strikes, we were able to move swiftly. That same day forty-five U. S. Navy planes hit a military barracks at Dong Hoi, just north of the DMZ. Delayed in take-off because the weather closed in, South Vietnamese planes struck the next day, twenty-four aircraft hitting another barracks at nearby Chap Le. Marshal Ky was in the right seat of the lead plane.

Once the machinery for the air strikes was functioning but before the planes executed the mission, I invited Bundy to fly with me to Pleiku to survey the scene and asked General Khanh to meet us there in order to obtain his approval of the reprisal. On the ground Khanh joined Bundy and me inside the *White Whale*. He was elated to indorse the proposal. While admitting that he anticipated no great military impact from it, he was happy to be able at last to strike back at the source of his country's unhappiness.

Outside the plane McGeorge Bundy seemed appalled at the shambles the attack had made of the advisory compound. He also appeared astonished at the rudimentary nature of the compound's defenses. As I had noted when escorting other civilian visitors, it was hard for the casual observer to comprehend the primitive countenance of insurgency warfare.

One who happened to be at Camp Holloway when the VC hit was the World War II soldier cartoonist Bill Mauldin. Kitsy and I had happened upon him a few days earlier in Hong Kong where we had gone for several days' rest. I had given him a ride to Saigon in my plane so that he could visit his son, a warrant-officer helicopter pilot stationed at Pleiku City. When the VC attacked, Mauldin tumbled from his bunk in his underwear shorts and dashed here and there helping tend the wounded. He flew to Saigon as soon as possible to file not only a cartoon, but a story. His son later served a second tour in Vietnam as a captain and aide to a division commander.

Having conferred further with McGeorge Bundy outside my presence, Ambassador Taylor recommended to the President that the United States and South Vietnam in effect move into Phase Two of the two-phase program against North Vietnam by way of the reprisal route. The ambassador urged "a measured controlled sequence of actions" against North Vietnamese military targets and infiltration routes in response either to major VC incidents or "a general catalog or package of VC outrages."

Probably at about the same time Ambassador Taylor was sending that message, Bundy and his colleagues who had accompanied him to Saigon— they included Assistant Secretary of Defense John McNaughton, White House Aide Chester Cooper, and chairman of the Vietnam working group Leonard Unger—were drafting their report to the President en route back to Washington. Bundy recommended much the same thing, though he called it a policy of "sustained reprisal." President Johnson promptly approved, so notifying Ambassador Taylor on February 9, although he was as yet unready for public announcement of his decision.

The new policy of reprisal bombing received a quick test. Apparently unawed by our reprisal for the Pleiku attack, the VC struck an even more telling blow on February 10. In the coastal city of Qui Nhon, an explosion destroyed a hotel used as an American enlisted men's billet. The entire hotel collapsed, killing twenty-three men, wounding twenty-one, and trapping others under the debris, the most American casualties yet incurred in a single incident.

The heavy rubble pinned one American soldier by a mangled leg underneath the collapsed building. The only way to extricate him was to amputate his leg, but American doctors were too big in stature to crawl through a narrow opening in the rubble to reach the man and perform the operation. A small Korean medical officer, Captain Un-Sup Kim, a member of a South Korean medical assistance team, volunteered to crawl at great personal risk into the rubble and do it. I subsequently decorated Kim and several years later was able personally to thank him again when as U. S. Army Chief of Staff I visited the Republic of Korea. Kim subsequently emigrated to the United States.

After we decided to strike in reprisal for Qui Nhon, our attempt to agree upon targets turned into a near fiasco—an illustration of the folly of running the minute details of a war ·by a committee of presidential advisers thousands of miles away, despite modern advances in communications technology. The explosion at Qui Nhon occurred just after 8 P.M. on February 10. Having received concurrence from the South Vietnamese government for a reprisal strike, my headquarters soon after midnight notified CINCPAC in Hawaii and the Joint Chiefs in Washington of the targets the 2d Air Division intended to hit. A few minutes later the Joint Chiefs proposed a different set of targets. Confused and sometimes contradictory messages passed back and forth through the night. At one point CINCPAC, apparently reflecting instructions from Washington, ordered that the South Vietnamese not be informed on the targets selected when in fact they were to participate in the bombing and were already deeply involved in the planning. Both Vietnamese and American pilots were awake all night, confused by orders and counterorders, so that when decision finally came after daylight on February 11, the pilots were exhausted.

Air strikes within the twenty-four-hour reprisal guidelines were nevertheless executed by U. S. and South Vietnamese Air Force planes at Chap Le and by U. S. Navy aircraft near Dong Hoi. In announcing the strikes publicly, the White House avoided using the word "reprisal" or specifically mentioning Qui Nhon. The strikes were in response to "further direct provocations by the Hanoi regime" and "continued acts of aggression." By avoiding tying the strikes to specific enemy deeds, the President sought to maintain freedom of action.

Two days later President Johnson elaborated on his decision to go to Phase Two. He announced publicly that under the code name "ROLLING THUNDER," the United States and South Vietnam were to engage in "a program of measured and limited air action" against military targets in North Vietnam south of the 19th parallel.

While recognizing that the decision reflected a major change in United States policy, I still saw no hope, in view of the restrictions imposed, that it would have any dramatic effect on the course of the war. There were to be, for example, only two to four attacks per week, each involving only two or three targets, and all south of the 19th parallel. That seemed to me a woefully weak way to "send a message," as Ambassador Taylor and others put it, designed to convince North Vietnamese leaders to desist. Yet as reflected in a cable from the Department of State, some in Washington officialdom saw the possibility of events reaching a "climax" within the "next few months."

The first strike under ROLLING THUNDER was scheduled for February 20, but the governmental crisis in Saigon occasioned by the attempted Phat-Thao coup prompted Ambassador Taylor to cancel it. Not until March 2 did the campaign begin.

A corollary to the decision to launch ROLLING THUNDER was a decision to bring American dependents home, thereby ending the long debate over that course. The President told us to get them out in a week to ten days. We did it in six.

Having long anticipated the order, the wives had already completed all but last-minute duties and had organized Vietnamese and American Red Cross teams to assist at Tan Son Nhut. One wife, Eileen Green, worked in Red Cross uniform until time for the last plane to depart, then collected her children, picked up two bags loaded not with clothes, which she deemed she could replace, but with her grandmother's silver, and climbed aboard. Several chartered Pan American planes left each day for the United States.

Kitsy insisted on taking the last plane, which by chance departed on Valentine's Day, and planned to live in Hawaii, at first in a small rented bungalow arranged for me by an old friend, retired Colonel Dick Ripple. As I saw her and our children aboard, I felt the sadness and uncertainty that all the others must have felt. Neither wives, children, nor husbands could know if we would ever be together again. As the plane climbed into the sky, I kept my eyes riveted on it until it became a tiny speck and disappeared. Even then I looked again in hope of catching another glimpse, sad but relieved that my loved ones were moving to safety.

More than any of the battlefield stresses or the decisions in Washington, the parting demonstrated that the war was changing. Just how it might evolve and how it might affect each of us personally, neither I nor anyone else could know.

Chapter VII
The Most Difficult Decision

As I had hoped, bombing the North boosted morale of the South Vietnamese, but as I had expected, it had no apparent effect on the will of North Vietnamese leaders to continue the fight. Graduated response simply would not work, particularly in the irresolute way Washington dictated that the campaign proceed.

Many Americans familiar with the devastation wreaked from the air on Germany and Japan in World War II no doubt visualized waves of giant bombers pummeling North Vietnam into submission. That was hardly the way it was. Instead of round-the-clock thousand-plane raids, Washington authorized only two to four raids a week and those by only a few dozen planes at a time, while dozens more went along for escort, diversion, flak suppression, and intelligence collection.

The number of planes in itself limited the effect, and for all the advances in technology since World War II, bombing was still a process beset by inaccuracy, particularly against the pinpoint targets selected in North Vietnam. The planes—mainly F-100s and F-105s—were essentially fighter-bombers, not the big Flying Fortresses and Superfortresses that did the job in World War II. Although Washington considered using the B-52s of the Strategic Air Command, the restricted nature of the targets and a concern about losing the big planes prompted a decision against it.

Interference from Washington seriously hampered the campaign. Washington had to approve all targets in North Vietnam, and even though the Joint Chiefs submitted long-range programs, the State Department constantly interfered with individual missions. This or that target was not to be hit for this or that nebulous nonmilitary reason. Missions for which planning and rehearsal had long proceeded might be canceled at the last minute. President Johnson allegedly boasted on one occasion that "they can't even bomb an outhouse without my approval." Fortunately, as time passed, the interest of the self-appointed air marshals in Washington gradually lessened, and the airmen gained greater leeway.

Bowing to the protests of vocal, wishful-thinking theorists in the academic community, the press, and the Administration, President Johnson in May 1965 ordered the first of what came to be periodic bombing pauses that the theorists claimed would prompt Hanoi to negotiate. That was folly. Why should the North Vietnamese negotiate when they were winning and when the only thing that might hurt them—the bombing—was pursued in a manner that communicated not determination and resolution but weakness and trepidation? The signals we were sending were the signals of our own distress.

Washington's timidity was an outgrowth of the advice of well-intentioned but naïve officials and of its effect on a President so politically oriented that he tried to please everybody rather than bite the bullet and make the hard decisions. To President Johnson's credit, he later realized his error. He subsequently told me that his greatest mistake was not to have fired, with the exception of Dean Rusk, the holdovers from the Kennedy administration, which he called "the Kennedy gang," a group whose loyalty to him as President he questioned.

Of the major civilian policy makers, only the Secretary of State, Dean Rusk, and one of his assistants, Walt Rostow, appeared to have any real understanding of the application of power. Even among ranking Pentagon civilians there existed an element of resistance to the President's policies: such men as Assistant Secretary of Defense for International Security Affairs John McNaughton; McNaughton's successor after his death in an airplane crash, Paul C. Warnke; Assistant Secretary of Defense for Systems Analysis Alain C. Enthoven; and a later Deputy Assistant Secretary for International Security Affairs, Townsend Hoopes.

Some of McNaughton's views, in particular, were incredible. On a visit to Saigon at a time when my air commander, Joe Moore, and I were trying to get authority to bomb SAM-2 (a Soviet-made missile) sites under construction in North Vietnam, McNaughton ridiculed the need. "You don't think the North Vietnamese are going to use them!" he scoffed to General Moore. "Putting them in is just a political ploy by the Russians to appease Hanoi."

It was all a matter of signals, said the clever civilian theorists in Washington. We won't bomb the SAM sites, which signals the North Vietnamese not to use them. Had it not been so serious, it would have been amusing.

Those officials and some White House and State Department advisers appeared to scorn professional military thinkers in a seeming belief that presumably superior Ivy League intellects could devise some political hocus-pocus or legerdemain to bring the enemy to terms without using force to destroy his war-making capability. Yet meaningful force is a necessary ingredient of international negotiations, and the North Vietnamese were particularly sensitive to its full implications. It was the only language they understood. Such gimmicks as bombing pauses and crippling target restrictions told them not that we understood how to use force but that we were insecure, obsessed with a paranoid concern for criticism from a segment of American and international public opinion that ignored the fact that the United States was not out to conquer but to repel aggression.

However desirable the American system of civilian control of the military, it was a mistake to permit appointive civilian officials lacking military experience and knowledge of military history and oblivious to the lessons of Communist diplomatic machinations to wield undue influence in the decision-making process. Over-all control of the military is one thing; shackling professional military men with restrictions in professional matters imposed by civilians who lack military understanding is another.

Perhaps the most wishful thinker of all was a perennial presidential adviser who, from long experience as ambassador to Moscow, where he had established a reputation for standing up to the Russians, should have been the most shrewd, W. Averell Harriman. That grand old statesman, who at the time was serving as ambassador at large, was apparently able to convince himself that Communist double-talk was a substitute for meaningful agreement. The toughness of the Vietnamese Communists escaped him. The folly of his thinking should have been apparent to anyone who took time to examine the nonsettlement he negotiated in Laos in 1962, which did nothing over the long run to stop the war there.

At a luncheon with Ambassador Harriman and the American ambassador to the Philippines, William McCormick Blair, during the Manila conference of October 1966, at a time when Russian supplies, including surface-to-air missiles, were pouring into North Vietnam, I listened in startled disbelief as Harriman said: "I can tell you, General Westmoreland, categorically, the Russians are doing everything they can to bring peace in Vietnam." As the enemy in 1968 was stalling at the Paris negotiating table, Harriman, according to the press, was "convinced there will not be progress in the political field until there is a reduction of violence." The way to do that, he said, was for the United States to reduce its operations. "If we take the lead," he said, "I'm satisfied that they [the North Vietnamese] will follow." Ease up on your opponent, he said in effect, and he will quit. The muse of history must have heard those remarks with as much incredulity as I experienced in reading them.

That the North Vietnamese in May 1968 finally reacted affirmatively to a halt in the bombing and agreed to come to a conference table did nothing to justify the policy of timidity. Having failed in an all-out effort to overthrow South Vietnam, the North Vietnamese needed time to recoup their losses, meanwhile sparing themselves further bombing. For more than four years they negotiated little more than the shape of the conference table, then in the spring of 1972 mounted the most powerful offensive to that time, a conventional, tank-supported invasion of South Vietnam. "When, without a previous understanding, the enemy asks for a truce," wrote Sun Tzu, "he is plotting."

Although I early opposed other than tit-for-tat bombing until the South Vietnamese were prepared to cope with North Vietnamese reaction, that view obviously changed once the North Vietnamese had committed sizable ground forces. Although the bombing of North Vietnam was outside of my jurisdiction, I used every appropriate opportunity to make known my dissatisfaction with the program then dictated by Washington. My views can be summarized by excerpts from a memorandum requested by President Johnson that I dictated while shaving and dressing on the final morning of the 1966 Manila conference:

> Thus far our air campaign to the North has been characterized by creeping escalation. This strategy has not influenced the will of Hanoi. The strategy has used air power inefficiently and expensively, and has achieved results far short of potential. In addition, a considerable and growing risk factor has been injected into the situation. The enemy now has a comprehensive air defense system under centralized control . . . [that] will result in mounting casualties as the war goes on—perhaps more than we will be willing or even able to sustain, given the present limitation on targets.

The time for a change in strategy, I went on, was at hand. I called for "shock action" against "lucrative targets" close to Hanoi and in Haiphong Harbor "that will hurt the enemy and convince him that our power does not have to be restrained."

That recommendation and numerous others brought no results. In the end it was predictably inevitable that the failure of the Hanoi authorities to knuckle under would bring disillusionment to those who had put so much faith in the bombing. That disillusionment led inexorably into another search for "something new" that might accomplish what the token bombing failed to achieve. The options left by then were few.

That the situation in South Vietnam was bad was at no time more apparent than as the token bombing began. In one of my more pessimistic evaluations, I reported in early March 1965 that if present trends continued, "six months from now the configuration of the . . . [South Vietnamese forces] will essentially be a series of islands of strength clustered around district and province capitals clogged with large numbers of refugees in a generally subverted countryside; and the . . . [South Vietnamese government] will be beset by 'end the war' groups openly advocating a negotiated settlement." While noting that the South Vietnamese people and their social and political institutions had displayed a "remarkable resiliency," I expressed concern "that we are headed toward a VC takeover of the country," probably within a year.

In view of the President's policy decisions, the only hope at the time for reversing the trend toward a Communist victory was air power, both the token bombing of the North and the use of American aircraft to support the

ARVN and hit the enemy's supply line in Laos. Thus my most pressing concern was the security of American airfields, particularly an air base at Danang that was essential to the air war against the North. Favorable action in Washington when I requested a U. S. Marine Corps HAWK missile battalion for Danang eased my concern over possible North Vietnamese air attacks, but the problem of ground security remained. Returning from an inspection of ARVN security arrangements at Danang in early February 1965, my deputy, Johnny Throckmorton, was concerned and recommended bringing in immediately an entire Marine Expeditionary Brigade of three infantry battalions with artillery and logistics support. While sharing Throckmorton's sense of urgency, I nevertheless hoped to keep the number of U.S. ground troops to a minimum and recommended instead landing only two battalions and holding the third aboard ship off shore.

Ambassador Taylor objected to bringing in American ground troops. Although some years earlier while in Washington he had recommended bringing in U. S. Army Engineers primarily to help in flood relief but also to provide an American ground presence, he had come to the conclusion by early 1965 that once the United States assumed any ground combat role, the South Vietnamese would try to unload more tasks. Sending the first U.S. ground combat troops would be a foot in the door leading to ever-widening commitment. He saw problems for the "white-faced" soldier trying to adjust to an Oriental environment, probably unable to adjust to the exigencies of guerrilla warfare in the same way the French had failed to adjust.

I shared Ambassador Taylor's reservations but to a lesser degree. The presence of American ground troops even on a static security mission could lead, I recognized, to pressure for a shift to a more active role and for more and more Americans. That would pose the very real danger of the South Vietnamese relying more and more on the United States, even though they potentially had the manpower to do the job themselves, so that eventually U.S. forces might have to bear the entire burden of the war amid a population grown as hostile to American presence as it had been to the French.

I saw my call for marines at Danang not as a first step in a growing American commitment but as what I said at the time it was: a way to secure a vital airfield and the air units using it, for which I saw no alternative, an airfield essential to pursuing the adopted strategy. So genuine was my concern that I apparently communicated it convincingly to Ambassador Taylor, for he reluctantly endorsed landing one of the two battalions I asked and eventually acquiesced in landing both.

Admiral Sharp at CINCPAC agreed with my two-battalion proposal, deeming it "an act of prudence which we should take before and not after another tragedy occurs." Washington on February 26 approved it, subject to South Vietnamese concurrence. The Quat government gave that readily.

At the last minute John McNaughton tried to substitute the Army's 173d Airborne Brigade, based in Okinawa, for the marines, apparently in an effort to keep the profile of commitment as low as possible. Airborne troops were more lightly armed than the marines and might be more readily withdrawn.

To that proposal Taylor, Sharp, and I all objected. Almost all contingency plans developed through the years for Southeast Asia involved using marines in the northern provinces of South Vietnam, and if any one of the contingencies should come about, I wanted to go with the plan. In view of a lack of logistical installations or support troops, a marine force trained and equipped to supply itself over the beaches was preferable to an airborne force lacking logistical capabilities. Since U.S. marines were already at Danang—manning helicopters supporting the ARVN, the HAWK battalion, and supporting engineers—sending more marines would avoid interservice confusion. Furthermore, the staying power of a more heavily armed marine force was better suited to a defensive security assignment.

In later months, after the American build-up, I stuck with the assignment of marines to the northern provinces. All the earlier reasons remained valid, particularly the marines' ability to make amphibious assaults and to supply over the beaches, capabilities of particular importance in the northern provinces for either defensive or, if necessary, offensive operations. Shorter land distances also were involved, which would help offset a relatively short range of marine land logistical capabilities.

Marine battalions were also heavy in infantry, consisting of four companies of over 200 men each, and the staying power that represented was important because of the proximity to North Vietnam and the likelihood of encountering greater numbers of North Vietnamese troops. I had not realized at the time that the marines were poorly trained in defensive warfare and were reluctant to dig in sufficiently for long defensive engagements, but that shortcoming could eventually be overcome. That the marines were basically an amphibious force might have argued at first glance for their commitment among the extensive waterways of the Mekong Delta, but few over-the-beach amphibious operations were destined to be launched there, and the other reasons for their commitment in the northern provinces were sound.

When the U.S. marines got word they were to land, it was like pulling the stopper from a bathtub. Any semblance of a low profile quickly disappeared. Under Admiral Sharp's direction rather than mine, the first of the two battalions stormed ashore near Danang on March 8 in full battle regalia as if re-enacting Iwo Jima, only to find South Vietnamese officials and U. S. Army advisers welcoming them and pretty Vietnamese girls passing out leis of flowers. One U. S. Army district advisory group composed of a captain, a lieutenant, and two sergeants greeted the marines good naturedly with a sign painted on a sheet: WELCOME TO THE GALLANT MARINES.

Because the marines' equipment included 8-inch howitzers capable of firing shells with atomic warheads, Deputy Ambassador Alexis Johnson was perturbed. Presence of the big pieces, he believed, might lead the enemy or the press to speculate on our using nuclear weapons. Since the marines had no atomic shells with them and since any number of American planes long employed in Vietnam had a similar capability, I saw no substance to his concern. Only after an exchange of messages with Washington did the controversy pass and the marines be allowed to keep their big guns. I did urge on the marines one concession to an Embassy quibble: changing the name of the marine contingent from the "Marine Expeditionary Force" to the "III Marine Amphibious Force" lest the brigade be associated in Vietnamese minds with the French Expeditionary Corps.

Circumstances of the landing led to the only sharp exchange I ever had with Ambassador Taylor. Word of the time of the landing got to me from the Joint Chiefs before it reached the Embassy, and even though I notified the Embassy, the word apparently failed to get to the ambassador in advance. He was visibly piqued, his upset accentuated because the marines had arrived with tanks, self-propelled artillery, and other heavy equipment he had not expected. "Do you know my terms of reference," Ambassador Taylor demanded sharply, "and that I have authority over you?" "I understand fully," I replied, "and I appreciate it completely, Mr. Ambassador." That ended the matter.

Although my concern about the Danang air base was alleviated, I remained disturbed about possible enemy action against other bases, notably a U. S. Army communications facility and a small airfield at Phu Bai, near Hué, not a good field but at the time the best we had north of the Hai Van Pass, and bases at Bien Hoa and Vung Tau. I asked Washington for an Army brigade for Bien Hoa and Vung Tau and another battalion of the III Marine Amphibious Force to come ashore and move to Phu Bai.

Still concerned about the Tan Son Nhut airport, I nevertheless believed strongly that it was essential in terms of pride and morale for the South Vietnamese themselves to be responsible for the security of their own capital region, of which Tan Son Nhut was a part. I decided we simply had to take the chance that the Vietnamese could do that job alone. I fervently hoped—as it turned out, wishfully—that additional American ground troops would prove unnecessary.

Meanwhile, President Johnson had called the U. S. Army Chief of Staff, General Harold K. Johnson, to the White House, where in no uncertain terms he charged him to go to Vietnam and determine what was needed to set matters right. Disappointed in the lack of results from the bombing of the North, the President and some of his advisers were letting their frustrations show. As General Johnson descended in an elevator with the President, following breakfast in the family quarters, President Johnson, towering over the Chief of Staff, thrust an index finger in his breastbone, leaned his face close, and said: "You get things bubbling, General."

I always had good relations with General Johnson, a dignified man of intellectual bent who had survived a long incarceration as a prisoner of the Japanese during World War II. When he arrived in Saigon on March 5, 1965, the situation on which I briefed him was at the time in some ways encouraging. Having bolstered morale of ARVN troops, the bombing of the

North had improved ARVN performance somewhat. Yet I saw that, as the bombing became routine, the effect on ARVN morale would be less and less, although stopping it would have considerable adverse effect. Because the dry season then enveloped much of South Vietnam, VC activity had decreased, but that was normal, since the VC always respected the ARVN's greater mobility during that season.

Yet there were for me seriously disturbing aspects. VC concentration in the I Corps Zone, the northern provinces, was increasing rapidly. More disturbing still were indications that the VC was planning to seize a large sector of the Central Highlands, there to establish a government to challenge Saigon's, and drive eastward to the coast to cut South Vietnam in two. The latter was a goal that had been long pursued by the Viet Minh in their fight with the French.

Indications that North Vietnamese units were moving south underscored my concern. There were reports that at least a regiment of the 325th North Vietnamese Division had been in the highlands since December 1964, as later proved to be correct, and soon after General Johnson's departure on March 12, positive evidence developed that the entire division had been there since February 1965. During the last days of the month portions of an ARVN regiment near an outpost called Dak To in Kontum province clashed with two North Vietnamese battalions and the able ARVN regimental commander was killed. The enemy's identity was not to be denied. How large a force the North Vietnamese intended to commit was the only question remaining.

It would take about a year, I deduced, to increase the ARVN to approximately 650,000 men, enough to counter the growing VC strength if not the North Vietnamese reinforcements. Meanwhile, the VC's demonstration, at Binh Gia in December 1964, that he was ready to move into Mao Tsetung's Phase Three, the big unit war; his concentration in the I Corps Zone and the highlands; and the possibility of large-scale North Vietnamese intervention made it obvious that the advent of the rainy season in the highlands and the Mekong Delta in May and June, only about two months away, would precipitate a crisis. Because the rainy season interfered with air support, it was always the enemy's best time for major operations.

Even if the bombing of the North should achieve the highly improbable goal of convincing the North Vietnamese to desist, I could see it happening in nothing less than six months, and I had maintained all along that success in the South had to accompany bombing in the North if conclusive results were to be expected. If President Johnson was determined to succeed in Vietnam, as General Johnson communicated to me, I saw no solution, while awaiting results from the bombing and expanded ARVN forces, other than to put our own finger in the dike.

General Johnson confirmed something that Secretary McNamara had written Ambassador Taylor before General Johnson's arrival, that President Johnson saw the bombing campaign as no substitute for additional actions within South Vietnam. As the President had indicated in his sharp message to the Ambassador at the end of December, he saw bombing the North as no cure-all in itself and raised the possibility of committing American ground troops in the South. He and others in his Administration were obviously coming to the conclusion that the United States had to take some further action in the South, find another "something new," if South Vietnamese collapse was to be averted before pressures against the North could take effect.

General Johnson's recommendations when he returned to Washington reflected much of my thinking. In addition to more U.S. aid and increased combat support, such as planes and helicopters, he asked creation of an international force for an anti-infiltration role along the DMZ, a step which I continued to support, and the commitment of an American Army division, either to defend the Bien Hoa-Tan Son Nhut complex or the Central Highlands. It was the latter that I wanted, plus the Army brigade I had requested earlier for Bien Hoa and Vung Tau.

To General Johnson I reiterated earlier requests I had made for logistical and engineer troops. If the numbers of U.S. troops were to increase, some kind of logistical apparatus had to be constructed for supporting them. How else to maintain them in a country lacking good highways, railroads, and telephone and radio communications and possessing only one major port and but three airfields capable of accommodating jet aircraft?

Since a logistical structure is not to be built overnight, I had asked months earlier, right after the Gulf of Tonkin incidents in the summer of 1964, for a logistical command and an engineer group (each about the size of a brigade), but without results. In response to another request I made in December 1964, the Defense Department had sent a team headed by Major General Richard D. Meyer and a civilian logistician, Glenn Gibson, to survey my logistical needs; in keeping with guidance from Deputy Secretary Vance, the team recommended only some ridiculously small augmentation, as I recall some thirty-nine people to be added to a tiny U. S. Army Support Command. I had repeated the request early in February but again without success.

While President Johnson approved more American military aid and combat support, he took no immediate action on the recommendation for an international force along the DMZ and an American division. Neither did he approve the logistical and engineer troops I needed. The latter was a cardinal error, for as long as any possibility existed of committing U.S. troops, logistical preparations should have been started. The long delay in providing engineer and logistical backup was an omission that was destined to plague us and to limit our capabilities for a long time.

Fortunately, about this same time Secretary McNamara did approve a much needed new airfield in the northern provinces along the coast south of Danang at a place that came to be known as Chu Lai. It got its name, incidentally, not from the Vietnamese language but from the way the Vietnamese pronounced the name of the U. S. Marine Corps commander in the Pacific, Lieutenant General Victor Krulak. Americans accompanying General Krulak on a visit to the site found the pronunciation amusing, and the name stuck.

Having learned from General Johnson that the President shared my conviction that a new step had to be taken to revitalize the effort in South Vietnam, I began the day after General Johnson's departure to make a detailed study of the situation and possible courses of action, both to crystallize my own thinking and to provide a basis for recommendations to Ambassador Taylor, Admiral Sharp, and my bosses in Washington. I sensed that we might be about to make a most momentous decision, one not to be undertaken without the most careful deliberation and analysis.

I predicated my study on the goals and strategy current at the time, on how to keep the South Vietnamese in the fight until the bombing campaign might convince the North Vietnamese to desist and how to make enough progress in the South to give the South Vietnamese the confidence and vitality to go it alone. The effect my proposals would have on the stability and effectiveness of the Saigon government was obviously integral to the considerations.

During 1964 we had expanded the South Vietnamese forces to the extent manageable and also substantially increased American advisers. That being done, a crash program to increase and upgrade the ARVN provided no assurance in itself of South Vietnam's survival. While a multinational, anti-infiltration force of approximately five divisions to be deployed along the DMZ and across the Laotian panhandle was desirable, I saw no possibility of getting authority to form it and overcoming inherent logistical problems in time to have the needed effect. Thus I saw no alternative, while proceeding with a realistic program to strengthen the South Vietnamese armed forces, to committing more American troops.

In addition to the Army brigade I had already requested to defend Bien Hoa and Vung Tau and the additional marine battalion for Phu Bai, I believed that if the enemy's designs in the Central Highlands were to be thwarted, I had to put an American Army division there, establishing in the process coastal logistical bases at Qui Nhon and Nha Trang to support military operations in the central region. I also proposed an additional battalion of marines at Danang and possibly a fifth to be added later to secure the new airfield at Chu Lai. Thus the proposed U.S. ground troop commitment would be the equivalent of approximately two divisions, or seventeen maneuver battalions.*

Intrinsic in my proposal was that American troops would be used in offensive operations. Whereas I saw the commitment as strategically defensive, aimed primarily at forestalling South Vietnamese defeat, the adage that

---

* A maneuver battalion is a combat battalion that can be maneuvered, either infantry, mechanized infantry, or armor, as opposed to a supporting battalion such as artillery, engineers, or aviation.

a good offense is the best defense was as applicable in Vietnam as it has been elsewhere throughout history.

The Army brigade at Bien Hoa and Vung Tau could provide a quick re-action force for the critical HOP TAC area; the Army division in the highlands could stage spoiling attacks to deny the enemy's objective of split-ting the country; and active operations by the marines could hamper the big VC build-up in the northern provinces. Yet if with this augmentation the strategy of punitive bombing still failed to achieve results by midyear of 1965, I warned, deploying even more American troops and forces from other countries should be considered. Intrinsic in that caveat was a concern for how many troops the North Vietnamese would elect to commit in the South.

I seriously studied an alternative proposal advanced by Ambassador Taylor as an experimental measure, that American troops be restricted to enclaves along the coast. By remaining in coastal enclaves, the theory had it, the Americans might secure critical areas while limiting their involvement and casualties, yet at the same time demonstrating to the North Vietnamese American determination to stay the course.

The ambassador's proposal was in many ways similar to one made not quite a year later by my long-time friend inexplicably turned critic of the conduct of the war, Jim Gavin. Writing in *Harper's* magazine in February 1966, General Gavin, in a broad-ranging letter, expressed the opinion that if the United States were to secure all of South Vietnam, far more forces than then deployed would be required, along with increased bombing of North Vietnam. That, he believed, might bring the Chinese Communists into the fight. Better, he wrote, to employ those American forces already in South Vietnam to demonstrate American resolve by holding a series of coastal enclaves while stopping the bombing and seeking a solution through diplo-matic means. Time has since shown that it took much more than that to prompt the North Vietnamese to engage in any kind of diplomatic negotia-tions, and even though the enclave theory was but a small part of General Gavin's over-all proposals, that was the part that press and public seized upon and remembered. Having espoused the theory, Gavin was stuck with it and for a long time tried to justify it publicly. At my invitation he later visited Vietnam for a first-hand look, but upon his return, he argued illogically that the logistical bases I had by that time established were ex-actly the enclaves he had been talking about.

Ambassador Taylor's proposal differed from Gavin's in that Taylor would authorize offensive operations in the vicinity of the enclaves and use American forces as a reserve for the ARVN up to fifty miles from the en-claves. Taylor also saw the enclave theory essentially as an experiment, albeit one that hopefully would succeed and thus obviate other measures. It would have the virtue, the ambassador maintained, of testing the effect of the presence of American troops on the traditional xenophobia of the Vietnamese.

I disagreed with the enclave strategy. As my staff study put it at the time, it represented "an inglorious, static use of U.S. forces in overpopulated areas with little chance of direct or immediate impact on the outcome of events." It would release few ARVN units for operations elsewhere and would have no effect on the critical situation in the Central Highlands. Most important of all, it would position American troops in what would be in effect a series of unconnected beachheads, their backs to the sea, essentially in a defensive posture. That would leave the decision of when and where to strike to the enemy, invite defeat of each in turn, virtually foreordain combat in densely populated locales, and limit the manpower base available for recruiting to expand the ARVN.

My operations officer, Bill DePuy, hand-carried my analysis and proposals to Washington near the end of March 1965 in company with Ambassador Taylor, who went at the President's behest to discuss what new steps should be taken. While they were away, the Viet Cong set off a bomb in Saigon that wrecked the hotel alongside the Saigon River that housed the American Embassy.

Feigning engine trouble, two men stopped their car in front of the building, jumped out, and ran. Vietnamese police guards ordered them to halt, then opened fire, killing both men, but seconds later the car exploded. A female American secretary and a U. S. Navy petty officer were killed and fifty-four other Americans wounded, including Peer de Silva, the CIA director in Saigon, who almost lost both eyes. Fifteen Vietnamese civilians on the street were killed and many in the vicinity wounded. Most of the injuries inside the building were from flying glass, employees having rushed to the windows at the sound of gunshots, and the blast caught them unprotected.

I had an appointment at the Embassy that morning, March 30, with Acting Ambassador Alexis Johnson. Had my schedule not been running late, I probably would have been in the lobby when the explosion occurred. I learned of it over my automobile radio when I was two blocks away. As I reached the scene, my first thought was to check on Ambassador Johnson and others in the Embassy, but I reconsidered. Since Ambassador Taylor was away, if Alexis Johnson was dead I would be the senior member of the U. S. Mission. Were there time bombs still to go off? I decided I should repair to my headquarters and its communications facilities.

From my headquarters I made sure that Army medics and military police were on the scene. With some difficulty I got the ambassador on the phone to learn that he was physically shaken but calm. My anxiety relieved, I dispatched a cable to Washington reporting the incident. Going to the Embassy, I found Johnson cut about the face but not seriously injured and brought him back to the security of my office. To have lost such a stalwart member of the U. S. Mission would have been a serious blow.

In the wake of the bombing, President Johnson asked funds to build a new Embassy. Located across a park from the Vietnamese presidential palace, it was destined three years later to be the scene of another spectacular VC sapper attack.

In Washington Ambassador Taylor found the President and most of his top advisers close to a decision to commit more American troops, but still wavering. Following General Johnson's visit to Vietnam, the Joint Chiefs had proposed committing two American divisions and another to be solicited from the Republic of Korea. This proposal and presumably my analysis were considered at meetings of the National Security Council during the first two days of April, which Ambassador Taylor attended. The ambassador apparently made his case well, for President Johnson endorsed his concept of enclaves as an interim measure and approved sending only two more American battalions, which would be the marine battalions I had recommended for Danang and Phu Bai, plus a contingent of engineer and logistical troops. Yet at the same time the President ended the strictly defensive posture of the marines, authorizing, in keeping with the ambassador's recommendation, offensive operations up to fifty miles from their bases.

As I read the President's decision, it was tentative, an experiment, as Ambassador Taylor had asked. Although the troops in the enclaves would improve security of the airfields, which was so essential, they would have no conclusive effect on the over-all battlefield situation, so that I was still convinced more would have to be done. Some of President Johnson's advisers were concerned that if American troops were deployed inland they might some day have to fight their way to the coast through mutinous South Vietnamese troops, an example of the paranoia that beset some officials in Washington.

The President's approval at long last of engineer and logistical troops seemed to presage additional combat troops later, although the President wanted to move step by step in the hope of carrying public opinion with him. Low key still was the watchword. Yet even if he did view the enclave strategy as tentative, a hurried call for a conference at Honolulu to work out details of the strategy made it clear that he was determined to give it an honest try.

In advance of the conference, the Departments of Defense and State jointly raised a number of proposals for Ambassador Taylor and me to consider. Some were typical of the detailed suggestions with which various Washington agencies constantly bombarded us. Many were incongruous and others we had long since tried and discarded, while the directions at times were so detailed as to constitute an insult to the intelligence. I often wondered how Eisenhower in Europe or MacArthur in the Pacific during World War II would have reacted to such minute instructions.

Send American recruiting experts to jazz up ARVN recruiting. . . . Integrate U. S. Army civil affairs experts into provincial governments. . . . Put fifty or so American soldiers in ARVN battalions to stiffen their backbones. . . . Distribute food directly to the troops and their families rather than through the ARVN command structure. . . . This specialized team or that one would arrive in Saigon all fired up with what they saw as new ideas. The bureaucracy in Washington seemingly was unable to comprehend that the embryonic South Vietnamese government and armed forces could absorb only so many programs at a time. At one point Ambassador Taylor cabled McGeorge Bundy: "Mac, can't we be better protected from our friends? I know that everyone wants to help, but there's such a thing as killing with kindness."

With Ambassador Taylor and Admiral Sharp, I met in Honolulu on April 20 with Secretary McNamara, General Wheeler, John McNaughton, and McGeorge Bundy's older brother, William, who was Assistant Secretary of State for Far Eastern Affairs. While accepting the strategic goal of breaking the enemy's will by denying him victory in the South, nobody saw any immediate hope of dramatic improvement in the ground war, which was essential if the North Vietnamese were to be persuaded to desist. To implement the approved restricted employment of U.S. troops and thus, it was hoped, bring about improvement, the conferees advocated sending nine more American battalions: one three-battalion Army brigade for Bien Hoa-Vung Tau and another brigade to establish enclaves at Qui Nhon and Nha Trang and three Marine battalions for the Chu Lai region. In keeping with a decision by the National Security Council when Ambassador Taylor was in Washington, we asked for representation from other countries: a battalion from Australia and three battalions from South Korea. Counting the four Marine battalions already ashore or approved, that would mean thirteen American battalions and four from other countries—the same number, seventeen, that I had asked in late March. Under the proposal American strength would total 82,000, that of other countries, 7,250.

Although the number of battalions was the same, I still obtained no force for the critical Central Highlands. Yet I could take some solace in that a brigade at Qui Nhon and Nha Trang would provide a measure of protection against the enemy's cutting the country in two, and the force that I hoped to get for Bien Hoa-Vung Tau, the 173d Airborne Brigade, might be used as a mobile reserve in event of crisis in the Highlands. Furthermore, the final report of the conference noted the possibility of further deployments, including an American airmobile division, which was the unit I wanted for the Highlands, and more Korean troops to bring Korean contribution up to division size.

Allied participation in Vietnam had long been discussed, since Washington saw Vietnam, like Korea, as a test of the Free World against Communist aggression. For long, even after President Johnson's call in early 1964 for "more flags," the United States concentrated not on troops but on economic and technical assistance, which by the end of 1964 fifteen countries other than the United States were providing; in February 1965 the Republic of Korea sent a task force known as the DOVE unit, built around an engineer battalion, to work on civic projects. The American news media, strangely, gave those contributions little visibility.

Serious discussion on obtaining troops from other countries began in December 1964, but the South Vietnamese at the time were apathetic if not opposed. They were sensitive, as their history would indicate, to having foreign troops on their soil. Yet when the need for more troops became pressing in March and April 1965, Ambassador Taylor readily secured South Vietnamese concurrence.

When Australia and the Republic of Korea agreed to send troops, I saw the possibility of creating the multinational anti-infiltration force for deployment along the DMZ, but for the time being I bowed to a more pressing need elsewhere. I wanted the Australian battalion to help secure Vung Tau and the South Koreans to provide security for port and base development along the coast. The force for the DMZ might be created when those jobs were completed.

The coming of more American troops and Free World (or "Third Country," as opposed to South Vietnam and the United States) forces inevitably raised the question of command arrangements. How to obtain the unity of command that military history through the years has shown to be essential? Should I press for a combined U.S.-South Vietnamese-Third Country staff? A South Vietnamese or an American commander? The United States would hardly sanction placing its troops under the South Vietnamese, yet the South Vietnamese for their part were just as sensitive. Having so recently achieved independence, they were jealous of their sovereignty while at the same time wary of providing any verisimilitude to Communist charges that they were puppets of the United States. No parallel with the situation during the Korean War existed, for even though the overall command in Korea was essentially American, it was under the aegis of the United Nations, which had no role in Vietnam.

I asked an officer who was completing his tour in Vietnam, Jimmy Collins, who spoke French and had good rapport with the Vietnamese, to stay and explore a concept of retaining two separate commands, American and South Vietnamese, but establishing a combined element responsible to both commands for international matters. The sensitivity of the Vietnamese became apparent early when during my first discussion on the subject with Generals Thieu and "Little" Minh, they professed to have heard of General Collins' assignment and were disturbed. The Saigon press was already speculating on the Americans taking control and was warning editorially against yielding South Vietnamese sovereignty.

Several factors other than Vietnamese sensitivity mitigated against a combined command. The South Koreans, too, were sensitive, anxious to have at least a façade of the same coequal status with the South Vietnamese that the Americans had. Most important of all, we were in Vietnam to help the Vietnamese, not to do the job for them, and to enable them to increase and improve their armed forces to the point when they could do the job alone. If we did it for them, how were they to learn? Junior and senior commanders alike learn to assume responsibility only from experience.

Even before commitment of American ground troops, we had already

had considerable experience with American combat-support units operating
with ARVN units. In normal practice the supporting element conforms to
the needs and wishes of the supported unit, and that had been working well.
The object in South Vietnam was to establsh mutual confidence between the
two commanders; once that was achieved, co-operation on the battlefield
posed few problems. I had already learned that I could influence the South
Vietnamese high command on military—if not political—matters by suggestion. That was how our advisers at lower levels also had been working.

Convinced that we could continue to handle command that way, avoiding
puppetry or proconsulship with only minimal loss of the advantages of
unified command, I dropped the concept of a formal unified command while
retaining Jimmy Collins as my liaison with the Vietnamese Joint General
Staff. Although the subject of combined command continued to arise from
time to time, I have no reason to regret my decision and seriously question
whether formal combined command would have been practically workable.
I never encountered serious disagreement with senior South Vietnamese
officers, and experienced but one at lower levels, that could not be solved by
frank discussion. In the final analysis, I had the leverage to influence the
South Vietnamese and they knew it, and both sides exercised a rare degree
of tact. Meanwhile, the South Vietnamese were able to develop their own
command channels and obtain the experience with command that is essential if a military force is ever to stand alone. In effect, we achieved unity of
command within the context of national sensitivities and our training mission.

On the matter of Third Country forces, the Australians, and later the
New Zealanders and the Thais, relinquished operational or tactical control
of their forces to me, while a civic action group from the Philippines ostensibly maintained an independent status, as did the South Koreans. Although
President Chung Hee Park of South Korea told me that he was "proud to
have my troops under your command," I respected the young republic's
desire to maintain its prestige and worked with Korean commanders on a
co-operative basis.

Assigning the South Koreans a separate tactical area of responsibility
afforded them a position of semiautonomy within broad guidelines. I also
had an excellent understanding with the able Korean commander, General
Chae Myung Shin, and whenever a problem posed difficulties at lower levels
we promptly and easily worked it out. An informal committee composed of
General Chae, the chief of the South Vietnamese Joint General Staff, and
me met infrequently to handle matters involving the Koreans and Vietnamese.

As the process of shipping American units got underway early in May,
controversy arose over just how they were to be employed. That came as a
surprise to me, for when President Johnson changed the mission of American units from a defensive posture and authorized them to engage in "counterinsurgency combat operations," that was to me a broad authority.

On May 8 I forwarded to Washington my concept of how operations were to develop. In Stage One the units were to secure enclaves, which I preferred to call base areas, and in defending them could operate out to the range of light artillery. In Stage Two the units were to engage in offensive operations and deep patrolling in co-operation with the ARVN. In Stage Three they were to provide a reserve when ARVN units needed help and also conduct long-range offensive operations. At the same time I pointed out that once the coastal bases were secure, the troops should move to secure inland bases and operate from those. I also recommended locations for the forces that had been discussed at Honolulu as possible future deployments, including an airmobile division. I particularly wanted a battalion to secure Cam Ranh Bay, just south of Nha Trang, one of the finest natural harbors in Southeast Asia.

Ambassador Taylor having approved my concept and copies having been forwarded through CINCPAC to the Department of Defense, the Joint Chiefs, and the Department of State, I assumed in the absence of any word to the contrary that Washington also approved. To make sure that assumption was correct, I suggested to Ambassador Taylor as he prepared in early June to leave for another conference in Washington that he check my interpretation with Secretary of State Rusk.

The ambassador's visit to Washington coincided with an imbroglio between the press and the Johnson administration over whether the mission of American forces in Vietnam had changed. The dispute had its genesis in a secrecy order which President Johnson had imposed on those involved in the decision in early April to sanction offensive operations up to fifty miles from the enclaves. Over the next few weeks reporters in Vietnam could see for themselves that the marines and the 173d's paratroopers were not sitting tight in their foxholes waiting for the enemy to come to them, which would have been foolish even for a strictly defensive posture. They could easily see that American units were patrolling in some depth and sometimes engaging in full-scale offensive operations. Yet the White House chose to meet the press's allegations obliquely.

Secretary Rusk admitted on television that "we don't expect these men to sit there like hypnotized rabbits waiting for the Viet Cong to strike," but he went on to intimate that they were outside their bases only to keep the enemy off balance and prevent major attacks against installations. The President's press secretary said flatly, "There has been no change in the mission of the United States ground combat units in Vietnam in recent days or weeks. The President has issued no order of any kind in this regard to General Westmoreland recently or at any other time." On the other hand, he explained, "General Westmoreland also has authority within the assigned mission to employ these troops in support of Vietnamese forces faced with aggressive attack when in his judgment the general military situation urgently requires it."

It was not falsehood, but it was a masterpiece of obliquity, and I was unhappy about it. To my mind the American people had a right to know forthrightly, within the actual limits of military security, what we were calling on their sons to do, and to presume that it could be concealed despite the open eyes of press and television was folly. This was either the start of or a contribution to a troublesome, divisive credibility gap that was long to plague the Administration and eventually to affect the credibility of some of my own pronouncements.

While the parameters for use of American troops remained in question, the long-anticipated step-up in enemy operations began with the start of the southwest monsoon and the poor flying weather of the rainy season. In early May a VC regiment—the first to attack as a regiment since the fight at Binh Gia five months earlier—did major damage at Song Be, capital of Phuoc Long province, along the Cambodian border north of Saigon. Only intensive air support and introduction of a fresh ARVN regiment brought to the scene by American planes and helicopters saved the town. Later in the month at Ba Gia, in the coastal province of Quang Ngai, a VC regiment virtually destroyed an ARVN battalion in an ambush and then dealt roughly with another battalion that tried to come to the rescue, the same action in which the American adviser, Captain O'Sullivan, performed so heroically. So heavy was pressure in the Central Highlands that government forces had to abandon several district headquarters towns. Overrunning a district town in Pleiku province, the VC began a siege of a nearby CIDG-Special Forces camp, Duc Co, that was to last more than two months.

Visiting Duc Co, I was so impressed with the heroism and dedication of a U. S. Marine Corps major, William G. Leftwich, Jr., that in my enthusiasm I called him "the best adviser in Vietnam." Major Leftwich had earlier received the Navy Cross for his extraordinary courage, despite serious wounds, in rallying an ARVN force to lift a siege of a district town along the coast, Hoi An. As a lieutenant colonel on a second tour in 1970, he was destined to die in the crash of a helicopter.

On June 10 battle again erupted in Phuoc Long province at the district town of Dong Xoai with an attack by portions of two VC regiments. The VC overran the CIDG-Special Forces camp outside the town, destroyed the first contingent of a reserve ARVN battalion arriving by helicopter, and prevented the rest of the battalion from landing. Two more relieving battalions were badly mauled before the Viet Cong two days later broke contact.

Throughout the fighting at Dong Xoai the enemy failed to take the district headquarters building, primarily because of the intrepid leadership of a Special Forces officer, Second Lieutenant Charles Q. Williams. Four times wounded, Lieutenant Williams nevertheless rallied the defenders, personally knocked out an enemy machine gun, and guided helicopters to the site to evacuate the wounded. He was subsequently awarded the Medal of Honor.

Meanwhile, the enemy stepped up pressure against roads and hamlets throughout the country, and MACV intelligence prognostications about North Vietnamese participation were gloomy. In addition to one North Vietnamese division already identified in the Highlands, the intelligence specialists saw the possibility of two more infiltrating into the country. One was probably already located just across the frontier in Laos.

ARVN losses were running unprecedentedly high. Having obtained authority from Washington to create a new ARVN division, I had to cancel plans and issue a moratorium on activating any more ARVN units. If existing units were to maintain an acceptable level of combat strength, all trainees coming through the pipeline had to be fed into them. The time I had hoped to gain by bringing in limited numbers of American security forces while building ARVN strength was obviously not going to be enough. A crisis was building, presaging the kind of semiconventional warfare the French had encountered in latter stages of their fight. Mao Tse-tung's Phase Three was coming up.

A few stop-gap measures were possible. In response to a decision made earlier by President Johnson, a number of U. S. Coast Guard boats arrived to join MACV's naval component in helping Vietnamese craft cut coastal infiltration. The U. S. Seventh Fleet's Task Force 77, composed of aircraft carriers, destroyers, and cruisers, began to provide air and naval gunfire support for American ground troops, particularly for the marines in the northern provinces where the troops were close to the sea.

Renewing a request I had made without success in March, I asked for strikes by the Strategic Air Command's B-52s against VC base areas. Earlier attacks by tactical bombers had proven relatively ineffective, so deeply had the Viet Cong dug in and dispersed their installations. It was also difficult to put enough tactical bombers over a dispersed target simultaneously to damage the enemy troops before they could flee.

The request approved, the first strike occurred on June 18 against an enemy base in War Zone D. Patrols investigating the damage brought back impressive reports. In the months to come use of strategic bombers for tactical support was to prove invaluable. Contrary to the carping of critics who likened it to employing a hammer to kill a fly, the B-52s became the weapon the enemy feared most. Flying so high they were beyond sight or hearing from the ground, they wedded surprise with devastating power.

Almost all B-52 targets were in the hinterland, usually far from any populated area, and usually consisted of troop concentrations or base camps. During the early months, Washington scrutinized every proposed target to the point of absurdity. When Clark Clifford, a member of the President's Foreign Intelligence Advisory Board, was visiting Saigon in 1965, I was particularly piqued over refusal to allow a proposed strike, presumably because somebody in Washington thought he spotted a thatched-roof shed of some kind in the aerial photograph of the target, which presumably indicated habitation. I asked Clifford to take back word that if Washington had no more confidence in me than exemplified in that case, somebody should come up with another commander. Interference eased after that.

In all my time in Vietnam there were only two cases of damage by the B-52s to populated areas. The first was in the vicinity of the Seven Mountains in the Mekong Delta in 1967 when several bombs fell out of the pattern and hit a village. The second was in early 1968 when the target was an enemy battalion in dense undergrowth near the Saigon River. One bomb fell out of the pattern and hit the outskirts of a village. The accuracy of the big bombers was almost incredible.

Even as the military crisis grew, new turmoil enveloped the political scene. Premier Quat had proven to be surprisingly effective, even adroitly squashing the feeble attempt at a *coup d'état* in May by the persistent Colonel Thao, but Quat's time in the Saigon game of musical chairs was almost up.

When Quat shuffled his Cabinet following the attempted coup, two of the ministers he proposed to dismiss refused to quit, and Chief of State Suu backed them, saying the Premier had no authority to fire ministers without the Chief of State's approval. Suu's motives were hard to decipher. He may have been standing on his rights, for the constitutional charter was vague on the issue, but more likely he was influenced by Quat's enemies, mainly militant Catholics, who saw a chance to get rid of Quat. Concern that the generals would intervene prompted Ambassador Taylor to delay his scheduled departure in June for Washington for several days, but General Thieu assured me the military men were content to let the politicians solve their own impasse.

With neither willing to give in, Quat and Suu both resigned and turned over the government to the military. The generals formed a ten-member Committee for the Direction of the State, with Thieu as chairman. Under sponsorship of the committee, a new government took over on June 19. As chairman, General Thieu was the Chief of State, while Marshal Ky served as Premier.

Ky's appointment disturbed Ambassador Taylor, primarily because he knew little about him except his former reputation as a gallant. Having dealt more extensively with Ky and having been briefed on his better qualities by my air commander, Joe Moore, I was less disturbed.

Like the ambassador, I had no way of knowing that the Thieu-Ky team was destined at long last to bring a measure of political stability to the country. The prospect at the time seemed to be more turmoil in the old pattern. The Thieu-Ky government was the fifth in the eighteen months since Diem's overthrow, and there had been three unsuccessful *coups d'état*. The growing military crisis was in many ways a direct result of the political instability. With governments coming and going as if Saigon was a revolving door, I could see little possibility of the South Vietnamese themselves overcoming the military crisis.

Ambassador Taylor's return from Washington failed to resolve the ambiguity I continued to sense in Washington's instructions on how American troops might be employed. The fracas in the United States between press and Administration that had occurred during Taylor's visit had apparently obviated more explicit directions.

Seriously disturbed by the trials of ARVN troops at Ba Gia and Dong Xoai and seeing the possibility that an occasion might soon arise where I would have to commit American troops if a major ARVN force was to be spared utter defeat, I queried Admiral Sharp as to my authority. He responded that I was the man on the ground and would "have to weigh the pros and cons," but he assured me that I had the authority. "I'm sure you realize," he added, "that there would be grave political implications if sizable U.S. forces are committed for the first time and suffer a defeat." Like me, Admiral Sharp was obviously mindful of the fate of Groupement Mobile 100 eleven years earlier.

The rumblings of the latest political crisis in Saigon had begun and the military crisis throughout South Vietnam was all too apparent when I made up my mind that if the United States intended to achieve its goal of denying the enemy victory in South Vietnam, Washington had to face the task realistically. Without substantial American ground combat troops, I concluded, the South Vietnamese would be unable to withstand the pressure from combined Viet Cong and North Vietnamese forces. Many senior South Vietnamese leaders, I knew, shared that view. The enemy was destroying battalions faster than they could be reconstituted and faster than we had planned to organize them under the ARVN's crash build-up program.

I was acutely aware of the gravity of my conclusion. Sizable American forces meant sizable American sacrifices, wounds, and deaths, probably extending over a long period of time, not months but years. I could see no quick victory even with American troops, but without them I saw quick defeat. I knew too that I was flouting the shibboleth of avoiding a ground war in Asia, yet I recognized that that shibboleth was subject to modification in terms of the nation's objectives, as it had been modified in the past.

During this critical period I reflected frequently on my talk in January 1964 with General MacArthur in his apartment at the Waldorf before my departure for Vietnam. Hopeful that the South Vietnamese could carry the burden of combat themselves, General MacArthur nevertheless saw the possibility that foreign troops might be required, in which case, he said, we should try to get as many Oriental nations as possible to help, particularly the Republic of Korea, the Philippines, and Nationalist China. Critics of the war later said that MacArthur categorically ruled out using American troops on the Asian mainland, but they were misquoting him. He had been referring only to land-locked Laos; if using American troops was the only way to save South Vietnam, he believed it would have to be done. In the general's mind, there was "no substitute for victory."

I was sharply conscious that I was a military man, charged not with making policy but with executing it. Yet if the National Security Council and the President deemed it in the interest of the United States to save South Vietnam from Communism, I bore the responsibility as the American military commander in Vietnam to advise from a military standpoint what had to be done to achieve that goal. Never in the Mission Council, chaired by the ambassador in Saigon, was there mention of pulling out and leaving the South Vietnamese to their fate. Like me, the others of the U. S. Mission were charged not with making policy or grand strategy but with executing it.

In a message on June 7 I told CINCPAC and the Joint Chiefs that enemy strength was increasing at a pace that the ARVN simply was unable to match and that I was convinced the North Vietnamese would commit whatever they considered necessary "to tip the balance." Without reinforcement by more American and Third Country troops, I said, the ARVN would be unable to stand up to the pressure.

At the time there were one Australian and nine U.S. battalions in South Vietnam. I asked for quick deployment of the others that had been discussed: nine Korean battalions, three U. S. Army infantry battalions, and the U. S. Army airmobile division, which when finally organized as the 1st Cavalry Division (Airmobile) had eight battalions. I asked also for an additional Marine battalion to bring the III Marine Amphibious Force to division size, more tactical air units, more helicopters, and more logistical troops. Those plus the battalions already in Vietnam totaled thirty-five battalions. Possibly because of subsequent additions worked out with the Joint Chiefs, which brought the total to thirty-four American battalions and ten from other countries, my message came to be known in Washington as "the forty-four-battalion request."

Both in that message and another five days later, I made clear my view that an enclave strategy was no answer. If South Vietnam was to survive, I cabled, we had to have "a substantial and hard-hitting offensive capability on the ground to convince the VC that they cannot win." The United States had to make an "active commitment" with troops that could "be maneuvered freely." The enemy's shift to big-unit war was drawing ARVN troops away from the heavily populated regions, leaving the people vulnerable to subjugation by local Communist forces and political cadres. American and Allied troops, along with the South Vietnamese airborne and marine battalions of the general reserve, would have to assume the role of fighting the big units, leaving the bulk of the ARVN free to protect the people. No more niceties about defensive posture and reaction, I intimated; we had to forget about enclaves and take the war to the enemy.

A few days later in mid-June I emphasized that I saw forty-four battalions as no force for victory but as a stop-gap measure to save the ARVN from defeat.

> The premise behind whatever further actions we may undertake . . . must be that we are in for the long pull . . . . [I] believe it is time all concerned face up to [the] fact that we must be prepared for a long war which will probably involve increasing numbers of U.S. troops.

That, I believed, would require some form of national mobilization and the public airing by Washington of a frank, objective, complete analysis of the problem and what we had to do about it.

As brought out in that message, I made no effort to deceive Washington as to how long I thought the job would take or how many troops would be required. To reiterate my conviction, I sent a message to the Joint Chiefs at the end of the month in response to a query they relayed from the President as to whether I thought the forty-four battalions would persuade the enemy to desist. "The direct answer to your basic question," I wrote, "is 'No.'" It would take until the end of 1965 to get all the forty-four battalions to Vietnam and "establish the military balance." For 1966, when I would hope to "gain and maintain the military initiative," I was unable to say what additional forces might be required. That depended on many variables, the most important of which was the resources the North Vietnamese might elect to commit. "Instinctively," I wrote, "we believe that there may be substantial additional U.S. force requirements." Again I repeated my call for some kind of limited mobilization, which I deemed "clear and pressing."

My proposal, I learned later, stirred sharp debate in Washington, as was to have been expected. While discussion progressed, the President as an interim measure granted me authority in June to commit American forces in support of the South Vietnamese "in any situation . . . when, in COMUSMACV's judgment, their use is necessary to strengthen the relative position" of the ARVN forces. Although that came fairly close to abrogating the enclave strategy, it still fell short of free maneuver, and what I might accomplish under the authority was limited by the number of troops at my disposal.

Under the new authority I proceeded with a plan I had been developing for the 173d Airborne Brigade, commanded by Brigadier General Ellis Williamson, to conduct a combined operation with the Australian battalion, an ARVN regiment, and two ARVN airborne battalions. On June 27 those forces (the airborne brigade had only two battalions at the time) made a limited three-day foray into War Zone D, the first time in years that any other than Communist troops had entered that fastness. It was an operation designed to prepare the Americans and Australians for moving into Stage Three operations as I had earlier outlined, while at the same time damaging and upsetting the balance of enemy troops that were in a position to hit the air base at Bien Hoa City. Several sharp engagements with the Viet Cong ensued, and American and Australian troops performed with distinction.

As part of the President's process of coming to a decision on my request for more troops, he sent a fact-finding team on a five-day visit to Saigon beginning on July 16. It was headed by Secretary McNamara, General Wheeler, and Henry Cabot Lodge, who at the end of July was to return for a second tour as American ambassador when Maxwell Taylor's agreed-on one-year tour reached an end.

To the visitors I could but reiterate the concerns and recommendations I had already transmitted to Washington. Although Ambassador Taylor confirmed my view of the seriousness of the military situation and agreed with using American troops to help, he and Deputy Ambassador Alexis Johnson both favored moving more slowly to give the South Vietnamese people more time to adjust to increased American presence. While I too saw that as a problem, I believed the need for help was immediate and that we would be able to demonstrate amply by word and deed that we were different from the French. Secretary McNamara must have shared my view, for his attitude throughout the conferences was one of acceptance of the forty-four-battalion concept and more as needed.

Indeed, even before Secretary McNamara's arrival, he asked my estimate of how many additional American and Allied troops would be required to convince the enemy he would be unable to win. In making the estimate, I was to avoid consideration of additional ARVN contributions, for he had no wish to pin success on such a variable. During his conferences with me in July in Saigon and at many another meeting over the months, he told me to ask for the troops that I needed to carry out my mission and not to restrict my requests. Nor was I to concern myself with economic, political, and public opinion problems. Leave those to him.

It was virtually impossible to provide the Secretary with a meaningful figure. In the end I told him only that I thought twenty-four more battalions in addition to the forty-four under consideration, plus more combat support and logistical troops, would put us in a position to *begin* the "win phase" of our strategy. That meant about 175,000 American troops at the start, followed by about 100,000. Yet I warned that VC and North Vietnamese actions well might alter the figures.

Which they did. Any number of times.

I based my reckoning on a concept of operations to be executed in three general phases:

Phase One: Commit those American and Allied forces necessary "to halt the losing trend" by the end of 1965.

Phase Two: "During the first half of 1966," take the offensive with American and Allied forces in "high priority areas" to destroy enemy forces and reinstitute pacification programs.

Phase Three: If the enemy persisted, he might be defeated and his forces and base areas destroyed during a period of a year to a year and a half following Phase II.

The authors of the celebrated Pentagon Papers used that estimate as a basis for saying that Westmoreland expected victory by the end of 1967. I had no such expectation and made no prediction whatsoever as to terminal date. The anonymous authors dated the "year to a year and a half" of Phase III from "the first half of 1966," which was a broad target date for Phase II to begin, not to end. In their suspect scholarship, they made no allowance for how long Phase II might take, nor did I in my concept make any prediction of how long it might take.

Having apparently studied the build-up question at considerable length with the Joint Chiefs before coming to Saigon, Secretary McNamara endorsed the forty-four-battalion concept and the follow-on force, although upping my estimate of twenty-four battalions to twenty-seven, for a total of seventy-one battalions, in keeping with prior deliberations by the Joint Chiefs. The Secretary also wanted the President to call the National Guard and Organized Reserve into service, a step that I saw as premature.

Although I wanted an expression of national resolve, I was conscious that without congressional legislation a Reserve call-up would be for only a year, and I knew that a year would not do the job in Vietnam without a massive, uninterrupted bombing campaign against North Vietnam, which I knew the Administration was not likely to approve. I well remembered the Reserve call-up by President Kennedy during the Berlin crisis, when strong pressures arose before one year was up, to bring the boys home, a recollection that President Johnson told me later that he shared. Provided there was an equitable draft without special exceptions for anybody but the most essential civilian workers, I believed the burden of the war could be shared by the whole spectrum of American youth over an extended period, and I was convinced that it would be a long war. A call-up of Reserves should be made only when the enemy was near defeat and more American troops could assure it.

Our July discussions in Saigon turned out, in a way, to be moot. During the second day the Secretary received a message from Deputy Secretary of Defense Vance telling him that President Johnson was considering a Reserve call-up and that he approved the forty-four-battalion proposal.

By the time the President in a press conference on July 28 announced his decision publicly, he had decided against calling Reserve units to active duty. Yet he had unquestionably reached the conclusion that he had to make a major effort in Vietnam with American troops. He made the decision, he said, in view of "the lessons of history":

I have today ordered to Vietnam the Airmobile Division and certain other forces which will raise our fighting strength from 75,000 to 125,000 men almost immediately. Additional forces will be needed later, and they will be sent as requested.

Chapter VIII
Evolution of Strategy

Explicit in my forty-four-battalion proposal and President Johnson's approval of it was a proviso for free maneuver of American and Allied units throughout South Vietnam. Thus the restrictive enclave strategy with which I had disagreed from the first was finally rejected.

Since the most serious and immediate enemy threat was in the Central Highlands, I deemed it essential as one of my first moves, which I had pointed out on several occasions in asking for the airmobile division, to deploy an American force there. I intended that a battalion of American marines temporarily secure Qui Nhon for the safe landing of the division. Although I anticipated using Route 19 to supply the division, supplies could go by air, which the airmobile division with its large numbers of organic helicopters was uniquely equipped to accomplish.

No exponent of the enclave strategy, Admiral Sharp nevertheless objected to deploying the airmobile division inland. He wanted to base the division itself at Qui Nhon and clear Binh Dinh province before moving inland, thus insuring a solid base for supply by road. He still was concerned also lest the enemy score a psychological victory against American troops *à la* Groupement Mobile 100. He also believed in using American troops to secure populated areas, whereas, in general, I saw that as a task for the ARVN, whose troops, by language, culture, and local knowledge, were better equipped for it.

At least one member of the Joint Chiefs agreed with Oley Sharp: General Wallace M. Greene, Jr., Commandant of the Marine Corps, one who sometimes made his points by an emotional raising of his voice. As a marine, Wally Greene thought in terms of beachheads. Visiting Vietnam, he tried to talk me out of my plan, but while I was determined that no American unit be subjected to the grim fate met in the Highlands by Groupement Mobile 100, I was convinced my plan was sound. Although a commander must observe caution, he wins no battles by sitting back waiting for the enemy to come to him. Given strong support within the Joint Chiefs by Bus Wheeler and Harold K. Johnson, I proceeded with my plan.

The enemy clearly was moving into the third phase of revolutionary warfare, committing regiments and subsequently divisions to seize and retain territory and to destroy the government's troops and eliminate all vestiges of government control. Yet at the same time the enemy's guerrillas, local forces, and political cadres at the hamlet and village level continued their small-unit war, seeking to terrorize and control the population and knock off small government outposts. The war at that point thus had two facets, yet the two were closely interrelated, both aimed at gaining control of the countryside and strangling the towns and cities. Neither facet could be ignored.

In an effort to explain this kind of warfare in simple terms, I occasionally likened the political subversives and guerrillas to termites persistently eating away at the structural members of a building, analogously, the structure of the South Vietnamese government. Some distance away hid the main forces, or big units, which—mixing my metaphor—I called "bully boys," armed with crowbars and waiting for the propitious moment to move in and destroy the weakened building. Only by eliminating the bully boys—or, at least, so harrying them as to keep them away from the building—was there a possibility of eliminating the termites or enticing them to work for our side, an essential though systematic and tedious process.

As I saw the three phases of my strategy, American combat troops were to be used at first to protect developing logistical bases, although some might have to be committed from time to time as "fire brigades" whenever the enemy's big units posed a threat, which was how I contemplated first using the airmobile division in the Highlands. In the second phase, we were to gain the initiative, penetrate, and whenever possible eliminate the enemy's base camps and sanctuaries. So long as the Communists were free to emerge from those hideouts to terrorize the people, recruit or impress conscripts, glean food, levy taxes, and attack government troops and installations, then to retire with impunity back into their sanctuaries, there was little hope of our defeating the insurgency. Invading the sanctuaries also might bring the elusive enemy to battle, affording an opportunity to destroy his main forces. In the third and final phase, we were to move into sustained ground combat and mop up the last of the main forces and guerrillas, or at least push them across the frontiers where we would try to contain them.

Two additional tasks were to be pursued throughout all three phases: pacification and strengthening the ARVN. By the time the war reached the final phase, I expected the bulk of the people to be under government control and protection and the ARVN to be so trained and equipped and in such numbers that the South Vietnamese alone could deal with any lingering opposition. In a later day that was to be called "Vietnamization."

An intrinsic goal in all these operations was to open roads and waterways, which were essential for moving troops, people, and commerce. Whenever the VC cut a road, they not only showed up the government's weakness but they also isolated communities and made the people vulnerable to propaganda and coercion. If the enemy controlled a road, he had a rich source of revenue from taxes levied on travelers.

In figuring on American troops to do a major share of the fighting against the enemy's big units, I had several considerations in mind. In the first place, the ARVN had greater compatability with the people than did American troops. Furthermore, since the enemy's large units would be met most often in his base areas or other remote regions, the greater mobility of American units would provide them with an advantage. Superior American firepower would be most advantageously employed against the big units, and using it in remote regions would mean fewer civilian casualties and less damage to built-up areas. The fewer Americans in close contact with the people also meant that much less provocation of the xenophobia of the Vietnamese, that much less opportunity for unfortunate incidents between American troops and the people.

That is not to say that American units were to conduct no operations in populated regions. Although South Vietnamese leaders asked at first that I restrict American presence to remote areas, I declined, unwilling to see my flexibility fettered and also conscious that American performance would set an example and a challenge to the face-conscious Orientals. So strong, too, was the enemy in some populated regions, such as the coastal sectors of the northern provinces, that American troops would have to stage major operations there. The same would obtain in Binh Dinh province and elsewhere. Hopeful that the South Vietnamese would gain pride and confidence by defending their capital, I still planned no major American commitment in Saigon or its close environs. I was similarly hopeful that amid the teeming population of the Mekong Delta the South Vietnamese also could do the job alone. Although the Delta was one of the incubators of the old Viet Minh insurgency and retained a considerable tradition of dissidence, the region was so far from North Vietnam and its supplies that few large enemy formations might be expected to be encountered there.

As events developed, so magnetized were press and television by the conventional fights between large units in remote regions that American contributions to the war in the populated areas often went unnoticed, which may have contributed to the notoriety of an implicitly critical phrase, "Westmoreland's big-unit war." In reality, despite my policy of using American units to oppose the enemy's main forces, more American troops were usually engaged on a day-by-day basis, helping weed out local opposition and supporting the pacification process, than were engaged in the big fights. Similarly, ARVN units also participated against the enemy's big units, particularly ARVN airborne, marine, ranger, and armor units, which I insisted on as a matter of policy.

Yet the very existence of large enemy units made it essential that American troops be prepared on short notice to drop what they were doing and move against a developing big-unit threat. When the troops moved away from the population, the guerrillas obviously gained a chance to recoup their losses, but I never had the luxury of enough troops to maintain an American, Allied, or ARVN presence everywhere all the time. Guarding against local resurgence would in the end be the responsibility of the militia —the Regional and Popular Forces—but it would take time to recruit, train, and equip them and provide sufficient leadership for them to do the job without setbacks.

Had I had at my disposal virtually unlimited manpower, I could have stationed troops permanently in every district or province and thus provided an alternative strategy. That would have enabled the troops to get to know the people intimately, facilitating the task of identifying the subversives and protecting the others against intimidation. Yet to have done that would have required literally millions of men, and I still would have had to maintain a reserve to counter big-unit threats. I never had any prospect of those numbers. In any case, it would have been perilous to ignore the undisputed military canon that to try to be strong everywhere is to be weak everywhere.

Noting the relatively small size of South Vietnam, some might have considered it practicable to seal the land frontiers against North Vietnamese infiltration, thus facilitating the task of rooting out the Viet Cong. Yet small though the country is, its land frontiers extend for more than 900 miles. In World War I close to 6 million Allied troops were needed to man the 455 miles of the Western Front. In World War II, 4.5 million Allied troops were needed to man a 570-mile Western Front. In Korea close to a million United Nations troops were needed to man a 123-mile front across the waist of the Korean Peninsula. To have defended the land frontiers of South Vietnam in similar density would have required many millions of troops, plus others to carry on the fight against the insurgency, numbers that it would have been absurd to contemplate. At peak strength in South Vietnam, achieved in early 1969, American troops numbered 543,400, Allied troops 62,400, and ARVN troops, including militia, approximately a million, for a total well under 2 million.

To provide at least some check, however inadequate, on enemy infiltration, I had to depend primarily on mobility. Employing only about 45,000 troops, the CIDG-Special Forces camps along the frontier provided bases for patrols that might detect major infiltration, to which units arriving by helicopter might react. The SOG teams operating in Laos harassed infiltrators and collected intelligence on enemy movements, as did both American and South Vietnamese long-range reconnaissance patrols operating within South Vietnam. When those patrols located enemy formations, I could react either with troops or with artillery and air strikes, including strikes by B-52s, although Washington's restrictions on operations in Laos and Cambodia for a long time limited the response there.

I continued for long to hope for an international force to man a line below the DMZ and across the Laos panhandle. One proposal that Deputy Ambassador Alexis Johnson and I worked out was that this be staged as a regional development project, with engineers extending Route 9 across the panhandle to the border with Thailand. To provide protection for the road construction, combat troops would be deployed, thereby providing an anti-infiltration screen. Yet after a first flurry of interest in an international anti-infiltration force in late 1964, officials in Washington never evidenced any more enthusiasm for it.

From the first I contemplated eventually moving into Laos to cut and block the infiltration routes of the Ho Chi Minh Trail, and in 1966 and 1967 my staff prepared detailed plans for such an operation. When Henry Cabot Lodge returned to Saigon in the summer of 1965 for another tour as American ambassador, he enthusiastically pressed for the move, and his eventual successor, Ellsworth Bunker, also supported it. Yet I recognized that blocking the trail would require at least a corps-size force of three divisions, and I would be unable for a long time to spare that many troops from the critical fight within South Vietnam. When at last, in 1968, our strength had increased sufficiently and the enemy had been depleted enough to make the move possible, President Johnson was so beset by war critics that he would take no step that might possibly be interpreted as broadening the war, which he had publicly announced he would not do.

In lamenting what came to be known, however erroneously, as the "big-unit war," critics presumably saw some alternative, for the essence of constructive criticism is alternative. Yet to my knowledge nobody ever advanced a viable alternative that conformed to the American policy of confining the war within South Vietnam. It was, after all, the enemy's big units—not the guerrillas—that eventually did the South Vietnamese in.

The enemy ultimately demonstrated that an enclave strategy was no answer, for enclaves would have done the enemy little damage, and he would negotiate, as he showed unmistakably, only when he was hurting. In 1969 a former Deputy Assistant Secretary of Defense, Townsend Hoopes, in a book titled *The Limits of Intervention,** called for an end of what he termed "hyper-aggressive search and destroy operations" and the adoption of a "modified enclave strategy" involving what he called "seize and hold" operations in the populated areas. That, plus a halt in the bombing of North Vietnam, he wrote, would lead the enemy to negotiate. The enemy's subsequent negotiating record scuttled that theory as thoroughly as it did the enclave theory, and neither theory took into account that while we sat in enclaves, however defined, the enemy's big units would remain free to wreak their will undeterred.

While Hoopes was presumably writing his book and I was the U. S. Army Chief of Staff, he talked with me. Since he mentioned my views only in footnotes, I presume he either had finished his work and merely wanted the

* New York: David McKay Co., 1969.

interview to provide verisimilitude or had no wish to present any conflicting point of view. I was later surprised when judges of the National Book Awards selected the book as one of the finalists in competition for the year's best nonfiction. That such a theoretically unsound work should receive serious consideration for such an award said something either about the judges' emotions regarding the war or about their knowledge of military operations.

Also writing in 1969, Sir Robert Thompson in *No Exit from Vietnam*† remarked that what he termed American "preoccupation" with the enemy's big units could produce no more than a stalemate. "In People's Revolutionary War," he noted, "if you are not winning, you are losing, because the enemy can always sit out a stalemate without making any concessions." With that I would agree, but not with Sir Robert's solution. He wanted to concentrate not against the big units but against the irregulars who, he said, provided the big units their sustenance. What he failed to recognize was that the situation in South Vietnam by the time American combat troops entered the country was different from the situation he had experienced in Malaya in the 1950s. Where there had been little outside support for the insurgency in Malaya, the big units in South Vietnam were no longer depending on ir- regulars for sustenance but on North Vietnam. From a military standpoint, it was the irregulars that were drawing support from the regulars. Although we were conducting simultaneous campaigns against the irregulars through- out South Vietnam, there could be no stamping them out entirely until the threat of the bully boys with their crowbars was substantially eliminated. With that achieved, both the campaign to uproot the irregulars and the pacification campaign would fall into place.

I elected to fight a so-called big-unit war not because of any Napoleonic impulse to maneuver units and hark to the sound of cannon but because of the basic fact that the enemy had committed big units and I ignored them at my peril. The big-unit war was in any case only a first step. As a former member of my staff in the Pentagon, Lieutenant General Richard G. Stil- well, wrote later, in likening insurgency to a boulder, a sledge first has to break the boulder into large fragments; groups of workers then attack the fragments with spalling tools; then individuals pound the chips with tap hammers until they are reduced to powder and the boulder ceases to exist.

In the early months of American involvement it was risky, even perilous, in regions where the enemy's big units might be met, to commit troops in less than battalion strength, and even then at least a brigade had to be avail- able in case of trouble. After our campaigns of 1966 and 1967 and after the enemy had expended his resources in a nationwide offensive in early 1968, I could commit companies and even platoons and multiple squad-sized pa- trols without major concern. The boulder was reduced to fragments, the fragments to chips. That the enemy could bring in another boulder from

† New York: David McKay Co., 1969.

outside the boundaries of South Vietnam and strike again, as he did in the spring of 1972 and finally in 1975, was another matter, one of the peculiarities of a war in which one side respected international frontiers while the other did not.

It was not enough merely to contain the big units. They had to be pounded with artillery and bombs and eventually brought to battle on the ground if they were not forever to remain a threat. That process led inevitably to the dramatic, often costly battles in the Central Highlands and along the DMZ that the American people looked at in horror on their television screens. Why fight for remote, jungle-covered hills, many asked, and then a few days later give them up? By moving American units from populated regions in order to find and fight the enemy in mountainous jungles, were we not letting the enemy call the tune?

The answers were multiple but none more important than the fact that, unlike the guerrillas, if we avoided battle, we would never succeed. We could never destroy the big units by leaving them alone. Besides, the terrain in the Highlands and below the DMZ was no less inhospitable for the enemy than it was for American forces; indeed, the helicopter made it possible to overcome the major obstacles posed by rugged terrain. That in fighting close to base areas beyond the Cambodian and Laotian borders and in the DMZ the enemy enjoyed a certain advantage in shortened lines of communications was evident, and along the DMZ he gained additional advantage from artillery located within the DMZ; but American mobility, firepower, and flexible logistical support more than balanced the equation. What was the alternative: relinquish the Highlands and the territory just south of the DMZ? Do that and you allowed him to push his base areas ever closer to the centers of population so that in the end you would be fighting among the population you were trying to protect.

In many cases, a specific hill or other piece of terrain had no intrinsic value except that the enemy was there or that he was using it as a stepping-stone to some objective among the population. Except along the DMZ, the enemy had almost no artillery, so that the high ground with its usual advantages of observation and command of surrounding territory had less long-term meaning than it would have had for a more conventionally armed force.

Nor did we have anywhere near enough troops even to consider holding all the commanding terrain. Once we had accomplished our goal of bringing the enemy to battle and inflicting heavy losses, in the process thwarting his objective and driving him back across the frontiers, what point in continuing to hold the high ground? Had we done that we would have ended up with little parcels of men spread all over the landscape, too few to deter enemy movement and too weak to defend themselves against determined attack. It was also important to avoid trying to hold positions too close to the Laotian and Cambodian borders, for in view of the proximity of large enemy forces just across the borders, that would have been inviting trouble.

To have held onto remote real estate after it had ceased to have meaning also would have tied up troops that might better be used rooting out the local guerrilla. That would have given support to the allegation that the enemy was luring us into the hinterlands to get us away from the population. If that was indeed his intent—and it certainly appeared to be—it was futile, for so great was American mobility that the troops could be returned quickly to the populated areas. Besides, the procedure was a blade with two edges. If the enemy did indeed lure us into remote regions, he at the same time afforded us an opportunity to bring him to battle and inflict the damage we had to impose if we were to achieve our objective of destroying his big units with minimum damage to the population.

The fight for a hill that attained perhaps the greatest notoriety was one that occurred after my departure from Vietnam, but it was a fight fairly typical of others that took place during my command. Part of the notoriety was attributable to the fact that somebody gave the hill a name that invoked images of a meat grinder or a butcher shop: "Hamburger Hill."

Hamburger Hill—in reality, Apbia Mountain—is a commanding feature near the Laotian border in the rugged A Shau Valley which points like a spear at a throat toward the cities of Hué and Danang. The enemy long controlled the valley after March 1966, when two North Vietnamese regiments attacked a lone CIDG-Special Forces camp there. Although normal practice when the enemy hit an outpost was to reinforce or counterattack, I simply lacked the forces in early 1966 to hold the valley against determined attack, so I withdrew the troops and abandoned the camp. With sufficient forces available in the spring of 1968, I directed a sweep back through the valley to end the threat it posed to Hué and Danang, and my successor, General Creighton W. Abrams, continued to conduct sweeps to deny enemy passage through the valley. On one of those sweeps in early May 1969, a South Vietnamese battalion and a battalion of the 101st Airborne Division found the enemy in strength on Apbia Mountain.

To have left the North Vietnamese undisturbed on the mountain would have been to jeopardize our control of the valley and accept a renewed threat to the coastal cities. A prolonged siege would have been costly and tied up troops indefinitely. The commander of the 101st, Major General Melvin Zais, quite properly ordered an attack.

The attacking American battalion was from the unit I had commanded in Korea, the 187th Airborne Brigade; the commander was Lieutenant Colonel Weldon Honeycutt, whom I had sent as a corporal to Officer Candidate School and who had later served as my aide. Honeycutt was a competent, experienced commander. For several days he pounded the hill with air and artillery strikes, but only after three unsuccessful infantry assaults did the North Vietnamese finally flee across the border into Laos, leaving behind a rear guard. The North Vietnamese lost 597 men killed, more than a battalion, a sharp defeat by any standards. The Americans lost 50 killed.

The outcry in the United States about the American casualties was vociferous, partly because a certain vocal element would condemn anything connected with the war and partly because the fight occurred at a time when Washington had announced that major American operations were to be phased down. Among the more intemperate critics was Senator Edward M. Kennedy, who on the floor of the Senate called the action "senseless and irresponsible" and implied that American commanders had ordered the assaults and "sacrificed" American lives only to assuage "military pride." That kind of criticism ignored reality and the purpose of the operations in the A Shau Valley.

Honeycutt's tactics at Hamburger Hill were aggressive, a feature of American tactics throughout the war. Aggressive tactics may produce sharp initial losses, but they save lives over the long run, for in a protracted battle, as in a protracted war, casualties inevitably accumulate. Allowed to drag on and on, the Vietnam war as a whole illustrates the point.

It was unfortunate that American strategy in Vietnam came to be known as a "search-and-destroy" strategy, for that misnomer fed a general American abhorrence for the destruction that warfare inevitably produces. A few graphic newspaper photographs and a TV shot of American marines setting fire to thatched-roof huts were enough to convince many that "search and destroy" was tantamount to a scorched earth. Yet in reality the operations were aimed at finding the enemy and eliminating his military installations— bunkers, tunnels, rice and ammunition caches, training camps, the essentials if his base camps and sanctuaries were to continue to provide havens from which he might emerge at times of his choosing to terrorize the people. Those surely are legitimate goals in any kind of war.

Given the elusiveness of the enemy and the junglelike nature of much of the countryside, some search-and-destroy operations failed to find the enemy. Because neither Americans nor South Vietnamese possessed overwhelming numbers, the cordons erected when the enemy was found were sievelike, and the enemy often escaped. Nor was it possible to occupy the sanctuaries permanently. Although we facilitated our later return by leaving behind airfields and manned outposts, foray after foray often had to be launched. To an impatient American press and public, that was frustrating, so that many looked on "search and destroy" as aimless and unrewarding.

That it was necessary on some occasions intentionally to raze evacuated villages or hamlets apparently fed the misunderstanding. So closely entwined were some populated localities with the tentacles of the VC base areas, in some cases actually integrated into the defenses, and so sympathetic were some of the people to the VC that the only way to establish control short of constant combat operations among the people was to remove the people and destroy the village. That done, operations to find the enemy could be conducted without fear of civilian casualties.

Although South Vietnamese authorities usually tried to provide comfortable facilities for the refugees, some hardship inevitably occurred, and the people understandably resented giving up their homes. Yet the alternative was to leave them exposed to the destruction of battle. By depicting evacuation of the fortified village of Ben Suc in the Iron Triangle early in 1967 as an act of inhumanity rather than the essential and—under the circumstances —beneficent act that it was, a correspondent for *The New Yorker* magazine, Jonathan Schell, added to the misunderstanding. That it was infinitely better in some cases to move the people from areas long sympathetic to the VC was amply demonstrated later by events that occurred when the discipline of an American company broke down at a place called My Lai.

The U.S. military strategy employed in Vietnam, dictated by political decisions, was essentially that of a war of attrition. Since the World War I battles of the Somme and Verdun, that has been a strategy in disrepute, one that to many appeared particularly unsuited for a war in Asia with Asia's legendary hordes of manpower. Yet the war in Vietnam was not against Asian hordes but against an enemy with relatively limited manpower. As the South Vietnamese government's control embraced more and more of the countryside, the enemy's recruiting base decreased and the VC had to depend upon the North Vietnamese to make good their losses. Although the North Vietnamese might constantly rebuild their units, they did so each time with manpower less adequately trained. Meanwhile, the continuing battle bought time to build up the ARVN and enable the government to solidify its position in the countryside.

In any case, what alternative was there to a war of attrition? A ground invasion of North Vietnam was out, for the U.S. national policy was not to conquer North Vietnam but to eliminate the insurgency inside South Vietnam, and President Johnson had stated publicly that he would not "broaden" the war. Because the number of American troops at my disposal would for long be limited, attacking the enemy inside Laos and Cambodia would be beyond my means for months, even years; I would grapple with restrictions on those operations when the time came, although I was destined never to overcome the restrictions. Meanwhile, I had to get on with meeting the crisis within South Vietnam, and only by seeking, fighting, and destroying the enemy could that be done.

An impatient people, we Americans seem to feel that once the first American troops arrive, the situation will quickly be set right and that once the President turns the faucet, the flow of troops will be swift and unrelenting. In an "area war," as the war in Vietnam was, there were no front lines to provide a gauge of progress. Reading every day of American troops fighting and winning, hearing pronouncements by national leaders that we were making steady progress, people unaware of how few American troops were actually engaged tended to see an early end that under the circumstances could not be. Even with large forces, a war of attrition can never be concluded swiftly.

Even had South Vietnam been a modern, fully developed country with adequate logistical facilities readily adaptable to military use, troop build-up would have been slow; for in view of world-wide commitments, the total numbers of America's armed forces were relatively small. In asking the first increment of American troops to meet the crisis, I had anticipated that not until the end of 1965 would all the first increment arrive. Even that pace involved a serious calculated risk, for men locked in combat cannot long survive without adequate logistical support. By the end of 1965, six months after President Johnson's decision to go beyond base security and enclave missions, American strength in Vietnam totaled 184,000. Included were only three full combat divisions—one infantry, one airmobile, one Marine— and three Army combat brigades, and a Marine regiment. The marines had an air wing, the Air Force two tactical fighter wings. Those were supplemented by an Australian battalion, a South Korean marine brigade, and a South Korean infantry division. All together, those forces represented forty-five maneuver battalions.

The Viet Cong and the North Vietnamese, meanwhile, had been rapidly building their strength. By mid-November 1965 MACV intelligence listed a possible nine North Vietnamese regiments inside South Vietnam and noted that since July regimental-size VC units had more than doubled, from 5 to 12. If that kind of build-up (forty-eight battalions) continued, I noted in a cable to Washington, it would be twice that planned for the second increment of American troops.

Concerned by that development, Secretary McNamara near the end of November flew direct from business in Europe to Saigon. In conferences with him, subsequent cables to and from Washington, a conference in mid-December with Admiral Sharp in Honolulu, and talks in Saigon during a visit from Generals Wheeler and Johnson, I formulated my concept of operations, deployments, and organization, and recommendations for the troops I considered we had to have to meet the changed enemy situation.

Under my plan of operations, every American division and separate combat brigade was to build a base camp, in effect a home station, which was essential for such rear echelon functions of the division as record keeping and maintaining reserve supplies. Conscious of the normal human tendency to make improvements in living arrangements, I had to maintain a constant vigil to insure that these camps remained relatively austere, both for reasons of economy and so that they could be moved if a division had to be redeployed far from the original base camp. Although tents were to be used at first, each camp eventually was to have semipermanent, cheap frame buildings, for over the long run those would be more economical than constantly replacing tentage that rotted quickly in the humid tropical environment. The region in the vicinity of each base camp constituted the unit's tactical area of responsibility, much as a unit in conventional warfare has a zone of advance. Unless called on to move elsewhere to engage large enemy forces or penetrate enemy sanctuaries, the unit was to patrol its zone, bring the enemy to battle, and in the process help South Vietnamese forces provide security for government ministries and the National Police engaged in pacification. The unit was also to assist in training the ARVN and to perform civic action, promoting self-help projects with the people such as digging wells and building bridges, schools, dispensaries.

When moving far from the base camp, a unit would leave behind a small security and house-keeping cadre. In the field the unit would erect fire-support bases to serve as protected artillery positions and as combat bases for patrols and for sweeps to find the enemy and his supply caches. Smaller fire-support bases might house artillery alone with a small security force. Artillery pieces were to be able to fire in any direction and, when sufficient artillery was available, provide interlocking fire with other bases.

As American forces increased, I established three corps-type headquarters with boundaries corresponding to those of the Vietnamese corps. In addition to commanding American units, each commander served as senior adviser to the Vietnamese corps commander. Neither technically being subordinate to the other, they co-ordinated all operations and logistical matters, much as I did with the Joint General Staff in Saigon. Practically, the role of adviser gave the U.S. commander controlling influence but not authority over the Vietnamese per se.

For several reasons I chose not to designate the American headquarters as corps. I wanted to avoid confusion with the four existing Vietnamese corps headquarters and also to emphasize that each American headquarters was supporting the Vietnamese—a force in the field supporting a corps, thus a "field force." Nor was the headquarters a corps in the usual tactical sense, since the commander had territorial responsibilities as well as tactical ones and eventually, I anticipated, would also be in charge of pacification.

Because the III Marine Amphibious Force at Danang already constituted a corps-type headquarters, it served as the American headquarters in the northern provinces alongside the South Vietnamese I Corps. A U. S. Army headquarters, the I (Eye) Field Force, Vietnam, located at Nha Trang served with the Vietnamese II Corps, responsible for the central provinces; and another U. S. Army headquarters, the II Field Force, Vietnam, at Bien Hoa served with the Vietnamese III Corps in the region around Saigon. Since I contemplated no major American deployment in the Mekong Delta, no comparable headquarters served with the Vietnamese IV Corps.

This organizational concept provided a flexibility that was essential, for who could predict exactly how the battle would develop? If necessary, for example, a field force headquarters might assume the role of a field army headquarters with one or more tactical corps subordinated to it. In later months, after introducing U. S. Army troops into the northern provinces to help meet an enemy threat, I found it necessary to put a corps headquarters within the zone of the III Marine Amphibious Force, to operate as a true tactical headquarters without advisory or territorial responsibilities, so that the flexibility paid off.

The first major fight involving American troops developed in August 1965, when U.S. marines at Chu Lai uncovered the presence of a VC regiment on the nearby Bantangan Peninsula, ostensibly preparing to attack the developing American base. The commander of the III Marine Amphibious Force, Lieutenant General Lewis W. Walt, acted with dispatch. Part of a regiment of the 3d Marine Division having just landed at Chu Lai, General Walt took advantage of the vessels that had put the men ashore to re-embark a battalion. Landing another battalion of marines by helicopter on the sandy peninsula to pin the VC against the sea, he sent the seaborne force ashore in the enemy's rear. Amphibious tractors and tanks provided close-in fire support, while a U. S. Navy cruiser that happened to be off-shore delivered devastating fire from 6-inch guns. It was the first amphibious operation of the war. Over several days the Marine battalions squeezed the black pajama-clad VC between them. When it was over, some 700 Viet Cong were dead while the others fled individually or in small groups into hills and mountains inland.

It was an auspicious beginning for American arms. Although I was destined in the future to have some anxious moments and some units were to take sharp losses, from this beginning until American withdrawal some seven and a half years later no American unit in South Vietnam other than a few companies on the offensive or an occasional small outpost ever incurred what could fairly be called a setback. That is a remarkable record.

One of those anxious moments involved first commitment of the U. S. Army's first airmobile division, the 1st Cavalry Division, whose big black and gold shoulder patch had become renowned in the Pacific in World War II and in Korea. The concept of a division capable of moving by air with its organic transport was new, an outcome of recent tests that had proven its feasibility, but the concept was still to be tried under fire. With the division scheduled to arrive in the II Corps Zone in September, in August I sent the 1st Brigade, 101st Airborne Division, one of only three U. S. Army brigades available at the time, to secure a site for a base camp for the division, while a battalion of American marines secured the landing beaches. Still expecting to use the division to meet the crisis in the Central Highlands, I located the base camp at An Khe, astride Route 19 midway between Qui Nhon on the coast and Pleiku, deep in the Highlands. As always, I made the final decision only at the last minute lest conditions should change. When the division reached Qui Nhon by sea, its combat troops were able to vault by helicopter to An Khe within hours after landing, and work was already underway on an airfield at Pleiku to facilitate operations in the interior.

The airmobile troops were still building their base camp, occasionally beating off inquisitive VC patrols, when the crisis I had anticipated began to materialize. Three North Vietnamese regiments—some 6,000 men—concentrated amid trackless jungle of elephant grass, scrub brush, and stunted trees near a CIDG-Special Forces camp at Plei Me, southwest of Pleiku. In late October one of the regiments surrounded the Plei Me camp, the first step—as revealed later by captured documents—in the enemy's plan for eliminating three CIDG-Special Forces camps in the area, capturing Pleiku, establishing control of the High Plateau, and pushing on to the sea to split the country in two.

The South Vietnamese defenders, with the help of massive air strikes, broke the siege of Plei Me, whereupon an ARVN armored task force pushed along a dirt road leading to the camp to re-establish ground contact. Yet it was obvious that the enemy had been only temporarily thwarted in his design on the camp. Going to the Highlands, I directed the commander of the 1st Cavalry Division, Major General Harry W. O. Kinnard, to find the enemy and seize the initiative from him.

For about a fortnight in late October and early November, the 1st Cavalry Division's 1st Brigade combed the jungle in the vicinity of Plei Me, making occasional contact with the enemy and determining that the North Vietnamese commander was assembling all three of his regiments in the Ia (which means "river") Drang Valley near the base of a rugged mountain mass straddling the Vietnamese-Cambodian border, the Chu Pong massif. From there he intended to try another attack on Plei Me.

At that point General Kinnard substituted a fresh brigade—the 3d— under Colonel Harlow Clark. Clark had commanded one of my companies in Korea and had been wounded in action there. Only days after his first action in Vietnam, that outstanding officer was destined to die in a helicopter crash.

The brunt of the fighting fell on the 1st Battalion, 7th Cavalry Regiment, commanded by Lieutenant Colonel Harold G. Moore, Jr., who as a second lieutenant had served with me in the 82d Airborne Division at Fort Bragg. Moore's battalion flew by helicopter into a landing zone covered with elephant grass interspersed with ant hills as high as a man's head, almost on top of two of the North Vietnamese regiments. The North Vietnamese quickly abandoned any attack on Plei Me and fell on Moore's battalion.

In fighting as fierce as any ever experienced by American troops, Moore's men with help from the rest of the 3d Brigade beat back first one North Vietnamese assault, then another, over a period of six days, November 14 through 19. B-52 strikes almost every day on and around Chu Pong Mountain marked the first use of the big bombers in direct tactical support of ground troops. As the fighting ebbed and all three enemy regiments retreated across the Cambodian border, they left behind over 1,300 dead. An enemy document captured later admitted heavy losses but rationalized them on the basis that the lessons learned were worth the cost of a hundred thousand men.

One who no doubt remembered the fight vividly was Specialist 4 Jack P. Smith. Cut off from his unit during a fierce engagement, Smith played dead for long hours at the base of a tree until he could at last make his way back to the American perimeter. He is the son of the ABC television news commentator, Howard K. Smith.

In a month of operations around Pleiku and in the Ia Drang Valley, the 1st Cavalry Division lost 300 men killed. The death of even one man is lamentable, and those were serious losses, yet I could take comfort in the fact that in the Highlands as on the Bantangan Peninsula, the American fighting man and his commanders had performed without the setbacks that have sometimes marked first performances in other wars. We had no Kasserine Pass as in World War II, no costly retreat by hastily committed, understrength occupation troops from Japan into a Pusan perimeter as in Korea. Nor could I ignore the dissimilarity between the outcome of the cavalry division's engagement and that of Groupement Mobile 100, which, like our cavalry, had just debarked at Qui Nhon and moved into the Highlands when the fighting began that ended in the unit's destruction.

In and out of Pleiku during the fighting, I made a point of being present when Colonel Moore and his battalion held a critique of the action. At the conclusion Moore held up an M-16 rifle, a newly developed, relatively light, fully automatic weapon. "Brave soldiers and the M-16," said Moore, "brought this victory."

Moore and many of his soldiers told me that the M-16 was the best individual infantry weapon ever made, clearly the American answer to the enemy's AK-47. Most American units at the time were equipped with the older M-14 rifle, which was semiautomatic and too heavy for the jungle. Convinced that Moore and his men knew what they were talking about, I asked Secretary McNamara as a matter of urgency to equip all American forces with the M-16 and then also to equip the ARVN with it.

Officials in the Department of Defense unfortunately disregarded the urgency of my request and failed to gear American industry to meet the need. Not until 1967 were there enough M-16s for all American troops, and only then was I able by degrees to begin equipping the ARVN. The ARVN thus long fought at a serious disadvantage against the enemy's automatic AK-47, armed as they were with World War II's semiautomatic M-1, whose kick when firing appeared to rock the small Vietnamese soldiers back on their heels. Armed with a light carbine, little more than a pea shooter when compared with the AK-47, the South Vietnamese militia were at an even worse disadvantage.

Just as the American press and some members of Congress during early stages of World War II criticized the M-1 Garand, which became the workhorse of American infantry during World War II and Korea, so critical attacks developed against the M-16. It was admittedly a weapon that had to be cleaned meticulously, and ordnance experts were able later to make some adjustments that improved performance; but from the first the M-16 in the hands of troops experienced in its use and care was a superb weapon. Yet as late as mid-June 1967 I still had to entertain a congressional committee sent to investigate it. So conditioned were the South Vietnamese by the controversy over the weapon in the American press that when I was able to begin giving the M-16 to the ARVN, some South Vietnamese military men were upset. Until convinced otherwise, they thought I was short-changing them with an inferior weapon.

When I was in Washington in May 1968, I found an opportunity to tell President Johnson personally of my concern about the lack of M-16s for the South Vietnamese forces. The President was shocked. He had known nothing of the Defense Department's failure to contract for the weapons in bulk. He promised to knock heads together. Rest assured, he told me, you will get your M-16s.

The slow production of the M-16 was a grave sin of omission. Like the failure to provide in advance for a logistical base, it slowed operations in South Vietnam and may well have added an extra year to the program to upgrade the ARVN to the point where the South Vietnamese alone might be expected to carry the fight.

In early February 1966 I flew to Honolulu to present my recommendations for further troop deployments to Admiral Sharp. From the 71 battalions agreed upon with Secretary McNamara the preceding summer, I considered it necessary to increase my request to 102, 23 to be Allied battalions and 79 of them American for a total American strength during 1966 of 429,000. As important as were the combat troops, I gave equal importance to building the support structure, which I had had to delay temporarily in the rush to meet the crisis with combat units. Unless we could obtain substantial increases in signal units, engineer battalions, aircraft and aircraft maintenance units, and port battalions, we would be unable to utilize the combat troops fully in sustained operations.

With news the next day that President Johnson was flying to Honolulu to meet with Chief of State Thieu and Premier Ky, the military conference changed to a summit meeting between heads of state. When the President arrived late on February 5, it was the first time I had seen him since I had met him at West Point when he was Vice President.

Having established residence in Honolulu, Kitsy was with me as I greeted the President. To my surprise the President said: "I have a present for you." Turning, he pointed to a charming seventeen-year-old, my daughter Stevie, whom Kitsy had already spotted and was embracing. The President had telephoned her boarding school and invited her to join him for the trip. It was indeed a present, for it was Kitsy's birthday. To the delight of television cameramen, Stevie rewarded the President with a hug and a kiss. The President told me later he was "in love with" my daughter.

In private talks with me, President Johnson seemed intense, perturbed, uncertain how to proceed with the Vietnam problem, torn by the apparent magnitude of it. Before I was to appear in a televised press conference, he seemed concerned about what I might say, although he telephoned me afterwards to tell me he had seen it and was pleased. At one point, he told me: "General, I have a lot riding on you." Subsequently, alluding to President Truman's problems when General MacArthur publicly disagreed with national policy during the Korean War, he cautioned, "I hope you don't pull a MacArthur on me." Since I had no intention of crossing him in any way, I chose to make no response.

On the second evening of the President's stay, he summoned me to his suite for discussions preceding an official dinner. Also present were Secretary McNamara, Secretary of State Rusk, Ambassador Lodge, Chairman Thieu, Premier Ky, and Minister of Defense Nguyen Huu Co. The session went on for three hours, delaying the dinner. Having reviewed my concept for fighting the war, the President persistently tried to get me to predict how long the war would last. I insisted that I could make no estimate more precise than "several years."

To the President, to the conference, and to the press I emphasized, as I had been doing in press interviews in Saigon, that it would be a long war. "The nature of the enemy is such," I said in my Honolulu press conference, "that we cannot expect him to be defeated by a single battle or series of battles. He will have to be ferreted out over a period of time, which will involve many campaigns, many operations." In my remarks to the conference, I concluded with a warning: "There comes a time in every battle—in every war—when both sides become discouraged by the seemingly endless requirement for more effort, more resources, and more faith. At this point the side which presses on with renewed vigor is the one to win."

President Johnson's apparent purpose in the Honolulu conference was, in addition to reviewing troop requirements, to meet the new South Vietnamese leadership, Thieu and Ky, judge their capabilities for himself, and emphasize the importance he attached to civilian programs aimed at bettering the lot of the South Vietnamese people and enlisting their support for the government. Among his entourage, for example, were the Secretaries of Agriculture and Health, Education, and Welfare, Orville L. Freeman and John W. Gardner, respectively.

I was impressed with the dignity and sincerity with which Thieu and Ky and their ministers conducted themselves during the meetings. While dedicating themselves to such broad principles as eradicating social injustice and building a better life for the people, in addition to defeating the insurgency and North Vietnamese aggression, they pledged specifically to formulate a democratic constitution, take it to the people for ratification by secret ballot, and on the basis of free elections create an elected government. Remarkably, in the years ahead, Thieu and Ky dutifully carried out those vows.

In the final meeting I was amused by the perplexity of the South Vietnamese when President Johnson intoned that the time had come "to nail the coonskins to the wall." There are no coons in Vietnam, and the Vietnamese were unfamiliar with the frontier tradition behind the remark.

In my official discussions with Secretary McNamara and General Wheeler, I learned that they endorsed my 102-battalion proposal, but they warned that without a call-up of the Reserves, which they considered unlikely, they would be unable to provide all the support units I needed. I would have to meet the requirements by help from the Air Force and the Navy, by contracting with U.S. civilian firms, and simply by making do.

Following the conference, Secretaries McNamara and Rusk established goals for 1966 as drafted by John McNaughton and Bill Bundy. Those goals, provided me in a formal memorandum, in effect spelled out the way the war was to be pursued, not only in 1966 but into the future. They set percentage goals for opening roads and railroads, for securing the population, and for pacifying four "high priority" regions. We were to insure continued defense of political and population centers and food-producing areas already under government control and of all military bases. Our military units were to destroy enemy forces at a rate at least as high as the enemy's capability to put more men in the field. They also set a percentage goal for the number of base areas or sanctuaries that the enemy was to be denied.

Nothing about those goals conflicted with the broad outline of how the war was to be fought as I had worked it out over months of consultation with South Vietnamese officials, Admiral Sharp, and the Joint Chiefs of Staff. Indeed, in setting the goals for 1966, senior civilian authorities acting for the President formally directed that I proceed as I had planned.

Despite that agreement at the highest levels, over the months to come lesser civilian officials in the offices of the Assistant Secretaries of Defense for Systems Analysis and International Security Affairs constantly sought to alter strategy and tactics with naïve, gratuitous advice. So, too, the Department of State from time to time tried to impose views differing from the agreed strategy. I found the latter particularly incredible: a civilian agency charged with foreign policy telling its ambassador in Saigon to prepare specific military plans! Although the cables went out over the name of Secretary Rusk, I suspect some of the self-appointed field marshals in the Vietnam Task Force were responsible.

In a cable in September 1965, for example, the department noted that since arrival of American troops, the enemy had launched few large-unit attacks and thus might be returning to protracted small-unit warfare. If that did occur, what were Ambassador Lodge's views on how to use American forces? If the VC did lie low, did we need more American troops? If we put in more troops, how to use them? "We would like for you," the message stated, "to develop specific plan for our joint consideration involving concentration of [South Vietnamese] forces on pacification and reliance on U.S. forces to handle large VC actions."

By nobody's rules were matters such as that valid considerations for the Department of State. Even if they were, what did they think we were doing in Saigon? Did the military do no planning, never look ahead? Would I, a military man, presume to tell a team of surgeons how to operate? What special audacity prompted civilian bureaucrats to deem they knew better how to run a military campaign than did military professionals? Is no special knowledge or experience needed? Had the would-be strategists taken the trouble to examine my cable traffic with the Joint Chiefs or had they consulted General Wheeler, they would have had their answers many times over.

To Ambassador Lodge's credit, he acknowledged that he was no military expert, although he had had military experience in Europe during World War II that afforded him considerable understanding, and he always consulted with me before replying to that kind of cable. Neither of us took those gratuitous queries very seriously, yet they were annoying in that they required long hours of staff work to frame replies that could have better been spent on other matters.

Chapter IX
Political Crisis

Probably no military commander in history ever had all the forces he wanted, which is one reason economy of force has long been one of the vital principles of war. A commander must accept the risk of diminished strength in one area in order to muster greater strength in another, either to attack the enemy or to defend a sector deemed more important or under greater threat. Recall the canon: to try to be strong everywhere is to be weak everywhere. Since the strength at my disposal was always limited, economy of force was an overriding consideration throughout the war in Vietnam but at no time more essential than in the opening months of the American build-up.

Protecting embryonic logistical installations and ports at Vung Tau, Cam Ranh Bay, Nha Trang, Qui Nhon, Chu Lai, and Danang and existing airfields at Bien Hoa and Phu Bai were vital assignments. For security of Saigon, its port, and Tan Son Nhut airport, I continued to rely on the South Vietnamese, both because I deemed them capable of doing it and because I believed it would contribute to their pride.

Even those troops assigned security missions participated in offensive operations. Only minimum numbers remained in static defense, while the bulk of the units pushed into the countryside, patrolling to find the enemy, attacking him, and preventing him from massing to hit the installations. Without a vast expenditure of manpower, providing leakproof defensive lines around installations or cities in the manner of Confederate trenches before Richmond was impossible.

Those assignments made, my next consideration was the population. While depending on the Vietnamese to protect Saigon proper, I needed American forces in the environs to help protect the surrounding population and prevent big enemy units from massing to move against the capital. The other priority areas were the densely populated coastal regions of the northern and central provinces.

One of the American units arriving in the fall of 1965, the 1st Infantry Division, the famed "Big Red One," I deployed north of Saigon to supplement the 173d Airborne Brigade; then, in early 1966, I positioned two brigades of the 25th Infantry ("Tropic Lightning") Division northwest of the city where a region of Cambodia known as the "Parrot's Beak" afforded the enemy a safe haven only thirty miles from the capital. A newly formed ARVN division went into position northeast of the city.

The South Vietnamese designated that unit the 10th Infantry Division. That was unfortunate, for the Vietnamese had learned from American soldiers, who had picked up the practice in Japan, to rate everything in descending order of value or importance by the numbers 1 to 10. Number 1 was top-notch; number 10 was beyond the pale. The 10th Division soon lived up to its mythical rating. The division commander, for example, made most of his decisions only after consulting his astrologist. Only with the passage of time and a switch to a new numerical designation, the 18th Division, did a new spirit evolve.

The first battles in the Central Highlands concluded, I moved the remaining brigade of the U. S. 25th Division to Pleiku to provide a permanent American presence in the Highlands. Two battalions landed from sea transports at Cam Ranh Bay and then moved by air to Pleiku, while the third flew from Hawaii direct to Pleiku. The preparations started as early as 1964 to build an airfield at Pleiku capable of handling large transport planes, even though the highway from the coast was often closed and cement and other heavy materials had to be flown in, thus proved judicious.

Because the North Vietnamese seemed determined to continue to fight for the Highlands, when the 4th Infantry ("Ivy") Division arrived in late summer 1966, I sent the bulk of the division there to establish a base camp on the red earth of the High Plateau. To avoid unnecessary shifting of troops, I transferred the brigade of the 25th Division already operating in the Highlands to the 4th Division, while sending a brigade of the 4th to the 25th. Because soldiers identify closely with their division, I was concerned lest the transfer adversely affect morale, but the effect proved to be minimal.

Unwilling to tie the 1st Cavalry Division permanently to the Highlands, since the division's unique air mobility made it an ideal reserve force, I temporarily shifted the cavalry to important Binh Dinh province where the division would contribute to thwarting the enemy's goal of cutting the country in two. Meanwhile, in late 1965, the South Korean Capital ("Tiger") Division relieved a battalion of U. S. Marines and the 1st Brigade, 101st Airborne Division, at Qui Nhon and began operations in the vicinity, complementing the work of the cavalry. The South Korean 2d Marine ("Dragon") Brigade performed a similar assignment for Cam Ranh Bay. Arriving in early fall of 1966, the South Korean 9th Infantry ("White Horse") Division operated in coastal sectors of provinces south of Binh Dinh.

The 1st and 3d U. S. Marine Divisions operated in the three southern provinces of the I Corps Zone, in the process securing Chu Lai and

Danang, while except for a U. S. Marine battalion at Phu Bai, I relied on the Vietnamese to defend the two northernmost provinces of Quang Tri and Thua Thien. In those provinces was the best of the ARVN units, the 1st Infantry Division. There, too, the semiclandestine political party, the Can Lao, exercised a strict regimen over the people that the VC found difficult to break. Yet because of the proximity of the DMZ and the North Vietnamese beyond it, I had to be prepared for the possibility that American troops would have to move north should the North Vietnamese push in strength across the DMZ.

Base camps established, all units were constantly on the offensive, seeking any enemy that might be encountered: guerrilla, local force, or main force. That is not to say that the men were constantly under fire, as they might have been in a prolonged conventional campaign. As often as not, the enemy was not to be found, so that the gnawing day-by-day, minute-by-minute dread of enemy fire or shelling was less a concern than in a conventional fight. Yet once the battle was joined, it could be as intense and as devastating as any ever fought.

As in conventional warfare, all operations had specific objectives, although they were usually enemy forces identified by intelligence sources rather than terrain features. As in January 1966, when an ARVN regiment, a Korean brigade, and the 1st Brigade, 101st Airborne Division, the only contingent of the famed "Screaming Eagles" destined to serve in Vietnam until later in the war, set out to find a North Vietnamese regiment believed to be in a river valley near Tuy Hoa, midway between Qui Nhon and Nha Trang, while at the same time keeping the enemy away from the region's rice harvest. Or in late March when contingents of the 25th Infantry Division, having completed a search for enemy units in southern reaches of the Highlands near Ban Me Thuot, cleared the road between Ban Me Thuot and Pleiku, Route 14, the first time anybody but the enemy had used that road in months. Or in the fall of 1965 when the 9th Marine Regiment south of Danang engaged in high-density patrolling, night ambushes, and protective cordons to keep the VC from poaching the rice harvest.

Operations might last weeks or even months, depending on the nature of the objective and the results or whether a unit had to be shifted to a more critical task. To facilitate identification in planning and reporting, all operations had a code name. When the 1st Cavalry Division early in 1966 began an operation called MASHER, President Johnson passed word that he objected to the name, probably because the connotation of violence provided a focus for carping war critics. The division commander, General Kinnard, hit on a new name that nobody could fault: WHITE WING. We later used names of American cities, battles, or historic figures.

During those early months, I was concerned with the tactical methods that General Walt and the marines employed. They had established beachheads at Chu Lai and Danang and were reluctant to go outside them, not through any lack of courage but through a different conception of how to fight an anti-insurgency war. They were assiduously combing the countryside within the beachheads, trying to establish firm control in hamlets and villages, and planning to expand the beachhead gradually up and down the coast.

The marines maintained that their approach was essential because of the proximity of densely populated hamlets and villages to their installations, particularly the air base at Danang, settlements that had been dominated by the Communists almost without challenge for at least fifteen years. Yet the practice left the enemy free to come and go as he pleased throughout the bulk of the region and, when and where he chose, to attack the periphery of the beachheads. With the enemy free to recruit in regions the marines had yet to enter and to operate in nearby hills with impunity, every subsequent move of the marines to extend the peripheries of the beachheads would become progressively more difficult and would make the beachheads more vulnerable. While the marines operated in that manner, the main force VC battalions in the I Corps Zone during 1965 had more than doubled, reaching fifteen by the end of the year.

I well understood the doctrinal approach behind the marines' methods. The very *raison d'être* of the Marine Corps is to provide an amphibious force capable of establishing shallow beachheads on hostile shores. By the very nature of their mission, marines are neither trained nor equipped for long, sustained operations, and it can be said that they were employed both in Korea and Vietnam on operations contrary to their mission simply because they existed and they were needed. Since by U. S. Marine Corps doctrine, for example, only the first elements of the assaulting force are to be delivered by helicopter, subsequent waves coming across the beach, the marines in comparison to U. S. Army units had few helicopters. That restricted mobility. Designed for short-haul beachhead supply, their helicopters were also more ponderous and ungainly than the Army's smaller, more versatile "Huey."

Understandably proud of an admittedly excellent close-support tactical air system, the marines long resisted the helicopter gunship. Their self-confidence also apparently made them reluctant to ask help, so that often I had almost to force them to accept U. S. Army support. Self-confidence and independence, however admirable, constitute a two-way street in command relationships. Whereas it is incumbent on the over-all commander to assure that his subordinates have what he discerns they need, it is also incumbent on the subordinate to ask for what he needs.

Rigidity in doctrine is no virtue, and problems exist to be overcome. I believed the marines should have been trying to find the enemy's main forces and bring them to battle, thereby putting them on the run and reducing the threat they posed to the population. As a first step I wanted General Walt to create a two- or three-battalion force capable of moving quickly by helicopter into enemy-dominated regions and more and more to join with the ARVN in operations large enough in numbers to punish the enemy's big units and disrupt their bases and supply caches.

Although there was no question that since I was commander of all American military forces in Vietnam, the marines were under my over-all command, I had no wish to deal so abruptly with General Walt that I might precipitate an interservice imbroglio. The III Marine Amphibious Force was a part of the Fleet Marine Force, Pacific, and thus remained for administration under the commander of the Fleet Marine Force, General Krulak. Furthermore, Wally Greene, the Marine Corps commandant in Washington, kept a watchful eye on every sparrow, and as a senior regional commander, General Walt had a mission-type order which by custom afforded him considerable leeway in execution. Rather than start a controversy, I chose to issue orders for specific projects that as time passed would gradually get the marines out of their beachheads.

In what may be called a pacification approach to anti-insurgency warfare, the marines achieved some noteworthy results, particularly with one of the more ingenious innovations developed in South Vietnam, the Combined Action Platoon. Composed of marine volunteers and Vietnamese militia, the platoon would move into a village and stay, getting to know the people, winning their trust, and working closely on civic action projects.* The first was formed in the summer of 1965 under Vietnamese-speaking Lieutenant Paul R. Ek. Although I disseminated information on the platoons and their success to other commands, which were free to adopt the idea as local conditions might dictate, I simply had not enough numbers to put a squad of Americans in every village and hamlet; that would have been fragmenting resources and exposing them to defeat in detail.

I admired the elan of the marines and had come to know it at first hand. I was one of few U. S. Army officers, if not the only one, ever to hold a senior position in a Marine command. It happened in Japan following the cease-fire in Korea in 1953 when Kitsy, after boarding a Japanese ship en route home, developed excruciating stomach pains and had to be transferred to a hospital ashore for an emergency operation and lengthy recuperation. So that I could be near her, I asked assignment to the closest American unit, which turned out to be the 3d Marine Division. As a young brigadier general I served, in effect, as an assistant commander of the division.

Now, in 1966, I unwittingly got into the bad graces of some marines and their ardent devotees in press and Congress when in writing Lew Walt's next-to-last efficiency report I noted, as required, what I considered a logical next assignment for him. General Walt had served me loyally and had a genuine appeal to the man in the ranks. Knowing Lew Walt's ability, I could give him only the highest recommendation. When the question of General Greene's successor as Marine Corps commandant developed a spirited contest among three candidates—Walt, Krulak, and Lieutenant General

* For an excellent account of one of those platoons, see F. J. West, Jr., *The Village* (New York: Harper & Row, 1972).

Leonard F. Chapman, Jr., all of whom I knew and respected—a newspaper article related that I had tried to intervene on Walt's behalf. Looking into the matter, I found it went back to that efficiency report in 1966 wherein I had indicated, without knowledge of whoever else might be considered, that General Walt was fully qualified to be Commandant of the Marine Corps. A telephone call to General Greene cleared it up.

For any commander, trying to anticipate the enemy's moves is an essential preoccupation. The need had been stamped indelibly on my mind during my cadet days by a tactical officer, a major with quiet, sympathetic manner, patient in counseling his young charges, who later became one of the nation's few five-star generals: Omar Bradley.

As a first classman-to-be on summer maneuvers, I commanded a battalion defending a hill. Against my ill-conceived defenses, the opposing troops succeeded. As the cadet battalion continued the maneuver, the umpire, Major Bradley, waited for me beside the road on horseback. As acting battalion commander, I too was riding. As I came abreast, he summoned me to join him.

"Mr. Westmoreland," he said, "look back at that hill. Look at it now from the standpoint of the enemy."

Turning, I became aware for the first time of a concealed route of approach that it was logical for an attacker to use. Because I had failed to cover it with my defense, he as umpire had ruled for the attacking force.

"It is fundamental," Major Bradley said calmly but firmly, "to put yourself always in the position of the enemy."

In a talk with President Johnson in his hotel suite during the Honolulu conference of 1966, he asked me if I were the enemy, what would be my next step. Because I had thought of that often, I was able to respond without hesitation: capture Hué.

To come to that conclusion required little perspicacity. As the ancient imperial capital, Hué was the symbol of a unified Vietnam. Taking it would have a profound psychological impact on the Vietnamese in both the North and the South, and in the process the North Vietnamese might seize the two northern provinces as bargaining points in any negotiations. Cut off from the rest of South Vietnam by high mountains traversed only by the narrow Hai Van Pass next to the sea and blessed with no ports or harbors, those two provinces posed serious defensive problems. The loss in March 1966 of the CIDG-Special Forces camp in the A Shau Valley, opening the valley to the enemy, made a North Vietnamese move on Hué all the more likely.

In addition, I had noted an article in the official North Vietnamese Army newspaper, *Nhan Dan,* telling of a North Vietnamese division that was rehearsing infiltrating by stealth over a distance of fifty kilometers or more, covertly assembling, then attacking by surprise. I immediately thought of Hué as a likely objective for such an operation.

Beginning in February 1966 intelligence reports began to indicate sharply increased North Vietnamese infiltration across the DMZ into the two northern provinces. As I watched developments closely, it became apparent that two North Vietnamese divisions were involved. They posed a clear threat to Quang Tri and Thua Thien provinces and to Hué.

That the North Vietnamese move into the two northern provinces involved an additional objective of drawing American troops away from the pacification effort farther south was a probability. Yet however that might hurt and however much more defensible a line through the Hai Van Pass than along the DMZ, I still would be unable to accept loss of those provinces. The psychological effect on the South Vietnamese, if not on the American people, would be catastrophic.

Nor did I see any reason to relieve the U. S. Marines of their responsibility for those provinces by shifting U. S. Army troops to the north. Although the ARVN had been defending in the far north, all of the I Corps Zone was General Walt's responsibility, and many of the factors that had prompted putting marines in the north in the first place were as valid for the two northern provinces as for the rest of the zone: in particular, that the sector was narrow enough to enable naval guns to cover almost all the populated area, that the marines' heavy organization promised defensive staying power, and that their ability to supply themselves over beaches removed some of the concern about lack of ports.

In preparation for an eventual shift northward, I directed planning to begin for upgrading the airfield at Phu Bai, reconstructing an airfield farther north at Dong Ha capable of handling big transports, and building a port for LSTs at Hué. At the same time I directed a search for a site for a new airfield to accommodate tactical bombers near Hué.

North Vietnamese infiltration fortunately was characterized more by deliberateness than by speed. Thus time, however indefinite, remained to improve facilities in the north before committing large numbers of American troops.

Well it was, too, for a new political crisis erupted in the northern provinces, centered on the old trouble spots, Hué and Danang. Had it coincided with a sustained North Vietnamese offensive, it could have resulted in loss of the northern provinces and might have done South Vietnam in. Many at the time feared it might do so in any case, for it was the most serious political turmoil to rock the country since the days of President Diem.

Not that all had been placid since the team of Thieu and Ky had taken over in June 1965. Following a decree two months later making a previously exempt class of students liable to military service, students joined by Buddhists began demonstrating in Quang Tri and Danang. Although the government modified the decree, demonstrations for a time persisted. The draft was not the real issue in any case. Students and Buddhists considered they had played the role of heroes in Diem's overthrow, yet only a military government in which they had no representation had been the result.

For all the best efforts of American Special Forces advisers, foment among the Montagnards also continued. In August 1965 FULRO supporters surprised a CIDG-Special Forces camp near Ban Me Thuot and carried off a store of arms, but swift ARVN reaction prompted the rebels to surrender. In December 1965 Montagnards seized a district capital, but again quick ARVN reaction squelched the revolt. Soon after the Honolulu conference of February 1966, Thieu and Ky moved to bring a Montagnard leader into the Cabinet as Special Commissioner for Montagnard Affairs. That appeared to diminish Montagnard unrest.

The serious crisis in the north developed in March 1966, after the military council that Thieu and Ky headed removed the I Corps commander, General Nguyen Chanh Thi. That was less the cause than the spark that students and Buddhists had been seeking to ignite their dissent and elicit support for their goal of ousting the military government in Saigon.

General Thi was in many ways like Ky. They looked somewhat alike: suave, wiry, mustached, flamboyant, swaggering. Both had infinite courage. Thi at one point had been prominently mentioned for Premier but had stepped aside in favor of Ky. Once a captive of the Viet Cong, Thi hated them to the extent that when he spoke of them a kind of malicious leer came over his face. Although his political ambitions may well have been limited, he gained a reputation among fellow generals for co-operating with the militant Buddhists, and every trip he made to Saigon promoted a degree of consternation lest he have some ulterior motive in mind.

Scarcely twenty-four hours passed following Thi's relief before thousands of student demonstrators took to the streets of Danang to demand Thi's reinstatement and denounce the Saigon government. The mayor of Danang made no effort to interfere. A hastily formed "Military-Civilian Struggle Committee" provided a controlling apparatus to increase the turmoil and bring Vietnamese soldiers into the movement. A few days later thousands of Buddhists staged a rally in Danang and joined the students in the streets. The movement spread to Hué where students seized the government radio station and filled the air with denunciations of the government. Anti-American banners in English, apparently designed to provoke incidents with American troops, appeared in the streets of both cities, and altars and statues of Buddha blocked traffic. An anti-American tone to the demonstrations increased, presumably in an effort to prompt Ambassador Lodge to put pressure on the government to grant the demonstrators' demands. For several days a general strike paralyzed Danang. To eliminate the possibility of incidents with Americans, General Walt put both Hué and Danang off limits to all U.S. military.

The specter of civil war hung over the demonstrations. ARVN troops in the northern provinces began to polarize around one side or the other. Men of the crack 1st ARVN Division were predominantly Buddhist, brought up to respect the bonzes, so how were they to react when the bonzes told them to turn against the government? By refusing an order to relinquish the I

Corps command and come to Saigon and by issuing militant statements from a refuge in Hué, General Thi fed the dissident fervor. It was a confrontation between two strong and stubborn men: Thi and Ky. The demonstrations showed no signs of decreasing.

I watched the crisis closely. With Ambassador Lodge's blessing, I conferred frequently with Thieu and other Saigon leaders and kept in touch by telephone and personal conferences with General Walt, his capable U. S. Army deputy senior adviser, Colonel Arch Hamblen, and an astute political adviser from the Embassy, Samuel Thomsen, who had had long experience in the northern provinces and was fluent in Vietnamese. American advisers and all American support, I directed, were to be withdrawn from any ARVN unit that ceased to follow government orders and helped the dissidents.

At my suggestion Ambassador Lodge underscored American concern by telling Premier Ky that 228 Americans in the I Corps region had died fighting for South Vietnam during the three weeks that this "foolishness"— my word—had been going on, and the American people were bound to be upset. I had an intelligence officer brief South Vietnamese government leaders on the growing threat in the I Corps Zone from VC and North Vietnamese, with the suggestion that the information be passed to the mayor of Danang, the militant Buddhist Thich Tri Quang, and others who might use their influence to quell the demonstrations.

Hoping to avoid sending troops and possibly provoking an armed clash, Thieu and Ky tried to meet some of the expressed dissatisfaction with the government. Within two months, they announced, a representative committee was to draft a constitution, and once that was approved by general referendum, elections would be held, possibly before the end of 1966. Yet if anything, that appeared to feed the dissidence. Demonstrations spread to Saigon, Pleiku, and Nha Trang, with demonstrators in Nha Trang burning the USIS Library. Some local ARVN commanders began to furnish the students arms and ammunition. Most disturbing of all, on the third of April 3,000 men of the 1st ARVN Division paraded in uniform through the streets of Hué behind their division band, shouting demands for the government's ouster.

Thieu and Ky promptly informed me they could wait out the crisis no longer. They were sending three battalions of South Vietnamese marines to the air base at Danang, used jointly by American and Vietnamese planes, in the hope that a show of force would bring Danang under control and Hué would follow. Because it was a domestic crisis, I denied use of American planes. The troops were moved by sea and in old C-47 aircraft previously given the South Vietnamese.

Alerting General Walt, I urged a neutral stance, but even that course, as Walt quickly discovered, was fraught with peril. When the South Vietnamese marines arrived, they found a dissident ARVN force of about 2,000 men under Colonel Dam Quang Yeu marching on the air base. Half of

Yeu's column had crossed a bridge several miles south of Danang when a U. S. Marine Corps company contrived to have one of its trucks break down and block the bridge. That gave General Walt time to arrange a conference with Yeu and elicit a promise to avoid attacking the air base if the Vietnamese marines made no move against the city of Danang.

Once out of General Walt's sight, Colonel Yeu nevertheless determined to make a show of force against the air base by setting up four artillery pieces where they could fire on the base. Walt sent Colonel John Chaisson, who later as a general officer served on my staff as director of the Combat Operations Center, to stop them.

Colonel Chaisson deliberately landed his helicopter under the muzzles of Yeu's artillery, two pieces of which were big 155-mm guns. As he talked with Yeu, U. S. Marine Corps fighter-bombers circled overhead, U. S. Marine artillery focused on Yeu's guns, and a U. S. Marine infantry battalion took up firing positions nearby. Rather than see American planes and lives wiped out by artillery the Americans themselves had provided the Vietnamese, Chaisson told Yeu, the Americans would open fire.

As Yeu refused to back down, his artillerymen began to uncase their shells and insert fuses in preparation for firing. Repeating his warning forcefully, Chaisson turned, boarded his helicopter, and took to the sky.

Under a sweltering noon-day sun a seemingly relentless tension dragged on. Nerves were tight when at last American marines watching through field glasses reported that the little artillerymen appeared to be halting their preparations to fire. Then they began to defuse the shells and put them back in their cases. The immediate crisis had passed.

An uneasy calm settled over Danang and Hué. Although General Thi remained at Hué, a new commander of the I Corps, General Nguyen Van Chuan, tried hard to ameliorate differences and convince Premier Ky that he should keep troops out of the cities. The governmental military council promised amnesty to all who had participated in the turmoil and promulgated a decree-law providing for free elections for a constituent assembly within three to five months. The Buddhists for their part agreed to suspend agitation but vowed to start again if the government went back on its promises.

I was hardly complacent. Buddhist chaplains in Pleiku province were openly proselytizing among the troops; Buddhists in the north were trying to organize junior officers within ARVN units; and some government leaders wanted to contrive an incident in the I Corps Zone as an excuse to move in with force and set matters right. Yet I saw no immediate crisis in the offing and took advantage of the hiatus to fly to Honolulu on May 12 for talks with Oley Sharp and some rest, however brief.

I was on the beach with my family when an aide called me to the telephone. It was Secretary Rusk in Washington. Ky, the Secretary told me, had air-lifted a task force of Vietnamese airborne troops to the Danang air base.

The troops had entered Danang and taken over the radio station, the mayor's office, and I Corps headquarters. General Chuan having been relieved as I Corps commander under pressure from the Buddhists, still a third had been named, General Ton That Dinh, but he, Ky believed, had fallen under the influence of the Buddhists. When Dinh refused an order to come to Saigon, Ky replaced him—I learned with some shock—with General Huynh Van Cao, the vacillating man who had served as such a poor introduction to South Vietnamese leadership when he had met my plane upon my arrival in Saigon.

The governing military council, I learned later, had elected Cao to the assignment over Cao's own objections. Had General Westmoreland been there, Cao told Americans, he would not have been required to take the job, for General Westmoreland had no confidence in him.

Once again the Vietnamese leaders had made their move while the American ambassador was out of the country on another periodic visit to the United States and, in this case, while I was also away. Yet had I been consulted, I would have approved the move of airborne troops to Danang. Despite the Buddhists' proclamations that all they were after was a civilian government, they were actually trying to get a government that they could dominate. Had Thieu and Ky given in to that, turmoil by Catholics, the religious sects, labor, whatever, would have been the result. Possibly even civil war. Thieu and Ky, I believed, were fully capable of handling the situation, and the American side was ably represented by Ambassador Lodge's deputy, William J. Porter, my own deputy, Johnny Heintges, and a chief of staff who probably had as much experience in Vietnam over the years as any American and in whom I had full confidence, Major General William B. Rosson.

I preferred, I told Secretary Rusk, to avoid rushing back precipitately lest I appear to display undue American concern over the action. Ambassador Lodge in Washington followed the same course, but after a day or so Secretary McNamara grew nervous and ordered me back. I flew into Saigon on May 20.

The ARVN command situation in the I Corps, I learned upon arrival, had turned into a comic opera. Both Thi and the newly relieved corps commander, General Dinh, were ensconced in Hué, with Dinh refusing to accept the fact of his relief and Thi assuming *de facto* command of the 1st ARVN Division. Dinh told an American adviser wryly that the worst the government could do to him was arrest his wife and children in Saigon, and that if that happened, he could get himself another wife.

While professing to any and all his utter reluctance to assume command, the new corps commander, General Cao, then in Danang, nevertheless accepted the challenge of going to Hué to try to bring the 1st ARVN Division into line. With him in a U. S. Army helicopter went the deputy senior adviser, Arch Hamblen. After talking with 1st Division officers, Cao and Hamblen were about to depart when a crowd of about a hundred students and a few soldiers swarmed toward the helicopter. Just as the craft began to take off, an ARVN lieutenant fired two shots from a .45-caliber pistol, striking the tail rotor drive mechanism. At Hamblen's signal, an American door gunner fired a short burst from his machine gun, killing the ARVN lieutenant. Despite the damage to the helicopter, the pilot managed to take off but had to land outside town and transfer his passengers to an escorting helicopter.

Poor reluctant Cao. Hardly had he returned to Danang when he came into conflict with Nguyen Ngoc Loan, chief of the National Police, sent by Premier Ky to command riot police helping to restore order in Danang. Loan—an Air Force colonel—insisted that Cao—an Army major general— authorize attacks on Buddhist pagodas, which were the main strongpoints left to the dissidents. Since Cao was himself a Catholic, he feared that if he ordered the attacks he would only exacerbate the situation. He refused.

As Arch Hamblen approached the I Corps command post, he looked through a window to spy Loan on his knees pleading eloquently with Cao while other officers milled about and someone behind Cao brandished a pistol near Cao's head. Hamblen rushed in. His arrival, Cao said later, saved his life. He attached himself to Hamblen and sought refuge in Sam Thomsen's office in General Walt's headquarters, from which he long refused to budge and where he spent most of his time praying.

He trusted no Vietnamese, Cao said, except his wife. He wrote me, begging "to become an American citizen, to join the Marines or the Army, to fight against Communists anywhere in the world."

Trying to follow instructions to maintain a neutral stance, General Walt still found that hard to do. The first incident arose in Danang on May 18 when U.S. marines guarding one end of a bridge over the Tourane River leading to important supply installations reported that dissident South Vietnamese troops at the far end had emplaced demolition charges to blow the bridge. Lew Walt himself went to try to get the South Vietnamese commander to remove them. While he distracted the Vietnamese at a conference in the center of the bridge, a marine engineer officer crept along the underpinnings, cutting demolition wires.

When at last Walt got a "thumbs-up" signal from the engineer officer, he broke off the fruitless discussions and gave the Vietnamese commander five minutes to remove his troops and the detonator. As minutes ticked by, the Vietnamese remained silent. When the time expired, he addressed Walt in English, which he had previously pretended to be unable to speak. "General," he said, "we will die on this bridge together." Raising his right arm, he brought it down smartly. As General Walt watched an ARVN soldier at the far end of the bridge drive the plunger down, he could but pray that his engineer officer had done his job well.

He had. As marines swarmed across the bridge to take possession of the other end, Walt gave the dismayed Vietnamese officer a glance of admiration, then turned and walked slowly off the bridge.

That evening ARVN dissidents gained control of an ammunition depot outside of Danang which contained tons of explosives that could do serious damage to the city and the air base. When loyal Vietnamese troops threatened an attack to take the depot, the dissidents vowed to blow it up. On my instructions, General Walt intervened. Perhaps impressed by Walt's earlier performance at the bridge, the dissidents agreed after several days of negotiations to neutralize the depot in a shared defense with U.S. marines.

With occasional street fighting continuing in Danang, Premier Ky ordered Vietnamese Air Force planes to attack remaining pockets of resistance. Aware that numbers of American civilians were still in Danang, General Walt tried to persuade the local Vietnamese Air Force commander to call off the attacks. He refused, citing direct orders from Saigon.

Learning that propeller-driven Vietnamese planes were taking off from the air base, Walt put four of his jets on alert. When the Vietnamese planes fired rockets at dissident troops near a U. S. Marine compound, three of the rockets hit inside the compound and wounded three marines. Ordering two jets into the air to orbit above the Vietnamese craft, Walt told the local air commander that if he so much as fired one more round, he would order the planes shot from the air. Not easily cowed, the Vietnamese commander sent four planes to orbit above the Marine jets. Just as determined, General Walt sent two more jets to form a fourth tier.

For two hours the aircraft orbited. At long last, Ky in Saigon backed down. The Vietnamese planes returned to the base.†

The attitude of Washington officials during the crisis was to me enigmatic. During first weeks of the foment, Washington decreed a hands-off policy, waiting to see which side appeared likely to triumph before showing the American hand. That was preposterous. While the Thieu-Ky government was admittedly military and had not been elected, it was still the government, certainly more capable of providing the stability essential to pursuing the war than a government founded by religious radicals who would be immediately challenged by other minorities. Presumably reflecting official thinking in Washington, General Wheeler asked my opinion about withholding all U.S. military and economic aid and withdrawing American troops into base camps, thereby, it was hoped, pressuring both sides to resolve their differences. That quite clearly was inadvisable unless the United States intended to withdraw completely from Vietnam, which was never discussed with me or, to my knowledge, ever considered by Washington.

As for Washington's view, officials there saw the events as much more tumultuous, much more serious than they actually were, partly because they got some of their information from flamboyant press and television reports. Tri Quang and other dissident leaders consciously used the foreign press to advance their cause. The press transmitted plaintive and distorted appeals

† For further details, see Lewis W. Walt, *Strange War, Strange Strategy* (New York: Funk & Wagnalls, 1970).

for help to President Johnson, the United States, the International Red Cross, whatever forum. Press and television were conveniently on hand for several immolations by monks in Hué, and when two members of the press arrived late for a nun's immolation, demonstrators co-operatively relit the fire.

Most newsmen on the scene took Tri Quang's word that the Vietnamese in the pagodas were unarmed. When Hamblen and Thomsen declined an invitation to go to Tri Quang's headquarters pagoda to parlay, several American newsmen decided to go themselves. As they approached the pagoda, a shot came from within, wounding one of the newsmen slightly. All beat a quick retreat.

In messages to Washington I urged calm and patience. Although I recognized that the internecine strife was embarrassing to Washington, I was concerned lest precipitate action exacerbate the situation. Thieu and Ky were facing a minority revolt not unlike earlier Montagnard rebellions, except larger and involving regular ARVN troops, and to fail to quell it would be to invite distrust and even further disorders throughout the country. I believed that in time other American officials and I could influence such leaders as Generals Thi and Dinh to desist, thereby isolating true militants such as Tri Quang. Meeting Thi at Chu Lai and holding out the promise of a trip to the United States for a medical check-up, I persuaded him to talk with Ky. Lew Walt accomplished the same with Dinh.

It was an advantage having a fearful General Cao hiding out in the American headquarters while still nominally in command of the I Corps, for it enabled Arch Hamblen virtually to command the I Corps. When Cao finally authorized attacks on the pagodas, they turned out to be, as expected, armed camps, but resistance quickly collapsed. Hamblen and Thomsen then went from one dissident ARVN unit to another with written appeals that Cao willingly signed urging the units to desist. One by one they gave in. By May 23 Danang was calm.

All these moves isolated Tri Quang, who had fled to Hué, and prompted him to step up the unrest there, including the sacking and burning the USIS Library and the U. S. Consulate; but those were throes of a dying cause. Almost all support by moderate Buddhists for the militants dissipated. General Cao at last returned to Saigon and the wife he trusted, while yet another new commander for the I Corps, General Hoang Xuan Lam, who earlier had commanded the 23d ARVN Division, ordered all troops away from the cities and back into the fight against the enemy, while the military council in Saigon eased tension by electing ten civilians to its membership. After an ARVN airborne force moved into Hué on June 15 and established control with considerable restraint, that city too was quiet.

The crisis in the north had temporarily set back the war against the Viet Cong. Although no truce had developed and ARVN troops in all cases had defended their installations, offensive operations against the VC were few. Possibly a half of the 1st ARVN Division had sympathized with the dissidents but only a handful from the 2d ARVN Division in southern provinces of the I Corps Zone. The crisis had blocked construction of an airfield I had planned near Hué. Because building the new airfield would involve moving about 2,000 graves, Ambassador Lodge asked me to abandon the project lest the dissidents seize on that to stir emotions further.

That an American public sending its sons to die in Vietnam saw these events in Danang and Hué as distressing is understandable, yet some form of political turmoil in a developing nation is apparently inevitable. Democracy and national cohesion are not to be achieved without growing pains, as the history of the United States itself painfully illustrates. Thieu and Ky obviously had to apply force if they were not to knuckle under, undermine their own government, and contribute to internecine warfare that, if the enemy was ready to capitalize on it, could have led to loss of the two northern provinces. The government and its troops, particularly the airborne troops at both Danang and Hué, acted with considerable restraint. So did American marines, who faced many a trying, provocative moment.

As the crisis ended, Ambassador Lodge aptly likened Vietnam to a man critically ill, yet so irascible that he throws pitchers of water at his doctor. That at least shows, Lodge continued, that he is getting better.

How much better no one could have discerned at that troubled time, yet in reality the end of the crisis marked the start of the brightest development yet on the Vietnamese political scene. The crisis in the north was destined to be the last of the violent political upheavals.

Chapter X
Semblance of Stability

The turbulence in the north had little effect on military operations elsewhere in the country where almost coincident with start of the political troubles, American troops began their first forays into the enemy's previously sacrosanct base areas. The fire-brigade phase had ended. We were moving early in 1966, as I had planned, into Phase Two, taking the offensive to the enemy.

For all my preference for meeting the enemy's big units outside the populated regions, most of the offensive operations well into 1966 were in or near populated areas simply because the VC regiments before American arrival had established themselves there, while most of the North Vietnamese units were still jockeying for position along the Laotian and Cambodian borders. Thus the 1st Cavalry Division's Operation WHITE WING (née MASHER) and two follow-up sweeps in Binh Dinh province involved a main-force VC regiment on the coastal plain and a North Vietnamese regiment that had moved into the sanctuary known as the Do Xa in rugged mountains overlooking the plain. Also in a populated region was the search by the 1st Brigade, 101st Airborne Division, for a VC regiment near Tuy Hoa. In conjunction with Koreans and South Vietnamese, the cavalry division staged one operation that ended in a classic encirclement maneuver in which more than 2,000 enemy troops were killed. By late fall 1966 the enemy's hold on the agriculturally rich coastal region had been broken and a splintered North Vietnamese regiment contained in the Do Xa, although as always continued sweeps would be required if an enemy that had long controlled the region was not to regain his posture.

Other operations radiating out from Saigon pushed back the VC threat to the capital and ended with the first large-scale penetration of a major base area. In close co-ordination, troops of the 1st Infantry Division, 173d Airborne Brigade, and the Australian battalion conducted a series of operations twenty to twenty-five miles northwest of Saigon, first sweeping the Michelin rubber plantation, which the VC had long roamed freely, then seeking command posts and supply bases in the Boi Loi and Ho Bo woods. Although this was home ground of the 5th VC Division, seldom did the enemy stand and fight. Contacts were usually with small groups fighting delaying actions, so that the number of enemy killed was small, yet our destroying installations that had taken months and even years to construct obviously interfered with the enemy's ability to operate in the same region again. The intelligence gathered from captured documents was also remunerative.

Whenever the VC thought they saw an advantage, they would precipitate a fight. A thousand-man VC force, for example, attacked a battalion of the U. S. 1st Infantry Division that was protecting engineers building a road, but the enemy fell back after losing 122 men killed. A VC battalion surrounded an American company and before reinforcements could intervene, killed 48 Americans. Although VC losses were double that, it was still a serious blow for such a small force.

In June two brigades of the 1st Infantry Division, in conjunction with an ARVN division, mounted a series of operations to open Route 13 from Saigon to rubber plantations in Binh Long province along the Cambodian border. The division's mechanized cavalry squadron equipped with light tanks and armored personnel carriers, either reconnoitering or opening the roads, triggered VC response on several occasions and led to sharp engagements that enabled the Big Red One to employ devastating artillery and air strikes. In the course of a six-week fight, all three regiments of the 9th VC Division, the unit that earlier had dealt the ARVN a severe blow at Binh Gia, absorbed heavy losses.

The ability of mechanized cavalry to operate effectively in the Vietnamese countryside convinced me that I was mistaken in a belief that modern armor had only a limited role in the fighting in Vietnam. Roads were poor, many bridges were too weak to support tanks, rice paddies constituted muddy morasses, much of the country was mountainous jungle impenetrable by tanks, and if armored vehicles churned up crops, we alienated the people we were trying to support. Yet much of the land was in fact solid terrain, and roads and bridges could be improved to accommodate tanks. While their use among rice paddies and mountainous jungle would be limited, their firepower and psychological impact elsewhere would be reason enough to employ them. Thus it was with enthusiasm that in September 1966 I welcomed arrival of the first armored unit equipped with the big Patton tank, the 11th Armored Regiment, known as the "Black Horse," commanded at the time by Colonel William Cobb and later by Colonel George S. Patton, whose colorful personality was much like that of his famous father.

Meanwhile, intelligence revealed that the enemy had apparently recovered from the beating in the Ia Drang Valley and was returning in strength to the Central Highlands. While the 3d Brigade, U. S. 25th Infantry Division, under Brigadier General Glenn D. Walker, located semipermanently in the Highlands, beat the bushes for the enemy, indications were that at least a full North Vietnamese division had come back across the border from Cambodia.

I called on the 1st Brigade, 101st Airborne Division, under Brigadier General Willard Pearson to join the search and later the entire 1st Cavalry Division, commanded by Major General Jack Norton. Patrolling relentlessly through the trackless jungle, catapulting from one hastily built hilltop fire-support base to another, those units through the summer killed close to 2,000 of the enemy; when the cavalry division returned for another sweep in October, a thousand more of the enemy would never make it into the populated regions. Confronted with that kind of pressure, the North Vietnamese were unable to mass for major attacks either against outposts or the provincial capitals of Kontum and Pleiku.

One of the more spectacular engagements developed in Kontum province at the end of May when paratroopers of the 1st Brigade of 101st Airborne marched to the aid of a small mountaintop outpost named Tou Morong, manned by local militia. Such a tight cordon had been drawn by a North Vietnamese regiment about the outpost that the militiamen and their women and children were unable to pull out. Going to their aid brought the enemy regiment to battle.

This was the action in which Captain William S. Carpenter, Jr., who as an All-American football player at West Point had been known as the "lonesome end," found his company in such distress that he called for an air strike on his own position. Unknown to Carpenter, some of the planes were carrying napalm bombs. In the strike twelve of Carpenter's men were burned, one seriously, but the stratagem saved the company. It was a heroic act, one deserving of the Distinguished Service Cross that Carpenter subsequently received, but unlike many another intrepid performance of American military men in South Vietnam that went unnoticed by the press, Carpenter's caught the newsmen's fancy. The reporters had it that Carpenter knew he was calling for napalm, and one embroidered on Carpenter's actual words, saying that when calling for the strike, he cried in the manner of a movie hero: "We'll take some of them with us!" A modest soldier, Carpenter was embarrassed by the furore. He later reluctantly answered my call to serve a stint as my aide.

When the separate 196th Light Infantry Brigade arrived in August 1966, I committed it on the fringes of War Zone C, where, it developed, the 9th VC Division was returning after absorbing replacements to cover the losses incurred in the fight with the 1st Infantry Division. With the VC came a North Vietnamese regiment. The enemy intended to attack a CIDG-Special Forces camp and lure relieving forces into ambush and counterattack.

Although the enemy in late October succeeded in overrunning a CIDG company moving to the camp's relief, in the process he revealed his presence. In consultation with me, the II Field Force commander, Lieutenant

General Jonathan Seaman, committed to the battle the 1st Infantry Division, then the 173d Airborne Brigade, and a brigade each of the 4th and 25th Infantry Divisions. The fight that ensued became known as Operation ATTLEBORO, which with 22,000 American and South Vietnamese troops was the largest of the war up to that time.

In operations lasting well into November, American artillery fired 10,000 rounds, and I again used B-52s as a tactical support weapon. The 1st Infantry Division made the deepest penetration yet into War Zone C. Falling back into Cambodia, the enemy left behind at least 1,100 dead and tons of supplies. A hero of the battle was a son of one of my former officer colleagues in the Pentagon, Major Stanley Meloy. In the two fights in War Zone C, the 9th VC Division was obviously crippled, for it was to reappear in combat only in the spring of the following year.

The enemy's obvious use of Cambodia as a sanctuary and refusal of Washington authorities to allow me to do anything about it was frustrating. Ostensibly because of mistaken strafing of Cambodian villages by South Vietnamese planes, Prince Norodom Sihanouk of Cambodia had broken diplomatic relations with the United States in May 1965 and in many a public statement revealed his sympathy for the Communists. Arms from Communist China had long been entering the country, and as early as mid-1965 my intelligence chief, Major General Joseph A. McChristian, had conclusive proof of at least seven major bases in Cambodia used by the VC and the North Vietnamese. They included the Parrot's Beak, thirty miles from Saigon, and the triborder area where the frontiers of South Vietnam, Cambodia, and Laos meet.

McChristian also had proof of major shipments of arms and other supplies to the VC through the Cambodian port of Sihanoukville, and some supplies were probably reaching the VC via international shipping passing through South Vietnam up the Mekong and Bassac rivers to the Cambodian capital of Phnom Penh. Cambodia was selling the North Vietnamese, for transmittal to the VC, 55,000 tons of rice annually, a major portion of the VC requirements, and the VC were buying almost double that amount direct from Cambodian farmers. By mid-1966 evidence was clear that extensions of the Ho Chi Minh Trail complex through Laos into Cambodia were facilitating entry of North Vietnamese troops into South Vietnam. It made little difference whether Prince Sihanouk conspired in these activities or merely looked the other way. The result was the same.

The benefit of these activities to the enemy and the detriment to American and ARVN forces were obvious. By diligent anti-infiltration work by the U.S. and Vietnamese navies along South Vietnam's coast, by bringing more and more of the South Vietnamese countryside under government control while protecting the rice harvest with military operations, and by SOG patrols and bombing of the Ho Chi Minh Trail in Laos, we were so damaging the enemy's supply system that had it not been for Cambodia, by late 1966, in McChristian's words, "the problems of logistical support, primarily rice, and internal distribution likely could have reached critical proportions." By maintaining base camps in Cambodia, the enemy could regroup, retrain, and mass his forces with impunity for strikes inside South Vietnam, thereby circumventing our efforts to forestall major attacks by pre-emptive attacks of our own.

On several occasions I asked authority to take such countermeasures as air and ground reconnaissance within Cambodia, "hot pursuit" when enemy forces broke off an engagement to retire across the border, raids by ground and air forces—including B-52s—against confirmed enemy bases, and air and artillery strikes against enemy weapons firing from Cambodia. As early as April 1966 I had asked specific approval to move a few miles inside Cambodian jungle to cut in behind the Chu Pong Mountain massif and trap North Vietnamese that had crossed into South Vietnam. I also proposed that the CIA buy up arms and rice in Cambodia by outbidding the VC. Yet even though the Joint Chiefs supported most of my proposals, the State Department almost always vetoed them, including the effort to outflank Chu Pong Mountain. For long all we could do to the enemy in Cambodia was drop propaganda leaflets on our side of the border whenever the wind was right to blow them across.

The State Department's policy was to woo Sihanouk, which seemed to us in Saigon to be naïve unless we could demonstrate unmistakably that we were going to succeed in South Vietnam, for Sihanouk clearly was out to play the winner. Part of the campaign to woo Sihanouk included a visit to Cambodia in late 1967 by Mrs. John F. Kennedy, the President's widow, ostensibly as a tourist to view ancient temples at Angkor Wat. That seemed to us in Saigon to be ludicrous.

Even if Sihanouk failed to respond favorably, the State Department maintained, it was better to tolerate the enemy's use of Cambodia than to spark Sihanouk's open collaboration with the enemy. I saw no possibility of that happening so long as we confined our retaliation to the underpopulated border region that the enemy had in effect appropriated, as he had in Laos.

Some Americans, however unwittingly, had already abetted Sihanouk's efforts to deny that the enemy was using Cambodia. In 1966 several American journalists toured Cambodia at Sihanouk's invitation, as did a so-called private group that included such presumably astute military observers as novelist Kay Boyle, Floyd McKissick of the Congress of Racial Equality, and Donald Duncan of *Ramparts* magazine. None saw any evidence of enemy activity. Much to the embarrassment of the Australian ambassador to Saigon, William Border, the Australian ambassador to Phnom Penh, who was officially representing U.S. interests there, also echoed Sihanouk's disclaimers. Sitting on incontrovertible facts in Saigon, I could only conclude that these people were either self-serving or easily deceived.

More disturbing was the attitude of the CIA. Possibly reflecting what Washington wanted to hear, the CIA long downgraded the extent and value of the enemy's use of Cambodia and of the port of Sihanoukville in particular. Contrary to Joe McChristian's convincing evidence on rice tonnages, the CIA at the end of 1966 maintained that the VC still depended for food "primarily on the South Vietnamese countryside." While McChristian could prove that over a thousand metric tons of Chinese Communist supplies, mainly military hardware, entered Sihanoukville during 1966, the CIA claimed that MACV was "overstating the significance of Cambodia to the Communists fighting in South Vietnam."

During a trip to Washington, the I Field Force commander, Lieutenant General Stanley R. ("Swede") Larsen, ran afoul of Washington's official stance on Cambodia. In a press conference General Larsen noted that in the Central Highlands American forces often pushed the enemy toward the border "where he disappeared to the west." Asked if that meant the enemy was using Cambodia, he replied: "One can draw no other conclusion." When a diligent reporter pursued the subject with Secretary McNamara, the Secretary said that evidence was insufficient to support that thesis. Asked to explain the conflict, Swede Larsen smiled. "I stand corrected," he said.

Following ouster of Prince Sihanouk in March 1970 by a cabal of military and civilian leaders, headed by Lieutenant General Lon Nol and disenchanted by Sihanouk's acquiescence in North Vietnamese presence in the country, hard evidence on the extent of Communist use of Cambodia became available. Sihanouk had decided in March 1965 to side with the Communists, and in 1966 he made a deal with the Chinese Communists for delivery through Cambodia of supplies for the Viet Cong, although the man who subsequently headed the successor government, Lon Nol, allegedly arranged without Sihanouk's knowledge for a 10 per cent cut for the Cambodian Army. From 1966 through 1969 the VC received 21,600 metric tons of military supplies such as arms and ammunition, including almost 600 tons of Soviet rockets, and over 5,000 metric tons of nonmilitary supplies such as food, clothing, and medicine, all of which was transshipped in Cambodian commercial trucks to VC bases along the Cambodian-South Vietnamese border. Using figures for the year 1968—the year of the enemy's highest expenditure of ordnance up to that time—the amount of arms and ammunition reaching the enemy through Cambodia was sufficient to meet the enemy's requirements at that level for at least eight years.

Through my years in Vietnam, for all my protests and recommendations, concessions permitting me to take countermeasures in Cambodia were few and feeble. I received authority in 1966 to conduct air and artillery strikes if fired on from across the border, but only if essential to preserve the integrity of American or South Vietnamese forces was I to pursue the enemy across the border into Cambodia. In the same year I gained approval for limited air reconnaissance, but if fired on, the planes were forbidden to fight back. Washington also finally authorized small ground reconnaissance patrols, but

The author in the summer of 1964 with Ambassadors Maxwell Taylor (center) and Henry Cabot Lodge.

The author in the summer of 1964, with General Duong Van ("Big") Minh (center) and the author's deputy commander, Lieutenant General John L. Throckmorton.

Mrs. Westmoreland, with Mrs. John
Klingenhagen (right), as a nurse's aide
Saigon, 1964.

U. S. Army Chief of Staff General Harold K. Johnson (right) talks with General
Cao Van Vien in December 1964. General Vien was subsequently head of the
South Vietnamese Joint General Staff. *(U. S. Army Photograph)*

In my state of undress, it occurred to me that I resembled a Montagnard.... This uld lead to a misunderstanding in the dark with armed soldiers on the alert infiltrators."

The author (right) following the VC attack on Camp Holloway, February 1965, with (from left) General Nguyen Khanh, White House adviser McGeorge Bundy, Lieutenant Colonel John C. Hughes, and Colonel John L. Klingenhagen.

The Honolulu conference, February 1966.

Admiral U. S. Grant Sharp (left), Commander
Chief, Pacific, and Major General Lewis W.
alt, commander of the III Marine Amphibi-
s Force, with the author in Vietnam in early
66. *(Marine Corps Photo)*

Lieutenant General Joseph H. Moore (left)
greets his successor as commander of the 7th
Air Force, Lieutenant General William M.
Momyer in June 1966.

The author with Lieutenant Colonel Mary Donovan of the 85th Evacuation
Hospital, 1966. (*Look* Collection, The Library of Congress. Copyright ©
Cowles Communications, Inc. 1966.)

Typical VC tunnel system.

A "tunnel rat" at work in the sector of the 25th Infantry Division near Cu Chi, in the III Corps Zone, August 1966. *(U. S. Army Photograph)*

The author aboard a helicopter over South Vietnam, October 1966. (*Look* Collection, The Library of Congress. Copyright © Cowles Communications, Inc. 1966.)

Bo Gritz with some of his Cambodians, including Nurse Toi, in 1966.

American marines in defensive positions alongside the Rock Pile, September 1966. *(Marine Corps Photo)*

The author in the field with an American infantryman during the rainy season, 1967.

unlike the authority granted SOG patrols in Laos, they were to fight only for self-preservation.

My every request to inform the world press of the enemy's use of Cambodia was denied until late 1967 after the Associated Press and United Press International revealed a visit by reporters to an enemy camp in the "Fish Hook" area of Cambodia, north of Tay Ninh province. Washington then approved my encouragement of press investigations. Only at that point could I make my first public mention of Cambodia as an enemy base.

On the chance that authority to move into Cambodia might eventually be granted, I had my staff in 1966 prepare a contingency plan for limited air and ground operations against the enemy bases and for a possible blockade of Sihanoukville and the Mekong and Bassac rivers, but that never went beyond the planning stage. In 1967 the Joint Chiefs pressed strongly for limited air and ground attacks against the bases, but the State Department opposed the plan and President Johnson disapproved it. Apparently in an effort to assuage the U.S. military, the President sent the ambassador to India, Chester Bowles, to Phnom Penh to try to work out something with Sihanouk. The only concession that Bowles obtained was Sihanouk's acquiescence if American forces should engage in "hot pursuit" or bomb in unpopulated areas along the frontier. Putting his hands over his eyes to demonstrate that he would see nothing, Sihanouk said: "We Cambodians do not like any Vietnamese—red, white, or blue." Yet even with Sihanouk's acquiescence, Washington refused authority to bomb inside Cambodia.

In early March 1967 I welcomed an invitation to attend a conference in Baguio, summer capital of the Philippines, conducted by the Department of State for its Far Eastern ambassadors, since it provided me an opportunity to explain the enemy's use of Cambodia and, I hoped, to elicit support for doing something about it. Most of the ambassadors—including my old friend, then ambassador to Japan, Alexis Johnson—appeared sympathetic, but either I failed to present my case well or the State Department was not to be moved by any evidence.

That attitude changed only in 1970 after the information obtained following Sihanouk's ouster confirmed what my intelligence people had been saying through the years. The fact that the VC and North Vietnamese were using Cambodian bases from which to attack South Vietnam, if not Cambodian complicity in supplying the enemy, was by that time fairly general knowledge.

President Nixon finally did something about it. He first authorized unannounced B-52 strikes beyond the Cambodian border against confirmed enemy bases in unpopulated areas. Then he granted authority for a limited ground invasion. Although the President accurately justified his order on the basis of saving American and South Vietnamese lives, he provoked indignant uproars from a segment of the press and the Congress, and the protests that followed resulted in a tragic confrontation between students and National Guard at Kent State University in Ohio in May 1970.

Nixon, they shouted, was widening the war, yet the enemy had long before brought the war into Cambodia and Lon Nol's Cambodian Government welcomed American and South Vietnamese intervention. Under the rationale espoused by the dissenters, the Allies in World War II would have been prohibited from invading France to get at Germany. Denying what your adversary is doing to you and turning the other cheek may make sense in social intercourse, but it can hardly be justified as a principle of war. Had the dissenting students, editorialists, and legislators been on the receiving end of some of those Soviet rockets or other lethal hardware that came through Cambodia, as were their compatriots in uniform, their indignation might have been considerably more muted. The Johnson administration's earlier policy of secrecy and lack of candor about the enemy's use of Cambodia may have contributed to the uproar.

One of the basic reasons the enemy turned to Sihanoukville and Cambodia as his primary source of supplies for his forces in at least the southern half of South Vietnam was a project known as MARKET TIME. Begun in the spring of 1965 under an able MACV naval component commander, Rear Admiral Norvell G. Ward, and pursued by his successor, Rear Admiral Kenneth L. Veth, it was a joint project of the U.S. and South Vietnamese navies to prevent the North Vietnamese from infiltrating supplies by sea into the hundreds of isolated coves that dot South Vietnam's extensive coastline. I decided to institute MARKET TIME after South Vietnamese planes during the first two months of 1965 found two big trawlers unloading arms and ammunition along the coast, clear evidence that screening by a fleet of South Vietnamese junks was inadequate.

By late 1966 close to a hundred high-speed aluminum-hulled Swift boats were patrolling the coast, supplemented by thirty-one 82-foot U. S. Coast Guard cutters and some fifteen U. S. Navy patrol aircraft, while farther off shore American destroyer escorts and minesweepers formed a second belt. Aided by Vietnamese junks and fire support from U.S. aircraft carriers and naval gunfire support ships, these craft searched close to 4,000 junks, sampans, and fishing boats every day. Whereas before 1965 the Viet Cong had received an estimated 70 per cent of their supplies by maritime infiltration, by the end of 1966 that had been reduced to a trickle of less than 10 per cent. Even so, an element of frustration was involved, for although vessels outside South Vietnam's territorial limits might obviously be transporting war supplies, probably headed for Sihanoukville, American and South Vietnamese craft had to operate scrupulously within the territorial limits. During these operations the South Vietnamese decorated a U. S. Coast Guard crew that sank a North Vietnamese trawler inside territorial limits, an unusual foreign decoration for coast guardsmen normally accustomed to operating close to American shores.

In a related program known as GAME WARDEN, 120 U.S. patrol river boats searched some 2,000 junks and sampans each day on South Vietnam's vast internal waterways, in the process interfering with VC tax collection and permitting freer movement of produce to the markets. That the searches troubled the VC was apparent from the number of attempted ambushes. The VC also floated signs down the rivers daring the boats to "come fight." A converted LST served as a mother craft for the patrol boats, and a fleet of U. S. Army helicopter gunships (later to be manned by U. S. Navy crews) was on call to help whenever the boats came under fire.

Powered by two water-jet engines capable of operating in shallow waters without damage from marine growth, unlike prop-propelled boats, the patrol boats were fast and maneuverable. The Navy had experimented with the Hovercraft air-cushion vehicle, but it had a plastic bubble to protect the crew from air turbulence that absorbed so much tropical sun even when air conditioned that the heat was intolerable. It was also so noisy that it telegraphed its approach to the enemy. The patrol river boats remained the workhorses of the inland waterways.

I was long concerned that the VC might sink a big vessel along the forty-mile course of the Saigon River to block the vital shipping channel between Saigon and the sea. The main channel ran through fifty square miles of mangrove swamps and thousands of tributary waterways, a region known as the Rung Sat, which was an ideal base from which the VC could operate against shipping. One of the most savage pieces of terrain in the world, the Rung Sat has almost no ground that is not subject to inundation from a six-foot tidal variation. The houses of the few villages in the region are built on stilts.

GAME WARDEN patrol boats operated frequently in the Rung Sat, as did small groups of U. S. Navy and South Vietnamese Navy commandos known as SEAL (sea, air, land) teams, which proved so effective that I asked for double the number to operate throughout the Mekong Delta. To break the VC hold on the region, I later shifted a battalion of the 1st Infantry Division to the Rung Sat where the men encountered some of the most unusual and trying conditions ever faced by the American soldier. Because the men spent hours and even days patrolling in water up to the waist, companies had to be rotated frequently to forestall foot and skin diseases. The men slept at night on air mattresses and at particularly high tides might awaken to find themselves afloat. Wooden platforms built above the high-tide mark served as helicopter pads. It was a strange war within a strange war, but it cut one of the main VC infiltration routes into the Saigon region and disrupted the enemy's organization. Even though the VC later hit an occasional ship with rocket, machine gun, or mortar fire, they never succeeded in blocking the shipping channel to Saigon.

The gamble I took in 1965 to meet the crisis threatening the ARVN by bringing in American combat troops before I had developed a logistical system to support them paid off, both because the American soldier adapts readily to exigencies and because engineer and logistical troops accomplished near miracles. Even though there were few support troops at first, the engineers and logisticians in less than two and a half years superimposed a modern logistical system on an underdeveloped nation capable of supporting one and a quarter million troops of various nationalities, while at the same time providing large amounts of supplies for the local population. Surely that was one of the more remarkable accomplishments of American forces in Vietnam.

Where there was but one deep-draft port at the start—Saigon, with its antiquated facilities—there were in the end seven, including Newport, built from scratch just upriver from Saigon to handle military cargoes while leaving Saigon for civilian needs. Where there were but three airfields capable of handling jet aircraft, there were in the end eight, plus eighty-four tactical airstrips that could accommodate propeller-driven planes, including transports, and hundreds of helicopter landing pads. Where there had been virtually no military storage facilities, there were in the end 11 million square feet of covered storage, over 5 million square yards of open storage, and 2.5 million cubic feet of cold storage. Where communications facilities had been limited and outmoded, a complex grid of radio and telephone facilities in the end linked every section of the country, while radio and submarine cable joined Saigon to Hawaii, Washington, and the world. Roads and bridges were built and rebuilt, canals dredged. The process was convulsive, but in a short span of time South Vietnam acquired facilities possessed by few nations other than the most highly developed.

A convulsive process like this inevitably leads to mistakes and expensive procedures that a less hurried approach would obviate. In the rush to get the first combat troops to Vietnam, for example, many units brought prepackaged equipment that turned out to be of no use in a tropical environment. For a while during 1966 ammunition stocks were low, forcing me to limit ARVN artillery to two rounds per day per gun, but no American unit ever wanted for necessary ammunition. An aerial shuttle from the United States patterned after the truck convoys of the "Red Ball Express" in Europe during World War II provided such critical items as spare parts and emergency supplies. Until dock and storage facilities could be increased, I had no choice but to hold ships for up to a month or more as floating warehouses, a costly expedient and one that American newsmen frequently criticized, but I was not going to be a party to shortchanging the American soldier.

One of the number of expedients used to expedite the construction program was a floating pier, a patented product of the DeLong Corporation. The piers were fabricated in the United States in sections and towed to South Vietnam, where they could be quickly emplaced. The DeLong piers helped turn Cam Ranh Bay into a major port in a matter of months and provided additional deep-draft facilities at Qui Nhon, Danang, and elsewhere.

Viewing the feverish construction activity throughout South Vietnam, a casual observer might have deduced that the Americans were concentrating less on the enemy than their own creature comforts. That was hardly the case. After the first influx of combat troops, priority did pass to support units as opposed to combat troops, but the number of support troops never exceeded 45 per cent of the total and by 1968 was down below 40 per cent. That compared favorably to a ratio of 43 per cent in World War II and Korea.

Once the early crisis of supply had passed, creature comforts were nevertheless a conscious part of the supply effort. Concerned about the effect of superimposing thousands of free-spending Americans on South Vietnam's tremulous economy, I tried to provide facilities that would keep American soldiers and their dollars on their bases and out of the towns and cities. A well-stocked PX, occasionally steak for dinner and ice cream for dessert, volley ball courts, and a few swimming pools—those might make good copy for a newspaperman or a Congressman looking for something to criticize, but they served an important purpose.

Although I established an over-all directorate of construction in MACV, first headed by Major General Carroll H. Dunn, all the military services contributed to the construction program, while ARVN engineers and engineers of Allied forces handled most of the construction for their own forces. Credit belongs also to a joint civilian contractor, Raymond International and Morrison-Knudsen (known as RMK). The partnership was joined later by Brown & Root and J. A. Jones (then referred to as RMK-BRJ), which handled much of the airfield and port construction, all effectively headed by the late Bert Perkins, executive vice president of RMK. The use of these civilian contractors and others, an unusual procedure in a combat zone, freed thousands of troops for other assignments.

At peak strength the civilian contractors employed 51,000 people. South Vietnamese civilians, Koreans, and Filipinos worked both for the contractors and directly for the military services, freeing further American troops. As an ancillary benefit, the South Vietnamese learned technical and supervisory skills. It might be initially amusing to watch a tiny Vietnamese, dwarfed by his machine, operating a big American bulldozer or roadscraper, but the Vietnamese learned quickly and worked efficiently. Washing the uniforms of American troops became a major cottage industry, as evidenced by many a green uniform spread on fence or shrubbery to dry.

Another civilian organization that proved to be a critical element in the supply lifeline was Pan American World Airways. The pilots and crews of Pan Am never said no, whatever the strain or danger. From the chairman of the board, Juan Trippe, to the gracious stewardesses, Pan Am proved a close friend of the man in uniform.

Maintenance of weapons and machines under tropical conditions was a serious and continuing problem. Obtaining construction materials for use in a country lacking natural resources involved lengthy shipments from the United States or elsewhere. The long monsoon seasons turned roads into morasses and inundated runways, while high tides and heavy surf limited over-the-beach supply. Yet for all these problems and more, the job was done and in a hurry. By late 1967 the vast construction effort was almost finished, and more than a million tons of supplies were coming through newly developed ports every month, all done in an underdeveloped corner of the world that is nineteen days by merchantman from San Francisco, thirty-four days from New York.

That a nation with no tradition of democracy could conduct a political campaign and free elections while engaged in a struggle for its existence was to me a most noteworthy achievement. That is what the South Vietnamese in 1966 and 1967 accomplished. Having promised President Johnson at Honolulu early in 1966 to begin the democratic process and having vowed at the conclusion of the Buddhist crisis in June to conduct elections for a constituent assembly, the first step toward election of a representative government, Ky and Thieu held to their commitment.

As registration for the election began, the Buddhists urged the South Vietnamese to boycott the election while the Viet Cong denounced the election procedure as a farce. The safety of those standing for election and even those who voted, said the underground VC radio, "could not be guaranteed." In some cases the VC confiscated identity cards which the people had to have to register. Yet for all the pressures, some five and a quarter million people registered, or about two thirds of the eligible electorate, and on election day, September 11, 1966, almost 81 per cent of those registered voted. Even the New York *Times,* usually quick to cavil, noted that "foreign observers who roamed freely on election day generally agreed there were few irregularities."

While the 117-man Constituent Assembly was at work drafting a constitution, another natural catastrophe tested the government's ability to provide for the people—a disastrous flood occurred in the Mekong Delta, leaving some 50,000 refugees, heavy livestock losses, and in some provinces destroying half the rice crop. Yet in contrast to the dawdling of General Khanh's government during the flood in the northern provinces in 1964, when the VC had profited, government agencies in the fall of 1966 provided emergency services with dispatch. As the waters subsided, I could detect no evidence that the VC had increased their hold on the people.

As I stood in the reviewing stand at the annual National Day parade in Saigon on November 1, 1966, I felt for the first time a genuine optimism over political developments. Much remained to be done, and the presidential election the following year was destined to produce some anxious moments, but the election of the Constituent Assembly was a solid start.

The VC fired fourteen rounds from recoilless rifles during the parade, reminder enough that a war remained to be fought, but Thieu and Ky were confident and despite rumors and press reports of conflict between them, I knew they made an effective team. An impetuous Ky recognized that he needed Thieu's restraining hand. Furthermore, the generals as a group had come to accept that the armed forces were the primary hope for stability in the country and that they had to maintain unity among themselves. The opening on the same day of a new presidential residence, Independence Palace, three years in the building, provided an impressive symbol of national pride.

I went to bed that night feeling good, confident at last not that the end of the war was at hand but that we had a solid substance to work with. No longer were we engaged in the frustrating exercise of trying to pick up beads of mercury.

In August 1966 I flew to Hawaii for another brief rest and conferences with Admiral Sharp. Upon receiving a telephone call from Deputy Secretary of Defense Vance telling me that President Johnson was contemplating inviting me and Kitsy to the LBJ Ranch in Texas, I told Vance that I thought it best for me to stay away from the United States lest I get involved in the political turmoil surrounding the war. My demurral was in vain. A second call informed me that the President wanted me to come.

The next day, Saturday, August 13, I flew with Kitsy, Captain Carpenter, and my faithful secretarial assistant, Warrant Officer Charles Montgomery, in the CINCPAC command plane to Bergstrom Air Force Base, near Austin, Texas, thence by presidential jet to an air strip near the Johnson ranch. The President and Mrs. Johnson greeted us. It was my first meeting with the First Lady, a gracious, charming, beautiful woman with genuine warmth.

It was my first encounter, too, with a favorite exploit of the President's: chasing deer about the ranch in his Lincoln Continental convertible. As dinnertime approached, Mrs. Johnson radioed to the ranch house to put steaks on, while we stopped by the road and had a drink from a bar mounted in a car belonging to the Secret Service.

At dinner the President asked his press secretary, Bill Moyers, to say grace. Moyers began in a voice so low that it was hard to understand him. "Speak up, Bill," the President said brusquely, "I can't hear you." "I beg your pardon, Mr. President," Moyers responded, "I wasn't talking to you."

My discussions with the President were cordial but hardly substantive, so that I was left to ponder exactly why he had insisted on the visit. The only significant exchange involved the possibility of another stand-down of the air campaign against North Vietnam. I strongly urged that he order no full halt to the bombing. North Vietnamese infiltration across the DMZ and continued infiltration through Laos made it essential that at least that part of the campaign directed at military movements continue. Although the President heard me with apparent interest, he made no commitment.

The next morning we accompanied the President and Mrs. Johnson to services in an Episcopal church in Fredericksburg, Texas. The press met us at the church and again upon our return to the ranch, whereupon we departed from the ranch air strip as the Johnsons waved good-by.

The trip back to Saigon was memorable in that Kitsy and the children—and our dog Hannah—flew with me not only to Hawaii but farther to take up new residence in the Philippines. Some weeks before, Ambassador Lodge had expressed surprise that Kitsy was residing in Hawaii not in government quarters but in a house I had purchased after she had left Saigon early in 1965. At Lodge's suggestion, Secretary McNamara had arranged for her to occupy old but reconditioned quarters at Clark Air Force Base in the Philippines. Although the people of Hawaii had been gracious and helpful, Kitsy and I both were anxious to keep the children out of the public eye and were concerned lest they be exposed to the vitriolic attacks of antiwar demonstrators. That was better accomplished in the Philippines, and the move also would afford me more opportunities to see my family over the long months still to come.

As we left Hawaii on a plane provided by Admiral Sharp, who had no love for animals on his aircraft, Kitsy unfortunately called out to Captain Carpenter, who, she failed to realize, was in the process of smuggling Hannah aboard the plane. Oley Sharp, who had come to see us off, looked up and must have seen what was happening, but he decorously said nothing.

I next saw President Johnson in Manila on October 24 and 25 when he convened another summit conference with Thieu and Ky, a follow-up to the earlier conference in Honolulu in February. It was an impressive assemblage that in addition to the representatives from the United States and South Vietnam included delegations headed by President Park of Korea, President Ferdinand E. Marcos of the Philippines, Prime Minister Harold Holt of Australia, Prime Minister Keith Holyoake of New Zealand, and Premier Thanom Kittikachorn of Thailand.

President Johnson's party included Secretary of State Rusk; Ambassador-at-Large Harriman; William Bundy, Leonard Unger, and Chester Cooper of the State Department; White House consultants Clark Clifford, Walt Rostow, and Robert W. Komer; John McNaughton of the Defense Department; and the Director of the USIA, Leonard Marks. Ambassador Lodge, Philip Habib, political counselor of the Embassy in Saigon, and I represented the U. S. Mission in South Vietnam. When I expressed surprise at the absence of General Wheeler and Admiral Sharp, the President confided that he intentionally wanted me to occupy the center of the stage as the senior military officer at the conference. I saw that as a kind display of confidence. Had he called me to his ranch to get to know me better in anticipation of that move?

My South Vietnamese counterpart, the Chief of the Joint General Staff, General Cao Van Vien, and I presented reviews of the military situation in South Vietnam. (As I concluded, an always thoughtful Dean Rusk slipped me a scrap of paper upon which he had scribbled, "Well done, Westy.") Yet the emphasis at Manila, as at Honolulu, was on social and pacification programs. The sessions confirmed something I had learned during a visit by Secretary McNamara to Saigon a few weeks earlier, that the President was considering some major change in the management of the pacification program. The surprise of the conference for me was a final communiqué in which the countries taking part promised to withdraw their troops from Vietnam not later than six months after the other side "withdraws its forces to the North, ceases its infiltration, and the level of violence thus subsides." Nobody consulted me on that.

The last session concluded, the President called me in the evening to the bedroom of his hotel suite to discuss with Walt Rostow, Ambassador Lodge, and Bill Moyers the possibility of his visiting Vietnam. He wanted to arrive, he told me to my consternation, at two o'clock the next afternoon.

Concerned about security arrangements, I saw no alternative but to tell him that was impossible. He was visibly piqued. Quite obviously, he said, I didn't want him to visit. "Dammit," the President said, "if that's the way you feel about it, I won't go."

I am sure the President was not unmindful of security, but his attitude left me no choice. I would be unable to complete arrangements by two o'clock, I told him, but I could make it by five. He accepted the change.

Since any leak of the President's plans would prompt cancellation, I deemed I had to be my own action officer in making the arrangements. Having instructed an assistant to alert my Chief of Staff, Bill Rosson, to be in my Saigon office early the next morning, October 26, I telephoned him at 7:15 A.M. I told General Rosson to assemble about 2,500 troops from all elements of the command for an awards ceremony at Cam Ranh Bay, which would also enable me to tell a cross section of the command about the Manila conference. To assure that senior commanders also would be present, I told him to assemble them for a briefing on the conference an hour earlier. Since I wanted the President to see a representative group of hospital patients, I told Bill Rosson under the guise of making room for anticipated casualties in an upcoming operation to move some Army patients from a hospital at Nha Trang to the Air Force hospital at Cam Ranh Bay.

I then flew to Cam Ranh Bay, arriving in midmorning, where I shared my cover plan with Joe Moore, Lew Walt, and the Field Force commanders, Jack Seaman and Swede Larsen. Flying back to Saigon, I told General Rosson the real plan, picked up the most senior members of the MACV staff, and headed back with them for Cam Ranh Bay. A plane carrying members of the press departed from Manila at about the same time, but a White House spokesman told the newsmen what was happening only after takeoff. It was a complicated cover plan, in effect for only a few hours, but it served the purpose of getting things moving without the security hazards of revealing the President's intentions.

Hardly had I landed again at Cam Ranh Bay than I received word that the President would arrive half an hour early. That, I learned later, was a common security practice, not out of any personal concern of the President for his own safety but out of concern for international complications should something happen on foreign soil. It left no time for a planned rehearsal, and even as the President's plane touched down, airmen were still putting bunting on the reviewing stand.

As I rode with the President in a jeep to review the troops, I told him that "no Commander in Chief in our history has ever had finer troops than these." I spoke with infinite conviction and sincerity and was pleased that he later publicly quoted my remark.

After speaking to assembled commanders at the officers' mess, the President went to an enlisted men's mess for lunch. A talented musician, Special Forces Captain Hershel Gober, who had become a favorite with his colleagues, played his guitar and sang original ballads about the war. Then a speeding ride to the presidential plane and my guest was gone, little more than an hour after he had arrived.

Chapter XI
Shift to the North

Just before the Manila conference, when Secretary McNamara visited me in Saigon, the basic purpose of his visit was to determine my views on additional troops for pursuing the war in 1967. Ask for what you need, McNamara told me; he would be the one to tailor the request to availability and economic and political reality.

Yet however tempting to ask the moon, I tried to exercise restraint. Since President Johnson's policy still was to confine the ground war within South Vietnam, there was no point yet in pressing for additional forces to move into Laos or Cambodia, although I continued to hope that eventually that authority would be granted. Sensitive to the political pressures already besetting the President, I realized that even stronger pressures would arise from a demand for vastly increased numbers. I was also conscious of the limited numbers of trained units still available in the United States.

Still concerned that the war would last well beyond the year that Reserve units might be employed without new legislation, I wanted at that stage to avoid a Reserve call-up. Most important of all was my conviction that, under the restrictions that had been imposed, the war still had a long time to run, so that I looked toward a well-balanced force that could be supported indefinitely by American manpower and industrial bases without undue degradation in the quality of noncommissioned and junior officers. I also had in mind the staying power of the American public.

As 1966 came to an end, the United States had 385,000 men in South Vietnam, but enemy strength continued to rise. Close to 60,000 North Vietnamese had entered the country during the year, the equivalent of five divisions, and the enemy's total combat strength exceeded 282,000. Although MACV's figures were higher than estimates of the CIA, I was convinced they were more nearly correct. My staff never inflated estimates of enemy strength for any reason, least of all to try to affect the American troop ceiling. Secretary of the Navy Paul Nitze had made such an accusation when he was a guest in my quarters in Saigon in June 1965, which shocked me, both because he made the accusation while a guest and because it seemed inconsistent with his reputation as a man of prudent judgment.

After detailed staff study, I asked for a troop increase of approximately 30 per cent, in the hope of leveling off with a well-balanced force of about 500,000 men. Conscious that that was minimal, I asked Secretary McNamara also to maintain for service in Vietnam a reserve in the United States the size of a corps—three divisions—ready for deployment as needed. That was important in view of the continuing build-up of North Vietnamese troops, the necessity to maintain pressure on the enemy, the need to expand the pacification program, the evident intent of the North Vietnamese to open a conventional type war in the northern provinces, and the possibility that a major enemy offensive might necessitate a large-scale counterattack.

Having decided in late 1964 to move into the third, or large-unit, stage of revolutionary warfare and to augment the VC with North Vietnamese units, the North Vietnamese never varied from the policy, although emphasis and methods within the over-all design sometimes changed. The eventual goal throughout was Saigon, but from the first the primary emphasis of the North Vietnamese focused on the Central Highlands and the central coastal provinces, with the basic end of drawing American units into remote areas and thereby facilitating control of the population in the lowlands. As in all the enemy's plans, there were underlying political or psychological objectives: to foster defeatism and war-weariness in the American people and to convince the South Vietnamese peasant that his government was bound to lose. A way of contributing to those objectives was to defeat a large American or ARVN unit à la Dien Bien Phu or Groupement Mobile 100.

It was the same strategy the Viet Minh had used to outlast the French, yet there were basic differences in the South Vietnamese opposition at this point that the North Vietnamese leadership seemingly failed to appreciate. As colonial masters, the French could never command the broad support of the people, but for all South Vietnam's political difficulties, it was possible for the government to attract support. That same condition made it possible to create an ARVN far more effective than the weak national army that had fought with the French, and a combination of the ARVN and American and Allied units constituted a military force far larger and more effective than the French Expeditionary Corps that at peak had had but 180,000 men. Because of the helicopter and other aircraft, Americans and Vietnamese also possessed a battlefield mobility heretofore unknown. A unit might be "lured" to the Central Highlands, as the North Vietnamese claimed, yet if that was to have any appreciable effect, the lure had to be maintained for a long time. In view of American firepower and mobility, that was hard for the enemy to do.

The local Viet Cong guerrillas posed in some ways a more difficult problem for me, for by harassing American and South Vietnamese installations with rockets, mortars, and sappers, they might tie down more and more troops on defense. Although those attacks made banner headlines, what price an air-tight defense of Saigon or Danang if the people in the countryside lay at the mercy of the enemy? Police in the most secure American city can never hope to foil every bank robber. When the VC early in 1966 began using a Soviet 122-mm rocket, they made defense even more difficult, for that rocket has an arclike trajectory like that of a round from a 105-mm howitzer and a range of well over six miles. By various methods—patrols, observation towers, radar, night vision devices, quick reaction from artillery and ground troops—we tried to reduce the number and effectiveness of those attacks; yet in the knowledge that some were inevitable, I resisted a natural inclination to commit more men to defense.

Despite sometimes catastrophic losses in the battles in remote areas, the enemy had persisted. Although I cannot know his thinking in detail, I am convinced he deluded himself as to how much he was accomplishing. His boasts of victories and casualties were exorbitant: some 70,000 to 80,000 American soldiers killed in a year, nineteen battalions of the American 25th Infantry Division annihilated (when the division had only nine battalions). Enemy estimates of American and ARVN losses often were excessive by as much as 800 per cent.

The high command in Hanoi must have known that claims like those were ridiculous. The fact that the North Vietnamese for long declined all American overtures to instigate negotiations—some of them supine—demonstrated that they were not unaware of what they had yet to accomplish. Having failed to gain control of all Vietnam at Geneva in 1954, they were convinced that military victories at least as significant as Dien Bien Phu had to precede negotiations. As one North Vietnamese general officer put it in the summer of 1966:

> Our basic intention is to win militarily . . . We must gain military victories before thinking of diplomatic struggles. And even when we are fighting diplomatically, we must go on with our war effort; we must multiply our military victories if we want to succeed diplomatically.

This was such a basic Communist tenet, so often proclaimed in other wars or confrontations, in other negotiations, that I found it hard to believe that many Americans, including some senior officials, saw it otherwise. Every little decrease in the tempo of enemy operations, any little let-up in the number of terrorist incidents, somebody in the United States saw as the North Vietnamese trying to send a signal to open negotiations. Were those Americans unaware that any number of clear, unmistakable channels for North Vietnam to send a signal were always open?

Yet more important, how could those Americans fail to understand that the enemy had no reason to negotiate? He was undergoing no excruciating pain—the policy of graduated response was seeing to that. Neither had he achieved anything on the battlefield spectacular enough to support a claim that he sat in the driver's seat. Without one or the other of those conditions, negotiation was nothing but a delusion for some American legislators, editorialists, academics, civilian bureaucrats, and an occasional film star to dally with for whatever amusement it provided them and whatever encouragement it afforded Hanoi.

The move of North Vietnamese divisions across the DMZ in the first half of 1966 into Quang Tri and Thua Thien provinces was a continuation of the strategy of drawing American units to remote areas. Yet it was, at the same time, a step toward trying to achieve a battlefield spectacular that might be used as a bargaining point at a future negotiating table and a psychological shock to the American people. Aware of those ends, I was nevertheless conscious of the requirement to protect the Vietnamese population, so that I saw no alternative to sending American troops to oppose the new threat.

Some programs to forestall or limit North Vietnamese infiltration in the north were already underway: bombing in the area just beyond the DMZ and in the Laotian panhandle; SOG patrols in the panhandle; and yet another program that had long been underway, which I named TIGER-HOUND—"tiger" for aggressiveness, "hound" for smelling out. Little O-1 aircraft reconnoitered inside Laos up to a depth of twelve miles and when they found something, they called in Air Force, Marine, and Navy fighter-bombers. If a fixed target was remunerative enough, I authorized use of B-52 bombers, although each mission had to be cleared first with the American ambassador to Laos, Bill Sullivan, who had a tendency to impose his own restrictions over and above those laid on by the Department of State. (We sometimes referred to the Ho Chi Minh Trail as "Sullivan's Freeway.") Both B-52s and tactical aircraft from time to time bombed the high Mu Gia Pass, inside Laos just northwest of the DMZ, which most of the traffic destined for the Ho Chi Minh Trail traversed. Although the bombing blocked the pass on occasion, it was impossible to keep it permanently closed.

The success of the TIGER-HOUND operations was possibly one reason the North Vietnamese opted in 1966 to send troops across the DMZ, that and the Buddhist crisis in Hué and Danang which they wanted to capitalize on quickly. After obtaining Washington's approval, I started a similar operation just north of and within the DMZ, known as TALLY HO.

Authorities in Washington were more reluctant for some reason to allow use of artillery and naval gunfire either in the DMZ or north of it. Near the end of 1966 I gained authority to fire artillery against enemy weapons firing from the DMZ, but not until February of the next year did my persistent pleas finally result in approval for pre-emptive fire. It took even longer to get approval for American and South Vietnamese ground troops to enter the DMZ, and even then the forays were restricted to forces which first became engaged below the DMZ. They might pursue as far as the demarcation line that split the center of the DMZ, but once contact was broken, they had to withdraw.

In response to the enemy build-up in the northern provinces, I flew to Danang on July 12, 1966, to confer with General Walt and the I Corps commander, General Lam. I told General Walt to move up a division, if required, into Quang Tri province and promised use of the Special Landing Force, a reinforced Marine battalion (later two battalions) held off shore as a floating reserve, which I might use for brief assignments without charge against the troop ceiling. I also promised priority on the use of B-52s. General Lam learned from his superiors in Saigon that they were prepared to give him up to five battalions of the ARVN's general reserve.

The North Vietnamese infiltration also prompted me to revive the idea of an international force to be deployed south of the DMZ. I developed a plan for a force to be called KANZUS, for Korea, Australia, New Zealand, and the United States. In Saigon the ambassadors from the nations involved were enthusiastic, but again the response from Washington was negative. I continued pushing for an international force even after I left South Vietnam to become the U. S. Army Chief of Staff, and I still believe using such a force at an obvious point of North Vietnamese infiltration would have had a world-wide psychological impact helpful in countering North Vietnamese refusal to admit that North Vietnamese troops were inside South Vietnam. Had an international force patrolled the DMZ in the spring of 1972 or in 1975, would the North Vietnamese have risked world opprobrium with conventional invasions?

Quang Tri province has towering mountains in the west, sandy coastal plains in the east. A sprawling Cua Viet River cuts off the northern third of the province. Where Route 1 crossed the Cua Viet, twelve miles north of the province capital of Quang Tri City, is the town of Dong Ha, where we maintained an air strip about ten miles south of the DMZ. Running west from Dong Ha is Route 9, a dirt road leading into Laos which passed a CIDG-Special Forces camp at the Montagnard village of Khe Sanh.

Using but one battalion at first as a reconnaissance force, the marines in July 1966 bumped rudely into North Vietnamese troops only seven miles from Dong Ha. Unlike the VC, the North Vietnamese stood and fought, prompting General Walt in the end to commit five more Marine battalions, including the Special Landing Force, while the South Vietnamese contributed five. Known as Operation HASTINGS, the engagement was the largest yet fought, although subsequently exceeded in size by ATTLEBORO in the fall of 1966 and others. In fighting lasting until the first week of August, the North Vietnamese lost close to 900 killed.

To guard against continuing North Vietnamese presence, General Walt left three Marine battalions in the north. Their patrols soon uncovered more enemy forces so that again Walt moved in reinforcements, to include an amphibious landing by the Special Landing Force on the coast between the mouth of the Cua Viet River and the DMZ. By the end of September, seven U. S. Marine and three ARVN battalions were involved and had added almost a thousand to the total of enemy killed. Some of the enemy units were clearly trying to straggle back to the DMZ. The marines had thwarted the enemy build-up before the North Vietnamese were ready to attack.

During frequent visits to Lew Walt's headquarters, I gained the impression that the marines in their supreme self-confidence, however admirable that might be, were underestimating the enemy's capabilities. Reviewing a war game in September that I had directed General Walt to conduct, I became convinced of it. They were particularly underestimating an enemy threat to the CIDG-Special Forces camp at Khe Sanh.

Aside from serving as a normal patrol base blocking enemy infiltration from Laos along Route 9, Khe Sanh was a base for many of the SOG operations into Laos, and its air strip was the takeoff point for TIGER-HOUND reconnaissance planes. Furthermore, I still hoped some day to get approval for a major drive into Laos to cut the Ho Chi Minh Trail, in which case I would need Khe Sanh as the base for the operation.

I expected a mass offensive in the northern provinces, I told General Walt and his staff, and Khe Sanh was a likely target for an enemy attempt within the next six months to replay Dien Bien Phu. I directed them to restudy the enemy's capabilities and ordered the U. S. Navy's Seabees to begin a crash program to upgrade the air strip at Khe Sanh to an all-weather field capable of handling C-130 transport aircraft, a project that I saw as a race against time, both because of approaching *crachin* weather and of possible enemy attack. I later wondered why the North Vietnamese made no effort to interfere with that construction and could only deduce that they wanted to let it proceed in the hope that eventually they could use the air strip themselves.

Meanwhile, recognizing the additional responsibilities placed on the marines by the enemy infiltration from North Vietnam, I explored the possibility of reinforcements. While directing contingency plans for emergency reinforcement, I sought forces for more permanent support.

Because much of Quang Tri province was in easy range of enemy artillery within or just north of the DMZ, I saw a series of American artillery bases as a primary requirement. I first moved there a battery of powerful U. S. Army 175-mm guns from a battalion already deployed near Saigon; then, as another battalion arrived in Vietnam, I sent that battalion north as well. These guns have a range of about twenty miles, so that from their new positions west of Dong Ha, they could fire into the DMZ and as far west as Khe Sanh. I also provided an incoming battalion of U. S. Army self-propelled 105-mm howitzers and, for control purposes, an Army artillery group headquarters.

Since large numbers of marines who had previously protected Danang had moved north, I reinforced the Danang defenses temporarily with a battalion, commanded by Lieutenant Colonel Michael Healey, of the 173d Airborne Brigade. Part of my rationale in transferring the battalion was to establish a U. S. Army force in the area as a basis for possible additional Army reinforcements. With that future course in mind, I also wanted the marines to develop arrangements for logistical support of U. S. Army troops, which the presence of Healey's battalion would require. I also arranged for moving the South Korean Marine brigade to Chu Lai to free some of the U.S. marines there for commitment farther north.

With those reinforcements General Walt was able to sideslip the entire 3d Marine Division to the north of the Hai Van Pass with headquarters at Phu Bai while the 1st Marine Division shifted to Danang. Those moves represented considerable improvement *vis à vis* the North Vietnamese threat, but I still believed more reinforcements might be required.

The only sure way of stopping enemy infiltration across the DMZ would have been to construct a conventional defensive line from the sea to the Laotian border, yet the thousands of troops that that would have required were simply unavailable and, besides, the North Vietnamese still could have come through Laos. I decided instead to construct what I called a "strongpoint obstacle system" built around a series of fire-support and patrol bases, designed to channel the enemy into well-defined corridors where we might bring air and artillery to bear and then hit him with mobile ground reserves.

Those bases, or strongpoints, were to occupy the few patches of high ground in the coastal region of Quang Tri province, thereby providing observation for directing artillery fire while at the same time denying the enemy direct observation and firing positions from which to hit our backup facilities, such as the air strip and unloading points for supplies on the Cua Viet River at Dong Ha. Because the North Vietnamese were building artillery positions within and just north of the DMZ with the obvious intent of bringing in big guns, bunkers and fighting positions in the strongpoints had to be sturdy and, because of the heavy rains in the area, provided with adequate drainage.

Of the forward strongpoints, the largest and most important were at Gio Linh astride Route 1 just below the DMZ and another a few miles to the west at Con Thien. Behind them were back-up positions serving as artillery bases and as a second line of defense: one at Camp Carroll, south of Route 9, a few miles southwest of the village of Cam Lo; another at Cam Lo; and several near Dong Ha. The marines subsequently erected another base farther west at the Rock Pile, a 700-foot chimneylike landform which blocked several valleys leading from the north and west. They also stationed a battalion at what became known as the Khe Sanh Combat Base. The CIDG-Special Forces camp shifted from Khe Sanh a few miles to the west along Route 9 close to the Laotian border at Lang Vei. The two outposts—Khe Sanh Combat Base and Lang Vei—together provided a degree of flank protection for the entire strongpoint obstacle system. A relatively simple defensive concept, it was one that the ARVN could in time take over, but I had to keep watch on the marines lest they make the bases big enough to accommodate their outsized battalions, which the smaller ARVN battalions would be unable to defend.

Work was beginning on the strongpoint obstacle system when I went to Clark Air Force Base in the Philippines in mid-September 1966 to confer with a representative of the Defense Department, Lieutenant General Alfred D. Starbird, who informed me that scientists had sold Secretary McNamara on a plan to create an electronic barrier to enemy movement running below the DMZ from the sea to the Laotian border and thence across the panhandle to Thailand. It was a noble idea: use advanced technology to spare the troops an onerous defensive task. It was also highly theoretical, but I got the impression that some of the people promoting it, if not McNamara himself, saw it as a cure for infiltration that would justify stopping the bombing of North Vietnam.

Known officially as Project JASON, the concept of a barrier line involved use of barbed wire, mines, electronic sensors, and fortified combat bases. As any experienced military man would know, the concept had a basic flaw in that no fence—electronic or otherwise—would be foolproof without men to cover it by fire, which raised the specter of tying down a battalion every mile or so in conventional defense. While co-operating with General Starbird and his scientists, I told the Secretary that I welcomed the devices but wanted to employ them in my own way. The scientists were thinking of a linear barrier; I wanted the devices spread in depth to help canalize enemy movement in between the strongpoint obstacles I was already constructing.

Secretary McNamara graciously agreed, but in a press conference in Washington he made the mistake of announcing grandiose plans for the barrier. Reporters promptly dubbed it the "McNamara Line" and the stories they quite understandably wrote told the North Vietnamese all about it. By the time the mines, wire, and sensors and bulldozers to clear the region of brush and trees were on hand, the North Vietnamese had moved artillery up to 152 mm in caliber into the positions they had previously prepared within and just beyond the DMZ. To have gone through with constructing the barrier, even in the modified form that I proposed, would have been to invite enormous casualties. Yet I wanted no formal announcement that we had abandoned the project, lest the enemy claim he had forced it.

While forgoing the idea of a wide swath cleared by bulldozers the whole length of the DMZ, General Walt and I settled for clearings in the vicinity of the strongpoints and intermittent barriers of wire, mines, and sensors. The sensors would provide early warning of the enemy's approach and the wire and mines encourage him to move along corridors of our choosing; but as I had originally contemplated, the final defense rested on planes, artillery, and mobile ground reserves.

Convinced that more troops eventually would have to be deployed to the north, I directed construction of a new airfield just north of Quang Tri City and docks along the Cua Viet River at Dong Ha. When completed by the

Navy's Seabees, those facilities multiplied cargo capacity in the two northern provinces some ten times and eliminated any danger that troops in the north might want for supplies should the enemy or monsoon rains close the Hai Van Pass.

Although American marines and their colleagues in the 1st ARVN Division had dealt the North Vietnamese infiltrators a severe blow at the end of September 1966, the North Vietnamese were persistent. As the new year, 1967, began, evidence mounted of continued enemy build-up within the DMZ, including an influx of artillery pieces, which finally prompted the State Department to relax its restriction on firing into the DMZ.

On March 20 the enemy dramatically illustrated the extent of his build-up. U.S. marines and ARVN troops in and around Con Thien and Gio Linh absorbed a thousand rounds of mortar, rocket, and artillery fire. The next day the enemy ambushed a Marine ammunition supply convoy only two miles from Gio Linh, while a few days later a Marine company near Cam Lo came under sharp ground attack. The war in the north was stirring up again.

To have at hand, if required, a U. S. Army force to take over the southern provinces of the I Corps Zone and enable more marines to shift north, I told my chief of staff, Bill Rosson, to assemble a special planning group to develop a provisional division-size task force of three brigades, with normal artillery, helicopter, and other support. The task force would draw on U. S. Army units from the II and III Corps zones, thus weakening those sectors slightly, but that was a risk I had to take. It was necessary to put the plan into effect sooner than I had anticipated. Named for General Rosson's home state, Task Force OREGON opened its headquarters at Chu Lai on April 20 with General Rosson in command, relieving in a matter of days the 1st Marine Division, which was moved to Danang.

When Army brigades without divisional attachment later arrived in Vietnam, I assigned them to Task Force OREGON and, with Department of the Army endorsement, redesignated it the "Americal Division." The designation derived from a division organized by General MacArthur under similar circumstances during World War II on New Caledonia. As in World War II, the new division replaced the 1st Marine Division.

The upsurge of North Vietnamese activity in Quang Tri province apparently presaged an enemy attempt to overrun the province, then to close on Hué. Although the effort began with heavy shelling of Con Thien, Gio Linh, and the backup positions, the first attack by enemy ground troops was to be at Khe Sanh.

Relative quiet having long prevailed at Khe Sanh, Lew Walt by April 1967 had substituted a company for the battalion that previously manned the combat base. From the base, located on a high plateau, the men of the company patrolled through elephant grass, bamboo thickets, and dense jungle covering nearby hills and mountains.

On the morning of April 24, a platoon-size Marine patrol brushed against a seemingly small enemy force on one of the plateau slopes, but when another Marine patrol came to relieve the first, at least a company of North Vietnamese attacked. Outnumbered, the marines lost thirteen men killed, but the bulk of the two patrols got away. They had made contact, it turned out, with a regiment of the North Vietnamese 325 C Division that had occupied several of the heights in the vicinity and was bringing in artillery for an assault to take the Khe Sanh Combat Base.

The patrol action triggered what became known as the "hill fights." Two battalions of the 3d Marine Regiment, flown in by helicopter and C-130 planes to the upgraded air strip, prepared to occupy three nearby peaks held by the enemy, Hills 861, 881 South, and 881 North.*

A long parade of Marine Corps fighter-bombers pounded the three objectives, and the 175-mm artillery pieces at the Rock Pile and Camp Carroll joined in heavy preparation fires. As the Marine foot troops began their climb, the crests were already scarred with ugly brown gashes, the trees splintered. Hill 861 fell fairly readily, but the fights for the two Hills 881 were as bitter and costly as many another in proud Marine Corps annals. North Vietnamese demolitions teams east of Khe Sanh severed Route 9, and on May 4 the North Vietnamese made a diversionary attack against the CIDG-Special Forces camp at Lang Vei. Local tribesmen and their Green Beret advisers beat off the attack without help, and the next day the marines secured the last of the three hills near Khe Sanh.

It was during this fighting that a new crisis of criticism developed in the American press over the M-16 rifle. Some U.S. marines, the press reported, were throwing away their weapons in disgust. Seriously concerned about the morale of the marines and about the effect this would have on the ARVN, to which I hoped eventually to give the M-16, I sent an inspection team to the I Corps Zone to investigate. As I suspected, the marines had been given the weapons without adequate instructions on how to maintain them, and the chain of command had failed to exercise proper supervision. The marines were reluctant in any case to give up their familiar M-14, a much heavier weapon less suited for jungle warfare but one requiring less care. Yet I considered it imperative, particularly if U. S. Army troops were to operate in the north and if the ARVN was to receive the M-16, that weapons be standardized.

Convinced that the M-16 was the better weapon for the locale, I talked at length with Lew Walt's successor, Lieutenant General Robert E. Cushman, Jr. General Cushman in turn passed the word down the chain of command, and as the marines came to appreciate the weapon's capability and lightness, for all the necessity for careful maintenance, they came to regard it as highly as did everybody else.

President Johnson later sent an old friend from Texas, Frank W. Mayborn, to investigate the M-16 for him personally. Mayborn was ostensibly

* Hills are designated by their height in meters.

merely accompanying a retired World War II general, Bruce Clarke, on an inspection trip to Vietnam, and it was only after their departure that I learned the true purpose of Mayborn's visit.

The maneuver to take Khe Sanh and thereby outflank the strongpoint obstacle system at least temporarily foiled, the North Vietnamese for much of the remainder of the year 1967 focused on the strongpoints, while General Cushman shuffled Marine battalions in and out of Khe Sanh. A company occupied Hill 861 while another held Hill 881 South. Patrols ranging the hills and jungle occasionally precipitated short fire fights, but for several months no new major threat to Khe Sanh developed.

The fight in the piedmont hills and the sandy coastal plain of Quang Tri province meanwhile was bitter. In one of the few instances during the war, American troops were subject to heavy, persistent enemy shelling. While a few grizzled Marine Corps veterans might speak disparagingly when comparing its intensity with some of the barrages they had undergone in World War II and Korea, time has a way of embroidering memories and, in any event, it was nerve-shattering and damaging enough to those marines caught up in it, as I personally found on several occasions when visiting the strongpoints. Air strikes, artillery fire, and continuous sweeps by marines outside the strongpoints usually forestalled enemy ground assaults on the bases, and American artillery and naval guns firing counterbattery undoubtedly cut down on the number of rounds the North Vietnamese could fire; but the fight was long and costly nevertheless. In the first enemy ground attack against Con Thien, launched by two North Vietnamese battalions in September 1967 preceded by a heavy mortar barrage, the defending Marine battalions lost forty-four men killed.

Con Thien appeared to be the primary objective. American TV commentators and newspapermen began to play it up as the long-awaited Dien Bien Phu, and, indeed, Con Thien was a dismal place where men seldom ventured far from a sand-bagged bunker or a hole in the ground and where heavy rains and mud often added to the drabness of the scene. Once when I flew in by helicopter, the pilot literally skimming the ground, the shelling made it difficult for me to get out. "General," one marine told me, " 'Charlie' apparently knows you are here." Yet as men have often done before under battlefield pressure, the marines at Con Thien lived and fought in relative good humor, accepting their hardships, dutifully executing their assignments.

By the first week of October 1967 the siege of Con Thien—if such it can be called—was over, broken by tenacious, aggressive marines and by a new concept in marshaling firepower known as SLAM, an acronym for seeking, locating, annihilating, and monitoring. The technique was developed by Joe Moore's successor as commander of the Seventh Air Force, General William W. ("Spike") Momyer. Momyer was a man of slight build, dependable, businesslike, a fighter for his convictions but nonemotional, logical, pragmatic. Under the SLAM concept, General Momyer marshaled the entire spectrum of heavy fire support—B-52s, tactical air, and naval gunfire—in close co-ordination with artillery and other ground fire.

After reconnaissance aircraft and other intelligence means fixed and defined the target, B-52s usually struck first, followed by tactical air, naval guns, and artillery. Long-range reconnaissance patrols then explored the target area to assess damage. Off and on for forty-nine days SLAM strikes pummeled the enemy around Con Thien and demonstrated that massed firepower was in itself sufficient to force a besieging enemy to desist, a demonstration that was destined to contribute to my confidence on a later occasion.

If comparable in any way to Dien Bien Phu, Con Thien was a Dien Bien Phu in reverse. The North Vietnamese lost well over 2,000 men killed, while Con Thien and Gio Linh continued to stand as barriers to enemy movement. Relinquish Con Thien, Gio Linh, and even Khe Sanh? Had we done that, the enemy would merely have moved his big guns forward, leading to other Con Thiens and Gio Linhs closer to the densely populated regions of the country.

The fighting in May 1967 included the first American sweeps into the southern half of the DMZ as far as the midway point marked by the little Ben Hai River. Conducted usually by two Marine battalions, sometimes augmented by ARVN units, the sweeps pushed the enemy across the Ben Hai or into the hills to the west, thereby relieving pressure on Con Thien and Gio Linh. Since the DMZ obviously would be a battleground for a long time, the marines co-operated with Vietnamese National Police in evacuating 13,000 residents from the area south of the Ben Hai River to the relative safety of refugee camps farther south.

Despite reinforcement by Task Force OREGON, the marines still could afford but one division for the two provinces north of the Hai Van Pass, for the 1st Marine Division was still engaged in the vicinity of Danang. Nor was I pleased with the semistatic defense that the shortage of troops imposed on the marines at Khe Sanh. Beginning in mid-1967, I began to plan for sending the 1st Cavalry Division from the II Corps Zone to the northern provinces, there to capitalize on that division's unusual mobility to operate around Khe Sanh as the division had done before in the Central Highlands. That might be a first step leading to a drive into Laos to cut the Ho Chi Minh Trail or a more daring project that the move of the North Vietnamese into and south of the DMZ invited: an amphibious hook putting troops ashore just north of the DMZ and moving others by helicopter and parachute behind the enemy to trap and destroy his ground troops, artillery, and supplies.

Yet like a drive into Laos, that hook might be executed only if I could talk cautious Washington officials into it.

The build-up that had enabled American forces to take the offensive during 1966 and make the first forays into the VC base areas continued through 1967 but at a more regulated pace. American strength during the year increased by just over a hundred thousand, which included the three brigades of the 9th Infantry Division, the 11th and 198th Light Infantry brigades, a regiment of the 5th Marine Division, and late in the year, headquarters and two more brigades of the 101st Airborne Division, bringing that entire division to the scene. By year's end over 3,000 helicopters were on hand and 28 tactical fighter squadrons.

Yet even so, the demands on American forces continued to be great. In addition to guarding against North Vietnamese infiltration across the DMZ, I had to continue to watch the Laotian and Cambodian borders for large-scale intrusion by the enemy's big units and to mount more operations into VC base areas. At the same time, if pacification was to make headway, American assistance to the ARVN in the small-unit war among the people had to continue.

To explain to my colleagues and to visitors the interrelationship between what were in effect two missions, I drew on a simple analogy. A boxer, I noted, must do two things at once: attack and defend. As he jabs and probes with one hand, he keeps his defense up with the other. When he sees a clear opportunity, he may take a momentary calculated risk by attacking with both fists. Not so the tactic of using both hands defensively. If he does that—"covers up"—he surrenders all initiative to his opponent. Nobody wins by defense alone.

While the defensive fight in the northern provinces and hundreds of small, essentially defensive operations among the people by squads, platoons, and companies proceeded, the first big offensive operation of 1967 was Operation CEDAR FALLS, a sweep in January into the Iron Triangle, that sixty-square-mile woodland haven for guerrillas operating against Saigon. It was a corps-size sweep involving the 1st and 25th Infantry divisions, the 173d Airborne Brigade, and the 11th Armored Cavalry Regiment.

With that many troops, the force was able to search the region methodically. Although the VC again fled or hid rather than fight, the American troops stayed for seventeen days, long enough to force those in hiding to surface. Some 700 VC were killed, while approximately the same number were captured or rallied to the government under the *chieu hoi* program. Possibly of greater long-range benefit, the troops found and destroyed a vast underground labyrinth of tunnels, command post, mess halls, munitions factories, and living quarters. That meant for the VC the loss of facilities that had been twenty years in the building.

The operation also produced more than 500,000 enemy documents, an invaluable intelligence find. It was from those documents that I learned that the Bob Hope troupe had been the enemy's target in the bombing of the Brink Hotel. The documents also included detailed maps of Saigon with all American headquarters, billets, and villas plainly marked, including mine.

Later in 1967, with all civilians evacuated from the Iron Triangle, teams operating Rome plows—big bulldozers equipped with a spike on one end of the blade capable of felling the tallest jungle trees—leveled the dense forest. In the same way that farmers with tractors or horse-drawn plows turn in the stubble of harvested wheat or oats, the Rome plows carved great hunks from the jungle and worked round and round the circumference until they reduced trees and brush to combustible rubbish, leaving the guerrillas no place to hide.

During February 1967 the same American units that had entered the Iron Triangle and more launched the biggest operation of the war to that time, Operation JUNCTION CITY, with twenty-two American and four South Vietnamese battalions, designed to do much the same to War Zone C as was done to the Iron Triangle. Aside from hope of trapping VC and North Vietnamese forces, an objective of JUNCTION CITY was to find COSVN, the enemy's over-all headquarters.

The plan was to erect a vast horseshoe of troops around three sides of War Zone C, then to sweep up the middle with armored and mechanized forces. Setting up the horseshoe involved a parachute assault by a battalion of the 173d Airborne Brigade, the only airborne assault launched by American troops during the war. In only two instances did the enemy stand and fight, and the staff of COSVN apparently escaped across the border into Cambodia. Yet as revealed later by defectors and captured documents, the operation forced the VC to relocate training facilities and other increments of their base areas inside Cambodia, farther from the population they were trying to control. Close to 3,000 of the enemy were killed.

Although the region was too large to level with Rome plows, it was possible to destroy some of the main enemy hide-outs. American engineers also constructed a bridge across a river leading into the area and built three airfields able to handle C-130 transport planes, thus facilitating re-entry on subsequent occasions. Although I wanted to leave behind an infantry brigade to harass any enemy that chose to return, the necessity to provide troops for Task Force OREGON in the I Corps Zone forced me to settle for CIDG-Special Forces outposts at strategic points. (Having anticipated need for these camps, we had prefabricated component parts available for rapid installation.)

JUNCTION CITY provided an example of the enemy's exaggerated claims. According to official North Vietnamese accounts, 13,500 American and South Vietnamese troops were killed; the actual total was 282. The North Vietnamese claimed 800 armored vehicles and 119 artillery pieces destroyed; actual losses were twenty-one armored personnel carriers, three tanks, and five artillery pieces.

Meanwhile, an experiment in U. S. Army-ARVN co-operation unfolded in the environs of Saigon, designed to supplement pacification, put local ARVN units on a more solid basis, and improve security for the capital. In an extended operation known as FAIRFAX, the 199th Light Infantry Brigade, commanded by the resourceful Fritz Freund, then a brigadier general, worked with the ARVN 5th Ranger Group. American and Vietnamese units paired off down to squad level in complete integration, a small-unit war characterized by hundreds of small night ambushes—sometimes an average of sixty per night—on roads and lanes, canals and rivers, and of operations to seal off a village or hamlet and search it methodically for VC, political cadre, and arms and supplies. It was the flares and tracer bullets generated by those little engagements that many a visitor to Saigon watched in the night from the rooftop restaurant of the plush Caravelle Hotel.

Operation FAIRFAX unquestionably improved the security of Saigon and resulted in more than a thousand VC killed. Yet as the months passed the South Vietnamese rangers developed a tendency to let the Americans do the job alone. By late fall of 1967 the American soldiers had taught about all they could to the Vietnamese in any case, so I arranged for an ARVN artillery battalion to be permanently assigned to the 5th Ranger Group, provided for adequate logistical support, and withdrew the U. S. 199th Light Infantry Brigade. From time to time I experimented with brigading smaller ARVN and American units, but those experiments and FAIRFAX convinced me it was better for South Vietnamese and American units to operate side by side in co-operation than to integrate. The South Vietnamese in the long run simply had to learn to stand alone.

In a periodic resurgence, contingents of North Vietnamese regulars early in 1967 emerged from the jungle canopy of the mountainous Do Xa to try again to regain control of coastal Binh Dinh province. The 1st Cavalry Division again reacted with a myriad of operations ranging from multiple patrols to battalion-size assaults that extended through much of the year. The enemy was soon fragmented, more than 3,000 killed.

At the same time Task Force OREGON—and later as the Americal Division—conducted similar operations in the two provinces to the north, Quang Ngai and Quang Tin, where, for all the earlier efforts of the 2d ARVN Division and U.S. marines, the Viet Cong were still strong and where another North Vietnamese division hid in the hills to the west. It was a slow process, a seemingly never-ending search for small, elusive enemy units, yet it was essential if the enemy was to be prevented from massing for large attacks and from working his will among the people. Sometimes North Vietnamese regulars emerged from the forested hills to precipitate larger fights, but they would soon break contact and retire. Rather than commit major forces to track the enemy down in the forests, I relied on long range patrols to locate him and call in air strikes.

Having long followed a policy of committing no American troops in the Mekong Delta (IV Corps Zone) other than support and advisory forces, I had begun in 1966 to consider how relatively small American numbers might bolster the ARVN effort there and set an example of tactical aggressiveness. Although the South Vietnamese had proven capable of containing the VC in the Delta, they seemed unable to eliminate them. Also influencing my consideration was an idea advanced originally by a U. S. Navy officer, Captain David F. Welch. In much the same way that U.S. forces in, for example, the Seminole War and the Civil War had used waterways to facilitate military operations, why could we not create special units equipped to utilize the extensive waterways of the Delta to get at the Viet Cong?

As planning proceeded on what eventually came to be known as the Mobile Riverine Force, I proposed to experiment with American forces among the dense population of the Delta by putting a battalion in populous Long An province, the closest of the Delta provinces to Saigon (although not actually in the IV Corps Zone). Long An was a province that Ambassador Lodge had long seen as pivotal: it was, the ambassador was inclined to remark, like Maine—"As Maine goes, so goes the nation." Since South Vietnamese leaders had long recognized that the presence of American troops put backbone into the ARVN units, they raised no objections; indeed, the local commander wanted not just a battalion of U.S. troops but a brigade of them. In adjacent Hau Nghia province, not properly a part of the Delta but with many similar characteristics, troops of the 25th Division through their operations against the VC and their civic action projects had had a remarkable impact on the ARVN garrison and the people. Yet several in the U. S. Mission were wary—Ambassador Lodge's deputy, William Porter, in particular, lest American troops upset the economic and social fabric of the province.

Since the Long An experiment would be a military move, it fell fully within my charge, yet in keeping with my usual practice, I made a point of keeping the Mission Council informed. I brought the 25th Division commander, Major General Frederick C. Weyand, and members of his staff to Saigon to brief the council on their experience in Hau Nghia. A tall, angular man with a sincere countenance, Fred Weyand on a briefing platform invited confidence. That he and his staff had explored every facet of their subject was quickly obvious. Most members of the council departed if not convinced they had thought up the idea of putting American troops in the Delta provinces themselves, then wishing that they had.

As the performance of the battalion in Long An met all expectations, plans proceeded for introducing an American division into the IV Corps Zone: the 9th Infantry Division, commanded by Major General George S. Eckhardt, my old World War II outfit that I had made a point of greeting when the men came ashore at Vung Tau. One brigade was to operate temporarily from a base camp east of Saigon called Bear Cat (another American attempt at inventing Vietnamese words). Another with the division headquarters was to be located in the northern Mekong Delta near My Tho, the capital of Dinh Tuong province, at a base to be created by dredging sand from the My Tho River, an arm of the Mekong. The third brigade was to be the Riverine Force, housed aboard barracks ships and barges of the U. S. Navy, capable of pulling up anchor and moving or being towed to other parts of the Delta. Planners from both my staff and U. S. Navy headquarters in Washington displayed impressive imagination on this project. Captain Welch trained and commanded the Navy component while Colonel William Fulton did the same for the Army brigade.

The base on the river was in itself a notable achievement. Rice paddies were excavated to provide a basin for river craft, while hydraulic dredges sucked up sand from the river bottom to fill in a square mile (640 acres) of inundated paddy. VC sappers sank one of the dredges in early January 1967, and during salvage operations, it ran into heavy seas off the coast and went down in deep water. Before all work was completed two years later, VC sappers had sunk two smaller dredges, and a third was destroyed when it inhaled live ordnance from the river bottom and blew up. For all those mishaps, Seabees and Army engineers created an island of sand that in the dry season was one of the dustiest places on earth, but it served the purpose. After consultation with my counterpart, General Vien, I personally chose the name for the base to symbolize American and South Vietnamese cooperation: "Dong Tam," which in Vietnamese means "united hearts and minds."

The Riverine Force quickly proved its worth. From the barracks ships, troops would go on operations to seek out the enemy in U. S. Navy armored troop-carrier boats, preceded by minesweeping craft and escorted by armored boats called "Monitors." Upon reaching the objective, the men would debark under the protective fire of machine guns, 40-mm guns, and 81-mm mortars mounted on the river craft. U. S. Army 105-mm howitzers on special artillery barges provided support. Iron grillwork around the boats provided protection against enemy rockets, causing them to detonate before hitting the body of the craft. Since the troops, like those in the Rung Sat, were in and out of water all day, they had to be rotated every two to three days to allow them to dry out, else "immersion foot" would become a major problem.

In the first year—1967—the Riverine Force engaged in five major actions and destroyed over a thousand VC. As operations began, ambushes from shore with the enemy using rockets and recoilless rifles were common, and the enemy was often encountered in battalion strength. As time passed, a sharp decrease both in the number of ambushes and the size of enemy forces attested to the success achieved. Sections of the Delta long given over to the VC were by the end of 1968 readily accessible.

Chapter XII
Pains of Nation-building

During Secretary McNamara's visit to Saigon in the fall of 1966, he told me he thought it inevitable that I would eventually be made responsible for pacification. President Johnson, he said, was aware of how fragmented the program was, how little executive and managerial ability the Embassy was devoting to it. Another visitor in October, Professor Henry Kissinger of Harvard University, apparently on a general fact-finding mission for the President, said much the same.

Ambassador Taylor's creation of the Mission Council in 1964 had lessened some of the fragmentation for a while, but as time went on the various American agencies slipped back into their old separate ways. As the American military effort expanded, so did programs managed by AID, CIA, and USIA, so that in time all agencies were competing for resources and scarce South Vietnamese manpower. Each agency still had its separate chain of command extending down into the provinces and its separate contact with its parent organization in Washington, where, as in Saigon, no one agency or person other than an overburdened President was pulling everything together.

As rumors spread that a change in pacification organization might be forthcoming, I made no pitch for the job lest I exacerbate already existing jealousies. I had always deplored the friction between the Army and the Navy in the Pacific during World War II and, on occasion, factionalism in the Pentagon. The very logic of the military's handling pacification, I believed, would eventually sell itself. The military had the necessary managerial experience and through senior officers and advisers had a rapport with the South Vietnamese military leadership and a mutual confidence born of a common military outlook that was hardly to be duplicated by American civilian officials. Also, military operations were an integral part of pacification, in that the final objective of all operations was to enable pacification to proceed. To be prepared when the time came, I quietly put a special staff group to work developing my ideas of a proper organization to handle the assignment.

Ambassador Lodge wanted no shift in pacification responsibility. It was not a problem of organization, he told Washington; it was a problem of security. Little could be done, he said, "economically, socially, psychologically, and politically for the 'hearts and minds' of men, if these men have knives sticking into their collective bellies." The ambassador was falling back on a long-standing disagreement with my so-called big-unit war and wanted the bulk of American troops assigned in support of pacification. Despite my numerous talks with the ambassador on the subject, it was near the end of his second tour before he finally agreed with me that there could be no security so long as the enemy's big units were free to strike when and where they chose.

The South Vietnamese were ahead of us in organization for pacification. Following the meeting in February 1966 with President Johnson in Honolulu, Thieu and Ky had renamed the pacification program, calling it "Revolutionary Development," which had appeal for the South Vietnamese in that it meant change in the social structure, and establishing a Ministry of Revolutionary Development to co-ordinate the pacification activities of all governmental agencies. A special school at Vung Tau trained fifty-nine-man Revolutionary Development (RD) teams which would move into a village, get governmental programs started, then eventually move on to another village. Some of the more imaginative work done in pacification was by the American adviser at that school, Major Jean A. Sauvageot, who worked hard to inculcate missionary zeal in the RD teams.

Ambassador Lodge attempted his own reorganization for pacification by calling on a former Air Force officer who had worked with the Filipinos during the Huk rebellion of the late 1940s and early 1950s, Edward G. Lansdale. Yet Lansdale's was an *ad hoc* staff with no institutionalization, and Lansdale himself, much to the disapproval of the Embassy's political counselor, Phil Habib, found it difficult to keep out of the South Vietnamese political scene. President Johnson then forced upon a reluctant Lodge the assignment of his deputy, Bill Porter, to head pacification, but Porter saw his job as one of co-ordination rather than directorship and found it impossible to strip the American civilian agencies of their independence.

Part of the pressure from Washington was attributable to the President's having assigned, following the Honolulu conference, one of his deputy special assistants to supervise pacification from the White House. Swinging his White House authority with abandon, this assistant, Robert Komer—"Blowtorch," Ambassador Lodge nicknamed him—began to prod the Embassy and the parent agencies in Washington relentlessly and abrasively. Bob Komer, I learned later, saw MACV as the answer to pacification, to which Secretary McNamara agreed and offered to lend the weight of his office to fighting the bureaucratic battle to get the shift of responsibility from the Embassy to the military.

The Embassy and the civilian agencies resisted with the tenacity of a cockleburr in a horse's tail, but President Johnson was determined to get results. In November 1966 he directed Ambassador Lodge to reorganize the U. S. Mission for pacification and put one man in charge. The President was giving the civilian agencies ninety days in which to make pacification work. If they failed, I was to get the job.

I promptly upgraded a staff section in my headquarters that had been handling support for pacification to become the MACV Revolutionary Development Support Directorate and put a brilliant young brigadier general in charge, William Knowlton. After a two-week delay ended by a prod from Washington, Ambassador Lodge created the Office of Civil Operations, or OCO, with Bill Porter in charge.

I felt sorry for Deputy Ambassador Porter. A frank, capable man with whom I shared a close and open relationship, he had to assume an impossible position. I gave him all help that I could, including assigning him, as military deputy, a polished staff officer who had commanded the 173d Airborne Brigade, Brigadier General Paul Smith. Yet the President obviously was going to dissolve OCO after ninety days. OCO was but a sop to the prideful creatures in the bureaucratic jungles of Washington and Saigon.

Because Bill Porter remained the deputy ambassador with the duties that job entailed, Washington was unhappy with Lodge's arrangement. Yet Lodge resisted assignment of a second deputy until Porter himself decided that one man had to devote full time to OCO. For that job Lodge chose L. Wade Lathram, who had been serving in Saigon as deputy director of AID.

Wade Lathram and OCO made an honest effort. At long last every civilian operation at province and corps level was placed under one man who was responsible up the chain of command to Lathram. At long last, too, civilian directors in Saigon dealing with pacification were located in one headquarters with the benefit of daily contact with each other. Yet the separate agencies continued to provide funds for their own programs, so that Lathram was hard put to transfer funds and resources from one program to another. OCO was working, but it would take longer than ninety days for it to achieve what President Johnson expected of it.

When Secretary McNamara told me in 1966 I was likely to get the pacification assignment, he intimated that I might receive even more responsibility, but he failed to elaborate. In mid-February 1967, after Ambassador Lodge had revealed a wish to retire, McNamara began to talk with the President about my assuming control of all American operations in Vietnam— civil and military—in the manner of General MacArthur in Japan. Whether there would have been an ambassador as well under such an arrangement was unclear. Then in late February McNamara specifically recommended to the President that I succeed Lodge.

The advantages of the arrangement in centralized control should have been obvious to all. Yet even as the discussion proceeded in Washington,

OCO officials in Saigon, on the theory of advancing pacification in certain areas, were trying to gain an official say in troop dispositions, which in view of the enemy's continuing buildup I simply could not accept. A military man in charge of civilian programs as well as military operations could integrate the two. In response to specific queries from General Wheeler, I suggested that if the President chose to name me ambassador, I should also have the title of Commander in Chief, U. S. Forces, Vietnam. I proposed three deputies: one for political affairs, one for economic and national planning matters, and one for military operations, the latter to have the title of COMUS-MACV and bear responsibility for all field operations. General Wheeler and Secretary McNamara were already discussing a military deputy and had in mind the current Vice Chief of Staff of the Army, General Creighton Abrams. That choice would have been infinitely acceptable to me.

Just after the first week of March, General Wheeler informed me that the President had turned away from the proposal, presumably swayed by Secretary of State Rusk, who apparently professed no objections to me personally but warned against complete militarization of the American effort. The President presumably was to decide what was to be done to integrate the civilian and military programs later in the month at a high-level conference on the island of Guam. He gave away the cast of characters but not the plot when in a public address a few days before the conference he announced that a diplomat who had had an earlier career as a successful businessman, Ellsworth Bunker, was to succeed Lodge. The current ambassador to Pakistan, an old Texas friend of the President, Eugene Locke, was to be his deputy. To head the pacification program, he named Robert Komer.

As the first order of business at Guam on March 20, President Johnson addressed assembled American airmen at Anderson Air Force Base. Because it was raining, the local host for the conference, Major General William Crumm, who headed the B-52 force on Guam, held an umbrella over the President's head. Watching handsome Bill Crumm, commander of the 3d Strategic Air Division, standing there like a statue, an impish thought passed through my head: one of the first things a young officer learned in the old Army was that an officer in uniform never pushes a baby carriage, never carries a large bundle under an arm, and never holds an umbrella. Nobody apparently had ever contemplated the situation in which Bill Crumm found himself.

Some of the arrangements for the conference were makeshift. Because the post guest house was small, many of the conferees had to stay in private residences vacated by their owners; I occupied the quarters of an Air Force major. Meetings were in the officers' club. From the building one could see the vast runway for B-52s stretching toward the ocean and out on the water beyond the runway a Russian trawler at anchor, presumably reporting to somebody every time a B-52 took off.

The new cast of characters—Bunker, Locke, Komer—was on hand, affording an opportunity for becoming acquainted with the South Vietnamese leaders who were attending the conference: Thieu, Ky, and others. In the course of the conference, Secretary McNamara talked to me about a four-star deputy who might take over when my tenure came to an end. We agreed that Creighton Abrams was the man. I told the President and McNamara that General Abrams' primary assignment would be to work with the South Vietnamese to move their armed forces toward self-sufficiency, much the same assignment that Johnny Heintges had been pursuing.

During the conference, I provided the group with a frank review of the military situation, including my assessment of the advantage the enemy gained from pauses in the bombing of North Vietnam. Concluding my remarks, I said that if the Viet Cong organization failed to disintegrate, which I saw as unlikely, and we were unable to find a way to halt North Vietnamese infiltration, the war could go on indefinitely. As I sat down, my audience was painfully silent. On the faces of many of the Washington officials, who had obviously been hoping for some optimistic assessment, were looks of shock. John McNaughton, in particular, wore an air of disbelief.

Aside from a general review of pacification, military operations, and South Vietnamese governmental programs, the basic subject at Guam was the organization of the U. S. Mission to assure a co-ordinated pacification program. I told the President I wanted to merge OCO and MACV's Revolutionary Development Support Directorate under MACV, with Bob Komer as my civilian deputy to supervise pacification. Having a civilian deputy in a military command was, I recognized, unusual if not unique in American military history. Yet the President by his earlier announcement had already decided that Komer was to be made available to me to assist in pacification, and I saw no solution to the problem of integrating civilian and military programs other than under the aegis of military command. Komer's presence also might salve the sensitivities of those in the U.S. civilian agencies who might resent military control.

On my plane en route back to Saigon and over the next two days, Bob Komer and I worked out a plan to merge OCO and MACV's pacification directorate into a MACV staff section to be headed by Wade Lathram, with General Knowlton as his deputy. It was an unusual arrangement, a civilian heading a military staff section with a general as his deputy, and a similar pattern of organization was to follow down the chain of command. The American side of pacification would have a single manager at each level from Saigon to district with one chain of command and one voice for dealing with the Vietnamese. Who headed the program at each level depended upon the best man available, not whether he was military or civilian.

Upon Komer's return to Washington, he outlined the plan to the President, but the President still delayed final approval. For personal reasons Ambassador Bunker was unable to go immediately to Saigon, and the President wanted the new ambassador to make the announcement of the change in Saigon. He also wanted Komer to orient his successor in Washington, Ambassador William Leonhart, who would keep an eye on pacification from the White House. Not until May 9, five days after Komer and General Abrams had joined the staff in Saigon, did the President formally approve the reorganization. Ambassador Bunker made the public announcement after his arrival in Saigon on April 25.

As my civilian deputy, Komer was to occupy a rung on the command ladder in some ways equivalent to that of General Abrams and was to have the personal rank of ambassador. Yet there was a difference in the two positions: Abrams was my deputy, or second-in-command, in all matters, while Komer was deputy *to* COMUSMACV for one matter only: pacification.

The Lord knows the President handed me a volatile character in Bob Komer. The nickname "Blowtorch" was all too apt.

To serve as a bridge between Komer and the military, which is a nice way of saying to keep Komer out of my hair, I nominated a smart major general who eleven years earlier had been adviser to Big Minh: George Forsythe. Not yet informed of the assignment, General Forsythe was at his desk in Hawaii when he received a telephone call from the White House. It was Komer, whom he had never met. "Hey, George," Komer blared into the telephone, "pack your bag. I'm going out to be Westy's deputy and run the war for him. You're coming along."

Bob Komer well understood that he had a difficult assignment. He could hardly have missed discerning the irritation some members of my staff felt over a civilian in the command structure. We had, some said, a political commissar. Komer was like a grain of sand in an oyster, and like an oyster, the staff set out to encase the irritant; but Komer was not about to be made into a pearl. He blustered, sometimes blundered, knocked heads together, wrote one caustic memorandum after another to any and all on whatever subject, including strategy. He was determined that everybody know he was there and what he was there to do. When an MP at MACV headquarters stopped his car to allow a vehicle with brigadier general's markings to proceed, Komer demanded a license plate with four stars, although he graciously accepted instead a special identification tag. I had to clamp down when I discovered he was using his old White House ties to send communications direct to the President with draft messages that he wanted the President to send back to the ambassador and me. I also had to convince him to be tactful with the Vietnamese, to speak bluntly only in private lest they lose face with their colleagues.

Yet Bob Komer was the man for the job. He pushed himself and his people hard. He had imaginative ideas, usually sound. Striped pants might work later, but at the start, abrasion was in order and Bob Komer worked overtime at that.

The new organization, which superseded OCO, was known as CORDS, for Civil Operations and Revolutionary Development Support. Because I recognized that pacification was a key to success, I gave CORDS my full support, on occasion surprising some of my military colleagues by overruling them on some matter involving resources, people, or responsibility in favor of Komer. I gave Komer high priority, for example, on the best officers, suggesting such men as Bob Montague, whom I had called on back in 1964 to get HOP TAC going. Because the pacification program had to have adequate military protection, I gave CORDS advisory responsibility for the militia—the Regional and Popular Forces—that had the assignment of local security. I also gave CORDS advisory responsibility for PHOENIX, a project aimed at identifying and excising the VC political infrastructure and run by the South Vietnamese primarily under direction of CIA advisers. Komer put PHOENIX together with assistance of William E. Colby, who was destined to succeed Komer and subsequently to be director of the CIA in Washington. If the guerrilla was to be divested of support from the people, the political control had to be neutralized.

To try to eliminate overoptimistic reporting on pacification, CORDS developed a new method known as the "hamlet evaluation system," or HES. In no way foolproof, the method nevertheless was an improvement in our continuing search for objective evaluation of a nebulous matter.

To provide further support for pacification, I convinced the South Vietnamese Joint General Staff to begin special training for all ARVN battalions and put the bulk of them on pacification duty That took considerable persuasion because most ARVN leaders saw fighting the enemy's big units as a more glamorous assignment. To counter the tendency of tactical training to deteriorate over long periods on pacification duty, refresher training teams went from unit to unit.

I also encouraged further experimentation with American units working with the ARVN. At a pineapple plantation west of Saigon, long given over to the VC, a company each of Americans and Vietnamese manned a fire-support and patrol base together. I pressed for countrywide adoption of a tactic first developed by U.S. marines, called "County Fair," which essentially drew a cordon around a village and maintained it for several days, meanwhile providing medical support for the people and giving the occasion a festive air with entertainers and government spokesmen. The police checked identity cards and searched the village to weed out VC guerrillas and infrastructure.

Another experiment was to attach a battalion of Vietnamese field police to an American division. Of marked success with the Regional and Popular Forces were training teams composed of an ARVN officer, an American officer, and three other American soldiers, all combat veterans, that lived with the small militia units for a month or more, then moved on to another unit. It was an adaptation of the Combined Action Platoons used by the U.S. marines but it made less demand on American manpower and was without permanent attachment to a Vietnamese hamlet

A cardinal principle in pursuing pacification was that it was primarily a South Vietnamese task. The Americans could only help with advice and resources. The goal was to provide the people with security, social justice, education, medical care, and economic opportunity, and in the long run only the South Vietnamese government could achieve that.

As additional men and resources poured into pacification, we abandoned the old spreading-oil concept, concentrating instead on localities where the VC were weakest, little islands of security that might grow and eventually merge. It was a slow process, always difficult to measure, but at long last pacification had the proper organization for making progress. Within a year dramatic improvements were to become apparent.

Soon after Ambassador Bunker's arrival, as political speculation over Vietnamese presidential and vice-presidential elections in September mounted, he asked me, in view of my long association with Chief of State Thieu, to act as the principal contact between Thieu and the U. S. Mission. As were others in the Embassy, the newly appointed ambassador was concerned lest conflict between Thieu and Ky over who was to run for President should bring political strife to Saigon again.

From the first I liked and respected Ellsworth Bunker. At our introductory meeting he asked that I call him by his first name, which I agreed to do but only in private. Seventy-three years of age at the time, Ambassador Bunker was an unflappable man who appeared to thrive in Saigon's sweltering heat and under crisis conditions, which he had already experienced many times in diplomatic assignments in such places as Brazil, Indonesia, and the Dominican Republic, the last in company with the deputy commander of the United States Army, Vietnam, Lieutenant General Bruce Palmer, Jr. Bunker was married to another diplomat, Carol C. Laise, U.S. ambassador to Nepal. When introduced at a performance of the Bob Hope troupe, Ambassador Bunker embraced his wife, "the first time in history," said Bob to the delight of the troops, "that two ambassadors have kissed in public."

Tall, white-haired, erect, seemingly aloof—some Vietnamese called him "Mr. Refrigerator"—the ambassador was actually warm and personable, something of a raconteur and a wit. At an Embassy dinner when my wife was visiting Saigon, he leaned over and said with the impertinence of a newlywed: "Kitsy, it's a shame you young people don't know anything about sex."

My military colleagues and I gained a staunch supporter in Ellsworth Bunker. Although his military experience was limited to artillery ROTC at Yale University fifty years before, he understood the application of power. The only way we were going to work ourselves out of a job in South Vietnam, he recognized, was to put more pressure on the enemy, and in messages to the State Department he supported my efforts to obtain approval to go into Laos and Cambodia. For that he got a rap over the knuckles.

When I began to discuss the upcoming elections with Thieu, he had no plans to run either for President or Vice President. I talked with him first on the subject in early May in his Spartan quarters at Tan Son Nhut, with his children running in and out. Although Thieu assumed Ky would run, he preferred a strong civilian candidate whom both the people and the armed forces trusted. He himself wanted only to make sure that he controlled the armed forces, which as Chief of State he did at the time. To that I agreed fully and so told him. It was hard to imagine the South Vietnamese armed forces without the capable and practical Thieu in a senior position of authority.

By urging Thieu to retain control of the armed forces, I unwittingly encouraged his running for President, for when the new constitution was promulgated, the President, like the American Chief Executive, was also to be Commander in Chief. With no strong civilian candidate available and Ky appearing to be the likely winner, Thieu became concerned lest Ky fail to retain him in a position of authority. Indeed, Thieu was concerned lest Ky as President prove unable to hold the armed forces together.

Thieu was honest and candid with me; I know of no case in which he tried to deceive me. The election process was still so rudimentary to the Vietnamese, he told me, that he saw no possibility of a strong political party emerging for a long time, and even if one did, he doubted the efficacy of civilian leadership in fighting the Viet Cong. Thieu liked Ky, yet he recognized, as I did, that Ky was impressionable, impulsive. Thieu on the other hand was a master of timing. He was patient, cautious, willing to take his time to block out his moves in advance behind the scenes, a deft handler of the leaders of the religious and sectional factions, although his caution was destined later to bring about his downfall.

Thieu and Ky both appeared to realize that if both ran for President they would split the vote that was favorable to a military candidate, possibly throwing the election to some minority figure. Contrary to rumors and numerous press reports, both assured me that there were no sharp differences between them, least of all to the extent of a feud, as the American press was reporting, apparently on the basis of speculation by some lower level officials of the American Embassy. Ky's impishness may have contributed to the speculation. It amused Ky, for example, to park his helicopter on the pad that he and Thieu both used so as to leave no room for Thieu's helicopter. If there were deep-seated differences between them, both men controlled themselves admirably.

Although Ambassador Bunker's policy was to avoid interference with the elections, he and other members of the U. S. Mission privately banked on Ky. The flamboyance and impetuosity that many had seen earlier as a drawback, most had by that time come to regard as "charisma." The South Vietnamese ambassador to the United States, Bui Diem, visiting Saigon and in close touch with the American Embassy, favored Ky, and his reports reinforced the view that Ky was the more suitable candidate. Meanwhile, rumor had it that first Ky, then Thieu, planned to engineer the return of Big Minh from exile in Thailand so that he could stand for President with either Thieu or Ky—however the story went at the time—running on the same ticket as Vice President.

I was alone among officials of the U. S. Mission in favoring Thieu over

Ky. I had watched Thieu progress through the years, as a division commander, chief of staff of the Joint General Staff, corps commander, Minister of Defense, then Chief of State and chairman of the Military Council. Although the Chief of State in those days was less visible than the Premier, Thieu as chairman of the Military Council wielded the real power, a fact even the ambassador apparently failed to appreciate. Among all possible candidates I saw Nguyen Van Thieu as the real hope for the country.

The Military Council met during the last three days of June to decide which of the two was to run. Although I was aware of the purpose of the meetings and that the sessions were long and emotional, extending far into the night, only after they were over was I able to piece together what happened.

Late in the evening of the second day, I learned, the generals concluded tentatively that Ky was to be their candidate for President with assurance that if he won, he would install Thieu as head of the armed forces. The generals were to sleep on the decision and confirm it the next morning.

At that next session Thieu electrified the others with the announcement that he had changed his mind. Rather than withdraw as a candidate, he said, he would resign his commission and run as a civilian.

That threw the council into turmoil. Nobody could live with such an arrangement. The corps commanders, in particular, were upset, each avowing in turn that under those circumstances, they would be unable to guarantee holding the armed forces together. Unlike the old days when *coup d'état* followed *coup d'état,* the generals were determined to maintain unity.

As both Thieu and Ky maintained their determination to run, tension mounted. It was late in the day when Ky finally broke the impasse. He would, he said, withdraw as a candidate and return to the Air Force.

That, surprisingly, was unacceptable to Thieu. He was happy only when Ky agreed to run on the same ticket as Vice President.

Of eighteen presidential and vice-presidential slates filed, the Constituent Assembly rejected seven on technicalities. Most of the seven were minor, little known candidates except for Big Minh, whose supporters entered his name despite his continuing exile. That left eleven. Slates were also filed for election of a sixty-member Senate at the same time as the President and Vice President.

Thieu and Ky rejected demands from some members of the Constituent Assembly and other candidates that because they were civil servants and would have an advantage as incumbents, they should resign their positions as Chief of State and Premier in advance of the campaign. Aware that incumbents in the United States conduct their campaigns while in office, an American could hardly take exception when Thieu and Ky declined to do so.

Having arrived at that decision, Thieu and Ky made every effort to run the machinery of the campaign and the election fairly. They lifted press censorship. At Thieu's urging, the Joint General Staff directed members of the armed forces to abstain from campaigning for him and Ky and to vote as individuals, not as a bloc. The Minister of Revolutionary Development directed the same for his pacification teams. Thieu and Ky called in province and district chiefs to direct that officials exert no pressure for any specific candidate. The government provided all candidates equal funds for campaigning, printed their posters and leaflets, provided transportation, arranged joint campaign appearances, and provided free radio and television time. To observe the elections, the government extended invitations to the United Nations, to all governments having diplomatic representation in Saigon, and to the international press.

For all those efforts, criticism and charges of unfairness were widespread, particularly by American newsmen. Investigating the allegations, Ambassador Bunker concluded that they were based on rumors, misquotation, and acceptance of statements by opposition candidates that anywhere else would have been dismissed as self-serving. Critics also tended to measure the campaign against perfection, something few long-existing democracies, including the United States, can claim.

When newsmen reported that if a civilian slate won, Ky would stage a *coup d'état,* the Ambassador asked me to investigate. I found no factual basis for the report. Ky himself denied it publicly and categorically. A number of other candidates, he told me, were trying to promote a split between him and Thieu. Thieu could be irritating; he had, for example, refused to permit Ky to appear with him on the American TV program "Face the Nation"; but Ky was determined to stick with him. An intoxicated American, Ky told me, had telephoned from New Mexico to urge that he stage a *coup d'état,* to which Ky had replied that those days were over in Vietnam.

At President Johnson's invitation, twenty prominent Americans from a variety of professions flew to Vietnam to observe the last few days of the campaign and the election. Because of a shortage of guest facilities, individual members of the U. S. Mission agreed to handle the housing and feeding of the American visitors. I was able to have two as my house guests: Governor Richard Hughes of New Jersey and Senator George Murphy of California, both of whom I found to be delightful companions. Senator Murphy in particular impressed me as an astute observer and a keen wit. It was a pleasure, too, to see again Henry Cabot Lodge, who accompanied the group.

Despite the usual VC country-wide terrorism—49 civilians killed, 204 wounded—the elections on Sunday, September 3, brought out 83 per cent of close to 6 million registered voters. The only serious difficulties were at three polling places in Quang Tri province, which terrorist attacks prevented from opening. The Thieu-Ky slate gained a plurality of 34.8 per cent. An avowed peace candidate, Truong Dinh Dzu, who had campaigned with a white dove as a symbol and advocated stopping the bombing of North Vietnam and VC areas and negotiating unconditionally with the enemy, was a surprising second with 17 per cent of the vote. There were unconfirmed rumors that peace groups in France and the United States had provided funds for Dzu's campaign.

The American observers and most of the foreign press agreed that the elections were free and fair. "These were clean elections," said Governor Hughes. It was, said the Reverend Edward L. R. Elson of Washington, D.C., later chaplain of the United States Senate, "a noble political exercise."

Yet carping continued, based mainly on the fact that no slate had won a majority. In a field of eleven slates, was that to be expected? Those Americans who criticized apparently forgot that they themselves have on occasion been ruled by minority governments. To one critic who avowed that the elections were rigged, Ky responded that if he had bothered to rig them, he would have made sure he got a bigger vote.

I myself found the elections a remarkable achievement, a culmination of the pledge Thieu and Ky had made to President Johnson at Honolulu early in 1966. Ky summarized the achievement well when he wrote the presiding officers of the U. S. Senate and House of Representatives:

> I take special pride in the fact that we have successfully started the course toward democracy and equality for a society which was imprisoned within the deep walls of feudalism, corruption, and intolerable social discrepancies. In spite of war, subversion, and several grave crises, my government has undertaken to organize five nationwide elections of vital importance within about a year's time: elections for the Constituent Assembly in September, 1966; elections for Hamlet and Village administration in April–May, 1967; Presidential and Senatorial elections in September; and elections for the Lower House in October. I do not know of any better way to warrant our determination to stay the course toward democracy.

Vice President Hubert Humphrey represented the United States at inaugural ceremonies on October 31. The administering of the oaths of office went without incident, but that evening during a reception inside Independence Palace, four rounds from 60-mm mortars that the VC had sneaked into the city inside a log exploded on the grounds, wounding the Vietnamese chauffeur of the commander of Australian forces, Major General Douglas Vincent. In the firing, one of the mortars blew up, killing a VC and several civilians in the vicinity. Those at the reception were unaware of the firing, although I did hear a few popping noises over the hum of conversation and a security officer later passed me a handwritten note telling what had happened.

Encouraged by progress in military operations and hopeful that the new arrangement under CORDS would speed pacification, I began in midyear of 1967 to put increased emphasis on upgrading the South Vietnamese armed forces with the goal of their assuming responsibility for more and more of the war. That involved expanding all the components, including the militia, which would mean more conscription, more equipment, and a more comprehensive training program.

When President Johnson decided in July of 1967 to limit further input of American troops, that made the project all the more important. Nor was it by coincidence that the renewed emphasis to upgrade the South Vietnamese forces began soon after the arrival of General Abrams to be my new deputy.

Abe was one of the U. S. Army's most experienced, capable, and admired leaders. Although newsmen often wrote that he had a "rough exterior," that was deceiving. Of a stocky build, often chewing on a cigar, he may have looked the part of a field soldier, which his record showed that he was, but he was generally soft-spoken, tactful, and polite, a devotee of gourmet food and classical music. His only characteristic that disturbed me was a tendency to erupt like a volcano, face crimson, fist pounding the table. So quickly would he regain his composure that I came to believe his outbursts were nothing more than a pose. Never can I recall after Abe's arrival making any decision over his disagreement. He was exceptionally well qualified to assist in the continuing task of upgrading the South Vietnamese armed forces.

The close association of American and ARVN units was part of the program, as, for example, in Operation FAIRFAX and mobile assistance training teams. At least one ARVN battalion participated in every large American operation, learning such techniques as fire control and use of tactical air support. Under a "buddy" concept, the 1st and 25th U. S. Infantry divisions began to execute joint operations with ARVN divisions serving in their vicinity, and other units took up the practice. I added 3,000 more American advisers to work with the ARVN and the militia.

Upgrading the militia—the Regional and Popular Forces—was also an integral part of the program. At my urging the South Vietnamese increased militia strength by 50,000 men. In the long run the militia would have to provide local security for pacification while the ARVN took over the war against the big units, for without the militia the ARVN would end up tied down in static defense.

However vital, improving the armament available to the ARVN was a slow process. Under the President's policy of guns and butter—but mainly butter—M-16 rifles, machine guns, mortars, radios, trucks, recoilless rifles, artillery pieces, all were hard to get. Not until well into 1968 would new items be available in any quantity for other than American troops. Only as 1967 neared an end did sizable shipments of M-16s for the South Vietnamese begin to arrive. I gave the first ones to the airborne and marines, which constituted the general reserves, and to the 5th Ranger Group for the protection of Saigon. I then assigned priority on all new equipment to the 1st ARVN Division to enable that division to provide more help to the U.S. marines in the northern provinces. Starting in November 1967, the 1st ARVN Division began to take over some of the positions in the strongpoint obstacle system below the DMZ. During the year U. S. Army Special

Forces advisers withdrew from a number of CIDG-Special Forces camps, leaving them entirely to the Vietnamese.

Those were important steps, but I was convinced that never would the South Vietnamese be able to assume responsibility for everything until they ordered a general mobilization. I had first urged that in 1966 but received little backup from the American Embassy, where Ambassador Lodge was apparently concerned about the effect of total mobilization on the country's shaky economy. I again pressed for it in mid-1967, this time with Ambassador Bunker's support.

Because of economic considerations and because of the limited numbers of American weapons and equipment available for the South Vietnamese, ARVN strength would be frozen at about 650,000 men, but under existing draft laws, actual strength was always below that. General mobilization as I envisioned it would make eighteen- and nineteen-year-olds available for service and would give the government full control of manpower and material resources. If the American people could see that the South Vietnamese were doing everything in their power to help themselves, sending additional American troops would be more acceptable.

Although both Thieu and Ky agreed that they needed general mobilization, they doubted that their government had the popular support to achieve it. They finally promulgated a mobilization decree in October 1967, but did nothing to implement it. As it turned out, mobilization would have to wait until the enemy shocked the government and the people into action.

Chapter XIII
On Public View

In the spring of 1966 Secretary McNamara had notified me that President Johnson was considering asking me to return to the United States to address the annual luncheon of executives of the Associated Press in New York. Questioning the propriety of returning for public appearances while the war continued, I balked. It was with reluctance that later in the year I went to the President's Texas ranch, but that involved no public appearance other than a single press conference, similar to those I held from time to time in Saigon and Hawaii. When Secretary McNamara supported my resistance to the New York speech, the President dropped the idea.

Not so the following year. The President sent word he wanted me to make the address at the press association's luncheon at the Waldorf-Astoria Hotel on April 24. This time he afforded no opportunity for me to express an opinion.

For all my reluctance, I appreciated the President's desire to keep the American people informed, particularly in view of manifold misinformation disseminated by antiwar activists. By providing a sober, authoritative explanation of the American role in Vietnam, I reasoned, I might contribute to thwarting North Vietnamese efforts to weaken American resolve. In any event, my Commander in Chief had ordered the job done.

As I prepared to return, the President made no suggestion as to what I was to say. The closest he ever came to that was in passing word on occasion through General Wheeler that he would welcome my stressing certain matters in my Saigon press conferences should I feel so inclined. In late February 1967, for example, in anticipation of a speech by Senator Robert F. Kennedy calling for another bombing halt, the President suggested that I might wish to express my views in advance.

In every case, including the inadvisability of a bombing halt, I believed in what I said, so that no compromise of my integrity was involved. A military commander surely has a right, even a duty, to speak out in support of national policy; it is when he seeks to alter that policy through public statements rather than through the chain of command, as MacArthur did in Korea, that he gets out of bounds. It was particularly easy to give my views on a bombing halt, for Senator Kennedy wanted to stop the bombing for a week and, if that failed to prompt the North Vietnamese to negotiate, to continue the halt indefinitely. If the stubborn mule refuses to eat one carrot, keep rewarding him with another, and another, and another.

To afford a chance to adjust to the time change between Saigon and New York, I went first to West Point, where I rested and spoke informally one evening to the cadets, then drove with Kitsy and my daughter Stevie to New York. Before the luncheon antiwar demonstrators outside the Waldorf set out to burn two effigies of me, but to their apparent chagrin, one failed to ignite. It was nevertheless sobering to see a representation of oneself go up in flames. Just a few weeks before when visiting a friend at Harvard University, Stevie had been attracted to what she took to be a campus bonfire, only to find it was her father being burned in effigy. Stevie did not tell me of the incident until several years later.

(Stevie sometimes displayed a maturity beyond her years. Invited to be queen of the annual Apple Festival in Winchester, Virginia, for example, she summarily declined. While her father was commanding American troops in a war that was for many Americans traumatic, she considered it inappropriate for her to engage in public frivolity.)

In my remarks at the Waldorf luncheon to the press association executives, I stressed the North Vietnamese support of the insurgency, the participation of North Vietnamese troops, the enemy's policy of terrorism and murder, our efforts to avoid civilian casualties, the courage of the South Vietnamese, the inspiring example of the American soldier. "Although the military picture is favorable . . . ," I said, "the end is not in sight." On that I elaborated later in response to a question: "It's going to be a question of putting maximum pressure on the enemy anywhere and everywhere we can. We will have to grind him down. In effect, we are fighting a war of attrition, and the only alternative is a war of annihilation . . ."

The military campaign, I noted in my formal remarks, was from the enemy's point of view only part of a protracted and carefully co-ordinated attack he was waging in the international arena, where, regrettably, I saw signs of success. "Through a clever combination of psychological and political warfare," I said, the enemy had gained world-wide public support "which gives him hope that he can win politically that which he cannot accomplish militarily." That, I noted, would inevitably cost lives.

Reflecting on a recent public burning of an American flag in Central Park, I decided to add an afterthought, not in my prepared text. Americans fighting in Vietnam, I said, were "dismayed, and so am I, by recent unpatriotic acts here at home."

Almost without exception, that last remark was the one that newsmen and critics stressed. The lead paragraph in the report of the speech in the

Washington *Post,* for example, read: "General William C. Westmoreland
. . . said today that antiwar protests in this country are encouraging the
enemy and costing American lives." A writer in the Washington *Evening
Star* said that I "lashed out at antiwar demonstrators." Senator Thruston B.
Morton of Kentucky said my use of the term "unpatriotic acts" without
differentiating between flag- and draft-card burners and legitimate acts of
dissent only added fuel to the controversy over the war. Although I subsequently said during a press conference in Saigon that I had no objection to
legitimate dissent, I doubt if I made any impression on ears that had no wish
to hear.

That afternoon in New York I continued my luncheon remarks in a
speech before the Council on Foreign Relations, noting with pleasure two in
the audience who had held key positions dealing with United States policy in
Vietnam, McGeorge Bundy and Mike Forrestal. Emphasizing the multiple
facets of the war—political, sociological, psychological, economic, and military—I concluded that the war was fundamentally political. Taking some
liberty with Clausewitz, I said, "War is an extension of politics, but politics
is also an extension of war."

Kitsy and I flew that evening to South Carolina to visit my mother and
sister in Columbia, where I accepted Governor Robert McNair's invitation
to address the South Carolina General Assembly and had the pleasure of escorting my aged mother into the chamber. I took the occasion to praise
South Carolinians serving in Vietnam and made the point that the black soldier had served "with distinction equal to his white comrades in arms." That
may seem an innocuous statement now that time has passed and change has
occurred, but in a chamber where I saw not a single black face except those
of the janitors standing in the rear, the words must have jolted some listeners.

That afternoon the University of South Carolina awarded me an honorary degree. Hardly had I begun my remarks when a young man stood and
shouted in protest. The placard he carried read "Doctor of War." Continuing to speak, I looked directly at him. He quickly retired, apparently less
constrained by my stare than by obvious disapproval of the rest of the audience. The protester, a chemistry instructor, later wrote me to apologize for
any personal affront occasioned by his demonstration.

In the audience was the university's football coach, Paul Dietzel. Follow-
ing the ceremony, we reminisced briefly over my effort to fulfill President
Eisenhower's charge to end the football doldrums at West Point by bringing
Dietzel to coach. The move had excited criticism in some circles at the time
because he left an unexpired contract at Louisiana State University, yet
Dietzel and I had conducted our negotiations with full knowledge and concurrence of LSU's president, Troy Middleton. Unfortunately, even a Paul
Dietzel was unable to overcome the advantage the Navy team enjoyed in
those years with its star quarterback, Roger Staubach.

Flying to Washington on April 26, Kitsy and I were guests of President and Mrs. Johnson in the White House for the night, another of several occasions when we were to be the recipients of their Texas-sized hospitality. At the first chance after arrival in the capital, I telephoned the Pentagon to get speech writers assigned to me, for shortly before leaving Columbia I had learned that the President wanted me to address a joint session of Congress on April 28. I would have no time to draft a speech myself.

The next day, April 27, I met twice with President Johnson in the Cabinet Room of the White House, along with Secretaries McNamara and Rusk, Deputy Secretary of Defense Vance, Undersecretary of State Nicholas Katzenbach, the Chairman of the Joint Chiefs, General Wheeler, and the President's adviser on national security affairs, Walt Rostow.

At issue in both meetings was the possibility of additional American troops for Vietnam. Encouraged by the military gains already achieved in just over a year and a half with relatively small American forces—the equivalent of just over eight American divisions—I saw the possibility, if considerably more American troops could be obtained, of stepping up operations and thereby speeding the end of the American role. I believed it would be worth a limited Reserve call-up, for if the added strength could speed operations, a Reserve call-up would at last be justifiable, particularly if I could get authority for a drive into Laos and possibly Cambodia and for an amphibious hook north of the DMZ. It has long been a proven military principle to reinforce success.

Before coming to Washington, I had submitted two plans for additional American troops beyond a strength of 470,000 already approved for 1967. One plan was for what I called a "minimum essential" force; the other, for an "optimum" force.

The minimum essential force, which I saw as necessary to continue and expand operations within South Vietnam, involved an additional 2⅓ divisions and 5 tactical fighter squadrons, which meant 80,500 additional troops, for a total of 550,500. The optimum force, which I saw as providing an even greater step-up of operations within South Vietnam plus an ability to take the war to the enemy in Laos and Cambodia, involved 4⅓ divisions and 10 tactical fighter squadrons, which with support troops would entail an additional strength of approximately 200,000 men, for a total strength of about 670,000.

In prolonged discussion of the two proposals, I discerned that the President was leaning toward a call-up of Reserves but that Secretary McNamara was reluctant, while nobody other than Walt Rostow expressed much enthusiasm for operations outside South Vietnam. Rostow commented that if additional forces were committed, they should be employed not for the usual operations but to gain some spectacular and visible advantage, as might be realized by an amphibious hook north of the DMZ. In the end it was clear that no decision on additional troops was to be immediately forthcoming.

As the discussion neared a close, Secretary McNamara wrung from me an estimate of how long it would take "to wind down our involvement" under each of my two plans. Assuming that the air war against North Vietnam and in the Laotian panhandle would continue, I said finally: "With the optimum force, about three years; with the minimum force, at least five."

I dislike predictions when dealing with anything as imponderable as war. Yet in retrospect I am struck by the accuracy—however attributable to chance—of the second prediction, for it was almost exactly my minimum force that the President eventually was to approve, and five years later all American troops were destined to be out of Vietnam.

That evening Kitsy and I moved to the home of General and Mrs. Wheeler in Quarters 6 at Fort Myer, the official residence of the Chairman of the Joint Chiefs of Staff. It was near midnight when a dinner with a number of distinguished guests ended and I could retire to my room to study the speech prepared for my delivery the next day, which I had reviewed that afternoon and asked to have revised. I was shocked. In only a few hours I was to go before a joint session of the Congress of the United States, yet the speech writers had failed to understand the changes I had asked them to make.

I had no choice but to rewrite major portions of the speech. The problem was for me to give my men in Vietnam the credit they deserved and to impart to the Congress and the American people the spirit and hope that I deemed necessary for successfully prosecuting the war, while at the same time avoiding an unduly optimistic account.

With Kitsy's help, I set to work. In time she had to give up, but I continued until at last I too was unable to keep my eyes open. I awoke again at 5 A.M. and with more help from a drowsy Kitsy finished the job.

While I dressed, a messenger hurried my final draft to the Pentagon. Typing was underway when I arrived to retrieve the manuscript for a quick rehearsal on a televiewer.

In what some reported as the first address to Congress by a battlefield commander during continuing hostilities, I said that the Allied forces in Vietnam would prevail. In this as in other remarks I consciously avoided using the word "victory," for the national goal was not to win a military victory over North Vietnam. We were instead providing "the shield of security behind which the Republic of Vietnam can develop and prosper." After warning that the enemy believed our Achilles' heel to be our resolve, I paid tribute to the American troops of my command:

> Our soldiers, sailors, airmen, marines, and coast guardsmen in Vietnam are the finest ever fielded by our nation . . . These men understand the conflict and their complex roles as fighters and builders. They believe in what they are doing . . . Backed at home by resolve, confidence, patience, determination, and continued support, we will prevail in Vietnam over Communist aggression.

The cheers and applause that interrupted and followed my address were heart-warming and encouraging. Although I recognized that I received the ovation in the name of the men I commanded, I nevertheless grew embarrassed as it continued. How to conclude it? I turned instinctively and saluted the presiding officers—the President of the Senate, Vice President Humphrey, and the Speaker of the House, Representative John W. McCormack—then repeated my salute to the legislators on both sides of the aisle. As I left the chamber, the applause continued.

Response to my appearance was predictably varied. Many congressmen and senators were laudatory. Others noted with pleasure that I had failed to remark again on dissent, and some questioned the propriety of my addressing the Congress while the war was still on, which, in effect, thrust me into the political arena in support of what was basically a controversial political decision. One of the more persistent critics of the war, Senator J. William Fulbright, chairman of the Senate Foreign Relations Committee, called it "a good speech." "From the military standpoint," he said, "it was fine. The point is the policy that put our boys over there." I subsequently invited Senator Fulbright to visit Vietnam, but he never came.

From the Capitol I went to the White House where the President hosted a luncheon in my honor. Guests included leaders of Congress, most governors, and members of the Cabinet. An old friend of mine and of the American serviceman from as long ago as North Africa in World War II, Miss Martha Raye, had hurried down from New York, where she was appearing on Broadway, to entertain us at the luncheon. Following remarks on the status of diplomatic overtures by Secretary Rusk, the President asked me to speak, which I did extemporaneously, seeking to explain in some detail the nature of the battle.

Later in the afternoon Kitsy and I flew for a brief visit with her parents in Fayetteville, North Carolina, then to Palm Desert, California, to call at President Johnson's request on President and Mrs. Eisenhower. It was a warm, friendly meeting. Showing us a portrait he had painted of his grandson, David, the former President told me that a few days earlier, after a round of golf, Bob Hope had told him he could understand why he was devoting more time to his painting than to his golf. "Fewer strokes," he said.

During the visit General Eisenhower said several times that my task was far more complex and difficult than his assignment in World War II. He had advised President Johnson, he said, to give me the men I needed to finish the job. At a White House meeting with the President and his Cabinet in 1966, General Eisenhower had remarked: "If force is going to do the bidding, you must commit the amount of force necessary to bring the conflict to a successful conclusion." He emphasized the simplicity of the directive he had received over twenty years before from the Combined Chiefs of Staff for the war in Europe: "You will enter the continent of Europe and, in conjunction with the other united nations, undertake operations aimed at the heart of Germany and the destruction of her armed forces."

General Eisenhower told me more than once that he lamented the restrictions Washington was apparently imposing on the conduct of the war in Vietnam.

A few months later, in July, when Secretary McNamara was in Saigon for further discussion of troop strengths and, I hoped, a decision on my request, I received a message telling of the death of my dear mother at the age of eighty-one. She had awakened, asked for a cup of coffee, drank part of it, then closed her eyes as if in sleep. She passed away as she had lived, quietly and serenely.

Kitsy and the children had reached Hawaii on the way back from a visit with my mother and Kitsy's parents, so I joined them there, and we flew together back to Columbia, where the funeral was conducted on July 12. I was gratified by the kindnesses extended to my sister and me by state officials, including the governor, both senators, and several members of the congressional delegation. A dear friend, former Secretary of the Army Robert Stevens, flew in from New York. Also present at the funeral was the man who had started my military career by appointing me to West Point, James F. Byrnes.

In one of the few messages President Johnson ever sent me directly, he offered his condolences and added: "Should be pleased to see you before your return to Saigon." While Kitsy and the children stopped with her parents, I flew up to Washington.

After a lengthy discussion with the National Security Council in the Cabinet Room, the President informed me that he had decided on the lesser of my two troop packages. A major consideration for him quite clearly was to avoid a call-up of Reserves. Opposition to my "optimum" force, which would require a call-up, had started with John McNaughton and Alain Enthoven and had spread to other civilian officials and eventually to Secretary McNamara. In the end even the "minimum essential" force was scaled down sharply, cut almost in half, providing me with just over 47,000 additional troops under a new troop ceiling of 525,000.

I was extremely disappointed, for I knew that failure to provide major troop augmentation would extend the time required to do the job. Yet I understood the pressures weighing on the President, and in submitting the two proposals, I myself had made clear that for the time being I could live with the minimum proposal. When the President at a news conference the next day noted that "we have reached a meeting of the minds" and that the numbers to be sent were "acceptable" to me, I agreed; but I made clear to him privately that I reserved the right to request more troops if required. War is too unpredictable to do otherwise.

President Johnson summoned me home again, along with Ambassador

Bunker, in November 1967, ostensibly for further consultations, but in reality for public relations purposes. Dissent in the press and the Congress was growing. Public antiwar demonstrations were increasing. In October, for example, some 35,000 demonstrators besieged the Pentagon. For a prominent Administration official to set foot on a college campus was perilous, as Secretary McNamara had painfully found out at Harvard University.

En route to Washington I again received an invitation from President Johnson to stay at the White House. Kitsy and Margaret were with me, Rip being in school in Hawaii and Stevie in Massachusetts, although Stevie later joined us for part of our stay. The President and First Lady could hardly have been more gracious. The first night, for example, they insisted that we have guests for dinner in our private upstairs dining room. We invited Kitsy's two brothers, Lieutenant Colonels Edwin and Frederick Van Deusen, and their wives and we all ate upstairs.

The next day, November 16, it was my special pleasure to attend a ceremony in the White House in which the President conferred the Medal of Honor on one of my soldiers, Staff Sergeant Charles B. Morris, who had served with the 173d Airborne Brigade. I had visited Sergeant Morris several times while he was hospitalized for wounds in Vietnam. Despite a serious chest wound, he had knocked out an enemy machine gun, continued to lead his platoon in a blazing fire fight, braved enemy fire to administer to his wounded, and despite a second wound, crawled beyond his platoon's perimeter to knock out another machine gun. A slightly built man, still not fully recovered from his wounds, he stood in the White House tall and proud. When the President invited me to say a few words, I extolled Sergeant Morris as representative of the stalwart American soldiers in Vietnam.

During the first days of my visit, I conferred with Secretary McNamara and General Wheeler and appeared before the Armed Services Committees of the Senate and the House of Representatives. I also taped an interview with Steve Rowan for CBS television. The second evening, November 16, at the President's last minute invitation, I dined with him and all Democratic members of the House of Representatives.

As I was shaving in preparation for the dinner, the President's daughter, Lynda Robb, asked if she could come in and talk. She was disturbed. During the day a reporter had asked her what the President would do if her husband, Chuck, were captured in Vietnam and held as a hostage. It was a cruel question. I tried to ease her concern by pointing out that when Chuck had been a rifle company commander he had been in some jeopardy, but now that he was serving on a regimental staff he was in a much more secure environment. She appeared relieved.

Before the President extended his invitation for dinner, Kitsy and I, at Mrs. Johnson's suggestion, had asked five couples who were close friends to have dinner with us in the upstairs dining room. They included Joe Moore and his wife, Virl—Joe had left Vietnam the preceding summer; Kitsy's godfather, Mike McConihe, and his wife, Margo; Mat and Pat Matheson; Elizabeth and Charles Balthis; and Cecil and Scotty Strong. Most of the ladies were distressed that the invitation had come too late to allow them to get to a hairdresser, but Scotty Strong, whose husband, an artillery officer, had been a close friend of mine since my days at Fort Bragg before World War II, was under the dryer when she got the news. She was exultant, the others envious.

Before dining privately, Mrs. Johnson joined Kitsy and our friends for cocktails. When someone commented on the beautiful decor of the room, she responded: "As with so many other details of this lovely house, we have Mrs. Kennedy to thank for this." No one could have been more gracious.

The dinner with the congressmen over, President Johnson and I joined the group in the upstairs dining room, where, I learned, Margaret—then age twelve—had returned after roaming like an inquisitive fawn through every corner of the White House. The President loosened his tie and slumped on the sofa with his feet on a low table. As he was about to depart, the men insisted on showing him what they had done to Kitsy's and my bedroom. To my surprise and the President's amusement, they had pushed the twin beds in the room together.

The next morning I awakened early to the ringing of a telephone. I reached for the bedside table, but couldn't find it. Sleepy-eyed, I groped about until I finally realized that in pushing the beds together, my friends had put the phone on the floor beneath them. I had no choice but to crawl under the beds groping for the telephone.

The President was on the line. As Kitsy later delighted in telling it, I stammered into the mouthpiece: "Yes, Mr. President. Yes, I'm awake, Mr. President. Not at all, Mr. President. I'll be right down, Mr. President."

The President wanted me to join him for breakfast. Come in your bathrobe, he said.

Breakfast with President Johnson, I soon learned, was a hectic affair. A big, imposing figure, he sat in his bathrobe in bed, facing a battery of three blaring television sets, each tuned to the news on a different network. (There was yet another set strategically positioned in the bathroom.) Aides came and went, bringing messages, asking signatures. Telephones rang incessantly. While the President ate in bed, I sat at his bedside and ate from a tray. Somehow we found an opening here and there for conversation.

On Saturday, November 18, I flew to Pittsburgh to a football game between the Military Academy and the University of Pittsburgh. (In the process I missed a White House meeting with the President and Ambassadors Bunker and Komer, which nobody had told me about.) As I entered the stadium, the Army coach, Tom Cahill, asked me to talk to the team. Thirty-two years before, I told the players in their dressing room, I led the Corps of Cadets into that same stadium, where Army incurred a sound defeat. When I returned as Superintendent, the best Army could gain was a tie. I expected them, I said, to do better. They did. They won.

At President Johnson's invitation, Kitsy and I flew by helicopter that evening to the presidential retreat at Camp David, Maryland, there to join Kitsy's brothers and their wives and her parents, Kay and Van. I had to interrupt my stay the next morning to fly to Washington and appear with Ambassador Bunker on a television show, "Meet the Press," but I returned for the night. No one could know, but it was the last time the Van Deusens were all to be together.

In Washington on Monday, November 20, I called on President and Mrs. Eisenhower, who were at Walter Reed Army Hospital for physical checkups, and that evening Kitsy and I joined the President and Mrs. Johnson for a family dinner, also attended by Senator Richard Russell of Georgia, chairman of the Senate Armed Services Committee. The President dashed off early to put in an appearance at a testimonial dinner for another senator. When he returned, Senator Russell had departed, and he invited me into the family living room where we talked until close to midnight.

Secretary McNamara, the President told me, was leaving the Defense Department to take "a big job." The President expected to appoint Clark Clifford ("a strong man") in his place. Some months later the President was to tell me that he was disappointed in the way Clifford handled the assignment.

The President suddenly became intensely serious. What would my men in Vietnam think, he asked, if he failed to run for re-election in 1968? Would they consider that their Commander in Chief had let them down?

Although taken aback, I responded that if the troops knew why he made such a decision, I was certain they would understand. His health, he said, was "not good," and he was weary. Lady Bird and his two daughters wanted him to retire. They had discussed the possibility of four more years in the White House at length and were against it. Noting that the Constitution made no provision for an invalid president, he alluded to the illnesses of Presidents Woodrow Wilson and Eisenhower.

Those were not the words of a man feeling his way, using his companion as a sounding board before making his decision, as some who would claim to have driven him from the White House would later profess. The President was tired; his wife was tired; he was concerned about his health. He had obviously made up his mind.

The subject, he reminded me tactfully, was "sensitive." I would never mention it, I said, until released by his own public announcement. Kitsy was subsequently as surprised by that announcement as anyone.

Shortly before the President announced his decision by tacking it as a postscript to a television address on March 31, 1968, he asked General Wheeler to telephone me in Saigon and tell me that he was about to act on the subject he had discussed with me in November. Alerted to expect a call, I was at the Embassy listening to the President's talk on a radio when the call came, delayed by difficulty in establishing connections. I was speaking on the telephone with General Wheeler when the President made his announcement.

I have never known a more considerate and thoughtful man than Lyndon B. Johnson.

On Tuesday, November 21, I made my most important public appearance during this visit—an address before the National Press Club in Washington. In that address I permitted myself the most optimistic appraisal of the way the war was going that I had yet made. The enemy, I noted, had not won "a major battle" in more than a year, by which I was referring to his overrunning the CIDG-Special Forces camp in the A Shau Valley in early 1966, which was a major battle only in that the long-term result was to give the enemy free access to the A Shau Valley. However, I added, "the enemy may be operating from the delusion that political pressure [in the United States] combined with the tactical defeat of a major unit might force the U.S. to throw in the towel."

I noted that we were currently moving into what I now called Phase Three, in which in addition to continuing to destroy the enemy, we were to increase our efforts to build up the Vietnamese armed forces. Then in a final Phase Four we would begin to "phase down" American units while turning over more and more responsibility to the Vietnamese, including the bases, airfields, and ports that we had developed. I called it my withdrawal strategy.

Only once during my period of command in Vietnam did I make a public prediction on how long American involvement might last and that only because two legislators—Representative Richard Ichord of Missouri and Senator Henry Jackson of Washington—had revealed to the press confidential testimony I had delivered before the House and Senate Armed Services Committees, which included an estimate of when withdrawal of American troops might begin. Even so, I never made a prediction as to when withdrawal might be completed. I repeated the estimate in the television interview with Steve Rowan of CBS and elaborated on it on the "Meet the Press" program and in response to a question following my address before the Press Club.

"In view of Secretary McNamara's ill-founded optimism a couple of years ago," the questioner asked, "aren't you uncomfortable when you say we may be able to withdraw troops from Vietnam in a couple of years?"

"My statement," I responded, "is to the effect that it is conceivable to me that within two years or less, it will be possible for us to phase down our level of commitment and turn more of the burden of the war over to the Vietnamese Armed Forces . . . Now, I make the point that at the outset this may be token, but hopefully progressive, and certainly we are preparing our plans to make it progressive."

As with my earlier prediction to Secretary McNamara, I am, in retrospect, impressed by the accuracy of the estimate, however much chance may have been involved. "Two years or less." Two years would have been November 1969. American withdrawals actually began three months earlier in August.

As I prepared to depart Washington, President Johnson telephoned me from his Texas ranch, where he had gone following my Press Club speech. He expressed appreciation for my visit and said he was making a White House plane available to take me to Hawaii. (That pleased my daughter Margaret. While we were in Washington she had taken a commercial flight to visit Stevie in Massachusetts, and upon her return announced that she preferred to fly "the other way.") The President was enthusiastic, he told me, about my plans to upgrade Vietnamese forces with the goal of beginning to withdraw American troops. He wanted to do all he could at the Washington end to expedite the project.

His officials in the Department of Defense failed to share his enthusiasm. Secretary McNamara—and later Secretary Clifford—never fully approved my goal of self-contained ARVN forces. Acting for Clifford as his deputy, Paul Nitze vetoed the engineer and logistical troops and their equipment that were essential if the ARVN was to be able to support itself, and delivery of M-16 rifles and other new equipment continued to be slow. I discerned that the cost-conscious McNamara and his top civilian aides never fully trusted the Vietnamese to do the job that I counted on them doing. They appeared to believe they could eventually convince the North Vietnamese to pull out, whereupon the ARVN with only minor strengthening could stand up to the Viet Cong.

Through the remainder of the Johnson administration, I never obtained approval for engineer and logistical troops for the ARVN. Only with the advent of the Nixon administration and new officials in the Pentagon was my withdrawal strategy of strengthening the ARVN to stand up to the total Vietnamese Communist enemy fully implemented. By that time it was billed as something new and given the name "Vietnamization."

Upon return to Saigon on November 29, I found President Thieu buoyed by my Press Club speech. The government printed it and distributed it widely among the ministries and the armed forces. For the first time, Thieu implied, he appreciated that I had confidence in him and the South Vietnamese and for the first time he discerned a goal toward which to work. I suspected my speech also told him the United States was not to stay in Vietnam forever.

Somewhat like officials in Washington, even those of us on the scene involved in day to day dealings with the South Vietnamese tended to become impatient and to expect too much from people who were essentially inexperienced in government. We sometimes failed to see what such a small thing as my remarks at the Press Club might mean to them.

Soon after the elections two months earlier, I had approved a suggestion from Bob Komer that his military deputy, George Forsythe, an old friend of Thieu's from the Diem days, talk with Thieu and, as the inimitable Komer put it, "get him off his ass." Thieu discerned immediately why Forsythe had come. "Are you going to give me the Franklin D. Roosevelt hundred-day speech?" he asked.

The Americans should remember, President Thieu went on, that he had to feel his way. "After all," he said with infectious ingenuousness, "this is the first time I have ever been President."

I next saw President Johnson near the end of 1967 after he visited Australia for the funeral of Prime Minister Holt, who had died in a swimming accident. He was to spend the night at Korat in Thailand and wanted Bob Hope, who was entertaining American troops in northern Thailand, to join him the next day for the flight to Cam Ranh Bay. For security reasons, I used Bob Hope's expected presence as a cover plan for assembling a cross section of troops.

At my request Bob rearranged his schedule with some difficulty and, in order to fly to Korat, got up at dawn, which to Bob was close to the supreme sacrifice. Yet all to no avail. When the President's pilots discovered they had erred in figuring the flight time from Cam Ranh Bay to Rome, where the President had an appointment with the Pope, they found it necessary to depart before Bob's arrival.

The changed schedule also meant that troops scheduled for a review and awards ceremony at Cam Ranh Bay were still assembling as the President's plane arrived without Bob Hope aboard. Stalling for time, I took the President to a hospital to award Purple Hearts and other decorations, thence when the troops were ready, to the reviewing stand.

The ceremony over, I asked the President's approval for the men to break ranks and gather around the reviewing stand where he might talk to them. The President warmed to the occasion, speaking with verve and enthusiasm as if he were on the campaign trail. When he finished, one of the men spontaneously called out, "Three cheers for the President!" The response was electric. "Hip, hip, hooray! Hip, hip, hooray! Hip, hip, hooray!"

As the President's plane disappeared in the sky, a soldier confided to me that he had enjoyed seeing the President, but he was disappointed. "I was expecting," he said, "to see Bob Hope."

While I had been in Washington in November, intense fighting had developed in the Central Highlands near a CIDG-Special Forces camp in Kontum province known as Dak To. Throughout my absence General Abrams kept me closely informed on the action, which I wanted to have for my personal interest and concern but also needed in order to answer questions from newsmen.

The fight at Dak To was the third engagement during the fall of 1967 that collectively came to be known as the "border battles." The first was near the village of Song Be in Phuoc Long province alongside the Cambodian border where on October 27 a North Vietnamese regiment attacked the command post of an ARVN battalion. Outnumbered four to one, the South Vietnamese nevertheless repulsed three assaults, then as the enemy began to fall back, left their positions to pursue. The North Vietnamese lost at least 134 men killed to 13 South Vietnamese.

The second began on October 29 at a drab little rubber plantation town, Loc Ninh, close to the Cambodian border in the adjacent province of Binh Long. Loc Ninh was destined through the years to serve as a tragic focus for enemy attack.

A heavy mortar barrage preceded a ground attack by a VC regiment against Loc Ninh's little band of defenders: three CIDG companies, a Regional Forces company, and a Popular Forces platoon. The VC got into the outer perimeter of the headquarters compound within the town before two reinforcing companies from an ARVN division helped the local troops drive them out. Two days later the enemy repeated the performance, only to lose heavily before again being forced to retire.

To sweep adjacent rubber plantations and pre-empt further attacks, a brigade of the American 1st Infantry Division joined the ARVN. Cleaning out rubber plantations was always a trying assignment, for long rows of evenly spaced trees afforded the enemy excellent concealment while leaving unobstructed fields of fire down the lanes formed by the interval between rows of trees. Nevertheless, eleven days after the first VC attack, the rubber plantations and Loc Ninh were calm again. The VC regiment lost at least 852 killed against 50 American and South Vietnamese dead, mostly South Vietnamese.

Meanwhile, a few miles south of Loc Ninh, where the Iron Triangle and War Zone C virtually merged, another brigade of the 1st Infantry Division encountered one of the most costly enemy ambushes of the war. As an American infantry battalion commanded by Lieutenant Colonel Terry de la Mesa Allen, Jr., whose father had led the Big Red One during World War II in North Africa and Sicily, searched the jungle for an elusive VC regiment, enemy fire suddenly erupted from all sides. Colonel Allen was among those cut down in the first burst. When the battalion's operations officer, Major Donald W. Holleder, who had been an All-America end at West Point in 1954, tried to reach the battalion to take command, VC fire killed him too. Although the VC lost 103 men killed, they took a heavy toll of the American battalion: 55 killed, 66 wounded.

Coming just before the inaugural ceremonies for the newly elected South Vietnamese government, the attacks at Dak To and Loc Ninh appeared to be an attempt to score a spectacular victory in order to embarrass the new government. That they might constitute more than that, a portion of a larger, more ambitious enemy strategy, began to be indicated by the extent of the enemy's commitment at Dak To in November and by intelligence gleaned shortly before that fight.

Through much of 1967 the 4th U. S. Infantry Division from its base camp near Pleiku City had been screening the steep, jungle-covered mountains of the Central Highlands against the presence of several North Vietnamese regiments known to be just across the border in Cambodia. U.S. engineers built a road deep into the jungle to support an artillery fire-support base created by leveling the top of one of the forested peaks. Yet contact with the enemy was sporadic, mainly in Pleiku province, until near the end of October when bits and pieces of intelligence revealed that an outsize North Vietnamese division controlling five regiments was moving northeastward into adjacent Kontum province in the vicinity of Dak To. In early November a defecting enemy sergeant said the division intended to capture Dak To and another camp under construction, Ben Het, which I had ordered built as a base for 175-mm guns in the hope that I could get approval to fire on the enemy's base camps inside Cambodia and southern Laos.

The CIDG-Special Forces camp known as Dak To lay on a valley floor close to a river, surrounded on all sides by peaks and ridges up to almost 6,000 feet in height with slopes covered by dense trees up to a hundred feet tall. If Dak To was to be defended, the high ground had to be secured, yet the little handful of Montagnard troops in the camp was sufficient only for local defense. Starting early in November, three ARVN battalions and two of the U. S. 4th Infantry Division began to push up the slopes.

Sharp contacts with North Vietnamese patrols revealed early that the intelligence findings were correct, prompting Bill Rosson, who was at the time commanding the I Field Force, to reinforce with the 173d Airborne Brigade. Hardly a day passed without heavy contact that afforded the American units remunerative opportunities to pound the North Vietnamese with artillery fire and strikes by tactical aircraft and B-52s.

The fiercest ground engagement developed on November 17 southwest of Dak To when a battalion of the 173d Airborne Brigade found a large enemy force entrenched on the slopes and atop a peak known as Hill 875. Trying to push up the slopes, the battalion incurred moderately heavy casualties so that the 173d's commander, Brigadier General Leo H. Schweiter, decided to replace it with another battalion. So intense was enemy fire that helicopters were at first unable to land, giving rise to erroneous press reports that the battalion was trapped. Suppressive artillery fire and air strikes in time enabled helicopters to put down.

It took five days to secure Hill 875, while a company from another battalion was heavily engaged holding nearby Hill 823, which was to be used as a fire-support base. An enemy battalion assaulted that company several times before falling back and leaving behind over a hundred dead.

As the fighting around Dak To ebbed toward the end of November and the North Vietnamese fell back again inside Cambodia, a total of sixteen ARVN and American battalions had become involved. The North Vietnamese lost 1,400 dead, their largest and most costly fight in the highlands since the Ia Drang Valley two years before. The ARVN lost 73 men killed, the Americans, 289. Dak To, Ben Het, and other camps in the area remained intact, while the enemy never got out of the hills into the populated regions below and a spectacular victory—if such he sought—continued to elude him.

A fortnight before the Dak To fight began, American troops had captured an enemy document that indicated a forthcoming offensive in western Kontum province. The goals were to annihilate a major American unit, force deployment of more American troops to the Highlands, destroy a large part of the "puppet" (South Vietnamese) army, and "make a concentrated offensive effort in co-ordination with other units in various battle areas throughout South Vietnam." The document stressed the need to overcome difficulties in supply in order to be able to carry out attacks in areas far from existing bases "in preparation for a prolonged battle."

If the document referred to Dak To, the enemy had failed to destroy any American or South Vietnamese forces. He had lured more American units to the Highlands, although they stayed less than a month. Dak To was possibly of greater portent if it was the opening round in "a concentrated offensive effort" throughout South Vietnam.

Something like that appeared to be in the offing. As early as August 1967 I had told newsmen in Saigon in an off-the-record background briefing: "Since heavy pressure [by American troops] began one year ago, it has been building cumulatively and the enemy has now reached a critical point which will probably require a momentous decision on his part. The leaders in Hanoi," I said, "are in the process of reassessing their strategy."

Whether the border battles presaged a major change in strategy remained to be seen. Meanwhile, American marines patrolling during December in the vicinity of Khe Sanh in the northernmost province of Quang Tri began to detect another North Vietnamese build-up around that combat base, and as Christmas approached intelligence reports noted a doubling of enemy truck traffic on the Ho Chi Minh Trail, a "frantic" enemy effort to move supplies into the DMZ and Laos. I expected, I told an interviewer in Saigon late in December, to see "an intensified campaign during the coming months."

When President Johnson in late December spoke with members of the Australian Cabinet, he reflected advice he had received from me. "The enemy is building his forces in the South," the President said. "We must try very hard to be ready. We face dark days ahead."

Chapter XIV
South Vietnamese and Allied Forces

Like most Americans who served in South Vietnam, I had at first only vicarious experience in counterinsurgency warfare. Although I had dealt closely with the local population during my service in post-World War II Germany, no earlier assignment had involved such an intricate interrelationship between the military and the political. I had had previous dealings with Orientals in Korea and Japan and considered that I had developed a certain understanding of them. Yet my colleagues and I in Vietnam were for a long time on what I called a "learning curve." There was no book to tell us how to do the job.

Taking my cue from the broad American role in South Vietnam—to help the South Vietnamese, not to do the job for them—I tried to cast myself in a support role, whenever possible paying deference to the Vietnamese as my hosts. I always walked or rode on the left of my South Vietnamese counterpart, the Chief of the Joint General Staff, General Vien, permitting him the military position of honor on the right. Seldom did I ask a senior South Vietnamese officer to come to see me; I instead called on him. I wanted to establish in the minds of South Vietnamese leaders that I recognized that they were running their country, that I was no proconsul or high commissioner summoning his subjects to the seat of power. In the process I hoped to give stature to my counterpart and other senior officials in the eyes of their own people. The Oriental's preoccupation with "face" is real.

That is not to say that I had no leverage with the South Vietnamese. I found that making a suggestion was usually sufficient to accomplish what I wanted, leaving my counterpart, General Vien, or Thieu, Ky, or whomever, to introduce the change as his own idea. Sometimes I capitalized on Fritz Freund's friendship with General Vien to have him plant an idea with Vien, whereupon Vien would suggest it to me and I would endorse it. I might have to wait a while for things to happen, but with one method or another, seldom was my patience unrewarded. Even conscription of eighteen- and nineteen-year-olds and national mobilization came eventually.

Subtle leverage was possible through the American advisers located at virtually every level in the South Vietnamese military forces from the battalion to the budget bureau in the Ministry of Defense. A particularly effective tool was the money provided under the Military Assistance Program, which I administered; if a unit was under par and failed to respond to my urging for improvement, I could simply withhold support for it until I could detect substantial change. On the battlefield tactical air and helicopter support could be used for leverage to encourage sound tactical plans.

Even regarding the relief of incompetent commanders, I usually got my way in the end. Indeed, General Vien frequently solicited my advice on commanders, and I tried to get to know them down to the level of the regiment. Like other Americans, I had to be careful lest I base my rating of a commander on his competence in speaking English. To devote continuing attention to leadership problems and development, I established a "leadership committee" under my personnel officer, at the first Brigadier General Donald H. McGovern. He would assemble periodically the senior American and South Vietnamese officers to review such subjects as criteria for commissioning noncommissioned officers, equitable promotion procedures, and the like.

Americans had to be careful lest they identify too closely with their South Vietnamese counterpart. "The best way to 'kill' a good Vietnamese officer," I told my commanders at one point, "is to put your arm around him and anoint him with U.S. holy water. If you publicly praise him too much, he will be considered an American boy and he will probably be eased out."

As it was the first time Nguyen Van Thieu had been President, so it was also the first time for almost all Vietnamese leaders to hold positions of authority. I often recalled General MacArthur's advice as I departed for Vietnam: treat them as you did your cadets. Cajole, guide, encourage. I sometimes pointed out that fifteen years earlier the South Koreans had been in much the same embryonic condition, and the presence and performance of Korean troops in Vietnam provided clear demonstration of the improvement that could occur in a short span of time.

So exceedingly polite are the Vietnamese that they will sometimes stray from the facts to tell you what they think you want to hear. That was no problem with General Vien and other officials whom I knew well, but I had to be careful of it on visits to the field. Even Vietnamese translators sometimes dressed up the remarks they were transmitting. In a village where I inquired about a program to increase pork production by giving a farmer a sow and a boar to breed pigs for sale, the translator said that the farmer who spoke to me was doing just that. My aide, Captain Robert B. McCue, who spoke Vietnamese, told me the farmer actually said he had sold the hogs and pocketed the money.

Although I never made ability to speak Vietnamese a requirement for an aide, anyone speaking the language impressed the Vietnamese, and it was often helpful. When another Vietnamese-speaking aide, Captain Richard D. Hooker, overheard two Vietnamese workmen speculating on who I was, he spoke up to tell them I was the commander of all American soldiers in Vietnam. "I thought he was an important gentleman," said one of the workmen. "Does he rank as high as the province chief?"

Cajolery and encouragement were sometimes insufficient. When I discovered, for example, that the ARVN had abandoned a program I had espoused of drawing officer candidates from men of demonstrated ability in the ranks rather than soliciting only the educated elite from the cities, I rebuked the Minister of Defense, General Nguyen Van Vy. The program was vital, I insisted, not just to provide incentive for the man in the ranks but as a part of the broad goal of social reform. I dealt just as firmly when I learned that the best Vietnamese SEAL teams were not fighting the VC but serving as bodyguards for Prime Minister Ky. Yet whenever I had to act commandingly, I did it in private to avoid embarrassing the Vietnamese official in front of his colleagues.

I made a point of keeping General Vien informed on every major move by American forces, and he carefully discussed with me his contemplated deployment of ARVN units. I conferred with the Minister of Defense, General Vy, at least once a month and with Vien every week, while also traveling frequently with Vien.

The South Vietnamese official whom I considered second in importance and ability only to President Thieu was the man who was my principal counterpart for most of my tour, Cao Van Vien. Never have I known a more admirable man: honest, loyal, reserved, scholarly, diplomatic. Unlike Thieu, who was from central Vietnam, and Ky, who was a northerner, Vien was considered a southerner, or *sudiste,* even though he had been born in Laos where his father was a merchant in Vientiane. Thieu and Vien were close friends, they and their families having shared a house together many years before when they were assigned to Hanoi.

Commander of the airborne brigade at the time of the coup overthrowing Diem, Vien had refused, even when threatened with death, to violate his oath of loyalty to the President and participate in the coup. He was imprisoned and for a time condemned to death, but so apolitical was he that he was at last released and returned to his command. Shot in the shoulder during an operation along the Cambodian border in the Mekong Delta, he rallied his paratroopers after an ambush and repulsed the enemy, a heroic action for which it was my pleasure later to award him the Silver Star. In the fall of 1965 he became chief of staff of the Joint General Staff and subsequently commanded the III Corps. When appointed Chief (i.e. head) of the Joint General Staff, he also acted for a while as Minister of Defense. My annoyance at a South Vietnamese tendency to give a man two jobs having finally gotten through to Thieu, Vien had his choice of the two and settled for Chief of the Joint General Staff, although retaining an equal status at the Cabinet level with the Minister of Defense.

Alone among the senior generals, Vien declined to move into the protected compound of the Joint General Staff, continuing to live in the same house in the Cholon district of Saigon that he had acquired as a major. There I came to know him and his charming wife socially over frequent sport-shirt informal dinners. Madame Vien had been known to be a close friend of Diem's controversial sister-in-law, Madame Nhu, and following Diem's overthrow consciously avoided the limelight. An astute businesswoman, she had inherited some money and, as Vien confided to me, was completely in charge of the family's finances. They had several children, among them a young daughter who played Chopin on the piano. The day medics removed a cast from a wrist I had broken in a fall while playing tennis, Vien thoughtfully invited me to a family dinner to celebrate.

Neither a drinker nor a smoker, Vien was a devotee of yoga and sky diving. On National Day 1967, he lost control of his descent because of winds aloft and landed on a street in downtown Saigon. I chided him that he was too important to his country to engage in that kind of daredeviltry, but he said it was good for the morale of the airborne troops. If he would stop jumping, I promised, I would arrange for helicopter pilot training. His eyes lit up, and he never jumped again. When he qualified as a pilot, I staged a simple ceremony to pin American helicopter wings on him.

Like many South Vietnamese generals, Vien disliked confronting subordinates with a direct order on a matter he knew to be sensitive. Wanting to shift two battalions of South Vietnamese marines from the II Corps Zone to Saigon, he issued no order to the corps commander but waited until the marines were moving by air within the corps zone, then directed the Air Force to change course for Saigon. To the corps commander's protest, Vien said, "So sorry."

Like Thieu and Ky, Vien deplored the corruption that permeated subordinate levels. Corruption was a perennial problem, partly because under the old mandarin system, it had become a way of life. It had long been established that a legitimate portion of an official's emolument was a cut of the funds and materials that passed through his hands. If a man rose to authority and then failed to use his position, say, to get his old father's tin roof repaired, the people saw him as cruel and inconsiderate. On the other hand, there clearly had to be limits if government leaders were to gain the trust and confidence of the people.

It was often difficult to get enough evidence on a corrupt official to obtain conviction, and if the courts acquitted a man, the government lost face. Rumors were sometimes so rampant that a man might be convicted by public opinion and have to be removed, but lacking solid evidence, the government could only transfer him to some other assignment.

That happened, for example, in the case of General Dang Van Quang, at the time commander of the IV Corps. Madame Quang was a flashily beautiful woman who appeared at formal events literally dripping with jewels. So ostentatious was her display of wealth that that was enough to convince countless Vietnamese that either she or her husband was corrupt. Thieu told me he had no evidence and deemed Quang so capable that at one point he had thought of him for the position of Chief of the Joint General Staff, but under the pressure of public opinion, he considered he had no choice but to relieve him. He made him publicly the government's chief planner, which was a nonjob, but he actually served as an adviser to Thieu.

In another case a division commander reputedly relieved for corruption was reassigned to be, of all things, the Inspector General. That was like getting a criminal off the streets by making him Chief of Police.

Many a relief for corruption was accomplished under the guise of inefficiency. Family ties, old friendships, and political realities added to the touchiness of relief, and American advisers had to exercise care in reporting corruption lest they get a reputation as spies and lose their leverage with their counterparts. Constantly harangued on the subject by the American press, I simply had to be patient, to recognize that it was a slow, tedious process for honest and responsible leadership to float to the top in place of men long ensconced through political appointment. I could take some negative solace in that even in long-established democracies, corruption or the specter of it is always somewhere just below the surface.

As with corruption, the South Vietnamese have greater tolerance for cruelty than most Americans. Having long experienced the calculated cruelty and terrorism of the Viet Cong—parading the severed head of an official through a village was commonplace—some South Vietnamese saw little point in observing niceties with prisoners of war. Yet responsible officials recognized—and I constantly stressed—that aside from humanitarian reasons, there were advantages in taking prisoners and treating them decently. Live prisoners can talk, constituting a basic source of intelligence, and word that prisoners and returnees under the *chieu hoi* program were well cared for would spread, prompting more to give up. There was also the hope—however vain—that the VC and the North Vietnamese would follow the example and treat their prisoners well.

As soon as possible after interrogation, American forces turned over all prisoners to the South Vietnamese, who held them in regional centers. Lack of security for those camps disturbed me, a concern that proved to be justified when in the summer of 1967 in the course of an attack on Quang Ngai City, the VC released over 1,400 prisoners. At my urging, construction was already underway on a central facility for military prisoners on Phu Quoc Island off the southwestern coast. That and improving the other camps eventually solved the problem.

Aware of the crisis when Communists held under similar conditions in Korea in 1952 revolted and took charge of part of a camp, I frequently checked on internal security in prisoner-of-war camps. I also made sure that the South Vietnamese abided by the rules for treatment of prisoners as provided by the Geneva Convention of 1949, for transferring the prisoners to the South Vietnamese did nothing to lessen American responsibility for those that American troops had captured. During the course of the war those amounted to 102,000. The camps were open to inspection by the International Red Cross, something never permitted by the North Vietnamese.

The South Vietnamese also had to build facilities for thousands of civilian prisoners. Those may well have been, as often charged, "political prisoners," yet the usual connotation of that term involves no acceptance of the fact that in insurgency warfare a civilian political cadre, even if unarmed, also constitutes the enemy.

Publicity in regard to allegedly harsh conditions for prisoners on another island, Con Son, off South Vietnam's southeastern coast, may have reflected on the military detention system, in that some people thought Con Son was part of the system. Con Son was, instead, the site of a long-established penal colony for civilian criminals. Advising the Vietnamese on that facility was the province of AID rather than MACV, but I did visit the island on one occasion, primarily to inspect a U. S. Coast Guard navigation-aid station. In the prison I noted some cells for solitary confinement, and conditions left much to be desired, but I saw no evidence of maltreatment.

Seeking a means for the Saigon government to communicate with the people, I proposed providing a television network for the South Vietnamese, which as a corollary could also provide entertainment for American troops in support areas. (Before a ground station could be built to serve the northern provinces, we transmitted television programs there by means of orbiting propeller-driven aircraft.) The government furnished sets for villages, and with Vietnamese and American channels, the medium was immensely popular. When some of the refugees from the village of Ben Suc slipped away from their refugee camp to return to Ben Suc, TV prompted them after a few days to come back. They said they missed seeing "Gunsmoke."

The Vietnamese delighted in ritual and specialized in ceremony. They much preferred putting on an elaborate display for a visitor to showing a true situation. Despite the threat of VC shelling, their National Day parades were impressive, and it was always a thrill to hear the spontaneous applause that greeted American troops parading in combat dress.

The South Vietnamese also took readily to the American military briefing. Theirs became so long-winded and formal that I soon adopted a technique of interrupting with questions designed to lead to discussions and break the formality. They themselves were reluctant to ask questions. After I spoke at a school for infantry battalion training instructors and invited questions, the leaders rebuked the men who spoke up, so that I had to insist that I genuinely wanted their questions. At later sessions the proper questions flowed freely, obviously planted in advance.

The South Vietnamese also participated in what I called "quarterly reviews of progress," begun in 1966. With General Vien I would go to each of the regional headquarters every three months for a detailed review of past events and future plans. The Vietnamese, I soon found, were reluctant to say anything critical in front of their colleagues, contenting themselves with pretty charts and flowery praise, so that I would have the generals stay behind for a private meeting in which I would insist that they deal forthrightly with personalities and real problems.

I made constant efforts to instill respect for South Vietnamese sovereignty throughout the American command. At American installations, for example, the saffron-and-red Vietnamese flag flew alongside the American flag. I stressed our hosts' sovereignty when addressing incoming troops and when conferring with commanders at every level. I directed that every American soldier carry at all times a small card listing nine rules of conduct, such as avoiding loud and rude behavior and display of wealth and privilege, treating women with politeness and respect, giving the Vietnamese the right of way, making friends among the people, trying to learn some of the language, and in general behaving as guests in the land. Nguyen Cao Ky said I should have added a tenth rule: don't sleep with the women.

Testy situations nevertheless arose, sometimes by accident, sometimes instigated by dissident Vietnamese, as in Hué when a student accused an American marine of tearing down a protest sign. One potentially more trying incident occurred in Saigon when, in the wake of a terrorist attack on an American installation, an American MP fired at a car that entered a restricted space in front of an enlisted men's hotel. No physical damage resulted, but the occupants of the car turned out to be General Doan Van Quang, chief of the Vietnamese Special Forces, and his family. Quang was irate until I telephoned to apologize.

More comic than trying in the end was the arrest one midnight by an American MP of a man near the Saigon docks who was wildly firing a submachine gun into the river. The MP confiscated the gun, handcuffed the man's hands behind him, and, as was the practice in arresting Vietnamese civilians, turned him over to the Saigon police. The man, it developed, was Colonel Van Van Cua, mayor of Saigon.

Cua was obviously intoxicated, either from drugs or alcohol, a condition for which he had some reputation. Although the commander of American housekeeping troops in Saigon, Brigadier General Robert Ashworth, hurried to the scene to apologize, Cua, weeping violently, refused to permit anybody to remove the handcuffs. Only Ambassador Lodge or General Westmoreland, he said, could do that.

General Ashworth returned to the police station later to find that although Cua still wore the handcuffs, he had changed from civilian clothes into uniform. Since he had had to use his hands for that, he had obviously had the handcuffs off and his continuing to wear them was nothing but a pose. When Ambassador Lodge heard of it, he nevertheless volunteered to do the honors of removing the handcuffs.

For a month or more Cua disappeared from public view. When he came back on the scene, he assured Ashworth that he held no animosity. Cua had apparently taken some kind of cure, for from that time on he displayed no problem with liquor or drugs and performed creditably as mayor.

Under agreements preceding American commitment in South Vietnam, the discipline of American troops was to be an American responsibility, which each service handled for its own people in accord with the Uniform Code of Military Justice. Although in previous recent wars American civilians in a combat zone were also subject to the code, Washington decided—and I concurred—that only in the most serious cases were American civilians to be tried by courts-martial and then only after the South Vietnamese government had waived jurisdiction. The policy covered only American civilian employees of the U.S. military and its contractors, not newsmen, businessmen, other visitors, or employees of U.S. civilian agencies, all of whom were subject only to Vietnamese authority. The Embassy staff, of course, had diplomatic immunity.

The arrangement appeared to please most American newsmen, who complained loudly any time they thought their rights were in jeopardy, but some reporters would have welcomed coming under the code, accepting the minor restrictions involved in exchange for the protection. In practice, an unruly newsman, particularly one who had come to know Vietnamese jails, preferred to be taken into custody by American MPs One of the few cases of courts-martial of an American civilian involved a merchant seaman in Danang who stabbed to death a fellow seaman. Several civilians were tried by the Vietnamese, mainly employees of military contractors.

As part of a continuing effort to lessen the impact of large numbers of American troops on the Vietnamese, I early sought a site for a new MACV headquarters outside of but close to Saigon. My office was located in a converted hotel on Pasteur Street, lacked adequate parking, and was so cramped and crowded that we had to have several annexes at other locations, which posed difficulties in day-to-day contacts among the staff and additional security problems. Close alongside a main thoroughfare, the headquarters buildings were particularly difficult to protect against terrorist attack, although the VC tried it only twice.

The first was part of the early wave of terrorism against Americans when a VC posing as an electrician placed an explosive charge in the ceiling of an office, but everybody had departed before the charge went off. The second was in February 1967, when the VC fired five Russian 82-mm mortar rounds from a house from which they had removed a portion of the roof. When they fled, they left behind a time bomb, which killed several investigating policemen. I was in my office at the time and presume the VC knew that. Although the mortar shells missed my headquarters building, one struck a passing truck, killing twelve ARVN soldiers.

The site I wanted was near Tan Son Nhut and the compound of the Joint General Staff, but Marshal Ky, then Premier, was saving the site for a postwar tourist hotel he planned to build. Much to the unhappiness of Ambassador Lodge, I had settled for an inadequate site within the city, across from a pagoda used by the militant Buddhists, which could have precipitated frequent confrontations; fortunately, the ambassador's and my combined pleas finally convinced Ky to change his mind.

The new MACV headquarters near Tan Son Nhut opened in August 1967 in prefabricated metal buildings. Meanwhile, headquarters of the United States Army, Vietnam, and its various logistical and combat support units, heretofore scattered in several locations, moved to a sprawling new base fifteen miles northeast of Saigon at Long Binh, near the town of Bien Hoa. My staff called the program to relocate away from the capital "Project MOOSE"—move out of Saigon expeditiously—which to the veteran of the Korean War had an amusing connotation, since "moose" had been the slang word for a Korean woman living with an American soldier. The relocations had the effect of moving thousands of American soldiers away from the population and reducing the likelihood of incidents, permitting return of many requisitioned buildings in Saigon to the Vietnamese, and cutting down on spending of piasters, the Vietnamese unit of currency.

Reducing piaster expenditures had long been of concern. In late 1966 Washington decreed that a "piaster ceiling" be imposed on American and Vietnamese military forces based on the amounts of piasters each had spent the preceding May. As worked out by the U. S. Mission's economic counselor, Roy Wehrle, and officials in Washington, the ceilings were designed to reduce the amounts of American dollars changed into piasters and spent on the local economy, either officially or by individual Americans, thereby, it was hoped, slowing inflation.

The goal was admirable, but the way Wehrle and officials in Washington proposed to accomplish it was not. Incoming American troops, Wehrle told me, would have to be reduced in number, and I should even begin to consider withdrawing some American troops. Sharp echoes of Wehrle's ideas from the Department of Defense convinced me that some of Secretary McNamara's advisers were using the piaster ceiling as a means of controlling the American build-up. If I was ever to bring the war to the point where the South Vietnamese could take over, I had to have more American troops. To let economics rather than military necessity dictate American deployments was unrealistic, a classic case of the tail wagging the dog.

Positive actions circumvented the Wehrle formula. By various programs I sharply cut the expenditure of piasters. Building up the Post Exchange system and recreational and entertainment facilities on American bases, prohibiting leaves within South Vietnam while providing short recreational visits to cities in easy range of air transportation outside Vietnam, moving troops and installations outside the cities—all these contributed to cutting down on piaster spending. Several savings programs for the troops also helped, such as savings bonds, pay options, and, upon enactment by Congress, 10 per cent interest on savings up to $10,000. Reducing the number of Vietnamese employees also helped, as did gradual completion of the building program for bases, ports, and airfields.

I set an initial goal of piaster spending of $20 per man per month and ultimately got down to $10. That success and arrival of a new economic counselor with a more flexible approach, Charles Cooper, brought an end to the ceiling before it could materially affect the troop build-up. Because various other factors temporarily froze any build-up of South Vietnamese forces—such as the need to fill up depleted units, develop quality before quantity, train new leaders essential to expansion, and await more recruits as more of the population came under government control—the ceiling had no effect on the size of South Vietnamese forces.

Another method of trying to control inflation was to flood the economy with American imports, thereby filling demand and lowering prices. South Vietnamese importers resisted this by leaving incoming merchandise to accumulate in warehouses at the Saigon port. By late 1966 the port was as clogged as it had been in the early days of American build-up when I had had to maintain ships as floating warehouses. So seriously did the congestion interfere with unloading military supplies that I sought and received authority for the military to take over the advisory role for the port from AID. Then to Premier Ky I proposed a decree to the effect that any merchandise left for more than thirty days would be picked up by ARVN trucks and sold at public auction. The congestion cleared miraculously.

Like Thieu and Vien, Ky would rate high on any list of capable South Vietnamese leaders. Another would be General Ngo Quang Truong, who first came to prominence as an airborne commander during the Buddhist uprising in Hué and Danang in 1966. He later assumed command of a demoralized 1st ARVN Division and quickly re-established it as one of the best ARVN units. He commanded the division for four years before becoming commander of the IV Corps and subsequently of the I Corps, in which position he was to be cast in an unfortunate role in the collapse of resistance in the northern provinces in 1975.

Two other excellent field commanders were General Nguyen Viet Thanh, who first drew my attention as a superb chief of Go Cong province and later as commander of the 7th ARVN Division, and General Do Cao Tri, former commander of the II Corps and later of the III Corps. Both were destined to die while serving as corps commanders in separate helicopter accidents in 1970 in Cambodia. Tri was a tiger in combat, South Vietnam's George Patton, and like Patton he was remiss in some aspects of human relations. In the days before American dependents departed in 1965, he embarrassed Kitsy and me by taking us to a cabaret in Dalat where the other ladies at the table were obviously Tri's mistresses.

No one was more conscious than I was when I first arrived in Vietnam of the deficiencies of the South Vietnamese armed forces, yet wringing one's hands was no solution. While the South Vietnamese fought for their existence, the Americans had to work with patience and persistence to help them create viable armed forces. Simply putting more South Vietnamese men in uniform and bringing in more American weapons and equipment weren't the answers. Nor was it just a question of teaching a man to march and shoot a rifle. Creating modern armed forces is a multifaceted task: personnel administration, care of dependents, logistical organization, training centers, military education, these and more. And almost everything had to be started from zero.

How rudimentary, even primitive, the equipment of the ARVN was for a long time is indicated by the fact that it was well into my tour before we were able to provide the troops with modern communications equipment. Having discerned soon after my arrival that lack of such equipment was a major contributor to deficiencies in combat, I hit on an idea for expedients. Around the start of 1965, I was able to divert sufficient funds to provide every squad and platoon leader with a brass whistle and every company with a bugle. That was no final answer to the communications problem, but it helped. Aside from practical use, the whistle became a kind of prestige symbol, and the bugle had a second use for ceremonies.

That by 1967 the South Vietnamese armed forces had progressed to a point where I could visualize a U.S. withdrawal strategy was a tremendous accomplishment. While doubling in size in something like three years, despite the thin veneer of leadership and having to do a large share of the fighting, the ARVN at the same time had held a politically troubled country together in the face of ever-increasing enemy strength. Few organizations in the world could have done so well.

Many Americans have a tendency to deprecate our allies. Many criticized French "frogs" in World Wars I and II, called our ROK allies in Korea "gooks." An American in one branch of the armed forces even deprecates other Americans in some other branch or even in some unit other than his own. The little ARVN soldier buried under a steel helmet designed for the stalwart American and weighted down with an M-1 rifle that even a six-footer might find burdensome could look ludicrous. Unlike the American male, the Vietnamese sees nothing embarrassing in a display of affection between men; two ARVN soldiers walking hand in hand was to Americans odd and effeminate. The statue at the entrance to the national military cemetery depicting a seated ARVN soldier was an apt representation, a passing American might jeer, of the ARVN on the attack; that a soldier at rest was appropriate for a cemetery escaped him.

The American news media contributed to a false image of the ARVN's performance. Serving an American public, the U.S. press and television understandably focused on American units, seldom covering ARVN operations unless something spectacular happened, such as heavy losses. Reading American newspapers, for example, one would have been hard put to realize that several ARVN battalions were in the thick of the fight around Dak To in November 1967. American newsmen gravitated to the big battles and found little interest in prosaic day-by-day operations in support of pacification. Raising hogs, planting improved strains of rice, or building schools had little appeal to the television cameraman or the reporter looking for headlines when compared with such subjects as desertion, corruption, or political machinations and demonstrations.

Following in the tradition of harshly critical American reporting established in the Diem days, few American reporters could find anything good to say about the ARVN. Limited messing and housing facilities with ARVN units discouraged newsmen from participating in ARVN operations, and so piqued by these newsmen's constant criticism were many South Vietnamese commanders that they did little to encourage their visits. One division commander refused to have an American reporter in his zone of operations. Many said better suffer in silence than try to change the unchangeable. One senior official said how presumptuous it was of some Americans to think the Vietnamese wanted them around forever when in fact it would be such a relief to be rid of the cynical criticism of the American press and Congress.

I convinced the South Vietnamese to conduct a daily press briefing similar to that held at MACV, but only two or three American reporters showed up the first day and seldom any thereafter. That was but one of my efforts to encourage American newsmen to report frequently and objectively on the ARVN. I tried, for example, putting American information officers as advisers in ARVN divisions. When I was in Washington for the Press Club speech in late 1967, I took the matter up in a special conference with the President. Yet I had no power over the press, and when the newsmen in the field failed to co-operate, the American people at home were left with the false impression that American soldiers were doing practically all of the fighting.

One of the harshest stories to come out of South Vietnam was a *Newsweek* article, "Their Lions—Our Rabbits," which implied that our North Vietnamese enemies would fight while our South Vietnamese allies would not. Aside from egregious factual errors, the entire thesis of the article was false. When it appeared in October 1967, the ARVN was already an effective force, although still lacking the transport, communications, and firepower of American units. ARVN casualties were running somewhat ahead of American casualties, which may be no foolproof gauge of competence but unquestionably demonstrates close and frequent contact with the enemy.

As part of the tendency to deprecate allies, many Americans also tend to see our enemy as twelve feet tall. The VC and the North Vietnamese were wily, tenacious, persevering, and courageous to the point of fanaticism—the way he supplied himself, for example, through the most primitive of methods: cargo bicycle, ox cart, corvée labor, elephant, sampan, floating supplies down rivers. Yet they were also human. They too blundered; they sacrificed themselves needlessly and often foolishly. Any American commander who took the same vast losses as General Giap would have been sacked overnight.

In evaluating the performance of the North Vietnamese soldier, Americans should have asked, "What choice did he have?" Many a North Vietnamese prisoner trembled in the conviction that his murder at the hands of his captors was inevitable, for that he had been taught to expect. Many captured soldiers had tattoos on their bodies bearing the slogan, "Born in the north to die in the south." They told of funeral ceremonies in their honor before they left their home villages. Their fatalism might benefit their performance in combat, but it was hardly a thing Americans are accustomed to fostering either in their own soldiers or in those of their allies.

The ARVN soldier had alternatives to dying and sometimes exercised them, as the desertion or AWOL rate often showed, yet hardly ever did an ARVN soldier defect to the enemy. Even during the early days of political turmoil, the bulk of the ARVN fought well, and in later years, as leadership at the junior level improved, they fought even better.

In keeping with my withdrawal strategy, I gave more and more responsibility to the ARVN. As Bui Diem, the Vietnamese ambassador to the United States, once put it: "One can sit beside the driver for weeks, months, or even years, but he will never learn to drive until he can take the wheel in his own hands."

Preparation of a "Combined Campaign Plan," an annual appraisal and projection of goals and methods relating both to military operations and pacification in Vietnam, provides an example. In 1965 and 1966 the Combined Campaign Plan was essentially an American document with South Vietnamese input. In 1967 it was the reverse. To emphasize the difference, I played on Vietnamese proclivity for ritual and staged a ceremonial signing of it. By 1968 the plan was almost wholly a South Vietnamese production.

A major project, essential to long-range development of the South Vietnamese armed forces, was to improve the military education system. A national military academy at Dalat, for example, was at first little more than a glorified officer candidate school offering only a two-year course. With Thieu's concurrence and over Ky's objections—Ky deemed it should await the end of the fighting—I upgraded the academy to a four-year institution modeled on West Point. By the time the first four-year graduates emerged in 1970, they were stalwart young men, not only well educated but physically strong after years of intensive training. They reminded me of the sturdy South Korean soldiers then in Vietnam, who themselves bore little resemblance to the ill-fed, ill-trained troops of the Korean War years.

I also directed special attention to the Command and General Staff College, changing it from a poor copy of the U. S. Army school at Fort Leavenworth to a course emphasizing the nature of warfare within South Vietnam, and I created a National Defense College in Saigon for study of governmental problems by senior ARVN officers who lacked exposure to national programs. Selected American advisers served in an officer candidate school and a noncommissioned officers' academy. I supported a military prep school in Vung Tau for the sons of officers and noncommissioned officers and of deceased veterans, from which the graduates went into the South Vietnamese Army, including some to officer candidate school and some to the military academy at Dalat. A large percentage of senior South Vietnamese field commanders took the U. S. Army's course at Fort Leavenworth, and at one time more than 900 South Vietnamese were undergoing military training in the United States. Through these measures the shortage of leadership gradually decreased.

Perennially short of troops in view of the multiple jobs to be done, South Vietnamese commanders resisted releasing battalions for refresher training, but I insisted that every battalion go through a refresher course after two years in the field. Separate branches such as the airborne, marines, Special Forces, and rangers had their own training centers.

Having both rangers and Special Forces involved duplication, but only after I departed did efforts to amalgamate the two pay off. The CIDG forces were essentially mercenaries paid by the Americans, and they were gradually absorbed into the Regional Forces. As the leadership base grew, I authorized increasing the airborne and marine brigades to divisions.

The ARVN gradually developed a good Inspector General's department, and teams of American and South Vietnamese inspectors made frequent unannounced visits to the field. I too dropped in often on ARVN units. That disturbed General Vien, who thought he always should accompany me, until I reminded him that I did not go as the American commander but as the senior American adviser.

The plight of ARVN dependents and discharged veterans was always disturbing. For a long time the wives and children of the soldiers lived under conditions well below those of the average peasant, and the soldiers' pay always lagged far behind the inflationary spiral. Funds gradually became available for improved housing, and establishing a post exchange and commissary system made it possible for these dependents to buy food at more moderate prices. The South Vietnamese PX-commissary was subsidized by the sale of American items, which produced capital for restocking it with items more familiar to the Vietnamese.

The practice of ARVN dependents living with or near the soldiers was a matter of considerable concern to me, for when the fighting began, the soldiers were often torn between defeating the enemy and looking after their wives and children. Yet over the long years it would have been impossible to hold the ARVN together under any other arrangement. The practice was nevertheless destined to contribute to the debacle that finally occurred in 1975.

For all my efforts, I was never satisfied with what was done for the Vietnamese veteran. Many were disabled and unable to work, and aside from humanitarian considerations, they were a potential political problem. It was bad, too, for the soldier's morale to know that upon discharge he might face a bleak existence. The veterans' program was for long under AID, but I eventually gained the ambassador's approval and South Vietnamese concurrence to make it a MACV responsibility. When General Omar Bradley, a former director of the U. S. Veterans Administration, visited Vietnam in 1967, I conferred with him on the problem. Yet for all General Bradley's advice and my insistence to South Vietnamese authorities, the plight of the veteran remained disturbing.

In consideration of South Vietnamese self-sufficiency as a primary goal, the only top-level joint agency that I sanctioned was a Combined Intelligence Center. That was essential because so much of the intelligence input had to come from the South Vietnamese, civilians as well as the military. As the months passed, and particularly as forays into the enemy's sanctuaries produced innumerable documents and as sophisticated photographic and computer equipment became available, the Combined Intelligence Center became a thoroughly professional agency. Primary credit for it belongs to my intelligence chief, Joe McChristian.

One of the more serious and nagging problems with the ARVN was treatment of the civilian population. By long tradition in Vietnam a man in a position of authority lords it over those beneath him, and wearing a uniform gave the South Vietnamese peasant his first taste of authority. That the soldier often had to scrounge for food compounded the problem, and that he usually was no native of the region where he operated gave him a sense of detachment. I had to stress proper treatment of civilians constantly, pointing out that co-operation by civilians was vital to gathering intelligence and that in the end only with the support of the people could the VC be eliminated.

Living in home neighborhoods, the Regional and Popular Forces posed little problem. The rangers and the airborne were the worst offenders. On several occasions I threatened to withhold funds for ranger battalions unless they changed their ways, and my endorsement of expanding the airborne to a division was made dependent on proper behavior with civilians. Gradual improvement in rations, including a combat or emergency ration designed for Vietnamese tastes, helped with this particular problem in all units.

As with American troops, I also stressed civic action projects for the ARVN, both to improve relations with the people and to give the troops a sense of participation in nation-building. To assure that the projects were needed, the ideas and approval of civic action projects had to come from the village or hamlet chief, and the people had to provide most of the labor. The idea was for the ARVN to help, not to do the job completely, for if people work for themselves, they take pride in what they accomplish.

It was no easy task to get the ARVN to participate in civic action. Under the French, the Vietnamese peasant had traditionally worked for the military, and the ARVN soldier was reluctant to reverse the process. It took almost a year to get the Minister of Defense to issue a directive requiring ARVN participation in civic action projects.

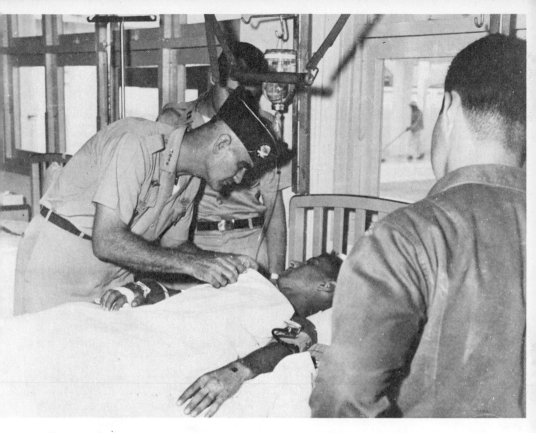

The author checks the wound of an American soldier in a hospital in South Vietnam.

Soldiers of the U. S. 4th Division evacuate a wounded comrade through the jungle near Cu Chi, in the III Corps Zone, during a fire fight in 1967. The men are wearing flak jackets. *(U. S. Army Photograph)*

The author in a favorite stance atop a jeep, talking to men of the 4th Infantry Division in March 1967.

Conferees at the Guam conference, March 1967. From left: Bui Diem, South Vietnamese Ambassador to the United States; General Nguyen Duc Thang; Foreign Minister Tran Van Do; Premier Nguyen Cao Ky; Chief of State Nguyen Van Thieu; General Cao Van Vien; General Nguyen Boa Tri; Nguyen Hu Co; Vu Quoc Thuc; the author; General Earle G. Wheeler, Chairman of the Joint Chiefs of Staff; Ambassador Ellsworth Bunker; William Gaud, Administrator, U. S. Agency for International Development; Secretary of State Dean Rusk (hidden); President Lyndon B. Johnson; Secretary of Defense Robert S. McNamara; Ambassador-at-Large Averell Harriman; Ambassador Henry Cabot Lodge; and Admiral U. S. Grant Sharp, Commander in Chief, Pacific.

Troopers of the 1st Cavalry Division in an air assault from a Huey helicopter in Quang Ngai province, April 1967. *(U. S. Army Photograph)*

The author with Ambassadors Robert Komer (left) and Ellsworth Bunker at Tan Son Nhut airport, May 1967.

The author introducing General Creighton W. Abrams to Premier Nguyen Cao Ky in May 1967.

A B-52 over Vietnam.

or General William J. Crumm, commander
e 3rd Air Division, in 1967.

A Monitor, "battleship" of the Riverine Force
in the Mekong Delta, 1967. *(U. S. Navy Photograph)*

The Westmorelands in the Philippines in 1967. From left: Stevie, Kitsy, Margaret, Rip, and the author. In the foreground is Hannah.

The author and Mrs. Westmoreland with former Governor and Mrs. James F. Byrnes in Columbia, South Carolina, 1967.

The author conducting a press briefing on his "two-fisted strategy" in the Pentagon, November 1967.

The author addressing a Joint Session of the U. S. Congress in November 1967.

Meanwhile, development of the South Vietnamese Air Force and Navy also proceeded. At the start the Navy was the most politically oriented of all the armed services; on one occasion a group of officers got up a petition demanding removal of the Chief of Naval Operations. Friction between officers who maintained traditions they had learned from the French and those who learned new ways under the Americans was for a time divisive. Yet all those difficulties gradually passed, and the main problem remaining was to persuade the American Navy to turn over greater responsibilities to the South Vietnamese.

Developing the Air Force was a slow process. Faced in the early days with severe restrictions on the use of American aircraft, we may have pushed the South Vietnamese too fast, thereby establishing a shaky base upon which to build. A perennial difficulty was finding enough young Vietnamese who were capable of absorbing the highly technical training necessary for them to become pilots and mechanics. Procurement of pilots was made more difficult by the practical requirement that they had to speak or learn English. Unlike the American Air Force, the South Vietnamese Air Force had responsibility for helicopters, which also had to have pilots and mechanics. Yet the South Vietnamese gradually absorbed new aircraft, such as the B-57 jet tactical bomber and the C-130 transport plane.

All things considered, I was convinced by the summer of 1967 that with a concerted effort to upgrade their armed forces with improved arms and equipment and to expand them, the South Vietnamese would soon be capable of assuming more of the burden of the war, which would lead eventually to a phased American withdrawal. The one big problem remaining was how to spur national mobilization and the drafting of eighteen- and nineteen-year-olds, and that had to await future developments.

No account of my stewardship in South Vietnam would be complete without recognition of the contributions of nations other than the United States. Thirty-four other nations contributed food, medicine, technical advisers, equipment, educational facilities, training, economic aid, and the like.* Four more—Australia, New Zealand, Thailand, and the Republic of Korea—also furnished combat troops, while a fifth—Republic of the Philippines—provided a civic action group that had its own security force of infantry, armor, and artillery. The total of foreign troops other than Americans was 68,800, more than fought under the banner of the United Nations in Korea.

That the United States openly solicited help from other nations apparently disturbed some critics of the war. Yet it is hard to find any war in

---

* Argentina, Belgium, Brazil, Canada, Costa Rica, Denmark, Ecuador, Federal Republic of Germany, France, Greece, Guatemala, Honduras, Iran, Ireland, Israel, Italy, Japan, Laos, Liberia, Luxembourg, Malaysia, Morocco, Netherlands, Norway, Pakistan, Republic of China, South Africa, Spain, Switzerland, Tunisia, Turkey, United Kingdom, Uruguay, and Venezuela.

which the powers involved made no effort to obtain allies. Of the five nations furnishing troops, the Republic of Korea offered troops in 1954, long before President Johnson issued his "more flags" appeal, and Australia and the Philippines were providing other types of assistance before the appeal. Nor do I find it untoward that the United States paid the costs for the Koreans and the Thais, for both South Korea and Thailand were already receiving funds and other support under the Military Assistance Program. The United States provided only an overseas pay supplement and heavy engineer equipment for the contingent from the Philippines, and the cost of all assistance furnished the Australians and New Zealanders was reimbursed by their governments.

It was sometimes necessary to help some of the foreign contingents even when no formal agreement had been reached by their governments and the United States. Visiting a newly arrived Spanish Army medical team in the sweltering Mekong Delta, for example, I found the men wearing woolen uniforms with high cadet-type collars. Those were their only clothes. When I returned to Saigon, I directed that U. S. Army fatigues be flown to them immediately. On a later visit the men thanked me profusely. The incident had made them feel they were part of the team.

The first contingent of Free World (or "Third Country") forces was a South Korean engineer battalion and an infantry battalion for their protection, the DOVE unit, which arrived in February 1965. I stationed the force in Bien Hoa province with the mission of building a circumferential highway around Saigon so that military traffic might avoid the bottleneck of the capital. I also wanted the unit in a relatively secure area lest a sudden avalanche of casualties precipitate political repercussions in South Korea. Although the highway was a long time in the building, it was demonstrably helpful during the heavy fighting of 1968 and 1972.

As the first South Korean combat troops arrived in the fall of 1964, President Park invited me to Seoul to hold discussions with his Cabinet and senior officers. It was then that he told me the troops were to be "under your command," which he repeated when he later visited South Vietnam, yet the Koreans wanted publicly to maintain an impression of coequal status. The agreement for assistance was negotiated between South Korea and South Vietnam, much as was the American agreement with South Vietnam, thus contributing to the posture of coequality.

I recall that visit to South Korea and two others—one as the U. S. Army Chief of Staff—with warmth and pleasure. The affection and gratitude that the South Korean people feel for Americans was everywhere apparent. On the last visit I was amused by the conduct of a stalwart young woman who served as my caddy when I played golf late one afternoon with the American commander in South Korea, General Mike Michaelis. As I made a good first drive, she called out, "Damned good shot!" On my next shot, a poor one, again she cried, "Damned good shot!" On a third try I topped my approach shot and ended up in water. Still she shouted, "Damned good shot!" It was the only English she knew.

All ROK combat units in South Vietnam were composed of volunteers. The Capital ("Tiger") Division was particularly effective, far different from the same division that had fought alongside my 187th Parachute Brigade in the spring of 1953 and had broken under attack by the Chinese. I had also fought in Korea alongside the 9th ("White Horse") Division, which also proved effective in Vietnam. The ROK marine brigade had command problems but fought well on defense. Because of a dictum from President Park, all ROK units were sensitive about keeping casualties down, which resulted in a deliberate approach to operations involving lengthy preparations and heavy preliminary fire. As General Abrams with his musical bent put it:

> . . . the kind of war that we have here can be compared to an orchestra. It is sometimes appropriate to emphasize the drums or the trumpets or the bassoon, or even the flute. The Vietnamese, to a degree, realize this and do it. The Koreans, on the other hand, play one instrument: the bass drum.

Yet since I used the South Koreans primarily for area security, including keeping a long stretch of Route 1 open, most operations involved small units where deliberateness was no real drawback and patience was an asset. The Koreans were particularly effective in cordon-and-search operations— surrounding villages by stealth, then allowing the people to leave and conducting methodical searches for arms and guerrillas. They were also good at persuading Vietnamese women or elders to convince their VC sons and husbands to return to the government under the *chieu hoi* program. One way was to let women previously evacuated go back to spend a night with their husbands, whereupon the men were usually more amenable to giving up.

A handsome, personable officer, frank and sincere, General Chae Myung Shin first commanded the Tiger Division, then all Republic of Korea forces in South Vietnam, close to 50,000 men. General Chae emphasized physical fitness, including tae-kon-do, the Korean form of karate, in which all limbs and the head serve as weapons, and introduced tae-kon-do in the ARVN and among Vietnamese youth as a civic action program. An advocate of ginseng tea, which reputedly promotes stamina, potency, and general good health, General Chae insisted on keeping me amply supplied. Although I learned to like it, any commercial I might do for it would fall somewhat short of its Korean billing.

Since General Chae and other senior and many junior ROK officers spoke English, communication with Americans presented few problems. Their forces having been created in the American image and according to U. S. Army doctrine, mutual military understanding was readily achieved. They tended to do everything exactly as the U. S. Army field manuals spell it out. In areas of overlapping responsibility, they usually co-operated amicably.

To some extent during my tenure and more later, the South Koreans tried to use their presence to get as much new American equipment as possible, trading off their participation in operations for new helicopters and artillery. From time to time I had to intervene to stop them from shipping brass from artillery shell casings back to South Korea to feed an industry in brass ornaments that had burgeoned during and after the Korean War. We were trying to salvage the brass so that it could be shipped to the United States and reused. The reputation of the Koreans for scrounging afforded one argument against a combined command, for under such an arrangement foreign officers would have made up part of the MACV staff. "Can you visualize," I would say, "a Korean major general as supply officer with keys to American depots?"

Aside from American soldiers, the Australians were the most thoroughly professional foreign force serving in Vietnam. Small in numbers and well trained, particularly in antiguerrilla warfare, the Australian Army was much like the post-Versailles German Army in which even men in the ranks might have been leaders in some less capable force. Under a succession of able administrative commanders—Major Generals Kenneth MacKay, Douglas Vincent, and A. L. MacDonald—and gifted field commanders—Brigadiers O. D. Jackson, R. L. Hughes, and S. C. Graham—a three-battalion task force with artillery, armor, and other support arrived in mid-1965 and served in the coastal province of Phuoc Tuy, southeast of Saigon, generally along Route 15 leading to Vung Tau. The Australians later furnished a Canberra light-bomber squadron and a guided-missile destroyer. Forces from New Zealand, which at first consisted of a 105-mm howitzer battery and subsequently two rifle companies, also arrived in mid-1965, operated with the Australians, and were of similar quality.

The toughest fight involving the Australians developed in late summer of 1966 when a company sweeping a rubber plantation bumped head on into an enemy force of 1,500 men. For three hours in a blinding monsoon rain that denied tactical air support, the company of just over a hundred men fought off one human-wave attack after another. As the Australians ran short of ammunition, Australian helicopter pilots braved enemy fire and the rain to resupply them. Because the heavy downpour deadened noise, two companies in armored personnel carriers were able to get close to the besieged company before the VC spotted them. As the relief force attacked, the enemy broke off the engagement, leaving behind 265 dead. The Australians lost 17 men killed, all but six in the first minutes of the encounter.

One ingenious project the Australians attempted had an unhappy ending. In an effort to secure a portion of Phuoc Tuy province, the Australians laid some 20,000 antipersonnel mines, but South Vietnamese militia that were charged with protecting the field failed to keep out VC infiltrators. The VC removed roughly half of the mines and used them for their own purposes throughout the province.

The Australians and New Zealanders jointly provided a squadron of the

Special Air Service, which is a cover name for ranger-type troops skilled in hand-to-hand combat and long-range patrolling. The exploits of those men were legendary.

Despite some antiwar sentiment in Australia, I gather that Australians were justifiably proud of their forces in Vietnam. Visiting Australia, Senator Fulbright reputedly shocked his listeners when he answered a reporter who asked what the Senator thought of the performance of the Australian troops. "I did not know," said the chairman of the Senate Foreign Relations Committee, "that you had any there."

The enthusiasm of the people of Thailand for combating Communist insurgency was well demonstrated the first day their government announced plans to send a volunteer force to Vietnam. In the capital of Bangkok alone 5,000 volunteered, including the son of the premier, who subsequently served in Vietnam.

The first contingent of the Royal Thai Volunteer Regiment, known as the "Queen's Cobras," arrived in the summer of 1967. I first provided the regiment an orientation period with the 9th U. S. Infantry Division southeast of Saigon, followed by a security mission in a portion of Bien Hoa province. The Thais subsequently expanded their force to 11,000 men to create the "Black Panther" Division, commanded by Major General D. Yose.

Having had only limited training, the Thais were less than aggressive on the attack, but as the VC soon discovered, they were tenacious on the defense. At midnight, shortly before Christmas 1967, for example, a VC battalion attacked one of the Thai companies. With the company commander was an American radio operator, Specialist 4 Ralph O'Connor. When I visited the site early the next morning, bodies of fallen VC lay all about. The Thais were excited over their performance and profuse in their praise of Specialist O'Connor, who had not only called in artillery support but had acted as an alter ego for the company commander.

Known as PHILCAG, a 2,000-man Filipino civic action group under Brigadier General Gaudencio V. Tobias arrived in October 1965 and operated close to the Cambodian border in Tay Ninh province. The Filipinos and Cambodians have historic ties, based on the Filipinos' having sent an expeditionary force to Cambodia in the mid-nineteenth century, and sometimes intermarry. Knowing that the Cambodian commander across the border had a Filipino mother, I positioned the Filipinos near the border in the hope some meaningful contacts might develop with the Cambodians. Although that failed to happen, the Filipinos did pick up valuable intelligence. Engaged in civic action work, including medical treatment, in the vicinity of Tay Ninh City, the Filipinos had a continuing project to clear portions of the Thanh Dien Forest for agricultural use and to build a refugee resettlement village. The force carried out the assignments well.

A sixth country wanted to send troops to Vietnam: the Republic of China. The head of state, Chiang Kai-shek, made the offer early in the war and reiterated it in 1964 after President Johnson's appeal. Recalling General MacArthur's recommendation to get other Oriental peoples involved in Vietnam, particularly the Nationalist Chinese, I would have welcomed Nationalist Chinese troops from a purely military standpoint; but I agreed with the Department of State that the likelihood of some form of Chinese Communist reaction to that made it prudent to decline. Nationalist China's contributions thus were small in number but big in quality: political warfare advisers, medical teams, agricultural and construction experts, two C-46 aircraft for refugee relief missions, and five LSTs.

Chapter XV
Reflections on Command

Under a panel of glass on my desk from the time I assumed command in Saigon I kept a quotation from Napoleon Bonaparte:

> A commander-in-chief cannot take as an excuse for his mistakes in warfare an order given by his sovereign or his minister, when the person giving the order is absent from the field of operations and is imperfectly aware or wholly unaware of the latest state of affairs. It follows that any commander-in-chief who undertakes to carry out a plan which he considers defective is at fault; he must put forward his reasons, insist on the plan being changed, and finally tender his resignation rather than be the instrument of his army's downfall.

As American commander in Vietnam, I underwent many frustrations, endured much interference, lived with countless irritations, swallowed many disappointments, bore considerable criticism. I saw any number of my proposals, which I was convinced were legitimate and would speed the conclusion of the American assignment, disapproved—such matters as troop strength, for example, minimum versus optimum force, drives into Laos and Cambodia, and so on. I took issue with the strategy of graduated response in the bombing of North Vietnam, with bomb halts, with holiday cease-fires. Yet I realized that air operations against North Vietnam were outside my jurisdiction, however much I might have thought they should have been part of it; and I saw the bombing policy not as leading to failure but only as delaying success.

Once the penchant of niggling officials in Washington for quibbling over B-52 bomb targets had passed, President Johnson and Secretary McNamara afforded me marked independence in how I ran the war within the borders of South Vietnam, and no commander could ever hope for greater support than I received from Admiral Sharp at CINCPAC and from General Wheeler and the other members of the Joint Chiefs. Yet a commander must recognize that political considerations will never allow total independence.

Politicians are too imbued with French Premier Georges Clemenceau's dictum, however erroneously quoted, that "war is too important to be left to the generals." A commander must learn to live with frustration, interference, irritation, disappointment, and criticism, as long as he can be sure they do not contribute to failure. I suffered my problems in Vietnam because I believed that success eventually would be ours despite them, that they were not to be, as Napoleon put it, instruments of my army's downfall.

Only once did the possibility of resigning enter my mind, and that was not because of a question of success or failure. That happened early in 1968 when I saw the Joint Chiefs for a time leaning toward a parochial decision favoring one of the armed services in a matter that I saw as the field commander's prerogative and one that, if taken, would have been detrimental to my command.

When my family left Saigon in February 1965, I continued to reside in the same villa on Tran Quy Cap. After Kitsy moved to the Philippines in August 1966, she would join me on the occasion of special functions, usually at the Embassy, flying over on an empty medical evacuation plane, flying back on a plane loaded with wounded which she would help to attend. Having my wife and family relatively close was a real solace over the years, a benefit that I persuaded Secretary McNamara to extend to other officers whom I asked to serve extended tours in order to provide continuity in key positions. It is often the soldier's lot to be separated from his family, yet I was grateful that the long separation could be ameliorated to some degree during my children's formative years.

The lady whom I first spied as a child with flying pigtails has contributed much to my career, including my service in Vietnam. She has been more than a wife, a companion, a sweetheart; as have so many service wives, she has been a colleague, sometimes performing unglamorous but necessary tasks, helping me to execute my duties, easing my cares and concerns. Some idea of the dislocation she has experienced through the years can be realized from the fact that between our marriage in 1947 and 1975, we have lived in 36 different houses, an average of more than one a year.

Kitsy is a remarkable person. The difference in our ages has meant that often when I have been the senior officer on a post, she has been considerably younger than many of the wives of other ranking officers. When I was a brigadier general, for example, commanding in a remote area of Japan, she was twenty-five while some other wives whose husbands were junior to me were old enough to have been her mother. Wives, like husbands, can entertain jealousies and other frictions, yet I know of no case where Kitsy's warmth and natural diplomacy failed her in her role as the boss's wife.

While I fought in Korea, Kitsy was left in Japan where she helped alleviate the problems of the families of the soldiers. Because I kept her closely informed on events in Korea, she was often able to dispel damaging rumors. When husbands were wounded, she comforted the distressed families. While she was in Vietnam, Hawaii, and the Philippines, she was near military hospitals and worked almost every day in them to help care for the wounded. Characteristically, she never told me of her work; I learned of it only from others. When I went on one of my trips from Vietnam to the United States, she flew to Japan where many wounded from Vietnam were treated and visited for long hours in every military hospital there. Once when she was in Vietnam she personally gave a red rose to every man in the hospital on Valentine's Day. On another occasion in Vietnam she was massaging the back of a badly wounded black soldier, who spotted her name tag and verified that she was my wife. "I always wondered," the soldier said, "what generals' wives did while their husbands were fighting. Now I know."

On another of Kitsy's visits to Vietnam to tour the hospitals, she developed a special rapport with another black soldier who had lost a leg. Returning to the Philippines, she came upon him again in a hospital there. A few weeks later, while she was accompanying me on a trip to Washington, she visited Walter Reed Army Medical Center, and there he was. "Ma'am," said the soldier, "you sure do get around."

During the course of his peregrinations through the hospitals, the soldier had established a friendship with another man who also had lost a limb. He asked Kitsy if there was anything she could do to keep them assigned to the same hospital. Kitsy made the request, and hospital authorities fortunately were able to grant it.

Raised an Army brat in a constantly changing scene, Kitsy has always been at ease in any company. While she enjoys formal affairs, she has such an air of informality that in her corner of the room ritual is soon dispensed with.

Kitsy was much impressed with the wives of Vietnamese officials. If the Vietnamese men, she liked to say, were half as strong as their women, the country would have no problem. She enjoyed their sense of humor, their propensity for earthy jokes. When she had difficulty deciphering the mixture of languages and getting the point, one or another of the ladies would take her aside and explain. Kitsy shares some of my lack of affinity for foreign languages; her attempts at French drew the same wry smiles as my attempts at Vietnamese.

Kitsy's sense of humor has brightened many an occasion. At a ceremony unveiling my official superintendent's portrait at West Point, the master of ceremonies asked her to say a few words. "This is the second time I have seen Westy unveiled," said Kitsy. "The first time was on our wedding night."

Not long after I became the U. S. Army Chief of Staff, the Secretary of the Army accepted my recommendation that the heads of the Army Nurse Corps and the Women's Army Corps be established as general officers. Soon after I had the honor of pinning stars on the first two female generals in the nation's history, Anna Mae Hays and Elizabeth P. Hoisington (and establishing a tradition by giving each a kiss on the cheek), Kitsy found herself at the hairdresser's beside General Hays, a widow. "I wish you would get married again," Kitsy said. "Why?" General Hays asked. "Because," Kitsy responded, "I want some man to learn what it's like to be married to a general."

Enjoying athletics, Kitsy had a great rapport with the cadets engaging in sports at the Military Academy. I recall one baseball game for which she might well claim to have provided the margin of victory—at least one player involved, William M. Boice, gives her the credit. It was Army versus Navy with the score tied at five to five in the bottom of the eleventh inning, with Army at bat. With one man (Joe Blackgrove) on first base, there were two outs. As Boice, the Army team captain, came to bat, Kitsy stood up in the stands and shouted for all to hear, "All right, Billy, you're the captain of the team. Now act like one!" Billy responded with a home run and won the game.

Kitsy shared my wish to avoid public exposure for the children. We relented only once, in 1965, when *Time* magazine named me "Man of the Year." Although we sanctioned a family picture, we were both pleased when the writer, Frank McCullough, granted our subsequent request not to use it. I recall only once, on a visit with me to Washington, that Kitsy agreed to a press interview and then because President Johnson encouraged it.

The kind of vitriolic attack that she and the children might expect to encounter was demonstrated on several occasions. Stevie's art teacher at Bradford Junior College baited her with antiwar lectures during class until Stevie finally stayed behind and informed him in strong words that she had enrolled to learn about art, not Vietnam. At a private dinner party in Honolulu, Kitsy was shocked when a lady across the table, wife of a state senator, suddenly rose, overturning her chair, and made derogatory remarks about the war in Vietnam, the military, and me. Kitsy could but watch in amazement as the woman strode from the room.

Asking no favors herself, Kitsy was nevertheless conscious that there were those in the Army as elsewhere who sought advantage by ingratiating themselves with those in authority or by putting them in their debt. When she asked a general officer who was traveling to Taiwan to purchase for her a jade figurine, the officer sent it to her without a bill. When her third try to determine the cost so she could reimburse the officer failed, she had it packaged and sent back to him. That officer later came under investigation for improper conduct in Vietnam.

Kitsy is deeply religious and, like many of us, genuinely admired and loved the Vietnamese people. At the private dinner in the White House in November 1967 that I missed, my friends told me she asked that they permit her to say the blessing. "Thank God," she began, "for our brave and strong nation and its courageous people." She went on to pray for Americans fighting in Vietnam and to ask blessings on what she called "our little country of Vietnam." "Dear Lord," she concluded, "do help us to be good citizens."

Like many a family of Army regulars, some of which had sons or fathers who served second and third tours in Vietnam, the war brought tragedy to Kitsy's family. The morning I was to be sworn in as the U. S. Army Chief of Staff, I received a message from General Abrams informing me that Kitsy's younger brother, Frederick, on a combat operation as a battalion commander, was missing and presumed dead after his helicopter was shot down and crashed in a river in the Mekong Delta. His body was later recovered, and he was posthumously awarded the Distinguished Service Cross.

Over the years Kitsy and President Johnson developed a real camaraderie, and the President on several occasions expressed thoughtful appreciation of her. In a hand-written note to me in late December 1967, for example, which accompanied a commendation, he wrote:

> I have never been so sure of any commendation I've ever given and am confident none has ever been more deserved, except perhaps the one I'm giving in this note to your Kitsy—for her endurance, tolerance, and her love for you and her willingness to continue to go along with her Com-in-Chief in his personal assignments. My affection to you both. LBJ.

On our trip to Washington in November 1967 Kitsy and I had Thanksgiving dinner in Hawaii with close friends, retired Lieutenant General and Mrs. Charles Herron, General Herron having been Department Commander in Hawaii when I served there as a young officer before World War II. As we sat down to our meal, General Herron, vigorous in his nineties, announced that he wished to read from the Book of Proverbs, thirty-first chapter. He read, in part:

> A worthy woman who can find?
> For her price is far above rubies.
> The heart of her husband trusteth in her . . .
> Strength and dignity are her clothing . . .
> She openeth her mouth with wisdom;
> And the law of kindness is on her tongue.
> She looketh well to the ways of her household,
> And eateth not the bread of idleness.
> Her children arise up and call her blessed;
> Her husband also, and he praiseth her, saying:
> Many daughters have done worthily,
> But thou excellest them all!

He read the selection, General Herron said, because to him it described my wife.

In living without my family in the Saigon villa, I took advantage of vacant bedrooms by having selected members of my staff who had recurring information of official value reside with me. They varied from time to time, but I sought whenever possible to have my command surgeon live there and a civilian scientist who joined my staff at my request.

For much of my tenure, my command surgeon was Major General Spurgeon H. Neel, Jr., known—how else?—as "Spurgeon, the Surgeon." He had been surgeon of the 82d Airborne Division when I had been the division's chief of staff, a man able to translate complex medical matters into layman's language. His living in my villa enabled us to discuss my command's medical problems frequently over meals and also allowed me to enjoy a gifted conversationalist well versed in many subjects.

While I never entertained the thought that the enemy might defeat us in Vietnam, I recognized that medical problems in a tropical environment well might do so. Except for medical ingenuity and a helping of luck, a little mosquito that usually emerged only at night and bore a virulent strain of malaria known as "falciparum," on which the usual malarial prophylaxis had no effect, well might have beaten us. During the winter of 1965–66, incidents of falciparum malaria among American troops in the Central Highlands rose alarmingly, and several men died. I myself contracted malaria in Sicily during World War II and know from personal experience how debilitating it can be. Although I have long prided myself on being able to sleep whatever my concerns, I lost sleep over that threat. I prayed over it.

When the U. S. Army Surgeon General, Lieutenant General Leonard Heaton, who was always co-operative, sent medical experts from Washington to help, someone learned of a drug known as "DDS" (diaminodiphenylsulfone), or dapsone, a leprosy suppressant. The French before us had noted that lepers who took the drug regularly in pill form seldom developed falciparum malaria, even those living in the Highlands where the mosquito carrier was indigenous. As cases of the disease continued to rise, I decided I would be unable to await extensive tests before turning to the drug. I took personal responsibility for ordering that everybody serving in the Highlands start taking the pill at once.

It worked. Taken in conjunction with the usual malarial prophylaxis, it reduced the incidence of falciparum malaria by at least half, lowered the incidence of relapse by some 37 per cent, and cut hospitalization time in half.

Doctors and nurses, even in uniform, I have found, are really civilian specialists. They need to be pampered, encouraged, made to know that their commander recognizes their vital importance. Every time I went into the field I visited at least one medical facility, both to see the patients and to talk with the doctors and nurses. No commander was ever served by more skilled and dedicated medical specialists, including the ward masters, who were senior noncommissioned officers trained as practical nurses.

I developed a special affection for the 85th Evacuation Hospital, one of the first hospitals to reach Vietnam. When I first visited it soon after its arrival in the fall of 1965, I discovered to my concern that the local commander had located it in tents several miles east of Qui Nhon in a region so rife with VC that everybody called it "Indian country." To so invite VC attack on an undefended medical facility with its patients, skilled doctors, and fifty female nurses was beyond my acceptance. I ordered that the hospital switch locations with a well-established engineer battalion inside Qui Nhon that was capable of its own defense.

The shift occurred just as the hospital began to be flooded with casualties from the 1st Cavalry Division's fight in the Ia Drang Valley in November 1965. While part of the hospital moved to Qui Nhon, the remainder cared for the influx of patients until facilities gradually became available at the other site. One of the operations at the tent site involved complex brain surgery on an officer who was a nephew of Senator Russell of Georgia.

As I had admired American nurses under austere conditions in Europe and Korea, so I admired the nurses in Vietnam, living in mud-surrounded tents, using outdoor latrines, eating from mess kits in rain or under blistering sun, seldom finding an opportunity for a bath.

Although the commander of the unit was a skilled neurosurgeon, Colonel Harold Murphree, so occupied was he with his medical duties that he in effect passed day-to-day administrative command to his head nurse, Lieutenant Colonel Mary Donovan. Colonel Murphree was also something of an amateur psychologist and recognized the good effect Mary Donovan's pleasant personality but forceful direction had on the rest of the staff. A small, gray-haired woman of Irish descent with a twinkle in her eye, she was on her last tour before retirement. Although the tropical heat reduced her to amorphous protoplasm, she refused to accept the fact and went on doggedly about her duties.

Medical personnel, I have observed, are discontent, even feel misused, when they are not occupied with their specialty. If casualties were few in one area, I encouraged Spurgeon Neel to transfer doctors and nurses to other, busier hospitals to help until they were needed again at their home base.

I unwittingly invited such discontent when in early 1966, upon learning that a North Vietnamese regiment was moving into the fringes of the Highlands near Ban Me Thuot and that heavy fighting might result, I ordered the 3d MASH (Mobile Army Surgical Hospital) to the vicinity. As always, I wanted a hospital located only a matter of minutes from the battlefield. Because the region was still insecure, I directed that the female nurses stay behind and despite their vehement protests, stuck to the decision.

When heavy fighting failed to develop and casualties were few, some of the doctors and male nurses at the 3d MASH became discontented. Some occupied their time by giving badly needed medical help in nearby Montagnard villages, but one vented his upset in a provocative television interview. He apparently failed to realize that I had been obliged to prepare for any contingency and was, in fact, delighted that the hospital had so little business. I subsequently used the 3d MASH as my reserve hospital, to be moved by air wherever needed throughout the country.

My other steady boarder at No. 60 Tran Quy Cap was my scientific adviser, Dr. William G. McMillan, on leave of absence from the University of

California at Los Angeles. Since I believed strongly in innovations, in trying anything that might ease the task, I wanted to exploit any technology that scientists might develop to help. A brilliant chemical physicist, Bill McMillan was at the same time practical and pragmatic.

I took advantage of Dr. McMillan's presence and later Ambassador Komer's to have them sit in on strategy conferences which I held every Saturday morning with senior members of my staff, to discuss intelligence and current and future operations and plans. In the hope of profiting from the backgrounds of the two civilians, far different from those of us in the military, I encouraged them to act as devil's advocates, to try to demolish the conclusions to which I might be leaning. That neither was a specialist in tactics, strategy, or other military matters was of no concern; indeed, that was the reason I wanted their views. I knew, too, that if they spoke out, they would generate candid and provocative comment from members of my staff. If a civilian of Bill McMillan's or Bob Komer's intellect questioned why we did things a certain way, it compelled us to re-examine our methods. I also had my command historian sit in on most of those conferences to provide historical background and precedent.

Conferences were to me a useful, even essential, tool of command, but it was important that they involve candid comment, discussion, and divergent views. It was necessary to strive constantly to disabuse the staff of any self-satisfaction or complacency, for which it had a natural tendency.

Usually once a month at a central location, either Nha Trang or Cam Ranh Bay, I conducted a conference of senior American commanders, which I saw as a vital exercise. If on my travels about the country I learned of some unusual method, some short cut, some effective innovation, I invited the commander involved to tell of his experience at the senior commanders' conference. So separated were the units in Vietnam, so varied the experiences in the different sections of the country, that I wanted all to share these experiences, each to learn from the other, to be stimulated, challenged by someone else's success. Because the political situation was so integral to the military, I frequently had a representative of the Embassy brief the commanders. On occasion I invited Australians, South Koreans, and South Vietnamese to speak, and sometimes South Vietnamese counterparts accompanied American commanders. The conferences were of particular value in counteracting the lack of institutional memory that resulted from rapid turnover of commanders and gave me an opportunity to share with new commanders the institutional memory that I myself had developed through my long tenure. Something that might appear to a newcomer to be a worthwhile innovation may well have been tried unsuccessfully several times before.

While I met with the senior commanders, my command sergeant major (the command's senior NCO and a member of my staff) conferred in much the same manner with other command sergeant majors. When possible I would meet with them to air problems that concerned me. On many field trips I took my command sergeant major along—Sergeant Major John M. Pavliga, later H. L. McCoy—to talk informally with noncommissioned officers and enlisted men, to get their views, learn their state of morale, hear their complaints.

Based on my previous command experience, I vowed that, whatever else, three things would be done well for the troops in Vietnam: food, mail, and medical care. Although it cost in terms of manpower, funds, and personal attention, I am convinced that it paid off, that the men knew I was watching those matters, and that they appreciated it.

Because of the nature of the war in Vietnam, the separation of units from each other, the numerous small, isolated installations, it was even more essential than in conventional warfare for the over-all commander to get out often into the field. On an average I spent four out of seven days visiting the troops. Although I could handle some of my paperwork on plane or helicopter between stops, long hours in the evening still were necessary. I dictated much of my correspondence to my loyal and efficient secretary, Warrant Officer Montgomery (and later to Warrant Officer Dick Sauer) while going to or from the office or airfield. On return trips from the United States or other points outside Vietnam, couriers would meet me at intermittent stops such as Guam or the Philippines with accumulated paperwork so that by the time I returned to Saigon I would be free for other duties. On every stop at Guam I tried to visit crews of the Third Air Force's B-52 bombers that gave us such excellent support.

Seldom did I ask a field commander to come to my headquarters in Saigon; I would instead go to him. My staff was fully competent to handle matters in my absence, and I wanted the field commander to remain at his post. If decisions involving the field command were to be made, better to decide them where the feel of the situation and all the facts were at hand. Taking a leaf from the methods of General J. Lawton Collins in World War II, I would have both the field commander and my operations officer write memoranda for the record of what we had decided, whereupon my staff would prepare the formal order as appropriate. Since my desk-bound staff officers had little opportunity to get away from Saigon, my visits enabled me to impart to them at least some feel for what was happening with the troops.

One of the more important benefits from my visits was the opportunity to uncover and solve problems on the spot, long before they might have come to my attention through the chain of command. On a visit to Dong Tam in the Mekong Delta, for example, I found that a previously programmed C-130 airfield was unnecessary and stopped it before work reached a point of no return. Having found facilities at a Vietnamese civilian hospital at Vung Tau overloaded and depressing, I was able to locate an incoming Korean military hospital there to assist. Finding at Cam Ranh Bay that engineers were short of drilling tools for breaking rock for runways, I was able to order more sent immediately instead of having to wait for a routine request to be processed.

To avoid the natural tendency for a subordinate command to make elaborate preparations for a command visit, I usually passed word of my coming only the night before or the morning of my visit. I tried to avoid a large entourage, traveling only with my operations officer, an aide, and sometimes the command sergeant major and a member of the press. Many times I arrived unannounced, a practice that kept units alert. To the concern of an occasional field force or division commander, I deemed it my prerogative to visit any subordinate command without prior notice to its higher headquarters. It was my policy to call frequently on headquarters two or more echelons below my own. If orders or suggestions emerged from the visits, the subordinate command had the responsibility of notifying the next higher echelon of command.

It was always interesting and inspiring to visit remote CIDG-Special Forces camps. On my first visit to a camp near the village of Ban Don along the Cambodian border in jungle-covered Darlac province, a Special Forces captain explained that he used elephants rented locally to carry supplies for his patrols. On another visit I inspected the herd. The day before, I learned, Lieutenant General William R. Peers, then commanding the I Field Force, had purchased a baby elephant and had it transported inside a Chinook helicopter as a gift for a Montagnard community that had been relocated at Edap Enang south of Pleiku City as protection against the VC. That may well have been a first—and possibly a last—for elephants.

I stopped on several occasions on the road to Dalat at a leprosarium at Di Linh, in Lam Dong province. A French priest ran it, a model of organization and cleanliness, with the help of French and Vietnamese nurses. The old priest had been a *poilu* in World War I and delighted in showing me pictures of himself in the trenches, medals, and other memorabilia. Throughout South Vietnam one encountered numbers of French citizens engaged in humanitarian projects.

One of the gratifications of my travels about South Vietnam was meeting officers and men with whom I had served over the years. I encountered hundreds of young officers who had been cadets when I was superintendent of the Military Academy and countless numbers of enlisted men who had served under my command. Most of the men had become senior noncommissioned officers or had been commissioned as warrant officers or officers. I was particularly pleased to see two former enlisted aides, Bob Bates and Aleksander Einseln, and a former driver, Dick Hendrickson, as officers and an old soldier friend, Harvey Batchelor, as a senior warrant officer.

My travels posed many a problem for my aides, particularly my preference for a split-second schedule that would obviate waiting. Once when I was scheduled to meet Secretary McNamara upon his arrival at Tan Son Nhut, my aide at the time, Captain Carpenter, had trouble prying me away from visiting the wounded at a hospital in Vung Tau. I became a little irritated, assuring Carpenter that I was watching the time and we would make it. We debarked at Tan Son Nhut just as the Secretary's plane was taxiing to a halt. "You see, Bill," I said smugly, "I told you we would make it." Not until several years later did Captain Carpenter reveal that he had radioed ahead to have the air controller keep Secretary McNamara's plane taxiing until we had landed.

As I had only limited numbers of troops at my disposal, it was essential for me to plan ahead constantly, to develop contingency plans for any eventuality, to have subordinate commanders forecast their situation and possible operations at least six months ahead. I tried to alert commanders weeks before an operation and often projected the possibility of a minimum number of troops being available so that when the time came and more were actually on hand, the commander would have a sense of relief. All plans included several options, with a final decision to be made on the basis of the situation just before the operation began.

If the enemy tried something and failed, such as the siege of Con Thien in the fall of 1967, I assigned a special group to study the action from the enemy's viewpoint for lessons he might have learned, on the theory that he would try again. A staff section known as J-5 developed multiple plans and critically examined our tactics and strategy. Since it was possible at any time to have a cease-fire or a political settlement, detailed plans had to be developed for those contingencies. Others were developed for possible Chinese Communist intervention, for an amphibious hook around the DMZ, for moves into Cambodia and Laos.

I was particularly pleased with three plans developed for Laos. I am convinced that two and probably the third would have succeeded, would have eliminated the enemy's steady flow of men and supplies through the Laotian panhandle, and would have materially shortened American involvement in the war.

The first was developed early in 1966 with major input by the commander of the 1st Cavalry Division, General Kinnard, who came to Vietnam excited over the possibility of a move into Laos after he had had talks in Washington with the Army Chief of Staff, General Johnson, a strong proponent of the maneuver. To help in the planning I called on Colonel Arthur D. Simons who was familiar with the dominant terrain feature in the southern part of the Laotian panhandle, the Bolovens Plateau, where he had earlier conducted operations for the CIA. It was Simons who later led a raid to try to rescue American prisoners of war in North Vietnam at Son Tay.

A basic feature of the plan was to establish an airhead* on the Bolovens Plateau with the 1st Cavalry Division, a technique I had often studied and practiced during my days with the 101st Airborne Division and the XVIII Airborne Corps and one that had been considered for the Normandy invasion during World War II. After becoming established on the plateau, the

* An island in hostile territory secured by paratroopers or helicopter-borne troops which can be supplied and reinforced by air and from which operations may be launched to expand the area or to harass the enemy.

cavalry division was to drive northward toward the town of Saravane, midway in the panhandle, then swing to the northwest in the general direction of the Mekong River town of Savannakhet. Meanwhile, the 3d Marine Division in Quang Tri province in South Vietnam was to push westward from Khe Sanh along the axis of Route 9 into Laos, cut the Ho Chi Minh Trail, and take Tchepone, a North Vietnamese communications center on Route 9 approximately twelve miles inside Laos. The 4th U. S. Infantry Division from the vicinity of Pleiku City in the Central Highlands and a South Vietnamese division from the A Shau Valley were to complement the other two drives by pushing generally northwestward into the Laotian panhandle. The neck of the panhandle being sealed, a portion of the force would remain behind to secure it.

That plan had gathered considerable dust when in early 1968 I directed the deputy commander of the United States Army, Vietnam, Bruce Palmer, to restudy the matter and draft another plan based on the assumption that troops could enter Laos from both South Vietnam and Thailand. Aware at the time of President Johnson's decision not to seek re-election, in my own counsels I anticipated a change of administrations in the election of November 1968, which might result in a change of policy permitting operations in Laos.

Under Palmer's plan, given the code name EL PASO I, no airhead on the Bolovens plateau was involved on the assumption that a Thai force with the help of the Royal Laotian Army would control the plateau. In view of increased North Vietnamese strength in the panhandle, not one but three divisions in South Vietnam—two American, one South Vietnamese—would drive generally westward along the axis of Route 9 to Tchepone, while another division drove eastward out of Thailand to converge with them on Tchepone. After reviewing General Palmer's first plan, I asked him to prepare another (EL PASO II) based on the possibility that no more than one reinforced division in South Vietnam would be authorized or available. In that case, four brigades were to follow the generally westward path from the A Shau-Khe Sanh region to Tchepone.

I tried to be flexible with plans and afford leeway to the local commander. In late 1966, for example, the II Field Force commander, Jack Seaman, had completed detailed plans for large-scale entry into War Zone C, an operation later executed, in February 1967, under the code name JUNCTION CITY, the largest operation of the war to that time. At the last minute my intelligence officer, General McChristian, developed new intelligence locating one of the enemy's regional headquarters along the Saigon River in the Iron Triangle. The information was so convincing that Seaman wanted to delay JUNCTION CITY and instead drive into the Iron Triangle, the operation that subsequently became known as CEDAR FALLS.

I was at General Seaman's headquarters at Bien Hoa for a briefing on the new plan when the 1st Infantry Division commander, my former operations officer, Bill DePuy, arrived. In either operation the 1st Division was to be involved. Not one to hold his tongue when he believed he was right, General DePuy was so sure that he had pinpointed a VC regiment in War Zone C that he argued strongly for proceeding first with JUNCTION CITY. Seaman told me later that he was convinced I would side with my former staff man, DePuy. He was surprised when I told him: "You are the commander; the decision is yours." CEDAR FALLS went first.

Once a month some member of my staff bearing no responsibility for pacification or operations—and thus hopefully objective—briefed me and my staff and occasionally the ambassador's Mission Council on measurement of progress. The briefing of necessity depended in large measure on statistics: enemy killed, weapons captured, miles of waterways and roads opened, villages pacified, percentage of population under government control, logistical installations completed, proficiency ratings of ARVN units.

Statistics were, admittedly, an imperfect gauge of progress, yet in the absence of conventional front lines, how else to measure it? Furthermore, Secretary McNamara and his Assistant Secretary of Defense for Systems Analysis, Alain Enthoven, constantly prodded for more and more statistics. How else, too, to judge whether we were meeting the essentially statistical goals that Washington officials had set at the Honolulu conference of 1966?

The most controversial of the statistics was the number of enemy killed, which was based on tally in the field and known as "body count." I abhorred the term. A WAC secretary in my Saigon office, Sergeant Betty Reed, told me years later that the only time during several years in my office she ever heard me swear was when somebody mentioned "body count." Yet the term was already so firmly established in the lexicon of the war by the time I arrived that there seemed little point in trying to change it. It had been introduced in the early 1960s to appease the American press whose members were questioning the validity of casualty reports, but it subsequently became a favorite whipping boy of the press.

Since conditions permitting count of enemy dead varied, it was hard to determine exactly how accurate the tally was. Because the press constantly questioned its accuracy, I directed several detailed studies which determined as well as anybody could that the count probably erred on the side of caution. Seldom, for example, were figures included on enemy killed by long-range artillery fire or air strikes, nor was there any way to determine how many later died of wounds. The best estimate of enemy wounded was that for every man killed, probably 1.5 were seriously wounded. A year after my departure from South Vietnam, North Vietnam's General Giap told an Italian news correspondent, Oriana Fallaci, that to that time the North Vietnamese had lost half a million men killed, a figure that squared well with our estimates.

A genuinely misleading statistic was that on American wounded. As established before my arrival, the policy was that every man who received the Purple Heart was reported as wounded, even though he might require no more than a Band-Aid before returning to duty. That made the American wounded figure appear to be much higher than arrived at under the practice followed in World War II and Korea of reporting only those wounded requiring hospitalization. In a three-year period (1950–53) in Korea, for example, wounded requiring hospitalization totaled 103,200. For a seven-year period in Vietnam (1961–67) hospitalized wounded totaled 56,000, but the official announcement of wounded, which included those not requiring hospitalization, was almost double that: 106,200.

So established was the practice of lumping both figures together that I believed a shift to listing only hospitalized cases would produce accusations of cover-up. Although I subsequently directed a practice of reporting both figures and differentiating between them, the press in general continued to report only the total, thus perpetuating the misconception.

As large numbers of American ground troops were committed, I seriously considered recommending press censorship. Yet I saw many obstacles. How, for example, to prevent reporters, including many from countries other than the United States, from filing their stories from some other country, as enterprising newsmen did during the fighting against the Moros in the Philippines at the turn of the century? Such cities as Bangkok, Manila, and Hong Kong were readily accessible. As for television, the very mechanics of censoring it was forbidding to contemplate. In any event, in the final analysis, the decision on censorship was not mine to make but the President's.

In the absence of censorship, I made special efforts to establish rapport with the newsmen, to demonstrate through candid exchange that I appreciated their responsibility to keep the American people informed and intended to help. So did Barry Zorthian, whose Joint United States Public Affairs Office provided a convenient central source of information. Zorthian held weekly background sessions, sometimes in his home, for selected newsmen. His office conducted a daily press briefing, in which someone from my headquarters participated; but daily accounts of actions that seemed much like each other, dull statistics, and the fact that the briefer was seldom personally familiar with the events he described eventually gave the session a bad name. Reporters who had been at the scene of an action would sometimes rise to tell, as they put it, "what really happened." They called the briefing the "Five O'Clock Follies."

To establish rapport was behind my practice of taking at least one newsman with me on my travels about the country. I instructed commanders at all levels to co-operate with the media and requested assignment of information officers with reportorial experience. They were capable: Colonels Lee Baker (Air Force), Ben Legare, and Roger Bankson, and Brigadier General Winant Sidle. Newsmen were free to hitch rides in official vehicles; to eat at nominal cost in official messes; and, when in the field, to billet with American troops. I tried at first to persuade the newsmen to organize an association so that we could deal on policy matters with a single spokesman, but when I came to know the intense competition that motivated them, I realized that was naïve of me.

The only restriction I imposed was to charge the individual newsman with responsibility for withholding information that might aid the enemy, particularly troop movements, and a duty officer was available around the clock to advise on security. Intentional or repeated noncompliance might subject the correspondent to loss of accreditation, which meant, in effect, denial of the use of American facilities. The MACV information officer had to impose that penalty only a few times in the four years I was in Vietnam, which, in view of the hundreds of newsmen involved, is a distinct credit to the press corps. One whom he had to discipline was Secretary Rusk's brother-in-law.

As was the case in the Remagen bridgehead on the Rhine during World War II, there are times when a senior commander must relieve a subordinate, yet it is one of the most serious decisions a commander has to make, involving in many cases an irreparably damaging effect on an officer's career. Done summarily in the heat of battle, it may in the end prove to be unjustified. Conscious of those facts, I tried to avoid direct, abrupt reliefs, but some reliefs were inevitable. When that was the case—as with a brigade commander in the 1st Division who demonstrated over a period of time that he was not sufficiently aggressive to command a brigade effectively—I tried to ease the officer out without fanfare. What point in embarrassing him needlessly?

When Bill DePuy assumed command of the 1st Infantry Division, he relieved a number of subordinates, so many that for a time I was concerned lest the morale of the division be impaired. The Army Chief of Staff, General Johnson, expressed displeasure. I watched the situation closely, but I had confidence in General DePuy's judgment, and the division in the end was the better for it.

Relieving a general officer poses a particularly trying dilemma. If an officer progresses through the United States Army's demanding promotion system to reach the rank of general, he is, except under most unusual circumstances, clearly competent, even if he may not be the best man for every assignment, and bad assignments inevitably occur. If he does prove to be less than effective in a particular position, it is best for the welfare of the troops and in the end for the officer himself that he be relieved or transferred. I found, for example, one commander to be too hotheaded for a division command and asked the Army Chief of Staff to move him to some other post outside my command.

Despite my efforts to avoid fanfare in reliefs, the press sometimes dramatized them, as was the case with a distinguished general officer well-known and popular within the Army. Since I wanted a general officer in command of separate brigades, I put him in charge of the 196th Light Infantry Brigade, even though he was an artillery officer who had specialized in missilery.

In the brigade's first action, admittedly a rough one, he committed his units piecemeal and lost control of parts of his command. Perhaps no one under the circumstances could have done better, and it may have been unfair in the first place to give an infantry brigade to one lacking in tactical infantry experience. With those qualifying factors in mind, I decided not on "relief," in the sense that would indicate I had lost confidence in the officer, but on transfer. He subsequently served with dedication and distinction as the artillery officer in the I Field Force, and was later promoted to major general.

As I was reluctant to go to Washington for public appearances, so I sought no public exposure for personal aggrandizement. I did believe it my duty, in view of the controversy surrounding the war and the critical nature of news reporting, to explain to the press and on television how and why we did things the way we did. Thus I followed a policy of making myself readily available for interviews.

I presume it was this exposure plus my appearances in the United States in 1967 that produced a minor and thankfully short-lived Westy-for-President boomlet. To me it was an unrealistic development and I refused to take it seriously. Yet some people forwarded me campaign buttons, and a number of speculative articles appeared in newspapers and magazines. No doubt seeking to honor a native son, the South Carolina General Assembly passed a resolution "to prevail upon" me "to enter the presidential race." To be mentioned for my country's highest office was flattering, but I already had a responsible job still far from finished.

I thought I had disposed of the matter in the question period following my National Press Club speech in late 1967 when a reporter referred indirectly to the political speculation.

"Old generals fade away," the reporter said. "What does a young general do?"

"He says good-by," I responded, "and thank you very much for your kind attention."

Lest I appear to consider myself seriously as a political candidate, I made no public statement on the matter until after I learned from General Wheeler that President Johnson was sensitive to the continuing speculation and wanted to know if I did, in fact, have political ambitions. I assured General Wheeler that I had none and took the first opportunity when a question arose on the subject at a press conference to state categorically that I had no political plans, intentions, or aspirations. The boomlet died immediately.

Political speculation was still underway when a journalist, Ernest B. Furgurson of the Baltimore *Sun,* renewed an earlier request that I co-operate in his writing a biography of me. That was impossible in view of my continuing duties; besides, I was reluctant to do anything that might sustain the political rumors. Yet Furgurson was already committed to a publisher and was free to write even without my co-operation. Thus I allowed him to travel with me on one of my field trips and provided him names of a few people with whom I had been associated in the past, but I could not grant him access to official files. Furgurson duly noted in the foreword of his book that I had neither solicited nor encouraged his effort.†

It seems to be an American custom to make anyone in the public eye a ready target for any carping critic. That I sought relief from my fourteen- to sixteen-hour day and seven-day week by an occasional set of tennis, played in the stifling heat of the lunch period, apparently disturbed some people, including columnist Jack Anderson, who wrote when I broke my wrist in a fall on the court in 1966 that I should have been "at the front." Wherever he thought that was. I recalled an earlier critical disclosure that when the Battle of the Bulge opened in December 1944, General Eisenhower was "on the golf course," which was technically true but only because his headquarters was in tents pitched on the links. A repatriated prisoner of war later wrote me that North Vietnamese guards taunted the prisoners that "Westy" would rather play tennis than fight.

Through the years I have found that no matter what the pressures, I can do my job efficiently if I get eight hours' sleep each night and some form of rigorous physical exercise two or three times a week. I got that exercise in Vietnam by playing tennis, first at the Cercle Sportif in Saigon, then later on courts at the headquarters of the Seventh Air Force at Tan Son Nhut.

Perhaps fate tried to convince me of something that Jack Anderson's criticism failed to do. Hardly had I recovered from the broken wrist when a hard ball hit the tip of a finger on my right hand and chipped the bone, so that again I had to wear a cast. I forced myself to learn to play left-handed, but apparently because my left leg was unaccustomed to the stresses of left-handed play, I strained a leg muscle while playing with Stevie on a visit to my family in the Philippines and had to keep the leg elevated in an ice pack for twenty-four hours.

When not going on field trips, I was in my office by 8 A.M., where one appointment followed another until seven or eight in the evening. I had dinner at nine, occasionally with guests. When with visiting congressmen, journalists, or churchmen, I invited junior officers from combat units, to give them, I hoped, a pleasant occasion and the visitors some feel for the fighting. After dinner, while sitting in bed, I dealt with paperwork until I fell asleep. If I woke early, I tried to finish the paperwork, and sometimes for breakfast I invited some officer with whom I wanted to confer but found no time for during the day.

On my desk at the office I kept a card sent me by an old friend that I enjoyed pointing out to visiting congressmen: "Cheer up. Things could be worse. You could have my job." Beside my bed at home I kept pictures of Kitsy and the children and several books: a Bible; a French grammar; Mao

† *Westmoreland: The Inevitable General* (Boston: Little, Brown and Co., 1968).

Tse-tung's little red book on theories of guerrilla warfare; a novel, *The Centurions,*‡ about the French fight with the Viet Minh; and several works by Dr. Bernard Fall, who wrote authoritatively on the French experience in Indochina and provided insight into the enemy's thinking and methods. I was usually too tired in late evening to give the books more than occasional attention.

Before such holidays as Christmas, New Year's, and Tet, the Vietnamese lunar New Year, I called on Thieu, Ky, and Vien, and over Christmas visited as many troops as possible while reserving New Year's for my family (if they were in the Philippines). Although I worked Sundays, I tried to attend church services. When I fell behind in that resolve, my command chaplain, Colonel Joseph Chmielewski, was quick to reprimand me.

One of the more inane controversies of the Vietnam war was that over use of nonlethal gases. There were three types: DM, a pepperlike irritant that causes sneezing, headaches, and nausea; CN, a tear-inducing agent that also irritates the skin; and the most common, CS, a tear-inducing agent that also irritates the nose and respiratory tract. All have only a temporary incapacitating effect, lasting from three to ten minutes with CN and CS and a half-hour to two hours with DM. All are similar to those used by police in riot control.

The United States first provided tear gas to the South Vietnamese in 1964 after an incident in which the Viet Cong forced villagers to precede them as shields in an attack. After that, the ARVN used it on two or three occasions before a press report in March 1965 sparked the controversy. North Vietnamese propagandists promptly claimed the United States was employing "poisonous chemicals." Some British Members of Parliament spoke out in protest, as did a number of American legislators, including Senator Wayne Morse of Oregon, who claimed the gas was among those "justly condemned by the general opinion of the civilized world." Senator Morse's usual companion in criticizing the war, Senator Fulbright, disagreed. He thought it "the most humane way to deal with the disorder."

For once I shared Senator Fulbright's view. Mingling with villagers was a common VC tactic, as was taking civilians with them into their caves and tunnels. Without tear gas our forces had but two alternatives: leave the VC alone or kill them and the civilians alike with bullets, shells, or explosives.

Upon instruction from Washington and because we had yet to develop equipment suited for using tear gas against the enemy's tunnels, I suspended its use temporarily. The controversy flared anew in September 1965, when the commander of a U. S. Marine battalion, Lieutenant Colonel Leon Utter, unaware of my order, used tear gas against VC bunkers and tunnels in which civilians also were hiding. The results were excellent. Over 400 people emerged, including women and children, none seriously injured.

‡ Jean Lartéguy, *The Centurions* (New York: E. P. Dutton, 1962).

Once the press picked up that story, I made sure that the Marine officer learned immediately of my restriction. My inclination was to congratulate him, but in view of my order, that was out of the question. Yet how absurd the restriction was was demonstrated a few days later in an action involving a nearby battalion. Denied the use of tear gas, the marines ordered a VC force holed up in a tunnel to come out or be destroyed by explosives. The VC failed to respond so that when the marines blew up the tunnel, they killed 66 VC. Had civilians been present, they too would have been killed.

Those contrasting examples at hand, I immediately asked shipment to Vietnam of blowers with which troops might flush smoke or tear gas into the tunnels. The first trial was by U.S. marines using smoke. Although the tunnel proved to be unoccupied, the smoke revealed the extent of the complex and aided in its destruction.

As the 173d Airborne Brigade early in 1966 was about to make a foray into the Iron Triangle with its vast tunnel system, I asked approval to employ tear gas. Although the State Department was still quibbling, Secretary McNamara authorized its use with the proviso that I brief the press in advance in an off-the-record session in which I would stress the humane aspects. Yet that was but a one-time approval. Not until two months later did I finally gain unrestricted authority to employ what was probably the most humane weapon at my disposal.

The holiday cease-fires that became a kind of tradition in Vietnam were of benefit only to the enemy. They came at Christmas, New Year's, Tet (January/February), and Buddha's birthday (April/May). As truck traffic from the North clearly revealed, the enemy used them to reinforce and resupply, and his forces withheld attack only as it suited their interests. Yet to many the United States would have appeared callous had we failed to go along with them. In an effort to keep them as brief as possible and so limit their value to the enemy, I would early agree on dates with the South Vietnamese and Allied commanders and suggest them to Washington officials before they themselves had set them. I got nowhere with a proposal to hinge agreement to the next cease-fire on the enemy's strict compliance with the previous one.

The American armed services and the officers and men representing them devised some of the most imaginative and successful expedients and innovations to cope with the unusual nature of the enemy and the war that any military force has ever brought to bear:

The Riverine Force, for example. And the slow old C-47 transport plane converted into a gunship with floodlights and rapid-firing Gatling-type "miniguns" and nicknamed variously "Spooky" or "Puff, the Magic Dragon," capable of maintaining nighttime vigil over isolated posts and delivering devastating fire. The Firefly, a helicopter with a floodlight. A swift, rocket-armed Huey Cobra helicopter gunship, which the officer who as a brigadier general first established the headquarters of the United States Army, Vietnam, Jack Norton, early urged me to push for with Secretary McNamara. Together, the Department of Defense and Bell Aircraft did a superb job developing the Cobra.

"Road Runner" operations, in which spotter aircraft in contact with artillery and fighter-bombers hovered over truck convoys to pick out enemy ambushes and in which the convoys in wooded regions made rapid dashes through likely ambush sites, guns blazing to keep the enemy down. Tracker teams using dogs to smell out the guerrilla; thirty-six dogs were killed in action, 153 wounded. Volunteer *chieu hoi* returnees, called "Kit Carson scouts," to lead to enemy arms caches and hideouts. A program called "Bushmaster," wherein a company established a secret base near enemy-used trails and supply routes, then sent out small detachments to conduct ambushes. I started a RECONDO school similar to the one I had established in the 101st Airborne Division, to train men for long-range reconnaissance patrols; when they found the enemy, they called in air and artillery strikes, and the intelligence they gathered was invaluable. A similar school trained ARVN troops. On one occasion men of the Special Forces parachuted a bulldozer into a remote area near the Laotian border in order to construct an air strip.

One of the more effective devices—the Rome plow for leveling the jungle and eliminating the enemy's hiding places—was in part an outgrowth of a chance encounter while I was swimming at the Kahala Hotel beach in Honolulu during a visit for a conference with Admiral Sharp. Recognizing me, B. K. Johnson, a Texan, introduced himself. He said he had cleared rain forests in the Australian bush by shattering big trees with a crane mounting a 5,000-pound steel ball on a chain. I sent an officer to Australia to see it and my engineers experimented with it, but others in the Army had by then discovered a more practical piece of equipment for our use, the Rome plow, with its bulldozer blade and a spike at one end that, with several stabs, could fell the largest tree. (It was named after the city in Georgia where it was manufactured.) I ordered a hundred immediately and ended with more than a thousand. It was a device the Vietnamese much admired, for in addition to eliminating enemy hideouts, it cleared vast acreage for cultivation.

Chemical defoliants also helped deny the enemy hiding places, particularly ambush sites along roads and waterways. Early in the war defoliants were also used to deny the enemy rice in remote areas that were VC-controlled, although as government control spread and areas of VC influence were less clearly delineated, the practice was less often employed. Some ecological damage may have resulted from the defoliants; how much and how permanent it is remains to be seen. Flying over much of the country as recently as 1972, I found Vietnam still a verdant land, which left me to question the truth of some of the more pessimistic allegations of permanent damage. The defoliants were a major factor in reducing the number of ambushes that were long so costly in American and South Vietnamese lives.

To keep Route 20 open as the lifeline for vegetables to move from Dalat to Saigon, engineers built mutually supporting fire-support bases that could be occupied whenever the VC acted up. We called them "Howard Johnsons."

In an effort to deter enemy movement on remote mountain roads, Dr. McMillan and his scientists tried an ingenious gimmick. They found a chemical solvent that when mixed with water and soil would turn the soil to slush, which as long as it was wet would not stabilize. At the start of the rainy season, they dumped tons of the solvent from C-130s on a constricted road in the A Shau Valley, but no substantial evidence was ever found that it proved effective in deterring movement.

Some of the electronic developments were impressive. By magnifying light from the stars, the "Starlight Scope" enabled men on outpost duty to see at night. "People Sniffers" could detect human presence, primarily from the odor of urine. The Mark 36 Destructor was a mine dropped from planes along roads in North Vietnam and Laos that once it was in position detonated if moved or if movement occurred near it. Little gravel mines, which took their name from their appearance, were sufficient to incapacitate a man who stepped on one, yet friendly troops could enter the area later because the mines self-sterilized in a few weeks. MSQ radar gave tactical aircraft a limited all-weather capability. Acoustic and seismic ground sensors listened in on enemy movements and in one case helped a reinforced company of the 25th Division north of Tay Ninh City to kill 250 of the enemy with virtually no loss. A more sophisticated version of Spooky, a converted C-130 aircraft, operated over the Ho Chi Minh Trail, equipped with the usual floodlights and miniguns and also with electronic equipment to eavesdrop on ground sensors. In hope of slowing traffic on the Ho Chi Minh Trail by mud, Air Force planes seeded clouds above the Laotian panhandle, but there was no appreciable increase in rain.

At the town of Nakhom Phanom just across the Mekong River from Laos in Thailand, a U. S. Air Force installation provided a communications and computer center to assemble data from aircraft orbiting above the Ho Chi Minh Trail and receiving signals from electronic sensors on the ground. Known familiarly as "NKP," or by the code name PEPPER GRINDER, the base was a landmark for all Air Force pilots.

Ordnance developments included "Beehive" artillery rounds that released thousands of little pellets that were markedly effective at close range, sometimes making the difference between life and death when isolated artillery units came under attack. Another newly developed form of artillery ammunition with tremendous fragmentation effect, known as COFRAM, was released for use during fighting at Khe Sanh early in 1968. A World War II development, napalm, a kind of jellied gasoline, helped get at the enemy in his dug-in base areas. The "Daisy Cutter" was a special bomb with heavy blast effect used to clear landing zones in the jungle. Although we experimented with burning out forested enemy base areas with incendiary bombs, getting fires started and keeping them burning in the damp jungle proved impossible.

In Europe during World War II, giant searchlights bouncing their beams off low-lying clouds created a kind of artificial moonlight useful for illumination in night attacks. Having seen that expedient, I tried it in Vietnam but with only limited success. During the dry season, rarely were there enough clouds, and during the rainy season, they were too all-enveloping. Continuous illumination with floodlights at some major installations, such as Tan Son Nhut, was more effective. So were searchlights mounted atop a 3,200-foot peak called Nui Ba Den—which means Black Virgin—that rises abruptly from flat terrain in Tay Ninh province; from that commanding position, the searchlights illuminated rubber plantations several miles away.

To beef up intelligence collection, English-speaking Vietnamese interrogation teams moved from one American unit to another to query prisoners soon after capture when they were more inclined to talk. A special American battalion quickly processed and analyzed aerial photography so that units in the field could get the information before the enemy situation changed. The commander of the 1st Marine Division, Major General Herman Nickerson, Jr., was convinced his men could locate enemy tunnels with divining rods.

Psychological warfare detachments operated throughout South Vietnam, distributing leaflets, broadcasting over loudspeakers, trying in various ways to persuade the enemy to defect. One unit tried playing plaintive North Vietnamese folk music at holiday periods. An ingenious commander of the 1st Brigade, 101st Airborne Division, General Pearson, who was for a time my operations officer, had his men photograph a co-operative prisoner with a Polaroid camera so that leaflets could be printed quickly for distribution before the man's unit left the vicinity. Yet despite a major and persistent effort, including bringing civilian psychological warfare experts from the United States, results were disappointing. Except for an occasional platoon-size group, most defectors were individuals. Mass surrenders never developed despite our intense psychological warfare efforts, which apparently could not overcome the enemy's intensive indoctrination.

By means of interlocking fire-support bases, artillery units could support each other. When a unit evacuated a base, a hidden platoon might stay behind to ambush inquisitive enemy who tried to move in. Companies of South Vietnamese guerrillas with American advisers operated far from any base, sometimes for a month or longer. "Hook" helicopters airlifted light and medium artillery. In "Eagle Flights," companies of Vietnamese or Americans in Huey helicopters swooped down swiftly upon a site where intelligence indicated an enemy presence or where accompanying helicopter gunships drew fire. These were, in effect, airborne raids on targets of opportunity. Every unit became proficient in air assaults by helicopter. With Department of the Army approval, I changed the structure of the American infantry battalion from three rifle companies to four, which, among other purposes, provided a company for base defense while still maintaining the triangular structure for operations outside the base.

Wooden or prefabricated steel observation towers were useful for spotting enemy mortars and rockets, particularly around base camps and cities. The M-113 armored personnel carrier, a tracked vehicle, operated well even in the muddy rice paddies. When covered with sand bags, a big metal container in which supplies and equipment were shipped made an effective pillbox or bunker. Boston whalers with outboard motors took some of the transport burden off helicopters in the Mekong Delta. The marines could quickly construct a tactical air strip with aluminum planking and an arresting gear as on an aircraft carrier. Because of the foresight of somebody among my predecessors, excellent tactical maps were available from a survey begun in 1956 and frequently updated. As early as 1965 I obtained an aerial delivery company to pack and deliver supplies by parachute; if all other methods failed, an isolated force still could be supplied. I kept the company centrally located at Cam Ranh Bay.

Targeting and employment of B-52 bombers gradually became ever more sophisticated. Those giant planes had a wing span of 185 feet, a length of 157 feet, and could carry a bomb load of 58,000 pounds in 500-, 750-, and 1,000-pound bombs. They could also carry canister-type bombs that could be timed to open when they were close to the ground and spray a cluster of small bombs. A radar sight enabled the bombers to achieve their remarkable accuracy. In the early days, once the planes had set out to hit a target, the mission could be aborted but not shifted to an alternate target, but with the introduction in the summer of 1966 of ground radar control, which could direct the big bombers over the target and also indicate the moment of bomb release, it became possible to change targets well after the planes had departed their bases on Guam and in Thailand.

Almost every mail brought a letter or two from some armchair strategist among the American public who thought he had the answer to our problems. Most were genuinely trying to be helpful, and some suggestions were expedients that we had already either tried or adopted. One man wanted us to mount the engines on B-52 bombers vertically so the planes could rise straight up, thereby eliminating the long flights from Guam and Thailand. Perhaps the most ingenious suggestion—if not also the most impractical—was that we inject all Vietnamese inside South Vietnam, including North Vietnamese troops, with a phosphorous solution so they would glow in the dark. All we had to do at that point, the writer averred, was keep the friendly Vietnamese inside their houses at night and go after anybody who glowed. My correspondent apparently failed to consider that if we had enough control over the VC and the North Vietnamese to inject them with the solution, why would we turn them loose? I was reminded of a story I had heard as a child that the way to catch a sparrow is to sprinkle salt on his tail.

As with contingency plans, it was essential to plan far ahead on almost everything, for the lead time often was long. When the enemy began using the 122-mm rocket with its vast six-mile range, I asked for prefabricated observation towers. Had there been no aerial delivery company, a number of encircled units would have been in serious trouble. If more troops were to be introduced into the northern provinces, more logistical facilities had to be built in advance. If Khe Sanh was to serve as a base for moving into Laos, or even if it was to be successfully defended, it had to have an airfield capable of accommodating transport aircraft. As the monsoons shifted from southwest to northeast or vice versa, I had to be prepared to move troops north or south to get maximum use from limited numbers. With so many things to be done with so few troops, I had to get involved in details that a supreme commander would ordinarily leave to subordinates. On many matters I was one of the few with a long institutional memory to bring to bear.

Having observed the graft and corruption in the U.S. military that occurred in World War II, which I had reflected upon on the long flight back from Europe, I knew I had to anticipate similar problems in Vietnam and try to circumvent them. People tend to forget that putting a man in uniform does nothing to turn him into a saint; he still retains his basic characteristics as part of a cross section of the American people, and wartime conditions pose many a temptation.

I was particularly concerned because of the large numbers of clubs and messes, which I encouraged as recreational facilities to keep the men away from the fleshpots. "There exists," I warned at a senior commanders' conference in September 1967, and on many another occasion, "a strong temptation for embezzlement." The Post Exchanges, intentionally well stocked to lower piaster spending and, again, to keep the troops out of the cities, afforded monetary temptations to which some men obviously succumbed; one had only to stroll Tu Do Street in Saigon to realize the quantities of American items that somehow found their way to sidewalk vendors. Currency manipulation added yet another temptation. "Be alert," I urged at another conference, "for crooks and grafters."

From the first I emphasized a large and active inspector-general system. "I want commanders and inspectors general," I said often, in the process mixing my metaphors, as was sometimes my penchant, "to keep their ears to the ground and be alert to smell out and solve problems while they are small." Every major unit had to have an effective criminal investigation system. "I insist," I said, "on maintaining high morality throughout the command."

I was deeply disappointed. In view of the large numbers who served in Vietnam and the multiple temptations, perhaps I should take comfort in that the vast majority remained honest and moral. That overwhelming majority is surely to be lauded. Yet if even one man errs, it is a stain upon the command. A mess manager in Saigon underpayed visiting entertainers and pocketed the difference. A finance office in Saigon harbored a ring of soldier crooks that falsified currency transactions and got away with $700,000 before they were caught.

The most sensational case broke in the summer of 1969 while I was Army Chief of Staff, a so-called "clubs and messes scandal" involving dishonesty in both Europe and Vietnam. As revealed by a Senate investigation, the U. S. Army's command sergeant major and seven sergeants had been involved in bribery, kickbacks, and smuggling. Also allegedly involved was a brigadier general, the personnel officer of the United States Army, Vietnam.

Uncovering a scandal and getting sufficient evidence for conviction are two different things. As Army Chief of Staff, I took such administrative action as I could against the guilty, including recommending to the Secretary of the Army (a recommendation that he accepted) to reduce the general officer to the grade of colonel and recall his medal for distinguished service. At congressional hearings the leader of the conspiracy, the sergeant major, implied that other senior officers and I had known of the irregularities and had done nothing about them, a brazen and despicable attempt to shift the blame. On the contrary, when I learned of irregularities, I directed a relentless investigation.

That dishonesty, immorality, and other irregularities have occurred in all wars was no excuse. Although I had hoped that Vietnam would be an exception and had worked hard to that end, it followed the pattern. What is the answer? Is human nature so fallible that even the best efforts inevitably fall short?

In addition to well-trained and motivated inspectors general and criminal investigators, the answer has to lie in an officer corps of the highest quality. Even with an officer corps schooled in and dedicated to the highest code of ethics, alert to policing its own and subordinate ranks, failures may still happen. Yet the striving for perfection must be constant. No military service—indeed, no nation—can long survive without constant search for that goal, constant policing, constant rededication when transgressions do occur.

Since a war of insurgency and counterinsurgency inevitably takes place in large measure among the civilian population, who constitute a conscious goal of the insurgents, it was essential from the first to do everything possible to avoid civilian casualties. I early formulated strict rules of engagement regarding ground fire, artillery fire, and tactical air strikes, rules designed to minimize civilian losses. That was one of the reasons for evacuating civilians from villages where they were intermixed with the Viet Cong, for forcing them to endure the indignity and hardship of refugee camps, for creating much-maligned "free-fire zones" where anybody who remained had to be considered an enemy combatant. I instituted a policy of updating, clarifying, republishing, and redistributing the rules of engagement at least every six months so that no incoming soldier or officer could plead ignorance of old regulations.

At a press conference in mid-1966, I said:

> Let one fact be clear. As far as the United States Military Assistance Command in Vietnam is concerned, one mishap—one innocent civilian killed, one civilian wounded, or one dwelling needlessly destroyed—is one too many.

On the card listing "Nine Rules of Conduct" that I provided all American soldiers, proper treatment of Vietnamese civilians was the central theme. By stressing civic action projects, I sought to get the troops involved with the people, to get them imbued with the concept that they were not there just to kill but to help the people to build. On a similar card for commanders, listing fifteen points of guidance, I stressed discriminate use of firepower, "particularly in populated areas." I required that all men entering Vietnam be indoctrinated in detail on the rules of engagement, the Nine Rules of Conduct, and provisions of the Geneva Convention on handling of prisoners of war. Another card issued to every soldier, "The Enemy in Your Hands," reiterated the rules of the Geneva Convention in regard to prisoners.

Having taught a course on the Geneva Convention and the laws of war at the Command and General Staff College in the late 1940s, I was sharply conscious of the responsibilities they placed on field commanders. Shortly after assuming command in South Vietnam in 1964, I called in my judge advocate general, Brigadier General George Prugh, and instructed him to form a study group to recommend what to do. From that study and from frequent later consultations emerged the strict MACV regulations.

My World War II experience also made me sharply conscious of atrocities. I recall the horror as troops of the 9th Division entered the town of Plomion in northeastern France and found the bodies of all the young men of the town. German SS troops had tied their hands behind them with barbed wire, lined them up against a wall, and shot them. I also later saw the horrors of the Nordhausen concentration camp.

In researching the records of my commanders' conference, I found few in which I failed to stress the necessity to forestall civilian casualties and property damage. I specifically required that whenever civilian casualties did occur or there was any incident that might be an embarrassment to the command or a source of friction with the Vietnamese, a report be submitted immediately to my headquarters and a subsequent report of investigation submitted to me by the most expeditious means.

Rules, regulations, cards, even indoctrination quite obviously would not forestall all civilian casualties in such a war. In the final analysis the commander on the battlefield had to weigh many factors, including the success of his mission and the protection of his men. Balancing those obligations against the possibility of property destruction and civilian casualties might be the responsibility of commanders at the lowest level, at platoon or squad.

Some casualties and property destruction were also bound to occur in villages and hamlets that the enemy turned into fortified camps. Human error also was a factor: a bomber pilot mistakes the target, an artillery forward observer reads the wrong map co-ordinates. Guns and machines can also err, as on one occasion I could personally attest. A rocket on a gunship escorting my helicopter was fired by mistake, killing a child and wounding another and the dead child's mother. Yet inevitability is no license, and a commander at whatever level must strive constantly to instill in his troops utmost care and respect for property and lives.

In December 1967 Ambassador Bunker called my attention to an article by Jonathan Schell on property destruction and civilian casualties in Quang Ngai province, which he had obtained prior to publication in *The New Yorker*. The accusations were shocking—some 70 to 80 per cent of houses in some areas destroyed, abject disregard for civilian casualties by callous forward air controllers.

So upsetting were these allegations that I wanted someone other than a member of my staff to investigate. At my request, Ambassador Bunker assigned the task to a senior Embassy official, James D. Hataway, Jr.

Hataway found Schell's report exaggerated. The author's style, Hataway noted, often led the reader to visualize destruction over a vast region when in fact the area described was only a few square kilometers. Except for a two-kilometer strip along Route 1, Schell wrote, for example, all houses the rest of the way to the sea were destroyed. That was patently misleading. Because the countryside between Route 1 and the sea was uninhabitable salt flats, there had never been any houses between the highway and the sea. Schell's report that forward air controllers engaged in grisly banter was, according to Hataway, quite representative, but he saw it as a kind of gallows humor, a kind of protective armor, in no way proof that the air controllers practiced wanton death and destruction.

Soldiers have employed gallows humor through the ages. What paratrooper, for example, singing the drinking song, "Blood on the Risers," really revels in the gory death of the man he is singing about? Gallows humor is, after all, merely a defense mechanism for men engaged in perilous and distasteful duties.

There was nevertheless truth enough in Schell's article to prompt me to go to Quang Ngai and talk with the commander of the Americal Division, who was responsible for operations in the province. Quang Ngai for more than twenty years had been under almost total VC control, and the civilian population was in the main militantly sympathetic to the VC. As much as anywhere in Vietnam, the VC in Quang Ngai province fortified the hamlets. Under MACV policy, if a defended hamlet was to be attacked, warning had to be given so that noncombatants—women, children, old men—might leave.

In my mind all precautions were aimed at careless or indiscriminate use

of firepower. Since murder is so obviously a major crime, surely it was unnecessary to put out a specific order saying American soldiers were not to
murder unarmed civilians. Similarly, if murder or other major crimes should
occur, those crimes even more than accidental deaths surely would fall
under my dictum that anything untoward was to be reported immediately to
my headquarters and investigation instigated.

Perhaps it was inevitable that some crimes of violence against civilians
would occur. At peak strength, 549,000 Americans were in Vietnam, but
because of constant turnover, a total of 2,594,000 served at one time or
another. Even the peak strength was the equivalent of the population of a
good-sized city, such as Buffalo, New York, or Cincinnati, Ohio, where
crimes of violence are a daily occurrence; and unlike the population of a
city, all the men in Vietnam were armed and operating in a hostile environment. Thus the remarkable fact may well be not that crimes occurred but
that they were as few as they were. During my tenure in Vietnam, thirty-one
men were tried for murder of civilians, seventeen for rape, and eleven for
manslaughter. Of the total of fifty-nine, thirty-six were convicted, a conviction rate, incidentally, above the average for American civilian juries.

Chapter XVI
The American Soldier

As the Christmas season of 1966 approached, an American U-2 reconnaissance plane returning to its base from a flight over North Vietnam exploded at 26,000 feet. Although the pilot ejected and was rescued, dense jungle along the Cambodian border swallowed the debris of the plane, leaving no trace.

My Deputy for Air, Spike Momyer, and his Air Force superiors in Washington were perturbed. Like all U-2s, the plane carried a highly secret "black box," the key to the high-level reconnaissance capability of the craft. That box could reveal sensitive technical information that might enable an adversary to devise measures to counteract the reconnaissance methods of the U-2. Although the box was rigged for self-destruction, there was strong evidence that the autodestruct mechanism had failed. The box had apparently gone down intact with the plane.

How to find the little black box? The plane had crashed in an enemy sanctuary up to that time unpenetrated by Americans or ARVN. Aerial photography of the double- and triple-canopied jungle revealed nothing. Although skilled Air Force technicians were able to estimate the general location of the plane in a cone-shaped area along the border northwest of Saigon, the cone encompassed approximately 440 square miles. Looking for the plane in that virtually trackless expanse would be like looking for a raft in thousands of miles of ocean, or, assuming the black box had blown clear of the plane, like looking for a chip of wood on that same vast sea.

I turned the problem over to the highly imaginative commander of the 5th Special Forces Group, Colonel Francis J. ("Black Jack") Kelly. Impossible was a word that Frank Kelly refused to recognize. He in turn assigned it to Captain James G. ("Bo") Gritz, the daring young commander of one of the first mobile South Vietnamese guerrilla forces to be organized. Each force consisted of a company of approximately 150 CIDG troops, in Gritz's case ethnic Cambodians, whom Gritz called his " 'Bodes." Gritz and eleven other Green Berets actually commanded rather than advised the guerrilla force, men who had volunteered to operate in remote areas for extended periods with only limited outside support.

Bo Gritz and his colleagues had little to go on other than a map marked with the cone as devised by the Air Force technicians, a look at a photograph of one of the black boxes, and the knowledge that they were moving into hitherto-unchallenged VC country. They knew too that their insertion into the jungle by helicopter was bound to alert the VC to their presence.

Almost from the start they had running brushes with the enemy, which inevitably produced casualties that had to be laboriously carried on litters and then daringly extricated by helicopters' dangling ropes, so as not to impair the force's mobility. It was a dangerous procedure in any case, for again it pinpointed the force's location. To disguise the operation as much as possible, fighter-bombers resupplied the men by dropping napalm containers as in a normal air strike, but instead of jellied gasoline, the containers held specially packaged supplies.

For close to three days Bo Gritz, his Green Beret colleagues, and his 'Bodes plowed through the jungle, cutting paths through vines and elephant grass, wading streams, following elephant trails, plodding uphill and down, trying always to maintain some kind of pattern to insure full coverage of the vast area they had to search.

Late on the third day the Cambodian scouts let out a whoop. Incredibly, they had found the fallen aircraft, but to Gritz's utter chagrin, the portion of the plane containing the black box was missing.

Because of various indications that somebody had been tampering with the wreckage, Gritz concluded that the VC had recognized the value of the black box and had made off with it. To a less determined man, that might have been undeniable proof that the mission was impossible. Not to Gritz. If the VC had indeed made off with the black box, he deduced, it was such an unusual event that every enemy soldier for miles around would know of it. The answer was to take a prisoner.

Late that afternoon Gritz and ten of his men set up an ambush on a trail that showed frequent and recent human use. Darkness had scarcely fallen when footsteps on the trail gave every indication that the ambush was to be rewarded. As the footsteps materialized into men, Gritz counted six. At his signal, the Cambodians opened fire, triggering the ambush. They did their job too effectively. As the firing died down, Gritz found that four of the VC were dead and the other two had escaped into the night, leaving blood trails.

Knowing that his force's position had been compromised, Gritz sent the main body of his guerrillas on to a bivouac area while he and his ten men waited the next night at the ambush site for the enemy that Gritz knew would come for the bodies of the dead. This time Gritz's orders were explicit. The 'Bodes were to kill all but the first two men in the column. To assure a live prisoner, Gritz and a trusted Green Beret sergeant would handle those two in hand-to-hand combat.

The men were barely in position for ambush when ten VC carrying AK-47s and AKSs moved up the trail as if on parade. At a prearranged signal, jungle quiet gave way to exploding claymore mines and chattering automatic rifles. Using CIA-supplied "zappers," telescopic, spring-steel billy clubs, Gritz and the sergeant jumped from their bamboo cover along the trail and attacked the two leaders. A Black Belt in tae-kon-do, Gritz overestimated the force of his blow and killed his man, but the trusty sergeant came through.

The prisoner was a youth of sixteen, injured severely in the fight with the sergeant. Having been in Vietnam for close to two years, Gritz spoke enough Vietnamese to convince the young VC that he was going to die from his injury. Only Gritz's doctor—the Special Forces first-aid man—could save him. It was hardly worth his while, Gritz said, to burden himself with a prisoner unless the prisoner could help him. Where was the black box? If the youth would agree to guide Gritz to it, the doctor would save his life.

Apparently convinced, the young VC agreed to help. The segment of the plane containing the black box was in his own base camp several miles away. He himself had seen them. The camp was heavily guarded, on full alert because of the ambush the previous night. The only way to succeed, said the VC, becoming ever more co-operative, was to move in by stealth by way of the camp's latrine area and make a surprise raid.

Concerned about the wives and children that almost inevitably shared such remote base camps, Gritz nevertheless deemed he had no choice but to take the youth's advice and shoot his way in. The escape the night before and the attempt to retrieve the bodies made the youth's warning plausible. Gritz chose a time of attack just before dusk, which would afford enough light for identifying noncombatants and for finding the black box, followed by darkness in which to get away.

Swathed in a big bandage, apparently harboring no doubts that the Americans had saved his life, the young VC made no effort to alert his comrades. Rifles blazing, the men of the Special Forces and their enthusiastic 'Bodes dashed into the camp. Surprise was total. The VC dived for holes and tunnels. Those men designated to find the black box had no trouble locating it. As darkness fell, the guerrilla force with the black box and the young VC in tow retraced its steps.

Having decided that he had gone far enough from the base camp to stop for the night in relative safety, Gritz told his men to make bivouac. It was, Gritz reflected, Christmas Eve. He had just looked at the luminous dial of his watch and observed that Christmas had come, when bursts from rockets and mortars erupted in the jungle. Green Berets and guerrillas alike scattered.

A standard precaution of designating an alternate assembly area whenever the little force went into bivouac paid off. When the men got together again after dawn, Gritz radioed for a helicopter to extricate his wounded, the prisoner, and the black box. He and the rest of the force would put greater distance between themselves and the base camp before asking extraction by the fleet of helicopters that would be required.

When Gritz and the main body of the guerrilla force were at last extracted several days later, Gritz went to Bien Hoa to seek out the young VC in a U. S. Army hospital to which he had been admitted. The youth, he found, had already been discharged. Nobody had realized he was a prisoner. As Bo Gritz told it: "They gave him a CIDG uniform and a carbine, patted him on the ass, and told him to go back to his unit."

Like many another soldier, airman, marine, and sailor in South Vietnam, Bo Gritz undertook any number of similarly unusual exploits. In many a man the Vietnam war and its strange nature brought out latent reserves of courage and ingenuity. Like thousands of other Americans, Gritz served voluntarily long beyond his normal tour—in Gritz's case, a total of four years.

Gritz's first assignment in early 1965, before the arrival of American combat troops, taught him the close interrelationship between the military and the political aspects of the war. He was a district and CIDG-Special Forces camp adviser located in the village of Sui Da in the shadow of an unusual terrain feature, the 3,200-foot Nui Ba Den Mountain. The mountain rises dark, forbidding, and alone from flat, sandy ground near Tay Ninh City. It is laced with caves, scarred by rock precipices sometimes 300 feet high, and marked by two peaks of lesser height than the crest. Here and there trees somehow find enough soil to grow. The mountain looked, said Bo Gritz, as if God had made a sandpile on a bed of asphalt and exploded it a thousand times.

For the people of Sui Da and nearby villages, Nui Ba Den had a strong mystique. During World War II, troops of the Cao Dai religious sect had held it against the Japanese. During the war with the French, the Viet Minh had never relinquished it. Then came the Viet Cong, commanded by a former Viet Minh, a Major Mung. ARVN rangers and airborne troops once tried to conquer the mountain, but after taking a hundred casualties in exchange for virtually no gain, they abandoned the effort. Gritz's CIDG troops refused to go closer to it than a highway that ran along the base. Even Gritz's South Vietnamese counterpart, Haimui Hai, whom Gritz thought was the bravest man he had ever known, looked on Nui Ba Den with terror.

Mung in late 1964 let the Americans have the boulder-strewn crest, where contingents of U. S. Army and U. S. Air Force troops established a radio relay station and a radar station, the spot where the Americans later added searchlights for illuminating nearby rubber plantations. Mung also let South Vietnamese Buddhists traverse a symbolic ninety-nine steps to reach a pagoda halfway up the mountain, where monks and nuns resided. The pagoda was the goal of religious pilgrimages.

Pleased with progress in pacification around Sui Da, Gritz believed he could score even greater gains if he could disprove the invincibility of the VC-held parts of Nui Ba Den. If he could secure the entire mountain, a group of Cham tribesmen who made their living as woodcarvers agreed to move their village there.

As Major Mung's generosity would indicate, the crest was of little value except as a communications site. It was too high for good observation and was often obscured by clouds, which sometimes interfered with the American use of it for searchlights. The best location for controlling the mountain, Gritz concluded, was a saddle between the crest and another peak. Known as Mui Cau, the saddle was about 1,500 feet high and afforded excellent observation on the approaches to Tay Ninh City and War Zone C.

Without telling the CIDG troops their objective, Gritz moved about twenty-five men to the base of Nui Ba Den just at dark. There Haimui Hai agreed to help convince the men to participate. At dawn two U.S. helicopters lifted them to the far side of the saddle. All day long under a blazing sun they worked their way over boulders and up steep precipices, men at times hoisting one another on their shoulders, sometimes pulling their way up on vines. The heat was stifling. Their drinking water exhausted, the South Vietnamese began to balk, to insist on turning back. Although Gritz convinced them the only way home was across Mui Cau, he recognized that without water he would be unable to make it.

Gritz said a little prayer. A few minutes later he was convinced God answered it. The point man spotted a stream of water the size of a quarter gushing from a crevice in a rock.

It was past noon the next day before the little force got close enough to the top of Mui Cau to make an assault. The VC were there, but their firing positions faced the other way. Gritz and his men had come in the back door.

For ten days Gritz held Mui Cau until his province adviser ordered him out. It was too big a drain on limited helicopter resources to keep the force supplied. You have proved you can do it, the province adviser told him; come on down.

A few days later the VC commander, Major Mung, issued a decree by means of pamphlets distributed in surrounding villages. The CIDG with their American friends, said Mung's message, had turned Nui Ba Den into a war zone. No longer were Buddhists to be allowed to visit the pagoda.

A delegation of Buddhist leaders called on Gritz to demand that he secure the pagoda. He tried. He could hold the pagoda itself, he found, but it was impossible to prevent costly ambushes along the ninety-nine steps leading to it. He finally had to withdraw.

Gritz had destroyed the myth of invincible Nui Ba Den, but in the end the achievement was hollow, for the Buddhists blamed him for the loss of the pagoda. Several times after I got to know Bo Gritz I called him from some other assignment to go to Tay Ninh to explain to some ambitious, newly arrived American commander why I sanctioned no attack on the whole massif. We had the crest; it would cost too much to seize and then secure the rest of it. In terms of relationships with the people, it would have been better all along to have left Nui Ba Den to Major Mung.

The job of the adviser in Vietnam was complex and trying. Men with little or no knowledge of Oriental culture suddenly found themselves charged, even while legitimately and primarily concerned with their own survival, with developing leadership among a people whose colonial rulers had never encouraged leadership. They had to adjust swiftly to social, political, and economic conditions totally foreign to their experience. Although in an advisory rather than a command role, they had to convince their South Vietnamese counterparts to do it their American way. Aside from communications problems posed by a substantial language and cultural barrier on both sides, some South Vietnamese leaders were stubbornly certain that their own way was better. Many a wily South Vietnamese officer tried to compromise his adviser, usually with women, to afford a fulcrum for assuring good reports on his unit or for avoiding interference with his corrupt manipulations. Even the best adviser was able to influence his counterpart only about 80 per cent of the time.

All the while, the advisers had to entrust their lives to strange troops whose inadequacies in the early months were all too apparent. That the VC in the early days had infiltrated ARVN units was also painfully apparent. Many an operation was betrayed from the inside, but how to find the culprit? So obviously rife with VC was one CIDG-Special Forces camp on the Mekong River near the Cambodian border that the American advisers manned a machine gun on a tower capable of firing on any point within the camp. Early in my tenure in Saigon a prolonged search for an ARVN soldier qualified to take secret cryptographic training in the United States finally produced a candidate, but shortly before he was to get on a plane, the South Vietnamese found he was a VC.

Although advisers had no command authority (except with guerrilla companies), it was the adviser who on many an occasion rallied ARVN troops from apparent defeat. If staff advisers were able to inject themselves into the planning for an operation, chances of success were considerably enhanced. Advisers provided an integral link between Vietnamese troops and American air, artillery, and helicopter support. They sometimes even played a political role. It can be said that during the crisis days of 1964, when coup followed coup, American advisers literally held the country together.

The adviser was on duty twenty-four hours a day, seven days a week, often under severe field conditions. Learning to live under the most primitive sanitation conditions was in itself trying. Although advisers drew some American rations, they ate most of their meals with the Vietnamese troops, which took considerable adjusting to when the main course might be rat or dog. Almost all advisers operating with troops had recurrent bouts of amoebic dysentery. The harsh conditions provided one of the strongest arguments for a one-year tour of duty, a policy that was in effect when I arrived, and I saw no reason to change it.

With the commitment of American combat troops, I decided on the same policy. Although it posed problems of continuity, the worst of those could be overcome by men voluntarily staying on and by my retaining some key personnel for longer periods and providing such incentives as government quarters for their dependents in the Philippines. All general officers served eighteen months or longer. A big problem developed when the year expired for many men in a particular unit at about the same time, posing a challenge to personnel managers. Voluntary extensions helped, plus transfers of experienced men to newly arrived units, but additional unit training still was essential after a large turnover.

In keeping with my belief that it was going to be a long war, the one-year tour gave a man a goal. That was good for morale. It was also advisable from the standpoint of health, and it spread the burden of a long war over a broader spectrum of both Army regulars and American draftees. I hoped it would extend the nation's staying power by forestalling public pressure to "bring the boys home."

While PXs, clubs and messes, and recreational facilities primarily helped keep troops out of the cities and reduced piaster spending, they were also good for morale. So too was the R&R (rest and recuperation) program, which provided a man an interim goal to break up his one-year tour. Troops went for a week to Hong Kong, Bangkok, Sydney, Tokyo, Manila, Singapore, Taipei, Kuala Lampur, Penang, and Honolulu. Since wives often met the men going to Hawaii, the troops called that particular R&R "rape and run." These creature comforts, plus other factors such as keeping men busy and informed, having them participate in civic action projects, and keeping complaint channels open, helped during the period 1964–69 to generate the highest morale I have seen among U.S. soldiers in three wars. It was only after 1969 that the psychological stresses and strains of an apparently endless war began to show.

Keeping the soldier's complaint channels open was of particular importance. Since a man is often reluctant to complain to his commander, he should have ready access to his chaplain and to the inspector general system. I trust that my emphasis on providing ways to air grievances had something to do with keeping letters of complaint to congressmen and senators at a minimum. Several veteran legislators told me they received far fewer complaint letters from servicemen in Vietnam than in two previous wars, although as war protests mounted and troop withdrawal began, that changed.

In an effort to demonstrate that the commander cared, I tried to meet every major American unit entering the country. Although I obviously was unable to talk with all the men, I spoke to representative groups. I took particular pride in greeting two units with which I had previously served, the 9th Infantry and 101st Airborne Divisions. The only major unit I was unable to meet was the 11th Infantry Brigade, the last major unit to arrive during my tour. It is ironic that a component of that unit was destined to get into trouble at a place called My Lai.

It was only after the start of American withdrawal in 1969 that serious morale and disciplinary problems arose. That was to be expected. Men began to doubt the American purpose. Why die when the United States was pulling out? As the withdrawal continued, men were idle; idleness is the handmaiden of discontent, and some local commanders allowed standards of appearance and discipline to become slack. Although antiwar demonstrations in the United States appeared to have little effect on morale in Vietnam before my departure, they clearly had an effect as America's purpose came into question. Only with withdrawal did serious drug problems arise. The same with "fragging," the slang word for killing officers and noncommissioned officers, usually with a hand grenade, a reaction based on grudges or done when a man was under the influence of alcohol or drugs. Fragging in one form or another has occurred in all wars but increases when a sense of unit purpose breaks down and *esprit de corps* fails and when explosives and weapons are loosely controlled. Anyone familiar with problems of morale and discipline among troops waiting for transportation home after World Wars I and II could hardly have been surprised. As the Army Chief of Staff, I was compelled to issue firm orders emphasizing the necessity of high standards of discipline and orderliness.

Also contributing to the problem of continuity and constant turnover was a process that some called "ticket punching." That was no conscious policy of trying to provide as many regular officers as possible an opportunity to get command experience on their records. It was instead a result of a natural desire of efficient young officers to hold positions of responsibility, to meet the challenges of command, and a similarly natural desire of higher commanders to want officers on their staffs who had had local command experience.

Although there were advantages in a commander holding the same job for a full year, such as cumulative experience and knowledge of his troops, broader experience was also worthwhile, and a man with command experience could make important contributions to staff work. An operations officer, for example, is usually better at planning operations if he has firsthand knowledge of what actually takes place at the fighting level. There were, in any case, enough good officers to take the place of those who moved on from command to staff. Yet there were also enough instances of poor commanders and officers who tried to gain advantage from turnovers to prompt me, when I became Chief of Staff in 1968, to develop a new system of officer personnel management with greater emphasis on specialization and the highest premium on selecting the best officers for a pool from which commanders would be drawn.

The average tenure for company and battalion commanders in Vietnam was six months. In World War II casualties and promotions produced a more rapid turnover than that.

At a press conference in Saigon in 1966, I noted: "In a war in which individual courage is a constant requirement and acts of heroism are a daily occurrence, I couldn't be prouder of the men our nation has given me the privilege of commanding in Vietnam. They are fighters and doers—tough combatants one day and compassionate, helpful neighbors the next; they have displayed amazing ingenuity in all endeavors." I took every opportunity to pay public tribute to the highly deserving men I had the privilege to command. Having fought in three wars, I am convinced the United States never fielded a more professional force than in South Vietnam during the years 1966–69.

Because both civilian and military educational facilities have improved over the years, the American soldier—by which I also mean airman, marine, sailor, and coast guardsman—was better educated than his predecessors. Since a limited, selective draft permitted close adherence to strict physical requirements, he was an excellent physical specimen. Although many were draftees, most were highly motivated. As demonstrated by the thousands who elected to serve extended tours, he often developed a kind of missionary zeal.

Some have called Vietnam the "working man's war." That refers indirectly to draft deferments for students. If a man had the money and could maintain his grades, he could defer service until he finished college and even graduate school, or could hire legal help to exploit other loopholes in the law and avoid service. Conversely, the man without funds for or interest in college filled the ranks in Vietnam.

While that policy might make sense in peacetime, once the fighting started it was wrong and indirectly was a reversion to the inequities of the Civil War when a man could buy a substitute. Although the policy seemingly did nothing to lower the splendid morale and performance of the average soldier in Vietnam, it had serious effects for the United States Army.

In the view of many, the policy contributed to antiwar militancy on college campuses in that young men feeling twinges of conscience because they sat out a war while others fought could appease their conscience if they convinced themselves the war was immoral. If nothing else, it made them more receptive to antiwar arguments. Antiwar militancy in turn put ROTC on the firing line, making it impossible for unpopular ROTC departments to provide officers in the numbers needed.

As a man finally completed his education and at last submitted to the draft, his level of education—sometimes master's degrees and doctorates—was often much higher than that of many career noncommissioned officers and officers. That created a serious communications gap. A by-product was a derogatory term for the regular soldier: "lifer."

One old sergeant allegedly met the problem head on when he lined up a group to police the company area. "You men with college educations," he directed, "pick up any trash that the wind can move: paper, small sticks, matches. You high school graduates, pick up heavier things: rocks, cans, big sticks. Now you uneducated guys, you stand there and watch these educated bastards and maybe you'll learn something."

Yet the situation was far from humorous, for the communications gap was real and the deferred man often brought his antiwar militancy with him when he finally got into uniform. Abetted by such activists as film star Jane Fonda, many tried to discredit authority by fighting haircut regulations, publishing and distributing underground newspapers, sponsoring or participating in protests, trying in any way possible to foment unrest. As Army Chief of Staff at the time, I was pleased with the unemotional manner with which the Army handled the problem, conscious that in time, as the men finished their service, it would inevitably pass.

One method of seeking to ameliorate the differences between noncommissioned officers and those men whose deferments had expired after they had received baccalaureate or graduate degrees was to set up advisory councils among the lower ranks. When used to complement the chain of command, those worked well. Since second lieutenants also were fresh off disturbed campuses, some commanders extended the advisory councils to include the new lieutenants. When one enterprising lieutenant set out to unionize all second lieutenants and prepared "demands" to be presented to senior commanders, the practice had to be discontinued.

As in all wars in all democracies, the Vietnam war produced deserters and others who fled the country to avoid service. I lament the fate of those young men, the disrupted lives, the separation from family, the loss of native land, and I lament the twisted emotion and logic that prompted them to leave. Yet how to condone or pardon their conscious flight from responsibility? When a man deserts, another man has to take his place; and there are legitimate ways in which a man who is a genuine conscientious objector can serve his country. Just because he might object to this or that particular war has no legitimacy, for if a man is allowed to pick and choose his war, the entire democratic system whereby all men share in a nation's responsibilities as well as its benefits breaks down.

The inequity of student draft deferments is dramatically and tragically illustrated by statistics on deaths in Vietnam by state in relation to population. A higher percentage of men served and died from states with generally lower incomes. The highest percentage of deaths per hundred thousand of population—39.8 per cent—was from West Virginia.

As I noted in speaking before the South Carolina General Assembly, the black soldier made a noteworthy record in Vietnam, the first war in which no vestige of the nation's long-standing social inequality was condoned. The number of black soldiers in Vietnam was roughly equivalent to the percentage of blacks in the armed services. Some complained that a greater percentage of blacks served in combat units. If that was so, it reflected chance and the effects of a man's technical skills rather than any conscious policy. The percentage of black soldiers killed was 13 per cent of all deaths, approximately the same ratio as there were blacks in the services.

Dating from the start of 1961 to the so-called Paris cease-fire in early 1973, the United States lost 46,397 killed in action in Vietnam. That made Vietnam the nation's fourth most costly war, behind the Civil War and World Wars I and II, yet it was also the longest war, and the percentage of men killed out of the total who served was the least of any of the four big wars. Another 10,340 died in Vietnam from causes other than combat, the least such deaths in the four big wars and only half as many as died from noncombat causes in Korea. Just over 13,000 of those killed in action, or approximately 30 per cent of the total, were U. S. Army regulars.

Possibly because the front line was nowhere and everywhere, death was no respecter of rank. Seven American general officers died: Major General Bruno A. Hochmuth, commander of the 3d Marine Division, in the explosion of a helicopter near Hué; General Crumm, commander of the Third Air Division on Guam in a mid-air B-52 refueling accident; Major General Robert F. Worley, deputy commander of the Seventh Air Force, when enemy fire downed his Phantom jet north of Danang; Major General Keith L. Ware, commander of the 1st Infantry Division, when his helicopter was apparently shot down near the Cambodian border; Major General George W. Casey, commander of the 1st Cavalry Division, in a helicopter crash in high mountains of central Vietnam; Major General John A. B. Dillard, commander of the U. S. Army Engineer Command, when enemy fire downed his helicopter in the Central Highlands; Brigadier General William R. Bond, commander of the 199th Infantry Brigade, by enemy small-arms fire when he landed his helicopter to help a besieged patrol.

The wounded American soldier who was admitted to medical treatment facilities had an excellent chance of survival. Of those admitted, 2.6 per cent died of wounds, which compares with 4.5 per cent in World War II and 2.5 per cent in Korea. In South Vietnam evacuation was so swift that many casualties reached a hospital in Vietnam that in earlier wars would have died before admission, which makes the percentage of men admitted to hospitals who survived all the more remarkable.

One factor contributing to high morale of the American units in Vietnam was the knowledge that if sick or wounded, the American soldier would receive swift and superb medical treatment. Because of the helicopter and use of the 3d MASH as a mobile reserve hospital, no man was ever more than a few minutes from medical treatment, although combat conditions on occasion might pose delay in his evacuation. Skilled doctors, surgeons, nurses, and wardmasters were on hand throughout the country and, as in other wars, upon their return to civilian practice, brought the benefits of their concentrated experience to the civilian community.

Although tropical diseases failed to impair American troops to the degree some had anticipated, disease still accounted for approximately two thirds of all hospital admissions. Despite preventive medicine, including dapsone (DDS), malaria was the biggest problem, followed by diarrheal and skin diseases, the latter consisting primarily of fungal and bacterial infections and immersion foot. Despite constant rotation of troops, immersion foot was always a problem in the water-logged Mekong Delta. Immunization forestalled some of the more exotic tropical diseases, such as cholera. Venereal disease, while prevalent, could usually be handled on an outpatient basis. Partly because of the one-year tour and partly because men were seldom exposed to critical danger for prolonged periods, neuropsychiatric disorders were relatively few, although the troop withdrawal period, with its drug, discipline, and morale problems, produced some increase.

From two small hospital facilities available when I first arrived, medical facilities kept pace with the build-up of American troops. Two hospital ships—the U.S.S. *Sanctuary* and the U.S.S. *Repose*—and a Navy hospital at Danang cared for Navy and Marine patients. The Air Force maintained a hospital at Cam Ranh Bay and several casualty staging facilities to care for patients being prepared for airlift to hospitals in Okinawa, Guam, the Philippines, Japan, and the United States. The Army had twenty-three hospitals throughout the country and several units of a system known as MUST, for "medical unit, self-contained, transportable." Those were equipped modular shelters that could be combined to form various types of field-treatment facilities and transported by fixed-wing aircraft or cargo helicopters to provide emergency hospital care almost anywhere.

The U. S. Army provided a share of medical support for all Allied forces, although the Australians and Koreans had their own hospitals. The U. S. Army maintained a convalescent center at Cam Ranh Bay for both American and Allied troops. When it became necessary to expand that center, I spared overtaxed engineer units by having the patients themselves do much of the work under engineer supervision, which provided a form of physical therapy and helped the men pass the time more constructively.

From the first, all American hospitals provided emergency treatment for Vietnamese civilians. The U. S. Army constructed three military hospitals for the South Vietnamese armed forces, and in 1967 two U. S. Army hospitals began to operate specifically for South Vietnamese civilians. When it became apparent that the Vietnamese disliked leaving their communities for hospitalization elsewhere, all American hospitals began to care for civilians whenever space was available. More than twenty Army, Air Force, and Navy teams traveled the country providing medical help for civilians, while ARVN medics, with the assistance of Special Forces medics, also treated civilians. Medical and dental care was a feature of the civic action projects of all American units.

One of the most incredible medical feats of this or any war was performed by Captain Harry H. Dinsmore, U. S. Navy, who volunteered to remove a live 60-mm mortar shell from the chest wall of an ARVN soldier.

Although the shell's impact fuse had been partially activated and the shell could have detonated at any time, Captain Dinsmore performed the delicate surgery calmly and skillfully, saving the soldier's life. He was subsequently awarded the Navy Cross.

Representatives of the American Red Cross served throughout South Vietnam and visited troops at even the most remote and isolated bases, including CIDG-Special Forces camps. Young women known affectionately as "Doughnut Dollies" were special favorites of the troops. The United Services Organization (USO) maintained clubs throughout the country.

Visits by American entertainers, writers, sports celebrities, and churchmen also boosted morale. Although MACV provided their transportation, food, and lodging, these people gave selflessly of their time, energy, and talents. For every celebrity who preferred to visit Hanoi, there were any number who opted for Saigon.

The grandest trouper of all was Martha Raye. Maggie, as the soldiers called her, visited Vietnam time after time, once for five months. Begging me to let her extend one stay over Christmas, she said she had no family to celebrate with at home; these gallant men were her family. She sometimes brought along an accompanist, other times enlisted the help of soldier entertainers instead. Once when she brought over a miniature edition of the Broadway musical *Hello, Dolly!* and performed in a steaming hangar, she collapsed and had to be hospitalized. When she was visiting a CIDG-Special Forces camp at Soc Trang, in the Mekong Delta, the VC attacked with mortars; Maggie pitched in to help with the wounded. She was under fire on several other occasions. Nobody contributed more of herself than that wonderful, generous woman.

Annual Christmas visits by another grand trouper, comedian Bob Hope, were tremendous favorites with the troops. Concerned about security of Hope and his troupe, my predecessor, General Harkins, had never approved a visit, but I considered the benefits worth the risks. Learning that he had been the intended victim of the VC attack on the Brink Hotel during his first visit in 1964 did nothing to deter Bob's coming again and again, and with him always a talented cast of entertainers. As Americans at home saw on their television screens in excerpts from the shows, the U.S. soldiers in Vietnam reacted to Bob and his troupe with the same enthusiasm and delight as others had before them in Korea and World War II. Although there were some anxious moments about security, no untoward incident developed.

At one dinner that I gave at my villa for the troupe, actresses Anita Bryant and Carroll Baker stripped all officers at the gathering of their insignia of rank, including my general's stars, as souvenirs. The next day I had to beg mine back when I found that I was unable to replace them.

Before one of Bob's visits, Marshal Ky enlisted my help to get Bob's measurements for a complete mandarin outfit. The robe fitted well, but the unique Vietnamese elder's hat was humorously small. Bob made the most of it for laughs.

One of the early visiting troupes was Mary Martin and the Broadway company of *Hello, Dolly!* The first night I had the entire cast for a social get-together at my residence, and the next night Ambassador Lodge had the principal players as guests at his home. The next day the producer, David Merrick, rudely lashed out at the ambassador in a press conference for failing to invite the entire cast. When Miss Martin and her husband came for dinner at my residence, she said she wished she could let President Johnson know that she and the rest of the company disapproved of Merrick's bad taste. I agreed to send her message through official channels. Probably because of the incident, I had some difficulty persuading Ambassador Lodge to go with me to the troupe's final performance to hear my words of thanks and to join an ovation at the end to Mr. Merrick, Miss Martin, and a superb cast.

The list of visiting entertainers was long and varied. Such as actors John Wayne, Robert Stack, Charlton Heston, Hugh O'Brian, Robert Mitchum, Raymond Burr, Don Defore, Jim Nabors; the team of Dale Evans and Roy Rogers; singers Jack Jones, Vic Damone, and Eddie Fisher; comedians George Jessel, Redd Foxx, Jerry Colonna, and Edgar Bergen; actresses Lana Turner, Julie Andrews, Jill St. John, Joey Heatherton, Nancy Sinatra, Anna Maria Alberghetti, Kay Stevens, Janis Paige, Ann Sydney, Connie Stevens, Phyllis Diller, Raquel Welch, Barbara McNair, Ann-Margret, Ursula Andress, and Fran Jeffries; Les Brown and his orchestra; dancers Jack Bubbles and the Nicholas Brothers; sports announcer Red Barber; Western entertainer Roy Acuff; golfer Billy Casper; any number of professional baseball and football players; Arthur Godfrey; Coach Woody Hayes of Ohio State University. The heads of major American veterans' organizations visited at least once a year. Israeli Defense Minister Moshe Dayan, who, I learned, went on patrol in enemy territory. The attractive columnist Ann Landers, who dispenses advice to the lovelorn; her stay of about an hour in my office set me up for teasing by some of my staff. Columnist Earl Wilson. Novelist John Steinbeck, who had been a war correspondent in World War II and was markedly impressed with the professional competence of American troops. A number of prominent religious leaders, including evangelist Billy Graham, theological writer Rabbi Richard Reuben, and Francis Cardinal Spellman, Archbishop of New York. (When Billy Graham, Bob Hope, and Cardinal Spellman were all visiting, I commented at a dinner for Cardinal Spellman that at last we had obtained Faith, Hope, and Charity.) I found Cardinal Spellman to be the most gentle, humble man I have known, but a tough man when it comes to principle. President Johnson's daughter, Lynda Bird, asked to come on one of the Bob Hope tours, but I vetoed the visit for security reasons.

Many lesser known entertainers from the United States, Australia, Korea, and the Philippines toured the circuit of clubs and messes. These young performers were working for pay, yet the enthusiasm and courage they displayed were nonetheless notable.

Two prominent visitors were killed: pianist and composer Philippa Duke Schuyler, when her helicopter crashed into Danang Bay, and Dr. Bernard Fall, by a mine when accompanying a Marine patrol near Hué along Route 1, which he had called in one of his books the "street without joy."

While welcoming visits by entertainers for the welfare of the troops, I also encouraged the coming of American political figures in the hope that their seeing at first hand the courage and dedication of their soldiers would afford them an understanding of the war that the press and television had failed to connote. The list of those who came was long, and some returned for second and third visits. The response to what they saw was in general enthusiastic, but there were exceptions and problems.

I cannot, for example, understand the about-face on the war of Michigan's Governor George Romney, except that as a man prominently mentioned as a presidential candidate he listened to too many antiwar dissidents and deemed it politically expedient to say he had been "brainwashed" while visiting Vietnam. I was also surprised to learn that Senator Charles Percy of Illinois, whose wife accompanied him, had on his own visited an insecure village and was for a time pinned down by VC mortar fire. Upon his return to Saigon, I tactfully scolded him for his bold actions in view of my command responsibility for his security.

In the case of Senator Stuart Symington of Missouri, a staunch supporter of the war, what he saw changed his views. Visiting an aircraft carrier, he was shocked by the extreme precautions imposed on attacking aircraft crews in an effort to avoid civilian casualties. Planes attacking targets in North Vietnam had to follow perilous, circuitous routes that exposed them much longer than necessary to enemy antiaircraft fire. While sympathizing with the objective of avoiding civilian losses, Senator Symington resented the additional danger that the policy imposed on American airmen. So long as Washington imposed restrictions like that, Senator Symington deemed he could no longer support the effort in Vietnam.

While several legislators came with preconceived ideas and left unchanged, none was as disappointing as Senator Edward Kennedy of Massachusetts, who made a five-day visit in late October 1965. I got the impression that Senator Kennedy embraced the refugee problem in Vietnam because it afforded an opportunity to be critical while achieving a pose of compassion, meanwhile avoiding specific commitment on the larger issue of the war itself.

Several young, idealistic, overbearing aides preceded Kennedy and by the time he arrived had located a refugee camp with probably the worst conditions to be found in the country. Although the senator's escort officer pointed out that a new camp for those refugees was under construction a few miles down the road and would soon be occupied, Senator Kennedy insisted on holding a press conference with television cameras present in the heart of the old camp. He obviously came to Vietnam with political malice aforethought and had no inclination to observe anything that conflicted with the pose he chose to assume.

As in other wars, the American soldier had his own particular jargon in Vietnam, some of it borrowed from television. The medical corpsman with Marine platoons was a "Ben Casey." Military police were "the fuzz." For long the favorite expression for anything that went wrong came from the "Get Smart" television show: "Sorry about that."

DEROS stood for "date eligible to return from overseas." Men approaching their DEROS were "getting short." When that date came, they departed by air on a "Freedom Bird" for the United States—known variously as "the world" or "land of the big PX." Some called Air Vietnam, the domestic South Vietnamese airline, after the pungent Vietnamese fish sauce, "Air Nuoc Mam."

Infantrymen were "grunts" who operated in the "boonies," short for boondocks. UH-1 helicopters were "slicks." The enemy was "Charley," from the words in the military phonetic alphabet for VC—Victor Charley. Some men shortened it even more to "Chuck." The Regional and Popular Forces (RFs and PFs) were "Ruff Puffs." The stockade, or jail, at the big base of Long Binh—the Long Binh jail—went by the President's initials, the "LBJ." The Vietnamese peasant lived in a "hootch." Reflecting earlier French influence, "beaucoup" was as much a part of the vocabulary as it was in World War II, and a hamlet or a village was a "ville." To be hit by enemy fire was to be "zapped." Anybody on our side was a "friendly."

As with soldiers through history, much of the wit was gallows humor, often shocking to the casual observer; Jonathan Schell so found the small talk and ditties of the forward air controllers in Quang Ngai province. A sign in the ready room of airmen who sprayed defoliants would have shocked ecologists: "Only You Can Prevent Forests."

An oft-heard tale of the travails of North Vietnamese supply would take long in the telling as the narrator recounted the troubles of a porter bearing two mortar rounds who travels from North Vietnam along the Ho Chi Minh Trail, up hill and down, attacked by air and artillery, bitten by ants, leeches, mosquitoes, sandals worn thin. When at last, months after departing the North, he reaches the mortar position deep inside South Vietnam, the crew quickly fires the two rounds. "OK," they tell him, "go back and get two more."

As a newly arrived senior officer walked with an experienced adviser along a low bank separating rice paddies, another story went, he saw a group of men wearing the Vietnamese peasant's traditional black pajamas, which the

VC also wore. "How do you know if they're enemy?" he asked. "If they salute," the adviser responded, "they're friendly. If they shoot, they're VC."

The ingenuity of the American soldier and his compassion for the Vietnamese was only exceeded by the diversity of the jobs he performed: computer expert, stevedore, bridge builder, aircraft, boat, or helicopter pilot, rifleman, artilleryman, door gunner, radiotelephone operator, bulldozer operator, the entire range of military specialties. The last included a new one, the "tunnel rat," men of small stature who volunteered to explore enemy tunnels with pistol and flashlight while trailing a telephone wire that served both for communications and measuring the length of the tunnel. The soldier did his job in a foreign, tropical, hostile environment in a war that was at once the most sophisticated in history and a return to the primitive, man pitted against man in a contest where wile and stamina might determine who would prevail.

So long did some American soldiers serve in Vietnam and so exemplarily that their records became almost legendary. Colonel Robert Schweitzer, for example, who served off and on from mid-1964 until mid-1971. A professional in every way, Colonel Schweitzer was wounded seven times and wore the Distinguished Service Cross, the Distinguished Flying Cross, three Silver Stars, the Soldier's Medal, two Bronze Stars, and twenty-one Air Medals. Or John Paul Vann, who served before my arrival as an officer and then returned at Ambassador Lodge's and my request as a civilian. No one better understood the Vietnamese than John Vann, but he had an affinity for sounding off to the press, particularly on the theory that the United States should assume over-all command in the manner of the French. He was senior adviser in the II Corps Zone when in mid-1972 he died in the crash of his helicopter in the Central Highlands, a victim, Radio Hanoi claimed, of VC fire. Or Lieutenant Colonel David Hackworth, who had four Purple Hearts from Korea and four more during over five years in Vietnam. He also had two Distinguished Service Crosses, nine Silver Stars, and nine Bronze Stars. As reflected by those awards, Dave Hackworth's combat record was unusual, but near the end he developed an affinity for personal publicity, sometimes spoke irresponsibly, and conducted himself with questionable ethics. He eventually retired prematurely from the Army.

To observe the American soldier—officers and men alike—was to be impressed with the dedication, determination, and day-to-day courage that he displayed. Although it was impossible to know all of those whose acts demanded recognition, I happily accepted the command responsibility of rewarding those that could be documented, for I agree with Napoleon's maxim, "A bolt of ribbon will win many battles." The importance of medals is indicated by the tradition of wearing them over the heart, which can be traced to medieval times when the Crusaders wore there the Christian cross, symbol of their fight to free the Holy Land from Islam.

Particularly stirring were the deeds of those 215 men who during the course of the entire war received the nation's highest award for valor, the Medal of Honor:

Such as Major Bernard F. Fisher, Seventh Air Force, who landed his plane on a fire-swept landing strip of a CIDG-Special Forces camp in the A Shau Valley that was under fierce attack in order to rescue a pilot who had crash-landed on the strip. Despite withering fire, he saved the pilot. He became the first Air Force officer in Vietnam to receive the Medal of Honor.

Such as Captain Robert F. Foley, 25th Infantry Division, who maintained the momentum of his company's attack by cradling a machine gun in his arms and despite painful wounds, charging the enemy. He personally saved several of his wounded men and singlehandedly destroyed three enemy machine guns.

Such as Staff Sergeant Webster Anderson, 101st Airborne Division, a black soldier from my home state, who, despite fire from enemy who had penetrated his artillery battery's position, climbed to an exposed position on the parapet from where he could direct devastating fire on the attackers. Wounded once by an exploding grenade, he picked up another to throw it back at the enemy, but it exploded and again wounded him grievously. He still refused evacuation until the attack was repulsed.

Or Lance Corporal Joe C. Paul, 3d Marine Division, who ran forward in advance of his platoon's position to attract the enemy's attention and fire until five wounded men could be evacuated. He fought from his exposed position until mortally wounded.

Such as Specialist 4 Robert F. Stryker, 1st Infantry Division, who threw himself full in the killing zone of a claymore mine, absorbing the blast with his body, shielding his comrades from the explosion, and dying in the process.

Or Lieutenant Colonel Joe M. Jackson, Seventh Air Force, who volunteered to fly his C-123 aircraft into the CIDG-Special Forces camp of Kham Duc to rescue a three-man air control team, even though the enemy had overrun the camp and small-arms fire and fragments from exploding shells in a burning ammunition dump made a death trap of the landing strip.

Or Engineman Second Class Michael E. Thornton, a member of a U. S. Navy SEAL team that attacked an enemy coastal base. He rescued his badly wounded lieutenant under fire, dragged him to the water's edge, inflated his life vest, and for two hours towed him out to sea until they were picked up by a patrol boat.

Or Captain Paul W. Bucha, 101st Airborne Division. When lead elements of his company moving through an enemy base area came under machine-gun fire from a bunker, he crawled forward alone and knocked out the weapon. As the men came under human-wave attack, he personally covered the withdrawal to the main company position and through an embattled night was the mainstay of the defense, despite a serious wound from a shell fragment.

Or Corporal Jerry W. Wickam, 11th Armored Cavalry Regiment, who personally charged three enemy bunkers, killing the occupants before falling mortally wounded from enemy fire.

Private First Class Clarence E. Sasser, 9th Infantry Division, who despite three wounds dragged himself about a helicopter landing zone through heavy fire to care for wounded colleagues.

Corporal Larry E. Smedley, 1st Marine Division, who charged an enemy machine gun and, although wounded and knocked to the ground by enemy fire, rose and continued his assault, eliminating the enemy weapon before he fell again with a fatal wound in the chest.

Many a U. S. Navy hospital corpsman who provided forward medical aid for American marines, such as Hospital Corpsmen Third Class Wayne M. Caron and Second Class David R. Ray, both of whom gave their lives while moving about in exposed positions to aid the wounded.

Others who threw themselves on grenades to save the lives of their comrades, such as Specialist 4 Daniel Fernandez, 25th Infantry Division; Private First Class Leslie A. Bellrichard and Staff Sergeant Frankie Z. Molnar, 4th Infantry Division; Privates First Class John A. Barnes III and Milton L. Olive III, 173d Airborne Brigade; and Specialist 4 Dale E. Wagrynen, 101st Airborne Division. Hospital Corpsman Third Class Donald E. Ballard threw himself on an enemy grenade to save marines around him but lived because the grenade failed to explode.

The list could go on and on.

Prisoners of war displayed a special kind of long-term valor. Aware that the fate of the prisoners was harsh, I assigned the task of trying to liberate those within South Vietnam to the 5th Special Forces. They tried on numerous occasions with courage and determination: in the U Minh Forest deep in the Mekong Delta on the Gulf of Siam; in War Zone C; in the An Lao Valley along the central coast; in the vicinity of the Seven Mountains in the Mekong Delta. Not one attempt succeeded.

It was an exercise in frustration, primarily because the Viet Cong constantly shifted the prisoners from one location to another. The only prisoners who got away were those the enemy released voluntarily, such as Private First Class Donald G. Smith and Specialists 4 James B. Brigham and Thomas N. Jones; or those who escaped on their own, such as Major James N. Rowe, who succeeded after more than five years of imprisonment.

Although hope of escaping from prisoner of war camps inside North Vietnam may have been vain, that failed to deter some Americans from trying it. One was Colonel Benjamin H. Purcell, who was deputy commander of a U. S. Army logistical support command at Danang when in February 1968 enemy machine-gun fire downed his helicopter and he was captured; five years of imprisonment followed, over three of the years spent in solitary confinement.

Determining from a guard that the camp where he was held was only ten kilometers from Hanoi, Colonel Purcell vowed to escape in hope of gaining asylum in the French Consulate in Hanoi. If nothing else, he realized, plotting the escape and shaping the tools to achieve it would occupy his mind. From a small piece of wire he fashioned a drill and from a flattened nail a chisel, and he set to work perforating a panel in the wooden door of his cell. As he drilled, he refilled the holes with morsels of bread colored with a gray paste made from toothpaste and soot against the day when the entire panel would be perforated and he would be ready to gouge it out. By rolling bread crumbs under the door, he lured a chicken to stand outside the door so that when a guard approached, the chicken's squawking would provide a warning.

One night after the camp had settled down, Colonel Purcell removed the panel and sneaked out into the courtyard. Timing his movements to avoid a pacing sentry, he made his way to a high wall surrounding the courtyard. Although it was topped with broken glass, he had little trouble climbing over and dropping down on the other side.

When daylight came, he was surprised to find that people he passed paid him scant attention, despite his obvious Western appearance. Since he spoke a little Vietnamese, he was able to ascertain that he was headed in the right direction for Hanoi, and a man from whom he asked directions offered him a ride on his bicycle. Yet that kind of indifference failed to last. Hardly had he dismounted when a policeman demanded his identification papers. Not much more time elapsed before he was back inside the POW camp.

Despite threats and physical abuse as a result of his attempted escape, Colonel Purcell determined to try again, but unfortunately, he was transferred to another camp some fifty miles from Hanoi. His plan was to get to the coast and, he hoped, steal a boat and follow the coastline to South Vietnam. That time he got out by removing a mat of barbed wire just above his cell door, but again he had little time to enjoy his freedom. He got only a short distance away from the camp before a guard accosted him and brought him back.

Primarily because of the risks involved both to the prisoners of war and would-be rescuers, no attempts were made to rescue prisoners held in North Vietnam until late 1970, after facts about the harsh treatment the prisoners had to endure became known. Although that was after I left Vietnam, I was closely involved as the Army Chief of Staff and a member of the Joint Chiefs in planning the raid. The objective was a compound at Son Tay, some twenty-three miles west of Hanoi.

Training for the raid began at Eglin Air Force Base in Florida in August, with volunteers from the Special Forces and the Air Force. As training began, aerial photographs of Son Tay showed clearly that the compound was occupied, but later, when the nearby Red River approached flood stage, photographs revealed that the prisoners' exercise court had grown up in grass, an apparent indication that the prisoners had been moved. The Joint Chiefs ordered the raid canceled.

In late fall of 1970, as the Red River subsided, new photo coverage revealed that the growth in the exercise court had disappeared. Did that mean that prisoners again were using the court? Was the compound reoccupied? I and the other members of the Joint Chiefs felt that the new photographs provided sufficient evidence to warrant a try.

The raid went off on November 21. It was perfectly staged; not a man was lost. The only trouble: the compound was empty. The exercise court, the raiders found, had been planted with grain, then harvested. That explained the changed appearance in the photographs.

While I was the Army Chief of Staff, I made a point in my travels about the United States of visiting the relatives of men who were prisoners or were missing in action. When after my retirement in 1972 the prisoners of war at last returned, I wrote to all who had served during my tenure in South Vietnam, including Staff Sergeant Richard R. Perricone, whose name was on a copper bracelet which I wore before his return as part of a nationwide campaign to remember the prisoners of war. The replies were often touching. "To you, sir," wrote Lieutenant Colonel J. Howard Dunn, Marine Corps, "I feel I can say that we served that particular tour of duty as we would have any other—with pride and to the best of our ability." Colonel Hervey S. Stockman, Air Force, wrote:

> Sir, we made no sacrifice. The great percentage of us were and are professional military airmen. If we didn't consider imprisonment initially as part of our military duty, we learned early that it is and that it must be dealt with just like other unpleasant duties. Some did it better than others, but ninety-nine plus percent . . . took to the task and upheld the honor of their country and service.

Chapter XVII
The Tet Offensive

Americans have nothing remotely like the Vietnamese Tet celebration that ushers in the lunar New Year. Even to say it is Christmas, Thanksgiving, and the Fourth of July rolled into one is insufficient to connote the importance the Vietnamese attach to the festivities. For weeks ahead, Vietnamese housewives bake traditional little cakes of sticky rice and wrap them in sweet-scented dong leaves. People lay in supplies of tea, candy, and rice wine, buy new clothes, decorate their houses with flowers. Relatives make arrangements to travel home to worship at the family altar and pay obeisance to ancestors. Visions of gifts of candy and five-piaster notes dance in children's heads. Nothing—not even a war for survival—must stand in the way of the Tet celebration.

The celebration begins on the eve of the lunar New Year: in 1968—a Year of the Monkey—the New Year's Eve would be Monday, January 29. That day, New Year's Day itself, and the day following are the most important of a week-long holiday, so festive that even Chinese merchants in Cholon, who seldom forego an opportunity to make money, close their doors. Possibly because the war was going well and an elected government wanted to demonstrate compassion for the people, the government in office during the Tet that ushered in that Year of the Monkey lifted a ban of several years' standing on shooting firecrackers. Fireworks to the Vietnamese are synonymous with Tet.

Seven months before the start of the Year of the Monkey—in July 1967—B-52 bombers flying unseen and unheard over thick jungle near the Cambodian border dropped their loads on an enemy military headquarters. One officer gravely wounded by fragments in the chest was a four-star general, Nguyen Chi Thanh, the senior North Vietnamese officer in South Vietnam. Despite hurried evacuation to Hanoi, General Thanh died.

Thanh's death occurred about the same time that North Vietnamese diplomats from around the world began to converge on Hanoi. Noting the dip-lomatic travels, many a wishful-thinking Western observer decided that this meant the North Vietnamese were at long last about to agree to negotia-tions. They were, indeed, about to make a momentous decision, but those who thought that involved negotiations overlooked the fact that the Com-munists never negotiate from a position of weakness.

The North Vietnamese in mid-1967 were in a position of weakness. After only little more than a year of fighting relatively sizable numbers of Ameri-can troops, Communist losses were mounting drastically, with nothing tan-gible to show for it. General Giap, the Minister of Defense, and others in the Hanoi leadership decided they had to devise a new strategy. The only senior official with firsthand knowledge of how disastrous it was to engage in con-ventional warfare against American firepower, the only senior official who might have argued against the new strategy, was beneath the earth: General Thanh.

The North Vietnamese decided, in effect, to go for broke, to mount a co-ordinated general offensive throughout South Vietnam, designed to achieve that objective peculiar to Vietnamese Communist insurgency, the general uprising. Ironically, Secretary McNamara was in Saigon manipulating a de-crease in even my "minimum essential" troop request at the same time the North Vietnamese leaders were making their big decision.

Whether the North Vietnamese leaders genuinely believed they could in-duce the people of South Vietnam to rise against their government is debat-able. They quite naturally depicted the objective in the grandest terms to their commanders and troops in the South, hoping thereby to enlist a su-preme effort no matter what morale problems might result from an un-successful *Friedensturm* (end-the-war offensive). What really mattered was to demonstrate that the Americans could win only at vastly increased cost, to inflict on the Americans a catastrophic Dien Bien Phu during an Ameri-can election year, and to gain some leverage—such as the two northern prov-inces of South Vietnam—with which to go to the negotiating table with an opponent whose resolve presumably would have been materially weakened.

Detailed planning followed in North Vietnamese and VC military head-quarters within South Vietnam and across the border in Cambodia. Then came the slow, laborious logistical build-up, a clandestine shift of arms and supplies forward to the vicinity of the towns and cities and people of South Vietnam. Then came, too, the attempt to lure American units to the border regions, at the same time demonstrating that any coming offensive whose preparations the Americans might detect was to be nothing new—just more of the same dogged disregard for losses in fights for border outposts that had achieved so little in the past.

Meanwhile, to weaken the will of the South Vietnamese people, so long accustomed to Western duplicity, the Viet Cong spread a rumor that the Americans were preparing to get out of Vietnam by arranging a coalition government with the VC. In the early fall of 1967 a VC agent told South

Vietnamese police that he had instructions from the Communist leadership to establish contact with the American Embassy. Washington officials, so long goaded by press, Congress, and antiwar spokesmen, leaped at the opportunity. Was this the long-awaited overture to negotiations? Yet nothing came of it other than what the VC wanted, to give substance to the rumor of American collusion with the VC that they were spreading.

To weave an even thicker mesh of deception, the North Vietnamese dropped word at a diplomatic reception in Hanoi on December 30, 1967, and at diplomatic posts elsewhere that if the United States stopped bombing the North, North Vietnam would "hold talks." Eager Washington officials fell over themselves to get the message, however Machiavellian it was. The North Vietnamese at last had said something definite, something on which to hinge negotiations—or so the eager officials deduced. The Communist government of Romania conveniently offered to serve as go-between. When a Romanian representative went to Hanoi in mid-January 1968, the United States demonstrated its good faith by halting the bombing in and around Hanoi during his visit.

The bombing halt fitted in nicely with plans of the North Vietnamese leaders to give their own people a memorable Tet holiday while denying one to the people of the South. Having previously announced a seven-day cease-fire for Tet, how better for the North Vietnamese to achieve surprise than by opening their grand offensive during Tet, a desecration of the sacred festival that the South Vietnamese would hardly believe possible? The Emperor Quang Trung in 1789 had pulled the same stunt against Chinese troops occupying Hanoi in support of a puppet government and routed them, yet that was hardly the same as sullying the holiday by Vietnamese attacking Vietnamese. Who in the South could conceive of that happening?

Lest the start of the offensive bring a return of the American bombers to spoil the celebration in Hanoi, the North Vietnamese Government decreed a change in the festivities. Instead of the start of the lunar New Year falling on Tuesday, January 30, it would fall on Monday, January 29, which meant the New Year's Eve celebration would begin on Sunday, January 28. That would give the North Vietnamese those important first three days of celebration before their soldiers in the South attacked after the true start of the lunar New Year, before daylight on January 31.

When I talked with news correspondents in Saigon in August 1967, informing them that I believed the time had come for the North Vietnamese to reassess their strategy, to make a "momentous decision," I was aware of none of those developments. I based my conclusions on logic. The enemy was hurting and he was winning no victories. As I remarked three months later in Washington, his only victory in over a year had been taking a CIDG-Special Forces camp in the A Shau Valley.

I considered that the enemy had four choices: he could quit, but that was hardly in keeping with Communist ideology or methods; he could return to guerrilla warfare, but combined American, South Vietnamese, and Allied strength would assure that he could accomplish little by that; he could go on the way he was going, which would be to rely on eventual American disenchantment with the war; or he could go all out to precipitate that disenchantment. If the decision he made was to be "momentous," it would have to be to go all out.

As the fall months passed, more and more indications developed to demonstrate that some kind of change, probably something big, was in the offing. The tenacity displayed at Loc Ninh in October and Dak To in November was unusual. So were a growing number of relatively small but aggressive attacks throughout the country. The number of *chieu hoi* returnees had dropped sharply. Prisoners were speaking of the coming "final victory." Enemy strength in the DMZ was increasing. Truck sightings along the Ho Chi Minh Trail increased by some 200 per cent.

At that stage the most logical course for the enemy, it seemed to me, was to make another and stronger effort to overrun the two northern provinces, coupled with lesser attacks throughout the rest of the country to try to tie down American forces that might be moved to reinforce the north. For a time I thought he might stage a major attack in the north during the Christmas season of 1967 in an effort to strike a psychological blow at American public opinion. Thus I directed a speed-up in planning for logistical improvements that would be necessary in order to reinforce the north, the most vulnerable part of the country. Although the enemy could cause trouble in other areas, it was only in the north that I saw a possibility of other than temporary enemy success.

While I was in Washington at the President's behest in November 1967, my deputy in Saigon, General Abrams, cabled me the contents of the enemy document captured near Dak To calling for "a concentrated offensive effort in coordination with other units in various battle areas throughout South Vietnam." I had discussed that document during a press conference at the Pentagon. The conference concluded with a question from Neil Sheehan of the New York *Times:* "Let me clear out one point. You don't think that the battle of Dak To is the beginning or the end of anything particular for the enemy?" To which I responded: "I think it's the beginning of a great defeat for the enemy."

The enemy's aggressive tactics during the late fall at Dak To and elsewhere contrasted sharply with an article by General Giap published in September 1967 in an official North Vietnamese journal. Giap proclaimed a protracted war of attrition and urged conserving forces. That, I concluded in the wake of the fall fighting, was camouflage, planned deception. It also conflicted with another document captured by men of the 101st Airborne Division on November 19 that appeared to be a broad outline for a major offensive, the long-heralded "final phase" of the war. "Central Headquarters," the document revealed, "concludes that the time has come for a direct revolution and that the opportunity for a general offensive and general uprising is within reach." A compilation in late November by the Saigon office of the CIA of various bits of evidence reinforced the case for a more aggressive enemy strategy.

At a party given by senior Vietnamese officers, General Tran Ngoc Tam, whom I had known since my first days in Vietnam, confided to me that he sensed that the enemy was planning some major move. It might be such a blow, he went on, that we might be unable to "win the victory."

As I noted in a cable to General Wheeler on December 20, the enemy "has already made a crucial decision concerning the conduct of the war," although I erroneously set the date of the "grave decision" as September rather than July. "The enemy decided," I continued, "that prolongation of his past policies for conducting the war would lead to his defeat, and that he would have to make a major effort to reverse the downward trend." Contrary to the Giap article, I noted, the enemy was exhorting his forces "to make a maximum effort on all fronts (political and military) in order to achieve victory in a short period of time." If the enemy was successful in "winning a significant victory" somewhere in South Vietnam, I concluded, "or gaining even an apparent position of strength," he might seek to initiate negotiations. I presume the information in that message was at least in part responsible for President Johnson's warning the Australian cabinet of "dark days ahead."

I nevertheless had no intention of sitting back to await the enemy's move. It would be better to get on with the fight, pre-empting with our attacks, it was hoped, any offensive the enemy had in mind and at least preventing him from pushing his bases forward from the border regions.

American units in the III Corps Zone began to move in December in preparation for renewed operations in jungle-covered northeastern Phuoc Long province that I hoped would pre-empt enemy attacks from War Zones C and D. I also projected a series of four operations, known collectively by the code name YORK, to sweep to the Laotian border in the four northern provinces, re-establishing control over the A Shau Valley and setting the stage for the invasion of Laos that I hoped a new administration in Washington would approve and possibly an amphibious hook around the DMZ *à la* the Inchon landing in Korea. Even if the enemy threat from the DMZ should materialize and forestall or delay the YORK operations, logistical preparation in support of them would help in meeting the threat.

Soon after nightfall on January 2, 1968, a sentry dog at a listening post outside the main defensive perimeter at Khe Sanh alerted marines in the post to movement nearby. Six men, making no effort at concealment, were approaching the listening post. Sent to investigate, a patrol headed by Second Lieutenant Nile B. Buffington saw that the men had green uniforms not unlike U. S. Marines. Buffington challenged them but got no reply. When he challenged a second time, one of the men made a move as if going for a hand grenade. The marines opened fire with M-16s.

The fire killed five of the men. A sixth, though wounded, got away in the darkness. All five of the dead turned out to be North Vietnamese officers, including a regimental commander and his operations and communications officers.

That encounter reinforced information from other intelligence sources to the effect that the North Vietnamese were again making Khe Sanh a focal point. Their 325 C Division had moved back to the vicinity of Hill 881 North while their 304th Division, which had fought at Dien Bien Phu, had crossed the border from Laos into positions southwest of Khe Sanh.

The commander of the U. S. III Marine Amphibious Force, General Cushman, began immediately to reinforce the two battalions of marines that had been serving as caretakers at Khe Sanh during the lull in enemy activity. Meanwhile, I ordered an intensive reconnaissance and intelligence collection effort and sent a special U. S. Army Special Forces long-range patrol unit to reinforce the marines. My Deputy for Air, General Momyer, began to put final touches on a plan to co-ordinate artillery, tactical air, and B-52 strikes around Khe Sanh, a SLAM operation like that first employed so successfully the preceding fall around Con Thien. I began to make plans for improving the effectiveness of Navy, Marine, and Air Force aircraft in the northern provinces by directing General Momyer to co-ordinate the total effort. Because Bob Cushman's headquarters already controlled more than three divisions, including the Army's Americal Division, successor to Task Force OREGON, I began to plan for introducing a U. S. Army headquarters into the I Corps region to control any reinforcements that I might send.

The apparent change in enemy strategy coincided with President Johnson's concerted effort to convince the American public that, contrary to many press reports and direful predictions of antiwar critics, genuine progress was being made in Vietnam. Although I received no instructions on what to say, my recalls to the United States to make public appearances during 1967 were apparently part of that effort. It was easy for me and my senior officers in Vietnam to fit in, however unintentionally, in the President's campaign, for we were in fact making substantial progress. The war *was* going well; the South Vietnamese were improving to the point they could assume increasing responsibilities; I could foresee the possibility of a start on American withdrawal in 1969.

The fact that the enemy had decided to change his strategy, "to make a maximum effort on all fronts (political and military) in order to achieve victory in a short period of time," did nothing to alter my estimates of progress. In the prior months of fighting, I had learned conclusively that it was when the enemy came out of hiding to make some major attack that American firepower could be brought to bear with tremendous effect. Even though we might incur some temporary setbacks if he came out of hiding to make a "maximum effort," it would be the beginning, as I had told Neil Sheehan, of "a great defeat for the enemy."

Although I subsequently alerted members of the press as intelligence on the enemy's plans became more definite, I made no concerted effort to prepare the American public for a U.S. debacle, for I saw no debacle in the making. I was confident that whatever the enemy attempted, American and South Vietnamese forces could eventually foil it. Even the warnings that I and others did issue via press and television generally went unheeded. Almost every year the American military command had predicted an enemy winter-spring offensive, and every year it had come off without any dire results for Americans or South Vietnamese. Was not the new offensive to be but more of the same?

Through Barry Zorthian and his Joint United States Public Affairs Office, the U. S. Mission on January 5 made public the document captured by the 101st Airborne Division in November in which the North Vietnamese Central Headquarters noted that the time might be near for "a general offensive and general uprising." The document gave no specific time for the all-out effort but did provide a key to its methods:

> Use very strong military attacks in co-ordination with the uprisings of the local population to take over towns and cities. Troops should flood the lowlands. They should move toward liberating the capital city [Saigon], take power and try to rally enemy brigades and regiments to our side one by one. Propaganda should be broadly disseminated among the population in general, and leaflets should be used to reach enemy officers and enlisted personnel.

Few American officials or reporters paid much attention to that document. Even those correspondents who reported it to their papers made nothing sensational of it. I could hardly fault them. Although I recognized that the enemy well might get into the towns and cities, since no impenetrable breastworks surrounded them, I knew it would be impossible for him to hold them. In view of American and South Vietnamese strength, for the VC and North Vietnamese to emerge from hiding throughout the country would be to invite catastrophic losses and certain defeat. The large enemy build-up in the DMZ and at Khe Sanh being an established fact, it would be much more logical and promising for him to stage diversionary attacks elsewhere while concentrating on creating something like Dien Bien Phu at Khe Sanh and seizing the two northern provinces.

Much of the attention of press, my own command, and Washington officials understandably focused on Khe Sanh. It was an obvious objective, essential to the enemy if he were to get behind the defensive posts facing the DMZ and move deep into Quang Tri province. Khe Sanh was isolated enough and bore enough similarities to Dien Bien Phu to excite armchair strategists. President Johnson, I learned later, had begun to develop a fixation about it. General Taylor had to set up a special White House Situation Room to depict and analyze American and enemy dispositions, complete with a large aerial photograph and a terrain model. The President asked General Wheeler to submit a memorandum on how Khe Sanh was to be defended, which led to the apocryphal story that the President had required the Joint Chiefs to "sign in blood" that Khe Sanh could be held.

In early afternoon of January 20 a North Vietnamese first lieutenant, La Thanh Tonc, appeared off one end of the airstrip at Khe Sanh, an AK-47 rifle in one hand, a white flag in the other and surrendered. He was piqued, Lieutenant Tonc revealed, because he had been passed over for promotion in favor of another officer whom he deemed far less qualified. While providing a detailed description of plans to capture Khe Sanh, he said preliminary attacks were to begin that night against marine outposts on Hills 861 and 881 South. They did.

The all-out attack, Lieutenant Tonc said, was to be made during the Tet holidays. Whether the lieutenant had his facts right about the main attack could never be fully established. A few days after his surrender, B-52 bombers struck a military headquarters in a limestone cave inside Laos, believed to be the North Vietnamese headquarters controlling the forces around Khe Sanh if not the entire northern region. It was obviously an important headquarters, for prisoners captured around Khe Sanh and in the DMZ reported having seen an important visitor there, believed to have been General Giap, coming and going. Following the attack, the radio traffic from the headquarters ceased for almost two weeks, there was evidence of considerable confusion in the North Vietnamese command in the north, and no major attack developed at Khe Sanh during Tet.

Elsewhere more detailed intelligence on the enemy's intentions had begun to emerge. On January 5 troops of the U. S. 4th Infantry Division had captured "Urgent Combat Order Number One," a detailed plan for attacks in Pleiku province to begin "before the Tet holidays." As the holidays approached, the division commander, Major General Charles P. Stone, put all American troops in the province on alert and stationed an American tank company as a mobile reserve within the town of Pleiku. He subsequently briefed me on his findings and alerted the Vietnamese II Corps commander, General Vinh Loc, who maintained an elaborate villa in Pleiku.

Vinh Loc was an enigmatic man, tall for a Vietnamese, a playboy, sophomoric, cantankerous, one whom I considered no better than marginally competent for such an important command as the II Corps. He once dressed up like a Montagnard king and led a contingent of Montagnards clad in loin cloths in a parade. To Charley Stone, Vinh Loc revealed that he too had some indications that the enemy was up to something, but that was not enough to prompt him to cancel plans to be in Saigon for the Tet holidays.

The alert of American troops nevertheless paid off early. Beginning on January 15, men of the 4th Division began to detect movement from beyond the Cambodian border of two regiments of the same North Vietnamese division that had fought in November at Dak To. Between January 15 and the start of Tet, 4th Division artillery and American bombers pummeled the enemy forces coming from Cambodia. So incapacitated were they that when the Tet offensive began, only one battalion was capable of executing its assignment.

Meanwhile, on January 10, a concerned Fred Weyand came to see me. Some time earlier I had promoted him from command of the 25th Division to command of the II Field Force and to the grade of lieutenant general. A former intelligence officer in the Pentagon, he had put together various bits of tenuous but disturbing intelligence and concluded that the enemy in the III Corps Zone was attempting to shift away from his border sanctuaries toward the population centers, including Saigon. Weyand thought I should cancel the projected pre-emptive attacks in Phuoc Long province near the border, which were awaiting the positioning of troops and the arrival of the dry season.

Weyand's information reinforced doubts that had already begun to arise in my own mind, and at my weekly strategy conference three days later, my intelligence officer, Brigadier General Phillip B. Davidson, who eight months earlier had succeeded General McChristian, presented much the same analysis. I agreed with Weyand and ordered the projected American attacks canceled so that American troops would be better able to react to enemy moves. American troops began shifting either to the vicinity of Saigon or along the corridors leading toward the capital from the border sanctuaries. Because of the threat in the north, I also canceled the first of the projected YORK operations and ordered the 1st Cavalry Division to begin to move from Quang Ngai and Binh Dinh provinces north into Thua Thien province. Those, as it turned out, were some of the more timely and critical decisions I made in Vietnam.

A major enemy offensive obviously was coming, to be launched, I believed, shortly before Tet, so that the enemy could take advantage of the Tet cease-fire and jockey his forces to exploit any gains achieved at the start. As I briefed the U. S. Mission Council on January 15, I saw a sixty-forty chance that the enemy would strike before Tet, probably on January 25. General Davidson, on the other hand, said his guess was forty-sixty that the enemy would maneuver during the cease-fire and then strike after Tet. Neither of us saw a high probability of an attack on the day of Tet, so harsh and disaffecting would be the psychological impact on the very people the enemy was trying to rally to his side.

Coincidentally, a new campaign developed in the United States aimed at halting all bombing of the North, presumably to further the negotiations at which North Vietnam had hinted as a cover for the coming offensive. The leading proponents of a halt, as reported by the press, were Senators Fulbright and Robert Kennedy. On January 22, in an interview with Howard Tuckner of NBC television, I spoke against a halt. I also noted: "I think his [the enemy's] plans concern a major effort to win a spectacular battlefield success on the eve of the Tet festival next Monday."

I transmitted much the same estimates through official channels to General Wheeler. In a message of January 20 I even included the Tet holiday as a possibility for the start of the offensive. "The enemy," I cabled, "is presently developing a threatening posture in several areas in order to seek victories essential to achieving prestige and bargaining power. He may exercise his initiatives prior to, *during,* or after Tet."*

So imposing was the threat that I went personally to President Thieu to try to get approval for canceling the customary cease-fire over the Tet holidays, or at least to reduce it from forty-eight to twenty-four hours. Neither my counterpart, General Vien, nor President Thieu would agree to a total cancellation. It would be too sharp a blow to the ARVN and the people, they said, to eliminate all observance of the nation's most important holiday and in the process give the enemy a propaganda club to be wielded against the South Vietnamese government. Upon my urging, Thieu did agree to shorten the cease-fire to thirty-six hours and promised that Tet leaves for ARVN troops would be limited and that a minimum of 50 per cent of the troops in all units would be on full alert.

As the Tet holiday drew closer, I became increasingly concerned about the build-up north of the DMZ and in Laos adjacent to the two northern provinces of South Vietnam and the advantage a cease-fire would afford the enemy for maneuvering his troops. Late reconnaissance revealed, for example, that the enemy was using bulldozers to construct a road in the A Shau Valley in the direction of Hué. At my urging, Ambassador Bunker asked Washington for approval to cancel the cease-fire entirely in the two northern provinces and, even if Washington halted the bombing in general, to continue bombing in the area immediately north of the DMZ, where the enemy was assembling. When Washington approved, I obtained President Thieu's concurrence.

To afford the enemy little time to adjust to the cancellation, the South Vietnamese Government was to delay announcing it until the morning of Monday, January 29, twenty-four hours before it was to have gone into effect. Yet the morning passed with no notice of the cancellation. I telephoned the Embassy to find that the South Vietnamese Government had provided its press office with a release but that the press office was shut tight, closed for Tet. President Thieu had departed to pass the holidays in My Tho, his wife's home town in the Mekong Delta.

Such a lackadaisical attitude on the part of the government was shocking and frustrating, yet indicative of the state of mind, the near euphoria, that envelops the Vietnamese at Tet. Seriously concerned, I telephoned General Vien several times during the day to gain his assurances that the armed forces would be on the alert. To Ambassador Bunker I explained that we had no choice but to announce the cancellation of the cease-fire in the north unilaterally. Barry Zorthian finally did it at a mission press conference in late afternoon.

Long accustomed to enemy truce violations, such as a major attack

* Emphasis provided.

against a unit of the 25th Division during a thirty-six-hour extension of the previous New Year's truce, granted at the insistence of the Pope in Rome, American troops experienced no letdown in vigilance. In addition to the shift of units closer to Saigon and the alert in the II Corps Zone, I ordered all units to maintain a mobile reserve for quick commitment. I also ordered an all-out effort throughout the country to collect intelligence. Some idea of the concern in my headquarters is apparent from a message that General Davidson, my intelligence officer, sent on January 21 to CINCPAC for transmittal to his wife, whom he had planned to see in Hawaii:

> Please tell Jeanne that I cannot meet her in Honolulu. Explain, please, within bounds of classification, the tense operational situation which prevents my coming. Thanks for everything. Regards.

On January 22 I cabled General Wheeler that the enemy might launch a multibattalion attack against Hué and also hit Quang Tri City. "I believe," I wrote, "the enemy will attempt a countrywide show of strength just prior to Tet."

At the strategy and intelligence conference on Saturday morning, January 27, General Davidson predicted major countrywide attacks and specifically named the towns of Kontum and Pleiku, although he ventured no starting date and pinpointed no other towns or cities. I was nevertheless becoming increasingly concerned about Saigon, partly because I had ended Operation FAIRFAX in December, redeploying the 199th Infantry Brigade and leaving defense of the environs of the city as well as the capital itself to the South Vietnamese. However much I considered that essential for their national pride, it nevertheless made for uneasy moments.

A day or two before Tet, I telephoned General Weyand and told him to move a squadron of the 4th Cavalry to the town of Hoc Mon, virtually within the shadow of the gates of Tan Son Nhut. Equipped with armored assault vehicles, the squadron would provide a ready mobile reserve with impressive firepower. No yes-man, Weyand expressed reluctance to part with the squadron and demurred. "Damn it, Fred," I said, "I know your views and have considered them. Now get with it!"

On Sunday, January 28, two days before Tet, ARVN security troops raided a house on the outskirts of the coastal city of Qui Nhon. They captured eleven VC, a tape recorder, and two tapes. The VC, the prisoners admitted under questioning, probably would attack Qui Nhon and other cities during the Tet holidays. The tapes were propaganda exhortations to be played over the presumably captured government radio station, urging the people and the armed forces to go over to the side of the "People's Forces Struggling for Peace and Sovereignty," to help smash "the dictatorial fascist regime of Thieu and Ky."

We thus knew that a major enemy offensive was coming. General Davidson was within a week of the opening date, probably closer than an intelligence specialist can normally expect to be. Phil Davidson's identifications and locations of all major enemy units were correct; no previously unidentified unit showed up, so that in that respect the case was unlike the intelligence failure in the Battle of the Bulge in World War II or intervention of the Chinese Communists in Korea in 1950. We had some warning of attacks on towns and cities, although we hardly could have expected to know the enemy's exact plans and nobody anticipated the extent to which attacks on towns and cities actually developed throughout the country.

As General Davidson put it to me later: "Even had I known exactly what was to take place, it was so preposterous that I probably would have been unable to sell it to anybody. Why would the enemy give away his major advantage, which was his ability to be elusive and avoid heavy casualties?" He was no doubt right. When I had asked Jack Seaman, commander of the II Field Force, in the summer of 1966 to prepare a war game based on the worst possible contingency in the region around Saigon, his staff had come up with almost exactly what did happen in 1968, but even though the appraisal alerted us to the possibility, we deemed it at the time unlikely.

Nobody in Saigon to my knowledge anticipated even remotely the psychological impact the offensive would have in the United States. Militarily, the offensive was foredoomed to failure, destined to be over everywhere, except in Saigon and Hué and at Khe Sanh, in a day or so, certainly nothing to compare with the six weeks required to defeat and eliminate the gains of the Battle of the Bulge or with the violence and extensive gains of the Chinese Communists' onslaught in Korea. The American people absorbed those psychological blows with little trauma. No one to my knowledge foresaw that, in terms of public opinion, press and television would transform what was undeniably a catastrophic military defeat for the enemy into a presumed debacle for Americans and South Vietnamese, an attitude that still lingers in the minds of many.

In retrospect, I believe that I and officials in Washington should have tried to do more to alert the American public to the coming of a major offensive. Through my reports to the Joint Chiefs, Washington civilian authorities knew all that I knew, yet they too failed to foresee the importance of preparing the American people for it. The order of the day at the White House remained low key. As a consequence, the offensive seemed to many in direct contradiction to President Johnson's campaign to demonstrate progress in the war, a refutation of my remarks at the Press Club two months earlier. Few bothered to recall that historically a force on the downgrade often tries to recover by means of some spectacular surge.

Yet what effect would more warnings have had when the U.S. press in Saigon treated every forecast as if the military command were crying wolf? My prediction to Howard Tuckner that the enemy was seeking a spectacular battlefield success was buried under speculation on the effect of a bombing halt. One of the few reporters who gave American readers any inkling of something unusual, Don Oberdorfer, subsequently of the Washington *Post* and author of an authoritative book on the offensive,† writing at the time in the Miami *Herald,* saw his story tied to a headline that concealed its impact: NEW HANOI GOAL: FORCE COALITION 'DEAL'?

"There is a growing hunch on the part of many [American officials]," wrote Oberdorfer from Saigon on January 12, "that the next month or two is likely to bring some critical—perhaps spectacular—moves on the part of the enemy. The next three weeks—from now until Tet, the Vietnamese lunar New Year—are considered particularly important." Having interviewed Fred Weyand, Oberdorfer reported on "marked changes" in Communist tactics, a shift of strength toward Saigon, North Vietnamese replacements in Viet Cong units, and Communist plans to attack in "mass formations."

Yet who would listen? How to alert anybody when press, Congress, and White House were preoccupied with Khe Sanh and the possible effect of a bombing halt on prompting the North Vietnamese to negotiate? The North Vietnamese had devised a clever scenario, including a threat to Khe Sanh and an ingenious hint at negotiations, and, however unwittingly, many Americans, including the press, Congress, academics, and even government officials, played the role intended for them as effectively as if they had had an advance look at the script.

For all the enemy's intricate planning for the offensive, something went wrong in the timing. At 12:35 on the morning of Tuesday, January 30, just over a half hour into the Year of the Monkey, Communist gunners fired six mortar rounds at the Vietnamese Navy Training Center in Nha Trang—and missed. An hour later, as Tet celebrants milled in the streets of Ban Me Thuot in southern reaches of the Central Highlands, setting off strings of firecrackers, a barrage of mortars and rockets hit the town, followed by a ground assault by two battalions. At about the same time, an enemy battalion attacked the little district capital of Tan Canh, adjacent to Dak To. A half hour further into the morning, three Viet Cong battalions moved against the provincial Highlands capital of Kontum City, while a battalion launched a ground attack at Nha Trang. Not quite an hour later, a ground attack at Hoi An, a district capital near the coast, south of Danang. At Danang a company of VC infiltrators hit the headquarters compound of the Vietnamese I Corps on the outskirts. At 4:10 A.M. two VC battalions attacked the outskirts of Qui Nhon, where, because of the warning two days before, the local commander had forbidden fireworks; infiltrators nevertheless briefly controlled the government radio station but had no tapes to play. At 4:40 A.M. the long-expected attack on Pleiku developed, which brought General Vinh Loc hurrying back from Saigon with more apparent concern for his villa than for the battle as a whole.

The VC at those eight towns and cities had in fact jumped the gun. Why

† Don Oberdorfer, *Tet!* (New York: Doubleday & Company, 1971).

was never explained. All eight were in the same enemy jurisdiction, known as Military Region 5, so that the regional headquarters may have been at fault. It could have been that the offensive was originally scheduled for the morning of January 30 but was changed to the 31st when the North Vietnamese decided to give their own people three days of celebrating in advance, and Military Region 5 failed to get the word. Or the destruction by B-52s of the North Vietnamese headquarters near Khe Sanh may have had something to do with it.

The warning afforded by the premature attacks was brief, but a warning nonetheless. "This," Phil Davidson said to me, "is going to happen in the rest of the country tonight or tomorrow morning." I agreed.

In midmorning of January 30 President Thieu announced cancellation of the cease-fire throughout the country. A short while later, through my chief of staff, Major General Walter T. ("Dutch") Kerwin, I sent a priority message to all American units, announcing the cancellation and directing that "troops will be placed on maximum alert with particular attention to the defense of headquarters complexes, logistical installations, airfields, population centers and billets."

Although announcements poured from the government radio all day on January 30, ordering all Vietnamese servicemen to return to their units, few made it. In isolated villages and hamlets many failed to get the word. Lacking transportation, others found it impossible to return for all their efforts. Still others deemed that in time of peril they should stay to protect their families. Effective strength at most ARVN posts remained at 50 per cent or very little more.

The enemy attacks that came on schedule before daybreak on January 31 thus were, in the main, no surprise. Assaults against specific installations within towns and cities did involve an element of surprise, for nobody could have discerned the exact enemy plan in each of the widespread attacks. Intelligence can seldom be that specific, and isolated installations were in no sense impregnable, however alert the guards. Nor was it possible among the teeming crowds of Tet revelers to screen out VC infiltrators with fake identification papers posing as civilians, those who would later rendezvous within the cities, pick up weapons and demolitions previously hidden by confederates, and launch suicidal attacks against such targets as radio stations, headquarters compounds, government buildings, and homes of ARVN commanders and government officials.

Or the imposing new six-story building on Thung Nhat boulevard in Saigon, the United States Embassy.

Tuesday, January 30, was a busy day. I either saw or telephoned every senior American commander in Vietnam to discuss the likelihood of immediate widespread attacks and went home late and tired. At around three the next morning, my current aide, Major Charles Sampson, woke me for a call from my headquarters. The attacks we had expected, and some we hadn't, were underway, including a sapper raid on the American Embassy.

I dressed and stood vigil by my home telephone. The attack on the Embassy was regrettable; but had the enemy controlled every inch of it, that would have had no effect on American military operations, and the Embassy staff had an alternate location elsewhere in the city. Of greater military concern were attacks on Tan Son Nhut, the nearby compound of the Joint General Staff, and others that began to develop in cities around the country.

A telephone call from Major Sampson to a fellow marine, a guard in the lobby of the Chancery, the main building of the Embassy, ascertained that the VC had failed to enter the Chancery. They had blown a hole in the wall of the Embassy compound, I learned later, to gain access to the grounds. Two Military Police guards, Specialist 4 Charles L. Daniel and Private First Class William E. Sabast, killed the first two VC to enter but themselves died in the exchange of fire. Two men of a jeep patrol who responded to a call for help also died: Sergeant Jonnie B. Thomas and Specialist 4 Owen E. Mebust. A fifth American, Marine Corporal James C. Marshall, who climbed atop a building to fire into the compound, also was killed.

It was a dramatic skirmish, the drama heightened by the fact that a skeleton night staff on duty inside the Chancery was in telephone contact throughout the fight with the State Department in Washington. Two members of the Embassy staff, Robert L. Josephson, a retired Army master sergeant, and George D. Jacobson, a retired colonel with long previous military experience in Vietnam, sat out the fight in an old French villa in which they lived within the compound. They were armed with nothing but a hand grenade and a bent coat hanger. When a platoon of Military Police entered the compound at dawn, one man tossed a .45-caliber pistol through a window just in time for Jacobson to kill a VC who was climbing the stairs to where he and Josephson were hiding.

With the coming of daylight a platoon of U.S. airborne troops landed on the helicopter pad on the roof of the Chancery, but by that time the fight was over. All fifteen VC sappers were dead, along with the five Americans and four Vietnamese employees of the Embassy, one of whom may have been a VC collaborator.

As soon as I learned that the airborne troops had landed, I drove by car to the Embassy. It was about 8:30 A.M. Like any battlefield, the compound was in disarray, bodies of Americans and Vietnamese still lying about. Yet unlike most battlefields, American reporters and television cameramen were seemingly everywhere. Their faces mirrored dismay and incredulity, as if the end of the world was at hand.

Entering the Chancery, I complimented the Marine guard to whom Major Sampson had spoken by telephone and made a telephone report to Philip Habib, then with the State Department in Washington. I then reported by telephone to Ambassador Bunker and recommended that all

Embassy employees report for work at the Embassy at noon. As I departed, Barry Zorthian asked me to hold a press conference on the scene. I took the opportunity to try to put the Embassy raid and the countryside attacks into perspective.

Contrary to rumor, I said, none of the Viet Cong had gotten inside the Chancery. Damage to the building was superficial. As for the big offensive throughout the country, the enemy, by coming into the open, was exposing himself to tremendous casualties. Fully conscious of American and South Vietnamese strength and ability, I had no hesitation in saying that the enemy was inviting defeat.

My efforts at perspective went for nought. The attack on the Embassy, Don Oberdorfer wrote later, "seemed to give the lie to the rosy projections and victory claims that Westmoreland and others had been dishing out." Oberdorfer said that the reporters could hardly believe their ears. "Westmoreland was standing in the ruins and saying everything was great."‡

That attitude on the part of the American reporters undoubtedly contributed to the psychological victory the enemy achieved in the United States. What would they have had me say, that the walls were tumbling down when I knew they were not? That the enemy was winning when I knew he was on the verge of a disastrous military defeat? When noting my statement that no enemy had gotten inside the Chancery, one reporter took pains to add that other sources—meaning rumor, but not so identified—said otherwise. Was the word of a professional military man who bore over-all military responsibility for the war in South Vietnam and who had personally gone through the Embassy building to have no precedence over rumor? Had the level of credibility and the art of reporting sunk to such a low?

In the race to drain every possible sensation from the Embassy story, reporters made little apparent effort to check facts, while basking in the praise of their home offices for their speed in beating the opposition. They sped unedited television film by air to Tokyo for transmission by satellite to the United States before facts were ascertained. Chet Huntley on the NBC Evening News had the VC inside the Chancery, the defenders in the compound outside. There was no report on Allied casualties in Saigon, said Huntley, "but they're believed to be high." Was that kind of gratuitous speculation justified? Was the long, costly American effort in Vietnam to be sacrificed to the idols of sensation and competition?

In the furor nobody took time to observe that even in conventional war, raiders can slip through the lines and do mischief in the rear. How much greater the opportunity in unconventional war. During the Civil War Yankee spies and raiders sometimes penetrated Richmond's close-knit ring of breastworks, and Saigon was no Richmond. The surprise was not that the VC attacked installations such as the Embassy but that they did it so few times.

‡ Oberdorfer, *Tet!*, pp. 33–34.

In the furor, too, few took notice that the VC also attacked the Embassy of the Philippines and with considerably more success. There they actually got inside the Chancery and occupied it for several hours. That had no more long term military result than if they had actually entered the American Chancery.

Elsewhere in Saigon, another small band of VC sappers attacked Independence Palace. Driven off, the thirteen VC—including a woman—holed up in an apartment house across the street, where to the delight of cameramen from all three American television networks, they held out for fifteen sunlit hours in living color.

A twelve-man VC force attacking Vietnamese Navy headquarters provided no footage because all but two died in the first few minutes of the attack. A stronger force broke into the South Vietnamese Government radio station, but government officials at a prearranged signal shut off power to the station and began transmitting from an alternate site. A VC battalion scheduled to liberate 5,000 prisoners in the main Saigon jail got lost and ended up fighting for its life in a cemetery a mile from its objective. Two VC battalions overwhelmed guards at headquarters of the ARVN Armored and Artillery Commands on the northern fringe of Saigon but found that the tanks they hoped to use had been moved elsewhere and the artillery pieces were useless without the breechblocks that the ARVN soldiers had removed. Another VC force occupied Phu Tho racetrack alongside Cholon and eventually had to be rooted out, but denial of that facility hardly posed any hardship. When an air observer called for artillery fire on VC pulling mortars in carts on the northwest fringe of the city, ARVN artillerymen plotting the reported co-ordinates found the targets were actually early morning players on the Saigon golf course.

More serious clashes developed at Tan Son Nhut and at the adjacent compound of the Vietnamese Joint General Staff. Up to three VC battalions attacked Tan Son Nhut and at one spot breached the defensive perimeter. A makeshift group of South Vietnamese airmen and airborne troops, assigned to protect Vice President Ky, filled the breach long enough for a squadron of the 4th U. S. Cavalry under Lieutenant Colonel Glenn Otis, the unit that I had earlier told Fred Weyand to move forward, to come upon the enemy from the rear. More than 325 VC died. As daylight came, planes, gunships, and artillery pounded the VC survivors, some of whom took refuge in a cotton mill just outside the air base. Searchers later found 162 bodies in the ruins.

A determined VC assault on the compound of the Joint General Staff well might have succeeded except for the intervention of a cluster of American MPs guarding a group of villas directly across the street from one of the gates the VC tried to penetrate. Used to house senior American officers and VIPs, the villas were known collectively as BOQ 3.

Just as the VC assault began and South Vietnamese Military Police at the

The author with President Lyndon
B. Johnson in the White House,
November 1967. (*Official White
House Photograph*)

The author escorts President Lyndon B. Johnson at Cam Ranh Bay, December 1967.

The author and Mrs. Westmoreland with actress Racquel Welch and actor Bob Hope during the Hope troupe's Christmas visit, 1967.

Defensive positions on the west perimeter of Khe Sanh in March 1968. *(Marine Corps Photo)*

Marine Colonel David E. Lownds (right) and Major General Rathvon McC. Tompkins at Khe Sanh, March 1968.

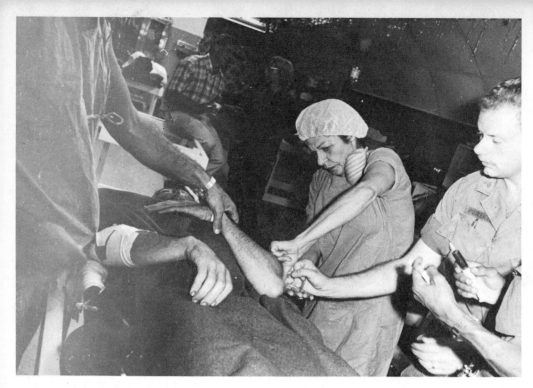

Actress Martha Raye assisting at a forward medical aid station in Quang Ngai province during the Tet offensive, 1968.

General Creighton W. Abrams, Deputy Commander, MACV, in 1968, presents medals to members of the Republic of Korea Capital ("Tiger") Infantry Division.

Artillerymen of the Australian Task Force stand ready beside their 105-mm howitzer at a fire support base in South Vietnam.

Infantrymen of the 25th Division with a scout dog in the Iron Triangle, 1968. *(U. S. Army Photograph)*

Soldiers of the 9th Division fighting near the Y Bridge on the southern outskirts of Saigon, May 1968. *(U. S. Army Photograph)*

One phase of civic action. Specialist 5 Fred Havens of Dayton, Ohio, provides medi[...] treatment for a South Vietnamese woman, M[...] 1968.

General Earle G. (''Bus'') Wheeler, Chairm[...] of the Joint Chiefs of Staff.

The Joint Chiefs of Staff meeting with President Richard M. Nixon and members of his staff in the White House in 1970. Around the table, from left: Air Force General John D. Ryan; Admiral Elmo R. Zumwalt, Jr.; the author; Commandant, U. S. Marine Corps, General Leonard F. Chapman, Jr.; Deputy Secretary of Defense David Packard; Secretary of Defense Melvin R. Laird; Vice President Spiro Agnew; the President; Admiral Thomas H. Moorer; and Dr. Henry Kissinger.

The author prepares to pilot a helicopter in 1971 during his tenure as Army Chief of Staff.

The author bids good-by to his staff upon retirement, June 1972.

gate opened fire, two American MPs passing by on jeep patrol also opened fire. Return fire killed them both, whereupon Military Police at BOQ 3 took up the fight, joined in time by some of the residents of the villas.

Answering a call from BOQ 3 for reinforcements, twenty-five American MPs in a truck and two jeeps headed up a narrow alley toward the villas. A VC rocket hit the truck head on, and fire from VC automatic weapons raked the scene as the survivors tried to find cover. An ambulance trying to reach the alley had to turn back when the VC fired a claymore mine. Sixteen MPs died in the alley. A few managed eventually to work their way to BOQ 3 to join their comrades and residents of the villas in firing sporadically across the street through the rest of the day. All could be grateful that the Viet Cong maintained their reputation for inflexibility and never turned from their objective of taking the South Vietnamese compound to assault undermanned BOQ 3.

General Vien, my counterpart, Chief of the Joint General Staff, meanwhile made his way to the compound from his home in Cholon through back streets, arriving at daylight at a gate as yet uncontested. Waiting at Tan Son Nhut were two companies of South Vietnamese airborne troops, all that remained uncommitted of two battalions that General Vien had been preparing to send to reinforce the I Corps when the enemy's premature attacks put everybody on the alert. Vien called those companies to the defense of the compound.

The fight for the compound continued through the day and into the night but with diminishing clamor. Those few VC who penetrated the walls were soon isolated and eliminated. Meanwhile, Vice President Ky moved into the compound from his quarters at Tan Son Nhut and an American helicopter with difficulty fetched President Thieu to the compound from his wife's home in My Tho.

The only attack specifically directed at an American installation in Saigon was that against the Embassy, obviously designed for the psychological effect that American newsmen helped it achieve. Some stray mortar rounds and small-arms fire hit some American BOQs, and Embassy security men spirited Ambassador Bunker from his villa in an armored personnel carrier, always on standby for such an eventuality, to a previously arranged hideout in another residence; but as was generally the case throughout the entire country, the real VC targets were South Vietnamese installations. Assassination squads also tried to kill South Vietnamese dignitaries. None succeeded, although in the Mekong Delta the VC for a time held the commander of the 7th ARVN Division, General Thanh, and his family hostage in the hope of promoting defection of the entire 7th Division; but General Thanh defied them.

The fact that so few American installations were hit anywhere—indeed, the VC often passed right by American installations to get at South Vietnamese compounds—gave rise to a belief among many South Vietnamese that the Americans and the VC were in collusion. No doubt encouraged by the Communists, the rumor was long in passing away, dispelled only by continuing involvement of American troops in the fighting.

The more prolonged Tet combat in Saigon developed in residential sectors where Viet Cong, in up to battalion strength in some cases, became well dug in. Although the ARVN began methodically to clean them out, in the process inevitably destroying sections of the city, I decided as a matter of military necessity to alter my policy of leaving the city's defense entirely to the South Vietnamese and over two days moved seven American battalions into the city or its outskirts to speed the mop-up. Other American battalions took positions on roads leading into the city lest enemy reinforcements seek to enter.

By February 5, six days after the predawn assaults began, Saigon was free of all but small enemy groups, although occasional skirmishes erupted as government forces encountered isolated VC trying to hide among the people. Unfortunately, on the second day of the fighting, an act of one South Vietnamese and the chance recording of it by still and television cameras handed the VC another psychological triumph that obscured the valor and determination that the Saigon police and ARVN troops displayed throughout the struggle in the city.

In the course of fighting near the An Quang pagoda, the chief of the National Police, Nguyen Ngoc Loan, summarily executed a VC prisoner with a shot in the head from his revolver. A still photographer, Eddie Adams, tripped his shutter just as the bullet slammed into the prisoner's head. An NBC television camera also recorded the event. The photograph and the film shocked the world, an isolated incident of cruelty in a broadly cruel war, but a psychological blow against the South Vietnamese nonetheless.

Going to my headquarters at Tan Son Nhut following my trip to the Embassy on January 31, I learned the extent of the enemy's offensive in other parts of the country. Either in the premature attacks, the main attacks, or additional attacks on the third day, some 84,000 enemy troops, mainly VC but interlaced with North Vietnamese replacements, hit thirty-six of the forty-four provincial capitals, five of the six autonomous cities, sixty-four of 242 district capitals, and fifty hamlets. It was an attack on a broad front.

The enemy penetrated in some strength into Saigon, Quang Tri, Hué, Danang, Nha Trang, Qui Nhon, Kontum City, Ban Me Thuot, Dalat, Phan Thiet, My Tho, Can Tho, and Ben Tre. In most cases militia and ARVN troops drove the enemy out within two or three days, in some cases within hours; but heavy fighting continued several days longer in Kontum City, Ban Me Thuot, Phan Thiet, Can Tho, Ben Tre, and Saigon, and in Hué the battle was protracted.

Having lost the lone CIDG-Special Forces camp in the A Shau Valley in 1966 and having lacked the forces to move back in, we possessed no block such as Khe Sanh against enemy infiltration through the A Shau Valley toward Hué. Under concealment of a low fog that the *crachin* weather featured at that time of year, at least eight VC and North Vietnamese battalions—equivalent to a division—infiltrated with the help of civilian accomplices into the old imperial city.

Of all the Communist targets in the Tet offensive, Hué—population 140,000, Vietnam's third city—may well have been the least prepared for what lay in store. Although I had reported to Washington on January 22 that a multibattalion attack might be expected at Hué, for some reason, I learned later, that information apparently failed to reach a small MACV advisory group in a little walled compound within the city. Except for some civilian officials, that group and a smaller U. S. Army advisory detachment with headquarters of the 1st ARVN Division constituted the only American presence in Hué.

Headquarters and two brigades of the 1st Cavalry Division arrived a few days later at a position north of Hué as part of my broad plan to reinforce the I Corps and my preparations for eventual mobile operations in the north. At Phu Bai, eight miles southeast of Hué, a quartering party had arrived as a preliminary to setting up an adjunct of my own headquarters to control the increased forces in the north until an Army corps headquarters could be organized, but the quartering party in no sense represented a functioning command. Also at Phu Bai was a rear echelon of the headquarters of the 3d Marine Division, getting ready to move north to join the rest of the division in the fight below the DMZ. And there was also a large U. S. Army communications installation at Phu Bai.

During the first day of the lunar New Year, January 30, there were strong intelligence indications of enemy movement toward Hué, but that information had to go first to headquarters of the III Marine Amphibious Force at Danang for analysis. By the time it got back to the little American advisory group in Hué, the time when it might have helped had passed.

There was, nevertheless, some last-minute alerting. The enemy's premature attacks elsewhere, when added to other fragmentary information, convinced the man who was responsible for defending Hué, General Ngo Quang Truong, commander of the 1st ARVN Division, that something was up. Most of Truong's troops were outside the city, but his division headquarters was in the Citadel, a walled portion of the city on the north bank of the Perfume River encompassing the palace and other buildings of the old imperial court. Truong alerted all his troops and ordered his entire division staff to spend the night in the headquarters.

Those precautions would facilitate the later fight and insure that the South Vietnamese held onto a portion of the Citadel, but they had little effect on the enemy's opening thrust. The enemy moved into Hué by stealth during the night. By daylight on January 31 the MACV advisory compound was under siege and most of Hué was in enemy hands, including much of the Citadel. The blue and red Viet Cong flag with yellow star flew from the

Citadel flagpole, the only time the VC succeeded in raising their flag over one of their Tet objectives.

As troops of the 1st ARVN Division moved to retake the city, the U. S. Marine commander, General Cushman, committed to the fight the only readily available force of American marines, a company of the 1st Marine Division. The remainder of that company's battalion entered the battle during the day. The marines early relieved the heroic little band that was still holding out in the MACV advisory compound.

As the fight began, Vietnamese and marines made do without tank, artillery, and air support, in the hope of sparing the venerable city, so rich a part of Vietnamese heritage; but as the enemy held on tenaciously, that policy proved too costly in American and South Vietnamese lives. President Thieu subsequently authorized whatever was necessary to retake the city.

Destruction inevitably followed. When ARVN troops pulled down the Viet Cong flag twenty-five days after the start of the fighting, much of the Citadel and of the residential part of the city south of the Perfume River were damaged. Contrary to reports in the American press, the palace and most of the other buildings of the imperial court still stood, but Hué nevertheless represented the closest thing yet in Vietnam to the destructive street fighting of World War II.

The pulling down of the North Vietnamese flag involved special intrepidity by a small fifty-man South Vietnamese unit known as "Tiger Force." As South Vietnamese troops neared the wall about the Citadel, General Truong, concerned about the morale factor of the North Vietnamese flag continuing to fly, ordered the Tiger Force to capture it. On a dark, rainy night, the men gained the top of the wall and proceeded along it in the direction of the flag, in the process hurling themselves over concertina barbed wire and past claymore mines. At long last they reached the foot of the flagpole and, despite enemy fire, pulled down the gold-starred North Vietnamese flag and ran up the saffron and orange colors of South Vietnam. All North Vietnamese resistance ended the next day.

Recapturing Hué involved eleven ARVN and three U. S. Marine battalions, while the 1st Cavalry Division operated north and northwest of the city to deny enemy reinforcement. A total of sixteen enemy battalions, equivalent to two divisions, participated. Over 5,000 of the enemy died within the city, another 3,000 in fighting nearby. The U. S. Marines lost 142 killed; the South Vietnamese, 384. During the fight to retake the city, my deputy, General Abrams, whom I had temporarily placed in command in the northern provinces, did a superb job of co-ordinating the efforts of the ARVN, U. S. Marines, and U. S. Army troops.

The final horror of the battle of Hué emerged only by degrees over the next weeks and months as hastily dug graves in and around the city gave up their grisly contents. During the invasion and twenty-five-day occupation, the Communists executed or buried alive more than 2,800 residents of Hué: civil servants, government officials, school teachers, ARVN and militia officers and men, policemen, priests, hundreds of males who appeared to be of military age. They also killed a number of Americans, including Stephen Miller, USIA representative; Courtney Niles, an official of NBC International; and several members of a U. S. Army communications team. The senior American adviser in Hué, a civilian, Philip W. Manhard, was captured and for a time shared a camp with the would-be escape artist, Colonel Purcell, before his eventual release in the final exchange of prisoners. Also murdered were a German doctor and his wife, two French priests, and several Filipinos.

In addition to committing U.S. troops to Saigon and Hué, I authorized commitment of limited numbers of American troops at Kontum City, Phu Loc, My Tho, and Ben Tre. In most cases the commitments were merely to speed the mop-up, although it can be said that American troops saved Ben Tre. The one case where intervention of American troops definitely saved a city was in the far north at Quang Tri City, not my doing but instead a product of the quick thinking of Ambassador Komer's military deputy, George Forsythe, who happened to be visiting the pacification team there.

After spending a night fighting as a rifleman to help keep North Vietnamese out of the MACV advisory compound, General Forsythe learned that an enemy force was approaching Quang Tri City from the southeast. The local ARVN commander had succeeded in building a defensive screen about the city everywhere but there. Flying by helicopter to the nearby headquarters of a brigade of the 1st Cavalry Division, Forsythe asked the commander, Colonel Donald V. Rattan, to send a battalion to fill the gap. Colonel Rattan replied that his brigade had orders to proceed with a mission against an enemy base area, but he volunteered to check with his division commander, Major General John J. Tolson, and recommend a change. The battalion arrived at the gap less than an hour before the North Vietnamese and in turning back the attack killed more than 400.

Many an American got involved in the fighting during the Tet offensive: advisers to ARVN units, isolated detachments, troops that intercepted enemy units moving toward their targets, Air Force pilots, helicopter crews, military police. Yet except at airfields used jointly by Americans and the South Vietnamese, such as that at Bien Hoa, the only major attack against an American base was a strike by a VC regiment at the extensive perimeter of Long Binh; under a superb officer, Colonel Frederic E. Davison, the 199th Infantry Brigade intercepted part of the regiment and then surrounded the rest soon after the attack began. It was later my pleasure as Chief of Staff to promote Davison as the first black general officer in the U. S. Army since World War II.

In the main, the Tet offensive was a Vietnamese fight. To the ARVN, other members of the South Vietnamese armed forces, the militia, the National Police—to those belonged the major share of credit for turning back the offensive. Some individuals failed; an occasional commander proved incompetent; but over all, when put to a crucial test, no ARVN unit had broken or defected. The South Vietnamese had fully vindicated my trust.

The destruction in Saigon, Hué, Ben Tre, and elsewhere was lamentable but an inevitable result of the enemy's decision to take the war to the people. Here at last was undeniable evidence of the damage that fighting among the population generated.

Except at Hué, most of the combat that could be considered part of the Tet offensive was over by February 11, a fortnight after it began, followed by a sharp flurry of local attacks, mostly with mortars and rockets, on February 18. From the premature start on January 29 through February 11, the Communists lost 32,000 killed and 5,800 captured, close to half the troops actively committed. American forces lost 1,001 killed; South Vietnamese and Allied forces, 2,082. By the end of February, as American and ARVN troops swept the environs of the towns and cities, the enemy toll rose to 37,000 killed. In only one case, at Hué, had the enemy held onto an objective for any appreciable length of time. Indeed, so short-lived was any success that most North Vietnamese units, which the enemy apparently withheld in order to exploit success, never got into the fight. Nothing remotely resembling a general uprising of the people had occurred.

It all added up to a striking military defeat for the enemy on anybody's terms.

In an order issued by COSVN, the VC headquarters, on February 1, calling for a continuation of the offensive, the enemy admitted failure:

> We failed to seize a number of primary objectives and to completely destroy mobile and defensive units of the enemy. We also failed to hold the occupied areas. In the political field we failed to motivate the people to stage uprisings and break the enemy's oppressive control.

Yet even though the South Vietnamese armed forces had scored an impressive victory, it would still have been possible for the government to throw it away. The offensive had disrupted the pacification program in the countryside, and the fighting had generated 600,000 new refugees. If the government failed to rejuvenate pacification and left the refugees to their fate, serious repercussions were inevitable.

The fighting had driven many of the pacification teams into the towns and cities, where reports that the enemy would momentarily renew his onslaught made them reluctant to return to the villages and hamlets. Yet as the enemy's continued efforts amounted to little more than a ripple when compared to the Tet offensive proper and as Ambassador Komer and his field representatives kept up the pressure, the teams gradually returned to their posts. In the end, the damage imposed on pacification by the enemy's offensive was far less extensive than originally estimated. Indeed, the fact that many among the VC political infrastructure had surfaced during the offensive in anticipation of a popular uprising meant in the long run that the task of pacification would be eased.

The refugee problem, however, had the ingredients of a genuine crisis. The government, from President Thieu down through the various ministries, appeared to be stunned. At a meeting of my staff well before the last of the enemy was rooted out of Saigon, I said we had to get the South Vietnamese to work the way Americans would in some natural disaster, an earthquake or a flood; we had to convince the President and the ministries that they had to operate around the clock.

Yet how to do it? Looking about the room, my eyes fell on George Forsythe. Recalling that in a previous assignment General Forsythe had gotten to know not only President Thieu but others who at that point constituted the government, I formed a task force under Forsythe to work closely with the Vietnamese. Ambassador Bunker volunteered to go with me to President Thieu to sell the plan. Bob Komer was to supervise the undertaking.

Thieu proved to be acutely aware of the problem. He provided General Forsythe an office in Independence Palace—an American first—and a counterpart in the Minister of Pacification and put Vice President Ky in over-all charge. To get the program off to a fast start, I made American engineers available and authorized their drawing extensively on American stocks of roofing, concrete, and other building materials. General Vien followed this up by making ARVN engineers available. Temporary refugee centers were soon rising, ruins being cleared to make way for new housing. American rice distributed free broke black market prices. In a matter of days the refugees could see that even though their existence was still difficult, their government was trying to help. Like the Vietnamese people through the years, the refugees displayed remarkable resilience.

Although the enemy had demonstrated that the government was unable to keep him out of the towns and cities, he had at the same time displayed his innate cruelty, his disregard for civilian lives and property and the sacred institution of Tet. The Tet offensive in the end proved to be the most galvanizing event to happen to the South Vietnamese since the insurgency began. Long reluctant to arm the people for self-defense lest the weapons fall into the hands of the enemy, the South Vietnamese Government at last realized that the people were begging for an opportunity to contribute. Long detached from the shooting war, residents of the towns and cities saw at last the life-and-death struggle in which they were involved. With only minor amendments, the National Assembly enacted the mobilization decree that the government had promulgated the preceding fall but had felt incapable of implementing. It provided at long last for the drafting of eighteen- and nineteen-year-olds.

The enemy had achieved in South Vietnam neither military nor psychological victory. For the South Vietnamese the Tet offensive served as a unifying catalyst, a Pearl Harbor. Had it been the same for the American people, had President Johnson discerned the same support behind him that Thieu did behind him, and had he acted with forcefulness, the enemy could have been induced to engage in serious and meaningful negotiations.

Unfortunately, the enemy scored in the United States the psychological victory that eluded him in Vietnam, so influencing President Johnson and his civilian advisers that they ignored the maxim that when the enemy is hurting, you don't diminish the pressure, you increase it.

During the course of the Tet offensive, I happened to think of a letter my father had written me in 1944 during the Battle of the Bulge, and I subsequently pulled it from my files.

> There is a tendency [he wrote] for some of the commentators to criticize Generals Eisenhower and Hodges for not having better G-2 [intelligence] and leaving that sector so weakly defended. I have an idea that either we or the Germans could concentrate enormous power at any one point and break through when and where desired. But after this strength has been spent, then what? These drives are like a bullet. At the muzzle of the gun it has great power but the time comes when this power is spent and the bullet is harmless.

My father was no military man, yet he had understood.

Chapter XVIII
The Battle for Khe Sanh

No single battlefield event in Vietnam elicited more public disparagement of my conduct of the Vietnam war than did my decision in early 1968 to stand and fight at Khe Sanh. The decision to hold onto that previously obscure little plateau in the rugged northwestern corner of South Vietnam was to my mind militarily sound and strategically rewarding, yet many who viewed it from a distance deemed it misguided and tragic. The decision generated one of the more caustic public attacks I encountered: a letter to the editor of the Washington *Post* on March 22, 1968, from the distinguished Harvard University historian Arthur Schlesinger, Jr.

Professor Schlesinger wrote that once the enemy had surrounded Khe Sanh, "a humane or intelligent leadership would have arranged for the immediate evacuation of the men." We stayed there, he believed, "Not for military reasons, but for political reasons: we stay because President Johnson deliberately committed American honor to holding Khe Sanh (and made the Joint Chiefs of Staff sign on in blood). We stay because Khe Sanh is the bastion, not of the American military position, but of General Westmoreland's military strategy—his 'war of attrition' which has been so tragic and spectacular a failure.

"President Johnson," Dr. Schlesinger concluded, "likes to compare himself with Lincoln—'sad but steady'—but he lacks one prime Lincolnian quality: that is, the courage to fire generals when they have shown they do not know how to win wars. Lincoln ran through a long string of generals before he got to Grant. It is not likely that he would have suffered Westmoreland three months."

President Johnson paid no apparent heed to Professor Schlesinger's advice, and I learned of it only after my return from Vietnam. By that time Khe Sanh had evolved as one of the most damaging, one-sided defeats among many that the North Vietnamese incurred, and the myth of General Giap's military genius was discredited.

Contrary to Professor Schlesinger's belief, to hold Khe Sanh was a military decision, my military decision, made without reference to the White House. In view of the harsh judgments of critics such as Dr. Schlesinger himself, it is understandable that President Johnson should seek assurance from his Joint Chiefs of Staff that Khe Sanh could be held, that the Joint Chiefs in turn should ask me to provide a daily report on the situation at Khe Sanh, and that President Johnson should ask that if I decided to evacuate Khe Sanh, I notify him in advance. To stand at Khe Sanh was nevertheless my decision, with which the President never once sought to interfere.

Professor Schlesinger was just as wrong in deducing that the war of attrition was my choice of a military strategy. A scholar of his eminence should have been aware of the tight civilian control exercised at the top level, of President Johnson's repeated public assurances that he would sanction no widening of the territory over which the war was fought. I would have liked to have known what alternative strategy Dr. Schlesinger proposed under the circumstances, if he had one.

"As a personal matter," General Wheeler added at the end of a cable dealing with Khe Sanh on February 4, "you should know that all of us, including the Commander-in-Chief, repose complete confidence in your judgment, your capacity of careful and prudent planning, and your ability to cope with the enemy in all circumstances. I say this to you because I do not want you to be misled and upset by untrue news media comments."

Khe Sanh will stand in history, I am convinced, as a classic example of how to defeat a numerically superior besieging force by co-ordinated application of firepower.

I first saw Khe Sanh soon after assuming command in mid-1964 on the inspection trip to the northern provinces that ended with the ambush of my plane on the airstrip in the A Shau Valley. The critical importance of the little plateau was immediately apparent, based on some of the same reasons that I frequently stressed in the months to come to General Walt and his successor in command of the III Marine Amphibious Force, General Cushman. Khe Sanh could serve as a patrol base for blocking enemy infiltration from Laos along Route 9; a base for SOG operations to harass the enemy in Laos; an airstrip for reconnaissance planes surveying the Ho Chi Minh Trail; a western anchor for defenses south of the DMZ; and an eventual jump-off point for ground operations to cut the Ho Chi Minh Trail. Relinquish Khe Sanh and you gave up all those advantages, while accepting the inevitability of carrying the fight into the populated coastal strip of Quang Tri province and affording the enemy an avenue of advance along the coast leading south.

As intelligence in late 1967 and early 1968 revealed another North Vietnamese build-up against Khe Sanh, I decided that reinforcing Khe Sanh and holding the more essential high peaks around it was the only feasible alternative to abandoning the base. After deliberate consideration, I ruled out abandoning Khe Sanh. To have done so would have been to co-operate with the enemy's grand design for seizing the two northern provinces and his constant efforts to carry the fight into the populated areas. Both General Walt and subsequently General Cushman agreed. None of us was blind to the possibility that the North Vietnamese might try to make of Khe Sanh another Dien Bien Phu, yet we were aware of marked differences in the two situations and were convinced we could hold Khe Sanh with a relatively small ground force if augmented by tremendous firepower.

Lest I overlook any possible peril, I carefully studied parallels between Dien Bien Phu and Khe Sanh. Being in a deep valley, Dien Bien Phu was more vulnerable than Khe Sanh, a plateau. The French at Dien Bien Phu had held none of the surrounding high ground; the U. S. Marines at Khe Sanh controlled the four key dominating terrain features: Hills 558 and 950, the latter commanding a river valley leading into Khe Sanh from the northwest, and Hills 861 and 881 South. The French had no artillery capable of supporting Dien Bien Phu from the outside; in addition to three 105-mm howitzer batteries, one 155-mm howitzer battery, and one 4.2-inch mortar battery inside Khe Sanh, the marines had support from sixteen powerful U. S. Army 175-mm guns at Camp Carroll, fourteen miles away but well within range.

The French post was remote and inaccessible by road; although destroyed bridges prevented use of Route 9 to Khe Sanh, the road could be opened even in the difficult *crachin* weather if ground contact turned out to be essential and adequate troops were put to the task. The French had limited air power; American air support, including B-52s, was massive. The airstrip at Dien Bien Phu was inadequate, and the French lacked aerial resupply capability other than by small parachutes; upgraded to meet contingencies in the fall of 1967, the airstrip at Khe Sanh could handle C-130 transports, and the aerial delivery company I had earlier stationed at Cam Ranh Bay could resupply the base both by huge cargo parachutes and by specially-packaged items disgorged from the rear of low-flying C-130s.

The French had no helicopters; ours were plentiful, including cargo helicopters. The French had no way of evacuating their troops; American marines could be evacuated either by air or by a relieving ground force. The only real similarity between Dien Bien Phu and Khe Sanh was the enemy's artillery, which was roughly comparable in both cases.

The weather at Khe Sanh was of some concern. The mists, low-lying fogs, and drizzling rains of the *crachin* last from October through April, and Khe Sanh is on the dividing line between the *crachin* and generally clear weather that prevails during the same period over the Ho Chi Minh Trail in Laos. While taking advantage of the weather in Laos, our aircraft would be handicapped at Khe Sanh, but B-52s, artillery, and tactical aircraft bombing by radar could make up for much of the disadvantage. The weather actually provided another argument for holding Khe Sanh—to prevent the enemy from taking advantage of the *crachin* and infiltrating the populated coastal region as he did in going through the A Shau Valley to Hué.

As the enemy build-up at Khe Sanh developed, almost every mail from the United States brought me letters warning that I was inviting another Dien Bien Phu and urging me to abandon Khe Sanh. The only ones taking the opposite tack of encouraging me to hold were French officers who had been involved at Dien Bien Phu.

Although confident of my position, I nevertheless asked my command historian, Colonel Reamer Argo, to study Dien Bien Phu in the hope of discerning tactics or methods that the enemy might employ at Khe Sanh and to survey the outcome of other historic sieges. In briefing me and my staff, Colonel Argo gave a gloomy presentation, pointing out that the besieging force at Dien Bien Phu, as at many another through history, succeeded primarily because the defenders lost all initiative. I knew that Khe Sanh was different, both because the tremendous air and artillery support available afforded us an effective tool for the initiative and because other American troops might be diverted to move either by air or overland to Khe Sanh if initiative became a matter of grave concern.

Argo's presentation nevertheless stunned my staff. Deliberately getting the attention of all, I said it was good that we had heard the worst. "But we are not, repeat not," I said in firm voice, "going to be defeated at Khe Sanh. I will tolerate no talking or even thinking to the contrary." With that I strode deliberately from the room.

There was another possibility at Khe Sanh: tactical nuclear weapons. Early in the fight President Johnson telephoned General Wheeler to ask if there might be a chance he would have to make such a decision, for he had no wish to be faced with it. Although I recognized the controversial nature of the subject and that employing tactical nuclear weapons would be a political decision, I nevertheless considered that I would be imprudent if I failed to acquaint myself with the possibilities in detail. Because the region around Khe Sanh was virtually uninhabited, civilian casualties would be minimal. If Washington officials were so intent on "sending a message" to Hanoi, surely small tactical nuclear weapons would be a way to tell Hanoi something, just as two atomic bombs had spoken convincingly to Japanese officials during World War II and the threat of atomic bombs induced the North Koreans to accept meaningful negotiations during the Korean War. It could be that use of a few small tactical nuclear weapons in Vietnam—or even the threat of them—might have quickly brought the war there to an end. No one could say so with certainty, of course, but surely a detailed consideration of the possibility was warranted. Although I established a small secret group to study the subject, Washington so feared that some word of it might reach the press that I was told to desist. I felt at the time and even more so now that to fail to consider this alternative was a mistake.

Although I gave General Cushman broad authority on tactical disposition of his marines and how many to employ at Khe Sanh, I directed that he commit no more than we were capable of resupplying by air. Cushman deployed three battalions comprising the 26th Marine Regiment and a battalion of the 9th Marines, supported by artillery, five tanks with 90-mm guns, and two platoons of Ontos tracked vehicles with 106-mm recoilless rifles. Also present was a CIDG company with Special Forces advisers. To assure ARVN participation in what I deemed to be an important fight, I insisted that the South Vietnamese contribute an ARVN ranger battalion.

The Khe Sanh defenders thus consisted of a reinforced regiment. In later weeks when I heard critics deploring the fact that the North Vietnamese were tying down sizable American forces that might be better employed elsewhere, I could but listen in wry amusement. There were two enemy divisions around Khe Sanh and part of a third waiting in the wings—15,000 to 20,000 men—facing one reinforced American regiment of about 6,000 men. The one South Vietnamese and four American Marine battalions represented only one sixtieth of the 299 U.S. and Allied combat battalions operating in Vietnam. How could anybody legitimately question who was tying down whom?

I had no illusions that Khe Sanh would be a brief fight lacking in American casualties, yet under the circumstances it was necessary to accept hardship and losses, as is so often the case in war. In one of my messages to General Wheeler, I expressed the hope that the American people would support a long, bitter fight. In general, the people did, despite a degree of theatrical hand-wringing and crape-hanging by press and television that I would hardly have believed possible. Virtually every television cameraman, for example, posed his commentator in the foreground of some awesome scene, such as a burning fuel dump or the wreckage of a C-130 that lay at the side of the runway. That one unfortunate C-130 became the world's most photographed aircraft.

The key to Khe Sanh was firepower. Having directed my Deputy for Air, General Momyer, to plan a two-part SLAM operation co-ordinating all available firepower, I gave it the code name NIAGARA to invoke an image of cascading shells and bombs. The first part was to be a comprehensive intelligence-collection effort using every available means to pinpoint the enemy by patrols, reconnaissance planes, radio intercepts, and electronic sensors. Part two involved carefully co-ordinated round-the-clock shelling and bombing by all available artillery and aircraft—Air Force, Navy, and Marine—and unquestioned priority on B-52 strikes. Throughout the fight I slept on a cot in the Combat Operations Center of my headquarters, a practice I began with the start of the enemy's Tet offensive, so I would be immediately at hand for any decision that had to be made on targets or troop deployments. (Disturbed at my lack of sleep, the Chief of Staff, Dutch Kerwin, asked Kitsy to take a returning medical evacuation plane from the Philippines to Saigon, the only way, he told her, he was going to get me to bed.)

In the course of just over two months—from mid-February to early April

—tactical aircraft flew an average of 300 sorties daily around Khe Sanh, close to one every five minutes, and expended 35,000 tons of bombs and rockets. B-52s flew 2,602 sorties and dropped over 75,000 tons of bombs. Marine howitzers within the combat base and the Army's 175-mm guns at Camp Carroll fired more than 100,000 rounds, or nearly 1,500 rounds per day. It was an awesome display of firepower; given the bomb-delivery capacity of the B-52s, one of the heaviest and most concentrated in the history of warfare.

In the face of that power, seldom could the enemy concentrate to attack *en masse,* and when he did, almost instantaneous reaction by artillery and tactical aircraft inflicted crippling losses. Nor was the enemy immune when he tried to move in close to the defenses. So confident were the marines of the accuracy of their supporting aircraft that they called for tactical air strikes within 400 yards of their positions, and B-52 strikes, which up to that time had always observed a safety margin of over 3,000 yards—more than two miles—hit within just over a thousand yards. As noted later by the commander of the combat base, Colonel David E. Lownds, whose luxuriant mustache made him a distinctive figure on television, "it shook the bunkers real good but to the best of my knowledge no bunker was ever destroyed nor any personnel injured."

The B-52 strikes awed many observers, including the commander of the 3d Marine Division, Major General Rathvon McC. Tompkins, an almost daily visitor to the base, a wiry little officer with an irreverent tongue. You could neither see nor hear the planes, noted Tommy Tompkins. "Then suddenly a long strip of earth just erupts, dirt and debris flying five hundred feet into the air. Then a few seconds later another nearby strip erupts the same way. One day I saw eight or ten North Vietnamese staggering out of the dirt of the first eruption, struggling for their lives, only to be engulfed by the second eruption. It was as if a little part of the world suddenly blew up from no apparent cause."

Among the keys to success of firepower at Khe Sanh were the electronic sensors, both those that could be sown from aircraft and others that could be left behind by close-in patrols. Early in the fight I directed that sensors earmarked for use as an extension of the old McNamara Line in Laos be shifted to the environs of Khe Sanh. The sensors enabled both air and artillery to get a fix on the enemy and prevent his massing for attack against the combat base.

The enemy shelling at Khe Sanh was sometimes intense but probably not so persistent as that at Con Thien the preceding fall. So awed, apparently, were the North Vietnamese by American firepower that they normally fired only four or five rounds at a time, then dived for cover lest some American observer had picked up muzzle blasts or telltale smoke. Over the weeks the marines learned that if they could hear the characteristic cough of a mortar shell leaving the tube, they had exactly twenty-one seconds to scramble for cover. If the firing came from a distance, men in one of the hilltop outposts could hear the shells whish overhead and radio a warning. The shelling over, someone would wave a pair of red underpants—"Maggie's drawers"— long the symbol for a miss on the target range.

I had firsthand experience of enemy fire when I made a flight into Khe Sanh to confer with the Marine commander, Colonel Lownds. While I was there, the North Vietnamese shelled the base, and as I flew out in my command helicopter accompanied by another helicopter known as a "chase ship," enemy small arms fire scored several hits on the chase ship, crippling it but not so much that the pilot could not continue the flight.

By one stratagem at Khe Sanh, Colonel Lownds may well have confused the enemy gunners. Since tall, conspicuous radio antennae marked his communications bunker as a lucrative target, he ordered fake antennae installed on every bunker within the combat base.

The enemy's most serious blow came not at Khe Sanh itself but at the CIDG-Special Forces camp nine miles away astride Route 9 at Lang Vei. Out of the darkness just after midnight on February 6 trundled nine Soviet-built PT-76 tanks accompanied by green-clad North Vietnamese infantry. (This was one of only two instances before the 1972 conventional invasion of South Vietnam that the enemy used tanks; the other was at Ben Het, another outpost near the Laotian border, in Kontum province in 1969, where the two enemy tanks that participated were knocked out.) In the melee that followed, the enemy drove the CIDG troops and their advisers, under Captain Frank C. Willoughby, from the camp.

The director of my Combat Operations Center, General Chaisson, awakened me twice before daylight to tell me of the fight at Lang Vei and the concern of Colonel Jonathan Ladd, successor to Colonel Kelly in command of the 5th Special Forces, about a relief force he had called for. Under established plans, the marines at Khe Sanh were to send a relief force if Lang Vei got into trouble, but twice the marines had turned down Lang Vei's call for help. They reasonably considered that a relief force moving by road was bound to be ambushed and that a helicopter assault in the darkness against a force known to have armor was too hazardous. Honoring the prerogative of the field commander on the scene, I declined to intervene until I could ascertain more on the situation.

Soon after daylight the next day, February 7, I called a conference of Marine Corps and Army commanders operating in the I Corps Zone and flew to Danang. There were a number of topics to be discussed at Danang, but of first priority was the crisis at Lang Vei. I directed General Cushman to provide helicopters for a relief force of CIDG troops with Special Forces advisers to bring out American and South Vietnamese survivors. Of twenty-four Americans at Lang Vei, fourteen got out; all but three of those were wounded. The other ten had been killed.

Nearly 6,000 military and civilian stragglers from the Lang Vei camp and an adjacent village, including a host of Laotian Ca tribesmen who had fled an earlier fight across the border, straggled down the road to seek refuge inside the defensive perimeter at Khe Sanh. Wary of enemy agents and unable to care for such a host inside the perimeter, Colonel Lownds kept them outside until Special Forces troops could arrive to screen and evacuate them to a camp set up outside Cam Lo, a prudent decision that the press chose to depict as an act of inhumanity. Evacuation was a slow process, much to the concern of Ambassador Sullivan in Laos, who sent cable after cable demanding that I fly the Laotians immediately to their capital Vientiane. To evacuate thousands, including women and children, by air in the face of enemy fire was no easy process. Even when all got away from Khe Sanh they had to be held for a time outside Cam Lo until aircraft could be spared for taking them to Laos.

The meeting with commanders at Danang, at which I ordered a relief force for Lang Vei, confirmed concerns that for some time had been troubling me. Quite apart from the assault on Khe Sanh and the presence there of two North Vietnamese divisions, the enemy threat in the north was real and disturbing: another North Vietnamese division was in the DMZ north of the Rock Pile, close enough to reinforce the enemy at Khe Sanh; another was just outside the gates of the vital Danang airfield; the equivalent of a reinforced division was at Hué; and two more were within the DMZ or just south of it near the coast—all together seven enemy divisions.

I had reinforced the marines in the I Corps Zone with the entire Americal Division and two brigades of the 1st Cavalry Division, and had shifted the Korean Marine Brigade northward to free marines at Danang. I also decided to reinforce further with a brigade of the 101st Airborne Division and directed development of a contingency plan for moving the entire division later. Yet General Cushman and his staff appeared complacent, seemingly reluctant to use the Army forces I had put at their disposal.

For almost two hours, I listened to reports of the various commanders, becoming more and more shocked at things that virtually begged to be done yet remained undone. Local decisions were urgently needed. I ended up giving direct orders myself to General Cushman's subordinate units, an unusual and normally undesirable procedure. The threat to the Danang airfield was of special concern. Why not use a brigade of Major General Samuel Koster's Americal Division at Danang? In exasperation I told Koster and the commander of the 1st Marine Division, Major General Donn G. Robertson, to leave the room and return only when they had worked out a viable plan for closely co-ordinated offensive action against the enemy threatening the airfield. They returned in half an hour with an excellent plan, all differences resolved.

Also disturbing was failure of the marines to provide tactical air support for the 1st Cavalry Division. Because the marines had their own tactical aircraft and air support system, a system of which they were justifiably proud, they furnished most of the close air support from Danang northward.

When moving the cavalry division into the northern provinces, I had admonished the commander of the 1st Marine Air Wing, Major General Norman J. Anderson, in General Cushman's presence, to make certain that the needs of Army divisions for tactical air support were satisfied. Visiting the cavalry division, I found that neither Anderson nor anybody from his Marine command had established contact with the Army division or arranged for direct communications for expeditious air support.

Having already become concerned about efficient management of tactical air resources in the northern provinces and having directed General Momyer to study the matter, I was convinced by this failure that I had to move immediately. To have several tactical air systems functioning in the same confined region—Marine Corps, Air Force, Vietnamese Air Force, and, on occasion, U. S. Navy—was simply too ponderous, too extravagant with resources, the situation too conducive to error. As I noted to General Wheeler, it was a "dog's breakfast."

Somebody had to be in charge, to allocate available tactical air resources other than helicopters where most needed and to co-ordinate their employment. Such a system had been worked out for the SLAM operation in support of Con Thien in 1967 and again for Operation NIAGARA around Khe Sanh, yet it was wasteful to have to set up a new system each time, and the SLAM arrangements had no effect on tactical air other than in the immediate vicinity of the defended base.

As I noted later in a cable to General Wheeler, it "became a matter of utilizing most efficiently available resources." While I recognized that Marine air doctrine was based on massive support of an amphibious beachhead, the situation in the northern provinces had long since changed from a beachhead to sustained operations over a large sector. Just as I had found it necessary to reinforce the marines with Army artillery, "it became necessary for the Marine air to lend a hand from time to time with air sorties to support Army units as a part of our over-all effort." In the same way that the marines controlled Army artillery units, so there had to be a single headquarters in charge of all tactical air in the north "to provide the required flexibility." It "made nothing but tactical and management sense" that the single manager should be my Deputy for Air, General Momyer. Yet when I directed General Momyer to set up such a system, the chorus of objections the decision precipitated was vociferous.

For all the pride of the Marines in their close air support system, I trusted that General Cushman and his air officer, General Anderson, would see the necessity of my move. Although a marine, my close staff associate, General Chaisson, had no trouble discerning it. Perhaps General Cushman would have accepted the decision graciously had it not been for the close supervision that Marine Corps headquarters in Washington exercised over anything involving the III Marine Amphibious Force. In this as in other matters, General Cushman's reaction came couched in the Marine Commandant's doctrinal terms.

In the Joint Chiefs of Staff the Marine Corps Commandant made a doctrinal issue of it. One meeting on the subject followed another. To my disappointment, the Army Chief of Staff, General Johnson, concerned lest a precedent be established that might lead to the Army's losing its helicopters to the Air Force, failed to support my position. Marine Corps pressure on Admiral Sharp at CINCPAC was heavy. It was one of my most exasperating exercises.

I had no intention of destroying the excellent air-ground co-ordination that the marines had developed. In general, the marines would continue to get most of their support from their own planes and would control their own helicopters, as did U. S. Army units. Yet with an entire Marine Air Wing in support of each Marine division, Marine ground troops got more support than the Air Force could provide Army units, and Marine aircraft often were capable of doing more. When not otherwise occupied, they could support Army units. Air Force planes on occasion provided the marines additional support, and it was not unusual for Army units to lend the marines helicopters.

As the Joint Chiefs in Washington continued to cavil over my decision, I sent one of General Momyer's assistants, Major General Gordon F. Blood, to CINCPAC in Hawaii to make sure Admiral Sharp understood the arrangement in detail. My efforts, I told Admiral Sharp, were designed "to bring to bear the maximum fire power on the enemy. This is not an Air Force maneuver designed to change roles and missions. The exercise is on my initiative as a Joint commander."

To my mind I owed it to the men I commanded and to the responsibilities I bore to use all resources available to me in the most effective way possible. Furthermore, it was my prerogative as field commander to employ my resources as I saw fit. If the Joint Chiefs intended to reverse my decision, I cabled General Wheeler, I wanted an opportunity to appear personally before them to explain "the practical problems faced by the responsible commander on the ground."

That was the issue—the one issue—that arose during my service in Vietnam to prompt me to consider resigning. I was unable to accept that parochial considerations might take precedence over my command responsibilities and prudent use of assigned resources.

Having Admiral Sharp's endorsement and lacking any directions from the Joint Chiefs to the contrary, I told General Momyer to work to perfect the system I had proposed. An improved over-all tactical air support system followed. The Air Force learned things from the marines that facilitated air support of U. S. Army units throughout Vietnam, and I suspect the marines may also have learned from the Air Force. The Joint Chiefs never acted to alter the arrangement. When I talked with President Johnson during a visit to Washington in April 1968, I found he had been misinformed about the proposal. Once I had given him the reasons for my action, he never mentioned the subject to me again.

Although I was planning to put a U. S. Army Corps headquarters in the northern provinces to control Army units as a subordinate command of the III Marine Amphibious Force—a possibility I had considered when I originally instituted the system of field force headquarters rather than corps—it would take time to organize a new headquarters. Yet with the rapid buildup of U. S. Army forces in the north, the need became acute. At the suggestion of my chief of staff, Dutch Kerwin, I decided as an interim measure to establish a branch of my own headquarters there.

Known as MACV FORWARD, the headquarters opened at Phu Bai, south of Hué on Route 1, in early February. Since many quick decisions would have to be made in my name, I asked General Abrams to take charge. MACV FORWARD, in close co-ordination with the III Marine Amphibious Force, temporarily controlled all American ground forces—Army, Marine Corps, and shore-based contingents of the U. S. Navy—in the two provinces north of the Hai Van Pass.

From the first, Generals Abrams and Cushman worked together harmoniously. It was in this context, for example, that General Abrams did such an excellent job of co-ordinating diverse forces in the retaking of Hué, which had been seized by the enemy during the Tet offensive. Yet they had to work in the face of any number of speculative press reports to the effect that the Marine Corps resented Army presence, that creating an Army headquarters demonstrated a lack of confidence in the marines, and that I was downgrading the III Marine Amphibious Force. General Cushman, some reporters had it, objected to my decision to stand at Khe Sanh but felt unable to face up to me on it. That and the other accusations were patently false, a marked disservice to everybody involved.

After a particularly blatantly speculative account by Bill Tuohy of the Los Angeles *Times,* I felt impelled to go to the northern provinces to hold a press conference explaining the true nature of the arrangement. Contrary to the false speculation, I noted, the reorganized headquarters was a first step in eventually upgrading the III Marine Amphibious Force to the level of a field army headquarters with a subordinate Army corps.

A month later, according to plan, the Army corps headquarters was placed under the operational control of the III Marine Amphibious Force and MACV FORWARD was phased out. Known at first as Provisional Corps, Vietnam, and later designed by the Department of the Army as the XXIV Corps, the headquarters and its troops were thenceforth under General Cushman, who also commanded what was in effect a corps of marines, so that the over-all command constituted a field army.

While General Abrams was still functioning as my alter ego at MACV FORWARD, I asked him to begin planning for the relief of Khe Sanh. Not relief in the sense of rescue, for the marines at Khe Sanh, backed by more than adequate air and artillery, never needed rescue, but relief in the sense of reopening ground contact and eliminating the enemy with mobile operations.

The more arduous fighting at Khe Sanh occurred on the hilltop outposts. The North Vietnamese obviously wanted the hilltops before assaulting the combat base itself, but in the face of marines displaying their traditional valor, they never came close. Somehow, despite long days of pea-soup weather and despite accurate enemy fire, helicopters kept the men supplied with such essentials as ammunition, food, and, especially, water. Particularly effective were big "hook" helicopters that dangled their cargo in big nets beneath their bellies. The traditional determination of the American soldier or marine in a support role to assure that his comrades in close contact with the enemy never lack for the tools of war and survival was never more heroically demonstrated.

The marines on Hill 881 South took an impish delight in taunting the enemy by raising the American flag on a makeshift flagpole every morning to the sound of a bugle. They blew the bugle, Captain Jack A. Brage told me later, so the North Vietnamese "would observe the colors being raised and know that the ragged, dirty, and tired marines were still full of fight and were there to stay." That the North Vietnamese responded with artillery and mortars failed to stop the practice. When the press reported that shell fragments were destroying the marines' flag, almost every mail for a time brought a new flag until eventually there were fifty-two on hand. That was typical of the heart-warming support that countless Americans provided, a welcome antidote to the skepticism of the press and the news of dissenters and demonstrators and people who paraded with candles around the White House.

Aware that the North Vietnamese had dug extensive tunnels to get at the French at Dien Bien Phu, I watched constantly for evidence that they might be repeating the tactic at Khe Sanh. My scientific adviser, Dr. McMillan, studied the matter and sent teams trained in seismographic techniques to Khe Sanh; but the enemy never did more than dig trenches leading toward the combat base. Since those were visible, they posed little threat.

No doubt because of the heavy American firepower, the North Vietnamese succeeded in launching only one major attack against the combat base and that in far less strength than intended. Patrols and electronic sensors picked up the enemy's assembly well in advance, then our planes and artillery went to work. Tribesmen in the region later reported coming upon bodies stacked along the trails near Khe Sanh in numbers from 200 to 500. The better part of a regiment was apparently destroyed, leaving less than a battalion to make the intended assault. During the night of February 29, the enemy launched three attacks against that portion of the perimeter held by the ARVN rangers—which may have said something about his respect for the American marines—but nobody got inside even the outer barbed wire.

Surprisingly, the enemy failed to try the one thing he could have done that would have posed a real problem for the marines at Khe Sanh. He presumably could have poisoned the little stream outside the combat base from which the marines drew their water, but he never disturbed it.

By mid-March it was apparent that the enemy was giving up at Khe Sanh, his attempted repeat of Dien Bien Phu an abject failure. The North Vietnamese began to pull back into Laos.

The withdrawal coincided with my own plans for re-establishing ground contact with the base. Although the marines were in no real peril, I was anxious to re-establish contact if for no other reason than to silence dolorous critics and allay President Johnson's concern. Yet a study of weather in the region over the preceding ten years revealed that not until about the first of April could I count on good weather for airmobile operations. Logistic preparations also had to be completed without slighting other on-going operations.

When on April 1 the 1st Cavalry Division under Jack Tolson launched Operation PEGASUS to re-establish ground contact, resistance was minimal. At the same time U.S. marines drove westward along Route 9, clearing and repairing the road as they went. So creditable was the work of the 11th Marine Engineer Battalion that I forwarded my personal commendation. As they neared Khe Sanh, men of the 26th Marines drove out of their base to establish contact with the 11th Engineers on April 6. Called to Washington at that time, I had the pleasure of announcing the link-up at a press conference on the White House lawn.

Spreading out from Khe Sanh in all directions, U.S. cavalrymen, ARVN troops, and U.S. marines learned something of the destruction American air and artillery had wreaked on the enemy. My staff estimated that the North Vietnamese lost 10,000 to 15,000 men in their vain attempt to restage Dien Bien Phu. The Americans lost 205.

I ordered the 1st Cavalry Division to turn south almost without pause from Khe Sanh and join the 101st Airborne Division and an ARVN regiment for operation DELAWARE, a drive into the A Shau Valley, so long an unchallenged enemy domain. Sufficient troops were at last available to deny the enemy undisputed use of the valley as a route to Hué.

Reinforcements in the I Corps Zone by that time totaled approximately 50,000 men, enough for the mobile operations around Khe Sanh that earlier had been impractical. Logistical facilities in the north also were finally sufficient to support extensive airmobile operations. To facilitate Operation PEGASUS, the 1st Cavalry Division had built another base—later named VANDEGRIFT—that could serve as a jump-off point for operations around Khe Sanh, but unlike Khe Sanh, that base was beyond the range of North Vietnamese artillery positioned inside Laos. SOG patrols and reconnaissance aircraft also could use the new base, and the massive bombing in the environs of Khe Sanh had opened up the forested terrain enough to facilitate airmobile operations. When General Cushman and General Rosson, the latter commanding the Provisional Corps, Vietnam, recommended evacuating Khe Sanh, I agreed in principle. Because of a decision recently reached by President Johnson, the sole remaining reason for holding it, as a base for a drive into Laos, appeared no longer valid.

I nevertheless disagreed with their recommended timing. Since operations were still to be conducted around Khe Sanh, why not hold onto the base long enough to use up the stocks of supplies that had been so laboriously transported there? Furthermore, I had learned by that time that I was leaving Vietnam. I decided to reserve the decision on Khe Sanh to my successor.

My successor, General Abrams, subsequently decided to evacuate Khe Sanh. The base no longer served to lure North Vietnamese soldiers to their deaths, and newly established Base VANDEGRIFT provided a launch platform for helicopter-borne operations around Khe Sanh and the necessary logistical support for them.

A postscript remained. When the North Vietnamese launched their conventional invasion in 1972, the South Vietnamese had nobody at Khe Sanh. The valleys leading down from the plateau into the populated coastal region to the east thus provided convenient avenues for the invaders. Holding Khe Sanh might not have saved Quang Tri province in 1972—there were many reasons why the bulk of the province fell—but it would have made the conquest considerably more difficult. Since the North Vietnamese still controlled almost all of Quang Tri province in 1975, Khe Sanh itself was not a factor in their final triumph.

As I reflect on the Tet offensive and Khe Sanh, two things come to mind: First, a statement I made on so many occasions that it became a kind of theme song, the necessity for endurance on the battlefield and patience at home. Second, the statement I made at the Guam conference in 1967 on the necessity to find some way to halt the enemy's infiltration through Laos or else the war could go on indefinitely.

The last two major operations in the northern provinces before I departed South Vietnam—Operation PEGASUS around Khe Sanh and Operation DELAWARE in the A Shau Valley—were primary examples of the most innovative tactical development to emerge from the Vietnam war: the airmobile concept. Although the airmobile concept can be said to have had its roots in the airborne techniques of World War II and the Army's first helicopter companies in the early 1950s, it can also be said to have been a direct outgrowth of a study board created in the spring of 1962 in response to a directive from Secretary McNamara for the Army to look into the possibilities of increased mobility in land warfare. It became known as the Howze Board after its president, Lieutenant General Hamilton H. Howze, a distinguished World War II commander. The findings of the Howze Board led in turn to creation of the Army's first airmobile division, known in the test phase as the 11th Air Assault Division and subsequently as the 1st Cavalry Division (Airmobile). It was my pleasure in 1967 to welcome General Howze to South Vietnam to see at first hand what had come about as a result of the study which he had conducted with such vision.

Beginning with the first helicopter support of ARVN units in the early 1960s, all airmobile operations in South Vietnam that went before Operations PEGASUS and DELAWARE were but prelude, for in those two operations American forces achieved a degree of co-ordination and sophistication in the flexibility and mobility of airmobile warfare never before known. PEGASUS involved close co-ordination of the airmobile troops with the fortifications of Khe Sanh and the massive firepower that had been mustered in support of that base. DELAWARE, by contrast, involved close co-ordination by American airmobile troops with an ARVN regiment in penetrating incredibly difficult terrain to prepare an airhead with tools and equipment brought in by air, then in linking up with other American troops advancing overland.

Flying into the remote A Shau Valley during Operation DELAWARE by helicopter with the 1st Cavalry Division's commander, Jack Tolson (whose pilot aide was Bill Mauldin's son who had survived the shelling of the Pleiku helicopter camp back in 1965), I was tremendously impressed with the professional competence of the airmobile troops. That same spring of 1968, with the backing of the U. S. Army Chief of Staff, General Johnson, I began converting the 101st Airborne Division to become the Army's second airmobile force.

Other tests and refinements of the airmobile concept no doubt lie ahead— surely much attention must be paid the possible effects on the concept of an enemy armed with sophisticated antiaircraft weapons—yet the operations in South Vietnam as exemplified by PEGASUS and DELAWARE will surely provide a firm base for further development.

Chapter XIX
An Alternate Strategy

During the last days of January and the first of February 1968 President Johnson telephoned General Wheeler several times, evincing his concern about Khe Sanh, seeking reassurance. In the course of one of those conversations on February 3, he asked General Wheeler to query me "if there is any reinforcement or help that we can give you."

Since the President asked the question in the context of Khe Sanh, I assumed he meant reinforcements for Khe Sanh. In my reply, I asked for another C-130 squadron, additional helicopters, additional air-drop equipment, a Navy Seabee battalion to help reconstruct Route 9, and—a perennial request—additional modern weapons for the ARVN.

Two days later General Wheeler noted indications that Washington might be inclined to send reinforcements in excess of the troop ceiling of 525,000, set in mid-1967. The alacrity, for example, with which Secretary McNamara had responded to my request for items related to Khe Sanh. That was encouraging, for despite my confidence that American and South Vietnamese forces would defeat the Tet offensive and would prevail at Khe Sanh, I was still concerned at that stage about what else the enemy might be planning for the northern provinces, and I wanted forces in quantities capable of counterattacking with maximum intensity at the appropriate time.

Only a few days after the Tet offensive began, in response to queries from Walt Rostow in the White House, I ventured that the enemy was engaged in an offensive in three phases. The first had begun in the fall of 1967, designed to seize remote regions along the border that might be expanded later. The second was the Tet offensive, the move into the towns and cities in an effort to destroy government control and incite a general uprising. The third was still to come, strong attacks against Khe Sanh and across the DMZ to try to seize the two northern provinces.

Washington, I soon discovered, was considerably more concerned than I was about what the third phase might bring. "There is a theory," General

Wheeler cabled, "which could be logical, that over-all enemy strategy is to attack and wear down the ARVN, thereby destroying them and ultimately gaining acceptance by the people of a coalition government which would request the withdrawal of U.S. forces from South Vietnam. In other words, the massive Khe Sanh build-up is an alternative threat to enforce a siphoning off of troops from the south, thereby reducing security of the population and affording opportunities to destroy ARVN units. Also, such a strategy could afford an opportunity to attack in force along the DMZ if you do not respond by a build-up of your forces in northern I Corps."

Shocked by the enemy's Tet offensive and perturbed about Khe Sanh and the dolorous reporting by the press, President Johnson suggested that I hold daily press conferences. That, I felt, would display undue concern, but I did schedule a conference on February 3 to try to put matters in perspective. Much as General Wheeler had suggested, a reporter asked if the enemy build-up against Khe Sanh was not a diversion for an attack against Saigon. Each, I responded, was a diversion for the other. The enemy's plan was a concerted, country-wide effort, and it made no sense to respond unduly to one threat while ignoring another. Yet each had to be met.

"Do you need reinforcements?" General Wheeler's cable continued. "Our capabilities are limited. We can provide the 82d Airborne Division and about one half of a Marine Corps division . . ." The United States Government, he went on, "is not prepared to accept defeat in South Vietnam. In summary, if you need more troops, ask for them."

While I feared no defeat at Khe Sanh or in South Vietnam as a whole, it was conceivable that the enemy could drive us back in the northern provinces, and it would be wise to prepare for the worst. With additional reinforcements, I could strengthen the north without risking further weakening of forces in the south, around Saigon, in particular. To General Wheeler I suggested that he send what he said was available: the airborne division and half a marine division. "It is conceivable," I noted, "that a six-month loan of these units would turn the tide to the point where the enemy might see the light or be so weakened that we could return them. . . ." Should the worst happen, should the enemy push us back in the north, the marines could make an amphibious landing near Quang Tri City and pass the 82d Airborne Division through the beachhead to cut into the enemy's rear, thereby preparing the way for retaking the northern provinces. Surf conditions in the north, I noted, would make such a maneuver possible beginning in April.

General Wheeler responded that the reinforcements might be sent before April, making them available "to assist in defense or pursuit operations." He was making no effort to sell me on reinforcements, he said. "However, my sensing is that the critical phase of the war is upon us, and I do not believe that you should refrain from asking for what you believe is required under the circumstances."

Those were encouraging words that confirmed my own convictions, yet in the past every troop request had undergone such detailed scrutiny and had evoked such alarm in the press that I may have become less than aggressive in my demands. With General Wheeler's encouragement, I made, on February 12, a formal request for reinforcements:

> If the enemy has changed his strategy, we must change ours. On the assumption that it is our national policy to prohibit the enemy from seizing and permanently occupying the two northern provinces, I intend to hold them at all cost. However, to do so I must reinforce from other areas and accept a major risk, unless I can get reinforcements, which I desperately need.
>
> I need reinforcements in terms of combat elements. I therefore urge that there be deployed immediately a marine regiment package and brigade package of the 82d Airborne Division and that the remaining elements of those two divisions be prepared to follow at a later time. Time is of the essence.
>
> I must stress equally that we face a situation of great opportunity as well as heightened risk. However, time is of the essence here too. I do not see how the enemy can long sustain the heavy losses which his new strategy is enabling us to inflict on him. Therefore, adequate reinforcements should permit me not only to contain his I Corps offensive but also to capitalize on his losses by seizing the initiative in other areas. *Exploiting this opportunity** could materially shorten the war.

General Wheeler promptly presented my proposal to the White House. Because of the time differential between Saigon and Washington, he did it on the same date as my message, February 12. The conferees, including the President and Secretaries McNamara and Rusk, deduced, General Wheeler informed me, that "You could use additional U.S. troop units, but you are not expressing a firm demand for them; in sum, you do not fear defeat if you are not reinforced." To which I responded that I was making a firm request, "not because I fear defeat . . . but because I do not feel that I can fully grasp the initiative from the recently reinforced enemy without them."

The Marine regiment and the airborne brigade, General Wheeler cabled back, would be deployed to Vietnam before the end of February. Those units arrived on time, but I never asked for deployment of the remainder of the two divisions.

A military commander must anticipate not only problems and likely moves by the enemy but also opportunities. He must be ready to exploit an enemy defeat, to reinforce success. In the case of Vietnam, I had also long considered it prudent to be prepared to exploit any change in American national policy in regard to conduct of the war.

In launching the Tet offensive, the enemy had markedly altered his strategy from a long, protracted war, to which up to that point my own plans and moves had been addressed, to a short-term, go-for-broke war. In the process

* Emphasis added.

he had incurred a severe, even traumatic setback. In view of his change and his defeat, was it not proper that our side, too, as I had cabled General Wheeler, consider a change in strategy, take advantage of the enemy's having come into the open, and strike boldly, breaking away from the long war of attrition that political restraints had for so long imposed?

There were indications that Washington also contemplated a change. "The critical phase of the war is upon us," General Wheeler had noted. The White House meeting on February 12 when General Wheeler had presented my request for reinforcements had also touched on the possibility of a change. Admiral Sharp at CINCPAC thought we ought to pressure Washington to lift the 525,000 troop ceiling.

There were also world-wide developments to consider. In Laos the North Vietnamese had captured a mountaintop radar station that was manned by American civilians trained by the U. S. Air Force and that was secured by CIA-supported Laotian irregulars; the loss sharply inhibited American air activity over Laos. In Korea, North Korean raiders had crossed into South Korea and tried to assault the Blue House, the presidential residence in the capital of Seoul; the North Koreans had also captured the American intelligence ship *Pueblo* and incarcerated its crew. Would the South Koreans have to pull their troops out of Vietnam to fight a new war at home? What of revived rumblings in East Berlin? Would the Middle East explode? General Wheeler and the others of the Joint Chiefs, I knew, were worried, conscious that the strategic reserve left in the entire United States for meeting any other crisis was less than three divisions. Nobody had pursued my request made in 1966 to create and maintain a three-division corps reserve earmarked exclusively for Vietnam.

In keeping with the necessity to plan ahead, and thinking of a change of strategy, I had directed my staff early in February to begin studying troop requirements for the coming year. In a cable on February 8, I told General Wheeler that the first priority was the modernization of the ARVN, but I added that I might require another American and another Korean division before the end of 1968.

General Wheeler told me to hold off on long-range requirements. As he had explained a number of times in regard to dealing with the Secretary of Defense and the White House, "we can handle only one problem at a time." A few days later I learned why he wanted to delay.

General Wheeler was coming to Saigon, to arrive on February 23. He came at President Johnson's behest for a first-hand evaluation, to achieve, he said, a "basis for coming up with a broad estimate of what we can expect in the future. By this I mean what strategies will be open to the enemy, what forces will he have available, what opportunities have been opened to us, what problems must we be prepared to face." The President, General Wheeler said, had to face up to "some hard decisions," what reinforcements to send to Vietnam, how to bolster the strategic reserve in the United States. He would await General Wheeler's return before making the decisions.

When General Wheeler arrived, I found him a tired man, seemingly near the point of exhaustion. He and his traveling companion, my old friend, Bill DePuy, at the time a special assistant to the Joint Chiefs for counterinsurgency, mirrored the gloom that pervaded official circles in Washington, a reflection of the doomsday reporting by press and television. The newspapers, General Wheeler recalled later, had given him the impression that the Tet offensive was "the worst calamity since Bull Run."

In the few weeks since the start of the offensive, much had taken place for the better in Vietnam: the enemy's heavy losses; markedly improved morale and confidence in the ARVN; firm moves by the government to bolster the ARVN, care for refugees, and drafting of eighteen- and nineteen-year-olds. But it was hard to get that viewpoint across to my visitors in three brief days. They tended to see matters through the veil of black crape that the press had drawn across their eyes. A rocket attack on Saigon during General Wheeler's first night, one round landing near his quarters, did nothing to help. On the theory that the enemy might be aware of where he was staying, he understandably asked to move in with me at the Combat Operations Center.

As Bus Wheeler and I conferred, we did so in the expectation that there was to be a reappraisal of American policy on conducting the war, presumably a new and broadened strategy. A change in strategy almost inevitably would involve a sizable call-up of National Guard and Reserves. In view of Secretary McNamara's coming replacement by a presumably hawkish Clark Clifford, that seemed a plausible possibility. The chairman of the House Armed Services Committee, Congressman Mendel Rivers, had publicly advocated a call-up.

Although I had earlier opposed calling the Reserves in the belief that the war would last long beyond the usual one-year tour for reservists and that extended service would produce cries to bring the troops home, the situation had changed. I was in much the same position as any battlefield commander at whatever level who must choose the optimum time to influence the battle by committing his reserve force; the enemy's losses in the Tet offensive had at last presented the right opportunity. I was convinced that with additional strength and removal of the old restrictive policy, we could deal telling blows—physically and psychologically—well within the time frame of the reservists' one-year tour. The time had come to prepare and commit the Reserve.

General Wheeler and I looked at the future in terms of a broad spectrum, from the worst that might happen to the brightest. The worst would involve collapse of the South Vietnamese Government, major additions to North Vietnamese strength in the South, and withdrawal of the South Koreans. The brightest would be continued stability in Saigon and improved performance by the ARVN, which would enable me with increased American forces and a new national policy to move boldly.

Some of the options we had in mind were:

—Finish the job of providing territorial security throughout South Vietnam and eliminating the enemy's base areas.

—Accelerate the bombing of North Vietnam and neutralize or destroy more remunerative targets, such as the port of Haiphong.

—Conduct ground operations to sever the Ho Chi Minh Trail.

—Raid the enemy's border sanctuaries in Laos and Cambodia.

—Launch amphibious and airmobile operations against North Vietnamese bases immediately north of the DMZ.

If I could execute those moves fairly rapidly following the heavy losses the enemy had incurred in the Tet offensive, I saw the possibility of destroying the enemy's will to continue the war. Indeed, a responsible member of the International Control Commission—the organization that had been created to police the Geneva Accords and was still around—had just returned from Hanoi and told me that the mood of the North Vietnamese leaders was one of dejection. The enemy, I theorized, had changed his strategy, gone all out, and his new strategy, like the old, had failed while generating—if we so acted—a new American strategy—a bold, damaging reaction. If there was anything to the business of "sending a message" to Hanoi, surely that was a way. Added to it would be the psychological impact of a Reserve call-up, a visible manifestation of American resolve to prosecute the war to a satisfactory conclusion, a profound discrediting of the enemy's hopes that the antiwar outcries presaged collapse of American will, a demonstration to the American people that their government intended to get the job done with dispatch. Even if the enemy still refused to buckle, the new moves would so weaken his forces in the South that I could accelerate my program to bolster the ARVN and withdraw American troops, leaving the war to the South Vietnamese.

To provide the capability of meeting contingencies or launching new moves, I and my staff deduced, there should be available for deployment, as needed, approximately the same numbers that I had proposed in my maximum or optimum force at the White House in 1967, that is, approximately 200,000 men. Quite obviously, not all could or should arrive at once: logistical preparations had to be made in Vietnam; a number of the new units would have to be mobilized from the National Guard and the Reserves, which involved a lead time of some six to nine months; and, as always, the monsoon seasons would dictate when the troops could be employed on the missions I intended. It was possible that not all the forces mobilized and readied for deployment would be needed.

I foresaw a first increment ready for deployment in May 1968, including a brigade of the 5th Mechanized Division, whose mobility with tanks and other vehicles could make a major contribution along the DMZ; an armored cavalry regiment; eight tactical fighter squadrons; and six battalions of the 5th Marine Division. A second, visualized as ready to ship by September, would include four tactical fighter squadrons and the rest of the 5th Mechanized Division. A third, programmed to be available at the end of the year but deployed when and if needed, would include three tactical fighter squadrons and an infantry division.

My intention was not to make a specific request for troop deployment. It was instead a field commander's input to consideration of mobilizing resources to meet any contingency or to pursue an alternate strategy. At the heart of it was the Joint Chiefs' concern to rebuild the strategic reserve in the United States. Basic to our understanding was that only the first increment—approximately half the total, or 108,000 men—would be earmarked for Vietnam and deployed upon specific request. The other two would reconstitute the strategic reserve and would be sent to Vietnam only if the North Vietnamese scored such successes that we found ourselves in trouble or if the President changed the strategy and approved a more aggressive policy for conducting the war.

It was a matter, as staff officers would put it, of getting troops in the rack, a request for readiness, for establishing a capability. You cannot deploy troops, however direly needed, that exist only on paper. Availability was the first thing; what would be done with them depended on what President Johnson or his elected successor decided in reappraising national policy. General Wheeler and I saw only a fifty-fifty chance that President Johnson would accept a more aggressive policy, but that seemed sufficient odds, in view of the rewards that might be realized, to justify an effort to promote a change.

The Chairman of the Joint Chiefs has a difficult job living with his civilian bosses, the Secretary of Defense and the President, striving to convince them in terms they can understand of matters that he views as military necessity and, in General Wheeler's case, within the concept of one thing at a time. One thing at a time was all he could hope to accomplish. Since Vietnam was the visible part of the iceberg, the part he knew was perturbing his civilian bosses, Vietnam rather than the strategic reserve was the context in which to present the request for additional troops. If he could gain authority to raise the troops, exactly what was to be done with them could be decided once the troops were actually available.

That decision and General Wheeler's view of conditions in Vietnam sharply influenced the report he forwarded from Honolulu en route back from Saigon to the Secretary of Defense and the White House, which I did not see at the time. Making no mention that I was considering more troops in hope of exploiting the enemy's defeat, nor making any allusion to the need to rebuild the strategic reserve, General Wheeler, probably as a tactic, emphasized uncertainty, that the enemy had "the will and the capability to continue" a high level of attacks. The enemy was recruiting extensively, he wrote, and bringing in more North Vietnamese troops. ARVN was in "a defensive posture around towns and cities" that soon might give the enemy the countryside by default. Tet, he said, had been "a very near thing." Westmoreland needed reinforcements, he implied, as an emergency measure.

I can hardly fault General Wheeler's approach. Imbued with the aura of crisis in Washington, he at least partially discounted the sanguine briefings I and my staff had given him. In any event, he saw no possibility at the moment of selling reinforcements in terms of future operations. Who among the civilians would appreciate a policy of exploiting the enemy's defeat, of reinforcing success? Having read their newspapers, who among them would even believe there had been success? Better to exploit their belief in crisis to get the troops, then argue new strategy later. One thing at a time.

The request may have been doomed from the first in any event, for it ran head on into another proposed new strategy. That was de-escalation, to include a bombing halt, that Secretary McNamara had begun to promote the preceding November. The cut-and-run people had apparently gotten to McNamara. Although the proposal put the departing Secretary in President Johnson's disfavor, he had nevertheless implanted an idea in the minds of a number of his civilian colleagues that was to prove persistent. It was easy, also, for many among the President's advisers to discern the incongruity between my public statements on the enemy's military defeat and General Wheeler's portrait of continuing crisis.

I obtained some idea of the machinery of the deliberations in Washington when General Wheeler, at the request of Clark Clifford, who was chairing a task force to make recommendations to the President on reinforcements, posed to me a series of questions: What military and other objectives are additional forces designed to advance? What specific dangers is their dispatch designed to avoid? What specific goals would they aim to achieve? Could the ARVN be further expanded?

The answers to all those questions, I believed, had been thoroughly presented when General Wheeler was in Saigon. Unaware of the crisis context in which the Chairman of the Joint Chiefs had presented the case for reinforcements, unwilling to accept that a crisis existed, and having had no word of any change in national policy, I was in no position to answer the questions in terms of the options that I hoped a change in policy and the reinforcements would enable me to exercise. Thus I was unable to make a strong presentation on behalf of the reinforcements. Like Ambassador Bunker and Admiral Sharp, I did press for relaxation of the restrictions on ground operations in Laos and Cambodia and for intensified bombing of the North. Oley Sharp put it well: "We are at a crossroads; either the U.S. uses its military power at full effectiveness with provision of adequate forces, or continues a campaign of gradualism and accepts a long drawn-out contest."

I was further confused when a subsequent message from General Wheeler informed me that he would be unable to fulfill my "request" because he lacked the troops. In the first place, I had made no request for immediate deployment other than a Marine regiment and a brigade of the 82d Airborne Division, and I well knew that additional troops were unavailable without a call-up of Reserves. Furthermore, in the past, any time that I projected requirements, usually on a calendar-year basis, the Department of Defense, the Joint Chiefs, and the services would study them in detail, whereupon Secretary McNamara would confer with me, examine alternatives, and arrive at a final recommendation for the President. I had no way of knowing that that was not to be Secretary Clifford's method.

Nor did I have any way of knowing that the man whom President Johnson had appointed as chairman of the committee to make recommendations on reinforcements, Clark Clifford, had turned dove and defeatist. Nor did the President have any way of knowing, for Clifford had something of a reputation as a hawk. When he did a complete about-face, the impact on the President must have been considerably stronger than if some admitted dove had come up with a similar conclusion.

Having submitted no request per se for deploying 206,000 troops, not even aware that the total of the three increments General Wheeler and I had discussed came to 206,000, and having thought I was dealing with top secret planning that would be made public only after a strategic decision had been reached, it was with considerable shock that I learned of a front-page article in the New York *Times* on March 10 that began:

> General William C. Westmoreland has asked for 206,000 more American troops for Vietnam, but the request has touched off a divisive internal debate within high levels of the Johnson Administration.

The only thing accurate about that lead was that an internal debate had developed. In any event, the story produced a shock wave of such dimensions that it registered on the seismograph of a presidential primary in New Hampshire. (Erroneously interpreted by political pundits, as it turned out, for time showed that most of those who voted against the President wanted to do more in Vietnam, not less.)

Ironically, even as the *Times* broke the story, the issue was all but dead. Two days earlier, on March 8, General Wheeler had notified me of "strong resistance in all quarters to putting more ground force units in South Vietnam . . . You should not count on an affirmative decision for such additional forces."

General Wheeler subsequently asked me to confer with him in a secret meeting at Clark Air Force Base in the Philippines. "The President," he told me, "says very bluntly that he does not have the horses to change our strategy." By "horses" he meant votes among his advisers.

The war, General Wheeler explained at the meeting on March 24, had become a political issue, with the prospect that the enemy might win in Washington as he had in Paris in 1954. The will of American politicians was faltering. Such antiwar senators as J. William Fulbright, Albert Gore, Frank Church, Robert Kennedy, and George McGovern were hounding the President. More important, a usually staunch Senator Richard Russell was against a call-up of Reserves, and a similarly staunch Senator John Stennis had joined the ranks of those who would support no increased effort. Press and television reporting on the Tet offensive had convinced many that the war was lost or could be brought to no satisfactory conclusion. The intellectual community and some who represented it in government were dead against the war and had no comprehension of the use of force.

Under those circumstances, the President had asked General Wheeler to tell me, making a major call-up of Reserves and contesting the enemy's geographical widening of the war was politically infeasible.† He felt he had no choice over the next few months but to try to calm the protestors lest they precipitate an abject American pull-out.

However much I regretted the decision, I told General Wheeler, I understood. The additional troops, I reminded him, were in the context either of a new strategy or of collapse of the South Vietnamese Government and armed forces. As it turned out, no emergency was involved. Indeed, the Saigon government had proven staunch and the Vietnamese armed forces had gained self-confidence. Ground contact was soon to be re-established with Khe Sanh. I did need the two units I had actually requested to be deployed, plus combat support and logistic back-up for them, in order to move quickly to the offensive in the North; but with that minimum help I could take the offensive throughout the country in due time while recouping the losses in pacification incurred during the Tet offensive. I could keep the brigade of the 82d Airborne Division, General Wheeler responded, but an Army mechanized brigade was to replace the Marine regiment. I would also be authorized 23,000 support troops, which would raise the troop ceiling to 549,000. Of essential importance, I also received authority to hire 13,500 South Vietnamese civilians to fill military jobs.

While I could live with the situation and continue to prosecute the war in terms of the old parameters, including gradually turning the war over to the ARVN, failure to provide large numbers of additional U.S. troops and exploit the enemy's losses with bold new moves seriously prolonged the war. Which makes it incredible to me that so many have tried to claim credit for turning the President around. The bombing halt that the President at last accepted got the enemy to a conference table in Paris, but it could not make him drink the bitter wine of real negotiations. And why should it have? He would do that only after he achieved some spectacular success or after he incurred unbearable pain. While Washington spared the bombs and the enemy talked but said nothing and agreed to nothing except the shape of the conference table, the war went on for four more years of American involvement. That is hardly anything to claim credit for.

As the month of May approached, indications were numerous that a renewed enemy offensive was about to begin. Apparently trying to achieve better co-ordination than in the Tet offensive, the enemy disseminated his attack plans widely, particularly in regard to operations against Saigon.

---

† To meet emergency requirements, the President did call to service 20,000 men in small specialist units and 2,600 individuals. Some 11,000 served in Vietnam, the rest in the strategic Reserve. All were inactivated by mid-December 1969.

Hoping to forestall the surprise and jolt that had occurred at Tet, I tried even more forcefully to keep General Wheeler and the press fully informed on what to expect.

Beginning on May 5 the new offensive turned out to be a sharply reduced version of the Tet offensive, apparently timed to precede start of talks in Paris ostensibly generated by President Johnson's halt in bombing the North. Except at Saigon and a few other places, it involved primarily attacks by rockets and mortars against towns, cities, and American installations. If the North Vietnamese had intended finally to make their bid for the two northern provinces of South Vietnam, they had waited too long; the shift of forces there from other sectors—which I consider a signal achievement—and reinforcement by the airborne brigade and the Marine regiment would have foredoomed even a major attack. The enemy accomplished nothing more in the north than mortar and rocket attacks and a strong thrust across the border from Laos against a CIDG-Special Forces camp at Kham Duc in Quang Tin province. Although General Cushman at first reinforced the camp, in my opinion it had none of the importance or defensive potential of a Khe Sanh, and I ordered evacuation, which U. S. Air Force pilots under the single-manager system of air support accomplished with incredible acts of bravery. An apparent renewed enemy offensive in the Central Highlands was aborted as a result of pre-emptive attacks by the 4th Infantry Division and the 173d Airborne Brigade, plus heavy B-52 strikes.

The most visible enemy effort was at Saigon, but it was this time more nuisance than threat, although it still produced some colorful television footage. American and South Vietnamese troops on the approaches to the capital intercepted and broke up most VC units. One enemy battalion worked its way by night to the vicinity of Tan Son Nhut, only to be destroyed by ARVN units in a nearby French military cemetery. Enemy mortar fire and rockets, including big 122s, struck the city. Small guerrilla bands of four or five men holed up in buildings, mainly in the Cholon district, and fought stubbornly until killed by South Vietnamese troops and police. At some places the VC deliberately set fires, mainly in the highly inflammable shanty towns of the poor, apparently trying to create an impression of a capital under siege.

Heavy fighting developed near a bridge over the Kinh Doi Canal along the southern edge of the city, known as the Y Bridge, where a VC force approaching the size of a battalion attempted to get into the city and did reach the outskirts. Reinforced by a brigade of the U. S. 9th Division under Colonel George Benson, the ARVN eventually routed the force, but in the process inevitably created destruction. It looked awesome on television screens and in newspaper photographs, but in the over-all context of the war the skirmish had little meaning.

The enemy no doubt would have mounted a larger effort in this May offensive—which American troops called "Mini-Tet"—but for the heavy losses in the earlier fighting and vigilance by ARVN and American forces. Yet the enemy had no real need at that stage to hold towns and cities or influence the South Vietnamese people to go against their government. He had but to demonstrate for the benefit of the conferees in Paris that he could still wreak visible damage, as his concentration on the fragile housing of the shanty towns revealed. He had already achieved the goal of unilateral de-escalation on the American side, stopping the bombing, halting rein-forcements, and denying an aggressive strategy and in the process had brought the Americans to the conference table while many Americans thought instead that they were bringing him there. He was free at that point to pursue a new strategy of talk and fight and, in the process, drag out the war.

During my visit to Washington back in November 1967, Bus Wheeler had raised the possibility of my reassignment. Under the provisions of a bill recently passed by the Congress, the tour of duty of the Chiefs of Staff of all services was to be limited to four years except in times of declared national emergency. Although the incumbent U. S. Army Chief of Staff, General Johnson, had been appointed under another law, it was still likely that he would retire after four years in the position, in July 1968. Both in November 1967 and again in a letter in late December, General Wheeler noted that I was "the obvious candidate" for Chief of Staff.

I heard nothing more on the subject until March 23, 1968, when General Wheeler telephoned from Washington to report that President Johnson had just announced in a news conference that I was to be the new Army Chief of Staff. In a message confirming the appointment, the President was gracious:

> Your appointment as Army Chief of Staff gives me great personal pleasure. I have never had higher regard or greater respect for any military colleague. It will be a source of uncommon strength to have you close beside me as we continue to press the struggle for peace and freedom in Vietnam.

When I met the next evening at Clark Air Force Base in the Philippines to hear from General Wheeler the President's decision against a new strategy, General Wheeler told me that in mid-January Secretary McNamara had suggested several possible candidates for the position to President Johnson but had concluded by recommending me. The President had agreed with the recommendation but for political reasons had elected to delay announcement.

The President wanted me to know, General Wheeler said, that I was his personal choice and that of Secretary McNamara and that McNamara's designated successor, Clark Clifford, agreed. Since the announcement came during the wailing period over the Tet offensive, the President urged me to ignore the inevitable press speculation to the effect that I was being "kicked upstairs." (Repatriated prisoners of war told me later that the North Vietnamese in their propaganda quickly took up that theme.) Those who did so speculate apparently overlooked the fact that in a three-year war in Korea the United States had four commanders while in an essentially eight-year war in Vietnam there were only two.

I received news of the appointment with mixed emotions. I had hoped to remain in Vietnam until the fighting ended, yet I was honored by the selection. In my own counsel I knew that with the decision against my proposed new strategy, the war was likely to go on for a long time still, and despite the amelioration provided by Kitsy's presence in the Philippines, I had been away from my family far too long.

The subject of my successor arose in early April when the President, after asking me to meet him in Honolulu, canceled the trip following the assassination of Martin Luther King, Jr., and subsequent rioting in several cities and asked that I proceed instead to Washington. As a guest again in the White House, I made my first acquaintance with the President's nine-month-old grandson, who toddled in and out of the room as we talked. Because he waddled when he walked and had body proportions similar to those of the Soviet Union's premier, the President called him "Khrushchev."

In the course of our conversations, the President asked my recommendation on my successor. I strongly urged Creighton Abrams.

During that visit I also seized upon one last opportunity to stress to President Johnson and his advisers, including Walt Rostow and Averell Harriman, that we were at that point in Vietnam in a position of unprecedented strength and that if we were to enter into negotiations, we should bear that in mind and negotiate accordingly. I also stressed the magnitude of the enemy's losses. Yet I sensed that the President was in no mood to accept that appraisal. The rioting in American cities and the mercurial nature of press reporting on the Tet offensive had left their mark.

Before I departed again for Saigon, I flew with the President in his helicopter over downtown Washington, where fires set in widespread rioting and looting were still burning. It looked considerably more distressing than Saigon during the Tet offensive.

Chapter XX
Chief of Staff

Although the position of Chief of Staff of the United States Army came into being following the Spanish-American War, the full authority and prerogatives of the position were some time evolving. During World War I, General Peyton C. March did much to enhance the position, but only with the tenure of the former American Expeditionary Forces commander, General John J. Pershing, did the Chief of Staff become uncontestably established as the supreme military authority of the Army. The Chief of Staff is the senior officer responsible to the presidentially appointed civilian Secretary of the Army. Appointed by the President with confirmation by the Senate, the Chief of Staff runs the headquarters staff in Washington and administers the Army through field commanders. I was fortunate when filling the position to be served by a highly competent staff headed by an able Vice Chief of Staff, General Bruce Palmer.

Following World War II the Unification Act of 1950 gave the Army Chief of Staff another responsibility: to serve as the Army's representative on the Joint Chiefs of Staff, a corporate body that provides military advice to the civilian Secretary of Defense, the National Security Council, and the President. The other members of the Joint Chiefs are the Chief of Naval Operations, the Chief of Staff of the Air Force, and a chairman from one or the other of the services nominated by the President and confirmed by the Senate. The Commandant of the Marine Corps sits as a member on matters of interest to the Marine Corps, a role usually broadly interpreted. In my capacity as a member of the Joint Chiefs, my principal assistant was a brilliant officer and close associate in many previous assignments, Dick Stilwell.

As senior officer of the Army, the Chief of Staff deals with such Army matters as discipline, logistics, management, training, and combat readiness, while as a member of the Joint Chiefs he is an adviser on policy and military operations. Although the dual role tests an individual's capacity, I find it a logical arrangement. In sitting on the Joint Chiefs, the senior officers of the services by the very fact of their responsibility for the effectiveness of their services lend knowledgeable authority to the policy-making and advisory roles of the Joint Chiefs.

As I became Chief of Staff on July 3, 1968, I considered that aside from my responsibilities with the Joint Chiefs, I faced two major tasks: to assure continued support for U. S. Army forces in Vietnam and to reorient, revitalize, and otherwise prepare the Army for meeting future roles in support of national policy, in the process repairing the erosion that was inevitable in the course of the nation's longest and most controversial war, a war in which the Army bore the major burden. Of those two tasks, the latter was the more complex, for even though American forces in Vietnam were not to reach a peak until early in 1969 and even though the last American troops were to leave only in early 1973, the mechanics for supporting Army forces in Vietnam had long been devised. It was the task of reshaping the Army for the future in the face of antimilitarism, racial discontent, budget restrictions, troop reductions, drug abuse, and other problems that would pose the greater tests of perseverance and ingenuity.*

As a kind of theme on which to hang objectives essential for restructuring the Army, I stressed what I called the "Four Ms": *Mission*—to attain a balanced Army responsive to all likely contingencies; *Motivation*—to enhance the dignity and pride of all in the Army; *Modernization*—to avoid obsolescence, make full use of technological advances, and build on the Vietnam experience; and *Management*—to make the most efficient use of public resources.

Since my task was to maintain a combat-ready Army in the face of declining public support, I deemed one of my more important responsibilities to be making the Army's role known and understood. I vowed to tell that story personally to public audiences in every state, plus Puerto Rico and the Panama Canal Zone, a goal which I achieved, usually in the course of visiting nearby Army installations.

Perhaps inevitably, my appearances sometimes brought out antiwar demonstrators. Some incidents were relatively mild, as in Nashville in the civic auditorium when about a dozen youths in the audience laughed or applauded at ridiculous times or shouted rude remarks, which I ignored. Or at Virginia Polytechnic Institute where somebody had erected a mock-up of a graveyard with crosses and placards, which I was unaware of until the president of the university apologized for it. At Kansas State University a student placed a Viet Cong flag on a balcony behind the rostrum, but several members of the football team removed him and the flag from the auditorium. At Lincoln, Nebraska, I simply walked through a group of about a hundred bedraggled demonstrators outside the hotel where I was to speak.

The undue attention paid to demonstrators by press and television struck

* Additional details on my tenure as Chief of Staff are available in the official report soon to be published by the Government Printing Office.

me when at Worcester, Massachusetts, I attended a fund-raising banquet for a South Vietnamese hospital in company with a long-time friend, my World War II chaplain, Father Edward Connors. Although several thousand dedicated people attended the banquet on behalf of a noble cause, the attention of reporters and cameramen focused on a couple of dozen youthful demonstrators outside the hall.

When I attended a football game at Pennsylvania State University, approximately a hundred demonstrators with the usual flowing hair and beards, disreputable dress, and crude placards surrounded the home of the university's president, Dr. Eric Walker, where I was a guest at a pregame luncheon. Among a group that sat down to block the driveway was a woman with a baby. After physically removing the demonstrators from the driveway, police loaded the guests into a bus for the trip to the stadium, and as a parting gesture, the demonstrators stoned the bus. A number of Penn State students wrote to apologize, and President Walker later informed me that an investigation revealed no involvement by university students.

At Ohio State University demonstrators surrounded the building where I spoke at the commissioning of ROTC cadets. My trusted security man, Warrant Officer Tom Taylor, moved my automobile to one entrance, where the demonstrators promptly converged, then whisked me through another door to another car. At the University of Cincinnati where I spoke at an assembly of Boy Scouts and their parents, Taylor used the same ploy. In Switzerland students, mostly American, organized an hour-long parade in front of my hotel in Berne with marchers bearing sensational signs and Viet Cong flags, much to the embarrassment of my official Swiss hosts, who had invited me to visit their army.

I sidestepped a potentially more serious incident at Yale University, where I was invited to speak under sponsorship of the Student Union, an organization long dedicated to free speech. The visit began with a pleasant informal session with leaders of the group, marred only near the end when a divinity student, with a wild look about him, announced that he had to conclude that I was crazy; but shortly before I completed dinner with a group of students at Mory's, Tom Taylor called me aside. City police had warned him, he said, that a mob of demonstrators assembled from various New England campuses intended to disrupt my speech by forcing entrance into the auditorium, pelting me with rotten eggs and tomatoes, and reading charges branding me a war criminal. Television cameras were already in place to cover the events.

I was prepared, I told my student hosts, to proceed with my address, no matter what the abuse, but I was concerned that the confrontation would reflect discredit upon the Student Union and Yale University and would be disrespectful of the United States Army that I proudly represented. While extending an invitation to members of the Student Union to visit the Pentagon for a serious group discussion, I deemed it prudent to cancel my speech. The students understood and apologized, but to my dismay the faculty adviser in an emotional outburst questioned my personal courage. Upon instructions from the Board of Trustees, the university's president, Dr. Kingman Brewster, Jr., later forwarded an expression of regret, and numbers of alumni wrote to express their concern, including the editor of the *Yale Alumni Magazine*.

However trying these incidents were, none of the agitation directed at me was as abusive as that heaped, on occasion, on panels of Vietnam veterans who visited several campuses upon invitation to explain the Army's role in Vietnam. The most serious incident occurred in 1970 at Cornell University where one member of a panel of officers was the much-decorated Colonel Bob Schweitzer. Early in the proceedings a young man mounted the stage and defiled the table in front of the officers with raw eggs and raw chicken giblets. For a time the audience thwarted all discussion by chanting obscenities. From time to time the Vietnamese wife of an alleged former AID official would jump to her feet and scream that the officers were liars. One young man seized the microphone and while waving pictures of injured infants, demanded to know "why you napalmed these babies." It was a grueling four-hour session under hot lights, but Colonel Schweitzer and his colleagues knew their subject and never lost their decorum. They performed as well on that strange battleground as they had in Vietnam.

That the antiwar activists were a small minority was amply apparent from the letters of support from individuals and organizations that filled my files, from the number and variety of invitations I received, from the warmth and enthusiasm of most in my audiences, and from the honors accorded me, which I accepted in the name of the troops I had commanded in Vietnam. One of the most moving events was a welcome home parade on November 11, 1968, in my home county of Spartanburg and in ceremonies in Columbia, the state capital, where a failing Jimmy Byrnes made his last public appearance. Bob Hope and his charming wife, Dolores, entertained that evening at a banquet hosted by Governor McNair.

It was my pleasure to address the national conventions of all the major veterans' organizations in various cities; speak before a joint session of the Nevada legislature in Carson City; participate with more than 30,000 others in honoring Vietnam veterans in Los Angeles where I was privileged to announce that a new USO building was to be named for Bob Hope; address a panel session of the American Bar Association on military law in St. Louis; deliver a Veterans' Day address in the Mormon Tabernacle in Salt Lake City; present the Davis Cup in Charlotte, North Carolina, to the American tennis team and a special trophy to a soldier, Stan Smith, who won the final match for the United States; present the outstanding football player award in the Liberty Bowl in Memphis to Joe Ferguson, subsequently quarterback with the Buffalo Bills; breakfast on St. Patrick's Day with men I have long admired, the New York Police Department; participate in laying the cornerstone of Eisenhower Hall, a new cadet activities building at West Point, and at Mrs. Eisenhower's request present to the academy the President's class ring, which, for fear of losing it, I wore from Washington to the ceremonies.

I was touched by a letter from a Mr. John Mischesko inviting me to visit his town of Mineville, a small mining community in upstate New York. The people of the town, Mr. Mischesko wrote, were proud of their men who fought in Vietnam; three had been killed and one had received the Medal of Honor. Yet in the atmosphere of doubt and dissent as depicted by press and television, many people were perplexed, wondering if their patriotic conduct was the proper course. No one ever came to see them. Would I please come?

In the spring of 1971 I was able to make the trip. The local chapter of the Veterans of Foreign Wars provided an honor guard, the high school band paraded, and ladies of the town prepared a delightful luncheon. It was always heart-warming to move among the people who constitute—however overworked the term—the grass roots of America. My friendship with that group of patriotic citizens continues.

During my travels I finally found an opportunity to get even with Bob Hope for the many quips he pulled on me at the lectern. At a dinner following Bob's receipt of an honorary degree at Ohio State University, I told of a happening following a dinner at West Point when a little old lady came to the head table and practically embraced me. "I've seen you so many times on television," she exclaimed. "Only somehow you don't look the same. You look much younger." After a pause, she added: "You *are* Bob Hope, aren't you?" It was hard for me to figure how she could have made such a mistake, I told the Ohio audience, because I was wearing my uniform. "Then it hit me," I said. "When the little old lady saw my profile, she noted my chin and thought it was a nose."

I also considered it important to become familiar with the U. S. Army's major installations, including overseas commands, and give them appropriate recognition. On visits to Alaska it was especially rewarding to get acquainted with the Eskimo Scouts, an element of the National Guard that mans outposts along the bleak Bering Sea. I spent a good deal of time visiting less familiar areas and was therefore able to return to Vietnam only in the summer of 1970. During the course of the visit, President Thieu hosted a luncheon and Premier Khiem a dinner, at both of which many former South Vietnamese colleagues were present. I also paid a sentimental return to my former residence at No. 60 Tran Quy Cap. My final visit to Vietnam was in early 1972, at which time a major Communist offensive obviously was soon to come.

In only one case during my service as Chief of Staff was it necessary to exercise my prerogative as military head of the Army to intervene on behalf of soldiers serving under the joint MACV command. That was in July 1969, when the commander of the 5th Special Forces Group, Colonel Robert B. Rheault, six other officers, and a noncommissioned officer were arrested in connection with the alleged murder of a South Vietnamese suspected of being a double intelligence agent. The eight were incarcerated in the Long Binh stockade under harsh conditions. I directed General Abrams as commander of the United States Army, Vietnam, as opposed to his other position as COMUSMACV, to release them pending disposition of charges. Later, because members of the CIA, presumably involved, would be unable to testify for security reasons, Secretary of the Army Stanley Resor ruled that a fair trial was impossible and dismissed the charges.

In another case involving an incident in Vietnam I was also compelled to get personally involved. That was in the spring of 1971 after approximately 50 enemy overran a fire-support base named Mary Ann, manned by more than 250 men of the Americal Division, resulting in 30 Americans killed and 82 wounded. It was a clear case of dereliction of duty—of soldiers becoming lax in their defense and officers failing to take corrective action.

I asked General Abrams to make known to me the results of his investigation. When I received his report with his recommendations for disciplinary action, I reviewed the case at length before submitting my recommendations to the Secretary of the Army, who under law was the responsible authority for dealing with disciplinary cases involving officers that were referred to the Department of the Army. Secretary Resor subsequently took disciplinary action against the division and assistant division commanders and four other officers.

As Chief of Staff I received a number of invitations from my counterparts in foreign armies to visit their countries, which the U. S. Department of State encouraged. While enabling me to establish rapport with senior military officials abroad, the visits also sometimes afforded contact with foreign heads of state and opportunities to inspect U. S. Army installations. Having Kitsy along on most of the trips was an indubitable asset in the social events that were inevitably associated with the visits.

Visits included a number of NATO countries, in most of which I observed NATO maneuvers: Britain, Belgium, Germany, Italy, The Netherlands, and Norway. Observing NATO maneuvers in Greece and Turkey, I was disturbed by an apparent lack of rapport between officers of the two countries, even though they were outwardly cordial in a ceremonial handshake on a bridge across a river that serves as the international boundary between their two countries. When unpredictable winds delayed the arrival of my plane in Spain, which I visited at the specific request of President Nixon, my hosts sped me perilously through the streets of Madrid at seventy miles per hour for an audience with Generalissimo Francisco Franco and his heir apparent, Prince Juan Carlos, whom I had entertained at West Point when he and Princess Sophia were on their wedding trip. (A joke current when I was in Madrid played on the Generalissimo's seeming indestructibility: One day television programs are interrupted for a special announcement. On comes an aged but hale Franco to announce the death of His Royal Highness Juan Carlos at the age of ninety-five.)

In Ethiopia, where I inspected a U. S. Army communications facility, an aged but alert Emperor Haile Selassie entertained me at a royal luncheon and sought my advice on the insurgency facing his country. Seated beside me, the Emperor's Foreign Minister made a great effort to assure me that his country's recent diplomatic recognition of Communist China had no anti-American connotations; the Emperor, he said, was trying to assuage Maoist-oriented insurgents across the Red Sea in Yemen who were supporting insurgency in the Ethiopian province of Eritrea. My stay in Iran, where the United States had a large military assistance program, included a long visit with the Shah, whose grasp of the role and potential of his country and the Middle East impressed me. He was particularly interested in the military utility of the helicopter.

In Taiwan I dined with an aged Chiang Kai-shek, who was distressed at American efforts to establish communications with Red China; addressing the staff and faculty of the National War College, I discussed the principles of Sun Tzu as the enemy was practicing them in Vietnam. In Singapore I was struck by Prime Minister Lee Kuan Yew's sensitivity to neighboring Thailand's weather-vane politics. In Indonesia I delivered a message from President Nixon to President Suharto explaining the necessity of our extending a promised quantity of military aid over a longer period than originally planned. In India, as guest of my counterpart, General Sam Manekshaw, I became acquainted with that country's volunteer army and its British traditions and had a particularly rewarding visit with the 9th Armoured Division and its colorful commander, Major General Gurbachon Singh, known as "Butch." My Indian hosts took me to the tiny protectorate kingdom of Sikkim to visit a division in the Natu La Pass, traditional invasion route from Tibet, where I observed Chinese Communist troops across the frontier. We walked the last few hundred feet to the crest of a peak well over 14,000 feet high; without supplemental oxygen, we had to stop every few steps for rest. My hosts for the evening were Their Highnesses the Chogyal (king) and the Gyalmo (queen), the former socialite Hope Cooke of New York. During a reception given by the king and queen, the leader of the opposition party urged me to initiate steps for the United States to take over protectorate responsibilities of his country from India; so absurd was the request that I may have been abrupt in my reply.

While in India I was impressed by the officers' friendliness to the United States and concerned at their information that trouble might be in the offing between East and West Pakistan. Although the East Pakistanis had religious ties with West Pakistan, the people allegedly leaned more toward association with India and longed to become an independent state (Bangladesh). When fighting did break out, I personally deemed it a mistake for the United States to support West Pakistan, and so stated in official counsels. Following a later conference with the President, Secretary of State William Rogers, and Henry Kissinger, it became obvious to me that Mr. Nixon had made commitments to West Pakistan which were associated with help in obtaining entree for Kissinger to Peking as the first step in establishing communications with Red China.

It was a particular pleasure to visit Australia, Korea, and New Zealand because of my association with troops of those nations in South Vietnam. I also made a supposedly secret trip to Cambodia to talk with an ailing Premier Lon Nol, who was recovering from a stroke, but doubted how secret the trip was when I found security troops lining the entire route from the airport into Phnom Penh. Lon Nol's primary interest appeared to be getting heavy tanks and long-range artillery. Although I wanted to go on for a first-hand look at the situation in Laos, Secretary Laird refused permission on the grounds that a visit from me might attract undue attention in the press.

After attending the Conference of American Armies in Rio de Janiero, Brazil, in September 1968, I hosted the conference the following year in Washington; but for lack of volunteer host countries, the conferences were discontinued until begun again in 1973. Now they continue to serve as a forum through which military leaders of the Western Hemisphere can become acquainted. I had particularly interesting associations with Lieutenant General Alejandro Agustin Lanusse, who was for a time President of Argentina, and Colonel Hugo Banzer Suarez, who became President of Bolivia. During visits to the Republic of Panama, I conferred at the request of the Department of State with General Omar Torrijos Herrera, who was taking a hard line regarding continued American control over the Canal Zone. Meeting on the Panamanian island of Contadora, I advised General Torrijos that the United States Senate would probably not ratify an agreement leaving control of the Canal Zone and use of the canal in doubt, but he held to his hard line.

As American society was changing, so it behooved the Army to be receptive to change, some of which was hard for some officers and noncommissioned officers with long service to accept. I early established a board headed by Lieutenant General William J. McCaffrey to review Army practices, policies, and traditions and recommend modernization. Were some practices out of date and unnecessary? In view of widespread use of air travel, could weekend leave policy be liberalized? Could food service better meet the needs of the soldier? Were soldiers being treated too much like immature young men? Should there be increased privacy in barracks? Could there be improvements in career management? How to improve training and make it more interesting? Was the education system for officers and non-commissioned officers responsive to the needs of the future? Because the Army's alumni can often be helpful in promoting acceptance of change, I hosted numbers of luncheons in the Pentagon for retired generals and others to discuss my conclusions following detailed staff studies.

Throughout I had to resist revolutionary, overnight changes advocated by enthusiastic young officers who were no doubt as impatient with the old regime as I had been at their age. They failed to appreciate that a big institution must achieve change without upheaval, that it is better to work gradually to achieve understanding through the chain of command.

Somewhat ridiculously, one of my toughest decisions as Chief of Staff was on haircut policy. To the youth of the day, long hair had become almost a way of life, a symbol of their times, an emotional issue. Yet to older officers, noncommissioned officers, and retirees short hair for the military man had long been synonymous with discipline. In any event, uniformity is a hallmark of a military organization and must be maintained. The anguish I underwent on the decision was almost farcical. In the end I settled for an increase in hair length that probably satisfied neither side completely but was acceptable enough to both to defuse the issue. Secretary Resor, who had several teen-age sons, was disappointed that I was not more permissive.

Haircut policy was but one of myriad problems, many of them volatile. The misuse of drugs, for example, had spread from civilian society into the Army and became a major problem, particularly in Vietnam, where the magnitude of the problem unfortunately caught the command by surprise. A serious dilution over the war years in the caliber of junior leaders contributed to this and other disciplinary problems. We eventually adopted a three-pronged approach to solving the drug problem that involved enforcement, education, and rehabilitation, with strong dependence on amnesty for the individual who would seek help. Experience showed that most young men could be saved for the service and for useful lives. A similar program addressed alcoholism.

Early in 1969 I developed an intuitive feeling that racial tensions were building throughout the Army and directed a thoroughly objective survey of conditions world-wide. A team of officers and noncommissioned officers headed by an outstanding black officer, Lieutenant Colonel James S. White, visited every major installation in the United States and abroad, then briefed senior commanders of each on their findings. Trouble was, indeed, in the offing. My anticipation came too late to avoid all conflict; but when trouble came, alleviating programs were already underway.

Dissent within the Army, usually fanned by outsiders, was for long a concern, even though limited to a few officers and men; it gradually decreased as the war in Vietnam wound down and dissidents completed their service. While the desertion rate during the war was high, it never equaled that of the Korean War. Of 2,400 Army deserters to foreign countries, 600 returned; and a survey revealed that most deserted because of personal problems, usually disciplinary, and that less than 10 per cent deserted for political considerations, including opposition to the war. Hundreds of young men took advantage of a conscientious-objector program to receive special medical training at Fort Sam Houston, Texas.

I directed special attention to modernizing and bringing more of an intellectual bent to the ROTC, which had shrunk seriously in numbers of cadets and which some academic institutions, among them some of the most prestigious, had abandoned. In some cases college or university history departments assumed responsibility for the ROTC's military history course; in summer encampments senior generals participated in national strategy seminars; and officers with graduate degrees headed the ROTC departments.

Educational facilities and opportunities for both officers and enlisted men were vastly expanded. College level courses were available at most major Army installations, and numbers of officers attended civilian institutions full time to obtain baccalaureate and advanced degrees. Noncommissioned officer academies provided career training courses similar to the institutional career schools for officers.

Reducing the strength of the Army in accord with congressional dictates was a complicated matter. Providing early discharges for some draftees helped, but corresponding involuntary reductions also had to be made in the ranks of officers and noncommissioned officers, many of whom had served with distinction. At one point the Congress unexpectedly imposed an arbitrary last-minute 50,000-man cut that proved thoroughly disruptive, forcing the Army to discharge, among others, specialists it had taken years to develop, with no time to train replacements.

Spurred by the so-called "clubs and messes scandal," the Army continued the campaign against corruption, instituting new fiscal and audit controls. Lest conditions in military stockades foment unrest, Secretary of the Army Resor and I retained a team of six prominent civilian penologists to investigate. Since barracks and other permanent facilities had begun to deteriorate while the bulk of the military budget was earmarked for Vietnam, I promoted a concentrated effort to upgrade them. As in civilian society, crime was a continuing problem, magnified by the high percentage of young people in the Army and heightened during the war by a tendency of civilian judges to forgive a man's dereliction in exchange for his enlisting in the Army, thus putting into uniform men with a penchant for trouble.

Throughout my tenure as Chief of Staff, the Army and the Reserves continued the historically traditional role of serving society. Providing disaster relief in hurricanes, floods, forest fires, blizzards. Handling the mail during a postal strike. Dropping feed by helicopter to cattle stranded by heavy snows. Giving emergency medical assistance. Overseeing vast civic works and conservation programs by the Corps of Engineers. Training sky marshals to discourage hijacking of commercial airliners. Assisting local law enforcement officials in civil disturbances. I was particularly proud of a plan for national contingency use that had as its purpose the education and development of unemployed youths while they worked at the same time to improve the environment; the Army would thus provide leaders and instructors as it had during the 1930s for the Civilian Conservation Corps.

Although National Guard troops were called upon more than a hundred times while I was Chief of Staff to assist in law enforcement, in only one case did the Army itself have to furnish troops: on May 9, 1970, in Washington to protect federal property and the functions of government when a dissident organization threatened to disrupt the government. When specifically charged with this kind of support mission by law and executive direction, the Army is impelled to look ahead, to anticipate where trouble may develop. In the volatile domestic climate of those years, to make sure that the Army would be prepared to support civilian authorities and the National Guard if necessary, I continued a special civil-disturbance directorate created by my predecessor and headed by Lieutenant General George Mather. The Army's preparations to be ready for such an assignment led to irate charges that the Army was spying on civilians. Although some involved in the program may have employed poor discretion on occasion, political authorities were fully aware of the Army's need to be alert to trouble and approved the concept, and any surveillance was in direct support of civil authority.

In the tragic confrontation in May 1970 between students and National Guard troops at Kent State University, I was appalled to learn that relatively untrained troops had been furnished live ammunition, which was contrary to policy even for experienced regular troops. I subsequently insisted on special courses for National Guard commanders with emphasis on restraint, for in the exercise of military assistance to civil power it is vital to use restraint even while providing a visible display of power.

However demanding the position of Chief of Staff, it had its lighter moments. I found time, for example, to improve my ability as a helicopter pilot. My former aide when I commanded the 101st Airborne Division, Tiger Honeycutt, who later fought at Hamburger Hill in Vietnam, had taught me the rudiments at Fort Campbell, Kentucky. Yet I felt a need for formal instruction and wanted to get my official wings, both for personal satisfaction and to demonstrate to others the importance I attached to the helicopter.

In off time, usually on weekends, I took lessons from Warrant Officer Charles Astrike at nearby Fort Belvoir, then went to the Army Aviation School at Fort Rucker, Alabama, to take qualifying tests and receive my qualification wings. Although I accumulated considerable flight time (including some in foreign helicopters when visiting other countries), I never asked for or received flight pay. It was with some satisfaction and keen awareness of change that I noted that my first mount in the Army had been a horse and my last a helicopter. In my retirement the thrill of piloting a helicopter is one that I miss most.

Perhaps my most ludicrous moment as Chief of Staff occurred in 1971 when I was conferring at my desk with another officer and the door burst open. In strode a disheveled stranger. That was odd, for my staff kept strict watch on all visitors, carefully regulating a crowded schedule and keeping the next appointees waiting in an adjacent "ready room." The stranger had obviously beaten the system.

The man strode with determination to my desk.

"Who are you?" I asked, accepting his outstretched hand.

"I am," the man responded, "Jesus Christ."

Although taken aback, I suggested he have a seat. After some banter about his prior military service, I asked him to state his business.

The stranger jumped to his feet. "I need your help," he shouted. "The porno movies and book stores on Fourteenth Street have got to go!"

It took some time for one of my aides to lure the man from the office with a promise of introducing him to someone better placed to help with the city of Washington's problems. It took even longer for my staff to get over the chagrin caused by the lapse in their security system. The visitor, it turned out, was an escaped inmate of a mental hospital in Washington.

Even before Richard Nixon was elected President in November 1968, one of his campaign pledges made it clear that the military services were to be faced with a strong new challenge. "Once our involvement in the Vietnam war is behind us," he said, "we should move toward an all-volunteer force." For an army that was required to maintain a large, balanced force and accustomed since 1940 to relying on selective service to fill its ranks (except for a brief period in 1947 when lapse of the draft law underscored the need for it), that was going to pose myriad problems. Even before the election I put to work a task force under a man who had handled his assignments well in Vietnam, George Forsythe, then a lieutenant general. He was ably assisted by my entire staff, especially my Deputy Chief of Staff for Personnel, Dutch Kerwin.

There are clearly military advantages in a volunteer force. It means less turnover in personnel, fewer newcomers to be trained, more professional leaders, and enhanced motivation. Yet there are disadvantages and concerns as well. The higher pay necessary to attract volunteers adds to the national budget, promotes inflation, and produces pressures to cut elsewhere. The size of the Army is determined less by security requirements than by how many men can be recruited—the old business of cutting the suit to fit the cloth. The Army may become the province of the less affluent and less skilled and fail to represent a cross section of the society. With the inducement of the draft eliminated, recruiting problems are magnified for the Reserves, whose maintenance at effective strength is especially vital if there are manpower reductions in the regular Army.

Yet I was sympathetic with the long-range goal of a volunteer Army and when the President made clear that he intended to move toward one by allowing congressional authority for selective service to expire at the end of June 1973, I did what I could to prepare the way. We doubled the size of the recruiting force and attempted to select fully qualified individuals to be a part of it. To free more men for field duty, we doubled the size of the

Women's Army Corps and authorized women to perform a broader range of duties. Where possible we hired civilians to replace soldiers, particularly for such tasks as KP.

As my tour as Chief of Staff neared an end and the deadline for a volunteer force approached, I urged the President, without success, to keep a selective service law on the books, one that could be implemented as required and that would serve as an inducement for enlistments. Although the services since my retirement have done an effective job of maintaining strengths near designated levels, the perils that I earlier envisaged still remain. A draft implemented by lottery only as required would bring men into uniform from all segments of the society, and a continuation of the principle of compulsory service to country would make a healthy contribution. With maximum efforts to attract volunteers, the draft would be sporadic and so small as not to be politically onerous.

In April 1969 the Department of the Army and a number of legislators and government officials received letters from a former soldier who had served in Vietnam, Ronald L. Ridenhour, alleging war crimes by American soldiers in an operation in March 1968, in the hamlet of My Lai (referred to as "Pinkville") in the village of Son My in Quang Ngai province. Involved was a component of the Americal Division's 11th Infantry Brigade.

Despite the obvious sincerity displayed by Ridenhour, I found it beyond belief that American soldiers, as he alleged, engaged in mass murder of unarmed South Vietnamese civilians. I directed an immediate check with MACV headquarters in Saigon. When the MACV inspector general reported that something untoward might have occurred, the Inspector General of the Department of the Army began an immediate investigation, which was subsequently pursued by the Army Criminal Investigation Division. It resulted in charges against four officers and nine enlisted men and trials of two officers and three enlisted men. Twenty-five former enlisted men were implicated, but since they had already been discharged from the Army, they were beyond the Army's jurisdiction.

Almost as deplorable as the events alleged was the possibility that officers of the 11th Brigade and the Americal Division had either covered up the incident or failed to make a comprehensive investigation. The developing evidence in the criminal investigation and the indications of command dereliction led Secretary Resor and me to arrange for an additional formal inquiry into the adequacy of the criminal investigation and the possible suppression of information. When I learned that some members of President Nixon's administration wanted to whitewash any possible negligence within the chain of command, I threatened through a White House official to exercise my prerogative as a member of the Joint Chiefs of Staff to go personally to the President and object. That squelched any further pressure for whitewash.

My first thought was to propose a civilian commission to enhance the credibility of the findings, but upon reflection I decided that the situation in Vietnam was so complex, the terminology and experience so alien to civilians, that it would be better to have a board headed by a military man assisted by civilian lawyers. To head the board the Secretary and I selected the former I Field Force commander, General Peers, who had a reputation throughout the Army for objectivity and fairness. Ray Peers had also been a division commander in Vietnam and thus was thoroughly familiar with conditions; he had never had jurisdiction over any activity in Quang Ngai province. Because he had entered the Army through ROTC at the University of California at Los Angeles, there could be no presumption that ties among brother officers from West Point would be involved. For the civilian legal counsel we obtained the services of two distinguished New York attorneys, Robert MacCrate and Jerome K. Walsh, Jr., who assisted General Peers but reported directly to Secretary Resor.

As a result of evidence developed by the Peers board, charges were brought against twelve officers, primarily involving dereliction of duty in suppressing information and failing to obey lawful regulations. These included the former Americal Division commander, General Koster, who at the time of the investigation was Superintendent of the Military Academy. Lest any findings reflect adversely on the Academy, he requested relief from that post.

Under usual courts-martial practice, the pretrial investigations would have been assigned to the Army commanders in whose commands the officers were serving. To simplify procedures and assure that all would be judged by the same criteria, I instead transferred all the officers associated with charges stemming from the Peers investigation to the First Army and assigned the investigation to its commander, Jack Seaman. I am sure it was for him a demanding assignment. After detailed review of the Peers board findings and further investigation, Seaman concluded that evidence was insufficient to bring any of the officers to trial for dereliction of duty except the former 11th Infantry Brigade commander, who was subsequently court-martialed and acquitted after a lengthy trial.

Even though the evidence as reviewed by a man of honesty and courage proved insufficient for trial or conviction, something had to be remiss in the Americal Division's chain of command if anything so reprehensible and colossal as the My Lai massacre occurred without some responsible official either knowing or at least suspecting.

It was true that at President Johnson's direction the 11th Infantry Brigade had been deployed to Vietnam before completing its training, in order to get the troops there in advance of an arrangement the President was hoping—vainly, as it turned out—to achieve with the North Vietnamese for a cease-fire and a freeze in troop strength. Although I committed the brigade in a quiet sector so training might continue, just over a month later the troops were caught up in the enemy's Tet offensive. It was also true that the unit at My Lai was part of a temporary or *ad hoc* task force lacking the unity of an established organization. Yet those were no more than mitigating factors, not excuses. Although the division commander did order an investigation, he made a basic error in assigning the investigation to the commander of the responsible unit, the 11th Infantry Brigade.

Contrary to my standing directive, not even the fact that an investigation, however perfunctory, took place was reported either to the intermediate headquarters, the III Marine Amphibious Force and the United States Army, Vietnam, or to my headquarters; and reference to my records reveals that I visited the Americal Division and the 11th Infantry Brigade on April 20, 1968, only a few weeks after the massacre, and nobody intimated to me that anything was under suspicion or even remotely remiss except a Red Cross official who complained about mail service.

As with civilian justice, the United States Army is committed to due legal process under which an individual must be presumed innocent until proven guilty. Indeed, the Uniform Code of Military Justice gives the accused extraordinary protection. The Army cannot bring a man to trial simply on the basis of unsubstantiated allegations, however plausible, however widely publicized. If pretrial investigation fails to produce substantiated evidence sufficient to warrant trial, the accused must be protected against prejudicial statements made during the investigation, for the investigation itself is no trial. Thus the full details of the Peers board, even as the proceedings of a grand jury, have been kept secret.

The U. S. Army does have another pretrial procedure not usually available to civilian authority: administrative review to determine if the performance of the person under investigation conformed to established standards of the military profession. If the charges against him are dropped, it means only that further criminal proceedings are unwarranted, not that his performance has been found adequate. As with the court-martial system, administrative review is not the province of the Chief of Staff but of the Secretary of the Army, although the Secretary has the benefit of the Chief of Staff's recommendations. As a result of administrative review, Secretary Resor took administrative action against two general officers of the Americal Division and eight others whose performances in connection with the investigation and reporting of My Lai were deemed to be below the standards expected of individuals of their positions, grades, and experiences.

In the criminal cases, acquittal resulted in all but that of a platoon leader, First Lieutenant William L. Calley, Jr. Charged with the murder of more than a hundred civilians, he was convicted on March 29, 1971, of the murder of "at least" twenty-two. He was sentenced to dismissal from the service and confinement at hard labor for life, but the latter was reduced by judicial review to twenty years and further reduced after my retirement by Secretary of the Army Howard Callaway to ten years, an action that President Nixon sustained. The case was subsequently and for a long time under judicial appeal in the federal courts.

Lieutenant Calley was legally judged by a jury whose members all were familiar with the nature of combat in Vietnam and well aware that even the kind of war waged in Vietnam is no license for murder. The vast majority of Americans in Vietnam did their best to protect civilian lives and property, often at their own peril. That some civilians, even many, died by accident or inevitably in the course of essential military operations dictated by the enemy's presence among the people was no justification or rationale for the conscious massacre of defenseless babies, children, mothers, and old men in a kind of diabolical slow-motion nightmare that went on for the better part of a day, with a cold-blooded break for lunch. I said at the time of the revelation: "It could not have happened—but it did."

Although I can in no way condone Lieutenant Calley's acts—or those of any of his colleagues who may have participated but went unpunished—I must have compassion for him. Judging from the events at My Lai, being an officer in the United States Army exceeded Lieutenant Calley's abilities. Had it not been for educational draft deferments, which prevented the Army from drawing upon the intellectual segment of society for its junior officers, Calley probably never would have been an officer. Denied that usual reservoir of talent, the Army had to lower its standards. Although some who became officers under those conditions performed well, others, such as Calley, failed.

An army has a corps of officers to insure leadership: to see that orders are given and carried out and that the men conduct themselves properly. Setting aside the crime involved, Lieutenant Calley's obvious lack of supervision and failure to set a proper example himself were contrary to orders and policy, and the supervision he exercised fell far short.

In reducing standards for officers, both the United States Army and the House Armed Services Committee, which originated the policy of deferments for college students, must bear the blame. It would have been better to have gone short of officers than to have accepted applicants whose credentials left a question as to their potential as leaders.

Some of the public sympathy that developed for Calley may be attributed to a rash of intemperate allegations that followed the revelation of the My Lai massacre. If Calley was guilty, why not also his superiors, including Westmoreland? Citing the Nuremberg and Yamashita trials of the World War II era as precedents, the chief proponent of such a concept, Telford Taylor, professor of law at Columbia University, who had been chief counsel for the prosecution at Nuremberg, pondered whether not only Westmoreland but also civilian officials in Washington should be tried for war crimes. On a television talk show promoting his book *Nuremberg and Vietnam: An American Tragedy,* he said that if the same standards had been applied to the My Lai trial that had been in the trial of General Tomoyuki Yamashita, "there would be a very strong possibility that they [myself and civilian government officials] would come to the same end as he did."†

† As reported in the New York *Times,* Jan. 9, 1971. See Telford Taylor, *Nuremberg and Vietnam: An American Tragedy* (New York: Random House, 1970).

His was an emotional outburst. Many a jurist as schooled in the law as Professor Taylor responded that the critics were ignoring two cardinal principles of the Nuremberg and Yamashita cases: intent and efforts to prevent war crimes. It was declared at Nuremberg, for example, that in order to establish a commander's criminal liability for atrocities there had to be ". . . a personal neglect amounting to wanton, immoral disregard of the actions of subordinates amounting to acquiescence."‡ In any event, while lamenting My Lai and any other war crime or felony with every fiber of my being, I am convinced that my actions in Vietnam and the efforts I made to forestall the kind of thing that happened at My Lai will stand every moral and legal test before both the bar of justice and the court of history.

During the investigations of the events at My Lai, it came out that within a few days of the action I had forwarded the 11th Infantry Brigade a commendation. It was based on the brigade's official report of 128 enemy killed at My Lai and four weapons captured. Why had such a disparity between killed and weapons failed to alert me that something untoward might have occurred?

The report on My Lai that reached my headquarters, where it was accepted in good faith, attracted no special attention for two reasons. As opposed to warfare against the enemy's big units, high body counts and low numbers of weapons collected in the war against the guerrilla in hamlet and village were not uncommon (the dead were presumed to be armed combatants, not civilians). To assure accurate reporting, I had had several reports like that investigated; the investigations revealed that guerrillas were adept at disposing of weapons in paddy or canal, and many guerrillas often were armed only with grenades and explosives. Secondly, in keeping with my desire to reward men and units for good performances, it was a practice in my headquarters either for me or my staff to select from among the volume of daily field reports those that appeared particularly noteworthy, whereupon numerous routine commendations would be prepared for my signature. Having passed up the chain of command, the reports gained added credibility from at least implicit endorsement of the intermediate headquarters: company, battalion, brigade, division, field force, and United States Army, Vietnam. We had to rely on the presumed and generally established veracity of the reports and the chain of command.

Despite excellent communications and speedy transport, no one person could know everything that happened in Vietnam nor be at the scene of every action. Any senior commander has to depend upon subordinates—especially commissioned officers—for local supervision. In naming General Koster the commander of the Americal Division I had acted not from personal knowledge of him but from the recommendation of the Army's Chief of Staff, General Johnson, and my deputy, General Abrams. I nevertheless

‡ See, for example, Waldemar A. Solf, "A Response to Telford Taylor's *Nuremberg and Vietnam: An American Tragedy*," *University of Akron Law Review*, Vol. 5, No. 1, Winter 1972.

had no reason to question Koster's ability—nor that of his subordinate commanders—to control his troops and comply with my regulations on reporting
irregularities that might be revealed following a routine survey of the battlefield, a normal duty of a field commander. Although the press on several
occasions alerted me to events warranting inquiry, not so on My Lai.

Over the years a number of other battlefield irregularities, some of which
were war crimes, were reported or alleged. The Army investigated every
case, no matter who made the allegation, with professionally qualified, non-
involved parties. Some investigations resulted in disciplinary administrative
action, some in courts-martial. Yet none of the crimes even remotely approached the magnitude and horror of My Lai, and many of the allegations,
principally those leveled by individuals testifying under the aegis of such organizations as the Vietnam Veterans Against the War and a so-called Citizens Commission of Inquiry into U. S. War Crimes in Vietnam, were
backed by no responsible evidence.

The terrible shame of My Lai and the failure of officer leadership that
was a part of it underscored my conviction that an army is the sum of the
caliber of its officer corps. Duty, honor, country—those are the watchwords.
Throughout my tenure as Chief of Staff, improving the officer corps was a
constant preoccupation: to bolster the Army's own officer education system
while at the same time taking advantage of cross-fertilization with the civilian educational environments; to create and keep open channels of communication so that curiosity, intellect, ingenuity, innovation, experimentation can find ready expression at all levels, particularly in the field; to
strengthen moral fiber so that the apparent inevitability of transgression on
the part of some may cease to be an inevitability.

In a series of command letters to the officers of the Army I stressed those
aspects of leadership that I considered to be imperative. "Absolute integrity
of an officer's word, deed, and signature," I wrote, "is a matter that permits
no compromise." If we were to achieve a modern volunteer force, we had to
produce a better Army, "one with greater pride, enhanced professionalism,
and increased capability—an organization that men of quality will want to
join and serve in for a career." The noncommissioned officer remains the
backbone of an army, and it behooves the officer to give him sufficient authority, responsibility, and counsel to assure that he does his job with pride
and ability. So too discipline remains the basic ingredient, the soul of an
army, discipline that results not from high-handedness but from "intelligent,
practical, and enlightened leadership; honest and forthright relationships
between the leaders and the led; and meaningful tasks, intelligently assigned
and successfully accomplished."

In a final command letter I stressed perhaps the most important point of
all. An officer's commission, I noted, reposes "special trust and confidence
in the patriotism, valor, fidelity, and abilities" of the officer. Old-fashioned
virtues may go out of style in a permissive society, but no army can long sur-

vive without them. The guardians of those virtues must be officers imbued with pride in the fact that they are invested with a special trust and confidence. Those who fail that trust are unfit to remain officers.

However reluctant to leave an army of which I had been a part for thirty-six years, I was fully and warmly confident in turning over my duties as Chief of Staff in mid-1972 to one as competent as Creighton W. Abrams. Aside from serving me with unusual ability as my deputy in Vietnam, Abe as my successor as COMUSMACV had executed an assignment unique in the annals of military history. While strengthening South Vietnamese forces in the trying and demanding task of Vietnamization, he at the same time broke contact with a still capable enemy and withdrew American forces. It was a signal achievement.

My only disagreements with the way Abe ran the war after my departure were what I deemed an undue preoccupation with the safety of Saigon and a lack of sensitivity to the enemy's capabilities in the two northern provinces. Where I had left defense of Saigon primarily to the South Vietnamese, he ringed it with American troops, presumably because of the high visibility even a minor incident in the capital commanded in the American press. When time came for the first American troop withdrawals in July 1969, Abe wanted the first pull-out to be the 3d Marine Division from the northern provinces, the region of South Vietnam that I considered to be the most vulnerable. After I protested to the Joint Chiefs of Staff and White House adviser Henry Kissinger, Abe reconsidered and named the 9th Infantry Division from the Mekong Delta instead.

As the time for my retirement approached, day-by-day responsibilities and decisions still had to be made, many of which would have effect well into the period for which my successor would be responsible. No retiring Chief of Staff could have had a more co-operative successor-designate. Where possible I deferred decisions, but on those that I considered pressing, I conferred with Abe, whereupon he studied and refined the programs and was ready soon after his takeover to implement, expand, and improve on them by his own innovative actions.

Although Abe came home from Saigon in June 1972, leaving Fred Weyand as the new MACV commander, there was a delay of several months before his confirmation because of election-year-inspired Senate hearings on an allegation that field commanders in Vietnam had exceeded their authority in taking the war to the enemy. The delay resulted in my Vice Chief of Staff, Bruce Palmer, acting temporarily as the Chief of Staff.

When Creighton Abrams died in September 1974, the first U. S. Army Chief of Staff to die in office, the Army and the nation lost a stalwart leader, a man of immense capability and achievement, a stellar patriot. However untimely his death, he left the Army under steadily improving conditions, for he had worked diligently to perform his demanding tasks. I salute the memory of a distinguished soldier.

Chapter XXI
The Continuing War

Soon after my return from Vietnam in the summer of 1968, I found it necessary to enter Walter Reed Army Medical Center in Washington for treatment of a recurrent intestinal upset apparently attributable to my long
months in Vietnam. Since former President Eisenhower was in an adjacent
suite, I found a number of opportunities to talk with him.

The political campaign of 1968 was in full swing with President Eisenhower pulling for his former Vice President, Richard Nixon. Knowing of the
former President's close relationship with Nixon, I took the opportunity to
tell him how important I considered the program to upgrade the South Vietnamese forces in composition and equipment so they could in time take over
the war, a program which the outgoing Administration—particularly Clark
Clifford and Paul Nitze—continued to neglect. When I reminded President
Eisenhower of my speech before the Press Club in 1967, when I had outlined a strategy involving turnover of responsibility for the war to the South
Vietnamese, he asked for a copy to pass along to Nixon.

Clifford's attitude toward Vietnam had gone beyond dovishness. He had
come back from a visit apparently convinced that the situation was hopeless, that South Vietnamese leaders wanted the war to continue merely to
insure American support for the South Vietnamese economy, that the only
recourse for the United States was to negotiate at any cost for the return of
prisoners of war and then get out. After he left the office of Secretary of
Defense in 1968, he attempted in a number of public statements to portray
himself as something of a hero in winding down the war, whereas in reality
his indecision, I am convinced, helped to prolong it.

Those meetings with President Eisenhower were destined to be among
my last. When he died in March 1969, I was privileged as Army Chief of
Staff to participate in final ceremonies in his honor, one of the nation's truly
great soldiers and statesmen.

At a reception in the White House for visiting heads of state and other
dignitaries following the funeral, it was my pleasure to make the ac-

quaintance of President Charles de Gaulle of France. Spotting his unmistakable towering figure across a crowded room, I was in the process of working my way toward him to introduce myself when I lost sight of him and he suddenly appeared at my side. He had been of the same mind. We had a brief conversation that revealed how closely he had followed the course of the war in Vietnam, for all his public criticism of the American position. He complimented me on my efforts, which hardly represented endorsement of my decisions, but neither did it suggest rejection.

My close relationship with President Johnson continued through his remaining months in office and into his retirement. I was again impressed with his thoughtfulness when he held a ceremony in the White House to award me the Distinguished Service Medal. He also attended ceremonies in the Pentagon in July 1968 when I took the oath of office as Army Chief of Staff. It was at the President's request that I prepared an official report on my years in Vietnam, published in 1969 by the Government Printing Office.

I was amused by an incident that occurred in late summer of 1968 when President Johnson, presidential candidate Richard Nixon, and I were all scheduled to speak on the same day in Detroit to the annual convention of the Veterans of Foreign Wars. Since I spoke in the morning, the President asked me to meet him when he arrived later at the airport. We were proceeding together into the city when a car carrying Nixon passed, heading for the airport. Recognizing the President's car, Nixon telephoned him on his car telephone. After an exchange of pleasantries, Nixon said he had given the veterans a "real hard line" on Vietnam. "Congratulations," President Johnson told him; he himself intended to do the same thing.

Not long after my return from Saigon, President Johnson told Kitsy that he understood that Quarters 1, the Chief of Staff's residence at Fort Myer, has a spectacular view of the federal city. When, he asked, was Kitsy going to invite him to a little family dinner?

Kitsy could hardly believe the President was serious. In any event, what did he mean by a "little family dinner?" She procrastinated until in another meeting some weeks later, the President repeated the question with obvious determination to have his way.

Kitsy finally concluded that a little family dinner might be construed to mean the President and Mrs. Johnson; their daughter Lynda (Luci was away); and because of the President's high regard for Bus Wheeler, the Chairman of the Joint Chiefs and Mrs. Wheeler. She invited them for the evening of October 8, 1968.

Delayed by business at the White House, the President was over an hour late, leaving Kitsy with considerable concern over how her dinner would fare. Yet all turned out well. The view from Quarters 1 was much as the President had pictured it, and the dinner proved to be a success, particularly when it came to a dessert that apparently was a presidential favorite: rum pie.

The President, having finished his pie, noted that General Wheeler had eaten only a few bites of his.

"Buzz?" the President whispered, getting the chairman's attention. He pronounced the nickname "Bus" as if it had to do with a bumble bee and used a tone of voice that seemed about to introduce some monumental business of state.

"Yes, Mr. President?" General Wheeler responded.

"Are you through with your pie?" the President asked.

"Yes, Mr. President."

"May I have it?"

"Yes, Mr. President."

Whereupon the President under the eaglelike gaze of Mrs. Johnson ate what remained of General Wheeler's pie.

I had returned to Walter Reed Medical Center the day after the dinner when, not quite a week later, the White House telephoned to determine if my condition would permit me to come immediately for a meeting. Because I was preparing to attend a scheduled birthday ceremony at Walter Reed for President Eisenhower, I asked if I might delay. When I reached the White House late, President Johnson was understanding and asked about President Eisenhower's health. He was always thoughtful and considerate of his predecessor.

Included in the White House meeting were Secretaries Rusk and Clifford, all the Joint Chiefs, Walt Rostow, and Senator Russell of Georgia, chairman of the Senate Armed Forces Committee. Under continuing pressure from antiwar critics, who had been joined by such close advisers as Vice President Humphrey and McGeorge Bundy, to halt all bombing of North Vietnam—the earlier halt involved only that part of North Vietnam north of the 19th parallel—the President was agonizing over the decision. A report from Averell Harriman and Cyrus Vance, the American negotiators with the North Vietnamese in Paris, made the matter imperative. In exchange for a total bombing halt, the negotiators reported, the North Vietnamese probably would agree to the South Vietnamese joining the negotiations, forego attack across the DMZ, and refrain from major attacks on cities or other major population centers of South Vietnam.

Senator Russell, the Chief of Naval Operations, Admiral Thomas H. Moorer, and I were skeptical. We were trading off an important military asset, I said, for a questionable political result. Once we stopped the bombing, the North Vietnamese might gradually erode the agreement but not so dramatically as to make it politically acceptable for the United States to resume the bombing.

A little over a fortnight later, on October 31, the President assembled another conference, including the Joint Chiefs and all members of the National Security Council. With others of the Joint Chiefs except for the chairman, General Wheeler, I was seated not at the conference table but along a wall. It was early apparent that the President was emotionally committed to stopping the bombing, although I sensed that he entertained no real expectation that the North Vietnamese would co-operate. He wanted to make a last effort before he left office to establish his niche in history as a man of peace.

One by one the President polled those at the table on stopping the bombing. The consensus of the response around the table seemed to be that if the North Vietnamese failed to co-operate, the bombing would be resumed, and nobody objected to a bombing halt. The President asked no opinion of those of us seated away from the table. Although I contemplated speaking up, so quickly was the business transacted that it was over before I could collect my thoughts.

That was a mistake, no matter that one lone objection might have carried no weight. As it turned out, Harriman and Vance had been putting words into the mouths of the North Vietnamese negotiators and deluding themselves that they heard expressions of agreement come back out. The Paris talks remained as sterile as ever while the war in Vietnam went on without change except for the added handicap for our side of unrestricted enemy movement, undeterred by bombing, throughout all of North Vietnam.

On two occasions following President Johnson's departure from office in 1969, I stayed overnight at his Texas ranch. During the first visit, I read drafts of several chapters of his memoirs; during the second I briefed him at President Nixon's request on Vietnam developments as seen from Washington. The second visit was in the fall of 1972, after I had written that I was to make a speech in Dallas and he had invited Kitsy and me to the ranch.

The former President was in a relaxed mood. We laughed about a sofa pillow embroidered with the words: "This is my ranch and I'll do as I damn please." In late afternoon, he took us on our second tour of the ranch in his big convertible. Stopping at a cottage down the road, he called out to three grinning young black boys: "Come on, boys; give the President a kiss." Each in turn planted a kiss on the President's forehead.

Continuing the drive, Johnson spotted a cow that had just dropped a calf. Using a telephone in his car, he called back to the ranch house, giving the brand number of the cow and directing that someone come out to check the birth. He had 13,000 head of cattle, he told me with pride, on 12,000 acres of land.

The President also telephoned to the kitchen for the cook to send sausage biscuits to a tenant house where he planned to stop. At the house Mrs. Johnson, the President, Kitsy, and I sat on the porch eating sausage biscuits, sipping a drink prepared by a Secret Service agent from a bar in a car that followed the President's, and waiting for the sun to set over the prairies.

"Let's have another drink," the President said after a while. "As the old Mexican says, 'It'll make us feel smart and rich.'"

The visit was a quiet, beautiful time, one that Kitsy and I will always recall with fondness. We shared memories, of what was, of what might have been. We shared a certain sadness, a certain frustration that for all our efforts we had been unable to shape events fully in the mold that we deemed was right. We also shared pride in having fallen heir to a part of history, however minor that part might turn out to be.

After dinner that evening, when conversation turned inevitably to Vietnam, Johnson remarked that early in the war he should have imposed press censorship, no matter how complex the problems that might have generated. The way it was, he said, the message of American resolve never got through to Hanoi. He spoke well of President Nixon and applauded his actions to force North Vietnamese leaders to negotiate seriously.

Excusing himself, the President left the room for a few minutes. When he returned, he noted casually that he had felt faint and had taken some medicine. He made no other reference to his health until we were alone at breakfast the next morning. He realized, he told me in confidence, that he could go at any time.

When Lyndon Johnson died only a few months later, early in 1973, Kitsy and I went to Washington to pay our respects as his body lay in state in the rotunda of the Capitol. That afternoon a telephone call from the White House informed me that, at Mrs. Johnson's request, President Nixon wanted me to represent him at the burial in Texas and place the presidential wreath on the casket. I changed my plans and accompanied Mrs. Johnson on Air Force One to Bergstrom Air Force Base in Austin. Kitsy followed in another plane, then we all went by motorcade in blizzard weather to the ranch.

The burial was a ceremony marked less by sadness than by pride. Sadness that the man at age sixty-five had died before he could savor the full joys of his retirement and his achievements, but consummate pride in the performance of one who had served his country honorably and selflessly in the Congress, in the vice presidency, in the presidency, one who had borne burdens of state as onerous as those of any who had gone before him. That pride engulfed me as I stepped forward to lay the wreath and salute the remains and the memory of Lyndon B. Johnson. My regret was that I had been caught in Washington without a uniform and was unable to render my final salute in the dress in which I had served him as my Commander in Chief.

As President Nixon came to office, new personalities and a new *modus operandi* entered into conduct of White House affairs and the war in Vietnam. For the first time all policy in connection with the war centered in a person other than the President, the President's adviser on national security affairs, the erstwhile Harvard professor whom I had known for a number of years, Henry Kissinger. No longer did initiative come from the American command in Saigon; it came from the White House and Dr. Kissinger. No more were there overly sensitive reactions to timid subordinates in the State and Defense departments, but fearless, skillful amalgamation of divergent opinions to come up with strong, definitive conclusions to present to the President. Pretending no expertise as a military tactician, Professor Kissinger was a historian and a negotiator, a diplomat with a feel for power, political strategy, and the nuances of international negotiations. As a historian, he was prone to say, he looked at events pessimistically, but as a diplomat, he had to take an optimistic view. President Nixon leaned on Dr. Kissinger not only for Vietnam policy but for all military problems, particularly the on-going strategic arms limitation talks (SALT) with the Russians.

The new Secretary of Defense, a former Wisconsin congressman, Melvin Laird, was an avowed and skilled politician. It appeared that he was under a strong mandate to make the Administration look good. When I suggested that he allow President Thieu to make the first announcement of Vietnamization—a term Laird took pride in having coined—he declined. Secretary Laird had a knack for coining words and expressions in order to give the connotation he sought, and others were amused when he chose to classify the renewed bombing of North Vietnam as "protective reaction," thereby presumably giving it a nonaggressive connotation.

When General Abrams, in keeping with the Secretary's guidance, dutifully submitted periodic withdrawal schedules, the Secretary always accelerated Abrams' proposed rate of withdrawal. He seemed obsessed with getting out of Vietnam for political reasons as soon as possible. He put such emphasis on withdrawal as to be virtually indifferent to what happened on the battlefield. The Joint Chiefs, for example, were surprised and perplexed when at a meeting with Secretary Laird on the day of North Vietnam's successful invasion of South Vietnam in 1972, he totally ignored that development and refrained from any mention or discussion of it with his military advisers.

Laird appeared to distrust the Joint Chiefs, seemingly unable to accept, as a consummate politician himself, that we were apolitical. He himself had frequent contacts with the Congress and had noteworthy success in bringing legislators around to his point of view. He operated according to a closely held "game plan," a blueprint of precise and skillfully devised political moves carried out by a small group of confidants. When Kissinger sought my views on the basis of my experience in Vietnam, the Secretary made clear his disapproval of my talking directly with Kissinger. Although the two were seldom together in my presence, Laird seemed to be concerned that Kissinger was exerting undue influence on policies of the Department of Defense.

As his principal assistant Kissinger accepted my nomination of an officer who had impressed me as a battalion commander in Vietnam, Colonel Alexander Haig, and was subsequently lavish in his praise of Haig's ability. Haig rose quickly first to one-star, then to two-star rank. When Kissinger and I spoke about Al Haig's future assignment, Kissinger agreed with me that he should in due time have an opportunity to command a division. Instead, in 1973, President Nixon summarily promoted Haig from two-star to four-star rank and designated him as Vice Chief of Staff of the Army. Since the President failed to obtain the endorsement of the then Chief of Staff, General Abrams, the appointment was awkward for Abrams, made all the more so when the White House set up a direct telephone line to the new Vice Chief. At the President's request, General Haig subsequently resigned from the Army to become the President's personal chief of staff in the White House.

I saw Haig's unprecedented promotion to four stars as a political move to make a man of rare ability and loyalty beholden to the President. By circumventing sound, well-established promotion procedures, the President did a disservice to the system and dealt a sharp blow to the morale of the Army officer corps. I am confident Al Haig would have preferred the traditional promotion route as followed by President Eisenhower in the case of his White House chief of staff, General Andrew Goodpaster.

Throughout the first Nixon administration, when I was Chief of Staff, the name of the game was re-election, with agencies encouraged to tone everything down, compromise if need be, but avoid unpleasant news. Expediency overshadowed principle. Dissident young officers intent on personal notoriety might exceed the bounds of propriety, truthfulness, even legality in writings and public proclamations, yet the Administration went to extremes to avoid confrontation. A Navy yeoman working in the White House might leak classified documents to a keyhole columnist without punishment, merely transfer. Two able men who served at separate times during that period as Secretary of the Army—Stanley Resor and Robert Froehlke—were under constant pressure to make things look good, but both staunchly resisted, Resor, in particular, with considerable success. It was distressing for me to have to watch disciplinary standards and principle set aside for public relations purposes.

Following overthrow of Prince Sihanouk in March 1970 and emergence of the Lon Nol government in Cambodia, it was Henry Kissinger who raised the possibility of at last invading Cambodia to attack North Vietnamese sanctuaries. In the absence of General Wheeler as Chairman of the Joint Chiefs of Staff and Admiral Moorer as the next senior member, I was the Acting Chairman. I recommended that the ARVN go in with American support from within South Vietnam. When Kissinger asked about using American combat troops, I said that obviously would enhance the chance of success, but I deemed it a policy decision that I was not sure the President was prepared to make.

A few days later, on May 1, when the President met with Secretary Laird and the Joint Chiefs in the Pentagon operations center, Nixon had made up his mind. He was ebullient. He was, he said again and again, going to "clean out the sanctuaries." You had to electrify people with bold decisions, he said. "Bold decisions make history," he exclaimed, "like Teddy Roosevelt charging up San Juan Hill, a small event but dramatic, and people took notice."

The President dominated the meeting, seemed to be in a hurry, and concluded abruptly. As he rose to leave, I interrupted. The President's unbridled ebullience and his obvious expectation of spectacular results required some adjustment to reality. I wanted him to be aware of the difficulties, that less than a month remained before the rainy season would limit operations of our vehicles, tanks, and planes, that with the numbers to be committed we lacked the capability to "clean out" all the sanctuaries. There was no discussion about limiting the duration of American participation in the operation; the President apparently decided that question after the invasion created an uproar among students, newsmen, and some members of Congress.

Despite all the limitations, the foray into Cambodia, which began April 30, achieved substantial results, although only part of the enemy's supply depots were destroyed. The troops failed to find the always elusive COSVN headquarters, which the President had unfortunately mentioned to the press as an objective. Although many of the enemy fled, some 10,000 were killed, quantities of supplies destroyed, and enough foodstuffs brought out to feed 25,000 men for a year. Only a permanent ARVN presence in Cambodia would prevent the Vietnamese Communists from rebuilding the sanctuaries, although reconstruction would take a long time. In the meantime, the level of combat in the provinces around Saigon and in the Mekong Delta dropped sharply. More important still, Lon Nol in Phnom Penh closed Sihanoukville to enemy supply ships.

Barring other ground forays into Cambodia, the only way to deter the enemy's rebuilding of his sanctuaries was by bombing. Having authorized bombing by B-52s beginning in the spring of 1969, the President continued the authority. The targets were the sanctuaries in the sparsely populated border region, as Prince Sihanouk had tacitly approved long before, so long as the raids were kept secret. Since Sihanouk's successor, Lon Nol, was actively fighting the Communists, there could hardly be objection to the raids continuing.

The President's policy of keeping the bombing of Cambodia a secret necessitated preparation of two files on the bombing, one as a cover naming targets within South Vietnam, the true file listing the real targets in Cambodia. Public revelation of the bombing by former airmen in 1973 caused a furor, no doubt partly because of the intimation of double-dealing in high places. Yet the targets were legitimate military objectives, as proven time after time by secondary explosions that the bombing triggered, and they were hit with at least tacit approval of the Cambodian government. I myself had assumed throughout that either the White House or the Secretary of Defense was following normal practice of keeping senior members of appropriate congressional committees informed.

With the closing of Sihanoukville to supply ships, with the bombing of supply depots, and with American and South Vietnamese naval patrols still sealing the coast, the North Vietnamese had to depend for supplies almost exclusively on the Ho Chi Minh Trail. Raiding the trail with ground troops was obviously the next step, so obvious that when it began in February of the following year (1971), the North Vietnamese were well prepared to oppose it.

Because of a prohibition on funds for American ground troops operating outside South Vietnam imposed by the United States Senate in December 1970, American ground troops were unable to participate in the operation, but the American command furnished much of the logistical, air, and long-range artillery support, primarily from a reactivated combat base at Khe Sanh. Not even American advisers were permitted to accompany ARVN units.

Despite rumors of the impending ARVN operation in Laos in the American and foreign press that may well have further alerted the North Vietnamese, the ARVN at first achieved quick gains. They penetrated as deep as twenty-five kilometers inside Laos and reached all assigned objectives, but then the North Vietnamese began intensive counterattacks. So heavy was the pressure and so intense the antiaircraft fire, in some cases denying resupply, that evacuation seemed the only recourse. Thus began that most difficult of all military operations, withdrawal in the face of strong enemy attack.

It was then that weaknesses in South Vietnamese preparations for the operation became evident. Command arrangements at the top were unsound, and the plan had been developed too quickly for adequate provision for close co-ordination between the ARVN troops and their American support. Long accustomed to working with American advisers, subordinate ARVN commanders had difficulty without them in arranging fire support and resupply. The senior American adviser and the over-all ARVN commander were functioning from different bases. Several senior ARVN commanders folded, prompting President Thieu to intervene and start issuing orders himself as far down as regiments, in many cases without General Abrams' knowledge.

Yet the ARVN soldier in general fought in Laos with tenacity and courage, and American helicopter crews and tactical airmen were superb. I was particularly touched by the intrepidity of two Americans whose actions came to my attention.

Sole survivor of the crash of a medical evacuation helicopter at an ARVN fire-support base, Specialist 5 Dennis Fujii supported the ARVN defenders for three days by directing armed helicopter and air strikes around the base, saving it from being overrun. An attempt by a fleet of helicopters to resupply the base and evacuate Specialist Fujii failed in the face of antiaircraft fire, but finally a lone helicopter made it through. As the craft lifted off with Fujii aboard, enemy machine-gun fire riddled it. Although the helicopter began to burn, the pilot managed to nurse it along to a landing at another fire-support base, also beleaguered. Pilot and crew were evacuated but Specialist Fujii again stayed behind. For two days he called in air support to help the ARVN defenders of that base. Twice wounded, he at last agreed to evacuation.

Known to ARVN troops only by a radio call sign "MUSIC 16," Captain Keith A. Brandt saved the lives of eighty-eight ARVN soldiers holding out in a bomb crater against an enemy force pressing them at little more than hand-grenade distance. Already having expended his ammunition in support of the defenders, Captain Brandt volunteered to guide a fleet of evacuation helicopters to the crater. As he made his approach, so intense was enemy fire that he had to veer off. "I've lost my hydraulics and my mast is on fire," he radioed, but with his helicopter trailing smoke, he made a second approach that led the rescue craft in. The job done, he again veered away. "I'm going to try to make the river," he radioed. The next message from MUSIC 16 was the last: "I've lost my engine and my transmission is breaking up. Goodbye. Send my love to my family. I'm dead." Yet he almost made the river. The helicopter exploded just before crashing into trees along the bank. Captain Brandt was posthumously decorated for valor.

Meanwhile, under a stream of enemy fire, the evacuation helicopters did their job. They came out heavily overloaded with many of the ARVN troops clinging to the skids. To those who knew how tenaciously the troops had fought and what peril and courage had gone into their rescue, it was bitter to see newspaper photographs with captions alleging cowardice and panic on the part of those who escaped.

In 1969 as American withdrawal picked up momentum, there were indications that the North Vietnamese were building for another all-out attempt against South Vietnam, to be launched whenever American numbers had decreased to a point where they would no longer be a factor on the ground. Although the U.S. command in Saigon assumed that if the enemy struck across the DMZ, President Nixon would authorize renewed bombing of North Vietnam, which would take care of the threat, I and others in Washington were less sanguine. I strongly urged strengthening the ARVN by creating another division for the northern provinces, and the National Security Council and the President agreed and so directed. With the help of American advisers, the South Vietnamese in time formed the 3d ARVN Division, which took position immediately south of the DMZ. Yet the action came at least a year too late, for the new division would have little time to gain experience before the North Vietnamese attacked. As I had in similar circumstances, General Abrams had insisted that the South Vietnamese first had to bring their existing units up to strength before he would provide resources for creating a new unit.

Positioning such an inexperienced division along the DMZ proved a serious miscalculation. When the North Vietnamese offensive began at the end of March 1972, following a build-up unhindered by American planes because of the bombing halt, the attack involved big Russian-supplied tanks, sophisticated antiaircraft missiles, and modern artillery, which had a predictable effect on untried troops.

Aside from the fact that the invasion struck the greenest ARVN division, the 3d, poor command arrangements made matters worse. There was no separate command over all troops north of the Hai Van Pass, as had been the case when American forces were there with, first, the Provisional Corps, Vietnam, and later, the XXIV Corps. Furthermore, the 3d Division commander, General Vu Van Giai, an experienced and brave officer, had no control over ARVN tanks and marines located in his sector. The newly formed 3d ARVN Division collapsed, opening the way to the enemy to Quang Tri City and posing a threat to Hué.

General Giai's lack of control of tanks and marines in his sector led to a fiasco at a bridge over a river along Route 1 north of Quang Tri City. Rather than fight with his back to the river, the tank battalion commander ordered his tanks to withdraw across the river. Having received separate orders to allow no one to cross the bridge, a contingent of marines refused to let the tanks pass. When the marines received orders to demolish the bridge, the tanks were left stranded and all were destroyed.

As the fight raged at Quang Tri City and, far in the south, at much-embattled An Loc where other enemy forces came across the Cambodian border, many observers were prepared to write off the South Vietnamese. The North Vietnamese had struck with all their strength in a conventional invasion that seemed destined to succeed where the Tet offensive of 1968 had failed.

Here, apparently, was the ultimate test of the long years of American effort to create viable South Vietnamese armed forces and of the decision taken by my predecessors many years before to organize regular units rather than light antiguerrilla forces. Even as the test developed, the last American battalions began to move, not to help in the fight but to complete American withdrawal.

As results of the test eventually demonstrated, the ARVN, for all of many errors in plans and execution, no longer required the assistance of American ground troops, although their success owed much to American tactical air support. Quang Tri City and much of Quang Tri province were lost, but the city itself, though in ruins, was subsequently recaptured and the threat to Hué turned back. American tanks dramatically airlifted from Japan in great U. S. Air Force C5A planes—three tanks to a plane—to replace tanks lost early in the fighting made a major contribution in the north. At An Loc the ARVN with the help of American air power held. The North Vietnamese offensive gradually ground to a halt.

In the face of clear North Vietnamese violation of whatever understanding there had been in Paris when President Johnson, on October 31, 1968, halted all bombing of North Vietnam, President Nixon resumed air and naval attacks against the North in April 1972. In the process he sanctioned the actions that should have been taken many years earlier, including B-52 strikes and mining—in effect, blockading—Haiphong Harbor.

A target that I recommended was perhaps North Vietnam's most imposing bridge, over the Ma River at Thanh Hoa, about eighty miles south of Hanoi. Ho Chi Minh himself earlier had dedicated the bridge with great fanfare, and when American bombs through the years failed to destroy it,

North Vietnamese propagandists pictured the bridge as a symbol of the country's invincibility. Ho Chi Minh having died in 1969 and new so-called "smart bombs" having become available, I saw destroying the bridge as a possible way to strike a blow at any lingering sense of invincibility that might exist in the minds of the North Vietnamese. The Joint Chiefs of Staff enthusiastically agreed. At long last the bridge that had defied destruction went down.

As I had reckoned all along, the bombing of North Vietnam failed to precipitate anything other than propaganda responses from the Soviet Union and Communist China. Yet so long as any chance of a Communist victory in South Vietnam remained, the North Vietnamese negotiators in Paris remained as obdurate as ever. With a prominent candidate for the Democratic nomination for President of the United States vowing, if elected, to overthrow the South Vietnamese Government, it was obviously in Hanoi's interest to hold out at least until the November election.

As the election neared, the fact that the polls showed that President Nixon was running substantially ahead of his Democratic rival was not lost on the North Vietnamese leaders. Their strategy apparently changed from awaiting the election to trying to get a settlement before President Nixon had a mandate for another term.

I had completed my four years as Army Chief of Staff and retired from the Army when in mid-October 1972 Dr. Kissinger announced that in secret talks outside the regular forum in Paris he and North Vietnam's chief negotiator, Le Duc Tho, were close to an agreement on a cease-fire in South Vietnam. While Kissinger was in Saigon twisting President Thieu's arm to agree with the questionable concessions made in Paris, President Nixon called me to Washington on October 20 to brief me on the development and to seek my advice.

I urged the President to delay action on the new agreement and to hold out for better terms. Although I had told him as early as two years before that the South Vietnamese were strong enough to accommodate a cease-fire, provided North Vietnamese strength in the South was not increased, I believed that continued bombing of North Vietnam and the blockading of Haiphong Harbor would in time force the North Vietnamese into meaningful concessions that might bring a genuine end to the war. The attempt by North Vietnamese negotiators at the last session in Paris to show how badly they wanted an accord by breaking into tears was nothing but a Machiavellian ploy. A few more weeks, or possibly months, would bring the concessions necessary for South Vietnam's survival. The President assured me that he was not to be pressured by the forthcoming election into premature signing of an agreement; he was confident he had the election won. Yet already the American public and the world had been led to expect an early agreement by Kissinger's announcement that peace was "at hand."

To the President I emphasized that it was vital that North Vietnamese troops be compelled to withdraw from South Vietnam. It was obvious that if they were allowed to retain the positions they had gained in their 1972 offensive, they would continue to pose an immediate threat to Hué, and their troop dispositions in the Central Highlands would outflank the entire northern two thirds of South Vietnam. Since the North Vietnamese had never publicly acknowledged presence of their troops in the South, a withdrawal agreement would have to be made in private, and safeguards against publicizing it would be difficult; but if South Vietnam was to survive, the matter had to be squarely faced. I also emphasized that we had to avoid forcing President Thieu into abject concessions that would brand him as an American puppet, cause him to lose face, and jeopardize his government. A repetition of the political instability of the early years would play into the hands of the Communists.

The presence of North Vietnamese troops in South Vietnam, I pointed out, was one of two North Vietnamese trump cards; the other was their holding American prisoners of war. Yet we too had trump cards if we would only use them: continuing the bombing, continuing our military and economic support of South Vietnam, and building up the South Vietnamese Air Force to the point that it could provide more effective support to the ARVN with tactical bombers and with transport planes for rapid movement of troops. Whatever the agreement, I assumed that American airpower would be available from outside South Vietnam to insure that the North Vietnamese abided by what they signed.

Although President Nixon told me he agreed with my expressed views, I left the White House feeling that the President was determined to reach an agreement soon, regardless of the long-range consequences for South Vietnam. In a White House briefing on the proposed agreement before I joined the President, I had been told as much. What we were really doing, it seemed, was pulling out and leaving the Vietnamese to settle their affairs between South and North. That in itself was not bad, but in doing so, we had an obligation not to leave South Vietnam at an inordinate disadvantage. The proposed inspection and policing arrangements for the agreement and a projected political accommodation between Thieu's government and the Viet Cong's Provisional Revolutionary Government were impractical, almost absurd, nothing more than a façade.

In the latter days of December 1972 and early in the new year, Dr. Kissinger achieved only a few improvements in the projected agreement, chief of which was a promise of withdrawal of all foreign troops, including North Vietnamese, from Laos and Cambodia; but he never obtained a promise of North Vietnamese withdrawal from South Vietnam. Thus a continuing eyeball-to-eyeball confrontation was inevitable. Whether the North Vietnamese would have honored an agreement to withdraw from South Vietnam is doubtful in any case; according to them, they were not even there. As amply demonstrated in their subsequent flagrant violations of other aspects of the cease-fire, they were not about to honor anything unless American bombs forced them to. The Paris agreement, which officially went into effect on January 28, 1973, thus had only two virtues: it ended the American involvement and brought the American prisoners of war home.

Whatever the sins of President Nixon in the closing months of his tenure in the White House, no one can legitimately accuse him of timidity about Vietnam. For all President Johnson's anguish over the war, he listened to too much faulty advice, and it was President Nixon who more realistically faced up to the necessity of applying concentrated force as the only thing the Communists understood.

The two Presidents had different styles. President Johnson counted the votes of his advisers before reaching a decision. President Nixon listened to his advisers but made his decisions independently, although he was prone to soften his position or back down when public clamor became great. Yet he made some hard and, in many circles, unpopular decisions concerning the Vietnam war, such as incursions into Cambodia and Laos, resuming the bombing of North Vietnam, and mining Haiphong Harbor. He made the decisions with courage and a realization that they had to be made if North Vietnam was to sanction any concessions. The alternative was to turn tail and run, leaving our hapless prisoners of war behind, and neither he nor the majority of the American people would have agreed to that. In the end the President apparently read the mood of the American people and the Congress and came to the conclusion that if he could bring the prisoners of war home, he could end the American involvement. The United States was hostage to its prisoners of war in Vietnam, possibly one of the few countries in the world that would have allowed itself to get into such a position.

No bells rang, no bands paraded, few turned out to cheer. Perhaps there could be no rejoicing after such a long, costly struggle, one that for all the sacrifice of American fighting men and for all their obvious dominance on the battlefield came to no conclusive end but kind of petered out. Yet the nation appeared to breathe a collective sigh of relief that the American role was essentially over, and there were a few heart-warming moments that did produce a kind of exultancy and seemed to pull the nation together: those touching times when at airports around the country the prisoners of war at last returned.

I liked the way columnist William S. White put it upon my return from Vietnam in the summer of 1968:

> . . . They say that in warfare there are to be no more parades. Maybe so. But in the memories of some . . . [the] unparalleled kind of heroism [exhibited in Vietnam] will pass in somber review long after the embittered nonsense of our days has become a shabby footnote to a time we shall all wish to forget.

Chapter XXII
No Substitute for Victory

As any television viewer or newspaper reader could discern, the end in South Vietnam, in April 1975, came with incredible suddenness, amid scenes of unmitigated misery and shame. Utter defeat, panic, and rout have produced similar demoralizing tableaux through the centuries; yet to those of us who had worked so long and hard to try to keep it from ending that way, who had been so markedly conscious of the deaths and wounds of thousands of Americans and the soldiers of other countries, who had so long stood in awe of the stamina of the South Vietnamese soldier and civilian under the mantle of hardship, it was depressingly sad that so much misery and shame should be a part of it. So immense had been the sacrifices made through so many long years that the South Vietnamese deserved an end—if it had to come to that—with more dignity to it.

As I have reconstructed those grim last days, primarily through talks with American and South Vietnamese officials who were there, including my former counterpart, General Cao Van Vien, head of the South Vietnamese Joint General Staff, the defeat was attributable to a variety of factors: the cease-fire agreement of 1973 that legitimatized the tactical position of the enemy, putting him in excellent position for later operations, while at the same time dictating dispersion of South Vietnamese forces; utter disregard by the North Vietnamese of the cease-fire agreement; overwhelming North Vietnamese strength in men and weapons; appalling shortages in the South Vietnamese military forces of spare parts and ammunition; a psychological malaise among the South Vietnamese born of the knowledge that American help was at an end while the enemy's suppliers persisted; a lack of detailed planning by South Vietnamese officials for that most difficult of all military operations, withdrawal in the face of a powerful enemy; the caution and indecision of President Thieu acting as his own field commander from Independence Palace; and the panic that feeds on panic.

For all the theatrical tears of North Vietnam's negotiators in Paris in 1972–73, the North Vietnamese leaders apparently never had any intention of abiding by the cease-fire agreement. The North Vietnamese were not alone in the first months in violating the agreement, for both sides were early involved in jockeying for position, but then came flagrant North Vietnamese violations: turning the old Ho Chi Minh Trail into a four-lane, all-weather supply route and building extensions deep into the Central Highlands, then pouring in more and more weapons and supplies and tens of thousands of North Vietnamese Army soldiers. It said something, too, about North Vietnamese intentions that when the Nobel Peace Prize was awarded to both Henry Kissinger and Le Duc Tho, North Vietnam's chief negotiator, Le Duc Tho turned his down.

As revealed by captured documents, Hanoi's leadership concluded in the summer of 1974, primarily on the basis of two new factors, that the time was at hand for a final major offensive to achieve victory, if not in 1975, then surely in 1976. One factor was the sharp cut by the United States Congress in aid to South Vietnam—to $700 million, half that requested by the Administration; the other was the governmental crisis in Washington occasioned by the Watergate scandal and President Nixon's resignation. Nor could they have failed to note also that the year before, the Congress had passed an amendment sponsored by Senators Case and Church to an appropriations bill prohibiting funds for any American combat action—air, sea, or ground—after August 15, 1973, without the express approval of the Congress.

As the North Vietnamese plan unfolded, the first phase was the conquest in January 1975 of Phuoc Long, a western province some forty miles north of Saigon where long years before the Viet Cong had captured a district capital and beheaded the district chief. The attack in Phuoc Long was a test to gauge American reaction.

President Thieu wisely decided not to reinforce Phuoc Long's defenders or to counterattack with his strategic reserves. The threat was not just to Phuoc Long but to the entire country, and Thieu's thirteen ARVN divisions were already thinly stretched in defense of it, their task made all the more difficult by the equipment and ammunition shortages. Furthermore, the harsh rationing of ammunition that Thieu felt impelled to institute because of the dearth of American aid remained in effect: 1 hand grenade per man per month, 85 rifle bullets per man per month, 4 rounds of 105-mm artillery ammunition per howitzer per day and 2 rounds for 155s. The defensive assignment was made still more difficult because the North Vietnamese, not being obliged to withhold anything for the defense of their own country, held the initiative, free to strike when and where they chose, only minimally deterred by a South Vietnamese Air Force hurting for spare parts and fuel for its planes and threatened by sophisticated Russian-supplied antiaircraft weapons brought into South Vietnam. The antiaircraft weapons included the most modern guided and heat-seeking missiles, including STRELA missiles that a panel of scientists under Dr. McMillan had long ago predicted to me the Russians might provide. These had begun to take a distressing toll not only of South Vietnamese planes but also of scarce trained pilots. In those circumstances Thieu had to retain his strategic reserves—the airborne and marine divisions—for some more vital objective than a remote, sparsely populated province such as Phuoc Long.

Yet the critical factor was not that Thieu opted against reacting, but that the United States did nothing. To the North Vietnamese the test case had proved its point. They obviously would have little need for further concern about American intervention.

The American failure to react was the culmination of fears that the South Vietnamese leaders had entertained from the time Henry Kissinger came to Saigon in the fall of 1972 to impel them to go along with the Paris cease-fire agreement. The prohibition on American combat action passed by the United States Congress in the summer of 1973 had underscored their fears, even though, according to General Vien, President Thieu had been promised by President Nixon in writing that in the event of a major North Vietnamese violation of the cease-fire agreement, the United States would "react vigorously." (Every member of the South Vietnamese National Security Council, Vien told me, had been provided a copy of Nixon's letter.) So too the cut in American aid funds added to trepidation, and even as combat raged in Phuoc Long province, visiting American legislators in Saigon made it clear that continuing American support was unlikely.

Late in 1974 Thieu and his senior officials had begun to face the likelihood that the South Vietnamese would be unable to hold onto everything. As developed in what General Vien called a "strategy of survival," their plan involved giving up almost all the Central Highlands and large portions of the central and northern coastal regions. In those coastal regions they would try to retain two types of enclaves, some for reasons of honor, such as the old imperial capital of Hué, and some for reasons of strategy, such as Danang, which might be used as a base for an eventual counteroffensive should the situation somehow undergo major improvement. The line of no withdrawal would extend diagonally across the country generally from Tay Ninh City near the Cambodian border northeastward to the coast at Nha Trang.

The loss of Phuoc Long province gave immediacy to the plan for withdrawal, but Thieu understandably vacillated. He was reluctant to come to a decision involving the sacrifice of so much of his country's territory and so many of its people, to face the political and psychological implications of giving up before the final fight started, to contemplate the virtual impossibility of caring for hundreds of thousands of refugees and evacuating tons of military supplies and equipment. Meanwhile, as the crisis began to develop, inadequate comprehensive planning had taken place at subordinate levels, planning that must be done in advance if an opposed withdrawal is to succeed.

The focus of the crisis appeared to be developing in the Central High-lands provinces of Kontum and Pleiku. There the extensions of the Ho Chi Minh Trail virtually encircled Kontum City and Pleiku City, helping, as it was learned later, eighteen North Vietnamese divisions to build up inside South Vietnam—some 400,000 men, four times the number that had been in the country at the time of the cease-fire—and two more North Vietnamese divisions were on the way. The North Vietnamese, intelligence indicated, were moving to cut the vital highways of the Central Highlands: Route 19 from Pleiku City to the coast, Route 14 connecting Pleiku City and Ban Me Thuot, and Route 21 from Ban Me Thuot to the coast. Considering the most immediate threat to be in Kontum and Pleiku provinces, the commander of the II Corps, General Pham Van Phu, moved two regiments to reinforce the regular garrisons, one provided by Thieu from the airborne division, the other a regiment of the 23d ARVN Division. That division's normal responsibility was defense of the town considered to be the Montagnard capital, Ban Me Thuot.

Before daylight on Monday, March 10, the commander of the 23d Division, General Phan Duy Tat, radioed from Ban Me Thuot to Saigon. The intelligence was apparently wrong, for the first strike came not in Kontum and Pleiku provinces but at the place whose defenses General Phu had weakened, Ban Me Thuot. Russian-supplied tanks, Tat reported, had surrounded his command post inside the town. Not a word of warning had there been from Montagnards manning the ring of Popular and Regional Forces outposts outside the town, the wily Montagnards apparently having decided to ride what looked to be a tide of victory for the North Vietnamese. Although Tat recognized that the North Vietnamese tanks were so close to his headquarters that air strikes against them might hit his headquarters, he was so desperate that he took that chance.

There occurred then what General Vien subsequently described to me ingenuously as the first of a series of "unfortunate incidents." Although the South Vietnamese planes knocked out several of the enemy tanks, they also knocked out the ARVN division's headquarters, killing the province chief and severing all communications to Saigon.

All resistance ceased in Ban Me Thuot on March 13. The next day President Thieu flew to Nha Trang to confer with the II Corps commander, General Phu. Sensitive to the need to keep the Montagnards on the side of the South Vietnamese, Thieu directed Phu to move the two regiments earlier sent as reinforcements in Kontum and Pleiku provinces to counterattack and retake the Montagnard capital, Ban Me Thuot. Because the North Vietnamese had by that time effectively blocked Route 14 connecting Pleiku City and Ban Me Thuot, the regiments would have to follow a seldom-used dirt road leading southeastward toward the coast at Tuy Hoa, then backtrack along Route 21 to get to Ban Me Thuot. Thieu also authorized withdrawal of all ARVN forces from the Central Highlands but only after plans for an orderly exodus were complete.

By coincidence, on that same day, I received a visit at Walter Reed Army Medical Center in Washington, where I was undergoing medical treatment, from the South Vietnamese ambassador to the United States, Tran Kim Phuong. When he told me something of the magnitude of the North Vietnamese threat and of the dire equipment and ammunition shortages faced by the South Vietnamese, I observed that if the South Vietnamese continued to try to defend their entire country, they faced the likelihood of defeat unit by unit. It would be better, I suggested, to withdraw methodically, inflicting in the process as many casualties as possible upon the enemy, eventually retiring to the vital area of Cochin China, the populous and productive Saigon and Mekong Delta regions. There the South Vietnamese might hold, husband supplies, and hope that the crisis would prompt renewed American aid. As over the next few days debacle enveloped South Vietnam, the thought crossed my mind that Ambassador Phuong might have transmitted my suggestion to President Thieu and that that had precipitated an order for withdrawal without benefit of essential and proper planning. It was with some relief that I learned later that although Phuong had passed a sleepless night considering whether to cable President Thieu my views, he had finally concluded it would be presumptuous to do so and decided against it.

It so happened that that afternoon I had an appointment at the White House with President Nixon's successor, Gerald Ford, in response to an earlier invitation from him to stop by. During the course of the meeting I expressed regret that the Congress had denied him the only means for influencing the situation in Vietnam, American bombers, but I recognized that the President would be unable to convince the Congress to remove that restriction and did not urge him to try. As fate would have it, President Ford as a member of the House of Representatives had helped shepherd the restrictive legislation through the Congress as a compromise providing a cut-off date of August 15, 1973, rather than one some time in June.

The debacle in South Vietnam began when General Phu inexplicably ordered an immediate withdrawal from Kontum and Pleiku provinces. The two reserve regiments that had arrived in the Central Highlands as reinforcements led the way, the one from the 23d Division anxious to get to Ban Me Thuot and counterattack in order to rescue the soldiers' dependents in the town. When word spread inevitably and quickly among civilians that the ARVN was abandoning the Central Highlands, the military columns were soon interspersed with tens of thousands of civilian refugees clinging to antiquated vehicles or plodding on foot with pitiful remnants of their possessions, trying by any means to make their way to safety.

The dirt road leading southeastward from Pleiku City 135 miles to the coast at Tuy Hoa wound through dense forests and cavernous defiles, and in some places bridges had been demolished or were in disrepair. Yet that was the only road still open to some 100,000 to 250,000 refugees and soldiers in a column that stretched for over 20 miles. To compound the refugees' miseries, defecting Montagnards sniped from the flanks, while North Vietnamese troops pressed against the rear of the column, pummeling the helpless masses with mortars and artillery. Then another of those "unfortunate incidents": planes of the South Vietnamese Air Force mistakenly bombed and strafed two battalions of the ARVN airborne regiment, virtually wiping them out.

Amid all the misery and confusion, the regiment of the 23d ARVN Division at last reached Route 21 and turned to the relief of Ban Me Thuot. It was too late. Twelve miles outside Ban Me Thuot the ARVN troops met civilians fleeing the conquered town. Their fervor for counterattacking to rescue their families was gone. Seeking their dependents among the refugees, the soldiers then had only one goal, to care for their wives and children.

Meanwhile, President Thieu had conferred with the commander of the I Corps Zone, the respected soldier, General Ngo Quang Truong, a man whom several American generals had told me they so respected that they would trust him to command an American division. Although the North Vietnamese were obviously massing to hit Quang Tri City and Hué in South Vietnam's two northern provinces, General Truong told Thieu he could hold Hué. While authorizing withdrawal from Quang Tri City, Thieu sent his reserves—the marine division and the rest of the airborne division—to help hold Hué and Danang and on March 20 went on national radio and television to announce that Hué was to be held at all costs.

By that time Thieu was out of touch with the local situation. A painful, fearful exodus of some 200,000 refugees from Hué down Route 1 over the Hai Van Pass toward Danang had already begun. Like the regiment of the 23d Division earlier, troops of the 1st ARVN Division—long one of South Vietnam's best—began to look not to the enemy but to the safety of their wives and children.

In the face of a collapse of authority, General Truong ordered withdrawal from Hué, possibly even as Thieu was issuing his caveat for defense of the city. Once Thieu's broadcast was over and word of Truong's decision arrived, the Premier, General Tran Thiem Khiem, ordered Truong to return to the defense of Hué with the help of the marine division, while on Thieu's order the remainder of the airborne division was to pull back for the defense of Saigon. In both cases it was too late. For the troops to buck the inexorable tide of pitiful refugees was impossible. In the process three of South Vietnam's most capable units were severely crippled: the 1st ARVN Division and the airborne and marine divisions forming the vital strategic reserves.

Danang was inevitably next, enveloped in a flood of terrified refugees and disorganized soldiers. Television viewers in the United States and elsewhere saw much of it happen. Panic, looting, indiscipline, brutality. Among the equipment losses were a score or more of planes at the Danang airfield, abandoned for lack of spare parts. It was a distressing sight, I am sure, like many another in the annals of warfare, the collapse of an army made all the more tragic by the misery and terror of desperate civilians fleeing for survival.

After Danang the defenses of one coastal city after another collapsed: Quang Ngai, Qui Nhon (where despite VC propaganda boasts, the only incident of a civilian uprising in support of the enemy developed), Tuy Hoa, Cam Ranh Bay, Phan Rang, Phan Thiet, beads on a necklace that had come unraveled. When it was over, six of South Vietnam's thirteen divisions had virtually disappeared, along with much of the Air Force and two thirds of the country. ARVN troops in the Mekong Delta and in the environs of Saigon, including those at Xuan Loc on the approaches to the important air base at Bien Hoa, might continue to fight with the same courage and determination most of the ARVN had exhibited since the days of the Tet offensive of 1968, but with the elite airborne and marine divisions rendered ineffective, the cause was virtually hopeless.

Barring major intervention by American bombers, which at that point was unrealistic to hope for, there was no alternative to surrender. Yet somehow there were those—particularly in the American press and Congress, who for so long had cried for negotiations, a "political solution"—who could still delude themselves that accommodation with the enemy was still possible. Get rid of Thieu, they demanded, then when that failed to bring any North Vietnamese response, get rid of Thieu's successor, the aging former Vice President, Tran Van Huong; but that failed to work either.

There seemed to be no end to the delusion that negotiating with the enemy was anything but surrender by degrees. The VC's Provisional Revolutionary Government long would have welcomed a "political solution" and probably still might have done so since a coalition government would eventually bring Communist control. Not so at that point the North Vietnamese. Why any concession at all when North Vietnamese military forces had already overrun almost all the country except for Saigon and the Mekong Delta, and total control was in prospect?

In the end poor Big Minh was coerced into abandoning his orchids and entrusted with the ignominy of abject surrender. I could not help wondering with sadness if Minh took with him to the ceremony the bamboo swagger stick with which his Japanese captors during World War II had knocked out his teeth, the ugly little memento that for Minh had become a symbol of what it was like for a country to lose its freedom.

There is, General Douglas MacArthur said, "no substitute for victory." For all who would face reality, the truth of those words was proven not only in South Vietnam but in all of Indochina.

The final collapse came in Cambodia on April 17, 1975, even before the end in South Vietnam. The Lon Nol government held out militarily almost until the end, but as I had discerned during my visit to Phnom Penh as Chief of Staff in 1971, there was really no hope for Cambodia. Even though President Nixon had looked upon Cambodia as an ideal example of the so-called

"Nixon Doctrine," whereby the United States would provide the means of self-defense but no troops, financial and military aid was not enough, in view of North Vietnamese support that as early as 1969 involved importing cadres of Khmer Rouge insurgents into North Vietnam for the same kind of training earlier provided VC cadres from South Vietnam. Although Prince Sihanouk had maintained a kind of perilous neutrality even as the Khmer Rouge gradually extended their areas of control and the North Vietnamese and VC used portions of the country for operations against South Vietnam, that kind of neutrality would have been short-lived even had Lon Nol and his colleagues not ousted Sihanouk. The brief incursions by American and South Vietnamese forces in 1970 did nothing to hasten Khmer Rouge successes; they would have come, unless there was major American commitment, in any case. The only real question was whether the downfall would be through a military or a political solution.

The North Vietnamese quite clearly would have preferred a less costly political solution in South Vietnam, Cambodia, and Laos, some form of negotiated or coalition government which they would in time have taken over. They achieved it only in Laos, an outgrowth of the American-sponsored Geneva Accords of 1962 that imposed a three-party coalition government of leftists, rightists, and neutralists, with no guarantees that the Communist Pathet Lao, bolstered by a continuing North Vietnamese presence within the country, would not in the end prevail.

It should be noted that when the North Vietnamese grossly violated the Geneva Accords of 1962, the United States in marked contrast to its later inaction in South Vietnam engaged in at least some reaction, with the tacit approval of the country's philosophic Premier, Prince Souvanna Phouma. Yet the reaction involved primarily CIA-sponsored covert moves that were in the long run ineffective. Although the CIA created an intrepid force of Meo tribesmen under General Vang Pao, the effort was essentially in support of a transitory force that should have been directed instead at rebuilding the Royal Laotian Army.

In 1971 I asked permission of Secretary of Defense Laird to go to Laos on invitation from the American ambassador, G. McMurtrie Godley, to survey the situation. The Secretary refused to grant me permission on the grounds that my presence in Laos might prompt speculation about increased American involvement. I was nevertheless able to meet with Ambassador Godley in Udorn, Thailand, across the Mekong River not far from the Laotian capital of Vientiane, and learned from him how perilous the situation was.

By 1971 Meo losses in the perennial fighting against the Pathet Lao and their North Vietnamese supporters on the strategic Plain of Jars in the northern part of Laos had become so heavy that widespread defections were becoming a serious problem. By early 1973 the Pathet Lao had achieved such gains that the neutralist premier Souvanna Phouma felt impelled to agree to a cease-fire (one the Pathet Lao never respected) and in 1974 to creation of a new coalition government, split equally between leftists and rightists, with minimum neutralist representation. It was only another interim step before Communist take-over.

Obviously aware of the intent of the United States Congress to abandon all of Indochina, Souvanna Phouma began more and more to give in to Communist demands. By March 1975 many rightist generals and politicians were fleeing the country, and with the fall of Cambodia and South Vietnam it was only a question of time before Laos too went Communist. Just when the final step took place is still fuzzy, but it was nevertheless by any definition a total Communist victory and an end to freedom in Laos. There was nothing left to show for a long and costly American effort.

No substitute for victory? A lack of determination to stay the course, to react with meaningful moves to the enemy's flagrant violations of solemn international agreements demonstrated in Cambodia, South Vietnam, and Laos that the alternative to victory is defeat.

Ignoring the restrictions that the United States imposed upon itself in conducting the war in Indochina, some observers have seen in the outcome some special military genius on the side of North Vietnam. They have in large measure attributed that alleged genius to my apparent counterpart, Vo Nguyen Giap.

In reality, General Giap was hardly my counterpart, for my position was never so exalted as Giap's. While he was apparently an influential member of his country's government, I was a field commander restricted to decisions and actions within the boundaries of South Vietnam, subject to the dictates of my country's government, and influential in policy matters only to the extent that Washington chose to act on my recommendations. Yet since Giap was for long his own field commander, there was enough direct confrontation between the two of us to enable me to some degree to analyze and judge his military performance.

A revolutionary comrade of Ho Chi Minh, Giap went into exile during the Japanese occupation of Indochina during World War II and studied at a Communist military school in China, where he apparently absorbed the teachings of Sun Tzu and of the pedagogue of modern revolutionary warfare, Mao Tse-tung. In Vietnam Giap organized an effective guerrilla army among mountain tribal groups, which served as a nucleus for the military forces of the Viet Minh and later the North Vietnamese Army. He was prominent in the Viet Minh's seizure of power and served from the first in Ho Chi Minh's government.

As revealed in speeches, writings, and deeds, Giap is a dedicated exponent of small-unit revolutionary warfare—guerrilla warfare—yet he also espouses what is considered the third stage of revolutionary warfare: attacks by big units. Giap moved too quickly into the big unit stage against the French and incurred a number of severe defeats before his eventual triumph at Dien Bien Phu. While acknowledging the courage and indefatiga-

ble stamina of the Viet Minh at Dien Bien Phu, one should also note that
the French defeat owed much to the blunder of French leaders in accepting
battle in a remote region where they had virtually no air support or resupply
capability. Time tends to obscure the fact that a tactical defeat for the
French was turned into strategic victory for the Viet Minh not so much by
what happened on the battlefield as by a lack of support in Paris for a seemingly interminable colonial war.

In the renewed war in South Vietnam beginning in the late 1950s, the
considerable success that Giap and the Viet Cong enjoyed was cut short by
the introduction of American troops. In the face of American airpower,
helicopter mobility, and fire support, there was no way Giap could win on
the battlefield.

Given the restrictions they had imposed on themselves, neither was there
much chance that the Americans and South Vietnamese could win a conventional victory; but so long as American troops were involved, Giap could
point to few battlefield successes more spectacular or meaningful than the
occasional overrunning of a remote fire-support base. Yet Giap persisted
nevertheless in a big-unit war in which his losses were appalling, as evidenced by his admission to the Italian journalist Oriana Fallaci that he had
by early 1969 lost half a million men killed. Ruthless disregard for losses is
seldom seen as military genius. A Western commander absorbing losses on
the scale of Giap's would hardly have lasted in command more than a few
weeks.

Deluding himself that American losses far exceeded those reported, Giap
further deluded himself by anticipating an uprising by the South Vietnamese
people during the Tet offensive of 1968. Military disaster for him followed.
He also deluded himself at Khe Sanh and erred in promoting battle in a
remote region away from the civilian population, which gave American
firepower free rein. His casualties at Khe Sanh were far in excess of those incurred by the French at Dien Bien Phu.

Giap's big conventional invasion across the DMZ at Easter 1972 was also
a major defeat. After early gains that surprise always insures, Giap retained
in the end only a portion of Quang Tri province and some remote border
regions, again at heavy cost in lives: in the entire campaign, possibly as
many as 100,000 dead.

General Giap insisted throughout that the North Vietnamese would win
because America's will to win would falter. In retrospect, one can discern
that the withdrawal of American troops that began in July 1969 was to Giap
a precursor of faltering American will, although it was not intended to be.
In keeping with the American objective of holding the line until South Vietnamese forces could develop to the point where they had a reasonable
chance of defending themselves, eventual total American troop withdrawal
was inevitable. This was executed in an orderly manner by August 1972.

Not long after that, following seven and a half years of controversial war,
cracks developed in American will. Forced in January 1973 by American

pressure to accept a cease-fire agreement that left well over 100,000 North Vietnamese troops inside South Vietnam and free access for tens of thousands more, South Vietnamese leaders surely had reason to believe that if their enemy seriously violated the agreement, the United States would intervene. Yet that was not to be.

In the face of that grave psychological blow for the South Vietnamese, it required no military genius to assure South Vietnam's eventual military defeat. Virtually unmolested by South Vietnam's crippled air force, Giap and his new field commander, General Van Tien Dung, were free to concentrate their twenty divisions against South Vietnam's overextended thirteen divisions. By concentrating in the Central Highlands—which Giap in his writings had long before noted was the key to solving "the problem of South Vietnam"—the North Vietnamese easily outflanked much of South Vietnam's territory and military forces. In that event, collapse of the defenders, even had they been much more experienced and possessed of much better leadership than had the South Vietnamese, was predictable.

Ironically, the North Vietnamese victory could have come much sooner. In view of the increasing commitment of American troops in the mid- and late 1960s, General Giap would have been well advised to abandon the big-unit war, pull in his horns to take away the visible threat to South Vietnam's survival, and thereby delude the Americans that they already had achieved their goal of making the South Vietnamese self-sufficient. President Johnson had given Giap that chance at the Manila conference of 1966 when he had announced that once "the level of violence subsides," American and other foreign troops would withdraw within six months. That would have been eight years before the eventual South Vietnamese defeat, long before the South Vietnamese armed forces would have had any claim to self-sufficiency.

Making that offer at the Manila conference may well have been an effort by President Johnson to rid himself of the albatross of South Vietnam, whatever the long-range consequences. For once the United States had pulled out under those circumstances and Giap had come back, what American President would have dared risk the political pitfalls involved in putting American troops back in?

Chapter XXIII
A Look Back

Anybody paying even perfunctory attention to provisos of the 1973 Paris cease-fire agreement, including the American who negotiated it under pressure for disengagement and return of American prisoners of war, Henry Kissinger, should have been able to discern the disadvantage to which we had condemned the South Vietnamese. Thus in noting that I was seriously perturbed over the agreement both while negotiations were in progress and after the agreement was signed, I make no claim to any particular clairvoyance.

In the fall of 1972 while negotiations for a cease-fire were underway, I prepared an article at the request of the editors of the New York *Times* in which I discussed the possibilities of a settlement in South Vietnam. After consulting with Henry Kissinger's office lest my remarks create some problem in Paris, I withheld the article from publication; but in view of the final denouement in Vietnam, I find some of my observations of interest.

"In my opinion," I wrote, "an early peace in Indochina is an illusion. And I also believe that a viable cease-fire is not a realistic prospect. . . ." It was hardly surprising, I noted, that the North Vietnamese would call for a cease-fire after having achieved advantages in their big 1972 offensive. Unless forced by the agreement to withdraw, they would gain at least de facto sovereignty over those portions of South Vietnam they had captured and would probably move their troops into those remote regions of South Vietnam, particularly in the Central Highlands, not then occupied by either side. That is what subsequently happened, in effect enabling the North Vietnamese to outflank almost the entire northern two thirds of South Vietnam.

I went on to insist, as I had in my talk with President Nixon in October, that it was vital to achieve withdrawal of all North Vietnamese troops from South Vietnam. If we would continue the bombing of North Vietnam and maintain mines in Haiphong Harbor, which had promoted the first meaningful discussions by the North Vietnamese, I believed we could obtain their withdrawal and attain our objective of assuring the South Vietnamese a reasonable chance for survival.

Upon first public announcement early in 1973 that a cease-fire had been signed, I reiterated some of those views to a reporter for the Charleston, South Carolina, *News & Courier* but asked that the interview not be made available to the national wire services lest my remarks in some way hinder public acceptance of the cease-fire. I seriously doubted, I said, that the North Vietnamese would halt their efforts to conquer the South. "I just hope," I remarked, "we don't in any way tie the hands of the South Vietnamese so they are prohibited from taking appropriate action to provide for the security of the people of South Vietnam."

In my view the United States had signed a solemn international agreement involving the fate of another country and in so doing had incurred a clear moral obligation to insure that the agreement was enforced. Under accepted practices of international law, when one side violates a treaty, the other is no longer bound by it and can take punitive action, including a renewal of hostilities. That was no doubt behind President Nixon's pledge that if North Vietnam violated the agreement, the United States would "react vigorously," which obviously meant with American bombs.

Yet when the need arose, that instrument had been put out of reach by the impotence that the Watergate scandal imposed on government in Washington and by the action of the United States Congress in 1973 in forbidding the funding of any American combat action without congressional approval. President Ford made no effort to obtain congressional approval for new combat action, nor did any of twelve nations other than the United States and South Vietnam that had comprised the international conference at Paris to guarantee the cease-fire agreement even bother to speak out against the North Vietnamese violations.*

Despite the long years of support and vast expenditure of lives and funds, the United States in the end abandoned South Vietnam. There is no other true way to put it. We not only failed to react to the gross violations by the North Vietnamese of a solemn international agreement; we also failed to match the material support that the big Communist powers provided the North Vietnamese. We failed even to replace all expended South Vietnamese arms and equipment, as we were entitled to do by terms of the cease-fire agreement; and it was clear, as South Vietnam began to collapse, that the United States Congress was about to eliminate all assistance.

Presumably reflecting the attitude of a majority of the American people,

* Communist China, France, the Soviet Union, Great Britain, the four members of the International Control Commission—Canada, Hungary, Indonesia, and Poland—and the four signatories of the agreement—North Vietnam, South Vietnam, the Provisional Revolutionary Government of South Vietnam, and the United States. By terms of the conference, the United States, North Vietnam, or any six signatories could reconvene the conference to deal with violations, but the United States apparently saw insufficient support among other signatories to justify a call to reconvene.

the Congress was tired of the Vietnam struggle. "Additional aid means more killing, more fighting," the press quoted Senator Mike Mansfield as saying. "This has got to stop sometime."

The killing could have stopped before it began, back in the late 1950s, had the South Vietnamese people and their leaders been willing to forsake freedom, to knuckle under to totalitarianism. The killing continued primarily because the North Vietnamese continued their aggression but also because millions of South Vietnamese preferred the possibility of dying to succumbing to Communism. Dating from the days of the Geneva Accords of 1954, the refugees had always flowed south, not north, and even those Americans who long maintained that the refugees were not fleeing the enemy but American shelling and bombing would have to admit that even after American shelling and bombing stopped, the flow was still always southward. So it was until the final deplorable end.

How could anyone genuinely believe that the South Vietnamese people had no desire to forestall the march of totalitarianism, to maintain their freedom—however imperfect—when for years upon years they bore incredible hardships and their soldiers fought with courage and determination to do just that? They carried on the fight under a government that many Americans labeled unrepresentative, repressive, and corrupt. No people could have pursued such a grim defensive fight for so long without a deep underlying yearning for freedom.

But as Sun Tzu put it, "There has never been a protracted war from which a country has benefited." Recall, too, the words of the Duke of Wellington to the House of Lords: "A great country cannot wage a little war." I myself had summed it up at the Honolulu conference of February 1966: "There comes a time in every battle—in every war—when both sides become discouraged by the seemingly endless requirement for more effort, more resources, and more faith. At this point the side which presses on with renewed vigor is the one to win."

The American people were tired of a war that had gone on for more than seventeen years, one in which their sons had been directly involved in a combat role for over seven years, one in which the vital security of the United States was not and possibly could not be clearly demonstrated and understood. Yet it need not have been that way.

Between 1963 and 1965, for example, when political chaos gripped South Vietnam and the lack of cohesiveness in the nation's heterogeneous society became clearly evident, the United States could have severed its commitment with justification and honor, though not without strong political reaction at home. Had not President Kennedy pledged the nation to bear any burden, meet any hardship, support any friend, and oppose any foe to assure the survival and the success of liberty? Indeed, Vietnam may have served a purpose for John F. Kennedy. Following his disastrous meeting with Khrushchev in Vienna in 1961, Kennedy allegedly told James Reston of the New York *Times:* "Now we have a problem in making our power credible, and Vietnam looks like the place." †

Even after introduction of American combat troops into South Vietnam in 1965, the war still might have been ended within a few years, except for the ill-considered policy of graduated response against North Vietnam. Bomb a little bit, stop it a while to give the enemy a chance to cry uncle, then bomb a little bit more but never enough to really hurt. That was no way to win.

Yet even with the handicap of graduated response, the war still could have been brought to a favorable end following defeat of the enemy's Tet offensive in 1968. The United States had in South Vietnam at that time the finest military force—though not the largest—ever assembled. Had President Johnson changed our strategy and taken advantage of the enemy's weakness to enable me to carry out the operations we had planned over the preceding two years in Laos and Cambodia and north of the DMZ, along with intensified bombing and the mining of Haiphong Harbor, the North Vietnamese doubtlessly would have broken. But that was not to be. Press and television had created an aura not of victory but of defeat, which, coupled with the vocal antiwar elements, profoundly influenced timid officials in Washington. It was like two boxers in a ring, one having the other on the ropes, close to a knock-out, when the apparent winner's second inexplicably throws in the towel.

Aside from making the grave error of graduated response, failing to exploit the enemy's defeat in the Tet offensive, and abandoning South Vietnam in the end, the United States made other serious strategic mistakes in Vietnam and Southeast Asia: waiting so long to make incursions into Laos and Cambodia and even when eventually doing so, reducing their effectiveness by restrictions; failing to demonstrate to the North Vietnamese that they were vulnerable just north of the DMZ; delaying so long in setting up a viable pacification organization in South Vietnam; going so slowly in re-equipping the ARVN, particularly with M-16s; failing to provide an international force along the DMZ; stopping the bombing of the enemy and thus facilitating the North Vietnamese build-up for the conventional invasion of 1972; failing to assure a strong ARVN chain of command in the northern provinces in anticipation of the 1972 offensive; not a strategic error in the usual sense but nonetheless of strategic impact, the policy of blanket educational draft deferments that created a working man's war and contributed to dissent at home.

Many of the errors could be traced to strong control of the conduct of the war from Washington, a policy born jointly of the failure of the Bay of Pigs invasion of Cuba in 1961, which demonstrated the perils of decentralization, and of the successful outcome of the Cuban missile crisis in 1962,

† As quoted by Neil Gillett, *Melbourne Australian Herald,* April 30, 1975.

which seemed to indicate that command from the White House was the only way to handle crisis and war in the nuclear age. Yet never was there created a central organization in Washington capable of exercising the necessary control; in the final analysis only the President could make a decision and then only after having listened to a host of sometimes conflicting voices.

Creating a unified command for all of Southeast Asia would have gone a long way toward mitigating the unprecedented centralization of authority in Washington and the preoccupation with minutiae at the Washington level. A unified commander provided with broad policy guidance and a political adviser would have obviated the bureaucratic wrangles that raged in Washington and resulted in military decisions strongly influenced by civilian officials who, however well-intentioned, lacked military expertise either from experience or study. Instead of five "commanders"—CINCPAC, COMUSMACV, and the American ambassadors to Thailand, Laos, and South Vietnam—there would have been one man directly answerable to the President on everything. Although that kind of organization might have created ripples within the service-conscious Joint Chiefs of Staff, the Joint Chiefs traditionally fall in line when the Commander in Chief speaks. Such an arrangement would have eliminated the problem of co-ordination between the air and ground wars that was inevitable with CINCPAC managing one, MACV the other.

Influencing many of the major decisions was an almost paranoid fear of nuclear confrontation with the Soviet Union and a corresponding anxiety over active participation by Chinese Communist troops. On those matters the President's advisers took undue council of their fears, for much of the time the Chinese Communists were heavily involved in their own internal problems—including the machinations of the "Red Guards"—and later the two Communist countries were preoccupied with friction along their common border, where the Soviet Union massed a threatening number of troops. Nor could the policy makers in the Departments of State and Defense conceive of the toughness and pertinacity of the North Vietnamese Communists. Surely they would back down in the face of threat or token commitment of forces by the world's greatest power; had not even the Russians backed down over Berlin and Cuba?

President Johnson's policy of guns *and* butter—pursuit of the "Great Society"—also exerted a strong influence. It further limited the President's strategic options, and it virtually foreordained the kind of long war that democracies are ill-prepared to sustain. When the President and his Administration failed to level with the American people about the extent and nature of the sacrifice that had to be made, they contributed to a credibility gap that grew into an unbridgeable chasm. A low-key approach means that some make sacrifices while most do not, and even those who make no sacrifice dislike it because their consciences trouble them. If a war is deemed worthy of the dedication and sacrifice of the military services, it is also worthy of the commitment of the entire population.

So too President Johnson erred in relying on the Gulf of Tonkin resolution as his authority from the Congress to do what he deemed necessary in Southeast Asia. When dissent developed in 1966 and 1967, he would have been well advised to have gone back to the Congress for reaffirmation of the commitment to South Vietnam, a vote either of confidence or rejection after the manner of the parliamentary system practiced in Great Britain and elsewhere. Given the American system of congressional elections every two years, a long undeclared war was bound to become a political issue. President Johnson with his normally keen appreciation for politics should have anticipated that and should have forced the Congress to face its constitutional responsibility for waging war.

By failing to level with the people and failing to impel the Congress to commit itself, the President allowed public opinion to become a leaden liability. Unlike Kennedy, Johnson did not have the background or style to carry public opinion with him, and he became a prisoner of it. If he declined to negotiate, when he well knew that the Communists entertained no idea of genuine negotiations except on their own terms, he appeared to many Americans to want the war to continue, however absurd that assumption might be. In the face of strident cries from the press, carping by legislators, and wild displays by demonstrators, he stopped the bombing when he knew that that would do nothing to stop the war but probably would prolong it. A most sensitive and conscientious statesman, President Johnson no doubt did his best; it was perhaps a situation beyond the mastery of any man.

In efforts to allay public outcry, authorities in Washington frequently made known to the world, including the enemy, through off-the-record press sessions or leaks to favorites in the media, what we were, or were not, going to do militarily; and some newsmen deemed any secret fair game for revelation. Both practices tended to deny us the advantages of flexibility, surprise, and strategic deception. They also provided the enemy critical response time and must on many an occasion have afforded him hope when otherwise his morale might have flagged.

How wrong were those who championed allegedly simple solutions. Get rid of Ngo Dinh Diem, some of these cried; yet that opened a Pandora's box of political turmoil seriously deterring effective prosecution of the war and leading directly to the necessity of introducing American troops if South Vietnam was not to fall. There were those who persisted in the belief that North Vietnamese leaders would negotiate seriously even though the United States removed all incentive for them to do so. That kind of reliance on stop-and-go actions, some kind of legerdemain, ran contrary to history, contrary to all logic. As one looks back, how empty those cries for negotiations. Yet up to the ignominious end there were still voices calling for negotiations, as if negotiations meant anything more than eventual surrender. If only the Americans would try harder to negotiate, make more concessions! It was a kind of music Hanoi obviously liked to listen to.

How short the memory of those who will not remember. As demonstrated clearly in Korea, coming to the conference table has no connection in Communist minds with ending the killing. For slightly over two years in Korea the Communists talked and fought at the same time. During that time more than two thirds of the 33,629 Americans who died in the war were killed. The record in South Vietnam turned out to be little different. Before President Johnson's partial bombing halt at the end of March 1968, which precipitated the start of negotiations in Paris, approximately 21,000 Americans had been killed in Vietnam. During the four and a half years while the Communists talked but still fought, 25,000 more men were killed, more than 50 per cent of the total of about 46,000 Americans killed in battle during the course of the war.

When President Nixon resumed the bombing and mined Haiphong Harbor in the spring of 1972, he was, to many a vocal critic, inviting the broader war with the Soviet Union and China that pundits had long predicted but which had never come. Yet by that time President Nixon had effected his rapprochements with those Communist nations, and their intervention again failed to develop. The critics still complained, for the President, they protested, was engaging in "saturation" and "terror" bombing. Yet by the casualty figures released by the North Vietnamese themselves—no strangers to exaggerations—the bombing represented the ultimate in precision against military targets.

Among those deploring the bombing was the previous Secretary of Defense, Clark Clifford. Writing in July 1972, he saw it as "a policy which assures continuation of the war." Yet the kind of bombing that should have been started as soon as a strong military and political base had been established in South Vietnam did in fact induce the Communists to make concessions that were considerably less attractive to them than those they had striven for at enormous cost for some seventeen years, and it did enable the United States to ransom its prisoners of war, even though in the end the Communists reneged on all else they had signed.

When the going got rough, many American officials sought refuge in simplistic solutions that made the going harder still, and yet they boasted that they had turned the President around. Those officials were no doubt honestly striving to do what they considered to be best. I can nevertheless lament seeing them extolled as having been right, when events quite clearly proved them wrong. I can also hope that in the future the nation's elected officials will recognize that if war is indeed too complex to be left to the generals, it is also too complex to be entrusted to appointed officials who lack military experience, a knowledge of military history, and an ability to persevere in the face of temporary adversity and vocal ferment.

I can make no such accommodation for those who burned draft cards and their country's flag, besieged the Pentagon, paraded the enemy's flag in the streets, encouraged others to break the law, fled their responsibility, and in general went beyond the bounds of reasonable debate and fair dissension.

None should escape the reality that his or her actions helped prolong the war.

Why should the enemy desist or even make concessions when Americans were falling over themselves to register their discontent and display how many concessions they themselves were prepared to make at whatever cost? A public pressure for alternatives that gave the impression that the United States alone stood in the way of peace was hardly to be read by the North Vietnamese other than as a sign of weakness, a lack of resolve. If nothing else, the dissenting voices of officials and legislators and the shouting in the streets provided a basis for North Vietnamese propaganda and distasteful grist to be fed helpless American prisoners of war. An American film personality visiting the enemy's capital, numbers of repatriated prisoners of war told me later, might be written off, but what about a former Attorney General of the United States?

The apparent climax to what William S. White called the "embittered nonsense of our days" came at the annual awards ceremony of the Motion Picture Academy of Arts and Sciences in 1975 when one of two gentlemen honored for a purported documentary on Vietnam called *Hearts and Minds* read a telegram from a North Vietnamese negotiator in Paris expressing gratitude to those Americans who had contributed to Communist success in "liberating" South Vietnam. It was absurd that the film was honored in the first place, for it was no documentary but pure propaganda. My own filmed remarks, for example, on the Oriental's value of life were used completely out of context, juxtaposed on scenes of Orientals wailing for their dead. Yet the greatest absurdity was that, in view of American sacrifices, an American would choose to go before a nationwide television audience to extol an enemy's victory and the collapse of an allied state to totalitarianism.

In view of the restrictions in numbers and combat policy imposed by Washington, the American military services can take pride in their accomplishments in Vietnam and assurance in the knowledge that it was not they that lost the war. Yet there are things the military could have done more effectively and others that with greater foresight might have been accomplished earlier.

Although the U. S. Army had anticipated guerrilla warfare and had organized a special warfare center at Fort Bragg to concentrate on studying and training for counterinsurgency warfare, the Army failed to pay sufficient attention to a combination of guerrillas, local forces, and invading regular troops. Similarly, the United States Government as a whole failed to anticipate the critical importance of economic and political factors. As events developed in South Vietnam, it took considerably more than Green Berets to deal with these.

Some of the myriad problems involved in fighting in an alien insurgency environment were anticipated. Most, though, had to be studied and adapted to on the scene: intelligence gathering in such an atmosphere; more expeditious techniques to control artillery fire; special applications of the Geneva Conventions; inflationary pressures on the local economy; language, unique customs, and mores of an unfamiliar population; jurisdiction over American civilians in the combat zone; command implications of troops of other nations; advisory relationships with the South Vietnamese. The U. S. Army in the future must encourage its officers to engage in more intellectual exercises, to analyze the lessons learned in Vietnam, and to anticipate future problems in all types of possible environments.

Tanks, for example, were far more useful than I had anticipated. (We brought in an armored unit only in September 1966, over a year after the first ground troops landed.) In early 1967 Major General Arthur L. West, Jr., and a team of officers and noncommissioned officers spent three months in Vietnam evaluating for me the operations of tanks and armored vehicles. I wanted to insure that we were using this expensive equipment most efficiently and to be prepared to handle the expected mass introduction by the enemy of hand-held antitank weapons—the PRG-2 and PRG-7 —being provided by the Russians. I also wanted an evaluation of the desirability of increasing the amount of armor in South Vietnam. The results of the study did prompt me to ask for more armor and mechanized units in my future troop requests.

Less parochial views relative to service roles and missions would have expedited development of the helicopter gunship, appreciable numbers of which were not available until 1969. More troops should have been trained earlier in long-range reconnaissance. Inadequate apparatus for locating enemy mortars, artillery, and long-range rockets made it necessary to turn to battlefield improvisation. The U. S. Navy might have earlier anticipated the requirements of riverine warfare. The U. S. Air Force might have foreseen the need for C-47 and C-130 gunships equipped with target-acquisition sensors. For long the accuracy of bomb delivery by tactical aircraft was little advanced over World War II, a serious deficiency in planning and weapons systems development. The U. S. Marine Corps should have altered its training and been prepared to modify its unit organizations in the likelihood of having to operate in a nonamphibious environment and participate in prolonged offensive and defensive operations.

Having observed many problems in the hurried logistical build-up in Vietnam, I as Chief of Staff encouraged a detailed study by a Joint Logistics Review Board, chaired by General Frank Besson, then commander of the Army Logistics Command. Under the so-called PUSH system in effect during the war, much of the material sent to Vietnam was not needed or even usable in that climate and in the type of war fought there. The findings of General Besson and his colleagues resulted in widespread changes in this vital aspect of warfare.

The lack of a unified command for all of Southeast Asia posed particular problems in the vital field of intelligence, for a proliferation of agencies was involved: MACV, the CIA, the Defense Intelligence Agency, the Army

Communications Agency, CINCPAC, the military intelligence services in Washington, and the component headquarters in Hawaii, plus the South Vietnamese Intelligence Service. Correlating those multiple agencies and coming to agreement on estimates was complicated and time-consuming, and, as the adage has it, when something is everybody's business, it is nobody's business.

That is not to say that I attach any validity to postwar claims by a former CIA intelligence analyst, who achieved considerable exposure in press and Congress with allegations that MACV consistently ignored his estimates, thus vastly underrating enemy strength and contributing to American losses in the Tet offensive. He claimed that while MACV estimated enemy strength at 300,000, actual strength was 600,000. Neither the man's own organization, the CIA, nor MACV could accept that figure. He was obviously including VC sympathizers and self-defense forces, including women and old men, who could in no sense be considered combat troops. We did not include those people in figuring the government strength; why include them for the enemy?

Nor was there any attempt at cover-up of true enemy strength as the same man has charged, to try to show the American people and the Congress that we were winning the war. The fact that the enemy committed only about 85,000 troops in the all-out effort of the Tet offensive would indicate that even MACV's figure might have been inflated and certainly does nothing to substantiate a figure of 600,000 or the wild allegation that using the lower figure contributed to American losses at Tet. That on some occasions Navy Secretary Paul Nitze and others could infer that we were overestimating the enemy in order to get more American troops while on other occasions critics could claim we were underestimating the enemy to make it look like we were winning would seem to indicate that in large measure the criticisms were self-serving.

Intelligence on enemy activities in Cambodia and on preparations within North Vietnam was especially difficult to come by, both because my headquarters was ill-equipped to deal with either locality under existing command arrangements and because other agencies had a tendency to assume somebody else was doing the job. The problem might have been handled by other than a unified command had each of the intelligence agencies been assigned as a "lead agency" on some particular aspect of intelligence, whereupon all other agencies would have assisted the lead agency in that particular field while in turn receiving assistance from other agencies in that aspect for which they served as lead agency.

The fact that the North Vietnamese incarcerated American civilian prisoners of war with American military prisoners raised an unusual question. In issues on which one man must serve as spokesman for the group, who is the senior—a Foreign Service Officer Grade 3 of the Department of State, a GS-12 employee of the CIA, or an Army lieutenant colonel? The three ranks are roughly equivalent. The fact was that, unlike the military, the civilians were not subject to the Code of Conduct for prisoners of war. Should not civilians who serve in a combat zone be subject to the same regulations as the man in uniform? It was disturbing also that as part of the Nixon administration's preoccupation with keeping anything controversial out of the newspapers, civilian officials bowed before emotional public opinion and dealt leniently with those who violated the Code of Conduct. If the Code of Conduct is to have validity, it must be enforced. If in view of Communist torture and brain-washing techniques the Code is too demanding, even though it is based on prisoner experience in the Korean War, then it should be revised. Any meaningful regulation should be realistic and enforceable.

It may be that I erred in Vietnam in insisting on a one-year tour of duty for other than general officers as well as enlisted men. Mainly regulars, the officers were so few in number that many had to go back for second, third, and even fourth tours, so that the disruption of family life or the threat of it was omnipresent. Two-year tours for all officers, including general officers, with a short home leave at the end of the first year would have reduced the disruption, but such apparent discrimination against officers might have added to the difficulty of procuring junior officers through officer candidate school and the ROTC. Perhaps an eighteen-month tour for all officers, as was always the case for general officers, might have been a workable compromise.

In my press conferences and public appearances both during my service in Vietnam and after my return, I recognized that it was not the job of the military to defend American commitment and policy. Yet it was difficult to differentiate between pursuit of a military task and such related matters as public and congressional support and the morale of the fighting man, who must be convinced that he is risking death for a worthy cause. The military thus was caught in between, and I myself as the man perhaps most on the spot may have veered too far in the direction of supporting in public the government's policy, an instinct born of devotion to an assigned task even more than to a cause and of a loyalty to the President as Commander in Chief. That is an ingrained tradition in the professional military man, and it can hardly be said that I gave more support to a Republican President than to a Democratic President, or vice versa. Sensitive to the necessity of troop orientation on the why, what, and how of an assigned mission, I felt impelled to give support in public to a national policy that I essentially believed in.

There were nevertheless times and circumstances when I declined to participate in what I discerned to be tendentious debate. When I was the United States Army Chief of Staff, for example, I received an invitation from an old friend of Kitsy's from her days as a student at Cornell University, the Reverend Robert Smith, to speak on Vietnam from his pulpit in an Episcopal church in Wilmington, Delaware. I was to be followed, I learned, by Dr. Benjamin Spock, baby doctor turned anti-Vietnam war activist, and the two of us later were to debate in the parish house. I considered such a confrontation inappropriate to the office of the Chief of Staff of the United States Army and respectfully declined.

Viewing the conduct and achievements of the military services in Vietnam in an over-all context, the record, for all the necessity of a long learning curve, was remarkable: the mammoth logistical build-up; various tactical expedients and innovations; the advisory effort; civic action programs; but perhaps most impressive of all, the accomplishment for the first time in military history of a true airmobility on the battlefield. The military man of the future will perforce truly think, live, and fight in the three dimensions of ground, sea, and air.

In the process he will be aided immeasurably in achieving the goal of better security with less expenditure of manpower—and thus economy of force —by the electronic sensor. Soldiers of the future may look back on the sensor employed in Vietnam as rudimentary and embryonic—much like the tank in World War I—but it was nevertheless sophisticated and useful enough to demonstrate a vast, even revolutionary potential. As Chief of Staff, I set up a program at Fort Hood, Texas, called STANO (*s*urveillance, *t*arget *a*cquisition, and *n*ight *o*bservation) to study new sensor equipment and integrate it into a system for battlefield exploitation of the new devices.

Another consideration for the future is the new accuracy of strategic bombers in a tactical role. The B-52s with their immense precision developed into the most lethal weapon employed in Vietnam, yet there were problems that were only gradually resolved. As the memory of those who did the job in Vietnam fades, the Army and the Air Force must work closely together to maintain and refine the techniques.

One of the least recognized accomplishments in Vietnam was in battlefield conservation, an element of the unglamorous yet vital field of logistics. So expensive has the hardware of war become that battlefield conservation is an essential element of battle, making economy of supplies an integral part of the principle of economy of force.

When I first took command in South Vietnam, so critical was the necessity to build airfields, ports, and bases that I asked for an engineer officer to head my logistics program, Major General Carroll H. Dunn; but as time passed, supply and supply management became of first priority, prompting me to employ a skilled manager, Brigadier General Henry A. Rasmussen. As Chief of Staff of the United States Army I inherited an expert logistician as Deputy Chief of Staff for Logistics, Lieutenant General Joseph M. Heiser, Jr., who earlier had headed the logistical command in South Vietnam. As the withdrawal of American troops began, General Heiser launched a logistics recovery program that saved millions of dollars in equipment and supplies. Provided impetus earlier by Secretary McNamara, the emphasis on savings permeated the entire Defense establishment so that in 1974 such a persistent critic of the military as Senator William Proxmire of Wisconsin could say on the Senate floor that ". . . the Department of Defense has faced and solved more management problems with greater success than any business in the world."

With television for the first time bringing war into living rooms and with no press censorship, the relationship of the military command in South Vietnam and the news media was of unusual importance. Yet for all my efforts and despite the sympathetic support of many newsmen, relations were in large part strained, a legacy of the Diem days exacerbated by the length of the war and the questioning by many of what constituted the national interest.

I was conscious that military commanders throughout history have had problems with the press. "Three hostile newspapers," wrote Napoleon, "are more to be feared than a thousand bayonets." During the American Civil War, General William Tecumseh Sherman, after seeking to hang a reporter for espionage, remarked: "I would rather be governed by Jefferson Davis than be abused by a set of newspaper scribblers who have the impudence of Satan. They come into camp, poke about among the lazy and pick up rumors and publish them as facts."

Some newsmen in South Vietnam did "come into camp, poke about among the lazy and pick up rumors and publish them as facts." On almost any subject a reporter could find a soldier or a junior officer willing to criticize or complain, which for centuries has been a healthy feature of soldiering, but how expert is the opinion of the man in the ranks whose perspective is narrow?

One problem was the youth and inexperience of many correspondents. Having little or no knowledge of military history, having seen no other war, and, like most in the military, having no ability in the Vietnamese language, some reporters were ill-equipped for their assignments. Short deadlines contributed to inaccuracy and some free-lance writers depended upon sensationalism to sell their wares. In general, journalism appears to nurture the pontifical judgment. I was on occasion reminded of General Eisenhower's remark to a publisher who had told him at length what was wrong with the conduct of World War II. "I thought it was only in the world's oldest profession," General Eisenhower said, "that amateurs think they can do better than professionals."

Another problem was constant turnover in reporters. Even dedicated veteran correspondents seldom stayed beyond a year to eighteen months, and some served only brief stints. (With a few exceptions—such as Joe Fried of the New York *Daily News* and the Mutual Broadcasting System, Robert Shaplen of *The New Yorker* magazine, George MacArthur of the Associated Press and later the Los Angeles *Times,* and Bud Merick of *U.S. News & World Report*—even dedicated correspondents seldom stayed beyond a year to eighteen months, and some served only brief stints.) Providing the press with background and perspective was like trying to paint a moving train.

Some of the harshest critics were newsmen in the United States who had never visited Vietnam. One such was the editor of the editorial page of the New York *Times,* John Oakes. I wanted Oakes and others of like mind to see Vietnam at first hand. When a friend of his, David Rockefeller, president of the Chase Manhattan Bank, was in Saigon early in 1966, I urged him to press Oakes to come. After he did visit later that year, I thought I discerned some softening in the generally hard line of the *Times* editorials.

Television presented special problems. Even more than the telegraph during the Crimean War and the radio in World War II, television brought war into the American home, but in the process television's unique requirements contributed to a distorted view of the war. The news had to be compressed and visually dramatic. Thus the war that Americans saw was almost exclusively violent, miserable, or controversial: guns firing, men falling, helicopters crashing, buildings toppling, huts burning, refugees fleeing, women wailing. A shot of a single building in ruins could give an impression of an entire town destroyed. The propensity of cameramen at Khe Sanh to pose their commentators before a wrecked C-130 and deliver reports in a tone of voice suggesting doomsday was all too common. Only scant attention was paid to pacification, civic action, medical assistance, the way life went on in a generally normal way for most of the people much of the time.

I tried throughout to avoid any vendetta with the press. The errors, misinterpretations, judgments, and falsehoods were sometimes annoying, and on occasion I resented the time that I and my staff had to spend clarifying or correcting news reports for our superiors in Washington. Yet there were positive aspects. In the constant search for the negative, the press served as a kind of adjunct to my Inspector General and informed me of many matters that I otherwise might have missed. In 1966, for example, a reporter came to me with a photograph of American soldiers dragging the body of a VC on the ground behind an armored personnel carrier, which enabled me to instigate an investigation with subsequent punitive action.

For every newsman who got his stories at the bar in the Caravelle Hotel, many more took the trouble and displayed the courage to get out with American troops, if not with the ARVN. By the time I departed Vietnam in mid-1968, eight American journalists had died covering the war, and one of the old hands, François Sully of *Newsweek* magazine, was subsequently killed in a helicopter crash. Perhaps the most consistently accurate and objective publication throughout the course of the war was a British periodical, *The Economist,* possibly because qualified historians were permanent members of its staff.

Reflecting the view of the war held by many in the United States and often contributing to it, the general tone of press and television comment was critical, particularly following the Tet offensive of 1968. As a respected Australian journalist, Denis Warner, has noted, there are those who say it was the first war in history lost in the columns of the New York *Times.* Lacking all but most limited access to the enemy, reporters often focused on the death and destruction inevitably produced by American and South Vietnamese operations. I sometimes wondered that if the same uncensored comment had been coming out of occupied France during the years 1942–44 when the Allies were bombing French railroads in preparation for the invasion of Normandy, whether Allied public opinion would have supported Allied armies going ashore on D-Day.

In an encomium to fellow newsmen, James Reston wrote in the New York *Times:*

> Maybe the historians will agree that the reporters and the cameras were decisive in the end. They brought the issue of the war to the people, before the Congress and the courts, and forced the withdrawal of American power from Vietnam.‡

Reston may well be right, but was the process right? Newsmen are supposed to report events, not influence or precipitate them. Like the young David Halberstam during his vendetta with Ngo Dinh Diem, many a newsman tried to usurp the diplomat's role of formulating foreign policy.

One cannot say that the government and the military, either American or South Vietnamese, made no mistakes in dealing with the press. While North Vietnam could speak with one controlled voice, the Americans and South Vietnamese used many, not always well orchestrated. So optimistic were some official spokesmen that they virtually invited the newsman to look behind their words. Military men are trained to regard their efforts positively, and it was not always possible for young officers striving for success on the battlefield to provide a truly objective account of their situation. War is an unpleasant business in any case. Still, journalists might have appreciated that the military has no obligation to make itself look bad and that optimism is in itself no sin. In the same vein American officials did themselves no credit when they publicly vented their exasperation with the press. However understandable Secretary of State Rusk's outburst against the press, in view of the frustrations he bore, newsmen were slow to forget it: "There gets to be a point when the question is whose side are you on."

In the past the vigilance of the press has often led to needed reforms in man's institutions, including the military. With the aid of the telegraph, for example, the press during the Crimean War promoted long overdue reforms in the British Army. Yet for all the journalistic criticism during the war in Vietnam, the press uncovered nothing in any way comparable. The press cannot even claim to have revealed one of the war's most shocking events, the slaughter at My Lai; the United States Army had already begun pretrial investigations of My Lai and had made a public announcement on the basis of charges against an officer who was involved when the press seized upon the story.

There can be no question that a free and independent press is an essential

‡ James Reston, "The End of the Tunnel," New York *Times,* April 30, 1975, p. 33.

component of the American form of democracy. So vital an institution is it, so basic, such a staunch bulwark of the American system, that it is well to tolerate some mistakes and derelictions, to make every effort to assure that total freedom and independence continue to exist.

Yet it is still a fact that in all professions one should meet certain standards, maintain certain norms. By extravagances and irresponsibility it is possible for the press itself to destroy its own credibility with the American people, so that even without government interference, this essential component of the American way could be seriously eroded or even destroyed. No society will long tolerate an institution that fails to maintain standards and confidence.

It may well be that between press and official there is an inherent, built-in conflict of interest. There is something to be said for both sides, but when the nation is at war and men's lives are at stake, there should be no ambiguity. In the process of backing into Vietnam, suspicions developed on both sides. If the nation is to wage war—declared or undeclared—a policy should be set to protect the interests of both press and government and avoid the ambiguity that characterized relationships in South Vietnam.

Even had South Vietnam survived as an independent nation, would a little corner of Southeast Asia have been worth all the American sacrifice? At least four presidents and numerous other Washington officials and legislators saw South Vietnam as the key to Southeast Asia and vital if the United States was to secure its interests in that region. Yet history may nevertheless judge that going into Vietnam was one of our country's greatest mistakes. On the other hand, history may judge that American aid to South Vietnam constituted one of man's more noble crusades, one that had less to do with the domino theory and a strategic interest for the United States than with the simple equation of a strong nation helping an aspiring nation to reach a point where it had some reasonable chance to achieve and keep a degree of freedom and human dignity. Even though American resolve fell short in the end, it remains a fact that few countries have ever engaged in such idealistic magnanimity; and no gain or attempted gain for human freedom can be discounted.

If only the Communists are to assist people of emerging nations, what hope is there for those who aspire to freedom? We may well be unable to afford to be the world's policeman, but neither can we afford to fail to live up to the responsibilities that the accidents of a bountiful land and a beneficent fate have placed upon us. We tend in this age of iconoclasm to disparage idealism, patriotism, and zeal; but if there are to be no more Vietnams, is there to be no more support of aspiring freedom, protection of the weak against the strong? What of John F. Kennedy's stirring pledge "to assure the survival and the success of liberty"? As many have observed, the price of freedom is never cheap, nor is even the survival of existing freedom. On the other hand, if there is ever to be another Vietnam, the American

people must be informed candidly why it has to be and the nature of the
sacrifices they may be called upon to bear.

Having failed to accomplish our objective in Southeast Asia, we can take
little solace in the fact that we delayed a Communist takeover for ten years.
On the other hand, there may well have been some pluses. Our stand in
South Vietnam may have encouraged Indonesia in its successful effort to
expel Communist influence. The Philippines were encouraged to suppress
their lingering Huk insurgency. Singapore became closely allied with the
West, and Thailand made significant economic progress, particularly in an
improved system of roads. Furthermore, despite the loss of South Vietnam, Laos, and Cambodia to Communism, the balance of power in Asia
may not have been materially altered for the near future. The United States
is still a Pacific power, and China has apparently moderated its policy toward its neighbors. Over those ten years, relationships between the great
powers have undergone marked change at the same time the other states of
Southeast Asia were gaining valuable time to create social and political institutions better equipped to cope with their own internal Communist
threats. This is not to say, of course, that the domino theory may not in the
end prevail.

If our vast expenditure of precious lives and resources is to have genuine
meaning, our nation must face up to overcoming any inclination to withdraw from world affairs. Many who were most vocally critical of the war
while it went on now seem inclined to cut off debate, to assure that there
are no "recriminations." There should be no witch hunt over Vietnam, but
before we close off debate, we should remember that whatever the mistakes,
we were in Vietnam for serious and moral purposes, and we should have no
fear of introspective analysis. Policy makers, planners, diplomats, military
leaders, politicians, bureaucrats, newsmen—all must search to discern the
mistakes and to heed the lessons of Vietnam so that in the end the bitter experience we have undergone can help us to become a better and stronger nation. As the thrill that swept the country over the outcome of the *Mayaguez*
incident off Cambodia indicated, Americans in general have no wish to look
upon themselves as losers.

As we strive to achieve an era of detente with the Soviet Union, we must
be certain in our consummate yearning for peace and disarmament that
we avoid the peril of unilateral concessions that would weaken our military posture. Above all, we must maintain national unity, never again to
lapse into the vitriolic divisions that beset our nation over the war in Vietnam. We must remember, as the scriptures and Abraham Lincoln have
told us, that a house divided against itself cannot stand.

Surely the American airman, marine, sailor, and soldier can look back on
his performance in Vietnam with unalloyed pride. Despite the final failure
of the South Vietnamese, the record of the American military services of
never having lost a war is still intact. Nor were the military services ever
anywhere near the distressful state that some hand-wringers tried to depict.

In the Army, for example, the rate of men absent without leave never came close to that of the Korean War until 1971, after the continuing withdrawal from South Vietnam had revealed a lessening of American resolve. A peak rate of desertions of 63 per thousand men in World War II, reached at the height of the war in 1944, was again never even approached during the war in Vietnam until 1971. The incidence of psychiatric problems during the war in Vietnam never reached even one third the number in World War II and was just over half that of the Korean War. For all the publicity given to men deserting and leaving the country because of moral convictions against the war in Vietnam, the number of those returning to society under President Ford's clemency program who gave opposition to the war as their reason for deserting was only 14 per cent.

Following World War II, reforms in the Army were imposed by an outside commission known as the Doolittle Board. During the latter part of the war in Vietnam, the Army itself undertook introspective analysis of its problems and as an institution began initiating changes and reforms. The changes may not have been as swift and revolutionary as some impetuous young officers might have wished; indeed, as the Army's Chief of Staff I intentionally worked methodically through the chain of command to achieve evolutionary rather than revolutionary change, for radical change can easily tear an institution apart. In retrospect, the military services may have listened too closely to the voices of those who were preaching despair, for all were soon re-established as the solid institutions that the American people have always depended upon. Those of us in the military may even have underestimated the degree of support the American people still afforded the military, for a recent public opinion survey revealed that the military services are among the public institutions that the people most trust.

For one looking back on thirty-six years of service in the United States Army, that is a rewarding thought. So, too, I am struck, upon reflection, by the unprecedented changes that occurred during those thirty-six years. From the World War I Stokes mortar and the Model 1897 French 75 artillery piece to sophisticated guided missiles; from the model 1902 rifle to the M-16; from carrier pigeons and Morse code telegraphy to walkie-talkies, computers, and sensors; from a private's pay of $21 a month and a second lieutenant's of $125 to today's private's pay of $344 a month and today's second lieutenant's of $634; through three wars and a number of police actions; from volunteer army back to volunteer army; and from isolationism to multiple international commitments. As one in the middle of the changes at various levels of command responsibility, I have always been impressed by the loyalty, flexibility, durability, and over-all effectiveness of the United States Army. The traumatic experience of Vietnam was no exception.

Among some of my military colleagues I nevertheless sense a lingering concern that the military served as the scapegoat of the war in Vietnam. I fail to share that concern. The military quite clearly did the job that the nation asked and expected of it, and I am convinced that history will reflect more favorably upon the performance of the military than upon that of the politicians and policy makers. The American people can be particularly proud that their military leaders scrupulously adhered to a basic tenet of our Constitution prescribing civilian control of the military.

As the soldier prays for peace he must be prepared to cope with the hardships of war and to bear its scars.

Acknowledgments

My appreciation for the kind assistance of the following:*

Lt. Gen. Milton B. Adams, United States Air Force; Lt. Col. Gene Arnold, Historical Branch, United States Marine Corps; Brig. Gen. Robert Ashworth; Col. Henry A. Barber III; Maj. Gen. Sidney B. Berry; Capt. Jack A. Brage, United States Marine Corps; Maj. Larry Budge; Lt. Col. Victor T. Bullock; Lt. Col. William S. Carpenter, Jr.

Also Staff Sgt. T. R. Carroll, United States Marine Corps; Mr. Richard W. Darrow; Maj. Gen. Phillip B. Davidson, Jr.; Brig. Gen. Oscar E. Davis; Mr. Vincent H. Demma, U. S. Army Center of Military History; Maj. Gen. George S. Eckhardt; Maj. Joseph H. Felter, Jr.; Lt. Gen. George I. Forsythe; Lt. Col. Raymond Fredette, Office of Air Force History; Mr. Bemis Frank, Historical Branch, United States Marine Corps; Lt. Gen. Daniel O. Graham; Maj. James G. Gritz; Mrs. Gail Guido, Office of Air Force History; Brig. Gen. Arch Hamblen; Lt. Gen. Joseph M. Heiser, Jr.; Lt. Col. Richard D. Hooker; Col. Arnold W. Johnson, Jr., M.D.; General Harold K. Johnson; Maj. Gen. Frederick J. Kroesen.

Also Brig. Gen. Theodore C. Mataxis; Lt. Col. Lloyd J. Matthews; Lt. Gen. William J. McCaffrey; Col. William McKean; Dr. William McMillan; Maj. Gen. H. G. Moore; Lt. Gen. Joseph H. Moore, United States Air Force; Maj. Gen. Spurgeon Neel; Lt. Col. Frederick E. Oldinsky; Maj. Gen. Frank A. Osmanski; Gen. Bruce C. Palmer, Jr.; Lt. Col. David Palmer; Lt. Gen. Willard Pearson; Col. Benjamin H. Purcell; Miss Martha Raye; Maj. Charles Sampson, United States Marine Corps; Col. H. Y. Schandler.

Also Lt. Gen. Jonathan O. Seaman; Mr. Henry I. Shaw, Jr., Historical Branch, United States Marine Corps; Maj. John Sherburne; Maj. Gen. Winant Sidle; Maj. Gen. John K. Singlaub; Mr. Samuel Thompson, Department of State; Brig. Gen. William A. Tidwell; Lt. Gen. John T. Tolson III; Maj. Gen. Rathvon McC. Tompkins, United States Marine Corps; Ambassador Viron P. Vaky, Department of State; and General Earle G. Wheeler.

* Unless another service is indicated, all officers are in the United States Army.

Glossary

An Quang   militant arm of organized Buddhists in South Vietnam.

ARVN (pronounced "arvin")   Army of the Republic of Vietnam, or South Vietnamese Army.

AID   Agency for International Development.

ATTLEBORO   code name for large joint operation in 1966 by American and South Vietnamese troops in War Zone C.

BARREL ROLL   code name for flights begun in December 1964 by American and South Vietnamese planes against North Vietnamese targets in Laos.

CEDAR FALLS   code name for large operation in 1967 by American troops in the Iron Triangle.

Chieu hoi   open-arms or amnesty program promoted by the South Vietnamese Government to encourage insurgents to rally to the government.

CIA   Central Intelligence Agency.

CIDG   civilian irregular defense groups. South Vietnamese tribesmen recruited in remote regions to work with advisers of the U. S. Army Special Forces.

CINCPAC   Commander in Chief, Pacific. Over-all commander of American forces in the Pacific regions, including Southeast Asia.

COFRAM   special U. S. Army artillery shell with tremendous fragmentation effect.

COMUSMACV   Commander, U. S. Military Assistance Command, Vietnam.

CORDS   Civil Operations and Revolutionary Development Support. Agency created in 1967 within MACV to co-ordinate the American pacification effort; successor to OCO.

COSVN (pronounced "cosvin")   Central Office for South Vietnam. Headquarters used by the North Vietnamese Communist party for political and military control in South Vietnam.

COUNTY FAIR a form of "cordon and search" in which American and South Vietnamese troops surrounded a village; while South Vietnamese police searched for arms, guerrillas, and political infrastructure, the villagers were provided entertainment and welfare services.

DELAWARE code name for American-South Vietnamese operation in the spring of 1968 in the A Shau Valley.

DEROS U. S. Army term meaning "date eligible to return from overseas."

DESOTO code name for U. S. Navy patrols in the Gulf of Tonkin.

DMZ demilitarized zone created by the Geneva Accords of 1954 along the 17th parallel dividing South and North Vietnam.

EL PASO I, II code names for proposed American-South Vietnamese ground operations in Laos.

FAIRFAX code name for joint American-South Vietnamese Army operations in 1967 to secure the environs of Saigon.

FARMGATE code name for early U. S. Air Force support of the South Vietnamese Air Force.

FULRO Front Unifié de Lutte de la Race Opprimée, or United Front for the Struggle of the Oppressed Race, a movement for Montagnard autonomy.

GAME WARDEN code name for a long-running project of the U. S. Navy to keep South Vietnam's internal waterways open.

HASTINGS code name for U. S. Marine Corps operations in conjunction with ARVN troops and South Vietnamese marines in Quang Tri province in summer and fall of 1966.

HES hamlet evaluation system. Method of rating hamlets and villages to ascertain the level of pacification.

HOP TAC code name for program begun in late 1964 to expand security in the region around Saigon.

JUNCTION CITY code name for large operation in 1967 by American and South Vietnamese troops in War Zone C.

JUSPAO Joint United States Public Affairs Office.

LEAPING LENA code name for small South Vietnamese patrols operating in Laos along the Ho Chi Minh Trail in 1964.

LST landing ship, tank.

MACV Military Assistance Command, Vietnam.

MARKET TIME code name for a long-running project of American and South Vietnamese navies to prevent North Vietnamese infiltration into South Vietnam by sea.

MASHER code name for an operation begun in early 1966 by American troops in Binh Dinh province; later renamed WHITE WING.

MUST   medical unit, self-contained, transportable.

NIAGARA   code name for a SLAM operation in the spring of 1968 in support of the Khe Sanh Combat Base.

OCO   Office of Civil Operations. Short-lived agency for co-ordinating the American pacification effort.

ONTOS   U. S. Marine Corps tank-killer vehicles armed with a 106-mm recoilless rifle.

OPLAN 34A   covert operations begun in 1961 by the South Vietnamese against North Vietnam.

OPLAN 37   proposal prepared in the spring of 1964 for American air operations in three phases involving attacks against enemy forces retiring into Laos and Cambodia, "tit-for-tat" reprisal strikes, and increasingly heavy bombing of North Vietnam.

PEGASUS   code name for operation to re-establish ground contact with the Khe Sanh Combat Base in April 1968.

PHOENIX   code name for a long-running program to identify and excise the Viet Cong political infrastructure.

PRAIRIE FIRE   code name for small American-South Vietnamese patrols operating in Laos along the Ho Chi Minh Trail, begun in 1965.

RECONDO   school to train U. S. Army troops for long-range reconnaissance patrols. A similar school was organized later for ARVN troops.

ROLLING THUNDER   code name for a long-running program of American and South Vietnamese air operations against North Vietnam.

SEAL   sea, air, land teams. American and South Vietnamese Navy commandos.

SLAM   seeking, locating, annihilating, and monitoring operations (U.S.) to co-ordinate reconnaissance and firepower resources in concentrated attacks by fire.

SOG   Studies and Observation Group. Component of MACV dealing with unconventional warfare.

TALLY HO   code name for air reconnaissance and attack immediately north of and within the DMZ; begun in 1966.

Task Force OREGON   U. S. Army force organized in April 1966 to provide reinforcements in the I Corps Zone, predecessor of the Americal Division.

TIGER-HOUND   code name for air reconnaissance and attack in the Laotian panhandle, begun in 1966.

USIA   United States Information Agency.

VANDEGRIFT   artillery fire support base built in 1968 by U. S. Army troops on the approaches to Khe Sanh and later manned by U.S. marines.

VC   Viet Cong. Contraction of a derogatory term meaning Vietnamese Communists.

WHITE WING   code name for an operation first known as MASHER by American troops in Binh Dinh province early in 1966.

YANKEE TEAM   code name for U. S. Air Force and Navy reconnaissance flights beginning in May 1964 over Laos.

YORK   code name for a proposed series of American-South Vietnamese operations to sweep the A Shau Valley and nearby border regions in preparation for possible operations in Laos.

Index

Abrams, Gen. Creighton W., 13, 213, 265, 368
  on Korean troops, 257
  personality of, 222
  as U. S. Chief of Staff, 381, 387–88
  as Vietnam Military Assistance commander, 151–52, 362, 381, 387, 390, 391
  as Vietnam Military Assistance deputy, 214–15, 222, 236, 313, 330, 345, 379
Acuff, Roy, 302
Agency for International Development (AID), 61, 69, 75, 210, 254, 366
  Con Son a responsibility of, 245
Airborne assault, only U.S., in Vietnam, 206
Airborne units
  South Vietnamese, 254, 399, 401, 402
  U.S., see under Brigades and Divisions
Aircraft, see ARVN—U.S. air support of; Helicopters; South Vietnamese Air Force; United States Air Force; specific types
Air division, U. S. Air Force, 2d, 74–75, 117
Airfields and airstrips
  construction of, 186
  new devices for, 283
Air forces, U. S. Air Force
  Third, 269
  Seventh, 75, 203, 277, 299
Airhead, definition of, 271n
Air-manager system, 343–45, 360
Airmobile division, see Divisions, U. S. Army—1st Cavalry
Air wing, U. S. Marine, 1st, 343
AK-47 rifle, 104, 158
Alaska, National Guard of, 367
Alberghetti, Anna Maria, 302
Allen, Lt. Col. Terry de la Mesa, Jr., 237
Allied troops, see Third Country troops
Ambushes, 101–2
  by Allied forces, 280, 282
  defoliation vs., 280–81
  of 1st Infantry's brigade, 237
  "Road Runner" operations vs., 280
  Sharp's fear of, 144
American Bar Association, 366
American Red Cross, 301
Amphibious force, U. S. Marine, III, 125, 140, 155–56, 166, 329, 342, 345
Anderson, Jack, 277
Anderson, Maj. Gen. Norman J., 343
Anderson, Maj. Gen. Orvil A., 21
Anderson, Staff Sgt. Webster, 306
Andress, Ursula, 302
Andrews, Julie, 302
An Giang province (South Vietnam), 52
An Khe (South Vietnam), 55, 102, 111, 156
An Lao Valley (South Vietnam), 307
An Loc (South Vietnam), 392
Annam, 49
Ann-Margret, 302
An Quang Buddhists, 46, 52
Antiwar demonstrations, 225–26, 231, 346, 364–66, 413–14
  at Kent State, 183–84, 373
  1970 Washington, 373
  Vietnam morale and, 296
Apbia Mountain, see Hamburger Hill
"Area war," 153
Argentina, 255n
Argo, Col. Reamer, 338
Armed Forces Council, 93, 96, 97
Armies, U. S. Army
  First, 22
  Eighth, 13, 14, 70
Armor, see Tanks

Army group, U. S. Army, 6th, 14
Artillery
  airlifting of, 282
  atomic, 124–25
  author's service in, 15–19, 20
  author's tactics for, 155
  on Cambodian-Laotian border, 238
  fire-support bases, 199, 281, 282
  new types of ammunition for, 281
  in 1966 War Zone C operation, 180
  in Quang Tri province, 196, 198, 199, 201, 203
    1968 Khe Sanh fight, 337, 339, 340
  Viet Cong's lack of, 155
ARVN, 240–55
  casualties of, 101, 137, 238, 251, 332
  communications equipment of, 250
  corps areas of, see Corps areas
  corruption in, 243–44
  dependents of, 253, 400, 401
  divisions of, see Divisions, ARVN
  draft for, 100–1, 241, 255, 333, 354
  fighting ability of, 99, 250–52
  general ranks in, 41n
  lack of self-criticism in, 246
  Laos invasion by, 389–91
  leadership of, 59, 85, 99, 241
    military schools, 252–53
  in May 1968 VC offensive, 360–61
  name of, 56
  1972 VC offensive and, 391–92
  1975 collapse of, 397–402
  pacification and civic action by, 216, 254
  poor training of, 59
  press briefings attempted by, 251
  rangers of, see Rangers
  self-contained, as goal, 234, 235
  Special Forces of, 78, 79, 253, 282, 289–90
  strength of, 58, 100, 147, 397
    1965 moratorium on new divisions, 137
  in Tet offensive, 323, 326, 328–33
  upgrading of, 99, 222, 234, 387
  U.S. advisers to, 59, 114, 222, 241, 294
    at battalion level, 111
    not in Laos invasion, 390
  U.S. air support of, 86, 101–2, 122–23
    author's 1965 authority, 110–11
  U.S. budgetary control over, 241
  U.S. command arrangements and, 133–34, 252
  U.S. newsmen and, 250–51
  U.S. supplies to, 186
  veterans of, 253–54
  volunteers in, 101
  weapons of, 59, 104, 158–59, 350, 397
A Shau Valley (South Vietnam), 61, 272, 281, 306, 336
  1966 operation in, 167
  1968–69 operations in, 151–52, 347–49
  Tet offensive and, 314, 319, 328–29
Ashworth, Brig. Gen. Robert L., 246–47
Associated Press, 419
Astrike, Warrant Officer Charles, 373
ATTLEBORO operation, 180, 197
Australia, 280, 370
Australian Air Force, 258
Australian Navy, 258
Australian troops in South Vietnam, 132, 133, 140, 154, 255, 256, 300
  description of, 258–59
  operations by, 141, 177, 258

B-52 bombers, 119, 147, 283
  accuracy of, 137–38, 283, 340, 418
  Cambodia raids by, 183, 389

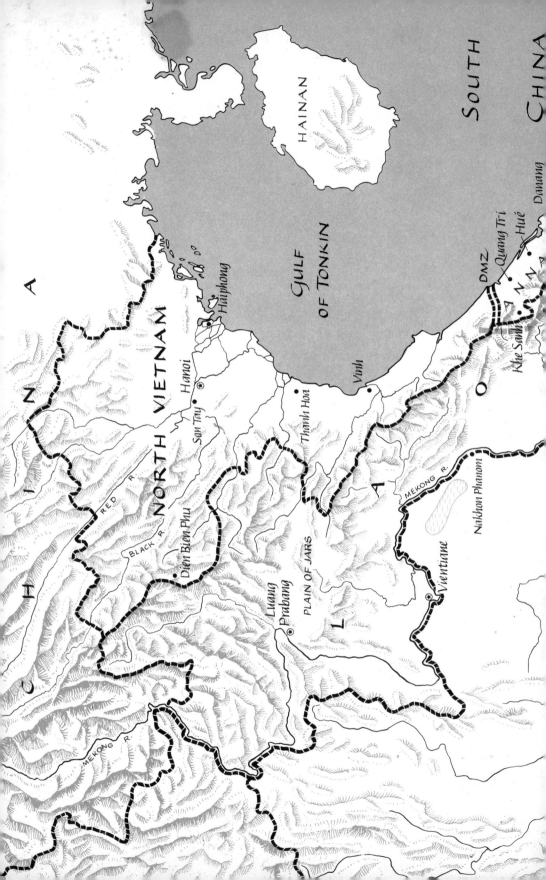